UN PEACEKEEPI

Civil wars pose some of the most difficult problems in the world today and the United Nations is the organization generally called upon to bring and sustain peace. Lise Morjé Howard studies the sources of success and failure in UN peacekeeping. Her in-depth analysis of some of the most complex UN peacekeeping missions debunks the conventional wisdom that they habitually fail, showing that the UN record actually includes a number of important, though understudied, success stories. Using systematic comparative analysis, Howard argues that UN peacekeeping succeeds when field missions establish significant autonomy from UN headquarters, allowing civilian and military staff to adjust to the post-civil war environment. In contrast, failure frequently results from operational directives originating in UN headquarters, often devised in relation to higher-level political disputes with little relevance to the civil war in question. Howard recommends that future reforms be oriented toward devolving decision-making power to the field missions.

LISE MORJÉ HOWARD is Director of the Conflict Resolution MA Program at Georgetown University.

UN PEACEKEEPING IN CIVIL WARS

LISE MORJÉ HOWARD

CAMBRIDGE
UNIVERSITY PRESS

CAMBRIDGE UNIVERSITY PRESS
Cambridge, New York, Melbourne, Madrid, Cape Town, Singapore, São Paulo, Delhi

Cambridge University Press
The Edinburgh Building, Cambridge CB2 8RU, UK

Published in the United States of America by Cambridge University Press, New York

www.cambridge.org
Information on this title: www.cambridge.org/9780521707671

First published 2008
Reprinted 2009

Printed in the United Kingdom at the University Press, Cambridge

A catalogue record for this publication is available from the British Library

ISBN 978-0-521-88138-8 hardback
ISBN 978-0-521-70767-1 paperback

CONTENTS

TABLES AND APPENDICES

ACRONYMS

ADEFAES	Demobilized Members of the Armed Forces of El Salvador
AG	South African Administrator-General
ANC	African National Congress (South Africa)
ARENA	Nationalist Republican Alliance
ASEAN	Association of Southeast Asian Nations
AU	African Union
CIVPOL	Civilian Police Division of a United Nations peacekeeping operation
CNRT	National Council of Timorese Resistance
CSCE	Commission on Security and Cooperation in Europe
DDR	Disarmament, Demobilization, and Reintegration
DPA	Department of Political Affairs
DPKO	Department of Peacekeeping Operations
DRC	Democratic Republic of the Congo
DTA	Democratic Turnhalle Alliance
ECOMOG	ECOWAS Monitoring Group
ECOWAS	Economic Community of West African States
FADM	Armed Forces for the Defense of Mozambique
FAO	Food and Agriculture Organization
FMLN	Farabundo Martí Front for National Liberation
Frelimo	Mozambique Liberation Front
FUNCINPEC	National United Front for an Independent, Neutral, Peaceful and Cooperative Cambodia
HDZ	Croatian Democratic Union
IDP	Internally displaced person
IMF	International Monetary Fund
INTERFET	International Force in East Timor
IOM	International Organization on Migration
KFOR	Kosovo Force (NATO)
KPNLF	Khmer People's National Liberation Front
MINUSAL	United Nations Mission in El Salvador
MINUSTAH	United Nations Stabilization Mission in Haiti
MONUA	United Nations Observer Mission in Angola

MONUC	United Nations Observer Mission in the Democratic Republic of the Congo
MPLA	Movimento Popular de Liberacao de Angola
NATO	North Atlantic Treaty Organization
NGO	Nongovernmental organization
OAU	Organization of African Unity
ONUB	United Nations Operation in Burundi
ONUMOZ	United Nations Operation in Mozambique
ONUSAL	United Nations Observer Mission in El Salvador
OSCE	Organization for Security and Cooperation in Europe
OSRSG	Office of the Special Representative of the Secretary-General
PLAN	People's Liberation Army of Namibia
PRK	People's Republic of Kampuchea (later known as SOC)
Renamo	Mozambican National Resistance
RPF	Rwandan Patriotic Front
RUF	Revolutionary United Front of Sierra Leone
SADC	Southern African Development Community
SADF	South African Defense Force
SDSS	Independent Serbian Democratic Party
SNC	Supreme National Council of Cambodia
SOC	State of Cambodia
SRSG	Special Representative of the Secretary-General
SWAPO	South West African People's Organization
SWAPOL	South West African Police
SWATF	South West African Territorial Force
UN	United Nations
UNAMET	United Nations Mission in East Timor
UNAMIC	United Nations Advance Mission in Cambodia
UNAMIR	United Nations Assistance Mission for Rwanda
UNAMSIL	United Nations Mission in Sierra Leone
UNAVEM	United Nations Angola Verification Mission (I, II, III)
UNCRO	UN Confidence Restoration Operation for Croatia
UNDP	United Nations Development Program
UNESCO	United Nations Educational, Scientific, and Cultural Organization
UNHCR	United Nations High Commissioner for Refugees
UNICEF	United Nations Children's Fund
UNITA	National Union for the Total Independence of Angola
UNITAF	Unified Task Force (US)
UNMIK	United Nations Interim Administration Mission in Kosovo
UNMIL	United Nations Mission in Liberia
UNMISET	United Nations Mission of Support in Timor-Leste

UNOCI	United Nations Operation in Côte d'Ivoire
UNOHAC	United Nations Office for Humanitarian Assistance Coordination
UNOSOM	United Nations Operation in Somalia (I, II)
UNOTIL	United Nations Office in East Timor
UNPREDEP	UN Preventive Deployment Force in Macedonia
UNPROFOR	United Nations Protection Force
UNTAC	United Nations Transitional Authority in Cambodia
UNTAES	UN Transitional Administration in Eastern Slavonia, Baranja, and Western Sirium
UNTAET	UN Transitional Authority in East Timor
UNTAG	United Nations Transition Assistance Group
USAID	United States Agency for International Development
WHO	World Health Organization
ZANU	Zimbabwe African National Union
ZAPU	Zimbabwe African People's Union

ACKNOWLEDGMENTS

When I began this project, I thought I would be writing a book about the sources of failure in UN peacekeeping. Before entering graduate school, I had been working at the UN, attending the daily press briefings from 1992 to early 1994, and most of what I heard was about disasters – in Bosnia, Somalia, Angola, and Rwanda. It wasn't until I started examining the UN's record from the viewpoint of a social scientist that I realized that there were numerous, unwritten stories of success. I therefore developed a research project aimed at finding the sources of success.

As I dove into the cases, I found myself on a tour of the world, tracking down the peacekeepers to ask them what they thought. I found six remarkable cases where UN peacekeeping in civil wars worked – in Namibia, El Salvador, Cambodia, Mozambique, Eastern Slavonia/Croatia, and East Timor. These are the main six stories that make up the heart of this book. There are other important attempts underway right now to create peace on the killing fields, and I only hope that some of the lessons from the successful missions will be applied elsewhere.

This book originated as a PhD dissertation at the University of California, Berkeley, and I owe many thanks to my dissertation committee members. Ernst B. Haas, my main mentor, was consistently challenging, brilliant, and unfailingly supportive throughout the entire process. I am extremely grateful for having had the honor and privilege of working with him, and I miss him dearly. My other committee members, George W. Breslauer, Steven Weber, and David D. Caron provided me with inspiration, constructive criticism, and excellent guidance.

I conducted interviews about this project in many different countries between 1997 and 2005. I would like to thank the following people for granting me interviews, sometimes multiple times: Karen Koning Abuzayd, Ahmed Salman, Martti Ahtisaari, Nahas Angula, Hedi Annabi, Babafemi Badejo, Pat Banks, Mark Baskin, Ben Ben Yahmed, Ivan Bettyar, Derek Boothby, Henry Breed, Tore Brevik, Prudence Bushnell, Hamish Cameron, Jose Campino Da Silva, Christopher Coleman, Roméo Dallaire, Manoel de Almeida e Silva, Alvaro De Soto, John Dooley, John M. Ebersole, Wilfried Emvula, Anna Frangipani-Campino, Hage Geingob, Marrack Goulding, Andrew Grene,

Fernando Guimaraes, Robert Hagan, David Harland, Brian Harlech-Jones, Julian Harston, Tunguru Huaraka, Zeljko Jerkic, Melissa Joralemon, Leonard Kapungu, Peter Katjavivi, Arjun Katoch, Peter Kessler, Asif Khan, Jacques Paul Klein, Peter Koep, Jean Krasno, Elisabeth Lindenmayer, Christo Lombard, Robin Ludwig, Jane Holl Lute, Frederick Lyons, Peter McDermott, Joel McClellan, Eric Morris, Madeleine Moulin-Acevedo, Nangolo Mbumba, Walid Musa, Alphonse Muynyaneza, Flemming Nielsen, Sadako Ogata, Bryan O'Linn, Ben Parker, Mark Pedersen, Wade Pendleton, Constancio Pinto, Tamara Pozdnyakova, Everett Ressler, Marie-Pierre Richarte, John Ruggie, Mike Sackett, John Shalikashvili, Mochida Shigeru, Hisako Shimura, Emma Shitakha, Andrei Shkourko, Lorraine Sievers, Haris Silajidzic, David Stephen, Ayaka Suzuki, Peter Swarbrick, Masimba Tafirenyika, Shashi Tharoor, Dmitry Titov, Andimba Toivo ya Toivo, Anil Vasisht, Adriaan Verheul, Friedhelm Voigts, Carl Von Hirschberg, Leslie Wade, Wolfgang Wagner, Wolfgang Weisbrod-Weber, Teresa Whitfield, Richard Wilcox, Derek Yach, and Fatemeh Ziai.

I owe many thanks to those who have read or provided me with helpful advice on various parts of this project over the years: Ivan Arreguin-Toft, Michael Barnett, Andrew Bennett, Michael Brown, Simon Chesterman, Martha Crenshaw, William Durch, Lynne Eden, Tanisha Fazal, V. Page Fortna, John Harbeson, Margaret Karns, Charles King, Mark Lichbach, Kimberly Zisk Marten, Steven Miller, Sally Morphet, Robert Rotberg, Donald Rothchild, Stephen Stedman, Leslie Vinjamuri, Paul Wapner, Carola Weil, and Marie-Joelle Zahar. I would like to thank my research assistants, Brenna Anatone, David Aten, and Mischa Sogut, and the students in my peacekeeping seminars at Wesleyan and Georgetown Universities for helping me develop my ideas. John Haslam, Jacqueline French, and the anonymous referees at Cambridge University Press provided first-rate comments and suggestions.

I am also very grateful to colleagues who created stimulating intellectual homes at the following institutions: the Department of Government and the MA Program in Conflict Resolution at Georgetown University; the Department of Government at Wesleyan University; the Center for International Development and Conflict Management at the University of Maryland, College Park; the Belfer Center for Science and International Affairs at the Kennedy School, Harvard University; the University of California's Institute on Global Conflict and Cooperation, Washington, DC office; and the Center for International Security and Cooperation at Stanford University. I am also grateful for financial support from UC Berkeley's Department of Political Science, the Berkeley Program in Soviet and Post-Soviet Studies, the Institute for the Study of World Politics, the Institute on Global Conflict and Cooperation, the National Security Education Program, and the MacArthur Foundation. And I was fortunate to receive awards for this project from the Soroptimist International, the Barnard College Alumnae Association, and the James D. Kline Fund.

Finally, I would like to thank my family. Pati, Mitzi, Leigh, Barb, Maia, Vito, Dick, and Brigitte make up the finest and most supportive close family that I could ever imagine, in addition to the numerous members of my extended family. Zoe and Julien were only ideas when I began this project, and I am very thankful to have such amazing, energetic, and inspiring little children. Most importantly, my husband, Marc Morjé Howard, has been my principal and most steadfast source of friendship, love, and intellectual inspiration. I dedicate this book to Marc.

Introduction: success, failure, and organizational learning in UN peacekeeping

Basic questions and the argument in brief

Civil war is the most important and troubling problem in international life today. Aside from the tragic killing and injury of innocent civilians, violent civil conflicts inspire lingering, seemingly intractable ills such as state collapse, corruption, dire poverty, rampant injustice, dislocation, environmental degradation, and disease, all of which may in turn instigate renewed and spreading conflict, international crime, and terrorist activity.

Given the extreme, cyclical, and burgeoning problems associated with civil wars, what mechanisms do we have to stop such conflicts? The most oft-used mechanism is United Nations (UN) multidimensional peacekeeping. Multidimensional peacekeeping operations endeavor to rebuild the basic institutions of the post-civil war state. These missions are large and complex, involving sizable political, military, police, refugee, humanitarian, electoral, and often human rights components.[1] Despite the UN's own problems, and despite the difficulties associated with peacekeeping, we simply have not yet invented better international mechanisms to bring order to the anarchy of civil wars. It is therefore of critical importance that we analyze and improve our understanding of UN peacekeeping. When has UN peacekeeping been successful? What are the sources of success and failure? How can the UN learn to engage better in peacekeeping? What are the types of learning in which the UN engages? These are the critical questions asked in this book.

The book sets out to answer these questions in a systematic fashion, using methods in comparative politics and international relations to construct the research design and carry out case study comparisons.[2] The most important

---

[1] "Multidimensional peacekeeping" is also sometimes referred to as "multifunctional," "multidisciplinary," or "integrated" peacekeeping. A civil war is a conflict where organized sides contend for power within a single recognized state, and where there are more than 1,500 casualties.

[2] Since I am examining a small universe of cases, I employ qualitative, comparative methods, including the methods of agreement and difference to construct the basic research design, structured, focused comparison to compare the cases, and a descriptive model of organizational change in order to build my own argument. On these methods, see Mill, 1843, Skocpol and Somers, 1980; George and Mckeown, 1985; Ragin, 1987; Dion, 1994;

nding is that UN peacekeeping tends to be more successful when the peacekeepers are actively learning from the environment in which they are deployed. In other words, rather than seeking to impose preconceived notions about how the missions should unfold, peacekeeping is at its best when the peacekeepers – both civilian and military – take their cues from the local population, and not UN headquarters, about how best to implement mandates.

The overall argument of the book is more nuanced. After studying and comparing the ten most complex cases of UN multidimensional peacekeeping, I argue that three conditions are necessary, and jointly they are sufficient, to explain success in UN peacekeeping. These three elements consist of, first, certain favorable "situational factors" of the country emerging from civil war; second, consensual but only moderately intense interests of the powerful members of the Security Council; and finally, "first-level" organizational learning on the ground, on the part of the UN peacekeeping mission. When this learning is inhibited, then the operation is unable to implement its mandate or help to construct new domestic institutions that will solidify the peace, even if the two other conditions for success are present. The first two conditions are modifications of arguments existing in the peacekeeping literature. The third factor has often been misunderstood, overlooked, or only partially explored. Therefore, I develop a descriptive model to depict first-level organizational learning in the field, within a given mission. I also develop a model of "second-level" learning, or learning that takes place at UN headquarters, in between missions, which is explored further in the concluding chapter.

Why another study of peacekeeping is necessary

This study focuses on what we can learn from the more *successful* cases of complex, multidimensional peacekeeping in civil wars. While the literature on UN peacekeeping has grown immensely since the end of the Cold War, only two edited studies to date have examined successful cases.[3] Most scholarly comparisons, as well as media attention and UN "lessons learned" reports, examine primarily the disastrous failures.[4] However, if one considers the civil

---

Collier and Mahoney, 1996; and George and Bennett, 2005. I draw on three main sources of data: (1) Over 100 interviews with central figures in peacekeeping that I conducted in New York City, Washington DC, Geneva, Nairobi, Zagreb, Sarajevo, and other parts of Europe, Africa, and North America. (2) Primary sources also consist of hundreds of UN documents collected at the sites mentioned above. (3) Secondary sources include the literature on peacekeeping, and case studies of each of the wars.

[3] Doyle, Johnstone, and Orr, 1997; and Krasno, Hayes, and Daniel, 2003.

[4] See, for example, Thakur and Thayer, 1995; Weiss, 1995; Mayall, 1996; Clarke and Herbst, 1997; Wesley, 1997; Moxon-Browne, 1998; Biermann and Vadset, 1999; Daniel, Hayes, and Oudraat, 1999; Jett, 1999; Walter and Snyder, 1999; Cousens, Kumar, and Wermester, 2000; Hillen, 2000; Boulden, 2001; Fleitz, 2002; Hawk, 2002; Cassidy, 2004; Whitworth, 2004; Berdal, 2005a; and Crocker, Hampson, and Aall, 2005.

war context of the interventions, the interesting question is not why the UN fails, but why it succeeds. Failure is to be expected. If we define failure as a continuation or worsening of the internal conflict, then failure is the status quo, when the UN enters a civil war.[5] If the status quo continues, then the UN, by almost any measure, fails. Failure can be caused by a variety of factors: the warring parties simply do not want to stop fighting and have the means to continue to fight; the major powers at the UN do not provide adequate funds or staff for the peacekeeping operation to function; or the UN is beset by internal rivalries and bureaucratic meltdowns. Success in civil war peacekeeping is unexpected and difficult because it involves external, multilateral actors who attempt purposefully to alter the actions of leaders and peoples in states emerging from war, as well as to restructure the institutions that enabled the outbreak of civil war. Moreover, as I develop below, there have been significant, surprising, but understudied successes in over half of the multidimensional operations.

While the lack of attention to success is reason enough to justify an additional study, another important factor is that the peacekeeping literature is largely descriptive. Most studies are not explicit about the reasons for choosing cases, establishing baselines for case comparisons, hypothesis testing, or categorizing and comparing causes.[6] Many studies have eschewed social science methods in part because, until recently, there simply have not been very many instances of UN peacekeeping in civil wars, rendering large-n statistical studies difficult to construct. But at the same time, even qualitative case studies have tended not to draw on important comparative case study methods.

There have, however, been many valuable contributions in the peacekeeping literature that advance our understanding of certain concepts (especially "first-generation peacekeeping" versus other types of peace operations), describe highly complex processes, suggest tentative hypotheses, offer "lessons to be learned" for both policymakers and warring factions, and examine specific relationships between, for example, the UN and some of its member states.[7]

---

[5] Peacekeepers are also often sent to the difficult cases, rather than the easier ones. See Fortna, 2004a, p. 281.

[6] These comments do not apply to the civil war termination literature, which I address below under the subheading "situational difficulty."

[7] "First-generation" peacekeeping refers to missions where peacekeepers are interposed between warring states and observe cease-fires between the states; first-generation, or "traditional peacekeeping" missions were the most common form of peacekeeping before the end of the Cold War. On traditional peacekeeping, see Burns, 1963; Claude, 1967; Rikhye, 1984; and James, 1990. The most significant other type of peacekeeping is "multidimensional peacekeeping" in civil wars. While some would quibble about different definitions and the evolution of different types within this category, I would argue that the most important distinction in UN peacekeeping is simply between the traditional military observer operations *between* states, and the more complex operations *within* states, which sometimes may include the important component of a transitional authority. On the definitions and different "generations," see Woodhouse and Ramsbotham, 2000; Thakur and Schnabel,

Some of the recent literature has focused on more general, theoretical issues in peacekeeping, such as the roles of psychology, norms, and culture.[8] There is also an important emerging literature on the issues of administrative control and military occupation.[9] Some of the basic substantive debates concern whether the consent of the parties is necessary, and the appropriate uses of force.[10] I contend that consent is necessary for success in multidimensional peacekeeping, as elaborated below, but that the capacity to use force should continue to be developed outside of the institutions of the UN, as I address in the conclusion of the book.

Case selection

In the post-Cold War history of UN peacekeeping, there have been thirty-five UN sponsored peacekeeping operations in civil wars.[11] While each operation has unique traits, those that are the most multidimensional should be considered as a group because they all enjoy an underlying base of Security Council support in having the UN, as opposed to regional organizations, or single states, intervene to try to end the civil crises.[12] The multidimensional

---

2002; Last, 2003; and Chesterman, 2004. On the processes of peacebuilding, peacemaking, and intervention, see Galtung, 1976; Fetherston, 1994; Brown, 1996; Last, 1997; Zartman and Rasmussen, 1997; Otunnu and Doyle, 1998; von Hippel, 2000; Woodhouse and Ramsbotham, 2000; and Paris, 2004. On relations between the UN and specific member states, see Coate, 1994; Jockel, 1994; Ruggie, 1994; Morrison and Kiras, 1996; Coulon, 1998; MacKinnon, 2000; Dobbins, 2004; Orr, 2004; and Perito 2004. On lessons learned, see, for example, Durch, 1996; Biermann and Vadset, 1999; Byman, 2002; and Goulding, 2003.

[8] See Britt and Adler, 2003; Callaghan and Schonborn, 2004; Whitworth, 2004; and Rousseau, 2005.

[9] See Bhatia, 2003; Chesterman, 2004; Fearon and Laitin, 2004; Marten, 2004; and Edelstein, 2005.

[10] On consent, see Ratner, 1995; and Daniel, Hayes, and Oudraat, 1999. On the use of force, see Pugh, 1996; von Hippel, 2000; and Findlay, 2003. On the issues of "when to intervene" and "ripeness," see Zartman, 1985 and 1995, and works on "preventive deployment" by Schnabel, 2002; and Sokalski, 2003.

[11] See Appendix I. There have also been some non-UN missions conducted by regional organizations such as NATO or ECOMOG, or single-state missions conducted by the United States or France, but these are not numerous and thus it is difficult to trace learning or lack thereof, especially *between* the operations.

[12] The group of multidimensional operations includes both those with and without the official title of transitional administration. Even the operations that did not have formal transitional authority were extremely intrusive (as in the cases of Mozambique or Liberia), while some operations that had the formal title of transitional administration (as in Cambodia) proved to be comparatively less deep in administrative capacity. All the missions studied here engaged in a very similar, large set of tasks, and thus can be compared as one group.

operations are also important to study, since they reflect the range of actions and capabilities that the UN has tried to develop over time. This helps us to understand which tasks the UN has been more, or less, effective at developing. Moreover one of the main positive aspects of multidimensional operations is their potential for integrating the many elements involved in ending highly complex civil wars.[13]

Ten of the thirty-five total post-Cold War operations in civil wars were highly complex in nature and were completed as of 2005, making a comparative evaluation of success and failure possible.[14] Of those ten, six were largely successful – Namibia (UNTAG), El Salvador (ONUSAL), Cambodia (UNTAC, which is a mixed success), Mozambique (ONUMOZ), Eastern Slavonia, Croatia (UNTAES), and East Timor/Timor-Leste (UNTAET). The high number of successful cases is surprising, even for peacekeeping experts, since most often the objects of analytic study and media attention are the four major cases of failure in Somalia (UNOSOM II), Rwanda (UNAMIR), Bosnia (UNPROFOR), and to a lesser extent Angola (UNAVEM II). This book demonstrates that the public and scholarly perception of constant failure in UN multidimensional peacekeeping is incorrect and seeks to shed light on the sources of success.

While the book focuses on the completed cases, there are also some very interesting and important newer cases of multidimensional peacekeeping underway, and the progress of these missions can be evaluated in light of what we have learned from the older cases. Large UN peacekeeping operations in Sierra Leone, the Democratic Republic of the Congo, and Kosovo all began in 1999. Most recently, the UN has embarked on another wave of multidimensional peacekeeping operations beginning in late 2003 through the summer of 2004, in Liberia, Côte d'Ivoire, Burundi, and Haiti. These two more recent waves of operations are explored as a group in Chapter 9, where the main findings of the book, concerning the sources of success and failure, are applied to the newer complex missions. In all cases, the factors of first-level learning, Security Council interests, and situational difficulty appear to be determining the outcomes, and learning – or lack thereof – remains an important and decisive factor. But how, more specifically, do we evaluate success?

---

[13] Dennis Jett argues that failure is caused by the over-ambitiousness or complexity of UN peacekeeping missions; see Jett, 1999, p. 6. While this may be true for some cases, civil wars have many different types of causes and consequences, and in order to end such wars, it has often been necessary to expand the scope of peacekeeping operations. As I demonstrate over the course of the book, the increase in operational complexity has in several cases increased the long-term chances of success in ending the civil war and creating a positive peace.

[14] I have excluded the operations in Haiti from a full-chapter analysis, since the conflict in Haiti has not been categorized as a civil war. I do, however, explore the most recent multidimensional peacekeeping operation in Haiti in Chapter 9, since its mandate is so similar to the other recent operations, even if the situation is somewhat different.

Measuring success and failure

Measurements of success in peacekeeping vary significantly. Many authors bemoan "difficult to apply" standards, and that "there are no easy answers" to the question of how minimalist or comprehensive measurements should be.[15] The difficulty in coming up with one set of standards is rooted in two problems: first, the problem of trying to devise a measure of peacekeeping success that includes both the interstate (traditional) and intrastate (often multidimensional) operations; and second, the extent to which phenomena outside the direct influence of the peacekeeping operation should be incorporated in the measures.

In looking to the first problem, interstate and intrastate wars are fundamentally different in nature, thus the ways in which the two types of wars end should be evaluated differently. In wars between states, while international negotiators might seek some formal agreement to help prevent the recurrence of war, there is absolutely no need to incorporate members from the warring factions into the new state, or to build institutions to ensure that domestic disputes do not re-escalate into violence. In intrastate wars, domestic institution-building is precisely what needs to happen if there is to be a stable, negotiated ending, rather than the total defeat of one side.

In terms of other scholars' measures of success, probably the most often cited are Paul Diehl's two measures of "limitation of armed conflict" and "resolution of the underlying conflict." But Diehl defines his indicators only in terms of *inter*state, traditional peacekeeping, thus questions of, for example, disarmament, power-sharing, and post-civil war state institution-building are overlooked. Also, as Charles King argues, the nature of the "underlying conflict" often changes over time so that "the factors that ignite wars are not the same as the forces that keep them going."[16] Moreover, the measures assess primarily the performance of the warring parties, and while this is of course important, it leaves out an evaluation of the third-party involvement.[17]

Turning to the second problem, should peacekeeping operations be held responsible for events that they do not directly control? Roland Paris argues in favor of a very high standard of success: stable and lasting peace supported by market democracy.[18] John Burton sets a similarly high standard for the construction of conflict resolution institutions that should be both permanent and robust.[19] A. Betts Fetherston and Robert Johansen argue on behalf of broad criteria for evaluation such as "world peace, justice, and the reduction of human suffering."[20] And Counsens, Kumar, and Wermester set goals for a self-enforcing cease-fire and peace, democracy, justice, and equity.[21]

---

[15] See, for example, Durch, 1996, p. 17; Hampson, 1996, p. 9; and Durch in Druckman and Stern, 1997, p. 154.

[16] King, 2005, p. 269.   [17] Diehl, 1994, pp. 33-40; and Johansen, 1994.

[18] Paris, 2004, Chapter 3.   [19] Burton, 1987 and 1990.

[20] Druckman and Stern, 1997, p. 152.   [21] Counsens, Kumar, and Wermester, 2000, p. 11.

Stephen Stedman and George Downs have suggested more minimalist, general measures of success including the following elements: (1) whether the violence ended, and (2) whether the peacekeeping operation exited the country in a manner such that the cease-fire was "self-enforcing."[22] But similar to the maximalist standards cited above, these measures potentially miss many of the results that arise from purposeful third-party action. Stedman and others argue that mandates vary from one operation to another, and thus that they do not amount to an objective standard for comparison.[23]

While it is true that mandates vary with each operation, and that at times certain provisions may appear open to different interpretations, the mandates tend to be written in fairly comprehensible language. Moreover, for the UN's multidimensional cases, the mandates outline many similar or even identical tasks. The mandates contain phrases such as "cease-fire observance," "civilian policing," and "elections monitoring" with little variation. While the basic meaning of the words is clear, the specific interpretation, methods of implementation, and the amount of resources necessary to fulfill the tasks varies.

In order to capture both the results of UN action as well as very important phenomena that might lie beyond the UN's direct control, I measure success in two simple but comprehensive ways. First, I examine success or failure in mandate implementation for the various tasks assigned to the mission. For each case, I compare the UN Secretariat's mandate, as expressed in peace accords and Security Council resolutions, with the Secretariat operation's interpretation and fulfillment of the mandate. It is not reasonable to expect that peacekeeping operations would be able to resolve civil crises beyond the standards set by the peace accords or Security Council resolutions, even though at times this has occurred. Success in mandate implementation is the most relevant and equitable standard to which the UN can be held, even if we might wish at times that standards set by the often hard-won, negotiated accords and Security Council resolutions were higher.

My second method of evaluation involves a broader assessment of the state of the country after completion of the UN intervention. This measure also takes into account the fact that sometimes the UN might fulfill its mandate, even though the conflict has not ended in a positive peace.[24] The evaluation incorporates some of the maximalist standards of institution-building and positive peace but does not go so far as to say that all missions that do not result in just, stable, market democracies are failures. Using the method of "structured focused comparison," I ask a series of questions for each case that explore the extent to which institutions that the UN attempted to monitor, reform, or create

---

[22] Downs and Stedman, 2002, p. 50.

[23] See Downs and Stedman, 2002, pp. 45-46; and Diehl's comments in Druckman and Stern, 1997, p. 152.

[24] Positive peace includes such factors as "human rights, economic fairness and opportunity, democratization, and environmental sustainability." See Barash, 2000, p. 129.

continued to function after UN guidance was withdrawn.[25] While the continued functioning or non-functioning of the institutions is beyond the UN's direct control after it has departed the country, local institutional capacity may result as a legacy of UN involvement, and it is therefore important to explore this dimension as well.[26]

The sources of success and failure

Once measures of outcomes are established, it is possible to study the causes of success and failure. There are generally three lines of argument presented in the peacekeeping literature.[27] First, many contend that situational factors within the conflict – mainly the will of the warring parties to stop fighting – determine the ease with which the war ends, regardless of what the UN does or does not do. Second, some claim that outcomes are the direct result of conflict or consensus in Security Council interest or "political will." Third, others argue that when the three rules of peacekeeping – consent, impartiality, and limited force – are followed, then missions are more successful.

Table 1 presents different hypotheses about the causes of success along the top row, and a list of the ten most multidimensional, completed cases in the far left column. The cases are divided into roughly two types, more successful and less successful, as indicated in the far right column. An unceremonious glance at the table quickly leads to the conclusion that none of the most common arguments – Security Council interest consensus/intensity, situational difficulty, or peacekeeping rules – holds up on its own for all of the cases. I argue that favorable situational factors (most importantly the consent of the parties), along with consensual but only moderately intense Security Council interest are both necessary but not sufficient conditions for success. In addition, I argue that a third, often unexplored, condition for success is first-level organizational learning in the UN Secretariat. Jointly, the three conditions are sufficient cause for the outcome of success, or if one or more of the conditions is not met, failure.

The situational difficulty

Many argue that the success or failure of a peacekeeping mission is the direct result of the "situational difficulty" of the civil war. "Situational difficulty" usually refers to various internal characteristics of the civil war that contribute

---

[25] This procedure was developed by Alexander George. See Appendix II, A for a list of the specific questions.

[26] Note that in Chapter 9, which examines the ongoing missions, this measure is not applied since the operations are still underway.

[27] Often these arguments are not elaborated separately, but listed together without being systematically explored to see how they link to, or cause, one another.

Table 1 *Mandate implementation: potential causes of success and failure*

Country (Dates)	Situational difficulty of civil war (10 easy, 1 difficult)	Security Council interest consensus	Security Council interest intensity	Peacekeeping rules followed (limited force, impartiality, consent)	Organizational learning (first level)	Outcome (of mandate implementation)
Namibia (4/89–5/90)	6	Usually	Moderate	Yes	Yes	Success
El Salvador (7/91–4/95)	7.5	Yes	Moderate	Yes	Yes	Success
Cambodia (2/92–9/93)	4	Usually	Moderate	Yes	Yes	Mixed Success
Mozambique (12/92–12/94)	7	Yes	Moderate	Yes	Yes	Success
Eastern Slavonia (1/96–1/97)	8.5	Usually	Moderate	No	Yes	Success
East Timor (10/99–5/02)	5	Yes	Moderate	Yes	Yes	Success
Angola (2/95–6/97)	6.5	Yes	Low/Moderate*	Yes	Some	Failure
Somalia (5/93–5/95)	3.5	Usually/No	High	No	No	Failure
Bosnia (2/92–5/95–12/95)	3.5	Usually/No	High	No	No	Failure
Rwanda (10/93–5/96)	6.5	Usually/No	Moderate*	Yes	No	Failure

to both the fueling and the eventual ending of the war. The most important characteristics, often cited in the literature, are the consent of the warring factions for the UN's operation, a detailed peace agreement signed by all sides, and the support or lack thereof from regional or neighboring (non-Security Council) states.[28] Of these factors, as will become clear in the following chapters, the consent of the warring parties appears to be the most decisive.[29] Other factors are also important; for example, a mutually hurting stalemate is often cited in the conflict resolution literature for determining when a conflict is "ripe" for resolution.[30] The number of fatalities and the duration of the war have been tested frequently in the civil war termination literature to see whether high or low scores tend to help or hinder the endings of civil wars; generally speaking, the fewer the fatalities and the less time a war endures, the easier it is to end it.[31] Finally, the state of the country's infrastructure is not often cited as a facilitating or detracting characteristic of ending civil wars. However, during my interviews with peacekeepers in the field, they often suggested that this factor is very important for determining how easy or difficult it is for a peacekeeping operation to function well.[32]

When one compares the overall measures of the situational difficulty, it becomes clear that scores and outcomes are uncorrelated.[33] For example, Namibia, a success by any measure, has a low situational difficulty score (meaning that it looked comparatively difficult to end, before the start of the operation), while Angola and Rwanda both had high scores, or looked fairly easy to end successfully, but both ended in failure.[34] I do not infer from these measures that situational characteristics are therefore insignificant for ending civil wars. Instead, I argue that certain permissive situational factors – especially the consent of the warring parties for the peacekeeping mission, the existence of a detailed peace agreement signed by all sides, and the support of regional powers – are essential components of this necessary but not sufficient factor

---

[28] See, for example, Marnika, 1996; Hillen, 1998, p. 176; Jablonsky and McCallum, 1999; Mersiades, 2005; and Whitfield, forthcoming.
[29] Werner and Yuen, 2005.
[30] On this point, see studies by Zartman, 1985 and 1995; and Kleiboer, 1994.
[31] See Bercovitch and Langley, 1993; Mason and Fett, 1996; and Fortna, 2004b. Note that Doyle and Sambanis have found inconclusive evidence that the longer a civil war endures, the more difficult it is to end. See Doyle and Sambanis, 2000, p. 787. However, most statistical studies argue that, quite simply, the longer a war goes on, the longer it goes on.
[32] There has also been some debate about whether ethnic, ideological, or resource-based civil wars are easier or more difficult to end in negotiated settlements. The results have been inconclusive, therefore, I have excluded this indicator. See Sambanis, 2001; Byman, 2002; Bercovitch and De Rouen, 2005; Collier and Hoeffler, 2005; and Humphreys, 2005.
[33] Appendix II presents a numerical summary of the different indicators, and the total score for each case, measured before the beginning of the UN peacekeeping operation.
[34] Several of the interview respondents noted that Angola and Rwanda appeared, before the start, to be "easy" operations, and thus the great powers did not think it necessary to devote significant resources to them.

for achieving success in multidimensional peacekeeping. Above all, if consent is not present at the outset of the operation, or if it diminishes after the mission begins, it must be created or re-created in order for the operation to succeed.

Recent findings in the civil war termination literature refute the "situational" argument in a different manner. They conclude that, in looking at a large number of civil wars in history, the situational specifics of a civil war are outweighed by the presence, or absence, of an external intervener. In other words, regardless of the circumstances of the civil war, this type of conflict tends to end in negotiated, stable settlements when there are third-party guarantees or intervention.[35] However, all of the cases that I address in this book include third-party intervention on the part of the United Nations, but with differing results.

The UN did not behave exactly the same way in each case, in part because of the differing circumstances of the civil wars. The numerical results of the situational difficulty, while fairly comprehensive, do not offer enough of a contextual, descriptive picture of the civil wars. Therefore, in the empirical chapters, I investigate the environment that the organization sought to influence by asking the same set of questions for each case. The questions concern the sources and history of the conflict, whether there was consent for the multidimensional peacekeeping operations, and other important factors such as the length of the conflict, the number of people killed, the number of refugees, and the state of the economy and infrastructure (see Appendix II, B). These questions are the most critical to answer in order to understand how difficult the UN thought the civil war would be to end through the mechanism of multidimensional peacekeeping, before the start of the operation.

Security Council interests

The other most often-encountered argument about how to achieve success in UN peacekeeping in civil wars is based on the conventional wisdom that there must be strong consensual support or "political will" among the five permanent members of the Security Council.[36] This argument is founded in part on the neorealist assumption that the UN is merely a venue for powerful states to achieve their goals in the international political arena. It is also found in the

---

[35] See, for example, Stedman, 1991; Licklider, 1993; Hampson, 1996; Doyle and Sambanis, 2000; and Walter, 2002. Fortna, 2004b focuses on peace agreements between states, but the findings support similar conclusions in the civil war termination literature, namely, that the content of peace agreements and outside assistance in constructing and maintaining those agreements have a greater influence on the durability of peace than situational factors in the war.

[36] For example, "political will" is mentioned nine times in former UN Secretary-General Boutros Boutros-Ghali's An Agenda for Peace and eight times in its Supplement. Many also discuss the necessity of great power consensus. See, for example, Oudraat, 1996; Biermann and Vadset, 1999, p. 363; and Malone, 2004. The five permanent members of the UN Security Council are China, France, Russia, the United Kingdom and the United States.

somewhat modified neoliberal school that the UN is merely an institutionalized bargaining forum and coordinating body.[37]

The actions and will of the Security Council are undoubtedly important for peacekeeping outcomes, even though they are moderated and influenced in interesting ways by situational factors and the actions of the UN Secretariat. I therefore devote a significant portion of each case study chapter to assess the degree of Security Council interest. I explore Security Council interest along two dimensions – "consensus" and "intensity." While all peacekeeping operations enjoyed a certain minimal level of consensual interest in having the UN engage in multidimensional peacekeeping, they did not all receive similarly strong or *intense* expressions of interest. In order to capture and describe Security Council *consensus*, I answer a series of questions about the nature of the Security Council debates, whether the resolutions were unanimous, and whether positions or interests changed during the peace negotiations or during the implementation period.[38]

There are basically three answers to whether there was Security Council consensus: "yes," "usually," and "no." If there were few debates, general agreement over the nature of the problem, unanimous votes on resolutions, and no significant changes in interests over the course of implementation, then we can say that "yes," there was a consensus of Council interest in the operation. If there were somewhat acrimonious debates, and some use of abstentions or the rare veto, but consensus for the most part, we can say that there was "usually" consensus. If, however, there were frequent, caustic debates with strong dissenting opinions, we can say that there was "no" consensus.

While consensus is one important dimension of Security Council interest, the depth or intensity of interest is also crucial to examine. In order to explore the intensity of Security Council interest, I count the number of resolutions and statements concerning each mission,[39] investigate whether there were other important items on the Security Council agenda at the time (dividing the Council's attention), and consider whether the Security Council mandates differed from the Secretary-General's mandate suggestions, and whether the Security Council / General Assembly provided the means requested by the Secretary-General for mandate implementation.

We can think of Security Council interest intensity in terms of being "high," "moderate," or "low." Security Council interest intensity is "high" when the

---

[37] While sometimes these assumptions are empirically justified, I argue in the concluding chapter that, increasingly, the UN Secretariat is behaving like an international actor in its own right.

[38] See Appendix II, C and D for the lists of questions. Note that these questions are of a purely descriptive nature. In other words, they do not explore all of the possible causal reasons for *why* the Security Council members voted the way they did, but rather *how* the great powers behaved and voted in the Council.

[39] I count this number and compare it with the extent of resources supplied, because sometimes the Security Council has made statements to the press in inverse proportion to the amount of material support granted to the operations.

Council meets frequently on the matter (as manifest in many resolutions and statements), when most of the means requested are provided, and when it alters mandates suggested to it by the Secretary-General.[40] Intensity can be said to be "moderate" when there is a combination of few resolutions with adequate funding. We can add a "*" to "moderate" interest intensity for the reverse: many resolutions but low funding levels. In both cases, the Council usually heeds the suggestions of the Secretary-General's office. When the Security Council meets rarely to discuss the matter, and few resources are provided, we can say that interest intensity is "low."

As demonstrated over the course of this book, the evidence from both the successful and the unsuccessful cases shows that Security Council consensus enables the UN operations to function but does not directly determine peace-keeping outcomes. Moreover, very high and very low levels of Security Council interest intensity tend to undermine the Secretariat's ability to implement mandates successfully. Close examination of all of the cases demonstrates that moderate levels of Security Council interest intensity, supported by consensus, are necessary but not sufficient conditions for success.

The "rules" of peacekeeping

Over the course of the last fifty years, beginning with the first explicitly labeled UN "peacekeeping" mission in 1956, three interrelated "rules" of peacekeeping have been established, namely, that all parties must consent to the operation, that the UN must not favor any given party, and that only a very limited use of force should be used by peacekeepers.[41] After the end of the Cold War, the UN began to move into the realm of *intra*state conflicts, and the new endeavors of peacekeeping, peacebuilding, and peace-enforcement were defined and delineated in former Secretary-General Boutros Boutros-Ghali's *An Agenda for Peace* in 1992. Peace-enforcement operations, authorized under Chapter VII of the UN Charter, opened the door to the UN's use of force in civil wars, which is often incompatible with the other rules of impartiality and consent.[42]

---

[40] Mandates for the implementation of peace agreements are often researched and written by members of the Secretariat in the name of the Secretary-General, and then amended and issued by the Security Council. When the Council ignores or significantly alters the suggestions made by the Secretary-General, this indicates that Council members have intense interests in the problem. In most of the successful cases, the Council simply heeds the Secretary-General's suggestions.

[41] The first official UN peacekeeping operation was the UN Emergency Force, dispatched to the Sinai peninsula following the Suez Crisis of 1956 (see Urquhart, 1987), although the UN Truce Supervision Organization, which has been monitoring the borders of Israel since 1948, was deemed the first UN peacekeeping mission some years after its deployment.

[42] A Chapter VI peacekeeping mandate requires that force be used only in self-defense, reliance on the host country for infrastructure support, and the fielding of a broad-based, neutral, international peacekeeping force that behaves in a generally pacific and conciliatory manner toward the parties to the conflict and toward the civilian population.

But a quick comparison of the operations and their success rates reveals that there is no simple, single-variable pattern that would lead us to believe that adherence to the rules of traditional peacekeeping translates into successful operations in civil wars. In looking to the "Peacekeeping rules" column on Table 1, we see that sometimes the rules in these intrastate crises were followed, while at other times they were not. Adherence to the rules (with the exception of "consent") does not appear to have a direct effect on the eventual outcome. However, I make the case in the concluding chapter that the UN ought not to be in the business of using force in order to maintain its legitimacy as a peacekeeping authority in international relations.

Organizational learning

The final, often-overlooked, factor for success is the ability of the UN Secretariat operations to learn during the process of implementing peacekeeping mandates. Table 1 shows that, of all the factors, organizational learning coincides most consistently with successful outcomes. The following chapters in this book attempt to demonstrate that this is not merely a coincidental, but rather a causal relationship. I explore two levels of organizational learning, with a focus on the "first level." Second-level learning refers to learning at UN headquarters, *in between* peacekeeping missions, while first-level organizational learning concerns learning *within* each peacekeeping operation, once it has been established in the post-civil war environment.

My argument about organizational learning, and indeed this study in general, is grounded in the theoretical tradition in international relations that recognizes the social construction of reality.[43] Constructivists generally argue that actors and structures are mutually constitutive, in contrast to neorealist and neoliberal assumptions that structures define actors' behavior.[44] Unfortunately, however, many theorists in the constructivist tradition eschew studies that look to policy results. Nevertheless, I am primarily concerned with outcomes that arise as a result of UN peacekeeping actions and policies. I study these outcomes while recognizing that leaders and members of the UN bureaucracy sometimes

In contrast, in a Chapter VII mandate, often referred to as "peace-enforcement," the UN mission views one or more of the parties to the conflict as adversaries. The commanders must take strategic initiatives to use force to secure positions; the mission cannot always rely on the support of the host country; and there must be a tight military command (i.e., not widely multinational) that is prepared for warlike battle.

[43] See, for example, E. Haas, 1990; P. Haas, 1992; Finnemore, 1996; Ruggie, 1998; and Wendt, 1999. As Ruggie (1998, p. 881) explains, the neoclassical constructivist school generally draws on pragmatic epistemological traditions, is concerned with pluralistic, social scientific causality, but recognizes that "insights will be temporary and unstable."

[44] See neorealist works by Waltz, 1979; Wohlforth, 2003; and Mearsheimer, 2003. For the basics of neoliberalism, see Keohane, 1984; Martin, 1992; Baldwin, 1993; and Simmons, 1994.

change their minds, policies, and organizational operations in response to new understandings of how to improve peacekeeping operations to end civil wars.[45]

First-level learning is defined here as *increasing ability to engage in multidimensional peacekeeping*. This definition has its roots in both the cognitive and the efficiency schools of the study of organizational change, and rejects arguments that equate learning with increasing complexity of thought. Similar to the cognitivist school, this approach begins with individual-level learning, mainly on the part of the Special Representative of the Secretary-General and his or her staff, and the ways in which experience in the field enables representatives of the UN to change organizational structures on the ground.[46] Changes in organizational structure in turn affect the actors in the organization, and, more importantly, actors and structures in the post-civil war environment. Organizational learning is in a sense a metaphor for individual learning, since individual learning is manifest as organizational change.[47] But unlike cognitivisits, and similar to efficiency-type explanations, the results of cognitive change are only understood to be learning if they enable the organization to engage better with its environment.[48] Both the cognitive and the complexity schools eschew improving ability as a component of learning.[49] However, I contend that improving ability must be linked to a definition of learning, if the organization in question purports to be goal-oriented. Without this link, if learning is merely a change in beliefs that results from experience or study (in the cognitive view), or increasing complexity of beliefs (in the complexity school), then the outcomes of this learning as reflected in organizational structures could be debilitating for the organization, leading to organizational dysfunction.

In the field during a peacekeeping mission, members of the organization learn innumerable daily lessons.[50] When aggregated, these lessons can amount to members of the Secretariat operation's learning *how* to implement the mandate.[51] This learning is then considered to be organizational learning when new

---

[45] Sometimes, of course, organizational change is misinformed, inappropriate, or otherwise inhibited, contributing to "organizational dysfunction," as discussed below.

[46] On the cognitive school, see George, 1979, p. 98; Tetlock and McGuire, 1985; Breslauer and Tetlock, 1991, p. 27; and Levy, 1994, p. 294.

[47] On this point, see Argyris and Schon, 1996, pp. 9-28.

[48] On efficiency, see Bennett, 1999, p. 83.

[49] On complexity, see Breslauer and Tetlock, 1991, pp. 32–34.

[50] George Breslauer and Philip Tetlock (1991, p. 6) make the apt distinction between "learning that" and "learning how." For example, one can learn "that" a stove is hot, but "how" to cook.

[51] In this book, the UN is treated as a non-unified actor, in that the major relevant components – the UN Security Council, and the UN Secretariat (specifically, its Department of Peacekeeping Operations) – are treated separately. However, from the perspective of the warring parties, the effects of the UN are generally perceived as if the UN were a unified actor.

ideas are manifest as change in organizational procedures, routines, strategies, structures, and goals.

This view of organizational learning, in contrast to the efficiency literature, focuses on the *process* of learning, or increasing ability; learning is not determined by the final outcome of the peacekeeping operation. The outcome of operations – be it success or failure – is considered to be separate from the independent variable of organizational learning.[52] In other words, it is possible that a peacekeeping operation could learn in the field, according to my definition, but not be a success in terms of mandate implementation due to other factors – inadequate Security Council interest, for example.

There are four basic indicators of first-level organizational learning. These consist of the organization's ability to (1) gather and analyze information; (2) coordinate among the different divisions of the peacekeeping mission; (3) engage the organization with its post-civil war environment; and (4) exercise leadership in such a way that the organization commands authority from all actors, even during crises.[53] Table 2 presents a summary of the preconditions indicating possible learning, as well as indicators of learning, or its opposite, organizational dysfunction. The preconditions represent structures that must be in place before the organization can engage in the learning process. Learning is possible if the preconditions are present, but the presence of these conditions does not ensure that learning will occur. I address each indicator below.

First, widespread mechanisms for gathering information are one of the most important preconditions for learning, while sound analysis of that information indicates actual learning. "Technical information" includes specific facts about, for example, numbers and types of potential voters, regions where mines are, groups of police who need retraining, where troops are, where refugees are, how many there are, and who is fighting whom. The UN Secretariat gathers technical information from different sources available to it, for example, from its ground operations, the specialized agencies, embassies, international and local NGOs, and local activists and newspapers. Extensive mechanisms for gathering and sharing technical information indicate possible learning; few mechanisms indicate dysfunction.

Once the basic information is gathered, it is used to analyze and define problems. Problem definition entails a political judgment about the *causes* of the technical information or, in other words, an evaluation of the motivations

---

[52] To continue the cooking metaphor, when one is learning how to cook, there could be certain indicators of increasing cooking ability that do not derive from the final outcome. Even after learning how to cook, not every dish would turn out to be fabulous, possibly due to factors beyond the cook's control.

[53] Inspiration for this descriptive model comes from Haas, 1990. This section also builds on the work of many scholars, for example, Deutsch, 1963; Allison, 1972; Simon, 1983; Etheredge, 1985; March, 1988; Leeuw, Rist, and Sonnichsen, 1994; Levy, 1994; Argyris and Schon, 1996; and Bennett, 1999.

Table 2 *Indicators of first-level organizational learning*

	Information	Coordination	Organizational engagement with environment	Leadership
Preconditions indicating possible learning	Mechanisms in place to gather technical information from a wide variety of sources	Peacekeeping operation takes charge of international organization coordination	Low level of headquarters engagement with daily decision-making; wide distribution of staff in field	Mission leadership is appointed early in the negotiation process and is familiar with the conflict
Indicators of learning	Problem definitions/political judgments based on technical information and derived from the field	Task prioritization is incrementally re-evaluated and re-aligned	Organizational profile tends toward integration with environment; organization is able to communicate intentions to local population	Mandate is interpreted as a "baseline"; leader of UN operations is able to alter incrementally the goals of warring elites; leader learns how to manage crises

and goals that create the factual evidence – for example, *why* parties are fighting, and what the changing goals are of the fighting organizations. Increasingly consensual definitions of problems based on information that comes directly from the field indicates learning; problem definitions that derive primarily from higher-level political discussions at UN headquarters indicate organizational dysfunction.

Second, frequent coordination meetings that include the various divisions of the UN peacekeeping operation, UN agencies in the field, and governmental and nongovernmental organizations are a precondition for learning. Learning occurs when the UN mission is the central coordinator of all (or at least most) related operations in the field and is able to rank and re-rank priorities based on field-level problem definitions. Conversely, organizational dysfunction results when different parts of the UN or other organizations are running parallel, hierarchical operations with divergent, or uncoordinated mandates and goals.

Third, in terms of organizational engagement with the environment, a wide distribution of UN staff in the field, among the local population, is a precondition for learning. Learning itself is indicated by two primary factors: the profile of the organization, and the operation's ability to disseminate information. The profile of the organization in the host country can range from "colonial" to "integrative." A colonial profile is one where staff stay on compounds, do not interact with locals, are heavily armed, and senior UN representatives are often involved in the daily decision-making (or micromanagement) of the UN operation. In contrast, an integrative organization engages actively with the local population, at lower, middle, and elite levels of society.[54] A learning organization will tend toward the integrative end of the continuum, whereas a dysfunctional organization often maintains a colonial profile. Another important aspect of organizational engagement with the environment involves the UN's ability to communicate its intentions to the local population, which indicates learning. The absence of an active UN information campaign indicates dysfunction.

The fourth and final indicator of learning relates to leadership. Preconditions for learning include the early engagement of the peacekeeping mission's leaders (preferably during the negotiation period), their familiarity with the civil war, and their prompt arrival in the field at the time of the cease-fire. Learning itself is indicated in three areas: mandate interpretation, altering the goals of the warring parties, and crisis management. In terms of *mandate interpretation*, when the Secretary-General's Special Representative of a peacekeeping mission interprets his or her mandate as a minimal plan of action, or "baseline," this is an indicator of organizational learning. Conversely, when the mandate is viewed as a "ceiling," or a constricting, inflexible guideline, the operation is not in a learning mode. Learning is also indicated when the leader(s) of the peacekeeping operation are able to *alter the goals* of the warring parties through

[54] Lederach, 1997, p. 39.

careful exercise of influence and authority, introducing new ideas in order to bridge political positions and unite interests. Altering goals often entails fostering the consent of the parties to allow the UN to intervene. A lack of ability to alter the goals of the contending sides incrementally indicates organizational dysfunction. Finally, each division of every peacekeeping mission will experience one or more important *crises*. Leaders of a learning organization are able to defuse the crises and alter operations in light of a new understanding of the demands of ending the civil war. In contrast, when several subdivisions of the peacekeeping operation are overrun by crisis, and operations cease to function, these clearly indicate organizational dysfunction.

The descriptive indicators that I present above and summarize in Table 2 apply only to the "first level" of organizational learning. In other words, they refer to each distinct operation, while it is in progress. This type of organizational learning is not based on learning discrete, concrete "rules of the game," because the game is constantly changing.[55] When the UN learns on the ground, it acquires the ability to adapt to the changing contexts of civil wars – the organization engages with its environment and invents mechanisms to understand it. Sometimes the organization may exhibit partial learning, when, for example, one or more of the components of learning are fulfilled, but not all four.

In sum, in the cases of successful mandate implementation, the military and civilian components had the ability to gather technical information, analyze and evaluate combatants' motives, coordinate the different international operations in the field, manage crises, alter the goals of the warring parties, and change the UN operations on the ground in light of new understandings of problems. At times, even when the Security Council expressed low levels of interest, and parties to the civil war were reneging on promises, the UN was able to learn, and the operations were successful at mandate implementation.

Although the descriptive model of first-level learning outlined above relates only to learning within a peacekeeping mission, I do not completely disregard comparative processes. I also examine a "second level" of learning, which is much broader, quite rare, and entails learning not within, but between missions. It begins with post-mission evaluation and organizational change at headquarters in response to evaluation. Second-level organizational learning can be defined as change in the organization's overall means, structures, and goals, in response to new understandings of problems and their causes. An important indicator of second-level learning, which also provides a link between the first and second levels, is improvement in the preconditions for first-level learning.[56]

Second-level organizational dysfunction is indicated when components of the organization are unable to define problems adequately, implement

---

[55] Again, the distinction between learning "that" and learning "how" applies.
[56] The preconditions of first-level learning are listed in Table 2.

strategies, or realize goals. An intermediate stage of less severe organizational learning, which could be called "incremental adaptation," is characterized by programs being transferred from one mission to the next regardless of the new context, and new programs or bureaucratic structures being added without adequate streamlining or questioning of the ultimate purpose of the collective endeavor.[57] In the conclusion to the book, I assess the extent to which it appears that second-level organizational learning, adaptation, and dysfunction have occurred in recent years.

Organization of the book

The core of this study is comprised of eight empirical chapters. Chapter 2 briefly explores the cases of peacekeeping failure in Somalia, Rwanda, Angola, and Bosnia. While the causes of failure are somewhat different for each case, I highlight the ways in which UN organizational dysfunction was similar across the cases. I then devote a chapter each to in-depth case studies of the six successful operations in Namibia, El Salvador, Cambodia, Mozambique, Eastern Slavonia, and East Timor/Timor-Leste (Chapters 3 through 8). Each chapter is divided into four main sections: an exploration of the situational difficulty of the civil war, an investigation of Security Council interests, an analysis of whether the UN peacekeeping operation implemented the components of its mandate and the effects of first-level learning or dysfunction, and an evaluation of the new state since the withdrawal of the UN's multidimensional peacekeeping mission. Chapter 9 explores the ongoing multidimensional missions and the mix of factors involved in shaping their potential outcomes; while there has been some first- and second-level learning in the missions, there has not been as much as one might expect, given the UN's extensive experience with this difficult type of peacekeeping. Chapter 10, the concluding chapter, recaps the basic argument that first-level organizational learning is a crucial component determining success and failure in peacekeeping operations. It also examines recent trends in peacekeeping and categorizes them in terms of second-level organizational dysfunction, incremental adaptation, and learning. I also apply my descriptive model of first-level learning or dysfunction to the current, non-UN operations in Afghanistan and Iraq, finding mainly first-level organizational dysfunction and a resulting lack of successful mandate implementation. But more generally, in terms of the overall picture of UN multidimensional peacekeeping in civil wars, my major finding is that there has been significantly more first-level organizational learning, or "learning while doing" than second-level learning between operations, and I explore the reasons for this condition.

[57] On "incremental adaptation," see Haas, 1990. On the sources of organizational dysfunction, see Gallarotti, 1991; and Barnett and Finnemore, 1999.

2

The failures: Somalia, Rwanda, Angola, Bosnia

Introduction

In Somalia, Rwanda, Angola, and Bosnia, UN multidimensional peacekeeping missions failed. For the purposes of this book, the main question for each case is whether the failure was an inevitable consequence of situational difficulties, namely, the lack of consent of the warring parties for the peacekeeping operation. Over the course of the following pages, I demonstrate that while lack of consent was undoubtedly one of the main factors driving the failures, in most of the cases, extreme Security Council interest or disinterest, combined with organizational dysfunction on the part of the UN Secretariat operation, were as important driving forces as situational factors. Moreover, often it appears that organizational dysfunction was indeed one of the main causes of failure. While organizational dysfunction itself is caused in part by the situation on the ground and by the Security Council's lack of support, or intense but not consensual interests, it is also caused in large part by internal processes that occur within the Secretariat, between clashing personalities and departments, and tensions between field offices and headquarters.

It is possible that an absence of any one of the three conditions for success can precipitate failure, but in all of the cases examined here, at least two, if not all three, conditions were not present. Although failure often has multiple causes, it is generally possible to judge which of the three sources of failure appears to be the strongest for any given case, based on evidence from the numerous assessments of the failures. I discuss each case below, with short sections devoted to the situational difficulty, the interests of the Security Council, and the lack of first-level organizational learning.

Somalia

The failed UN multidimensional peacekeeping operation in Somalia is not a particularly instructive case when trying to determine which of the three main causal factors is more important for failure, since all three clearly contributed to the failure, according to almost all assessments of the operation. First, the situation of state collapse made international intervention very difficult because there were no legitimate leaders from whom to obtain consent.[1] Moreover the person who became the center of international attention, Mohamed Farah Aideed, never consented to the UN's multidimensional operation. Second, the Security Council, led by the United States, was either too interested, and then not interested enough, in the operation. The Council at first expressed extremely high interest intensity, helping to appropriate over $2 billion to the effort. But after the deaths of the American troops, the Council became extremely disinterested in talk about, or funding of, the operation. Third, the UN Secretariat operations were in a pattern of first-level organizational dysfunction from very early on and never recovered. In other words, all three factors contributed in significant ways to the failure. However, I argue that there is enough evidence to suggest that had the external actors behaved differently, it is possible that the UN could have been more successful at implementing its mandate. I briefly illustrate the role of each of the three factors below.

First, in terms of the situational difficulty, Somalia is a country made up of many different pastoral and nomadic clans, all of which share a common language (Somali), religion (Islam), and ethnic background. Under colonialism, the Somali people were divided between several different states: British Somaliland, Italian Somaliland, and French Somaliland (Djibouti); thousands of Somalis also lived and continue to live in Ethiopia and Kenya. The British and Italian Somalilands were united upon independence in 1960. After several years of struggle to form a functioning central government, Mohamed Siad Barre took the state by force in a bloodless coup, ushering in an era of severe authoritarian rule that was at first supported and armed by the Soviets. But with Soviet support of the coup in neighboring Ethiopia, Siad Barre shifted allegiances, coming to enjoy support and abundant arms from the United States. This support was used to bolster Siad Barre's attempt to conquer Ethiopian territories inhabited by Somalis during the Ogaden war of 1977–78.

The events leading up to the civil war in 1991 were complicated, as was the war itself, and this brief account offers a simplification of the state of affairs.[2] By 1990, several armed political factions (clans) within Somalia had emerged that sought to challenge Siad Barre's rule, the most powerful of which, the Hawiye Habr Gedr, was led by Aideed.[3] In January 1991, Siad Barre and his entourage fled the country after Aideed's attacks, marking a new era of inter- and intra-clan warfare. Mohamed Ali Mahdi, a businessman from the north, member of the Hawiye Abgal clan, and leader of the United Somali Congress, was "elected" president of Somalia during a peace conference in Djibouti in

---

[1] Babafemi Badejo, interview with the author, Nairobi Kenya, February 15, 1998.
[2] For example, there were at least fifteen clan factions fighting in the war, but I focus only on the two most powerful here.
[3] Duyvesteyn, 2005, p. 41.

mid-1991. But Aideed immediately challenged his leadership. Aideed saw himself as the rightful ruler of Somalia, after having driven Siad Barre from power. While there were several other important figures and clans involved in the civil war, it is crucial to recognize the importance bestowed by international actors upon these two central figures, Aideed and Ali Mahdi. It is also important to note that there is considerable disagreement in the literature on this case about the extent to which Somalia was in a state of total political chaos and Hobbesian anarchy after Siad Barre's fall. Some claim that the clans created and used the state of anarchy with the purpose of gaining greater power for themselves, while others argue that there were in essence fluid or in fact almost no centers of authority.[4] Both views have merit: at the time of international intervention in the war in Somalia, while the clan structures were undoubtedly fluid and shifting, there had emerged several leaders, two in particular, with whom the international actors sought to negotiate. These leaders in turn used the international negotiations to enhance their domestic standing and solidify their otherwise weak and shifting bases of support.

At the outset of the international interventions, Somalia was in a state of political collapse and experiencing a severe crisis of authority and legitimacy. Over 200,000 people had starved to death of famine, and between 30,000 and 50,000 civilians had been killed in fighting from November 1991 through March 1992.[5] The central infrastructure had been destroyed, and the economy was in a state of almost total breakdown. While Ali Mahdi consented to external intervention in the crisis, Aideed agreed at first, but then withdrew his consent, as I describe below in the section on the Unified Task Force (UNITAF) and the United Nations Operation in Somalia (UNOSOM).

Turning to the second factor contributing to the failure, the UN Security Council became interested in intervening in the crisis, as many have argued, in large part because the war and famine had gained significant attention from vociferous human rights organizations and the media.[6] The Council authorized three different peacekeeping operations in Somalia: UNOSOM I (April 1992–March 1993), UNITAF (December 1992–May 1993), and UNOSOM II (March 1993–May 1995). UNOSOM I was a simple, limited UN peacekeeping force; UNITAF was a US-led multinational force that had Security Council authorization; and UNOSOM II was a UN multidimensional "peace-enforcement" mission, and took over the responsibilities of both prior missions.

Between 1991 and 1995 there were numerous attempts to convene peace talks, including by one count, seventeen national and twenty sub-national

---

[4] For the first argument, see Wesley, 1997, p. 70, and Laitin, 1999; for the second, see, for example, Hirsh and Oakley, 1995, and Lyons and Samatar, 1995, p. 7.

[5] Menkhaus, 1997, p. 55; Clarke, 1997, p. 5.

[6] On this point see, for example, Minear, Scott, and Weiss, 1996, pp. 53–57. See also Strobel, 1997.

efforts.[7] The first UN peace talks paved the way for UNOSOM I. As I describe below, other early peace talks appeared to be on the right track but were overtaken by higher-level political demands at UN headquarters, and as a result, failed.[8]

Nevertheless, sixteen of the seventeen decisions made by the Security Council between 1992 and 1994 regarding Somalia were unanimous with no abstentions.[9] The number of resolutions was high relative to other peacekeeping operations except those in Cambodia and the former Yugoslavia. The mission's budget dwarfed all others of the time: UNOSOM I and II had a combined budget of almost $2 billion. In other words, there was generally consensus of Security Council interest in the Somalia operations, and those interests, led by the United States, can be characterized as intense given the sizable budget. But the United States' interest dropped quickly after the deaths of American troops in October, as described below.

It was in 1992 that many large UN peacekeeping operations began. The UN had sent 20,000 troops to Cambodia, 12,000 to Croatia, several hundred to El Salvador, several thousand to Mozambique, and was planning to increase troop deployments for all of these operations. The war in Bosnia also began during the spring of 1992, and it eventually came to overshadow all of the other conflicts. UN member states were stretched for resources and troops in unprecedented ways.

Nevertheless, powers large and small pledged to assist the international efforts in Somalia. While none of the permanent five members of the Security Council sent troops for UNOSOM I, France and the United States did send troops to fight in UNOSOM II. In terms of interested European powers, France, Germany, Belgium, and Italy all sent troops to assist the United States with its UNITAF operation (called "Operation Restore Hope" by Americans). But, as Gérard Prunier describes, this effort was "somewhat paradoxical" in that it appeared in hindsight that the "intervention under US leadership was a case of the blind leading the blind."[10]

The United States under the Bush I administration became interested in providing humanitarian support to relieve the suffering of the Somali people in the afterglow of the successful US intervention in the Gulf War. While the US government was largely uninterested in the first UN mission, UNOSOM I, this disinterest gave way rather quickly to more intense, but contradictory interests,

---

[7] Menkhaus, 1997, p. 60.

[8] At one point, Italy, while not a member of the Security Council, sponsored its own separate peace talks with Aideed, publicly defying UN command and policy and indicating a lack of coordination within some of the negotiating efforts.

[9] On one resolution, S/RES/946, 30 September 1994, the United States abstained. This was a resolution to extend UNOSOM II's mandate for one month and to consider UN withdrawal.

[10] Prunier, 1997, p. 145.

after the crisis of Somalia became known to the American population.[11] In fact, in a highly unusual move, the United States in essence took over the UN proceedings on Somalia, writing the first draft of both the Security Council resolutions for UNITAF and UNOSOM II. The US plans for UNITAF were devised mainly at the Pentagon, with almost no input from civilian diplomatic organs. The strategy therefore, as many have argued, had no political basis or goals. The goal was merely to provide humanitarian support and exit the country within three months.

The United States has come under extreme criticism on many fronts – from academics, its own military, the media, humanitarian NGOs, African leaders, and US allies – for its dealings in Somalia. It has been criticized both for its interest and lack of interest, but in general, for overall poor leadership in the crisis.

Finally, we turn now to UN organizational dysfunction in Somalia, which resulted in mandate implementation failure. From the outset, the operation was riven by divisions between headquarters and field, and between UN and US policymakers. UNOSOM I, a simple operation designed to oversee a cease-fire and the delivery of humanitarian aid, did get off to a promising start. After the peace negotiations between Aideed and Ali Mahdi, Algerian senior diplo-mat Ambassador Mohamed Sahnoun was appointed to direct UN activities in Somalia in April 1992. From the outset, Sahnoun's strategy was to negotiate with the various clans and sub-clans; he also had the ear of Aideed, which no subse-quent negotiator would enjoy. While Sahnoun worked to build the confidence of the various factions, he was dismayed by the lax approach of the UN Sec-retariat in taking the initiative during several opportunities to establish peace, and he was angry about the flagrant abuses of some UN relief agencies; more-over, he was not silent in his criticism of the UN both on the ground and at headquarters.[12] Tension between Boutros-Ghali in New York and Sahnoun in Somalia escalated and eventually erupted. Sahnoun had worked during most of the summer of 1992 to reach an agreement between Ali Mahdi and Aideed to have 500 UN peacekeepers deployed in Somalia to protect human-itarian aid convoys. It had been exceedingly difficult to convince Aideed that the UN and its troops would remain impartial, and to gain his approval for the 500 troop deployment. As the troops deployed, Boutros-Ghali sponsored a Security Council Resolution to deploy another 3,000 troops without first consulting Sahnoun or the warring factions. The Security Council approved the measure, which infuriated Aideed and undermined Sahnoun's negotiat-ing strategy. Sahnoun was forced to resign. After this, Aideed would turn

[11] On President George H. W. Bush's "Thanksgiving Decision" to provide humanitarian relief to Somalia, see Hirsch and Oakley, 1995, p. 43; and Woods, 1997, pp. 157–58.

[12] David Stephen, interview with the author, Nairobi, February 18, 1998; and Walid Musa, interview with the author, Nairobi, February 23, 1998. See also Sahnoun, 1994.

against all UN efforts.[13] Sahnoun had developed "a special relationship with Aideed . . . the dismissal of Mr. Sahnoun . . . seems to be the turning point of the UNOSOM mission, and perhaps of the entire UN operation in Somalia."[14] While Sahnoun's general approach was to take the time to listen and try to comprehend what the parties wanted, why they wanted it, and to negotiate with them at length, his successor, Iraqi Ambassador Ismat Kittani, took the opposite approach by often seeking to impose quick solutions that had been decided upon in New York, rather than in the field.[15] UN humanitarian relief operations faltered, since it was impossible to protect food convoys throughout the country with a mere 500 lightly armed peacekeepers, and the United States decided to step in with its own force.

In December 1992 the US-led UNITAF operation deployed in Somalia with 38,000 multinational troops, the vast majority of whom were American, with the sole goal of opening up supply routes for humanitarian relief delivery. The operation was led in part by former US Ambassador to Somalia Robert Oakley. The warlords had been in control of humanitarian aid routes for some time before the beginning of UNITAF. With the limited goal of immediate relief, in order to deliver that relief, Oakley "necessarily became hostage to the order that the warlords could provide, as this order was the key to the humanitarian effort."[16] Oakley came to rely on the warlords for the protection of humanitarian aid, which furthered the control the warlords already had over aid deliveries. As a result, the warlords' political control was strengthened, even though the United States would have preferred to reinforce more-representative and less-violent political forces. Moreover, an incentive arose for the warlords to wait to challenge each other more forcefully until the end of the powerful UNITAF's term, and the deployment of the weaker UNOSOM II force under UN command.

Three months later, after securing some supply routes and delivering much-needed aid, but achieving nothing in terms of ending the war, operations were handed back over to the UN under the name of UNOSOM II. The mandate for UNOSOM II, drafted by members of the new Clinton administration, was deeply conflicted. On the one hand, the mission was to perform broad multidimensional peacekeeping tasks such as bargaining with the parties in order

---

[13] Aideed apparently mistrusted the UN Secretary-General from the outset, especially because Boutros-Ghali had been the former Minister of Foreign Affairs for the Egyptian government, which had supported Siad Barre, Aideed's first enemy. In addition, Aideed was angered when, in the summer of 1992, an aircraft with UN markings was discovered delivering money and arms to Ali Mahdi. The UN-chartered plane was not working for the UN at the time, but the event nearly caused negotiations to break down even earlier.

[14] Lalande, 1995, p. 74.

[15] As explained in an interview with an expert on Somalia working in the UN, who preferred to remain anonymous, Nairobi, February 1998. See also Menkhaus, 1997, p. 55.

[16] Laitin, 1999, p. 162.

to achieve a peace plan, restoring law and order, establishing administrative councils, and preparing for an election. But on the other hand, the force was also endowed with Chapter VII peace-enforcement strength, authorizing "all means necessary" to protect humanitarian relief efforts and actively disarm the combatants. Not only was the mandate drafted with conflicting imperatives, but it appears that the UN had devised almost no plan for how to interpret or implement the mandate: "The Secretariat delayed active participation in transition planning until very late in the day ... The upshot was a tardy, half-realized operation with a double dose of problems."[17] Troops were slow to arrive, as were funding, logistical support, and civil administrators. There were unclear chains of command, and poor inter-operability between the troops.

The first major catastrophe came on June 5, 1993, when, after inspecting an Aideed weapons storage site without his consent, twenty-four Pakistani troops were killed and fifty-six wounded. Shortly thereafter, the United States decided to send in US Army Rangers who would operate separately from UNOSOM II command. From August through September 1993, the Rangers repeatedly raided Aideed's compounds, trying forcibly to remove his weapons. But then the second and final catastrophe hit. On October 3, during a raid on an Aideed compound, eighteen US Rangers were taken hostage and killed; one was dragged through the streets of Mogadishu in front of live TV cameras, creating instant popular antipathy in the United States for the operation.[18] While UNOSOM II troops tried to rescue the Rangers, they had not known about the operation until just before it took place, and they therefore arrived too late to be able to save the US troops.

UNOSOM II experienced all aspects of organizational dysfunction. In terms of gathering information and integrating with its environment, one UN Security officer who worked for UNOSOM II noted: "The major problem with the UN on the ground in Somalia is that they didn't use the intelligence information that was available to them."[19] Not only did the UN not gather information, it also did not effectively disseminate it, which led to misperceptions on the part of Somalis about the UN's purpose: "The intervention of the muscular UNOSOM II force against the will of some of the parties led to a widespread perception among the Somalis that the UN was planning to invade the country."[20] Many

---

[17] Durch, 1996, p. 326.
[18] For a lively account of these events in great detail, see Bowden, 1999.
[19] Hamish Cameron, interview with the author, Nairobi, 1998. This sentiment has been echoed in many accounts of the UN operations in Somalia. For example: "The mission was hampered by a lack of quality intelligence: much of its human intelligence proved inaccurate or was deliberately misleading; and the American signals intelligence technologies were often inappropriate for the low-tech militias and the maze-like nature of Mogadishu." Wesley, 1997, p. 76. Durch (1996, p. 335) agrees: "The management of intelligence information was a difficult problem."
[20] Wesley, 1997, p. 73.

clan leaders viewed UNOSOM II as "another armed group." Thus, UNOSOM II became a party to the conflict that it had set out to end. Coordination problems among the various UN operations and between the UN and other international actors in Somalia were numerous. And finally, UN leadership in the field was not unified or effective at problem-solving, and it was often compromised by both the United States and by UN headquarters in New York.

UN documents about this case do point to some minor accomplishments despite the organizational dysfunction: humanitarian relief was provided, seeds for future harvests were distributed, thousands of children were vaccinated, schools outside of the urban centers were rehabilitated, local governing structures were resurrected, and some divisions of UNOSOM II began to assist with judicial and prison reforms.[21] These successes, however, were outweighed by the continuation of state collapse and clan warfare during and after the departure of the UN.[22] In March 1994, in light of the failures, the United States announced that it would withdraw its troops from Somalia. The Europeans quickly followed suit. With a severely weakened UN force, and casualties mounting on both the UN and the Somali sides, the UN gave up in March 1995 by withdrawing UNOSOM II. Over a decade later, the fighting in Somalia continues.

Did the difficult nature of the war in Somalia necessarily lead to the outcome of extreme failure on the part of the external interventions? Given that there had been progress toward peace especially early on, under the leadership of Sahnoun, and that the US and UNOSOM II interventions could quite conceivably have been better designed in terms of overall strategy and tactics, there is reason to believe that the outcome of such extreme failure was not inevitable.

Rwanda

The other three cases of failure discussed in this chapter pale in comparison to the failures of the international efforts during the Rwandan genocide. As hundreds of thousands of ethnic Tutsis and thousands of politically moderate Hutus were being slaughtered, the Secretariat was unwilling to acknowledge the scale of the "massacres," as was the Security Council. At the height of the genocide in late April 1994, the Council voted, counterintuitively, to reduce the size of the dysfunctional United Nations Assistance Mission for Rwanda (UNAMIR) from 2,500 to 270.[23] This vote proved to be one of the primary historical signals of the failure, but what were the deeper causes? Each of the three crucial causal forces were important and are examined here: the situation

---

[21] See *The United Nations and Somalia*, 1996, pp. 55–58; and United Nations, 1995.

[22] Menkhaus, 2004.

[23] S/RES/912, 21 April 1994. In actuality, the force only dropped to about 450 troops, but 270 was the number cited in the resolution.

of civil war in Rwanda, disinterest on the part of the UN Security Council, and organizational dysfunction in the UN Secretariat.

In 1992 and through most of 1993, the UN Security Council and Secretariat launched more peacekeeping operations in civil wars than ever before in the history of the organization. But with the Somalia debacle, enthusiasm to continue the wave of new, large, multidimensional peacekeeping operations quickly subsided. It was in this context that the civil war in Rwanda was coming to an end. Both of the warring sides had signed the long-negotiated and detailed Arusha Agreement, and both sides requested UN oversight of the implementation of the agreement. In other words, in terms of the situational difficulty before the start of the UN mission, since both sides consented to the peacekeeping operation, it appeared that the mission would not be difficult in comparison to the operations where not all parties had granted consent.[24] Fatefully, the Security Council voted to launch UNAMIR on October 5, 1993, only two days after the deaths of the US Rangers in Somalia.[25] None of the members of the Council was willing to challenge the United States on its new disinterest in funding and fielding multidimensional peacekeeping operations in civil wars. This disinterest would prove catastrophic for Rwandan Tutsis and moderate Hutus when, six months later, they would become the victims of genocide. Below I address first the situational difficulty, and then I turn to a combined discussion of the joint actions of the UN Secretariat and Security Council.

The civil war in Rwanda of the 1990s began with the Rwandan Patriotic Front's (RPF) invasion in October 1990 in retaliation for repeated government-sponsored massacres of ethnic Tutsis. The RPF was made up mainly of Tutsis, many of whom had been living in exile in neighboring Uganda since being forced to leave Rwanda in 1959. Rwanda had been colonized by Germany in 1890, and then by Belgium after World War I. Both the German and Belgian colonial powers strengthened and formalized Tutsi rule over the Hutu majority by placing Tutsis in many state administrative positions. In 1959, the Hutu majority rose up against the Belgian colonial administration, drove out hundreds of thousands of Tutsis, and eventually gained independence from Belgium in 1962.[26] In 1973, Major General Juvenal Habyarimana staged a successful coup and held one-party, authoritarian control over the country until his death on April 6, 1994 – the day marking the beginning of the genocide.

During the spring and summer of 1993, peace negotiations had been taking place between the government and the RPF in Paris, and then in Arusha,

---

[24] Roméo Dallaire, dinner conversation with the author, Hanover, New Hampshire, April 4, 2003.

[25] S/RES/872, 5 October 1993.

[26] Rwanda's population in the early 1990s was over 7 million, approximately 85 percent of whom were Hutu, 14 percent Tutsi, and 1 percent Twa. Another 600,000 or more Rwandan Tutsis were living in exile in Uganda. United Nations, 1996, p. 341; the CIA, World Factbook, 2005; Adelman and Suhrke, 1996; and McNulty, 1997, p. 26.

Tanzania.[27] In an attempt to demonstrate good faith during the negotiations, the Rwandan government under President Habyarimana proposed to open the political system to other political parties, including to the RPF, in order to end the stalemated civil war. By late July, the government and the RPF formally agreed to a power-sharing arrangement, and detailed plans for its implementation, by signing the Arusha Agreement of August 4, 1993.

In terms of other factors making up the situational difficulty before the start of the UN peacekeeping operation, the basic infrastructure of the country had not been completely destroyed, and regional actors were generally supportive of the peace process.[28] During the peace process, a new political force (sometimes referred to as "Hutu Power"), had been gaining strength. The movement's destructive potential was, for the most part, unrecognized by the Rwandan government under Habyarimana, the RPF, or the UN. The new movement was fiercely resistant to political changes in favor of reconciliation.

After the signing of the Arusha Agreement, and the deployment of the small UNAMIR multidimensional peacekeeping mission, the extremist movement in Rwanda gained force. The movement, which culminated in a well-planned genocide, was made up of the following groups: members of Habyarimana's government who were unwilling to open up the political sphere to other parties and most certainly not to the Tutsi-dominated RPF; *Interahamwe* and *Ipuza-mugambi* militias numbering 50,000 (who had originally been trained mainly by the French); the Gendarmerie or rural police (also trained by the French); the government's Forces Armées Rwandaises who were less involved in the planning and execution, but did take part; and finally, ordinary peasants who carried out most of the genocidal killing after "years of indoctrination in the 'democratic majority' ideology and of demonization of the 'feudalists.'"[29] The extremists waged a genocide that lasted approximately 100 days and killed approximately 800,000 people.

The Security Council's disinterest and UN Secretariat's organizational dysfunction, which preceded and continued during the genocide, must be considered in tandem (unlike other sections of this and other chapters, where each factor is treated separately), because the action and reaction between the two corporate actors happened quickly and repeatedly.

When the Security Council considered fielding UNAMIR, it was in the throws of reconsidering UN multidimensional peacekeeping altogether after the failures in Somalia. The Council did not recommend adequate funding, nor did countries provide adequate troops, given the extensive mandate assigned to UNAMIR. UNAMIR was mandated under Chapter VI to observe the

---

[27] On the peace process and the accord, see Prunier, 1995, pp. 149–52.
[28] Tanzania was especially helpful, as the talks were held there. Uganda and Burundi were still somewhat involved on the side of the Tutsis.
[29] Prunier, 1995, pp. 239–47.

cease-fire, contribute to the security of Kigali, monitor the integration of a new army, investigate non-compliance with the Arusha Agreement, oversee polic-ing, monitor human rights, monitor refugee repatriation, assist with landmine removal, assist with the coordination of humanitarian aid, and assist with preparations for elections.[30] UNAMIR was also given strict orders not to use force except in the limited case of self-defense. While the Secretary-General had recommended that the force be charged with collecting weapons as a way to enhance security, the Council did not include this provision in the mandate.[31] The mission was to implement all of these tasks with a mere 2,548 military troops and 60 civilian police. The budget, from October 1993 through April 1994, was little more than a paltry 35,000,000.[32] The results were astonishing. The "Independent Inquiry on Rwanda," set up in 1999 by Secretary-General Annan to examine the UN's actions during the genocide, and led by the former Prime Minister of Sweden Ingvar Carlsson, dramatically summarizes:

> The mission was smaller than the original recommendations from the field suggested. It was slow in being set up, and was beset by debilitating admin-istrative difficulties. It lacked well-trained troops and functioning materiel. The mission's mandate was based on an analysis of the peace process which proved erroneous, and which was never corrected despite the significant warning signs that the original mandate had become inadequate. By the time the genocide started, the mission was not functioning as a cohesive whole: in the real hours and days of deepest crisis, consistent testimony points to a lack of political leadership, lack of military capacity, severe problems of command and control, and lack of coordination and disci-pline.[33]

The Special Representative of the Secretary-General for UNAMIR was Jacques-Roger Booh Booh, former Minister of External Relations of Cameroon, and the military commander was Canadian Major-General Romeo A. Dallaire. On January 11, 1994, Dallaire had sent an important fax outlining the details of plans for genocide, but the now-infamous "black file" was basically put aside. Dallaire's fax described information obtained from a high-level official in Habyarimana's government, who had decided to inform on the plans for genocide, with which he disagreed, in return for protection from the UN for his family.[34] The informant explained that radical elements within Habyarimana's government, over which Habyarimana had no control, were actively planning to re-ignite the civil war. They plotted to kill Belgian peacekeepers to provoke Belgian withdrawal; were compiling extensive lists of Tutsis and political ene-mies for "extermination"; and were indoctrinating and training thousands of

[30] S/RES/872, 5 October 1993.
[31] Carlsson, Sung-Joo, and Kupolati, 1999, p. 4; and Dallaire, 2004, Chapter 3.
[32] Woods, 1997, p. 379.   [33] Carlsson, Sung-Joo, and Kupolati, 1999, p. 21.
[34] Gourevitch, 1998a; and Dallaire, 2004.

Interahamwe militia to do the killing. The informant also explained the location of a weapons cache, which Dallaire wanted to raid. This fax was all but dismissed at UN headquarters. A fax with the name of Kofi Annan, then head of the UN's Department of Peacekeeping Operations, but signed by his aide Iqbal Riza, told Dallaire simply to notify Habyarimana of the information, notify the Belgian, French, and US governments of the warning, and not to raid the weapons cache.

Three months later, everything that the fax predicted came true and worse. President Habyarimana was killed, paving the way for a coup by radical forces in the government. The next day, Prime Minister Agathe Uwlingiyimana, who was being protected by Belgian peacekeeping troops and UN Volunteers, was killed as were several other Rwandan government officials who were supposedly being protected by UNAMIR troops. Ten Belgian peacekeepers were brutally massacred, and soon thereafter the Belgian government made the unilateral decision to withdraw completely, which gutted what there was of the UNAMIR operation. As the disaster unfolded, UNAMIR obeyed repeated UN headquarters' instructions not to use force. The mission took actions to protect civilians, against headquarters' recommendations, but these attempts were subverted by France, Belgium, the United States, and Italy, which had all instructed their troops only to evacuate their own nationals.[35]

In April 1994, Secretary-General Boutros-Ghali was touring Europe and did not come back to headquarters in New York until a week after the alarming reports of civil violence had begun to enter the Secretariat. Numerous questions from the field and from various governments were asked of the Secretary-General and the Department of Peacekeeping Operations (DPKO), but left unanswered.[36] Finally, the Secretary-General returned to New York and produced a report to the Security Council.[37] In this report, Boutros-Ghali presented the Council with three alternative courses of action. The options, roughly speaking, were to withdraw altogether, send in a massive Chapter VII operation, or simply reduce the size of the operation on the ground in an attempt to maintain some kind of international presence while saving the lives of UN peacekeepers. The Secretary-General did not indicate which option he and the Secretariat recommended. The Security Council was not ready to abandon Rwanda altogether (with strong lobbying against such action from

[35] Power, 2002, Chapter 10.
[36] For example, after the ten Belgian peacekeepers had been killed by extremists in early April, Willie Claes apparently called the Secretary-General to discuss what should be done, but Boutros-Ghali nonchalantly replied that he would "get back to him in four or five days." Barnett, 1997, p. 560. At headquarters in New York, member states with peacekeepers on the ground were desperately trying to find out through DPKO what was going on, but DPKO was not answering the phone or returning calls. See Adelman and Suhrke, 1996, p. 90.
[37] S/470, 20 April 1994.

Nigeria, the Czech Republic, and New Zealand); but it was also not prepared to field a large peacekeeping force. Nor was it supplied with any sort of plan from the Secretariat for how a peace-enforcement operation could be conducted. The Secretary-General's report did not mention that some UNAMIR troops had begun to protect civilians against genocidal attacks, which was outside of UNAMIR's mandate, but which, General Dallaire maintained, was the morally appropriate action to take – civilian protection could have been included as part of a new mandate, but it was not.[38] The report also did not mention genocide. It is possible that a formal declaration of "genocide" would have forced the hand of the Security Council to take actions to stop the genocide.

In terms of specific member states of the UN, the United States and Belgium actively advocated the immediate withdrawal of the operation. The United Kingdom was also against strengthening UNAMIR, arguing that a stronger force was "not feasible because of the lesson drawn from Somalia that conditions on the ground could evolve rapidly and dangerously."[39] The United States and other members of the Security Council also complained that they were under constant pressure to save money in face of a mounting billion dollar UN peacekeeping debt.[40] In contrast, the more numerous but less powerful Non-Aligned Movement in the General Assembly was in favor of strengthening UNAMIR, arguing that it was the UN's duty to intervene. The discussions about how to act delayed decision-making during the height of the genocide. In the end, the vote to downsize UNAMIR was unanimous.[41]

The Secretariat and major powers had information about the nature of the genocide and the tactics of its perpetrators, but they did not use this information to define the problem or shape their interests.[42] They defined the problem not as systematic, well-planned genocide, but as chaotic civil war and ethnic massacres. Such definitions justified the policy of withdrawal, since it was argued that there was nothing possible that internationals could do in the face of such chaos.[43] According to political scientist Michael Barnett, who was working at the US Mission to the UN at the time, many members of the UN also felt that another failed UN peacekeeping mission would bring about the downfall of

---

[38] Instead, the resolution gave UNAMIR the mandate only to "monitor and report on developments" on the safety and security of civilians.

[39] Carlsson, Sung-Joo, and Kupolati, 1999, p. 15.

[40] Carlsson, Sung-Joo, and Kupolati, 1999, p. 29.   [41] S/RES/912, 21 April 1994, para. 8c.

[42] As Vaccaro (1996, p. 377) explains, "The failure [of UNAMIR] was twofold: not enough accurate analysis was available to the Council, and the information that was reported seems to have fallen on deaf ears."

[43] Many students of UN decision-making in UNAMIR maintain that if the problem had been defined in terms of genocide from the outset, this would have necessitated swift action under Article II a and b of the 1948 Genocide Convention. See for example, Adelman and Suhrke, 1996, p. 72; Vaccaro, 1996, p. 377; Barnett, 1997, p. 576; and Barnett 2002.

the organization, and thus they chose to remain concerned about the genocide, but not do much, rather than potentially sacrifice the reputation of the whole UN.[44]

Belatedly, the evidence from the ground became so overwhelming and horrifying that pressure mounted to change the arguments and interests of the members of the Secretariat and the Council. The Secretariat finally issued a report on May 13 that labeled the violence in Rwanda as genocide and urged the Council to take immediate action.[45] The Security Council was divided about how to respond. The United States and United Kingdom were not in favor of intervention. The US government had recently issued Presidential Decision Directive 25, which set out a new non-interventionist policy for the United States Meanwhile, France also suggested low numbers of troops. Rwanda, a member of the Council since December 1994, voted against a UNAMIR II troop increase and a Chapter VII arms embargo.[46] Nevertheless, the Council did finally vote to sponsor UNAMIR II, granting it a mandate to protect civilians, with 5,500 peacekeepers.[47]

After a month of the Secretary-General asking for troop contributors, only a few countries were willing to provide several hundred peacekeepers for the new mission, but the number came nowhere near 5,000. Since no countries were willing to provide troops, the Security Council authorized France's swiftly deployable "Opération Turquoise," with a Chapter VII mandate, for two months until the UN could cobble together a force. While France might have taken the lead in UNAMIR II, such a move was unacceptable to many countries, since France had clearly been an ally of the Hutu government.[48] Opération Turquoise was narrowly supported by the UN Security Council with ten votes in favor, and a very rare five abstentions filed by Brazil, China, New Zealand, Nigeria, and Pakistan.[49] Note that the Council voted to field UNAMIR II, a Chapter VI operation, at the same time that it endorsed Opération Turquoise under Chapter VII, with peace-enforcement powers; the mandates of the two operations were completely at odds with one another. In other words, the Council's decisions were not always consensual, nor were they consistent with one another. We can characterize the Council's interest intensity as "moderate*" which denotes that while the Council did not endorse a mandate with adequate resources, it did pass many resolutions on the matter.[50]

---

[44] Barnett, 2002.   [45] S/565, 13 May 1994.   [46] S/RES/918, 17 May 1994.

[47] S/RES/925, 8 June 1994. Note that China and the United States changed the wording in the resolution from "genocide" to the weaker "acts of genocide."

[48] Waugh, 2004, p. 72. Some analysts have even argued that France was in part responsible for the genocide, since the French had been instrumental in training the *Interahamwe* and rural police. See McNulty, 1997.

[49] S/RES/929, 22 June 1994.

[50] "Moderate" interest intensity is indicated when the Council provides adequate resources but does not vote often. In this case, the opposite was true, which is why the * is added

Opération Turquoise arrived in Rwanda just after the RPF had gained new strength and was forcing the Hutu militias and Forces Armées Rwandaises into retreat. By July 17, over 1 million Rwandans, mainly Hutu, had crossed into what was then Zaire, fleeing the RPF's rapid advance, and eventually helping to spark an enormous, protracted civil war in the Democratic Republic of the Congo. By July 18, the RPF had gained control over all of Rwanda with the exception of the French "humanitarian zone" protected by well-armed Opération Turquoise troops. Rwanda continues to be governed mainly by Tutsi elite, although ethnicity is no longer recognized as an official marker. While most of the Hutu refugees have returned, and formal tribunals, truth, and reconciliation processes are underway, Hutu extremism and Tutsi political domination continue to plague Rwanda.

There is an important debate in the literature on Rwanda about who was more responsible – the Security Council or the Secretariat – for international inaction in the face of the genocide.[51] I contend that undoubtedly both share responsibility, but that the Secretariat in some ways bears more. The UN Secretariat and its leader, the UN Secretary-General, are supposed to play an agenda-setting and advocacy role in the UN system. The Secretary-General is meant to provide moral leadership, and the Secretariat's DPKO and the Department of Political Affairs are supposed to plan for and implement international peace agreements. The Secretariat can often set its own mandate and agenda and request Security Council approval. As Barnett explains, "the Secretariat's agenda-setting influence was potentially enhanced in this case because few, if any, member states had independent sources of information, and they therefore relied heavily on the Secretariat for intelligence and policy recommendations regarding UNAMIR's future."[52] However, during this crisis, the Secretariat, namely Boutros Boutros-Ghali's office and the DPKO, which was headed by Kofi Annan at the time, with Iqbal Riza in charge of the Rwanda file, "gave the impression of distance and aloofness from the emerging tragedy."[53] This only reinforced the disinclination among many member states in the Security Council to propose a greater role for UNAMIR.

Angola

Between 1988 and 1999, the UN fielded four separate peace operations in Angola. By the start of the third and most multidimensional peacekeeping mission, the parties had signed a long and hard-negotiated peace accord, the Security Council was more interested in funding this mission than its precursors

---

to the label "moderate." The Council passed ten resolutions concerning Rwanda in 1994 out of seventy-six total. In other words, it voted often but did not recommend adequate resources.

[51] See, for example, Berdal, 2005b.   [52] Barnett, 1997, p. 560.   [53] Barnett, 1997, p. 559.

(even though its interest in Angola was still rather low in intensity), and the UN appeared poised to learn on the second level from its past mistakes in Angola and success in nearby Mozambique. Nevertheless, the multidimensional operation, authorized under Chapter VI of the UN Charter, was unsuccessful in implementing its mandate. The failure of this operation stems from a negative interaction of all three basic causal elements examined in this book. One of the parties, UNITA (National Union for the Total Independence of Angola), was unwilling to sustain its consent for the peace process due in large part to the UN's dismal past record in Angola. The absence of consent deepened when, as in the past, the UN was unable to follow through on its security guarantees in a timely manner as promised in the peace accord. The UN, in turn, was unable to implement its guarantees because of weak Security Council support and internal dysfunction within the peacekeeping operation. I address below each of the three primary sources of failure – the situational difficulty, Security Council disinterest, and UN first-level organizational dysfunction.

First, Angola has a long history of unconstructive external involvement in its internal affairs. The country was "discovered" by the Portuguese in 1483. Later, under Portuguese rule, millions of Angolans were sold into slavery and the countryside was mined for its abundant natural resources. In the 1960s, at least four different indigenous parties began fighting for independence from Portugal, which was finally won in 1974.[54] The Portuguese swiftly departed Angola, extracting human and material resources, and leaving a devastated country in their wake. A rushed independence agreement cited the need for a transitional coalition government, but independence was granted "to the people," with no framework, means, or details for the transfer of power, dis-armament procedures, governing bodies, or elections. Moreover, since blacks were for the most part not granted access to education, there were few qual-ified civil servants remaining in Angola who could manage the new govern-ment. A weak Marxist-Leninist regime came to power, but civil war quickly enveloped the country. The civil war was worsened by external intervention, as Angola became a proxy site for the Cold War. The USSR and Cuba sup-ported the MPLA (which also benefited from Chinese weapons), while the United States, some European countries, and Apartheid South Africa supported UNITA.

With the end of the Cold War, many expected that peace would finally come to this southern African country, after three decades of debilitating warfare. More than 500,000 people had been killed out of a population of some 11 million; 3.5 million people were internally displaced, 300,000 were refugees, over 70,000 had become amputees (the highest per capita in the world at the

---

[54] Only the Movimento Popular de Liberacao de Angola (MPLA) and Uniao Nacional para a Independencia Total de Angola (UNITA) remained strong by the time of the third UN peacekeeping mission.

time), and upwards of 10 million land mines littered the country.[55] What infrastructure had been developed under colonial rule was all but destroyed. The battle of Cuito Cuanevale in November 1987 marked a major military stalemate, paving the way for the first round of negotiations. These resulted in the first UN peacekeeping mission, the United Nations Angola Verification Mission (UNAVEM I).

UNAVEM I successfully oversaw the withdrawal of 50,000 Cuban troops from Angola in 1988. Subsequently, in 1991, Portugal, the United States, and the Soviet Union negotiated the "Bicesse Accords" between the governing MPLA and UNITA. The accords did not, however, include provisions for an adequate transition process with third-party guarantees to ensure that both sides adhered to their promises. The UN was slowly drawn into the process of monitoring the implementation of the accords, namely by monitoring the elections, under a new peacekeeping operation, UNAVEM II. UNAVEM II was established in May 1991 and was to be a "small and manageable operation."[56] The Security Council did not want to field another massive peacekeeping mission and thus allotted only 350 unarmed military observers to monitor the demobilization of over 200,000 troops, and a mere 400 electoral observers to monitor elections in a country that is as large as France, Spain, and Germany combined. The UN Secretariat reluctantly went ahead with the operation, but it did not fare well. The sorely understaffed, under-funded UNAVEM II in effect merely staved off fighting for a time, allowing both sides to regroup and prepare for possible battle if the election outcome was not to their liking. Jonas Savimbi, head of UNITA, lost the elections by nine percentage points, declared them to be fraudulent (there were few reliable mechanisms in place to prove him right or wrong), and the most vicious fighting of the war ensued. Upwards of 300,000 people were killed while, as during the Rwandan genocide, the UN and the rest of the international community merely observed. The international involvement, namely through this dysfunctional UN peacekeeping mission, created a situation far worse than ever before during the war.[57]

From September to October 1993, the permanent five members of the Security Council appeared to be somewhat more serious about finding a solution to the ongoing war in Angola, and they authorized peace negotiations to resume under the direction of UN Special Representative of the Secretary-General, Maître Alioune Blondin Beye of Mali. The "troika" made up of Portugal, Russia, and the United States, which had been active during the Bicesse negotiations, observed these negotiations as well. With this support, Beye saw through the drafting of the extremely lengthy and multidimensional Lusaka Peace Accord in October 1994. The accord was drafted at a time when UNITA had been losing territory to Angolan government forces, and many observers contend that

---

[55] Jackson, 1996; Hare, 1998, p. 11; and Jett, 1999, p. 95.   [56] Anstee, 1999, p. 592.
[57] For a masterful account of UNAVEM II and its problems, see Anstee, 1996.

Savimbi agreed to participate in the peace process partly in order to maintain control over his remaining territory.[58] The Angolan government appeared to agree with the analysts, since almost immediately after the agreement had been reached, the government launched an offensive against UNITA in Uige and Huambo in an attempt to consolidate government hold over the provincial capitals before the final signing and official cease-fire took hold. In response, Savimbi did not attend the signing ceremony in November 1994. He claimed that he could not rely on the UN to guarantee his security (which was not unwarranted) and sent a representative in his place. While the Lusaka Peace Accord was very detailed, and both sides consented to it and to UN oversight, these otherwise favorable situational conditions were tinged with ambiguity as to the depth of consent.[59]

Second, in terms of Security Council interests, the Council's decisions on Angola have reflected a certain consensual ambivalence toward the conflict. All decisions have been unanimous, reflecting a basic level of consensus. However, on the one hand, the Council mandated that the UN missions maintain neutrality toward both parties, but on the other hand, the Council voted in favor of sanctions repeatedly against UNITA, in 1993, 1997, and 1998 – the first occasions in history when a nongovernmental entity has come under UN sanctions. Moreover, while the Security Council voted in favor of having the Secretariat oversee disarmament in Angola, during the Lusaka peace process, Russia and China continued to supply arms to the Angolan government; the United States sold military aircraft and bought (and continues to buy) massive quantities of oil, also from the government; and many European and African countries continued to buy diamonds from UNITA in exchange for weapons.[60]

In general, the United States, as the most powerful member of the Security Council, was ambivalent from the start of the Lusaka peace process about whether a peace could be brokered at all.[61] The United States was also very

[58] Jose da Silva Campino, interview with the author, New York, October 16, 1997.

[59] Rothchild, 1997, p. 141.

[60] Economist, 1999; Human Rights Watch, 1999; and Fowler and Mollander, 2000. Dealing in arms with the government was morally questionable, but buying UNITA diamonds was illegal under the UN sanctions against UNITA. The Netherlands, Bulgaria, Romania, and Ukraine were cited repeatedly as buyers of diamonds from, or weapons suppliers for, UNITA. Zaire under Mobutu was a major UNITA trading partner, and Togo, Burkina Faso, and Zambia were all cited by the Security Council as supplying fuel and weapons to UNITA. See S/203, 10 March 2000. Moreover, the diamond company De Beers purchased approximately $3 billion in UNITA diamonds between 1993 and 1998. See Angola Peace Monitor, 2001.

[61] Note that Angola ranks number seven on the top ten list of countries from which the United States imports crude oil as it has for many years (Iraq ranks number six). See US Department of Energy, 2005. Clearly, access to Angola's oil falls within the United States' definition of protecting national self-interest. However, the war never severely disrupted oil production or exports, which means that the United States never came under anything but moral pressure to help end the war.

concerned about the potential cost of a large UN operation that might not be successful, which in effect discouraged others from supporting it and added to delays in troop deployment.[62] The delays in UN deployment created uncertainty for both parties and incentives not to cease fire or disarm. Thus, uncertainty on the part of the United States and the Security Council fostered only greater uncertainty on the ground, creating a downward spiraling process.

In looking at the Security Council's resolutions on Angola, it would appear that Angola was a low priority on the agenda from 1994 to 1996, reflected in few resolutions concerning the conflict, and although $383 million in funding for the first twelve months was approved, the mandate for UNAVEM III was too extensive, considering the amount of resources available.[63] By 1997–98, when the operation started failing, the Council met more often to discuss the situation, but it also voted to downsize the mission rather than providing more funding. Thus we can say that while interest intensity was generally low to moderate at the outset, it shifted to a "moderate*," when the Council met frequently about the problem but did not provide adequate resources to solve it.

Third and finally, in terms of organizational dysfunction, UNAVEM III experienced problems from the outset. Its mandate was very broad, including the following tasks: monitoring the cease-fire; verifying the withdrawal, cantoning, demobilizing, and disarming troops; collecting and supervising UNITA arms; verifying movement of government forces and overseeing the establishment of a new army; verifying the extension of the state administration to UNITA-controlled areas; monitoring the Angolan National Police; verifying the withdrawal of mercenaries and the disarming of civilians; cantoning the rapid reaction police; providing security for UNITA leaders; coordinating and facilitating humanitarian activities; clearing mines; and supporting, verifying, and monitoring presidential elections.[64]

The operation was authorized by the Security Council in February 1995, three months after the parties had signed the Lusaka Peace Accord, but the peacekeepers did not arrive until that summer. The peacekeeping force was authorized at almost 7,000 military personnel, 350 military observers, 260 civilian police, and 420 civilian international staff (bolstered by 300 local staff and 75 UN Volunteers). Note that while there were many peacekeeping troops, the civilian affairs division was comparatively very small, given the tasks it was supposed to fulfill.

---

[62] Paul Hare, the main US negotiator, cites concerns over peacekeeping costs on several occasions in his book. See Hare, 1998.

[63] In 1994, of 76 resolutions, 6 concerned Angola; in 1995, 3 of 63 concerned Angola; in 1996, 5 of 56; in 1997, 7 of 53; and in 1998, 11 of 72. See also Dzinesa, 2004, p. 654.

[64] United Nations, "Angola-UNAVEM III," 1997.

The delays in the arrival of the peacekeeping troops encouraged cease-fire violations on both sides. And while eventually the troops did arrive, their deployment was reportedly "mainly for cosmetic purposes, largely in provincial capitals and without relation to the cantoning areas for demobilizing troops or to routes of retreat in case fighting broke out again . . . the largely self-imposed limitations made the military contingent less effective than they could have been."[65]

Rather than pursuing a more comprehensive, and possibly more effective, military strategy, Special Representative Beye was under strict orders from the Security Council and Secretariat headquarters to maintain UN impartiality toward the two sides, even though it was clear that UNITA, and Savimbi in particular, was not complying with promises made in the Lusaka Protocols. There were three important obstacles that UNITA presented to the UN and to the peace process. First, Savimbi delayed cantoning his troops for many months past his deadline. In January 1996, US Secretary of State Madeleine Albright visited Savimbi in person to encourage him to demobilize. Soon thereafter, Lynda Walker, the British Minister of Overseas Development, met with Savimbi to try to convince him to do the same. He did eventually comply, cantoning tens of thousands of troops. However, as became abundantly evident later, he did not canton his elite forces and did not surrender most of UNITA's best weapons. Second, UNITA and the international mediators experienced great difficulty in devising a power-sharing role for Savimbi in the new government, and in turning UNITA into a political party from a war machine. Eventually, while some UNITA deputies were included in the government, Savimbi refused to give up his stronghold in Bailundo and move to the capital, Luanda, in order to assume his position as leader of the opposition. Third, the UN was supposed to oversee the extension of the government's civilian administration to UNITA-controlled areas. While the government made numerous attempts to extend its bureaucracy peacefully, in the end it resorted to force in an attempt to try to govern the diamond-rich regions controlled by UNITA.

Despite these obstacles, and a very limited interpretation of what the organization was authorized to do, UNAVEM III did eventually manage to move into something of a first-level learning mode, and to implement some of the tasks in its mandate. Humanitarian coordination and civil-military relations within UNAVEM III became smoother over time.[66] The military division redeployed in a way that would make oversight of troop cantoning easier. The military and civilian divisions saw to it that close to 70,000 UNITA soldiers were cantoned, nine UNITA generals and 11,000 UNITA troops joined the new national army. Bridges were repaired, roads de-mined, and a Government of National Unity and Reconciliation including both UNITA and MPLA leaders was formally

[65] Jett, 1999, p. 85.
[66] Jose da Silva Campino, interview with the author, New York, October 16, 1997.

ushered into power in April, 1997. These successes, however, were tempered by more significant failures.

In May 1997, Zaire's dictator Mobutu Sese Seko was chased out of his country by armed opposition forces, opening up the potential for UNITA to lose its most important external diamonds and arms link. At the same time, the Angolan government saw an opportunity to try to claim the diamond-rich territories in the northeast. By the next month, intense fighting had broken out in Zaire, exacerbated by UNITA armed forces' attempts to keep the opposition, led by Laurent Kabila, from power. Meanwhile, in Angola's northeast, fighting also broke out between government forces and UNITA. As one analyst explained: "The intensity of the fighting demonstrated not only that UNITA still controlled major portions of the country, but that it had hidden a major military capacity from the UN."[67]

Despite the evidence of a faltering peace process, the Security Council voted in June 1997 to end UNAVEM III on time, and to replace it with the much smaller United Nations Observer Mission in Angola (MONUA). In its resolution to end UNAVEM III, the Security Council also commended the operation on its successes.[68]

In June 1998, the Council voted for a third time to impose sanctions on UNITA. This time, the sanctions resolution was more specific about international monitoring mechanisms for UNITA's diamond trade, which was still providing the organization with an estimated $500 million each year.[69] UNITA leaders in turn declared the UN resolution "an attack" on UNITA and began a physical counterattack. UN observers, peacekeepers, and aid workers were shot at and detained; two UN planes were shot down; and UNITA began to regain regions that the government had established control over after the peace deal.[70] By December 1998, Angola had returned to full-scale civil war. In February 1999, the UN terminated its observer mission, since there was "no longer peace to keep in Angola."[71] In September 1999, after a major government offensive, UNITA lost most of its conventional capacity to wage war and turned to guerrilla tactics.[72]

After two and a half more years of brutal fighting, in February, 2002, Savimbi died in battle, marking the end of the war in Angola. Within a matter of weeks, the Angolan government reached out to a defeated UNITA, began troop reintegration into the regular army, and political reconciliation and

---

[67] Jett, 1999, p. 163.   [68] S/RES/1118, 30 June 1997.

[69] Economist, August 23, 1997; Jett, 1999, p. 163. However, the Security Council did not formally establish an investigative body until May 1999. The ban on Angola's trade in rough diamonds became the foundation for what would eventually become the "Kimberley Process Certification Scheme" in 2002, an attempt by fifty-four governments, NGOs, and the diamond industry to crack down on "conflict diamonds." See Wright, 2004.

[70] Economist, 1999.   [71] Angolan Mission Observer, 1999.

[72] Angola Peace Monitor, 2001.

incorporation of what remained of UNITA as a political organization.[73] Steps toward reconciliation between the Angolan government and UNITA have transpired without international oversight or assistance and appear to be proceeding at a slow but steady pace. After decades of war, but with vast diamond and oil wealth that no longer need be spent on fighting, Angola could be poised for recovery.

The analytic literature on Angola is not very well developed, reflecting the disinterested and disheartened views of many states, multilateral organizations, and scholars alike. Generally there is some debate about the extent to which Savimbi, or the UN, was the primary cause of the failures of the Lusaka peace process.

Human Rights Watch, for example, singles out the UN Security Council and Secretariat. One report contends that rather than confronting the parties' warlike actions more directly, UNAVEM III "turned a blind eye. . . . The UN's practice of ignoring the two parties' deceptions and depredations and its own lack of transparency . . . encouraged both parties to regard the peace process with contempt, and both the Angolan government and UNITA . . . determined that war was their preferred outcome."[74] There is substantial evidence that the Security Council and UN Secretariat could have performed better. The UN had two chances to help Angola in a transition to peace, but both times the transition period merely allowed both sides some reprieve from fighting, in order to regroup and prepare for more war. Moreover, the UN's inability to follow through on security guarantees for Savimbi, and the delayed arrival of the UNAVEM III operation, meant that Savimbi could not put his trust in the UN.

Most analysts contend, however, that Savimbi, the obstinate leader of an extremely entrenched and powerful military organization, with access to important natural resources to sustain his fight, lies at the heart of the UN's failure and the long duration of the war in Angola.[75] This view has been supported by the moves toward peace and rebuilding in the wake of Savimbi's death.[76]

Bosnia-Herzegovina

The UN's many peacekeeping operations in the former Yugoslavia were, at the time, the most elaborate and cost-intensive in the history of the UN.[77] The

[73] Hare, 2005, p. 230.   [74] Human Rights Watch, 1999.
[75] See, for example, Hodges, 2004, Chapter 7; Hare, 2005; and Le Billon, 2005.
[76] World Bank, 2005.
[77] The total operational costs in Bosnia and Croatia were approximately $5 billion – more than twice as expensive as any previous peacekeeping mission. There were over 200 deaths of peacekeepers, approaching the 230 mark reached in the operation in the Congo from 1960 to 1964. At its peak of activity in the fall of 1995, the total number of UNPROFOR troops deployed was almost 24,000.

causes of failure of some of the operations have been recounted and debated in many books and articles.[78] Rather than attempting to recap what has been presented exhaustively in the literature, I focus mainly on the event precipitating the collapse of the multidimensional UN Protection Force (UNPROFOR): the fall of the "safe areas," especially Srebrenica, in July 1995. First, I will briefly describe the situational factors of the war at the outset of the peacekeeping operation, and outline the various nonconsensual interests of the members of the Security Council. I then turn to a discussion of the final and disastrous failure in Srebrenica. While UN peacekeepers stood aside, the Army of the Bosnian Serb Republic staged a massacre of genocidal proportions resulting in the deaths of over 7,000 Bosnian Muslims, and the ethnic cleansing of over 40,000 people.

First, in terms of situational factors and Yugoslav history, Yugoslavia came into being in the wake of World War I, with the collapse of the Ottoman and Austro-Hungarian empires. A popular movement arose among the Serbs, Croats and Slovenes, all southern Slavic ethnic groups formerly divided between the two empires, resulting in the creation of the Kingdom of Serbs, Croats and Slovenes in 1918. In 1929, the Kingdom was renamed "Yugoslavia" (literally, "South Slav Land") by Serbian King Alexander, in an attempt to supercede ethnic divisions and unite the country. When World War II broke out, the fighting in Yugoslavia was mainly between the pro-socialist partisans and the nationalists (rather than between ethnic groups). In 1948, Marshal Josip Broz Tito, leader of the partisans during World War II and President of one-party Yugoslavia, broke off relations with Stalin and the Soviet Union, and in 1956 he helped to create the Non-Aligned Movement in the United Nations. Tito was a strong leader on the world stage, and a resolute but popular leader within his own country. He oversaw a delicate "balance" between the major ethnic groups of Yugoslavia, while trying to promote multiethnic "Yugoslav" nationalism. After Tito's death in 1980, a rotating presidency came into power, with representatives of each of the six republics taking turns at the helm. By 1991, this arrangement proved inadequate for managing the unity of the Federation when Slovenia and Croatia declared independence in June. The Yugoslav People's Army first invaded Slovenia in a quick but failed attempt to coerce the republic to stay in the Federation, and then it moved on to Croatia (described further in Chapter 7 of this book) and Bosnia.

The causes of the war have been well debated in dozens of books and articles. While many analysts make claims to have found "the single" most important cause, the war has complex and multiple causal roots. The "ancient hatreds" thesis is one of the most popular arguments, which holds that the ethnic groups

---

[78] See, for example, Gutman, 1993; Magas, 1993; Denitch, 1994; Kaplan, 1994; Woodward, 1995; Silber and Little, 1996; Rhode, 1997; Holbrooke, 1998; Burg and Shoup, 1999; and Bose, 2002.

in the former Yugoslavia have been hating each other since time immemorial.[79] This argument has been discredited by dozens of other analyses, which point to evidence that Yugoslavia would never have come into existence and stayed together for seventy-three years if there were not a popular basis for the union, that the ethnic groups had not fought each other in ethnic terms before World War II, and that the intermarriage rate between the groups was extremely high – approximately 30 percent in urban areas.[80] Other analyses point to the role of instrumental domestic elites in their quest to hold onto power, the rise and erosion of a Yugoslav national culture, political economic institutions that gained separate force within each of the republics, relative deprivation fueling animosity between wealthy and poor republics, and international actors who fueled different sides of the war.[81] Each of these factors contributed significantly to the outbreak of the war.

When 12,000 lightly armed UNPROFOR peacekeepers arrived in Bosnia, war had not yet broken out there. The peacekeeping operation did not have a mandate from the Security Council or the warring parties to try to stop the fighting if it began. The operation did not enjoy the consent of all of the parties (especially the Bosnian Serbs), there was no peace agreement to try to implement, and there was no stalemate on the battlefield. Other situational factors, however, appeared to favor the operation: there had been few fatalities, the war in Slovenia and Croatia had not endured for very long, and the infrastructure was well-developed with little damage. When the mandate to protect the "safe areas" was handed to the Secretariat by the Security Council in June 1993, these broad situational factors still obtained.[82]

Turning to the interests of the members of the Security Council, interest in the war in Bosnia could be characterized as high in intensity, and usually, although not consistently, consensual. Of the remarkably high number of ninety-two Security Council resolutions in 1993, twenty-four concerned the former Yugoslavia.[83] In general, from 1992 through 1995, the various conflicts in the former Yugoslavia dominated the Security Council's agenda.[84] In all of those years, more resolutions were passed regarding this conflict than any other, and resolutions regarding the conflict in Bosnia in particular were

---

[79] See, for example, Doder, 1993; and Kaplan, 1994.

[80] See Wachtel, 1998; Burg and Shoup, 1999.

[81] For one example of each of these types of analyses, listed in order, see Gagnon, 1994/95; Wachtel, 1998; Crawford, 1995; and Woodward, 1995; see also Rathbun, 2004, and Oliver, 2005 on the role of international actors.

[82] S/RES/836, 4 June 1993.

[83] Of these, eight concerned Bosnia-Herzegovina specifically. During 1993, a rare five resolutions, all concerning the former Yugoslavia, were not unanimous votes. On one resolution, Pakistan and Venezuela abstained; China alone abstained on three, and Russia and China together abstained on one.

[84] In 1992, of 73 total resolutions, 26 concerned the former Yugoslavia; in 1994, of 76, 12 were about the area, and in 1995, of 65 total, 24 related to the former Yugoslavia.

also numerous. The Security Council tended to allocate significant funds to the former Yugoslav peacekeeping operations, although not enough to sustain a "peace-enforcement" force. Many argued that such a force was necessary in order to secure the peace *before* any attempt at "peacekeeping," which usually entails maintaining and implementing a peace agreement.

The members of the Council had different and shifting definitions of the problem. For example, at the outset, the United States defined the problem as one of ancient ethnic hatreds, which led policymakers to argue that intervention would be futile, but then the United States shifted focus to instrumental elites, especially Slobodan Milosevic.[85] France tended to see the conflict as one of tensions between instrumental elites and publics where all sides shared similar guilt, and thus advocated the equal treatment of all sides. Germany and most of the European Community defined the war as one of aggression fought by Serbia to create a Greater Serbia.[86] China was against international intervention in what it perceived as an internal matter. The Non-Aligned Movement saw the conflict as one of Serb aggression, and thus supported the UN's use of force, and lifting the arms embargo, which, its members argued, was disproportionately hurting the Bosnian Muslims. Each of the definitions gave rise to different military strategies. While the military on the ground came up with its own problem definitions and strategies, these rarely corresponded with those being devised at headquarters in New York, in large part because of the difficulties in coming to a consensus about the basic nature of the war.[87] In the "safe areas" in particular, this disjuncture in problem definition meant that the areas were viewed by some as havens where the Bosnian forces could and should rest and regroup while being protected from Bosnian Serb attack.[88] Others, however, felt that the areas should be neutral territory, free of troops, where only humanitarian aid should be distributed. These debates provided the backdrop for the creation of the contradictory "safe areas" mandate.

In the wake of the swiftly deteriorating humanitarian situation in Bosnia-Herzegovina in early 1993, which was brought on mainly by Bosnian Serb attacks on isolated pockets throughout Bosnia, the Non-Aligned Movement sponsored a Security Council resolution to protect Srebrenica as a "safe area,"

[85] Christopher, 1993.

[86] While Germany was not a permanent member of the Security Council, it was a very influential member of the "Contact Group," which was the international negotiating team made up of representatives from France, Germany, Russia, the United Kingdom, and the United States (and eventually Italy).

[87] There were also, of course, problems of command, as there are always, when peacekeepers are supposed to be working to further the policies of an international body but feel more loyal to their home government and its policies.

[88] Especially since the arms embargo was not going to be lifted officially for the Bosnian Muslim forces.

under Chapter VII peace-enforcement provisions.[89] A weak version of the pro-posal was approved, which did not specify the boundaries of the safe area, nor did it specify the terms or methods of demilitarization from within, and protection from without.[90] Soon after, the safe area concept was extended to Tuzla, Zepa, Gorazde and Bihac.[91] In light of continued attacks on these areas, and increasing pressure from the Non-Aligned Movement, the Security Coun-cil passed another resolution to fortify protection of the areas.[92] This third "safe area" resolution, sponsored by France, Russia, Spain, the United King-dom, and the United States, included the mandate to deter attacks, monitor cease-fires, occupy several points on the ground, and promote the withdrawal of Bosnian government forces. Pakistan and Venezuela, as members of the Non-Aligned Movement, abstained on the measure, fearing that the mandate was not matched by adequate means. The resolution was *not* based on a formal report from the Secretary-General, thus the specifics of implementation were not planned in accordance with the formulation of the mandate. Indeed, in an informal working paper, the Secretary-General expressed his severe reserva-tions about UNPROFOR's ability to deter attacks without sufficient numbers of peacekeepers.[93] The safe area resolutions were adopted while also ignoring the professional advice of UN military ground reports.[94] Two weeks after resolu-tion 836 was passed, the Secretary-General responded to the Security Council's decision by requesting, on behalf of UNPROFOR under the direction of French General Jean Cot, 35,000 troops in order to carry out the mandate.[95] But the Security Council voted to provide only 7,500.[96] The modalities of implemen-tation were left up to the Secretary-General and his operations on the ground.

   The Security Council made decisions about the "safe areas" that were almost completely divorced from a vision of implementation. The decisions often reflected political debates that were driven by internal politics in Washington, Paris, London and Moscow. The UN's "Report on the Fall of Srebrenica" is crit-ical of the Council's decisions: "The efforts of Members Sates to find compro-mise between divergent positions led to the UNPROFOR mandate becoming

---

[89] The town of Srebrenica had a population of about 7,000 before swelling to about 30,000 after Bosnian Serb forces overran Cerska and Konjevic Polji in early March 1992. The Srebrenica municipality had a population of about 37,000 before the war – 73 percent Bosnian Muslims, 25 percent Serbs, and 2 percent Yugoslavs. By the spring of 1993, the town was on the brink of humanitarian disaster. See S/25519 letter from the Secretary-General transmitting a letter from the High Commissioner for Refugees concerning the situation in Srebrenica.

[90] S/RES/819, 6 April 1993.   [91] S/RES/824, 6 May 1993.   [92] S/RES/836, 3 June 1993.

[93] Annan, 1999, "Report on the Fall of Srebrenica," paras. 58, 77, 81, 492. This report was drafted mainly by David Harland, the civilian head of UNPROFOR in Bosnia from 1994–95, and written in the name of Secretary-General Kofi Annan.

[94] Owen, 1995, p. 161; and Annan, 1999, para. 58.   [95] S/25939, 14, 16, 17 June 1993.

[96] S/RES/844, 18 June 1993.

rhetorically more robust than the Force itself."[97] In the words of David Owen, the Security Council's decision to reinforce UNPROFOR troops in the safe areas with 7,500 troops instead of 35,000, as the military units on the ground had requested, was

> the worst single decision taken by the Security Council during my tenure as Co-Chairman of the ICFY [International Conference on the Former Yugoslavia]. The "safe area" mandate was a totally inconsistent one: for the areas to be safe, they had to be demilitarized, then defined, and then defended by the UN. As it was, in the absence of consent and cooperation it was impossible to fulfill the mandate, and Serb attacks into, and Muslim attacks out of, "safe areas" continued.[98]

Finally, in terms of UN organizational dysfunction while trying to implement the "safe areas" resolutions, the problems were diverse and numerous. Broadly speaking, there were three types of tensions pulling apart the safe areas operations: (1) whether humanitarian aid workers should be under armed protection, (2) problems of leadership arising between Boutros-Ghali and different UNPROFOR military commanders, and (3) tensions on the ground between UNPROFOR and the Bosnian government forces.

First, the United Nations High Commissioner for Refugees (UNHCR) and other relief agencies had been carrying out relief operations since 1992 that depended on the consent of the warring factions. The UNHCR, the strongest and most active of the humanitarian agencies, sought to bargain on its own with the warring parties, using the rules of impartiality and non-use of force in order to secure consent to get supplies through to needy populations. The humanitarian workers were spread out over the country and vulnerable to attack if any warring factions were to view them as hostile. For this reason, throughout the operations, Sadako Ogata, head of the UNHCR, was against the use of force by UNPROFOR, since this could leave her operations, and others similar to hers, open to attack. However, not all of the UN agencies or member states agreed with this position. Most felt that armed protection of humanitarian convoys was necessary, and that "close air support" from NATO would be appropriate.

Moreover the mandate for the safe areas stipulated a military approach both to disarming Bosnian government forces from within, and protecting civilians inside the territories from surrounding hostile Serb forces. The concept of a safe area necessitated armed involvement, and non-neutral activity, both to disarm and to protect. While the Security Council voted unanimously to construct safe areas, it did not spell out what would happen to the humanitarian mandates

---

[97] Annan, 1999, para. 43.
[98] Owen, 1995, p. 355. See a similar statement made by the Pakistani representative to the UN Security Council in Annan, 1999, para. 71.

that were based on consent, nor did it specify how the Secretariat was to protect the areas, given so few forces at their disposal.

Second, within the Secretariat itself, tensions often arose between Secretary-General Boutros-Ghali in New York and the military commanders on the ground. Command on the ground was changing frequently (generally every six months), and thus the UNPROFOR command was frequently divorced from policymaking. One person working for the UN on the ground described the ground-headquarters relations in regard to the safe areas mandate and its implementation as "Kafkaesque."[99] The Secretary-General's report on Srebrenica also states that UNPROFOR suffered from "command and control problems . . . throughout its history."[100] Extreme examples of difficulties arose in March 1993, when French UNPROFOR Commander Philippe Morillon declared that the UN would protect the inhabitants of Srebrenica, who were under frequent Serb attacks, without first consulting UN headquarters in New York.[101] Then again, in January 1993, General Jean Cot repeatedly ignored or challenged the plans of his superiors at headquarters, in particular the wishes of the Secretary-General.[102] And lastly, after the fall of Srebrenica in July 1995, the Dutch Battalion "did not report . . . fully the scenes that were unfolding around them following the enclave's fall . . . This failure of intelligence-sharing was also not limited to the fall of Srebrenica, but an endemic weakness throughout the conflict, both within the peacekeeping mission, and between the mission and Member States."[103] In other words, there were debilitating tensions in command and control, between the leadership in the field and headquarters, which led to poor communication and information-sharing and disastrous results of decision-making processes.

Finally, there were also often conflicts, rather than integration, between the UN forces on the ground and the Bosnian government regarding the safe areas.[104] The Bosnian government had understood that the UN was intervening in these areas to protect civilians, but instead, the UN operations in the safe havens, given the lack of reinforcement troops, wound up creating large refugee camps where people could be minimally fed, clothed, and sheltered, but not necessarily protected from Serb attacks. Indeed, the UN mandate as carried out meant that the UN in effect was creating large pockets of potential victims (often evacuated from other areas – thus the UN was seen as contributing to the goals of the ethnic cleansers), attempting to disarm them, and then not

---

[99] David Harland, interview with the author, Sarajevo, June 11, 1998.
[100] Annan, 1999, para. 471.   [101] Morillon, 1993; and Rhode, 1997, p. xv.
[102] Preston, 1994.   [103] Annan, 1999, para. 474.
[104] There were also tensions between the UN and the Bosnian Serb forces, as the Bosnian Serbs had understood that the safe areas were supposed to be completely demilitarized. Instead, reports that the bases were being used as places for rest and re-fueling for the Bosnian government forces provoked the anger and retaliation by the Serbs. See Woodward, 1995, p. 321; and Durch and Schear, 1996, p. 237.

protecting them from attack. These policies inspired no love for the UN on the part of the mainly Muslim civilians, not to mention the Bosnian government and its military. The results of organizational dysfunction within the UN were deadly.

On July 7, 1995, Bosnian Serb forces attacked the safe area of Srebrenica. UNPROFOR's Dutch commander requested that NATO provide close air support, but he was denied that request from within the UN.[105] The next day, the Dutch peacekeepers began to withdraw to protect themselves, but they were fired on by Bosnian government troops in an attempt to force the UN to call in NATO airstrikes against the Bosnian Serb forces.[106] The threat/request was denied because of "poor visibility." After many more requests for air support, Dutch and American F-16s struck two Serb tanks, but the attack was quickly called off for fear of the safety of the Dutch peacekeepers on the ground.[107] By July 10, 15,000 Muslim men of fighting age had disappeared from Srebrenica, and many were massacred.[108] In all, upwards of 40,000 Muslims were "ethnically cleansed" from the area.

Two weeks later, the safe area of Zepa came under attack. There, a small Ukrainian contingent of UNPROFOR was held hostage by Muslim forces who threatened to kill the peacekeepers unless NATO struck the Serbs from the air. The desperate hostage-taking attempt proved to be in vain, as the enclave was overrun and ethnically cleansed by July 25; over 100 people were massacred. When Gorazde, the largest of the safe areas, came under similar attack, it was defended by NATO airstrikes.[109] In the other safe areas, geographical or local defenses were enough to ward off attacks. The assaults on the safe areas precipitated the downfall of UNPROFOR and end of the war. NATO responded to the attacks in August 1995 with "Operation Deliberate Force," bombarding Serb positions around Bosnia; at the same time, the Croatian government expelled its Serb population from Serb-occupied territories in Croatia. These events severely crippled the ability of Serb forces from all of the former Yugoslav republics to wage war, eventually forcing Milosevic to the bargaining table in Dayton, Ohio. Bosnia remains in a state of negative peace with international forces continuing to oversee its security and smooth functioning of the state.[110]

---

[105] Under the "dual key" arrangement, NATO could only use air power when requested by the UN to do so.

[106] Fifty-five UN troops were also held hostage by Bosnian Serb forces ostensibly to protect the Serbs against airstrikes.

[107] On July 21, the Dutch contingent withdrew.

[108] The International Red Cross estimates that over 7,000 people are still missing, most of whom are presumed dead.

[109] Some wondered why UNPROFOR's new Rapid Reaction Force was not used to ward off these offenses. The Rapid Reaction Force was designed not to come to the aid of civilians, but rather to protect UNPROFOR troops and humanitarian convoys.

[110] Friedman, 2004; Chandler, 2005; and Gallagher, 2005.

The problems that beset the UN's policies in the safe areas are a classic example of organizational dysfunction and its potentially tragic results. The Secretariat was unsystematic in its information gathering, analysis, and information
dissemination. The Security Council was unable to come to a consensus about
the definition of the problem, in part because of the lack of advice from the
Secretariat. There was poor coordination between humanitarian and military
divisions, between headquarters and the field, and between the UN mission
and the local government. Rather than engaging in a constructive way with
the population and elites, the mission antagonized both Bosnian Muslims and
Bosnian Serbs. And finally, UN Secretariat leadership was not well exercised
either in the field operation, or at UN headquarters. This overwhelming picture
of organizational dysfunction was caused in part by poor and contradictory
decision-making in the Security Council, and a belligerent, genocidal, Bosnian
Serb army, but the failings of the Secretariat are undoubtedly an important part
of the picture.

Conclusion

In each of these cases, there were generally three primary factors at play working
to cause the failure of the peacekeeping operations. Often the situational difficulty, especially nonconsent of the parties before the start of the peacekeeping
operation, appears to drive the failure, but this is not always the case. I argue
that in Somalia and Angola in particular – the two cases where nonconsent of
the parties is most often invoked as the reason for the failure – it is possible that
consent could have been maintained if members of the Security Council had
behaved differently, or if the UN peacekeeping operation had functioned better.
In Somalia, early UN efforts to obtain consent from Aideed were effective, but
they were thwarted by tensions between UN headquarters and field operations;
in Angola, consent was forthcoming from both parties until it became clear
that the UN could not oversee the maintenance of the cease-fire or guarantee
Savimbi's safety.

The early failure in Somalia foreshadowed the other failures, since it created a
pervasive sense of doubt about the possibility for peacekeeping success among
the members of the Security Council, especially within the most powerful
member, the United States. This doubt drove the Council to become less inclined
to field large and potentially more effective peacekeeping forces, and it became
more skeptical of the abilities of the Secretariat. Meanwhile, important cases
of success, as discussed in the following chapters, were ignored even though
greater recognition could have potentially countered the Council's reservations.
In terms of second-level learning between missions, only the simple, negative
"lessons" of Somalia were applied during the Council's decision-making about
the conflicts in Rwanda, Angola, and Bosnia. Even though the preconditions
in Rwanda and Angola were radically different from the other cases – namely,

that there were detailed peace agreements signed by both sides, and both sides had consented to the UN peacekeeping operation – the Council decided not to take risks by fielding large forces. The failure in Somalia led many members of the Council to become extremely risk-averse, which negatively affected the ability of the UN to alter the situations on the ground. But Security Council interests also appear to have arisen in response to other factors than what happened in Somalia. Lack of consensus on the nature of the problems, driven most likely by domestic political considerations, compelled the Council to draft contradictory resolutions that were next to impossible to implement. Partly as a consequence, in each of the cases, the UN Secretariat fell into a state of organizational dysfunction.

In the cases of failure, the Secretariat was often experiencing organizational dysfunction, with the exception of some organizational learning in Angola. When the Security Council handed down mandates that were contradictory, the Secretariat did not insist on clarification or simplification. The contradictions were often between UN Charter Chapters VI and VII mandates. A Chapter VI peacekeeping mandate requires that force be used only in self-defense, reliance on the host country for infrastructure support, and the fielding of a broad-based, neutral, international peacekeeping force that behaves in a generally pacific and conciliatory manner toward the parties in the conflict and toward the civilian population. In contrast, in a Chapter VII peacekeeping mandate, often referred to as "peace-enforcement," the UN mission views one or more of the parties in the conflict as adversaries. The force commanders must take strategic initiatives to use force to secure positions; the mission cannot always rely on the support of the host country; and there must be a tight military command (i.e., not widely multinational) that is prepared for warlike battle. In Somalia, Rwanda, and Bosnia, the peacekeeping operations were given directly contradictory mandates under both Chapters VI and VII. In addition, in Angola, which was under a Chapter VI mandate alone, the neutrality of the peacekeeping force was questionable given that at the same time the Security Council had imposed Chapter VII sanctions against UNITA.

In none of the cases did the Secretariat dare to challenge the Council when the Council handed down contradictory peacekeeping mandates, even though it potentially could have. While the Secretariat is beholden in many ways to the Council, it is also undoubtedly an actor, both in a moral and practical sense, during the formulation of mandates, and especially during their implementation. Within the Secretariat, the failures are almost always attributed to the Security Council and to the warring factions. However, to be charged with implementation of mandates means that the Secretariat is accountable, in part, for the outcome of the mandate implementation. As I demonstrate in the following chapters, the Secretariat often bears responsibility for successes as much as it does for failures.

3

Namibia: the first major success

Introduction

The United Nations Transition Assistance Group (UNTAG) in Namibia was the UN's first attempt at engaging in multidimensional peacekeeping since the downfall of the Congo operation in 1964. Ending in March 1990, the mission differed from all previous UN peacekeeping operations in that its primary means and purpose were political (in overseeing a democratic transition after decades of civil war and colonial rule), rather than military (where monitoring a cease-fire is the primary task). The mission also brought about the innovation of several important peacekeeping mechanisms that are still in use today, namely, a western "Contact Group," an elaborate "information program," and most significantly, UN "civilian policing" in its current form. Overall, the operation was successful on two fronts: first, in terms of implementing the Security Council Resolution 435 mandate; and second, by creating the conditions for the ongoing political stability of post-independence Namibia.

In this chapter, I argue that UNTAG was able to "learn" as an organization on the ground, during mandate implementation, and that this was a primary cause of the operation's successful conclusion. While fortuitous "situational factors" and moderate Security Council interests were also important conditions, organizational learning lies at the heart of UNTAG's success. At critical moments during the implementation of the peace accords, UNTAG took its cues from local, rather than higher-level political forces in the Security Council. In other words, the implementation was not micromanaged from the political center in New York. This configuration enabled the UNTAG to integrate better with its environment, and to learn from it.

Situational factors

The war in Namibia progressed over time from a guerrilla war of independence to a civil war, as South Africa increasingly developed indigenous Namibian forces to fight against the South West African People's Organization (SWAPO). The internal Namibian conflict would be the primary definition and focus of

An earlier version of this chapter was published as "UN Peace Implementation in Namibia: The Causes of Success," *International Peacekeeping*, Vol. 9, No. 1, 2002.

UNTAG, and early efforts of the "Contact Group."[1] But the war was also part of a larger regional struggle fought between South Africa and its neighbors. The regional conflict was the United States' preferred definition of the problem. Third-party disagreements over the basic nature of the problem, and methods to solve it, led to the temporary dissolution of the Contact Group, and a ten-year delay in implementation of the 1978 peace accord. But before addressing these events, I turn to a brief historical overview of Namibia.

Namibia is unlike most countries in the world, in that it experienced essentially all of the most horrific political ills of the twentieth century – genocide, colonialism, and apartheid. Formerly known as South West Africa, Namibia is sparsely populated, measures about one and a half times the size of France, and has two large deserts encroaching on much of the land – the Namib in the west, and the Kalahari in the East. In the late 1800s it was colonized by Germany, during which time the Germans committed genocide against the Herero and Nama tribes.[2] After Germany's defeat in World War I, South Africa occupied the territory. South West Africa was then under British control for a brief period, later to be reoccupied by South Africa in 1920, which administered it under a League of Nations C mandate. After World War II, South West Africa was slated to fall under UN Trusteeship, but South Africa refused to relinquish control.

In 1966, the United Nations General Assembly declared South African rule illegal, and named SWAPO the "sole and authentic" representative of the Namibian people. In 1971 the International Court of Justice also ruled against South Africa's mandate. But international declarations and rulings did not induce South Africa to give up its claims on Namibia. By the late 1950s, South Africa had already institutionalized its system of apartheid in Namibia and considered it a fifth province, governed by a South African "Administrator-General." South Africa's economic interests in Namibia's diamond and mineral mines, plus a desire to protect the minority white way of life, led to increasing tensions. The year 1966 marked the first armed battle between SWAPO and South African forces at the SWAPO camp in Omgulumbashe, Namibia.

South Africa's ban of opposition movements in its own country and sur-rounding territories sparked approximately thirty years of war in the region, with separate, but at times interrelated, struggles in Angola, Mozambique, Namibia, South Africa, and Zimbabwe.[3] With the fall of Portuguese colonial rule in 1974, Angola and Mozambique became independent and quickly fell

---

[1] The "Western Contact Group" was set up in 1977 to aid in the (unsuccessful) imple-mentation of an early UN Security Council resolution on Namibia. Its members were the United States, the United Kingdom, France, West Germany, and Canada. For an excellent description of the group's early achievements see Karns, 1987.

[2] The genocide occurred in response to the tribes' resistance to colonization, between 1904 and 1908. On the genocide, see Caroll, 1967.

[3] See Nujoma, 2001; and Mandela, 2004.

victim to internal fighting; both countries became fertile training ground for "Marxist" Namibian guerrillas.

Meanwhile, the South African government sought to oppose the rise of SWAPO by building up both South African-sympathetic indigenous administrative structures and military forces in Namibia. In terms of the civilian administration, South Africa sought to establish an "internal government" in Namibia. This began with the December 1978 and November 1980 elections to ethnically based "Representative Authorities."[4] As one scholar explains, people elected to the head of the Representative Authorities were

> well-paid politicians provid[ing] themselves with luxurious cars and homes, and a top-heavy bureaucracy [was] spawned. Ethnic administrations soon became breeding grounds for enormous waste, inefficiency, and corruption, while the White administration retained its generous tax base and its extensive, under-utilized facilities, protecting them by a policy of rigid racial segregation.[5]

Thus, some elites from various ethnic groups in Namibia were reaping the benefits of cooperating with South African-influenced rule.

Ethnic divisions, while downplayed in most of the literature on Namibia, are partially relevant for understanding some of the Namibian internal political battles during the 1970s and 1980s, and even some tensions today. Ovambos make up the largest ethnic group (about 50 percent), and were the founders of SWAPO. Alienation from what has been perceived as Ovambo nationalism in SWAPO helped to convince leaders of several other ethnic groups to support the South African-imposed Representative Authorities. Some also united in the multiracial Democratic Turnhalle Alliance (DTA) – formerly the second largest political party in Namibia, and one that is still struggling to rid itself of its identity as the "colonial collaborator."[6] Part of the DTA's political platform during the 1980s included the claim that the party would protect Namibia from the spread of socialism as promulgated by SWAPO. Thus, through various ideological, ethnic, and instrumental means, South Africa built support for its administrative structures in Namibia.

Another aspect of South Africa's strategy to maintain its authority in Namibia was to build up indigenous military forces to fight against SWAPO and its "People's Liberation Army" (PLAN). Under the 1980 legislative proclamation AG8, Namibians of fighting age were forcibly conscripted into the South

---

[4] The Representative Authorities had been established under AG8, the South African-controlled Administrator-General's Proclamation of April 1980. See *Official Gazette Extraordinary of South West Africa*, 1980.

[5] Harlech-Jones, 1997, p. 29.

[6] Dreyer, 1994, p. 109. The DTA garnered significant financial support from South Africa during the 1970s and 1980s.

West African Territorial Force (SWATF), which was designed to fight alongside the South African Defense Forces (SADF) against SWAPO in the north.[7] By 1986, "officially, 35,000 [SADF] troops were stationed in Namibia, with unofficial estimates indicating the much higher number of 80,000."[8] Joining the SADF, by 1989, the SWATF had grown to over 30,000 troops, about half of whom were non-white Namibians. In addition, 7,000 to 10,000 Namibians[9] were put into well-paying "counterinsurgency" units, under the South West African Police (SWAPOL), including the infamous Koevoet or "crowbar" unit – a multiracial group, notorious for its brutal and indiscriminate use of force.[10] The build-up of these forces meant that up to half of those fighting against SWAPO were indigenous Namibians, coming from a wide swath of groups and regions. During the 1980s, the war of liberation from South Africa took on more of the quality of a civil war, with Namibian political groups and military forces fighting each other for control of the state.[11]

Battles over the victors of Namibian (and Angolan) independence continued until late 1987 and early 1988, the fiercest of which were waged in northern Namibia and parts of Angola. In late 1988, a military stalemate was reached in Angola, with the battle of Cuito Cuanevale. The large costs to South Africa of supporting the military operations in Angola and Namibia, coupled with the anti-apartheid international economic sanctions, and the growing mobilization of church groups, students, and workers in Namibia and South Africa, led the South African government to back down on its military campaigns.[12] This, in addition to the exit of the P. W. Botha administration, the release of Nelson Mandela, US pressure to remove Cuban troops from Angola, and Soviet pressure on the African National Congress and similar organizations to back away from the strategy of armed struggle, culminated in an opening in the Namibian negotiations.[13]

---

[7] This rule provoked massive protests within Namibia, and a 5,000-person refugee exodus to the front-line states. See *Official Gazette Extraordinary of South West Africa*, "Proclamation by the Administrator-General for the Territory of South West Africa. No. AG8." Windhoek, 24 April 1980.

[8] Dreyer, 1994, p. 161.

[9] Reports on these numbers vary widely. These are taken from Cliffe, 1994, p. 33.

[10] According to Wren, 1989, the Koevoet were said to be responsible for the majority of Namibian deaths.

[11] In all approximately 11,291 of SWAPO's People's Liberation Army (PLAN) fighters, 2,000 civilians, and 715 South African security forces were killed in the Namibian battles, while between 44,000 and 90,000 Namibians were made refugees out of a pre-independence population of 1.4 million. See Steenkamp, 1989, p. 185; Ntchatcho, 1993, p. 65; and Brown, 1995, p. 37.

[12] Costs were estimated at R 4 billion in 1988. See Price, 1991, p. 277.

[13] Note that Cuba had upwards of 50,000 troops in Angola, fighting against UNITA.

Security Council interests

This opening in the negotiations had been a long time in the making. As far back as 1978, the UN Security Council had agreed to the basic principle of a UN-assisted Namibian independence process, with a decision in favor of Security Council Resolution 435. But disputes remained over which groups would determine the outcomes of Namibian independence. The rough international political division over Namibia was between, on one side, South Africa, the Namibian "internal parties," and at times the Contact Group, and on the other, SWAPO, the UN General Assembly, the non-aligned states in the UN Security Council, and the front-line states.[14] The UN Secretariat's UNTAG mission, mandated by 435, was supposed to be impartial, even though both South Africa and SWAPO accused UNTAG of favoring the other side.[15] South Africa and its supporters on the Security Council, namely the United States, the United Kingdom, and West Germany, favored a South African-administered independence process.[16] This would insure that western investments in Namibia would remain secure, as some feared possible nationalization of major industries in a SWAPO-driven independence.[17] These three western states, along with Canada and France, were also members of the Contact Group. The Contact Group innovation was designed as an ad hoc multilateral forum, which would put international diplomatic pressure on the South African government to release its grip on Namibia.[18] The Contact Group brought South Africa to the negotiating table and drafted three 1978 documents, which created the basic framework of UNTAG's peace implementation mandate.

[14] The front-line states included Tanzania, Zambia, Angola, Mozambique, Botswana, and Zimbabwe (since its independence in 1980), plus Nigeria. The group was founded by the Tanzanian President Julius Nyerere with the aim of coordinating African policies on the liberation of Southern African countries.

[15] Prior to setting up its offices in Namibia, UNTAG was seen by South Africa and the DTA as favoring SWAPO, because of the UN General Assembly's support for SWAPO. The General Assembly supported SWAPO financially for many years, including the construction of the United Nations Institute for Namibia in Angola, set up to train Namibian exiles and refugees.

[16] West Germany was a non-permanent member of the Security Council in both 1978 and 1988 – the two years when many of the significant international debates about Namibia took place. At one critical point, the Council held a ten-in-favor (out of fifteen total) vote on a resolution to condemn South Africa for holding illegal elections to the Namibian Representative Authorities. In a rare move, the five Council members who were also in the Western Contact Group abstained, signaling support for South Africa. See S/RES/439, 13 November 1978.

[17] "All Five [Contact Group members] had strong economic interests in maintaining their relationship with South Africa." Vergau, in Weiland and Braham, 1994, p. 30.

[18] See footnote 1.

Mandate

The documents included first, the Contact Group's Settlement Proposal of April 10, 1978, second, the Secretary-General's report of August 29, 1978, and finally Security Council Resolution 435.[19] First, the Settlement Proposal called for free and fair elections to pave the way for a transition to Namibian independence. The proposal included the mandate for the Secretary-General to appoint a Special Representative, who "will have to satisfy himself at each stage as to the fairness and appropriateness of all measures affecting the political process at all levels of administration before such measures take effect. Moreover the Special Representative may himself make proposals in regard to any aspect of the political process."[20] This resolution placed the Special Representative at the center of all operational decision-making. Finnish diplomat Martti Ahtisaari was chosen for the position in 1978, after his appointment as the UN General Assembly's Commissioner for Namibia starting the year before. Ahtisaari had previously held diplomatic posts in Africa, serving as Finnish Ambassador to Tanzania, with accreditation to Zambia, Mozambique, and Somalia. Ahtisaari would eventually become the UN Under Secretary-General for Administration before serving as Special Representative, and later, the President of Finland.[21]

The Settlement Proposal included a very specific timetable for the implementation of the elections, with explicit tasks that the UN, the South African government, and SWAPO were to fulfill. The elections were to create an independent Namibian Constituent Assembly, which would draw up a constitution immediately after being elected, and govern as the independent Namibian "National Assembly" from then on. All adult Namibians would be eligible to express political views, form political parties, and vote by secret ballot without fear of discrimination. Before the election campaigns, all discriminatory or restrictive laws were to be repealed, all refugees welcomed back into the country, all hostile acts were to cease, and all political prisoners were to be released. An independent jurist was to be appointed to oversee matters concerning the release of political prisoners and detainees.

While the above provisions concerning the elections were basically clear, some uncertainties remained, many of which were cleared up five months later in the Secretary-General's report S/12827. For example, Secretary-General Javier Pérez de Cuéllar requested specific numbers of forces based on estimates of the numbers of South African forces in the country. He united the civilian and military components of UNTAG under one Special Representative. He also broadly defined the military component's ability to use force in self-defense,

---

[19] See S/12636, 10 April 1978; S/12827, 29 August 1978; and S/RES/435, 12 July 1982.

[20] S/12636, 10 April 1978, para. 5.

[21] Ahtisaari has also since played important roles in peace negotiations across the world, in Bosnia, Banda Aceh, Iraq, Central Asia, and is currently the lead UN negotiator for the Kosovo peace talks.

including "resistance to attempts to prevent it from discharging its duties under the mandate of the Security Council," and he estimated the pull-out date to be one year from the start date.[22] The conditions for ensuring free and fair elections were also further elaborated and grouped in a logical order. However, the report did not address a number of issues including: the start date of the operation; how and whether SWAPO would be restricted to base; the process of disarmament; police, judicial, and constitutional reform; reform of the civil service; economic reform, including the question of land redistribution; the specifics of financing the operation; and the extent to which the UN would be "controlling" or merely "supervising" the elections. These uncertainties, while potentially hindering the operation, actually helped the Special Representative define the mission based on the realities of 1988 when the operation began, rather than 1978, when the accord was initially drafted.

Finally, Security Council Resolution 435 of 1978, a rather brief document, accepted the previous proposals, reiterated the objective of the withdrawal of South Africa's "illegal administration" of Namibia, welcomed SWAPO's readiness to sign a cease-fire, called on South Africa to sign, and later included an annex on broad constitutional principles. Other than the constitutional principles, it did not attempt to address the thorny issues listed above.

The 435 vote was not unanimous. In a mild diplomatic counter to the western initiative, the USSR and Czechoslovakia abstained while China did not participate in the vote. As the Soviet Ambassador to the UN at the time, Anatolyi Adamishin, explains: "We [Soviets] did not hate 435, we only considered it unbalanced . . . Our African friends asked us not to veto it because it was better than nothing. So we agreed. Later our friends reproached us, requesting that we do something about it because it gave too many advantages to South Africa. But by then it was too late."[23] But the resolution also gave many advantages to SWAPO, namely the possibility of internationally supported majority rule and independence. While it appeared that conditions were ripe for implementation of 435, both sides remained resistant to setting a cease-fire date, believing each was being pressured by its allies to concede too much.

Linkage

The beginning of implementation was then further delayed after the 1980 US presidential elections. The new Reagan administration replaced the Carter foreign policy team and introduced a strategy of "linkage" as a way to end the conflicts in Southern Africa. According to Chester Crocker, former US Assistant Secretary of State for African Affairs, South Africa declared that it would agree to Namibian independence only after Cuban troops had been withdrawn from Angola. The Reagan administration also wanted to ensure that Namibia

---

[22] S/12827, 29 August 1978, para. 20.   [23] Weiland and Braham, 1994, p. 21.

remained free from the spread of communism, and that this could only be assured if Namibian independence were linked with Cuban troop withdrawal.[24] Meanwhile, in the UK, Prime Minister Margaret Thatcher was eager to join in the "ringing assault on socialism," through the US-proposed "constructive engagement" with South Africa.[25]

Although the linkage policy may have been created with the best of intentions, it caused the Namibian peace process to falter. France, under the socialist government in 1983, temporarily suspended its participation in the Contact Group to protest against the linkage policy.[26] Later, West Germany and Canada followed suit. In addition, as one analyst explains, "SWAPO, Angola, and the other front-line states decried linkage and constructive engagement. All saw the new US positions as indications that the United States supported South Africa and its policies, including apartheid."[27]

While the fighting in Namibia intensified over the 1980s, there were some Security Council debates over clarifications and amendments of 435, especially concerning ways to draw South Africa into the process. The front-line states, the Contact Group, and SWAPO all agreed that the South African Administrator-General Louis A. Pienaar and the UN Special Representative Martti Ahtisaari would exercise joint authority over Namibia during the transition period. In addition, the UN attempted to increase its status as impartial by discontinuing General Assembly funds to SWAPO and suspending SWAPO from General Assembly observer status. Constitutional reforms were also agreed to, whereby personnel in the civil service would retain their positions upon independence. This would help to ensure that whites maintain their socioeconomic positions in post-independence Namibian society.[28] These provisions were offered in large part to convince the South African government of the UN's commitment to impartial implementation of the peace accord.

By 1988, all sides appeared ready to begin active negotiations again, due in large part to the changing international circumstances, and the stalemate on the battlefield in Angola. The Non-Aligned Movement, which had five members on the Council in 1988 and seven in 1989, and the USSR favored a process whereby SWAPO would have more control over the terms of independence.[29] Considering the fact that in order to pass a Security Council resolution there must be at least nine votes out of fifteen in favor, the divide could potentially have deadlocked the Council. Rather than trying to secure a Security Council

[24] Crocker, 1992, pp. 63–66.   [25] Urquhart, 1987, p. 307.   [26] Vance, 1983, p. 126.

[27] Papp, 1993, p. 173. Brian Urquhart (head of UN peacekeeping until 1986), UN Secretary-General Javier Pérez de Cuéllar, and former US Ambassador Donald McHenry have all spoken of the negative effects of linkage on the peace process in Namibia.

[28] S/15287, supplement to Security Council Resolution 435, 12 July 1982.

[29] In 1988, Algeria, Nepal, Senegal, Yugoslavia, and Zambia, all members of the Non-Aligned Movement, were on the Council. In 1989, there were seven non-aligned countries on the Security Council: Algeria, Colombia, Ethiopia, Malaysia, Nepal, Senegal, and Yugoslavia.

resolution, the cease-fire negotiating process briefly left the UN altogether, reverting back to the domain of the Contact Group.

South Africa insisted on excluding SWAPO from all negotiations, a demand to which the United States assented.[30] Subsequently, the Protocols of Geneva and Brazzaville, and the Tripartite agreement were all signed in 1988 by Angola, Cuba, and South Africa, under the mediation of Chester Crocker. These agreements set dates for Cuban and SADF troop withdrawal from Angola, UN verification of the withdrawals, SWAPO deployment to north of the 16th parallel in Angola, and a "Joint Commission" between Angola, Cuba, and South Africa (with the United States and USSR as observers) as "a forum for discussion and resolution of issues regarding the interpretation and implementation of the tripartite agreement."[31]

These agreements mentioned Namibia only in passing. The United States and United Kingdom defined the war primarily as a regional one. Once the official cease-fire was signed – but not by the excluded SWAPO – and the Cuban troop withdrawal secured, they thought that the internal problems in Namibia would basically work themselves out, with minimal UN assistance. However, more third-party mediation and eventual peacekeeping was necessary, given SWAPO's exclusion from the process and the potential for deepening civil war within Namibia.

UN assistance restarted when Secretary-General Pérez de Cuéllar pieced together a cease-fire agreement between SWAPO and South Africa. Each party signed identical letters to Pérez de Cuéllar, pledging to abide by Security Council Resolution 435, and the date of April 1 for the cease-fire. To the end, South Africa refused to legitimate SWAPO by signing an agreement directly with the party.

Consensus

Thus during the 1980s, there was a rather low degree of Security Council *consensus* as to the members' interests in the area, the nature of the problem, and what to do, as evidenced by the creation and dissolution of the Contact Group. After 1980, the United States, unlike most other Security Council members, defined the problem as a regional one. This definition arose out of an ideological interest in stopping the spread of communism, and economic interests that were

---

[30] "Crocker had the policy [of] only talk[ing] to governments." Vergau, in Weiland and Braham, 1994, p. 80. Chester Crocker defends this policy by insisting that "opening the door to non-state parties" would mean an "endless" list of parties with which to deal. But others in the Contact Group, mainly members from West Germany, countered that SWAPO was the only significant non-state warring party in Namibia, thus it should have been included. See Weiland and Braham, 1994, pp. 78–79.

[31] "The Protocol of Brazzaville, 13 December 1988"; "The Protocol of Geneva, 5 August 1988" (reproduced in S/20566, 4 April 1989); and "Agreement Between Angola, Cuba and South Africa, 22 December 1988" (reproduced in S/20346, 22 December 1988).

assumed to be better protected by a South African-sympathetic Namibian elite. In contrast, states in the Soviet bloc and the Non-Aligned Movement maintained that they were more interested in the problems of colonialism, apartheid, and negation of the basic human rights of the majority of the population in Namibia; the Soviet bloc was also, of course, interested in furthering its own ideological and economic interests in the spread of socialism. By 1988, the crumbling of communism and apartheid paved the way for the beginning of UN implementation of the 1978 peace accord.

The convergence of ideological interests was also bolstered by the fact that as early as 1978, all sides had essentially agreed to a formula whereby the UN would *oversee* a Namibian independence process that would actually be *administered* by the South African-supported government in Namibia. It had taken nearly ten years for the permanent five members to agree on what to do in Namibia. The tenuous consensus in 1988 ushered in the three important agreements on Cuban troop withdrawal from Angola; the start date of the UNTAG operation in Namibia was an additional, but less prominent, part of these agreements. Overall, we can thus say that "usually" there was Security Council consensus about what to do in Namibia. But before turning to the specifics of the implementation process, we must first discuss Security Council interest *intensity*.

Intensity

In 1988, the Security Council did not have all that much on its plate, especially compared to what was to come over the next four years. The Council adopted twenty resolutions during the entire year. The majority of these concerned the Middle East and the Iran–Iraq conflict. Namibia briefly flashed on the radar screen in September, but again, western member states had chosen to negotiate through the Contact Group, outside the realm of the UN or the Security Council.

In 1989, the negotiations shifted back to the UN forum. The Council adopted twenty resolutions again, but this time one-fifth had to do with Namibia, which meant that more Council time was spent on this conflict than any other peace and security issue. Most of the debates were over UNTAG's size and budget. The western powers argued that the main problem had been solved (Cuban troop withdrawal from Angola), and that UNTAG's budget should be cut severely, mainly by halving the UNTAG military component from the original estimate of over 7,500 troops.[32]

---

[32] In Chester Crocker's memoir, *High Noon in Southern Africa: Making Peace in a Rough Neighborhood* (1992), he devotes less than a page to the UN implementation process in Namibia (see p. 484). This is symbolic of the extent to which implementation of the Namibian mandate was of low-level importance to the United States. Once the Cuban

In contrast, the non-aligned countries argued that the situation on the ground in Namibia had changed for the worse, in that there were many more South African-trained and sympathetic police and Security Forces fighting against SWAPO in a civil war. They argued that this new ground situation necessitated *more* of an UNTAG presence rather than less.[33] The Secretariat, represented by Secretary-General Pérez de Cuéllar, split the difference. It recommended that troop levels be kept at the original number in reserve, but that only 4,650 be deployed. The formal cease-fire and implementation start date was set for April 1, 1989. But the debates in the Security Council and the General Assembly dragged on until March 1, which meant that UNTAG would not be fully operational until well into May 1989. The budget for the operation was cut from approximately $700 million to $416 million, but none of the implementation tasks were removed.[34] By April 1, the official start of the cease-fire, UNTAG had only a handful of people on the ground. This inadequate presence helped precipitate the violent clashes of early April, which almost led to the downfall of the operation, as discussed below.

In all, the intensity of Security Council interest in Namibia in 1988–89 could be characterized as "moderate." By 1989, the Security Council's interest in Namibia had intensified, as manifest in the increased number of debates and resolutions on the subject, but this increased intensity did not translate into an increase in support; rather, the proposed budget was cut nearly in half.[35] The moderate level of interest in the Namibian operation, while potentially undermining the operation's effectiveness, appears to have worked to the benefit of UNTAG. It meant that much of the important day-to-day decision-making in UNTAG took place on the ground, in Namibia, in relation to the needs of the operation, rather than at headquarters, in relation to great-power concern over the details of the operation.

Organizational change and mandate implementation

How did the UNTAG mission learn in Namibia during the twelve-month implementation of its mandate? Learning was possible in part because all of the

troop withdrawal had been acomplished, the United States became, fortuitously, uninterested in the Namibian problem. The United States had "a regional strategy and was not explicitly concerned with internal conflicts." Weiland and Braham, 1994, p. 78.

[33] See Pérez de Cuéllar, 1997, p. 308.

[34] See United Nations, 1996, p. 228. It is entirely possible that the drastic cut in the military division might not have been very detrimental to the overall operation, as it forced the organizers of UNTAG to resort to more creative uses of their budget.

[35] During the implementation phase, the Security Council did not often address the efforts in Namibia, essentially leaving the operations to the Secretariat. Only two resolutions were passed – S/RES/640, 29 August 1989, and S/RES/643, 31 October 1989 – both of which were sponsored by the non-aligned countries and are discussed further in the section on civilian policing.

preconditions for learning were satisfied. The leaders of UNTAG were granted broad authority over the general operation, and in particular over the actions of the South African Administrator-General, as detailed in the 1978 Settlement Proposal. UNTAG organizers had been involved in the planning of the mission from the outset of the negotiations and were well versed in Namibian politics and society by the time of the implementation. While UNTAG had a clear and centralized chain of command, it was also spread wide throughout the vast country, in order to engage the organization directly with its environment. The spread of the organization allowed it to learn about the needs and worries of ordinary Namibians, while teaching them about the coming elections, political parties, and democratic governance. The preconditions made organizational learning possible.

The four central components of the mission included (1) overall establishment of UNTAG offices, (2) military disarmament and civilian policing, (3) refugee return, and (4) preparations for, and the holding of, elections.[36] Each of these components confronted crises or changing circumstances on the ground and dealt with them appropriately, as discussed below.

Establishment of the UNTAG offices amidst renewed fighting

On April 1, 1989, the day that the UN operation was to begin, between 300 and 500 PLAN fighters emerged on the Namibian/Angolan border. Koevoet, SWATF, and SADF forces began to fire at the PLAN, believing their intentions to be aggressive.[37] SWAPO responded by sending reinforcements southward from Angola, to aid the PLAN fighters. The South African side requested of the UN that SADF forces, many of which had already been restricted to base, be released to fight in the battle. The SADF declared that their forces on the battlefield were outnumbered, that SWAPO was acting in violation of the Geneva Protocol, and that SWAPO's PLAN must be stopped with force. Martti Ahtisaari, UN Special Representative of the Secretary-General, was in Namibia but unequipped to take control of the situation. There were not nearly enough UNTAG forces in Namibia to enforce a cease-fire (only 300 military observers had arrived several

---

[36] A separate component of the operation was the office of the "Independent Jurist." This person was to oversee the release of political prisoners and detainees and offer legal advise to the Special Representative when needed. In total, the Independent Jurist oversaw and made recommendations for only sixteen cases of prisoners held by South Africa. As for the issue of SWAPO detainees, in the 1970s and 1980s, up to 2,000 SWAPO members were detained by their comrades under suspicion of spying on behalf of South Africa. In 1989, members of the Special Representative's office visited all purported sites of detention and found them to be empty. However, the issue of detainees remains a sore political issue even today. See Groth, 1995; and Saul and Leys, 2003.

[37] Many reports on this subject have been made, and most conclude that the PLAN fighters were not expecting to fight. Rather, they were expecting to be rounded up and confined to base by UN peacekeepers.

days earlier), moreover, UNTAG never had the capability to stop forces from fighting. Ahtisaari convinced Secretary-General Pérez de Cuéllar to allow some SADF and SWATF troops to leave their bases to counter the perceived military attack being waged by PLAN fighters. After nine days of fighting, more than 300 PLAN fighters and civilians and thirteen SADF soldiers were killed. It looked as though UNTAG had failed even before it began. After these events, South Africa and SWAPO had reason to pull out of the hard-won agreements, as both had violated those agreements by breaking the cease-fire.

There are three basic arguments as to the cause of the April 1 fiasco; all are in part valid. First, some argue that UNTAG could have prevented the incursion, but that the budgetary and deployment delays precipitated the event.[38] Second, some SWAPO representatives argue that because SWAPO was not involved directly in the cease-fire negotiations, they were acting under Security Council Resolution 435, the original UN peace plan, which indicated that the PLAN troops would be confined to bases both in and outside of Namibia. The PLAN were simply doing what they thought they should, by entering Namibia in order to be confined to base.[39] Finally, others argue that it was simply a lack of compliance on SWAPO's part.

As the fighting wound down, negotiations ensued, with South Africa emboldened by SWAPO's blunder. By April 9, 1989, on Mt. Etjo, several miles to the north of the capital Windhoek, Angolan, Cuban, and South African representatives met with members of the UN (with US and USSR representatives observing), to reconfirm their commitment to the peace agreement.[40] Representatives of the United Nations knew that the SWAPO debacle in the north would be a perfect excuse for the South Africans to revoke their adherence to 435, ask the UN to leave, and proceed with South African plans for Namibian "independence." Presumably, a South African-controlled process would not be fully democratic and would enable a power shift to the minority in Namibia who were sympathetic to South African rule. The South Africans, however, remained at the bargaining table, signaling to Special Representative Ahtisaari that the South Africans were serious about adhering to the internationally legitimate plan for independence. Apparently, pressure from Prime Minister Thatcher during a visit to Pretoria in early April played a large role in convincing the South Africans to uphold the UN framework.[41] A humbled SWAPO, while not a signatory to the declaration, accepted it. The hasty declaration

---

[38] See Chand, in Weiland and Braham, 1994.

[39] Several PLAN fighters interviewed by the UN maintained that they were following orders to surrender weapons upon arrival in Namibia, and only began fighting when attacked by SADF troops.

[40] These were the representatives who made up "the Joint Commission" established in the Protocol of Brazzaville.

[41] This information comes from Martti Ahtisaari, President of Finland, interviewed by the author in Kulturanta, Finland, July 10–12, 1998; and Carl von Hirschberg, retired

called for PLAN troops to gather at specific "assembly points" in Namibia, where they would immediately be escorted to camps north of the 16th parallel in Angola by UNTAG observers and observers from the South African Administrator-General's office. In all, only several hundred PLAN fighters at most ever made it to the assembly points; in the end, over 5,000 were confined to base in Angola.[42]

The crisis appeared at first to weaken the position of the UN, as the non-aligned countries and the Organization of African Unity (OAU), previously strong backers of the operation, began to accuse Ahtisaari of siding with the South Africans.[43] Secretary-General Pérez de Cuéllar and Marrack Goulding, head of UN peacekeeping, received considerable criticism in New York for the way Ahtisaari handled the crisis, and insisted that black African interests be better represented. Headquarters thus proposed that a Deputy Special Representative from one of the front-line states be added to UNTAG in the field; in a matter of weeks, Joseph Legwaila of Botswana joined the mission, and the internal UN crisis passed rather quickly.[44]

In retrospect, Ahtisaari holds that he was not particularly worried that the UNTAG military component was not on the ground to stand between the two sides during the April 1 crisis. UNTAG was not organized to perform such a task, and the seemingly pro-South African move to allow SADF forces to leave their bases also helped to convince South Africa that the UN was more even-handed in its outlook than assumed. As a consequence, the South Africans were more willing to compromise with UNTAG and, eventually, SWAPO.[45]

With SWAPO forces withdrawn, and South African forces in Namibia demobilizing, the stage was set to begin the practical tasks of peace implementation. Within a few weeks UNTAG deployed, eventually including 1,500 civilian police, 2,000 civilians, and 4,500 military, from 109 states. UNTAG attempted to accomplish much more than its mandated tasks. Most significantly, the leadership of UNTAG sought to change Namibian *society*, and to interact directly with the Namibian *people*, not simply with the political elites.

Mandate interpretation

As early as 1978, Ahtisaari had been intimately involved in designing the operational plan for UNTAG but was unable to begin actively performing his duties as Special Representative until 1988, due to the delay in Namibian independence. He and his colleagues, after years of visits to Namibia, and interaction with the

Ambassador of South Africa and former Deputy to the South African Administrator-General, interviewed by the author in Kulturanta, Finland, July 11, 1998.
[42] Dreyer, 1994, p. 191.   [43] Goulding, 2003, p. 166.
[44] Sir Marrack Goulding, telephone interview by the author, July 1, 1999.
[45] Interviews with Ahtisaari; and Thornberry, 2004, p. 111.

Namibian elite in exile and South African officials, were in position to figure out the practical and political aspects of mandate implementation, which were inextricably combined. An unpublished UN report on Namibia explains:

> While the central feature of UNTAG's overall mandate was the supervision of free and fair elections for a Constituent Assembly in a transition to independence acceptable to the whole international community, the SRSG [Ahtisaari] had decided that such free and fair elections could take place only if no less than a major change in the overall atmosphere of the country had first taken place; so that the Namibian people could feel free, and sufficiently informed, to express genuine choice as to their future.[46]

Since 1978, Ahtisaari had been pushing for "a massive active intervention by UNTAG to change the political climate in the country."[47] In order to achieve success, racial tensions and military and police violence would have to be curbed through creative means. It was envisioned that UNTAG would

> interpose itself as a source of authentic and objective information in a country which had been starved of this for many years . . . UNTAG would have, as a condition precedent to its success, to ensure that its legitimacy and authenticity were accepted throughout the country. The establishment of UNTAG's legitimacy, in turn, depended upon the perception of its effectiveness in dealing with the problems confronting the implementation, and upon its reputation for objectivity and integrity. Thus a closely integrated and coordinated operation was required.[48]

The obstacles to achieving these objectives were numerous. The 1.4 million people in Namibia were widely dispersed and disparate. The majority had endured decades of colonial oppression, civil war, racial discrimination, and deliberate campaigns of misinformation.[49] With an approximate 38 percent literacy rate, the UN had to resort to many creative means to communicate with the population. And of course, the April 1 crisis had increased mistrust on all sides just prior to the UN's full deployment.

Office of the Special Representative of the Secretary-General

The first step was to establish UNTAG's physical presence throughout Namibia. This was coordinated and administered through the Office of the Special Representative of the Secretary-General (OSRSG).[50] There were three interrelated divisions of the political side of the operation: the OSRSG, UNTAG "centers," and the information program.

---

[46] Unpublished UN Report No. 2, p. 14, para. 30.
[47] Unpublished UN Report No. 2, p. 6, para. 12.
[48] Unpublished UN Report No. 2, p. 6, para. 13.   [49] Heuva, 2001.
[50] The Director of the OSRSG was Cedric Thornberry. See Thornberry, 2004.

The OSRSG was responsible for the political direction and overall coordination of the operation.[51] Each morning, representatives of different UNTAG components would meet to share information and discuss strategies. The first meeting of the day was between the main heads of UNTAG – the Special Representative, his Deputy, the Force Commander, the Commissioner of the Police, and the Director of the OSRSG. Top-level political concerns and developments of the last twenty-four hours would be discussed. The second was a lower-level "co-ordination meeting," where liaison officers (with the UNTAG Centres, governmental representatives and observer missions) would brief the UNTAG press spokesman, and military, police, and civilian heads.

It is important to note that almost all UNTAG staff were members of the international civil service who had volunteered for a rotation in UNTAG. Since 1978, Ahtisaari had in mind specific individuals to fill key positions and was able to recruit others over the course of the ten-year delay in implementation. Ahtisaari was also very conscious of the importance of recruiting women and maintaining a careful gender balance.[52] In addition, by the time the operation finally began, Ahtisaari had become the UN's Under Secretary-General for Administration. Thus, he had knowledge of, and access to, the most talented UN staffers.[53]

Relations with the Administrator-General

Although UNTAG attempted to establish itself as an independent force, it was also set up to monitor the workings of the office of the Administrator-General, Louis A. Pienaar. Pienaar's office was the main legal authority in the country; however, Ahtisaari's office potentially had the power to override decisions, since each step in the independence process "had to be fulfilled to the satisfaction of the Special Representative."[54]

The Administrator-General's office sought to thwart UNTAG's operations in a variety of ways, most of which were bureaucratic. For example, the "Status of Forces Agreement" between South Africa and the UN set out the legal and logistical conditions under which the UN could function.[55] Despite careful advanced planning between the two delegations, South Africa often breached

---

[51] Where previous peacekeeping operations had employed two political officers, this operation had 100.

[52] As Louise Olsson (2001, p. 97) describes, "many of the women in the civilian UNTAG staff took it upon themselves to adapt their work to meet the local needs of both women and men."

[53] It is also important to note that approximately 40 percent of the staff of the operation were women. It was a conscious policy choice on the part of Ahtisaari and Thornberry to include more women in the operation than in previous peacekeeping operations, and more women in key decision-making positions.

[54] S/RES/435, 12 July 1982.   [55] S/29412/Add.1, 16 March 1989.

the agreement. UNTAG personnel were often caught up in bureaucratic hassles including being provided with inadequate lodging, facilities, vehicles, and means of communication, as well as being presented with unauthorized customs duties and taxes, and problems securing diplomatic pouches.[56] When such problems could not be solved within Namibia, Ahtisaari would call officials in South Africa and UN headquarters, threatening Pienaar and his administration with political sanction and/or bad press; usually the Administrator-General's office would quickly acquiesce.

Regional and district centers

In order to establish UNTAG as a legitimate authority with all Namibians, Ahtisaari's strategy was to have the staff of the forty-two district and regional offices interact as much as possible with the local population.[57] They were to strive for "moral" rather than merely "executive" authority by helping to create "a new atmosphere and climate of reconciliation."[58] In the "eyes, ears and voice" of UNTAG, as the district and regional centers have been called, staff members knew well the overall mission objective and the time frame. But other than these restrictions,

> [S]taff were provided with broad guidelines, rather than detailed recipes, on how to execute their functions. This required that district staff initiate and adopt a *modus operandi* which took into account the diversity of their respective areas . . . Daily reports were fed to Windhoek which not only permitted the flow of information, but also allowed for adjustments in both policy and working methods . . . Staff were in constant contact with the local population and thus had instant feedback on their own performance permitting adjustment as necessary.[59]

Moreover, there was a decentralized system of interpreters, whereby UNTAG staff were allowed to seek out and hire interpreters on the spot as needed. The combination of well-structured, widely disbursed offices with flexible mandates provided an efficient and legitimating framework for information-gathering and political coordination.

[56] Unpublished UN Report No. 1, p. 1.
[57] The original plan called for nine district centers in the north, but early in the operation it became clear that there were simply too few offices in this populous, war-torn region, thus another three were opened (Unpublished UN Report No. 1, p. 20, para. 42). In all there were thirty-two district, and ten regional centers.
[58] Ahtisaari, in Weiland and Braham, 1994, p. 67; Thornberry, 2004, p. 376.
[59] Unpublished UN Report No. 2, pp. 36–37, paras. 75–77.

Information program

One of Ahtisaari's most important tactics was to raise public consciousness of what UNTAG was doing and why, as he had "essentially to build up and rely upon a moral authority rather than direct executive or enforcement powers."[60] Thus, once in Namibia, he made the information program an integral part of his office and operation.[61] A mandate for this program was not specified in any of the settlement documents, but Ahtisaari realized that some type of political information program would have to be instituted in order to "change the atmosphere."[62]

The population was poorly informed and prone to rumor and exaggeration. For example, some white Namibians feared that UNTAG would take over the administration of the territory, redistribute land, and destroy their businesses and communities. Some members of all races were under the impression that UNTAG was a political party. Many were also fearful of voting, as there were rumors not only that the ballot would not be secret, but also that one's hand could be permanently marked or even cut off when it came near the ballot box.[63]

In order to counter the mis- and dis-information, the staff resorted to diverse and creative methods. For example, after church services, UNTAG staff would discuss their operations with thousands of Namibians on a weekly basis.[64] They would also meet with community leaders, unionists, student groups, political groups, traditional groups, veterinarians associations, and farmers unions.[65] Many of these meetings would last up to four or more hours. The staff's tenacity paid off, as "reports of intimidation decreased, numbers of peaceful political rallies (almost all were monitored by the civilian staff) increased, and dialogue, at all levels, commenced."[66]

Ahtisaari and his staff also sought frequent contact with local and international radio, television, and newspapers, by holding press conferences every day. But the South West African Broadcasting Commission continued to operate as a source of disinformation. Rather than shutting down the Broadcasting Commission, UNTAG used SWABC facilities to counteract disinformation on the Broadcasting Commission's own airwaves. Starting in June, UNTAG began running two radio programs each day, during the peak listening hours,

---

[60] Unpublished UN Report No. 2, p. 38, para. 81.   [61] Thornberry, 2004, pp. 187–88.
[62] For a more thorough analysis of the information programme, see Lehmann, 1999, pp. 28–50.
[63] Nangolo Mbumba, Minister of Finance, interviewed by the author in Windhoek Namibia, July 23, 1998. After voting, election observers did stamp people's hands with indelible ink, visible only under ultraviolet light, in order to prevent people from voting twice.
[64] Approximately 90 percent of Namibians are Christian, and many attend church regularly.
[65] See Wren, 1990.   [66] Unpublished UN Report No. 2, p. 34, para. 70.

in English, Afrikaans, and thirteen other Namibian languages. In all, UNTAG produced 202 radio programs and 32 television programs. The staff also used T-shirts, posters, and skits to relay their messages, producing and distributing approximately 600,000 visual items. Many items included slogans such as "Namibia: Free and Fair Elections," "Your Vote Is Secret," and "It's Your Chance to Choose for Namibia." More detailed messages explained what political parties were, how to create and join them, the rights of all citizens in a free and democratic society, how citizens should expect to be treated by a legitimate police force, how to register complaints, and step-by step procedures for voter registration and voting.

Within a relatively short period of time – nine months – UNTAG managed to inform the new citizens of Namibia about what was to happen in the November elections and beyond. "In moments of tension or crisis, UNTAG used its leverage as impartial observer to promote interaction among the parties and to present factual evidence of the actual situation on the ground."[67] Ahtisaari maintains that a major reason why he was able to establish a trusting and smooth relationship between UNTAG and Namibians was because he had a trusting and solid relationship with his staff. The Special Representative was also given the power to answer only to the Secretary-General, thus he alone was in total political charge of all aspects of UNTAG. Aside from the decision to appoint a Deputy Special Representative, changes in the operation, and the specifics of how to implement various tasks, were generally the domain of UNTAG in the field, not Secretariat headquarters or the Security Council, which worked to the benefit of the operation. As Cedric Thornberry, Director of the Office of the Special Representative, explained:

> There is no real *feeling* in the Secretariat for people in the field, though, paradoxically, there is an element of envy. "Paradoxically" because any staff member can volunteer for such duties – though, of course, few are qualified to do so. One reason is that there's no rotation, no self-interested sense of solidarity with those on the front-line, so field personnel prompt, at best, equivocal responses.[68]

Over time, and in relation to needs in the field, Ahtisaari realized that he needed to increase both the number of UNTAG centers, and the information program in general, neither of which could have been determined at headquarters before the start of UNTAG. Both increases, as well as the substantive uses of the offices, required tremendous commitment and adaptability on the part of the UNTAG staff. Alterations in operations, such as suggestions for new aspects, means, and targets of the information program, were initiated from the Special Representative's office, based on recommendations he had received through the numerous channels of information available to him. In other words, the

[67] Unpublished UN Report No. 2, p. 32, para. 66.   [68] Thornberry, 2004, p. 293.

UNTAG central offices were managed, and derived their success, primarily from the field, rather than from UN headquarters.

Military demobilization and civilian policing

The military and policing sections of UNTAG, while less successful at "over fulfilling" their mandates, did nevertheless accomplish many of their designated tasks, even with reduced financial support for the military component. The most fascinating organizational changes, born of sheer necessity on the ground, were in the civilian policing division, or "CIVPOL" – never before had the UN sought to engage in such policing tasks in a peacekeeping operation. This section first addresses the efforts at military demobilization, followed by the innovation of UN civilian police monitoring.

The military component

The UNTAG military component had three main tasks: (1) restricting to base and disarming SADF and SWAPO troops, (2) monitoring SADF withdrawal out of Namibia, and (3) demobilizing the Namibian regular and territorial units who fought against SWAPO (mainly the SWATF), dismantling their offices, and collecting and guarding their weapons.[69] At the time of the cease-fire, there were approximately 32,500 non-SWAPO forces to disarm and demobilize, only about half of whom could be withdrawn from Namibia to South Africa. There are no reliable estimates of how many SWAPO forces were in the country, as they were mainly guerrilla troops and moved in and out of the civilian populations essentially without detection.

According to UN Security Council Resolution 629 of January 16, 1989, the SADF "demilitarisation" was to follow a strict timetable, including cease-fire and restriction to base by April 1, and incremental withdrawal to be complete by mid-November, 1989. Despite the partial remobilization of SADF forces after the events of April 1, by mid-May they were confined to base. By November (after the elections), the last troops departed for South Africa.

In the same month, SWAPO's PLAN guerrillas, about 5,000 of whom had been confined to base in Angola, were released and the camps closed down. The troops wound their way across the border, often as unarmed refugees returning in civilian clothing. Demobilizing the PLAN was far more complicated than the SADF. As Force Commander Prem Chand explained:

---

[69] Four subsidiary tasks included (1) transferring SADF civilian functions (in communications, schools, and hospitals) to parts of UNTAG, and then to the new Namibian government, (2) providing communications, security, and logistics for the UNTAG civilian and military components, (3) monitoring borders, and (4) ensuring the security of returning refugees and exiles.

Dealing with SWAPO's forces was an entirely different and more difficult exercise. Firstly, as with guerrilla forces in general, PLAN were scattered across extensive areas where there had been fighting, strafing, bombing. They were also extremely well dug in, in camouflaged bunkers and trenches, i.e., there was no question of clear-cut bases, and SWAPO could not provide us with the detailed organizational tables containing the details of personnel, weapons, and ammunition, something that is standard for a regular army.[70]

Rather than attempting to figure out the specifics of where the PLAN functioned, UNTAG set up several bases in Angola, as mentioned above, where PLAN members were grouped, disarmed, and then released as civilians. In other words, UNTAG essentially overlooked the presence of the PLAN in Namibia, in line with South Africa's demands during the drafting of the peace accords. South Africa did not want to legitimate the PLAN by recognizing its existence in an international setting. Fortunately for the UN and the South African Administrator-General, after April 1, the PLAN did not seek to disrupt the transition process. This was not surprising, as it was in the PLAN's best interests that SWAPO win the elections by non-violent means, so that former combatants could legitimately be re-employed in the Namibian regular army, as many eventually were.

In terms of the task of disarmament, two months before the November elections, most heavy arms were gathered, stored, and transported across the border to South Africa by South African troops accompanied by UNTAG monitors. However, there was no reliable mechanism to account for small arms.[71] The UN's original plan was to set up collection and storage sites in three or four sections of the country. But in the end, only one large collection site was established in Windhoek, the reason being that the UN did not have enough resources; its military presence was small, and weapons collection and storage is "relatively man-power intensive."[72]

SWATF demobilization was also completed in September, although its former members continued to receive pay until February 1990. Continued pay was offered as a carrot to allow demobilized troops time to find new employment in Namibia. Often these troops came from less-developed communities and would rather have remained employed, even under a racist force, in exchange for high salaries. As Harlech-Jones explains,

> When the payment of salaries to former permanent soldiers for the SWATF ceased in February 1990, almost ten thousand more men joined the ranks of unemployed and unremunerated Namibians. Many thousands of

[70] Prem Chand, former Force Commander of UNTAG, in Weiland and Braham, 1994, p. 93.
[71] There is widespread belief today that many of the small arms used to fight the war are still in the population.
[72] Chand, in Weiland and Braham, 1994, p. 99.

Namibians had been taught to fight and kill in the South African Army, in the SWATF, and in SWAPO's PLAN. But few had gained skills that could secure their prosperity in peacetime.[73]

By the end of UNTAG's mission, in the "spirit of reconciliation," PLAN and SWATF forces were integrated in equal numbers into the Namibian army. While some remained unemployed and continued to unite periodically in small groups to demand employment from the SWAPO government, they no longer constitute a significant destabilizing force.

Thus, while the major tasks of restricting SADF and PLAN to base, monitoring SADF withdrawal, demobilizing the SWATF, and reintegrating PLAN and SWATF into the Namibian army were basically successfully completed, the tasks of small arms collection, and PLAN demobilization, were left by the wayside. In the case of disarmament, it is believed that more could have been done with greater resources, whereas in the case of demobilizing the PLAN, the task essentially took care of itself.

In general, two processes worked to reduce the centrality of UNTAG's military component. First, the severe decreases in the military budget, due to the decreased military threat. Second, UNTAG's military component was more isolated from Namibian society than its political components, which meant that the military division was less visible and less noted, even though eleven of its members were killed in the line of duty. While the military division did have civilian functions, and fulfilled them well, its presence was overshadowed by the other, more prominent political components of UNTAG.

CIVPOL

In contrast to the concrete military tasks, those of the Civilian Police were vague, and thus more open to redesign during the process of implementation. CIVPOL's tasks were not spelled out in the Settlement Proposal, although South Africa essentially agreed to an outline of the idea described only in these terms: "The Special Representative shall make arrangements when appropriate for UNTAG personnel to accompany the police forces in the discharge of their duties."[74] Thus the idea of UN civilian policing, as it is currently understood, was born.

The primary functions of these UN "personnel," later named CIVPOL, as outlined by Steven Fanning, the Police Advisor, were to help enforce the law impartially, ensure that people could express their views without fear of harassment or intimidation, and ensure an electoral process that was free from manipulation or interference, by monitoring closely the actions of South West African Police (SWAPOL).[75] Even though one can list these tasks, they overlap and are open to a wide range of interpretations. Further attempts at clarification

---

[73] Harlech-Jones, 1997, p. 32.   [74] S/12636, 10 April 1978, para. 9.
[75] Fanning, in Weiland and Braham, 1994, p. 104.

revealed that CIVPOL was to play a "civilian," "political," and "psychological" role.[76] CIVPOL were placed under direct control of the civilian Special Representative, not the military division. Police functions were "seen in traditional terms, involving a high level of contact and interaction with the general public, and thus conceptually quite distinct from those of the military."[77] As for their psychological role, CIVPOL were to "maximize the visibility of the UN in Namibia. Local people needed to trust that the presence of the UN police would guarantee their freedom of political movement."[78]

In 1978, the Secretary-General had requested 360 police monitors for approximately 3,000 Namibian police. But by the mid-1980s, the number of police had risen sharply to over 8,000.[79] In addition to the increase in numbers, at the time that the settlement proposal was drafted, the elite and brutal Koevoet was not in existence. By 1989, the Koevoet numbered about 3,000 of the 8,250 SWAPOL.[80] Given the change in the situation on the ground, the Special Representative, with the support of the Secretary-General, and the non-aligned and Soviet bloc states on the Security Council, sought to augment UNTAG's civilian police numbers. In January 1989 the number was increased to 500.[81] In the wake of the April 1 events and the purportedly brief redeployment of some of the Koevoet, the number was further increased by 1,000.[82] And again, in light of persistent police "intimidation and abuse," especially in the north, another 500 CIVPOL were added in September, for a total of 2,000, just in time for the elections.[83] Governments of thirty-four UN member states had loaned civilian police. In terms of deployment, forty-nine stations were set up by September; thirty of these were in the northern region. Often the CIVPOL were housed near or with the UNTAG district and regional centers, and shared some equipment with the military division.

It was clearly difficult to develop CIVPOL, both conceptually and practically. Most of Namibian society had a deep mistrust of the police, and the leaders of UNTAG wanted to make sure that it would not be associated with the repressive force. As Colin Leys explains, from 1978 onwards, "the militarization of Namibian society had one clear effect on policing: it finally ended any pretence that the police upheld the rule of law."[84] But UNTAG also was to have "no direct responsibility for maintaining law and order in Namibia."[85] UNTAG did not seek to acquire these responsibilities because most of its troops were not familiar enough with Namibian law and society. CIVPOL needed to be taught

---

[76] Unpublished UN Report No. 2, p. 58.
[77] Unpublished UN Report No. 2, p. 58, para. 141.
[78] Unpublished UN Report No. 2, p. 58, para. 142.   [79] Jaster, 1985, pp. 41 and 75.
[80] Unpublished UN Report No. 2, p. 64, para. 158.
[81] S/20412, 23 January 1989 in response to S/RES/629, 16 January 1989.
[82] S/20658, 26 May 1989, and Security Council Resolution 640, 9 August 1989.
[83] S/20872, 28 September 1989, and Security Council Resolution 643, 31 October 1989.
[84] Leys and Saul, 1995, p. 135.   [85] Unpublished UN Report No. 2, p. 57, para. 140.

by the local police all manner of activities, even while seeking to impart the principles of "even-handed," "non-discriminatory," and democratic policing to their SWAPOL counterparts.

CIVPOL troops would monitor SWAPOL by accompanying them on foot and vehicle patrols, monitoring them during political gatherings, reading their paperwork, and observing their behavior in police stations. It was important that CIVPOL remain identifiably distinct from SWAPOL, thus they traveled in separate vehicles, flew the UN flag, and wore distinctive clothing. They sought to interact with SWAPOL, and to report any abuse of power first to the UNTAG Station Commanders, District Commanders, the Police Advisor, or finally all the way up the chain of command to the Special Representative.[86] The primary method of oversight was political – SWAPOL officers would be warned by their superiors, sometimes even by officials in South Africa, to desist from wrongdoing or non-compliance with CIVPOL. At one point, the Special Representative had a SWAPOL commander fired, but in general the threat of, or actual, firing was reserved only as a last resort.

Given the novelty of their task, the quick expansion of the CIVPOL force, and the diverse cultures represented in the CIVPOL, there were of course wide-ranging problems within the operation. For example, approximately one-third of CIVPOL did not have driving skills; there was only one vehicle for every three officers; almost all vehicles were not equipped with communication devices; the radio system for the force was not fully operational until late in the summer; there was often not enough housing for the increasing numbers of CIVPOL; and many did not speak compatible languages with each other, or with the local population. The working language was often Dutch, since many CIVPOL members were Dutch, and Afrikaans and Dutch are fairly mutually intelligible, allowing SWAPOL and CIVPOL at least a minimum level of communication.[87]

Aside from the internal difficulties, and problems with the SWAPOL regular police, CIVPOL also experienced significant resistance from the Koevoet. The only two Security Council resolutions passed during the UNTAG operation related directly to efforts to stem Koevoet "paramilitary" and "counterinsur-gency" activity.[88] UNTAG was subject to considerable misinformation about the Koevoet units and deception on the part of the offices of the South African Administrator-General. Koevoet was supposed to have been confined to base or disbanded by December 1988. However, as the Secretary-General's report to the Security Council of October 6, 1989 states:

---

[86] SWAPOL attempted to thwart CIVPOL's activities by using a wide variety of methods. For example, SWAPOL would not provide accurate patrol schedules or rosters, hid information, and played "cat and mouse" games such as driving over terrain that they knew CIVPOL vehicles could not handle.

[87] English was also widely spoken within UNTAG, and increasingly so in Namibia. English is now the national language of Namibia.

[88] Security Council Resolutions 640 and 643 of 1989 demanded Koevoet disbandment.

Although ostensibly members of SWAPOL, many of the ex-Koevoet personnel continued to operate in the same manner as they had before the disbandment of Koevoet. This included the use of armoured personnel carriers known as "Casspirs" mounted with heavy machine guns. UNTAG received many complaints of intimidation and other unacceptable conduct by ex-Koevoet personnel, and UNTAG police monitors were on a number of occasions themselves witnesses of such behaviour.[89]

In response to Koevoet abuses, a "Task Force on Koevoet" was created on the suggestion of Special Representative Ahtisaari, and with the approval of Secretary-General Pérez de Cuéllar and the Security Council. The force was a combined CIVPOL and military effort, which gathered information about Koevoet members and activities. Some suggested that all Koevoet be incarcerated rather than disbanded. Ahtisaari maintained that to do so could potentially cause problems upon their eventual release and guessed that their less-organized, politically unmanaged violence would dissipate over time.[90] While this plan did eventually succeed, on October 30, 1989, just days before the elections, ex-Koevoet units were also disbanded in an official "demobilisation parade."[91]

Aside from the Task Force on Koevoet, Special Representative Ahtisaari and Police Advisor Fanning created other new divisions within CIVPOL over the course of the operation. For example, they created an "Investigations Unit" to "gather information required by the OSRSG on the progress of sensitive cases."[92] They also created a "Forward Investigation and Co-ordination Centre," which countered rumors and gathered information on potential disruptions in the independence process in the north.[93] This center could be thought of as the functional equivalent of an intelligence unit, except that its mission was to keep the peace rather than fight a war.

In addition to monitoring the police, CIVPOL also escorted refugees back into the country, provided protection for the UNTAG civilian staff, and functioned as election monitors during the elections. In addition, before and after the elections, they devised a police retraining program for the new Namibian police force. The newly constituted police force was to be based on the British model of "policing by consent," where such principles as a more bureaucratic approach to upholding the rule of law, policing with minimal force, fair treatment, and service, were central. But even under the climate of goodwill in the post-election period, this transition was extremely difficult.

---

[89] S/20883, 6 October 1989.   [90] Weiland and Braham, 1994, p. 114.

[91] But of course the problems with Koevoet did not end there. Throughout the election period there were reports of intimidation by "DTA supporters" who were former members of the Koevoet. After the elections, the ex-Koevoet were widely vilified.

[92] Unpublished UN Report No. 2, p. 74, para. 191.

[93] Unpublished UN Report No. 2, p. 74, para. 192.

The problems stemmed from lack of funds and means to retrain or otherwise employ former police and combatants. The UN's four-week training course reportedly graduated less than 200 police.[94] However, approximately one thousand ex-PLAN and SWAPO members were sent for police training in Zambia. These, along with several thousand others, were integrated into the Namibian Police, the Ministerial "Home" Guard, the Border Guard, Protection Officers, and a new National Defence Force. After the UNTAG operation ended in March 1990, about 500 former CIVPOL and military forces stayed in Namibia on bilateral arrangements with the new Namibian government to continue to provide security and to assist the new government with the creation and training of the Namibian Police. Within two years, the Namibian Police had essentially changed society's relation to the police – people no longer feared the police. There remains, however, widespread criticism of incompetence.

To summarize, the military division of UNTAG had fairly straightforward tasks to carry out. Despite drastically reduced funding, the force was able to accomplish most of the goals set out in its mandate. As for CIVPOL, both its mandate and the methods to fulfill it were more vague, political, and creative. "The role of the UNTAG police turned out to be far greater than had been envisaged. This importance became more evident each day the operation progressed."[95] There is no doubt that CIVPOL helped enforce the law impartially, ensured that people could express their views free from harassment or intimidation, and safeguarded an electoral process that was essentially free from manipulation or interference.

CIVPOL successfully played its civilian, political, and psychological roles, despite substantial problems within the organization of the force, with SWAPOL, and with the Koevoet. The UNTAG police even helped to create new, albeit somewhat unsatisfactory, police–society relations in Namibia, and engendered an important new dimension in contemporary UN peacekeeping.

Refugees

One task that was not new to the UN was refugee assistance. The "three Rs" – repatriation, resettlement and reconstruction – in Namibia were overseen by the UNHCR, as an integral part of UNTAG's civilian operations. UNHCR's mandate came from the 1978 Settlement proposal, paragraphs 7 (c) and (d), which granted all Namibian refugees voluntary, peaceful return, with full amnesty, through suitable entry points in time for participation in the elections. UNHCR also went to great lengths to obtain direct tripartite agreements in the form of signed protocols between UNHCR, SWAPO, Angola, and Zambia. The UN expected that between 40,000 and 100,000 Namibian exiles and refugees would

[94] Leys and Saul, 1995, p. 138.   [95] Fanning, in Weiland and Braham, 1994, p. 103.

return, many of whom were in Angola and Zambia; in the end, the UNHCR handled papers for the voluntary return of 42,736 returnees.[96] Working on a strict timetable, the refugee resettlement process was unprecedented for its smooth organization. All accounts attest to the remarkable cooperation between UNHCR, UNTAG, SWAPO, the Administrator-General's office, the countries where the refugees had been staying, several international organizations (IOM, UNICEF, WHO, FAO), and finally, the Council of Churches in Namibia.

The major obstacles in the repatriation process involved (1) security and protection of the returnees, (2) amnesty, and other legal matters, (3) financing the operations, and (4) coordination of reintegration. UNHCR's work with other organizations in each of these areas was extensive. First, as Nicholas Bwakira, the former head of the operation explains, "UNHCR was part and parcel of UNTAG's objective not only to hold free and fair elections but also to create the very political and social conditions which would make such an election possible."[97] Unlike in later operations, relations between UNTAG and UNHCR remained highly cooperative.[98] UNTAG police and military were present at all reception centers.

As became abundantly clear in most of the other divisions of UNTAG, success depended on engaging with the local population and drawing on its strengths. For refugee repatriation, UNHCR turned to the Council of Churches for help with locating refugees, establishing air and land re-entry points, and organizing reception centers.[99] As Heinz Steegmann, the head of the Council of Churches in Namibia for Repatriation, Resettlement and Reconstruction, explains, "For many [returnees] the churches and the church represented a source of safety and trust . . . The safest places were churches, even when it meant that the facilities would be more primitive [than empty military barracks evacuated by the SADF]."[100] Churches also worked as vehicles for communication between the local population and returnees. Again Steegmann explains, "To overcome the rampant fear and mistrust we kept reiterating the message that 'It's your

---

[96] Ntchatcho, 1993, p. 62; and Unpublished UN Report No. 2, p. 99. Some have argued that the 100,000 number was severely inflated, and worked to discredit UNHCR's otherwise remarkable operation. See Weiland and Braham, 1994, p. 140.

[97] Bwakira, in Weiland and Braham, 1994, p. 120.

[98] "The coordination of activities between UNHCR and UNTAG was exemplary. Whereas UNHCR was entrusted with humanitarian tasks, the complex of problems of a political nature were dealt with by UNTAG. The combined approach enabled the operation to be completed successfully." Unpublished UN Report No. 2, p. 113, para. 300.

[99] While the Council of Churches played an integral role, it was never a part of the official mandate. The organization established air entry points, border points, reception centers, and over seventy other centers for monthly ration collections. Unpublished UN Report No. 2, pp. 106, 109, 110.

[100] Steegmann, in Weiland and Braham, 1994, p. 128.

people who are coming home. We wish to help them and therefore need your cooperation.' "[101] As Special Representative Ahtisaari explained,

> Quite frankly, I hardly could have imagined any other organization that could have handled this very sensitive task [refugee resettlement] in the fashion that the churches did. I believe that after the very difficult start that we had, the churches helped to get the overall operation back on track. They did as much as high-level politicians, the Security Council, and UNTAG. I want to go on the record as stating that I do not think that we would have succeeded without them.[102]

The Council of Churches committee, along with UNHCR, managed to recruit thousands of volunteers to work in the reception camps and mission stations (which were mainly churches). These activities paved the way for the return and resettlement of many refugees – a primary precondition for holding fair elections. The campaigns of UNTAG, UNHCR, the churches, and SWAPO, to convince people who were disbursed in over forty countries to come back, was successful.

The second obstacle, which relates to conditions under which returnees felt safe to come back, was the issue of amnesty. The South African Administrator-General's (AG) office interpreted the paragraph concerning amnesty in Resolution 435 to mean full amnesty for political prisoners, but only temporary amnesty for civil crimes. After months of haggling that eventually escalated to high-level political threatening, the AG backed down. In terms of other legal matters, the AG's office, much to the chagrin of returnees and UNTAG, maintained control over visas, immigration, health checks, customs, and other legal issues relevant to returnees. But it is unlikely that UNHCR would have had the funds or knowledge to carry out these tasks independently. The UNHCR monitored the AG's work closely and brought missteps to the attention of the Special Representative's office.

The third issue the mission faced was budgetary. In 1989 the UNHCR requested $58 million for an estimated 58,000 returnees ($1,000 per person, including reintegration funds).[103] But in the end, the budget was cut to $36 million. As Bwakira, the head of UNHCR in Namibia, explained, "I remember arriving in New York on 18 December, there was a major article on the front page of the *New York Times* calling for a cut in the budget. As a result UNHCR reduced the budget by 17 million dollars, or the amount set aside for the reintegration/rehabilitation program."[104] UNHCR raised its funds through voluntary contributions, thus the budget stood outside UNTAG's projected budget of $416 million. In the first few weeks of the campaign, UNHCR had

---

[101] Steegmann, in Weiland and Braham, 1994, p. 129.
[102] Ahtisaari, in Weiland and Braham, 1994, p. 121.
[103] Unpublished UN Report No. 2, p. 105.
[104] Bwakira, in Weiland and Braham, 1994, p. 126.

raised more than half of its budget, and fearing that it would raise too much money, stopped the campaign. In the end, however, the agency did not manage to raise enough to fund its projects, especially those concerning rehabilitation – the fourth and final obstacle in the returnee operations.

Many UN-system organizations took up some of the slack by assisting with reintegration. For example, the "WFP [World Food Program] provided food for the returnees for one year," WHO took care of vaccinations and health certificates, FAO and UNICEF distributed seeds and tools, and UNESCO aided in educational planning.[105] One of the most successful operations was the "comprehensive tracing system" set up several months before the beginning of the operation by UNHCR and the Council of Churches; of the 43,000 returnees, all but 200 were reunited with their families or friends. Despite these efforts, deeper plans for programs concerning cultural understanding, educational training, and psychological assistance as part of rehabilitation were cut short due to lack of funds.

But even if UNHCR had been able to gather more funds for rehabilitation, it is not clear that they would have been able to manage this process as well as the one that has been organized and managed by the churches and the new, democratically elected Namibian government. The process of bringing a war-torn society together is not something that can easily be conducted by outside organizations, and today, the issue of rehabilitation is simply no longer pressing in Namibian society.

In short, UNTAG's mandate stipulated that Namibian refugees must return voluntarily in order for the elections to be considered fair. The mandate did not specify the method of return, nor did it aspire to achieve successful reintegration. UNHCR's methods for determining repatriation and resettlement relied heavily on the Namibian churches and the AG's office. Again, as with the other divisions of UNTAG, refugee repatriation efforts set standards of performance higher than outlined in the mandate. UNHCR also took its cues for action primarily from local, legitimate organizations (such as the churches), or unavoidable ones (such as the AG's office), while fostering state-level diplomatic negotiations with the countries where the refugees resided, in order to see through the operation.

Elections

Holding elections was the central purpose and primary goal of the UNTAG operation. Creating the conditions for, and managing, the elections was arguably the international community's most important contribution to the process of implementing peace in Namibia. Once UNTAG offices had been established in over 200 locations, police monitoring mechanisms in place,

---

[105] Unpublished UN Report No. 2, p. 101.

refugees resettled, and military demobilization underway, the procedures for the elections unfolded with only a few moments of difficulty, and according to a strict timetable. There were five basic steps in the process: (1) clarification of the legislative framework, (2) registration of voters, (3) registration of parties, (4) the electoral campaign, and finally, (5) the vote itself.

First, fair representation was a hotly debated issue. Early in the independence negotiations, South African-sympathetic parties had put forth various proposals, which in effect would make white votes carry more weight than black votes. After serious negotiations, Administrator-General Pienaar and Special Representative Ahtisaari struck an agreement, with SWAPO's somewhat reluctant consent. Based on a system of proportional representation, in order to adopt a constitution, there would have to be a two-thirds majority approval of the Constituent Assembly, rather than a simple majority, as SWAPO had hoped.

Other electoral procedures were drafted by the Administrator-General's office, but they could not be issued without the approval of the Special Representative. This meant that the UN "ultimately held the upper hand and could always prevail if it was sufficiently persistent."[106] The rules were then published in the "Official Gazette," which was in turn widely distributed. Another tool that the UN employed to keep the Administrator-General's office in check was a phrase from a 1989 Security Council resolution that "all proclamations conform with internationally accepted norms for the conduct of free and fair elections."[107] At every step, the UN consulted international elections experts whose recommendations were then transmitted to the Special Representative and Administrator-General's offices, pre-empting possibilities for fraud or unfair practices.

Second, concerning the registration of voters, the South Africans were worried that SWAPO would seek to register Angolans who were members of ethnic groups that spanned across the northern border. Similarly, SWAPO feared that Namibian refugees might have trouble voting (especially if they were born abroad), and that South Africans might be brought in to tip the vote to the side of SWAPO's main competitor, the DTA.[108] In the end, the voting registration rules included provisions for the following: the age limit was set at eighteen; anyone with one Namibian parent could vote; anyone who had resided in the country for four years and signed an affidavit that they planned to stay after independence could vote (this meant that 450 South African civilian officials, military, and police would participate in the election); anyone born or residing

[106] Szaz, in Weiland and Braham, 1994, p. 143
[107] Szaz, in Weiland and Braham, 1994, p. 143.
[108] Note that in the final vote, one of the most eyebrow-raising outcomes was in a district not bordering Angola, but South Africa, where 263 percent of the estimated eligible voters registered. Cliffe, 1994, p. 124.

in Walvis Bay could register, but only *outside* of the Bay;[109] and finally, returnees
with proper UNHCR documentation were permitted to register.

In order to ensure that as many people as possible were registered, UNTAG
and the Administrator-General's office set up 36 permanent registration centers, 33 temporary, 110 mobile registration teams, and 3 helicopters (for remote
rural areas), and the registration period was extended for one week.[110] The
Administrator-General's office had estimated 685,000 eligible voters, but in the
end, over 700,000 registered, or 105 percent of the eligible population, demonstrating the inaccuracy of the Administrator-General's census predictions.

Third, in terms of registering political parties, at the outset, over forty-
five groups expressed interest in registering. However, in a country with a
population as small as Namibia's, it was clear that this high number would
only foster the creation of a fragmented Parliament. Thus, the Administrator-
General and the Special Representative agreed to two requirements for party
registration: over 2,000 signatures, and a deposit of 10,000 rand (about $4,500).
In the end, ten parties registered, seven of which were voted into the Constituent
Assembly.

Fourth, the campaigning began only in late September, delayed by negotiations over the repeal of discriminatory legislation. Under the 1978 Settlement
Proposal, all discriminatory legislation was to be eliminated before the elections.
However, there was considerable resistance to the repeal of AG8 – the mandate
for the controversial Representative Authorities – since many ethnic group representatives argued that this would lead to a chaotic administrative situation
just before the elections. Special Representative Ahtisaari, after consultations
with legal advisors and SWAPO representatives, agreed to allow some of the
laws governing the Representative Authorities to stay on the books for a few
more months. As soon as the Constituent Assembly had been established after
the elections, AG8 was repealed.

There were also disputes over incidents of intimidation, harassment, and
violent crimes committed by both sides, but mainly by DTA supporters. UNTAG
set up regular meetings between the parties to deal with tensions as they arose,
averting them to the extent possible before they escalated. In order to bolster this
approach (after the UN Secretary-General Pérez de Cuéllar's visit in July), an
innovative "Code of Conduct" was signed between nine of the ten competing
parties. Once the code had been distributed, UNTAG offices would receive
complaints of abuses of the code and report them to its policing divisions or
a new Commission for the Prevention and Combating of Intimidation and

---

[109] Ownership of Walvis Bay, Namibia's only deep-water port, was an unresolved holdover
from the earlier negotiations. The UN recognized the port as South African territory in
Resolution 435, but in 1994 it reverted to Namibia.
[110] The UNTAG electoral teams consisted of 238 election supervisors to monitor their counterparts in the Administrator-General's office on a 1:1 ratio.

Electoral Malpractice, otherwise known as the "O'Linn Commission."[111] The O'Linn Commission also investigated complaints and brought cases to trial. The new electoral institutions apparently functioned well together, forming in effect a new and temporary legal entity governing elections. As Paul Szaz, former Legal Director of the OSRSG, explains, "Unlike most elections, violence decreased over time, from a high level during the summer preceding the formal campaign to negligible significance immediately before the balloting."[112]

Despite the overall reduction in violence, there were some rather serious disruptions in the process even up to the time immediately preceding the vote. For example, several days before the elections, South African Foreign Minister Pik Botha held a press conference announcing falsely that SWAPO forces had again amassed on the Angolan side of the border, and were preparing to invade Namibia. CIVPOL, along with the UNTAG military and district and regional centers, quickly determined that the reports were false and widely publicized South Africa's duplicity. Also, in response, the Security Council issued a statement "deploring South Africa's false alarm of 1 November, and calling on South Africa to desist from any such further actions."[113] Unlike the similar-sounding alarm of April 1, 1989, this time, UNTAG had information mechanisms in place to establish the veracity of the reports, and pre-empt a possible armed clash through diplomatic means.[114]

The vote took place between November 7 and 11, 1989. UNTAG staff were at a 4:5 ratio with Administrator-General counterparts at most polling stations. UNTAG employed 1,758 electoral supervisors from the UN system, of these, 358 military served as ballot box supervisors – one for each polling station. In addition some 1,038 police monitors participated with a minimum of two UNTAG police in each polling station.

With 97 percent voter turnout, of the seventy-two seats in the Constituent Assembly, SWAPO won forty-one and the DTA twenty-one. The remaining ten seats were divided among five smaller parties. Given that the adoption of a constitution required a two-thirds majority, SWAPO and the DTA would either have to cooperate with each other, or abandon the constitutional process. SWAPO immediately documented its primary ideas, and much to the surprise of all, the DTA accepted the SWAPO proposal as the working draft Constitution. The Constitution was adopted on February 9, 1990, only eighty

---

[111] Named after its Chairman, Bryan O'Linn, then an Acting Judge of the High Court. This commission also worked with the Churches Information and Monitoring Services, which compiled hundreds of election-related abuses. Bryan O'Linn, interviewed by the author in Windhoek Namibia, July 29, 1998.

[112] Szaz, in Weiland and Braham, p. 150.

[113] *Yearbook of the United Nations*, 1989, Vol. 43, p. 804.

[114] In another example of pre-election disruptions, Anton Lubowski, the most prominent white member in the SWAPO leadership, was shot to death in front of his house on September 12, 1989.

days after the convening of the Constituent Assembly. While not a requirement, the Constitution was formulated and adopted by consensus:

> Our Constitution is the product of serious internal political negotiations. We debated every aspect until we reached a consensus . . . we never had to vote on a single issue even though we were a collection of political parties from across the spectrum – a racist party at one extreme and SWAPO at the other. . . . Our Constitution is at once our victory, our shield, and our guide for the future.[115]

The document is based in large part on the 1948 Universal Declaration of Human Rights, making it exceptionally broad-minded when it comes to human rights.

There were, however, two major absences from the judicial reform process. First, the Constitution stipulated that no ancestral land claims would be honored. This has generated continued land alienation and poverty among the large portions of the population that rely on subsistence farming to survive.[116] New legislation to regulate the problems with land reform has been slow to develop; however, land disputes in Namibia remain much less controversial and violent than, for example, in Zimbabwe and South Africa.

The other basic problem concerns the civil service. Civil servants under the South African-controlled administration were for the most part allowed to keep their positions while the new government has built up its own parallel structures. This process has been criticized both for creating too large a state, and as "an overdrawn policy of national reconciliation."[117] Nevertheless, as the Deputy Minister of Trade Wilfried Emvula declared: "Better to live with a bloated civil service than a civil war."[118]

These overdue processes of land and civil service reform are working to create a newly bifurcated country. The political elite has become part of the upper class, while most ordinary citizens still have few possibilities for advancement. Despite these problems, the Constitution remains a negotiated document, founded in an atmosphere of "give and take," which has set the tone for the future of Namibia.

Namibia since UNTAG

In the years since the end of the UN's peace implementation efforts, Namibia remains at peace. There is no ongoing widespread military confrontation,

---

[115] Gurirab, in Weiland and Braham, 1994, pp. 171–72.
[116] Wade Pendleton, Professor of Sociology, University of Namibia, interviewed by the author in Windhoek Namibia, July 30, 1998. See also Bauer, 1998.
[117] Weiland and Braham, 1994, p. 176.
[118] Wilfried Emvula, Deputy Minister of Trade and Finance, interviewed by the author in Windhoek, Namibia, July 28, 1998.

nor is the level of crime or private violence high.[119] According to Freedom House's 2005 ratings (on a 1–7 point scale, one being the most positive), Namibia was given a 2 for political rights, a 2 for civil liberties, and is rated "free."

There have been several national and local elections since the one overseen by the UN. In the 1992 regional elections, both SWAPO and the DTA received support from all regions (although SWAPO more so from all), indicating a waning north–south political bifurcation. In the 1994 and 1999 national elections, former President Sam Nujoma, a popular personality among both advocates and foes, won by a wider margin than in 1989, with very high voter turnout.[120] Nujoma ran and won again in the December 1999 elections, after he and his supporters saw through a controversial amendment to change the Constitution in order to allow Nujoma to run for a third term. Nujoma promised not to seek a fourth term, and in the fall of 2004, Hifikepunye Pohamba, the SWAPO candidate, won the presidency by a wide margin. Although Pohamba was anointed by Nujoma, it is significant that Nujoma stepped down at all, considering the precedent in many African nations where leaders have converted their terms in office into lifetime appointments.

In terms of international affairs and its effects on domestic politics, Namibia's contentious decision to intervene in the war in the Democratic Republic of the Congo on the side of Laurent Kabila, in partnership with Angola and Zimbabwe, and against the Congolese rebels and their UNITA allies, provoked major protests both within and without the country.[121] Most importantly, within Namibia, the move, combined with dissent over Nujoma running for a third term, inspired a split within SWAPO. The younger members of SWAPO led by Ben Ulenga, the former Minister of Tourism, founded a new social democratic party, the Congress of Democrats, in 1998. Despite its youth, and retaliation from older SWAPO members who saw the split as disloyal, the party faired comparatively well in the December 1999 and 2004 national elections, coming out ahead of the DTA both times as the second largest party in Parliament.[122] This split can be viewed as a step toward a peaceful opening, albeit still small, of the political space in Namibia.[123]

---

[119] Crime in Windhoek is reportedly on the rise. There have also been low-level disputes in the Caprivi Strip, but they do not suggest that Namibia might relapse into war.

[120] Rotberg, 1995.

[121] Namibia withdrew its 2,000 troops in June 2001, after signing the Lusaka Peace Accord.

[122] In the 2004 National Assembly elections, SWAPO won 75 percent of the vote, the Congress of Democrats just over 7 percent, and the DTA 5 percent. In other words, SWAPO remains the hegemonic party in Namibia, even though opposition is starting to grow.

[123] It is also interesting to note the growth of women's participation in politics since independence. In 2004, 29 percent of the members of the Namibian parliament were women, which is very high both on the African continent and in the world. See Bauer, 2004; Geisler, 2005; and Becker, 2006.

In terms of the economy, Namibia's GDP has been growing faster since independence than before. Diamond mining and offshore gas exploitation have grown. The population is now at about 2 million, and GDP per capita (purchasing power parity) stands at approximately $7,800, which is relatively high but masks significant inequalities.[124] Namibia remains economically dependent on South Africa and economically stratified internally, between a growing rich non-white and white class, and a large, poor, black underclass. Thus, while the political forms of apartheid have been outlawed, economic divisions persist.

However, Namibians have had remarkable political successes, many of which stem from the first elections and constitution drafting, facilitated by the United Nations.[125] In the words of Namibia's Prime Minister Hage Geingob, "UN diplomacy in Namibia played a major role in the independence process. Namibia today is the child of international solidarity. It's because of the UN connection that we've been so successful."[126] Moreover, often in peace processes, it is the minority side that feels it has been unjustly treated, and is ready to resume conflict. But as Dirk Mudge, former leader of the DTA opposition party, attested after independence: "When people ask me about political stability in Namibia, I say that I can see no possibility whatsoever of any group, and I am not talking about individuals, wanting to take over the government by any means other than democratic ones. I say this without fear."[127] Thus, for the most part, the outlook for Namibia remains decidedly positive.

Conclusion

In looking to the causes of the successful peace implementation in Namibia, this chapter has investigated three types of influences over the outcome: first, the context of the civil conflict at the time of implementation, second, external interests, especially the UN Security Council's, in seeing through the operation, and finally, field-level organizational learning during the course of implementing the UN mandate. While organizational learning was in part enabled by the two other conditions, if the organization had not been able to learn, it is unlikely that the operation would have been so successful.

The evidence from this case suggests that the warring parties' consent for peace implementation is not always present but can be created and sustained. A second major finding is that, contrary to the common assumption, high levels of Security Council interest do not necessarily make for successful UN peacekeeping operations. At critical moments during the implementation of

---

[124] *CIA World Factbook*, 2005; and Suzman, 2003. HIV/AIDS has also become a devastating epidemic in Namibia, pushing life expectancy rates down significantly and hampering economic and social growth. See Otaala, 2003.
[125] Dale, 2005.   [126] Interviewed by the author, Windhoek Namibia, July 30, 1998.
[127] Mudge, in Weiland and Braham, 1994, p. 164.

the peace accord, UNTAG took its cues from local, rather than higher-level political forces. In other words, the implementation was not micromanaged from the political center in New York. This configuration enabled UNTAG to integrate with its environment, respond directly to the political needs of Namibian society, and carry out a successful operation.

UNTAG's clear, centrally organized command structure in the field was also widely distributed and allowed for creativity and flexibility on the part of its staff in seeking contact with Namibians. The members of UNTAG accurately assessed problems and dealt with them through political means by setting up mechanisms to decrease tensions. The organization derived its political judgments from field-level information. The components of the organization worked together to interconnect their operations, and at the same time the leadership incrementally re-evaluated and reprioritized the centrality of each component as the operation progressed over time. The organization engaged and integrated with its environment, and was able to communicate its intentions to the local population. And finally, the leadership interpreted the mandate as a "baseline," rather than an idealistic, but potentially unachievable goal. Moreover, the mission faced several crises, including the SWAPO debacle on April 1, resurgence of the Koevoet, and the South African challenge on November 1, but each of these crises was quickly and adequately defused.

Many of the innovative strategies devised in the Namibian context – such as civilian police monitoring and training, the information program, regional and district centers, and the electoral code of conduct – would later be replicated in other parts of the world. The mission sought to create and support rules for the peace consolidation process through the legitimate means of compromise and persuasion, which have set the tone for ongoing political processes in Namibia. While UNTAG's year-long stay did not drastically alter the economic standing of most Namibians, it did tip the balance toward the consolidation of peace, and the structures and principles of democratic rule.

4

El Salvador: centrally propelled learning

Introduction

The United Nations Observer Mission in El Salvador (ONUSAL) was established in May 1991, in the midst of the Salvadoran civil war, before the brokering of a cease-fire or a final peace agreement. The mission had been invited, under Chapter VI of the UN Charter, by both sides of the conflict – the Salvadoran government and the opposition, the Farabundo Martí Front for National Liberation (FMLN) – to monitor the abysmal human rights situation in the country. After the warring sides signed the peace accords in January 1992, ONUSAL expanded to include significant civilian police, military, and later elections-monitoring divisions. Specialists in Central America have argued that, as of the mid-1990s, "of the UN's internal peacemaking efforts since the end of the Cold War, its work in El Salvador stands out as the most unambiguously successful."[1] While I would argue that the UN was comparatively more successful in Namibia, because of the results of its widespread engagement directly with the population, there is no question that the peacekeeping mission in El Salvador was successful, both in terms of implementing its mandate, and in terms of helping to reform and create domestic institutions that would ensure the future peaceful development of El Salvador.

I argue that the operation was a success in large part because the UN mission functioned as a learning organization over the course of shaping and implementing its mandate. But unlike the other successful cases, the impetus for organizational learning in ONUSAL came largely from headquarters, since the central political figures of the UN operation had their offices there, rather than in El Salvador. I explain this anomaly over the course of the chapter.

Situational factors

The war in El Salvador was one of the twentieth century's longest-running civil conflicts in Latin America.[2] Extending over twelve years, it took the lives

---

[1] Stanley and Holiday, 1997, p. 22.
[2] While the civil war in Colombia was waged on and off for more years, the war in El Salvador was the longest-running "formal, high-intensity civil war." See Torres-Rivas, 1997, p. 215.

88

of approximately 75,000 people and created well over a million refugees and internally displaced persons.[3] El Salvador's civil war began in the early 1980s, even though its origins extend back to the early 1930s, with the onset of authoritarian rule and military ascendancy in the political sphere.[4]

There is surprising consensus among most analysts about the nature and causes of the civil war. First, it was fought over ideology and economic inequality (rather than over ethnic or national identity). Throughout this century, but especially between the 1960s and 1980s, the disparity between the wealthy and the impoverished increased dramatically, manifest most directly in radically disparate land distribution.[5] In a small, densely populated country, a very small number of affluent families held enormous social, economic, and political power.[6]

Second, in order to maintain their standing, the "oligarchy" tended to support the militarization of the political sphere. Over the years since the 1930s, while not necessarily unified, the army, security forces, paramilitary forces, and police had come to dominate political life, committing grave human rights violations including torture and massacres.

Throughout the 1960s and 1970s, the oppression of the peasantry, as well as crack-downs on the Catholic Church, worked to form an unanticipated, broad bond between various sectors of society; segments of the Church, the Christian Democrats, the Communist Party, and the universities formed opposition groups.[7] Fearful that the uniting organizations would bring about communist rule, a group of junior military officers carried out a bloodless coup in 1979.[8]

The civil war itself was sparked in the spring of 1980, when, as he was saying mass, Archbishop Oscar Arnulfo Romero was assassinated by extreme rightists. In the months after his tumultuous funeral service, disparate opposition parties

[3] Estimates on the exact numbers vary. See Wood, 2003, Chapter 1. Lungo (1996), writes that up to 750,000 people were internally displaced, while 1-million immigrated to the United States, p. 194. *The UN and El Salvador*, 1995, indicates slightly lower numbers, p. 7, para. 14.
[4] See Montgomery, 1995; Stanley, 1996; and Wood, 2003 for authoritative accounts. For a discussion of the history with a neo-Marxist bent, see Torres-Rivas, 1997. For a discussion that includes more conservative views, see Gettleman, Lacefield, Menashe, and Mermelstein, 1986, with introductory comments by Ronald Reagan and Jeane Kirkpatrick.
[5] According to Montgomery (1995, p. 23), "In 1986, 51 percent of the rural population had no land, whereas in 1961 the landless had been 11.9 percent." See also Kowalchuk, 2004, p. 189.
[6] "It used to be said that about 85 percent of the land belonged to fourteen families" explains del Castillo (1997, p. 344). In 2005, El Salvador had a population of 6.7 million people in a country slightly smaller than the size of the US state of Massachusetts. See *CIA World Factbook*, 2005.
[7] Brockett, 2005, Chapters 3 and 8.   [8] Stanley, 1996, p. 133.

began to unify, culminating in the formation of the FMLN in December of 1980.[9]

Supported by Cuba, the Soviet Union, and Nicaragua's newly elected Sandinista government, the FMLN sought to destabilize and delegitimatize the Salvadoran government through a campaign of terrorist attacks on government officials as well as on the Salvadoran physical infrastructure.[10] In 1981, the FMLN launched the "final offensive" military campaign, hoping to trigger a popular overthrow of the government. But the government, with emergency military matériel and financial support from the United States, effectively countered the offensive, driving the FMLN into the countryside and mountains, from which the ensuing guerrilla war was waged. For its part, the government and various paramilitary organizations sought to frighten people in the countryside away from supporting the FMLN through brutal, public assassinations and sweeping military campaigns.[11] While the Christian Democrats nominally ruled the country for most of the 1980s, the El Salvadoran Armed Forces, along with the death squads associated with the rightist party the Nationalist Republican Alliance (ARENA), waged brutal warfare. These groups were supported financially, and sometimes were trained by members of the US military.[12]

There were many internal and external players involved in the peace negotiations. Intrastate conflicts in the region had at times crossed the borders between El Salvador, Nicaragua, Guatemala, and Honduras.[13] As early as 1983, concerned countries in the region – Colombia, Mexico, Panama, and Venezuela – united to form the "Contadora Group," which was supported by a UN Security Council resolution, and engaged in a series of "consultations" with Costa Rica, El Salvador, Guatemala, Honduras, and Nicaragua.[14] While the discussions, which focused mainly on Nicaragua, did not progress visibly for El Salvador, they provided a certain regional and international momentum to resolve internal disputes in Latin America.[15] Adding to this momentum, as

---

[9] Note that in December 1980, four US Church women were raped and assassinated, prompting the United States to cut off aid (temporarily, until President Reagan came into office in January 1981) to the Salvadoran government and Armed Forces.

[10] Recent scholarship has questioned the extent of Soviet backing. See Stokes, 2003.

[11] Argueta (1983) provides a heart-wrenching, novelistic account of these campaigns. Wood (2003) argues that the military campaigns served to strengthen the FMLN, since the people most likely to join the insurgency were those who had close relatives killed by the military.

[12] ARENA was founded in 1981, and led by the extreme-right figure, Roberto D'Aubuisson.

[13] Note also that the 1969 "Soccer War" between El Salvador and Honduras added to the land squeeze in El Salvador, when 100,000 landless peasants were forced to return to El Salvador from farms in Honduras.

[14] S/RES/530, 20 January 1983. See *The UN and El Salvador*, 1995, p. 8. Two years later, the Contadora regional effort expanded to include Argentina, Brazil, Peru and Uruguay.

[15] The Esquipulas I and II agreements, signed in Guatemala, were the cornerstone of the regional peace effort.

Fen Osler Hampson explains, "Democratic governance took hold in country after country in Latin America in the 1980s, providing a base for regional support of real democratization in El Salvador."[16]

It is necessary to note that, in terms of regional actors, later on in the negotiations, an informal "friends" group would form, including Colombia, Mexico, Spain, and Venezuela, with the occasional support of the United States. This group was smaller than the unwieldy and, for El Salvador, largely ineffective, Contadora effort. In a book chapter reflecting on the negotiations, the top negotiator and Personal Representative of the UN Secretary-General in El Salvador, Alvaro de Soto, explains that "the 'friends' mechanism also had the purpose of preempting rival initiatives that might confuse the negotiation."[17] The "friends" always deferred to de Soto, while assisting him in exerting pressure on the warring sides to strike deals with each other, and conform to commitments. Thus, while there were interested regional actors, the mediation and implementation was centralized in the UN, with Alvaro de Soto as the lead figure.[18]

Between 1982 and 1989, in the midst of the civil war, six Salvadoran elections were held, but all were boycotted by the FMLN. In 1989 Alfredo Cristiani of ARENA was elected, winning out over the more extremist ARENA leader Roberto D'Aubuisson. Cristiani, a US-educated member of the landed aristocracy, sought to shift ARENA away from its paramilitary roots, and toward a free-market ideology.[19] The election of Cristiani turned out to be a windfall for the peace efforts. ARENA had traditionally enjoyed the support of the military, and thus stood a good chance of enforcing any military concessions that would need to be made in order to conclude peace talks.

In the same year, a major ideological shift occurred within the FMLN. The emergence of glasnost and perestroika under Mikhail Gorbachev in the USSR pulled the proverbial ideological rug out from under many armed resistance groups including the FMLN, and, similar to the ideological shift in ARENA with the election of Cristiani, internal opposition to the prospect of negotiating gave way to more moderate views.[20] In September and October of 1989, the FMLN and the government held their first talks aimed at working toward a negotiated settlement to the armed conflict. But shortly after the talks, an explosion in a Union Hall during a meeting killed several people, including a prominent leader of the national trade union. In response, the FMLN waged a renewed all-out offensive that brought the fighting for the first time directly

---

[16] Hampson, 1996b, p. 79.

[17] De Soto, 1999, p. 366. He is referring here mainly to an effort by the Venezuelan government to "hijack" the negotiations, just as the UN had been making progress. See pp. 368–69.

[18] A Peruvian diplomat, De Soto served as Personal Representative of the UN Secretary-General until February 1992, when he became the Senior Political Advisor to the new Secretary-General, Boutros Boutros-Ghali.

[19] LeVine, 1997, p. 229.

[20] See Wood, 2000.

to the capital, San Salvador. Apparently in counter-response, several days after the start of the offensive, on November 16, 1989, six Jesuit priests, their house-keeper, and her daughter were assassinated at gunpoint on the grounds of the José Simeón Canas University of Central America.[21] The murder of the Jesuits sparked international outrage against the anti-FMLN militias, especially from within the US Congress, as charges were made that the group responsible for the murders had originally been trained by US personnel.[22] Meanwhile, the FMLN offensive continued, and although it did not overthrow the government, it demonstrated that the FMLN could not be defeated militarily.

Taking these points into consideration, it appeared that by 1989, the stage was set for resolution, but it was not entirely clear how this would come about. The FMLN's list of demands included the establishment of a provisional gov-ernment until elections could be held, fundamental changes in the 1983 Consti-tution, land reform, and the purging and reorganization of the El Salvadoran Armed Forces; but the government categorically refused to accede to any of these points. Rather than trying to negotiate on the substantive points, when the FMLN and the Salvadoran government met for talks in Mexico and in Costa Rica in September and October of 1989, they agreed simply to schedule further talks. While the last round of major fighting occurred after the autumn 1989 negotiations, both sides kept to their agreement to continue talks that would be facilitated by a "credible third party" – the United Nations.[23] Furthering this commitment, both the FMLN and the government of President Alfredo Cris-tiani wrote separate letters to the UN Secretary-General in December 1989 and January 1990, requesting his assistance in future negotiations, and welcoming mediation by his Personal Representative, Alvaro de Soto.[24]

In terms of the conditions that might hinder peace implementation, by the end of 1989, El Salvador was in shambles. Aside from the destructive fighting that had consumed much of the country, a 1986 earthquake caused extensive damage, especially to San Salvador's infrastructure.[25] To make matters worse, there had been a dramatic decline in coffee prices over the 1980s, culminating in the breakdown of the International Coffee Agreement in the summer of 1989.[26] This dealt a further crushing blow to El Salvador's economy, since its major export crop was coffee.

---

[21] For a masterful account of this episode, see Teresa Whitfield's *Paying the Price: Ignacio Ellacuría and the Murdered Jesuits of El Salvador*, 1994.

[22] The election of George H. W. Bush to the presidency also brought about a more pragmatic anti-communist stance in US foreign policy.

[23] Hampson, 1996b, p. 73. The quotation is from a senior Salvadoran official who was present at the talks.

[24] *The UN and El Salvador*, 1995, p. 12.

[25] The earthquake destroyed approximately 50,000 homes. Vickers, 1992, p. 31.

[26] del Castillo, 1997, p. 345.

In terms of more specific, political obstacles to peace implementation, the FMLN had established its own means of arms production, and thus could potentially have continued fighting indefinitely, suggesting a mutually hurting stalemate. Moreover, while the warring sides were expressing more moderate views rhetorically, they remained far apart on every substantive issue to be discussed in peace talks. In addition, the parties had asked the UN to set up the first stage of a peacekeeping mission, through human rights observation, in a country where there was "no peace to keep."

Security Council interests

From 1989 to 1995, the Security Council did not, for the most part, exhibit either intense or conflicting interests toward the peace negotiation process, or toward the UN peacekeeping mission in El Salvador. This is most directly manifest in the fact that at no point in the operation did the Security Council come to a resolution that was not first formally requested by the Secretariat, the warring parties, or regional actors. Thus rather than being at the forefront of determining the definition, scope, and direction of the mission, the Security Council had more of a responsive, but supportive profile.

In terms of the United States, as the most powerful member of the Security Council, its involvement with El Salvador had, prior to ONUSAL, been extensive, but varied over time. From 1980 to 1992, according to a RAND study, US aid of all types to El Salvador approached $6 billion, making the country one of the top five recipients of aid for the period; approximately 75 percent of this aid was dedicated to the military.[27] This is the clearest indication that the United States was helping to fuel the war, while hoping for a decisive victory for the anti-socialist parties. But over time US policy changed, especially with the changing of administrations. President Jimmy Carter had decided to approve of low levels of military aid in 1979, which he cut after the four American churchwomen were killed by Salvadoran death squads. With the election of President Ronald Reagan in 1980, aid was restored and augmented dramatically. By 1989, a Congressional effort, spearheaded by the Democratic Senator from Massachusetts Joseph Moakley, to stop aid to El Salvador in protest of the murder of the Jesuits as well as other human rights abuses was gaining momentum. That year, the new US President, George H. W. Bush also supported decreasing aid. The retreat worked to propel forward the negotiation and peace implementation processes, since the Salvadoran Armed Forces no longer had sufficient external means to continue the fight.

In term of policy goals, in the early 1980s, US policy followed a strategy of "Low-Intensity Conflict," whereby the armed fight against the FMLN and

[27] See Schwartz, 1992; and Murray and Barry, 1995, p. 215.

the spread of communism was coupled by support for democratic reforms.[28] Throughout this time, the United States was supportive of the goal of a complete military defeat of the FMLN, rather than negotiation. To justify the policy, President Reagan explained:

> Central America is a region of great importance to the United States. And it is so close – San Salvador is closer to Houston, Texas, than Houston is to Washington, DC. Central America is America; it's at our doorstep. And it has become the stage for a bold attempt by the Soviet Union, Cuba, and Nicaragua to install communism by force throughout the hemisphere.[29]

The US policy of supporting military defeat of the FMLN, coupled with assistance for democratization had contradictory results on the ground: political advances in terms of democratization were outweighed by the increasingly strong military and its human rights abuses. With doubt mounting about the effectiveness of US policy in El Salvador, the United States began to change its positions, remaining on the sidelines during the negotiations.[30]

The United States supported the peace process by allowing the United Nations and interested regional actors to pursue negotiations and peace implementation without attempting to restrict those processes. In fact, the FMLN "grew to appreciate the critical and ultimately positive role played by the United States in the peace process."[31] Representatives of the United States also made important political gestures in support of the peace process. For example, the Chairman of the Joint Chiefs of Staff Colin Powell traveled to El Salvador in April 1991, marking the first direct US contact with the FMLN. Under Secretary of State Bernard Aronson quickly followed on his heals; Vice President Quayle spoke at the signing of the Chapultepec Accord; and the United States and USSR issued eight joint statements at critical moments supporting the signing and implementation of peace accords.[32] During the implementation of the accords, the United States also used the threat of withdrawing aid as a leverage instrument to ensure that the Salvadoran government carry out its promises. Thus over time, the United States dramatically changed its position, from being a direct supporter of the war in El Salvador, to bolstering the peace efforts.[33]

The other members of the Security Council – the USSR, France, China, and the United Kingdom – played nowhere near as central a role as the United States, both during the war, or during the peace process, but it is still important to

---

[28] See Montgomery, 1995, p. 148; and Barry and Preusch, 1988.
[29] Gettleman, et al., 1986.   [30] LeVine, 1997, p. 251.
[31] According to interviews with FMLN representatives, paraphrased in LeVine, 1997. Note that unlike SWAPO in Namibia, the United States agreed to allow the FMLN to participate in the negotiations.
[32] Statements were released in August, 1987; December 10, 1989; October 18, 1990; January 5, 1991; March 16, 1991; August 17, 1991; December 3, 1991; and January 8, 1993.
[33] Smyth, 1992, p. 4.

explore their positions toward the conflict. The USSR apparently supported the
FMLN militarily through the 1980s; however, by the late 1980s the FMLN had
built up a significant army of its own, becoming more independent not only
from the Soviet Union, but also from Cuba and Nicaragua.[34] According to one
analyst, the FMLN had four primary sources of arms: the international arms
market (where arms were purchased with ransom money), voluntary contributions from people in countries such as Germany, the FMLN manufactured
many of its own arms, and the theft of US-donated arms from the Salvadoran
Armed Forces.[35] When the formal negotiations began in November 1989, the
FMLN waged its final large-scale offensive, ignoring calls from the USSR for
a negotiated settlement. According to one FMLN representative, "the Soviets
were not a factor in the negotiations."[36]

USSR

France also had somewhat of a historical involvement in the Salvadoran
conflict. With the rise of the socialist government in 1981, much to the dismay
of the United States and others, France "recognized El Salvador's guerrilla-led
opposition as 'a representative political force' entitled to take part in negotiations."[37] In a joint statement with Mexico issued to the Security Council, France
lent its support to FMLN attempts to pressure the Salvadoran government into
accepting a negotiated solution to the civil war, which, by that time had already
consumed 22,000 lives.[38] But with the passions of the Cold War subsiding, and
the socialists in co-habitation with the Gaullists from 1986 to 1988, France kept
to the background in the negotiations.[39]

FRANCE

Similarly, China did not voice any public opposition in the Security Council
regarding the UN-led process, even though it may have had some cause to do
so. First, China tends to be opposed to using the Security Council to forward
western notions of human rights, especially concerning issues of intervention
in sovereign states. Second, for years, the Republic of China (Taiwan) had been
supporting the Salvadoran government and even increased diplomatic and
economic cooperation through 1990–94, much to the dismay of the People's
Republic of China. In return, El Salvador has consistently supported Taiwan's
independence, and voted in favor of it during UN Security Council membership
votes, where China has always vetoed. Despite potential cause for objection,
there was little from China.

China

With the rise of Thatcherism beginning in 1979, the United Kingdom was
sympathetic to the United States' cause of fighting the spread of socialism,
whether in El Salvador, Namibia, or elsewhere. During the 1980s, the United
Kingdom was fighting its own battles in the region, in the Falkland Islands

UK

---

[34] Stokes, 2003.   [35] Montgomery, 1995, p. 117–18.
[36] Quoted in Hampson, 1996a, p. 136.   [37] Wright and Herron, 1981.
[38] Dickey, 1981.
[39] Note also that West Germany's Social Democrats were sympathetic to the FMLN's cause,
and the former West German Chancellor Willy Brandt, as head of the Socialist International, went so far as to give financial and moral support to the guerrillas. Koven, 1981.

(Malvinas), and in little-mentioned Belize, on the side of Belize. The UK was also assisting US efforts in El Salvador by providing funds earmarked for El Salvador to the World Bank and the Inter-American Development Bank, in the face of objections from Britain's Labour Party, West Germany, the Netherlands, and Canada.[40] But the UK did not counter UN Secretariat moves once the peace process was underway.

Aside from the permanent members of the Security Council, it is necessary to note the extraordinary amount of support that the UN operation received from Spain. In 1986, with the re-election of the socialist Prime Minister Felipe Gonzalez, and admission to the European Community, Spain sought to position itself more strongly as a bridge between Latin America and Europe. While the main issue on its foreign policy agenda was economic cooperation between the two continents and debt relief, by the time of ONUSAL's formation Spain offered the largest contributions, especially in terms of police and military personnel, of all the European nations.[41] Spanish representatives were in the first small UN human rights observer group sent in 1989. As ONUSAL got underway, its military and police divisions were headed by Spaniards and included almost two hundred Spanish troops and police; Spain also helped to set up the Public Security Academy. Spain also provided $50 million in aid to El Salvador in 1992, and more in 1993.[42] Moreover, Spain was one of the most prominent members of the "Group of friends."

Consensus

While during the 1980s several countries on the Security Council opposed each other's policies toward El Salvador for ideological reasons, by the 1990s, the major sources of debate had evaporated, and the Council expressed remarkable consensus around UN efforts to end the war in El Salvador through a negotiated settlement. All of the votes in the Security Council between 1991 and 1993 were unanimous, with no abstentions.[43] The three most important resolutions were 639 of May 20, 1991, to begin human rights verification, 729 of January 14, 1992, to include the police and military divisions, and 832 of May 28, 1993, to include the elections division, and again, all votes were unanimous. During each of these votes, there seems to have been little disagreement among the members over whether to adopt the Secretary-General's recommendations and plans, as all were adopted without modification. Finally, Council interests do not

---

[40] According to one report, these funds came to $16 million in 1982, making the UK the second largest supporter, after the USA, of the Salvadoran government at the time. See Chapman, 1982.

[41] See *The UN and El Salvador*, 1995, p. 175.   [42] *Inter Press Service*, December 16, 1993.

[43] Note that Cuba was a non-permanent member of the Security Council in 1991, but according to the official records and news reports of the time, Cuba did not attempt to block or modify any Security Council resolutions.

appear to have changed from 1991 to 1995; if they did, it was not manifest in the peace implementation. Even if there were some minor disagreements behind the scenes during ONUSAL's tenure, we can say that "yes" there was Security Council consensus.

Intensity

In January 1992, at the time of the most critical vote over whether to expand the mission to include police and military divisions in ONUSAL, the Security Council had more on its plate than ever before. The expansion of the ONUSAL mandate was swept in on a wave of new, similar, multidimensional missions. In February alone, aside from ONUSAL, the UN began important, complex missions in Yugoslavia and Cambodia. Moreover, the large operations in Somalia and Mozambique would also begin that year; recently begun operations that were still underway included those in Angola, Western Sahara, and Iraq–Kuwait. The Security Council issued comparatively few statements or resolutions that specifically concerned El Salvador, or Central America in general.[44] And the Security Council mandate often reflected the wishes of the Secretary-General and his advisors.

As for supporting the operation financially, as usual, funds were amassed in a special account through apportioned assessment of UN member states. The Security Council, the Advisory Committee on Administrative and Budgetary Questions, and the General Assembly all voted to provide essentially all of the funds requested by the Secretary-General, coming to a total of $107,003,650 – an average budget at the time for a peacekeeping mission of such a size and mandate.[45]

To summarize, while over the 1980s members of the Security Council differed in their interests and positions in the Salvadoran conflict, and fueled opposite sides in the war, by the time of the negotiations in 1989, interests had converged. All five permanent members expressed unanimity over the principles of the final peace negotiations and UN-led implementation, as did the rotating non-permanent members. This consensus, however, did not translate into particularly intense Security Council action. The combination of scant Security Council formal attention, as manifest in few statements and resolutions, combined with roughly adequate resources indicate a "moderate" level of Security Council interest intensity. El Salvador was not a top priority for the Security Council, in part because the operation was not in constant operational

---

[44] In 1989, one resolution and one statement on Central America were released; in 1990, none; in 1991 there were two resolutions and one statement; in 1992, three resolutions and two statements; in 1993, two resolutions and four statements; in 1994, two resolutions, two statements, and one letter to the Secretary-General regarding post-ONUSAL arrangements.

[45] *Yearbook of the United Nations*, 1993, p. 331 and United Nations, 1996, p. 737.

crisis. Moreover, at the time, the Security Council had many, new, difficult missions to oversee, most significantly in Bosnia and Cambodia. The somewhat detached, but supportive interests of the Security Council worked to provide the UN with the political space in which to implement its mandate.

Organizational change and mandate implementation

How did ONUSAL learn over the course of implementing its mandate? The learning, as with all of the other successful missions, was based in individual-level learning about how to implement the mandate, which was then reflected in organizational change. First-level organizational learning was enabled by the support of the Security Council, regional actors, and the fighting parties. But this support was not simply extant, as an underlying feature of the process at all times – it was actively cultivated by members of the Secretariat operation. Thus, there was an interactive process of garnering support for the UN operation, which enabled the organization to learn and eventually succeed in its mission.

The UN mission in El Salvador had a very different organizational structure from the other successful missions. The Secretary-General and his Personal Representative kept the operation close to the heart of the organization, at headquarters in New York. The center of political decision-making was in the Secretariat. The key figure pressing the parties to comply with the peace accords was not the Chief of Mission, also known as the Secretary-General's Special Representative; most often, it was the Secretary-General's *Personal* Representative, Alvaro de Soto. However, suggestions for operational changes did most often flow from the field to headquarters. There is no doubt that part of the reason why the mission had such close ties to UN headquarters is that El Salvador is close to New York geographically. Many UN officials who were involved in the operation cite the quick plane ride and no time zone difference as a reason why officials in New York were able to engage so directly with the operation. In addition, the fact that Secretary-General Pérez de Cuéllar and his Personal Representative, de Soto, were both Spanish speakers from Latin America assisted in that they could communicate directly with the adversaries, and shared some common cultural understandings.

The way in which the UN sought to alter the root causes of the war was to focus on elites, by bargaining with the leadership of the two major warring parties, removing from the negotiations figures at the elite level who supported the armed conflict (especially in the Armed Forces), as well as altering Salvadoran institutions that contributed to the war. While different divisions did attempt to reach out to the society at large, especially the human rights, CIVPOL, and elections divisions, they did not seek to alter the political mind-set of Salvadoran society. This had in large part to do with the assumption that people in El Salvador did not require the intensive training in democratic and electoral politics that was needed to bring about successful elections in, for example,

Namibia. El Salvador had a relatively high, 71 percent literacy rate; it had also been relatively prosperous compared to other countries in Central America.[46] Moreover, many observers both in and outside the UN system assumed that the ruling party, ARENA, would remain the majority party, but that the more exclusive institutions of the state needed to be changed. These factors worked to free the UN operation to focus on altering behavior and institutions at the elite level.

Unlike all of the other successful cases, the UN began its ground operation *before* the declaration of the cease-fire. This does not mean that ONUSAL was trying to *enforce* or coerce the end of the conflict, but that members of the Secretariat, especially de Soto, were using diplomatic maneuvers to *mediate* an end to the conflict beginning in 1989. Mediation efforts were supposed to end with the signing of the Chapultepec Accord in January 1992 but in fact continued sporadically until the end of the UN peace operations in 1996. From May 1991 through 1995, the UN was also *verifying* implementation of the peace deals. The activities of mediation and verification are very different. In the process of mediating peace deals, the mediator learns of many politically sensitive acts that, according to the organizers of ONUSAL, should not be subject to verification standards. Therefore, the Secretary-General and his advisors thought it best that, while the UN as an organization was engaging in both types of activities, different individuals within the organization should perform the different tasks. Thus de Soto was not considered for the position of Chief of Mission of ONUSAL verification, but he did remain the mediator, shuttling between the parties at each instance when they were having difficulty fulfilling promises that they had made in the peace accords.

The position of Chief of Mission, often termed the Special Representative of the Secretary-General, changed hands three times throughout the course of ONUSAL. This meant that unlike the other successful cases, the Special Representative was not involved throughout the course of the operation as the top UN representative and central international political figure. The mission was originally headed by Iqbal Riza, a Pakistani diplomat who had served in the UN for at least twenty years. Riza has been described as a "model Special Representative," who took directives well from headquarters, and who kept headquarters well informed, but who was a "prickly" person who did not always get along with de Soto. Riza was called back to headquarters after less than two years on the job, to become the deputy to Kofi Annan, the new Under Secretary-General of the Department of Peacekeeping Operations.[47] Riza was Chief of Mission from July 1991 through March 1993; he was followed by Augusto Ramírez-Ocampo from April 1993 to March 1994, and Enrique ter Horst from April 1994 to September 1995. The second Special Representative, Colombian

---

[46] *CIA World Factbook* 1997, and US Department of State, 1998.
[47] Note that Riza also played an important, if controversial role in the UN mission in Rwanda.

diplomat Ramírez-Ocampo, was reputed to be less of a team player, not a particularly good manager, and interested in putting a positive face on the mission even though the purpose of the mission was to exert pressure on the parties by drawing attention to the ways in which they were not living up to their obligations. Ramírez-Ocampo left the mission between the first and second rounds of the presidential elections, in order to pursue his political career in Colombia. By most accounts ter Horst, a Venezuelan diplomat, jurist, and longtime UN employee, was the most effective of the Special Representatives. He actively sought compliance with the accords, mediated disputes himself, and after initial poor relations between ONUSAL and the United Nations Development Program (UNDP), integrated UNDP aid with the tail end of ONUSAL operations in order to create a smooth transition from the "peacekeeping" to the "peacebuilding" and development phases.[48]

ONUSAL went through three distinct phases of operation, from a small human rights monitoring group in July 1991 with just over one hundred members, expanding in February 1992 to include Police and Military Divisions totaling over 800 international and local staff, and finally adding an Electoral Division, from late 1993 to April 1994, augmenting the total staff with another 900 short-term electoral observers.[49] Even though not all aspects of the accords had been implemented by the time of the elections, there was pressure from both within the UN system and from the Salvadoran government to close ONUSAL after the elections.[50] De Soto sought a compromise solution, whereby the mission would be downsized, renamed, and come under the authority of the less powerful UN General Assembly, rather than the Security Council. The new operation, "MINUSAL," extended from May 1995 through April 1996 and was directed by Enrique ter Horst until October 1995.[51] After April, this mission was downgraded again to "ONUV," with a staff of only eight members and three civilian police, lasting until it closed offices with little fanfare in December 1996. The gradual phasing-out of the operation allowed for continued attention to the implementation of the accords, even after the major institutional changes had been completed.

According to the Chapultepec agreement, ONUSAL was supposed to be verifying implementation alongside the domestic body, the Peace Consolidation Commission. The Peace Consolidation Commission, however, was unable to function most of the time, since it included representatives from all political

---

[48] Note that integrating the UNDP more thoroughly with peacekeeping efforts has become standard practice in recent peacekeeping operations.

[49] United Nations, 1996, p. 737.

[50] The pressure from within the UN system originated in the DPKO, which was fielding more missions than ever before, and was extremely short of personnel. Moreover, the Security Council wanted to shut down even the successful operations after the debacle in Somalia.

[51] MINUSAL stands for "The United Nations Mission in El Salvador." ONUV stands for "The UN Verification Office."

parties but was supposed to make decisions by consensus. Several analysts explain: "This makeup generally created deadlock, since . . . three parties generally sided with the government and . . . three did not."[52] In the end, "final decisions [were] either made by the government or worked out in bilateral negotiations between the government and the FMLN, with ONUSAL mediation."[53]

Mandate creation

Unlike some other UN peacekeeping operations, the UN was intensely involved prior to the ONUSAL operation, in the peace *negotiations*. The Secretary-General's Personal Representative, de Soto, was a direct signatory to many of the peace accords.[54] Over time, de Soto gained legitimacy with all sides as the most authoritative UN figure in the peacemaking and peacekeeping processes.

The initial mandate for the UN to assist in the peace negotiations came directly by request from representatives of the warring parties in 1989.[55] But this initial request was followed by three more years of arduous negotiations during which, with the assistance of de Soto, the FMLN and the Salvadoran government signed seven different peace plans, culminating in the Chapultepec Accord of January 16, 1992.

The Chapultepec Accord gave greater detail to many of the provisions set out in the previous accords, including, most significantly, an ambitious and extremely detailed timetable with over 100 deadlines for demobilization, weapons collection, reintegration of former combatants, police reforms, and other related issues. Unlike many other peacekeeping operations, the UN was granted extremely broad powers to investigate and bring to light human rights abuses; indeed, the cause of furthering human rights would be the cornerstone of the operation. However, the Chapultepec Accord dealt mainly with the police and military aspects of ending the war. Judicial reform and land reform were included, but not nearly to the extent that the FMLN and the UN negotiators had been advocating.

ONUSAL was expected to oversee the patrolling of "public security zones"; help to set up the new National Public Security Academy; post ONUSAL military observers inside El Salvadoran Armed Forces and FMLN troop barracks; and monitor all movement and supplies in and out of all barracks and bases. A

---

[52] Stanley and Call, 1997, p. 129.   [53] Holiday and Stanley, 1993, p. 25.

[54] De Soto was also personally responsible for arranging many of the talks and the international conferences that preceded some of the talks.

[55] Convincing the FMLN to request UN assistance proved quite difficult. This was especially the case after the April 1st 1989 debacle in Namibia, which the FMLN wrongly interpreted as the United States' attempt to control the UN in Namibia by allowing the SWAPO infiltration to be crushed by South African forces. The FMLN feared that the United States would have similar power over UN actions in El Salvador, and that any perceived or actual FMLN offensive might be countered by both the government and a US-manipulated UN.

new national body comprising government, FMLN, and major political party representatives, the Comisión Nacional para la Consolidación de la Paz (hereafter referred to as the Peace Consolidation Commission) was set up as a supervisory forum for the implementation of the accords.[56] The Peace Consolidation Commission was to "evaluate the progress" of implementation of the numerous provisions in the accord, and "transmit its conclusions and recommendations to the Chief of ONUSAL," but the Peace Consolidation Commission was never a well-functioning mechanism.

The mandate for the UN operation was granted by the warring parties and ratified by the UN Security Council, but the UN Secretariat played a significant role in the mandate's formulation. This is because the UN functioned as mediator during the peace negotiations, using the technique of a "single negotiating text." In other words, UN negotiators would draft the text of various aspects of the peace proposal, present the drafts to both sides, and then revise in light of suggestions. The parties did not generally draft their own documents, which meant the proposals often flowed from the UN Secretariat's agenda.

Throughout the processes of drafting the peace accords and formulating the UN's mandate, the UN Secretariat was at the center of the negotiations, supported by regional actors and the superpowers, encouraging the two sides to negotiate with each other. The Secretariat incrementally and consistently proposed options for conflict resolution to the parties and to the Security Council. For its part, rather than blocking or altering Secretariat proposals, the Council, while cautious, allowed the Secretary-General's office to move forward in its pursuits.

Mandate interpretation

The Chapultepec Accord of January 1992 granted the UN power to verify implementation of the agreements in non-binding terms. In other words, the UN could make recommendations and offer technical support to authorities. But as many analysts and practitioners argue, "The UN pushed that mandate to the limit . . . [even though] at the time of the negotiations it was not expected to play an activist role beyond verification."[57] By the summer of 1993, the UN came to describe its method as "active verification," where it would put pressure on Salvadoran political elites by making "concrete and specific recommendations to be implemented by the parties."[58] Alvaro de Soto, at UN headquarters,

---

[56] While falling far short of an interim government, the Peace Consolidation Commission was the first step toward bringing all parties, including the FMLN, into the political fold.

[57] Johnstone, 1995, p. 19. One analyst, writing from a human rights perspective, has argued that the mission "made a restrictive interpretation" of its mandate, see Acuna, 1995, p. 39. But most others argue that ONUSAL exceeded its mandate from the very inception of the operation. See, for example, Montgomery, 1998, p. 122; and Stanley and Holiday, 1997.

[58] A/47/698-S/26033, 2 July 1993, paras. 324 and 325.

appears to have been at the center of the authority and legitimacy that the Salvadoran parties granted the UN. As he describes, "We were able to exert pressure through shame, cajoling, and persuasion. We got very far using these tactics. Especially when you compare the mandate of this mission with the more robust mandates of other missions."[59]

The authority, legitimacy, and trust bestowed upon the UN was seen by some to stem from the UN's ability to provide guarantees to both sides. As a representative of ARENA explains: "Neither side trusted the other and no Salvadoran body could do it [verify implementation of the accords]. The country's institutions were too weak. So it was obvious the UN would put itself a bit above Salvadoran institutions . . . [The mission] was a guarantee for each side."[60]

The primary tasks in ONUSAL's mandate included human rights monitoring, civilian policing, military demobilization and reintegration, land and economic reform, and finally, elections monitoring. Each component is evaluated below.

Human rights

The human rights division was the cornerstone of ONUSAL. Human rights were the first point of entry for the UN into the Salvadoran conflict, and one of the main institutions created during ONUSAL: the National Advocate for the Defense of Human Rights, remained strong even after ONUSAL's departure. However, as in all peacekeeping operations, there were in-built tensions from the start of the mission, and nowhere were these manifest more than in the institutions that the UN attempted to create to protect human rights. The tensions were of two kinds. First, the tension between "impartiality" and "verification" was manifest in the UN's dual pursuit of peace as well as justice for human rights abuses. Investigating human rights violations necessitates accusing leaders of abuse, but at the same time, the UN's mission was predicated on remaining "impartial," and on fostering the consent of the parties so that they would carry out the provisions to which they had agreed in the various peace deals. The second type of tension was in the UN's desire to construct functioning *UN institutions* in El Salvador to monitor, investigate, and call attention to past and present human rights abuses, while attempting to create independent, *Salvadoran* human rights protection structures. By the end of the mission, both of these tensions were essentially resolved.

This section on human rights investigates first the ONUSAL human rights office, and the extent to which it fulfilled its mandate as set out in the peace

---

[59] Alvaro de Soto, interview with the author, UN Headquarters in New York, January 20, 1999.

[60] David Escobar Galindo, Salvadoran poet, university president, and ARENA representative in the peace talks, as quoted in *Improvising History*, 1995, p. 7.

accords and Security Council resolutions. It then goes on to examine the two human rights commissions (the Ad Hoc Commission and the Truth Commission), the Salvadoran Human Rights Advocate Office, and finally, the UN's attempts to reform the system of justice as it pertains to the protection of human rights.

ONUSAL and human rights monitoring

ONUSAL originated as a human rights, rather than cease-fire, monitoring mission. The first human rights monitoring mandate stemmed from the July 1990 San José Agreement, where the UN was charged with the powers to "verify the observance of human rights in El Salvador," "receive communications" from any individuals or groups, "visit any place or establishment," "hold meetings" anywhere, "interview" any individuals or groups, collect information by "any means it deems appropriate," "make recommendations to the Parties," support judicial authorities in order to improve human rights protection, "carry out an educational and information campaign on human rights," and "use the media to the extent useful for the fulfillment of its mandate."[61] ONUSAL intended to investigate alleged violations of human rights and humanitarian law. In turn, both parties agreed to comply with all norms of human rights protection, assist the mission in its work, and ensure the security of the mission's members. The early mission's mandate was somewhat difficult to understand, as it did not "include making public statements on what it had observed";[62] it also did not necessitate that the UN bring about a reduction of human rights abuses, even though its presence in the country most certainly had this effect.

The mandate set forth in the San José Agreement also stipulated that the UN would "take up its duties as of the cessation of the armed conflict."[63] This agreement was intended, therefore, to assist in restructuring the post-conflict state and was "not conceived to deal with violations of human rights . . . resulting directly from the armed conflict."[64] But both parties requested earlier UN deployment, in the middle of the peace negotiations, even as both were continuing to renege on, and thus undermine, the peace agreements. For example, aside from intensified warfighting during the autumn of 1991, the government continued to torture and execute political prisoners, and the FMLN continued its assassinations and forcible recruitment of minors while at the same time signing peace accords promising to end such actions.[65] In other words, both parties were "spoilers" of the peace accords from very early on, while appearing willing before the international public to end the war.

---

[61] See A/44/971-S/21541, 16 August 1990.
[62] A/46/658-S/2322, 15 November, 1991, para. 4.   [63] A/44/971-S/21541, 16 August 1990.
[64] Acuna, 1995, p. 37
[65] See The UN and El Salvador, 1995, p. 17; and Americas Watch, 1992, p. 7.

Given this appearance of willingness, the UN Secretary-General Pérez de Cuéllar sent an initial exploratory group, which found "the existence of a widespread desire in all sectors of opinion in El Salvador that the UN should commence the verification of the [San José] Agreement as soon as possible, without awaiting a cease-fire."[66] Upon the Secretary-General's repeated suggestion to the Security Council of early deployment, the Council eventually voted unanimously to establish ONUSAL "throughout the length and breadth of the country."[67]

ONUSAL began preparations in El Salvador for its human rights monitoring mission on July 26, 1991. By October 1, ONUSAL was established in four regional offices (San Salvador, San Miguel, Santa Ana, and San Vicente) and two subregional offices (Chalatenango and Usulután), with a staff of 101 international civil servants from twenty-seven countries, "including human rights observers and advisers, legal advisers, educators, political affairs officers, military advisers, police advisers, administrative support, and communications personnel."[68] It concentrated its activities in the five regional departments most affected by continued armed conflict and sought contacts with the parties, human rights groups, and different organs of the state. In addition, it conducted meetings with "the main political, judicial, and military authorities, making frequent visits to mayors' offices, departmental governments, military and police units, law courts and other public entities."[69] Representatives also held coordination meetings with members of the FMLN in order to escort them in and out of the country to peace talks in Mexico and New York.

By the end of its first month of operation, the mission had received more than 1,000 complaints of human rights abuses from people in widely different sectors of society.[70] This suggested that ONUSAL was establishing some measure of authority within the country; however, there were of course problems. Some "extremist groups" apparently did not understand the mission's mandate, and accused the UN of being partial to the FMLN. In response, the mission published its mandate widely in the daily newspapers, putting a quick end to these particular public accusations.[71]

But the mission did not widely publicize the human rights abuses that it observed. There was a sentiment within the mission that public outcries would not support the UN's purpose of "impartial" verification, especially given the fact that other organs of the UN were still trying to negotiate a final peace deal. Rather than employing public shame, ONUSAL's major method, for which it has been criticized by nongovernmental human rights groups, was to inform

---

[66] A/46/658-S/2322, 15 November 1991, p. 2.
[67] The UN and El Salvador, 1995, p. 18; and S/RES/693, 20 May 1991.
[68] The UN and El Salvodor, 1995, p. 18.
[69] A/46/658-S/2322, 15 November 1991, para. 4.
[70] The UN and El Salvador, 1995, p. 19.   [71] A/46/658-S/2322, 15 November 1991.

the parties and UN headquarters of abuses by both sides. In the early stages of the mission, this was done in rather ad hoc fashion, as the leaders of the operation sought ways to normalize organizational routines while exerting leverage over the parties.

By October 1992, a new director of the human rights division created a three-step "systematic investigatory procedure." The office would first collect complaints of alleged human rights abuses; second, it would investigate the complaints using the ample powers of inquiry granted by the mandate; and third, report on the findings while making recommendations to the parties for ways in which behavior and institutions should be changed. One year later, these reports began to include analyses of past trends and predictions about future potential difficulties, thus making it easier for UN headquarters to exert pressure on the parties while presenting them with facts from the past, and suggestions for the future reform.

By mid-1993, at least three prominent politicians were killed under suspicious circumstances, suggesting that politically motivated killings were on the rise. In light of these and other death-squad-style murders and violence against Salvadoran citizens, ONUSAL redirected its appeals toward public pressure for human rights compliance. The expanded mission began "publicizing the parties' records in implementing the recommendations of both the truth commission and the human rights division."[72] The mission also began to use innovative means of conveying its human rights message to the Salvadoran people more directly, through the use of radio, television ads, posters, and even a puzzle for children, the pieces of which comprised the articles of the Universal Declaration of Human Rights.[73] Moreover, Secretary-General Boutros-Ghali stepped in to set up a "Joint Group for the Investigation of Politically Motivated Illegal Armed Groups," which included the UN's Head of the Human Rights Division, the Salvadoran Human Rights Advocate (explained below), and two appointees from the Cristiani government. While the group had only a six-month mandate, and no indictment powers, it did produce a report that named, albeit in secret appendices, alleged death-squad funders, organizers, and members. And while none of these people were brought to justice, the report appeared to have the effect of stemming the tide of political killings in the months leading up to the elections.

Within the first few months of ONUSAL's establishment in El Salvador, the mission and other human rights groups observed "clear signs of a significant decline" in human rights abuses related to the armed conflict.[74] These abuses declined even further after the formalization of the January 1992 Chapultepec Accord. By 1993–94, the human rights division would expand its activities beyond its original mandate in response to ad hoc requests to mediate land

[72] Johnstone, 1995, p. 27.   [73] *Improvising History*, 1995, pp. 51–52.
[74] S/23580, 19 February 1992.

disputes, observe demonstrations, and participate in police training activities. It also formalized its methods for reporting on human rights abuses, coming to be called "active verification." Over time, the structure of the division and the interpretation of its mandate changed, as leaders of the mission sought new means of exerting pressure on the parties in order to gain compliance with human rights commitments. The mission was criticized by different groups for being both too partial and too impartial, and it responded to these criticisms by altering organizational routines appropriately. By all accounts, even though this result was not expressly written into the mandate of this division, the human rights division contributed to bringing about marked declines in human rights abuses, and toward strengthening domestic institutions.

The Ad Hoc and Truth Commissions

National and international human rights action in El Salvador was not solely the domain of ONUSAL's human rights division. Whereas ONUSAL focused on monitoring human rights abuses as they occurred, two other significant commissions were established to report on human rights abuses of the past. All three divisions were charged with recommending ways in which institutional changes might be made, in order to protect human rights better in the future.

The Ad Hoc Commission came about as a UN-proposed compromise. During the New York peace negotiations and afterward, the FMLN had been insisting on an all-out purge of officers of the *tandona* class of 1966, while the military advocated a "self-purge" system.[75] This issue was one of the most difficult of all to negotiate, for it struck at the very heart of one of the primary centers of military and political power: the Salvadoran military elite. After intense negotiations, both sides agreed to a three-member commission of prominent Salvadorans who were charged with evaluating the conduct of 2,293 active-duty officers.

Much to the surprise of ARENA, the Ad Hoc Commission wrote a report recommending the discharge or transfer of 102 active-duty officers. Before the report was released to the public, the Crisitani government began to protest its recommendations, reporting fears of a possible coup. In order to avert a potential major political crisis, Under Secretary-General for Special Political Affairs (in charge of peacekeeping) Marrack Goulding and Alvaro de Soto flew to El Salvador to negotiate a "recalendarization" (or delay) of implementation.[76] As Ian Johnstone remarks:

---

[75] In 1966, a *tandona* ("big class") of 45 officers graduated from the Military Academy, taking over the Armed Forces high command in 1988. Over twenty members of the *tandona* were named in the Ad Hoc Commission's report. See Murray and Barry, 1995, p. 46.
[76] McCormick, 1997, p. 293.

The Secretary-General accepted that the report should remain confidential and was flexible on the pace of implementation but drew a firm line on the need for full compliance. After the initial delay, he refused President Cristiani's request to let some of the top officers remain in their posts until normal retirement, but carefully refrained from demanding action by a specific date – effectively putting the matter on hold until the truth commission reported in March. Thus the UN deftly handled the situation by insisting on compliance with the recommendations, but not in a way that would have destroyed President Cristiani's ability to keep the military in check.[77]

During implementation of the Ad Hoc Commission's recommendations, the UN managed to balance its aspiration on the one hand to encourage the Salvadoran government to acknowledge past and prevent future human rights abuses, while on the other, maintaining consent for the peace process. But the other human rights commission, the international Truth Commission, upset this balance somewhat.

Both of the warring sides consented to establishing the Truth Commission in the Mexico Agreement of April 27, 1991. A compromise designed by UN negotiators, the three top international commissioners were appointed by the UN Secretary-General, with the consent of both parties, and had a mandate to establish the truth about the most egregious acts of violence perpetrated by both the government and the FMLN. The Commission's recommendations regarding institutional change were to be binding, although the implementation schedule was flexible.

The Truth Commission's 250-page report was released in March 1993, shocking the ARENA government. After receiving over 22,000 complaints of serious acts of violence from various sources, including testimonies from over 7,000 individuals, the Commission highlighted the most celebrated cases, as well as those that were exemplary of patterns of abuse. The Commission named officials in the Salvadoran government and Armed Forces who were responsible for the 1980 assassination of Archbishop Romero, the 1981 massacre of over 500 people in El Mozote, and the 1989 slaying of the six Jesuit priests; it also named those in the FMLN who were responsible for the killing of four US marines in San Salvador in 1985. To the surprise of many in the government, the Commission estimated that 95 percent of the serious acts of violence were committed by the Salvadoran military, security forces, and death squads, primarily against civilians; only 5 percent were thought to be committed by the FMLN.

The international Truth Commission did not recommend prosecution for any of the individuals named, since much of the Salvadoran judicial system was implicated in the report and could not be expected to render justice reliably. Instead, the Commission issued a long list of suggestions for institutional

[77] Johnstone, 1995, p. 33.

reform, the most controversial of which included the resignation of all members of the Supreme Court, the disqualification of all named political figures
from holding or running for public office for ten years, and the dismissal of all
named Armed Forces and members of the civil service.

Reaction among the top leadership in El Salvador was outrage. General
René Emilio Ponce, the person named as the "intellectual author" of the Jesuit
murders, decried the report declaring that it had "exceeded the authority"
granted to it in the peace agreements, and that it was "unjust, incomplete,
illegal, unethical, partisan, and insolent."[78] Similarly, the infamous president of
the Supreme Court, Mauricio Gútierrez Castro, named the report a "stupidity"
and declared that "only God" would remove him from his post before the end
of his term.[79]

Even though both sides had agreed to uphold the findings of the Commission, the Cristiani government granted amnesty to everyone named in the
report. Further undermining the international jurists' recommendations, both
the government and the FMLN decided not to abide by the ten-year ban on
holding public office – Villalobos, the FMLN leader, was named in the report,
but had already begun to make preparations for his election campaign.

Thus, similar to the findings of the Ad Hoc Commission, the issuing of the
Truth Commission's report put the UN again in the position of trying to promote the implementation of a document by which the parties were unwilling
to abide. This is another example of the organization trying to strike a balance
between accusing officials of human rights abuses while attempting to remain
impartial, and ensuring consent for a peace process. In the end, the report
appears to have had a lasting impact on Salvadoran society. Most importantly,
the report laid to rest the debates about who was responsible for some of the
most notorious murders and massacres of the civil war period; it also con-
firmed the findings of the Ad Hoc Commission, naming many of the same top
100 generals, which eventually assured their discharge from service. Moreover,
portions of the report have been used to write the history books that Salvadoran
children use today.

The Human Rights Advocate

While ONUSAL's human rights monitoring division and the Ad Hoc and Truth
Commissions were temporary institutions, the primary new and lasting institution that resulted from the peace accords to oversee the protection of human
rights was the National Advocate for the Defense of Human Rights, commonly
referred to as the Human Rights Advocate or Ombudsman. This office, however, was largely ineffective for several years after its inception, due primarily
to the inexperience and lack of commitment of the officials heading the office;

[78] Popkin, 1995, p. 210.   [79] Popkin, 1995, p. 211.

thus for the first few years of its operation, the majority of human rights complaints fell to the ONUSAL's Human Rights Division. Indeed, for about three and a half years, ONUSAL enjoyed greater legitimacy and a higher profile than this Salvadoran institution.[80]

As ONUSAL prepared to end its mission in 1994, it sought to impart its expertise and accumulated experience to the Ombudsman's office but without great results. In April 1995, a new, pro-active Advocate, Dr. Victoria Aviles, was elected. Dr. Aviles was very receptive to cooperating with ONUSAL's reduced mission, "MINUSAL," in order to promote her office's work. Authority and legitimacy shifted from the UN to this reinvigorated institution, as the office began to receive more and more complaints from Salvadoran citizens, and to engage in active investigations of the police, judiciary, and military. Her office also sought to prevent abuses by anticipating land disputes, and working with the police and the Public Safety Ministry on training and dispute resolution. As one analyst explains, "From 1996 through 1998, public opinion polls showed that the [ombudsman] office was regarded as the institution in the country which most contributed to protecting human rights, more than the police, courts, or even non-governmental human rights organizations."[81] Thus, in this instance, the UN's aspiration of creating indigenous institutions to carry out the roles that it had previously played appears to have been realized.

Broader judicial reforms

Before the peace agreements, the Salvadoran judicial system was highly centralized, politicized, and corrupt. In 1994, a new Supreme Court assumed power and was "by far more professional, politically independent and pluralistic than its predecessors."[82] In April of the same year, sixteen constitutional amendments were proposed, largely based on recommendations of the Truth Commission. The United Nations sought to press a reluctant government, and a reluctant FMLN opposition, to approve of the reforms, but both sides remained recalcitrant. Finally in 1997, Alvaro de Soto was brought in to "break the log jam."[83] He managed to persuade the parties to agree to fourteen of the proposed constitutional amendments, including, among others, a reduction of the period of judicial retention, indemnification of victims of judicial mistakes, a new procedure for selecting the National Council on the Judiciary, and new guarantees of *habeas corpus*. Nevertheless, the courts remain overly centralized and inefficient, judges tend to be poorly trained, and there is poor coordination between the police and the judiciary.[84] In the case of broader judicial reforms, the parties were agreeing to reforms only with the assistance of the United Nations, and then implementing their agreements only when members

---

[80] Popkin, 1994, p. 2.   [81] Call, 2002, p. 407.   [82] Spence et al., 1997, p. 18.
[83] Spence et al., 1997, p. 20.
[84] Stanley and Loosle, 1998, p. 15; Ladutke, 2004, pp. 228–29.

of the UN, primarily Alvaro de Soto, traveled down to El Salvador in order to press the parties to conform with their commitments. After the end of the UN's mandate, however, lasting reforms do not appear to have taken hold.

To summarize, at the time, ONUSAL was "the most extensive human rights verification operation ever undertaken in any country . . . and a process unprecedented in the history of United Nations Peacekeeping."[85] ONUSAL's human rights mandate was rather modest, but was interpreted by the organizers in very broad and active ways. Over the course of this active verification, ONUSAL's human rights division experienced two types of tensions: between accusing human rights abusers while remaining impartial, and between the UN's attempt to create functioning UN institutions, while trying to create indigenous institutions that were to serve largely the same purpose. Both of these tensions were eventually resolved. The ability to manage crises, adequately define and redefine problems, coordinate means, incrementally alter goals of the warring parties, engage the organization with the local population at an appropriate level, all indicate organizational learning.

Civilian police

The civilian police, or "CIVPOL" division of ONUSAL experienced resistance to its development from the outset of its establishment. CIVPOL faced obstructions from international donors, from other parts of ONUSAL, from the local policing forces, and finally, from the Salvadoran government. Nevertheless, CIVPOL did manage to learn while in the field, fulfilled its mandate, and even accomplished quite a few tasks beyond its duties as laid out in the peace accord.

The Chapultepec Accord included dozens of specific institutional changes that were to be made in policing, in order to convert repressive police and internal security forces into a single modern force, based on the principles of professional, apolitical, community- and rights-based policing. The new police force, called the National Civilian Police, unlike its predecessors in El Salvador, was to be categorically separate from the military. ONUSAL's CIVPOL was mandated to assist in the selection of candidates for, and the creation of, a new police training academy (the Academia Nacional de Seguridad Pública). It was also tasked with "ensuring a smooth transition" and sending a group of specialists "to accompany officers and members of the National Police in the performance of their duties."[86]

In the face of a rather under-specified mandate, the potentially largest task of which was to "ensure a smooth transition," a multinational force of 631 officers was suggested by the UN Secretariat and authorized by the Security Council. The vision of the operation was similar to that in Namibia: CIVPOL

---

[85] United Nations, 1996, p. 429.
[86] A/46/864-S/23501, 30 January, 1992, Chapter II, National Civil Police, no. 7 A, para. e.

would establish offices near central and regional police headquarters, and would accompany the Salvadoran National Police in their daily activities. Interpretation of the mandate would also eventually include on-the-job training for the fledgling National Civilian Police, as well as actual policing in the FMLN-dominated ex-conflict zones, where a severe security gap developed in the six months between the time that Chapultepec was signed and a new National Civilian Police created. Despite large ambitions on the part of the UN in general and the CIVPOL division leadership in particular, civilian policing was not one of the favorite projects for donors, and only 314 police observers were ever deployed.[87]

While CIVPOL were fewer in number than expected, those who did eventually arrive were reputed to have adequate language skills, good equipment, and standard professional qualifications (unlike some of the CIVPOL in previous and future UN peacekeeping operations), which helped to overcome some obstacles the force was to face.[88] The first obstacle was internal to ONUSAL. The mandates, and interpretations of the mandates, of the Human Rights and CIVPOL divisions overlapped, creating friction and competition between the two divisions. Both divisions were tasked with receiving and investigating human rights abuses, but the organization had been set up such that the offices of the human rights and CIVPOL divisions were in separate buildings, and each had separate, parallel, and vertical reporting mechanisms. Rather than sharing tasks and information horizontally, the two divisions tended to clash. This situation eventually ended when the new Chief of Mission, Enrique ter Horst, took over from Ramirez-Ocampo in April 1994, integrating the two divisions, and empowering regional coordinators to command personnel of both divisions.[89]

The second type of obstacle was more profound and came from the Salvadoran government and the Salvadoran policing forces. In the accords the three main Salvadoran police forces – the National Police, the National Guard, and the Treasury Police – were to be replaced by one National Civilian Police. The last two were to be abolished while the first was to be phased out more gradually, operating under UN monitoring, until the new National Civilian Police could be trained and established throughout the country.[90] At every step, the Salvadoran government created impediments to these major institutional transformations. For example, upon agreeing to abolish the National Guard and the Treasury Police, many members of these forces were simply transferred to the National Police.[91] In May 1992, the UN protested this practice, which was in violation

[87] Stanley and Call, 1997, p. 125.   [88] Stanley and Loosle, 1998, pp. 4–5.
[89] Costa, 1995, p. 381.
[90] The new National Civilian Police was to be composed of 20 percent former FMLN, 20 percent former National Police, and 60 percent new recruits.
[91] Stanley, Vicker and Spence, 1993, p. 17.

of the accords, and sent de Soto and Goulding to El Salvador to exert pressure on the government, which worked.[92] In another example, the government had been refusing to fund the new police training academy adequately and provide proper facilities. Salvadoran officials claimed that they had been promised international funding for this major project, and thus were unwilling to devote government funds. As a result, the creation of a new police academy to train the new police force got off to a late and halting start. However, with the assistance of the UN, and bilateral aid from Spain and the United States, within two years (by 1994), adequate numbers of basic police agents and officers had been trained in order for the National Civilian Police to be viable. There were many other examples of the Salvadoran government reneging on promises to create and sustain a new, civilian-controlled National Civilian Police, including the appointment of a former Army captain as the sub-director for operations, and the formation of irregular public security units containing members of the former repressive, Executive Anti-Drug Trafficking Unit and the Special Investigative Unit. However, with each of these obstacles, the UN devised ways to induce the government to change its practices. The pressure more often than not emanated directly from UN headquarters. But at the same time, the well-trained CIVPOL assisted greatly in advancing ground-level problem definitions and solutions. As one analyst states:

> The main role of the CIVPOL division was to prevent the National Police from acting in an openly politicized and abusive manner during the peace process and to assist in maintaining public safety in former conflict zones. It carried out these functions successfully. Its general mandate to ensure "smooth transition" implied a broader role for the UN in helping to diagnose and solve public security problems as they arose, as well as assisting the new National Civilian Police in its development.[93]

Indeed, during the National Civilian Police's first six months of operation, it became one of the most trusted institutions of El Salvador, and "one of the most important venues for national reconciliation."[94]

In sum, the UN CIVPOL, with severely reduced numbers than originally mandated, managed to accomplish its tasks as set forth in the peace accords. Like other divisions, members of CIVPOL interpreted the mandate broadly, seeking not only to verify implementation of the accords, but also to assist more directly in institution-building. While there were coordination problems between the CIVPOL and the human rights division, stemming from overlapping mandates, these were eventually resolved by ONUSAL's Special Representative. Problems encountered between the UN and the Salvadoran parties were resolved by the intervention of de Soto from UN headquarters, similar to the pattern in other

[92] See S/23999, 21 May 1993.   [93] Stanley and Loosle, 1998, p. 16.
[94] Stanley and Call, 1997, p. 116.

divisions. While some analysts have criticized CIVPOL for not recognizing and tackling the question of crime early enough, which has contributed to the advanced crime levels of today, even critics maintain that "human rights groups, international observers, and Salvadoran analysts all agree that the human rights performance of the National Civilian Police remains superior to that of the old security forces . . . [and police] abuses are often reported by fellow National Civilian Police officers, something unheard of in the old regime."[95] Others also express that, "There is no doubt that El Salvador has a police force that, far from inspiring fear in the general public, is a source of confidence and security."[96] Centrally propelled learning in the ONUSAL's CIVPOL operation made fulfillment of the mandate possible, which in turn brought about a major transformation in Salvadoran policing.

Salvadoran Armed Forces reform and FMLN reintegration

By many accounts, ONUSAL's military division was one of the most successful aspects of the mission. Militarization was seen as one of the root causes of the conflict, therefore much of ONUSAL's attention was devoted to discontinuing both the military's, and the FMLN's, armed hold over the country. Above all else, the FMLN sought military reforms during the negotiations and implementation of the peace accords. The Salvadoran Armed Forces, in conjunction with the government and at the insistence of the UN, for the most part conceded to FMLN demands in return for an end to the civil war.

ONUSAL's military division was responsible for the following tasks: monitoring the cease-fire; supervising the separation of forces and troop quartering; counting troops and weapons; weapons collection at specified sites and investigations of any violations of this provision (i.e. weapons outside of collection locations); exercising control over troop movement (if any troops were to leave bases or barracks, they had to have ONUSAL approval and were often accompanied by ONUSAL troops); verification of all supplies moving in and out of bases; concentration of all FMLN arms, munitions, mines, and other military equipment; destruction of all FMLN weapons; minefield clearance; and finally, the Chief Military Observer of ONUSAL was to be the Chairman of a "Joint Working Group," made up of one representative from each of the parties, which was to "facilitate application" of the agreement.[97] The Chapultepec Accord also included an extremely detailed annex of all of the bases where the Salvadoran Armed Forces and FMLN forces were to be concentrated, and dates by which concentration and demobilization should be completed.

Many analysts have commented on the significant role that Spain played in the military division. While ONUSAL's military division included troops from

[95] Stanley and Call, 1997, p. 118.   [96] Costa, 1995, p. 368.
[97] A/46/864-S/23501, 30 January 1992, Chapter VII.

ten different countries, approximately 80 percent of the force, as well as the
Chief Military Observer, were from Spain. This large Spanish presence, while
unsettling for some Latin Americans who likened it to a neo-colonial force,
worked to offset the perception among the Armed Forces that the ONUSAL
mission was biased in favor of the FMLN. As one military analyst explains:
"Cooperative relations between Spanish observers and the Salvadoran Armed
Forces had existed for many years prior to ONUSAL's military operation and
provided a basis of trust, thus contributing to the continued perceived legitimacy of the mission."[98] During the demobilization process, both sides would
often stall, accusing the other of reneging on commitments made in the peace
accords. The perceived neutrality of the military division, not to mention its
wide disbursement throughout the country and language facility, worked to
defuse many of these disputes. However, it was often necessary to call on Alvaro
de Soto (or Marrack Goulding) at UN headquarters to fly down to El Salvador to mediate the most difficult disputes, and to propose new timetables, or
"recalendarizations" of the implementation schedule.[99]

By the start date of the cease-fire on February 1, 1992, unlike in some other
operations, the military division was at its maximum strength of 368 in El
Salvador.[100] This was due in large part to the fact that there were 131 fully
equipped UN troops in Nicaragua who were no longer needed for the mission
of the United Nations Observer Group in Central America and were simply
moved to El Salvador on January 24 for the start of the expanded ONUSAL
mission.[101] Once in El Salvador, 268 members of the division were quickly
distributed throughout the country to monitor troop activity, maintaining the
wide distribution until mid-December 1992, when the demobilization process
was completed.[102] UN military offices were co-located with the human rights
offices, facilitating coordination between the two divisions and making any
digressions easier to detect, investigate, and thwart. In all, while there were some
delays in demobilization, the cease-fire was never broken. The maintenance of
the cease-fire is attributed to the widespread presence of ONUSAL monitors,
especially in the most tense former combat areas and the sixteen "friction"
zones monitored by the Salvadoran Armed Forces.[103]

There were numerous delays in the demobilization timetable. Whenever
the ONUSAL ground mission could not convince the parties to agree to new
schedules, they called on headquarters for assistance. The first of these incidents occurred in the first month after the cease-fire date. The military was
resisting implementing several of the dozens of stages in the demobilization of
its forces, including most importantly demobilizing the National Guard and

[98] Fishel and Corr, 1998, p. 51.   [99] Goulding, 2003, Chapter 13.
[100] United Nations, 1996, p. 443.   [101] United Nations, 1996, p. 421.
[102] McCormick, 1997, p. 285.   [103] Fishel and Corr, 1998, p. 52.

Treasury Police.[104] At the same time, the FMLN protested against inadequate concentration facilities, forced evictions from some of the land that its members occupied and lived on, and government non-compliance with demobilization. While the Chief Military Observer was able to work out disputes regarding the fifteen FMLN concentration sites, through the mechanism of the Joint Working Group, ONUSAL had to request that Under Secretary-General Marrack Goulding intervene in March 1992, in order to exert more pressure on the sides to comply with their commitments. In a report he later drafted and in an addendum to the first of the semi-annual Secretary-General's reports to the Security Council on ONUSAL, Goulding's criticism of the Salvadoran government's lack of compliance worked to embarrass the government internationally, and increased donor pressure on the Cristiani administration to comply with its commitments.[105] Within a month after the May 1992 report, the government and the FMLN agreed to the first "recalendarization." The FMLN demobilized the first 20 percent of its forces, and the government agreed to key legislative changes, including provisions to recognize the FMLN as a political party upon its final stage of demobilization and weapons destruction. The two sides would come to at least two more similar deadlocks, where, in August and November of 1992, Marrack Goulding, later with Alvaro de Soto, would fly from New York down to El Salvador to mediate revisions in the timetables. The basic thrust of the disputes were over the FMLN's concerns that it would not be granted adequate land, while the Salvadoran Armed Forces resisted downsizing and purging.

One analyst provides a description of an example of how ONUSAL managed to exert leverage over local authorities to changes their practices. In San Miguel from September to November of 1991, ONUSAL had been receiving complaints that local underage boys were being recruited for service in the Armed Forces. The regional UN coordinator, Nguyen Dong,

> traveled to the army's national training center in La Unión to present its commander with a list of names. In the first meeting the commander virtually denied that forced recruitment of underage boys was taking place and put the list in his drawer. On the second visit the commander took the list and released five boys a few days later. By the third visit, the commander was willing to search immediately for the boys in question and release them within twenty-four hours. By November, according to Nguyen, the problem was significantly reduced [and eventually] ended.[106]

In general, there was a pattern in the military division of ONUSAL officials exerting pressure on local officials, while headquarters representatives, namely de Soto and Goulding, exerted pressure for reform on higher-level officials.

[104] *The UN and El Salvador*, 1995, p. 26.
[105] See S/23999/Add.1, 19 June 1992; and Holiday and Stanley, 1993, p. 423.
[106] Montgomery, 1995, p. 245.

The Salvadoran Armed Forces eventually decreased in numbers from approximately 63,000 to 31,000 in one year, ahead of the anticipated two-year schedule.[107] As explained above in the section on human rights, the Ad Hoc Commission report stipulated that over 100 of the top officers be purged from the Armed Forces for human rights abuses. While the Armed Forces were extremely reluctant to do this, after the release of the Truth Commission report which reaffirmed the Ad Hoc recommendations, the Cristiani government came under enormous pressure from the UN Secretary-General, the United States (with a visit from Colin Powell, Chairman of the US Joint Chiefs of Staff), and members of the Contadora and Friends groups to comply with the findings. Cristiani eventually complied, thus beginning the restructuring process of the Armed Forces from its previous internal security functions, to the new, more traditional role of the external, national defense of El Salvador.

Similarly, the FMLN no longer poses a threat to the peace, since it has been converted from a guerrilla fighting force into a political party; this transformation has not, however, come about without difficulty. Often the ONUSAL mission was put into the de facto position of assisting the cause of the FMLN by pressuring the government to conform with its promises in the peace accords. As de Soto explains, "the FMLN had only two concessions to make, to stop fighting and to disarm, whereas the government had to agree to a lot of reforms in exchange."[108] In order to maintain pressure on the government, the UN was often seen as siding with the FMLN. However, on one very important occasion, ONUSAL and the Security Council had publicly to accuse the FMLN of "the most serious violation of the peace accords."[109] In its haste to help transform the FMLN into a political party, ONUSAL had accepted FMLN guarantees that it had turned in all of its weapons for destruction, and demobilized the last of its 12,000 troops in December of 1992.[110] However, an explosion of an FMLN arms cache in Managua, Nicaragua, on May 23, 1993, revealed that while the troops may have returned to civilian life, not nearly all of their arms had been surrendered. A sub-group of the FMLN, the Fuerzas Populares de Liberacion took responsibility for the cache that included a large supply of rifles, bullets, explosives, grenades, mortars, rockets, and surface-to-air missiles.[111] In response, the UN Secretary-General expressed his personal concern to the FMLN: "Such a deliberate attempt to mislead me places my credibility in doubt and raises in my mind very serious questions of confidence."[112] The Salvadoran government even went so far as to suggest that the FMLN, as a political organization, should be disbanded under a law that prohibited armed groups from becoming

---

[107] There were likely fewer Armed Forces troops than initially reported, which means that the decrease in number might not have been this dramatic. See "Reluctant Reforms," 1993, p. 33.

[108] De Soto, 1999, p. 380.   [109] *The UN and El Salvador*, 1995, p. 42.

[110] S/25812, 21 May 1993.   [111] S/26005, 29 June 1993.   [112] S/26005, 29 June 1993.

political parties.[113] But the FMLN agreed to demonstrate its commitment to the peace process by destroying the weapons in Managua and, moreover, by revealing over 100 other weapons collections, and allowing ONUSAL's military division to destroy them.[114] The FMLN agreed to this measure because it had guarantees from the UN that the Cristiani government would not be allowed to disband the FMLN, or otherwise flagrantly exclude the party from the postwar political process.

Overall, there is no doubt but that ONUSAL's military division fulfilled its tasks as set forth in the Chapultepec Accord.[115] Through the use of creative means, and coordination with the Human Rights division, the military division oversaw a successful cease-fire that was never breached, troop concentration and demobilization, and weapons collection and destruction. In the end, the Salvadoran Armed Forces numbers were cut by half, its top brass purged, and new civilian oversight of the military and its training academy was formally instituted.[116] While the ONUSAL military division and Special Representative were able to deal with some crises on their own, the major periods of deadlock were again broken by the intervention of de Soto (and Goulding) from UN Secretariat headquarters.

The military division engaged in centrally propelled first-level learning. Its troops were widely distributed in the field, were in place before the cease-fire date, and the military division offices coordinated closely with other divisions. When crises or delays arose, the mission defined problems adequately and engaged the organization at the appropriate level to overcome the crises – headquarters often exerted pressure on higher-level Salvadoran officials, while regional coordinators focused on local-level officials. Organizational learning enabled the mission to succeed in implementing its mandate.

Land and economic reform

After troop demobilization, the reintegration of ex-combatants into society was seen as a key element in the transition to the consolidation of peace in postwar El Salvador. The Chapultepec Accord sought to specify the means of reintegration through a National Reconstruction Plan, which included infrastructure

---

[113] *The UN and El Salvador*, 1995, p. 42.
[114] *Managing Arms in Peace Processes*, 1997, pp. 133–34.
[115] The only task not explored in this section is the de-mining mandate. For this task, ONUSAL's military division coordinated efforts with UNICEF, the Organization of American States, and the Inter-American Defense Board. In addition to educational programs with UNICEF designed to protect mainly children from accidents, the de-mining program removed over 10,000 mines and explosives from some 425 minefields. This, for the most part, eliminated the problem of mines in El Salvador. See S/1994/561, 11 May 1994. Also, *Managing Arms in Peace Processes*, 1997, p. 135.
[116] Williams and Walter, 1997, p. 183.

development, retraining and short-term salaries for combatants, and most significantly, a land transfer program. National reconstruction and land transfers
were to be implemented by the government, funded primarily through international donors, and verified by the Peace Consolidation Commission. ONUSAL
was not mentioned in this section of the accord, and the UNDP was authorized
only to advise the government and provide technical assistance. The chapter of
the accord regarding the land transfer program was not as meticulously mediated or drafted as most of the rest of the document; the mandate was overly
specific on some points, but not specific enough on others, leading to serious
disputes between the government and the FMLN about its implementation.[117]
The implementation went though a series of delays and restarts. After an early
change in the mandate to include ONUSAL verification, on many occasions
disputes were resolved as a result of direct UN mediation and "active verification."

By most accounts, in 1992 implementation of land reform looked to be
extremely difficult to achieve. Most Salvadorans thought that this would be
the most difficult of all parts of the accords to implement – more so than the
reform of the FMLN, the police or the Salvadoran Armed Forces.[118] Land,
mainly in former combat zones, had been occupied by "landholders" during
the war, many of whom were sympathetic to the FMLN. The "landowners,"
on the other hand, were generally government supporters. Under the land
transfer program, the government agreed to buy occupied land from willing
landowners, and to provide credits to the landholders to purchase the land on
which they had been living.[119] If landowners did not want to sell their occupied
land, they would have to wait to reclaim it until the government could relo-
cate landholders to other farming plots. In 1992, beneficiaries included about
15,000 government soldiers, 7,500 FMLN combatants, and 25,000 landholders.
In a country with a population density of approximately 260 inhabitants per
square kilometer at the time, the most dense in all of Latin America, finding
enough land for all those who wanted to farm was going to be difficult, not
to mention the political resistance on the part of government bureaucrats who
were loath to carry out a program that would benefit primarily the FMLN and its
supporters.

By the end of 1992, the land transfer program, dubbed "the land for arms"
deal, had come to a halt. The government had not begun the land program
as stipulated in the Chapultepec Accord, and the FMLN retaliated by refusing
to go forward with its troop demobilization. The two sides deadlocked over a

---

[117] See del Castillo, 1997, pp. 346–47.
[118] According to an October 1992 poll, 37 percent agreed that land transfers would be the most
difficult part of Chapultepec to implement, while 20 percent thought that demobilization
of FMLN was most difficult. See del Castillo, 1997, p. 348.
[119] The average plot of land was 4.01 manzas (6.82 acres), costing 25,649 colones ($2,948).
See Spence et al., 1997, p. 37.

number of technical, financial, and political issues. As Boutros-Ghali explains: "ONUSAL, concerned at the consequence of further delays in initiating the transfer of land, which was supposed to have begun by 1 May 1992, became progressively more involved in the land issue."[120] By October, it appeared that ONUSAL leaders would not be able to mediate the dispute from the ground, and called on the UN Secretary-General. On October 13, 1992, Boutros-Ghali proposed compromises for both sides, with UN oversight of the implementation of the new agreement.[121]

After this episode, members of the UN stepped in to mediate numerous other land-related disputes. For example, in November 1992, in Cuidad Barrios, the cease-fire was nearly breached during a dispute between FMLN former combatants returning to what they said was their land, and government troops who had been "demobilized" into the National Police. The Special Representative of ONUSAL at the time, Iqbal Riza, along with the Archbishop of San Salvador intervened to defuse and resolve what could otherwise have been a deadly controversy. In another example, in May 1994 the program had been paralyzed for six months because the FMLN was having trouble finalizing a list of beneficiaries, while the government was running into financial difficulties. Here, the UN Secretary-General himself stepped in to mediate and end the dispute. And again, the UN intervened in September 1994 when the advocacy group "Demobilized Members of the Armed Forces of El Salvador" (ADEFAES) occupied the National Assembly and other government affiliates, demanding their fair share of land and postwar benefits. This settlement held for only four months, when in January 1995, the group took over parts of the Department of La Paz, and later the National Assembly again. While the government's initial reaction was to respond to the strikers with violence, the Special Representative of the ONUSAL mission at the time, Enrique ter Horst, helped to mediate a settlement. In the end, the government yielded to ADEFAES demands by including 5,000 former members of the paramilitaries in regular retraining and other social programs.[122]

After serious delays, land was successfully transferred to 98.9 percent of the beneficiaries by the end of 1996.[123] This amounted to only approximately 10 percent of the country's farming land, but it did provide a source of employment for many former combatants.[124]

---

[120] S/24833, 23 November 1992, para. 55.
[121] Letters were issued between all sides to make these agreements, but they were not issued as formal UN documents. See *The UN and El Salvador*, 1995, pp. 257–64.
[122] For a more complete account of all of these episodes, see del Castillo, 1997, pp. 351–57. For a description of the ADEFAES difficulties, see Murray and Barry, 1995, p. 53. See also Spence et al., 1997, p. 37; and Wood, 1995, pp. 96–98.
[123] A/51/693, 25 November, 1996.
[124] In terms of the economic and developmental aspects of reintegration, like many multidimensional peacekeeping operations, the ONUSAL mission was not mandated, nor did it

To summarize, at first ONUSAL was not mandated to assist in the land transfer program. However, as it became clear that this program was a controversial and extremely important element in the implementation of the peace accords (not to mention the eventual consolidation of peace in El Salvador), the organizers of ONUSAL became more involved, interpreting the mandate broadly to include, eventually, "active verification" of the program. Over time, with assistance from headquarters when needed, ONUSAL succeeded in defusing potentially serious disputes before they became violent. ONUSAL was functioning in an organizational learning mode, which enabled the mission to verify the successful implementation of the land transfer program.

Elections

Progress in the many areas in which ONUSAL was working set the stage for the elections, even though elections monitoring was not originally one of the major components of the ONUSAL mandate. As happens only every fifteen years in El Salvador, in March 1994, elections were to be held simultaneously for the Presidency and for the Assembly, as well as for the 262 Mayoralties and 20 Deputies to the Central American Parliament.[125] In January 1993, the Salvadoran government formally requested that the UN verify the complicated elections. The Secretary-General subsequently reported to the Security Council that "it is my intention to enlarge ONUSAL to include an electoral component for the purpose of observing and verifying the Salvadoran general elections."[126] The Security Council agreed to the expansion of ONUSAL to include a fourth major division for elections, endorsing the view of the Secretary-General that "the general election of March 1994 should constitute the logical culmination of the entire peace process in EL Salvador."[127] While these elections would not, in the end, be the culmination of the peace process as there were still land

seek, to play a significant role in these areas. Instead, other UN affiliates such as the World Bank, the IMF, and UNDP, as well as other organizations such as USAID, the European Union and the Inter-American Bank, worked to fund many projects under, for example, the Water Agency, the Hydroelectric Commission, the Ministry of Public Works, and the Social Investment Fund. See "Land, Peace, and Participation," 1997, p. 3; and Murray et al., 1994.

[125] The 1983 Salvadoran Constitution, the central legal document still in effect during the peace process albeit amended during that process, clearly stipulates when elections are to take place: every five years for the presidency, and every three years for the Legislative Assembly. These stipulations were not changed during the peace process, which meant that the process took place in the shadow of the future elections.

[126] S/25812/Add. 1, 24 May, 1993. Note that the document is later phrased less assertively, in the form of a request, but we see here again that in El Salvador, it is the Secretariat urging the Security Council to act, not the other way around.

[127] S/RES/832, 27 May 1993, para. 5.

and police reforms to implement after March 1994, the elections proved an important step toward strengthening Salvadoran democracy.

The mandate stipulated that the UN simply "observe and verify" the process before, during, and after the elections. However, the organizers of ONUSAL knew that the central obstacles to the elections were an incomplete and inaccurate voter list, and a lack of voter registration cards for approximately one-third of the potential voters (an estimated 786,000 people).[128] They thus interpreted the mandate to include logistical and technical support for the fault-ridden voter registration process, even though these are not mentioned in the official mandate.[129]

ONUSAL's task was enormous, especially given that it had constantly to battle with the Supreme Electoral Tribunal – a state organ that was only nominally independent from the ruling ARENA party. In addition, ONUSAL's difficult mission was made more so by internal problems within the Electoral Division, especially early on. The Electoral Division was run by the well-respected Spanish sociologist Rafael López Pintor, who had some, but not extensive, experience with elections monitoring, and did not assume his post until September, 1993, almost four months after the division had already begun its work.[130] He was in charge of a staff of only thirty-six people deployed throughout the six regional offices (expanded by 900 for the days just before and after the elections; there were also some 3,000 other international observers on election day). By the time López Pintor arrived, many of the staff in the regions had already set up their sub-organizations, since there had been only minimal central coordination, training, or guidelines. As one analyst who worked for the division explains: "The Electoral Division . . . evolved on an ad-hoc basis at the regional level; headquarters did not develop a master plan until very late, and even then it failed to implement the plan fully."[131]

The master plan involved two important steps. First a massive attempt at registering hundreds of thousands of people in time to vote, and second, observing campaign practices. First, in terms of registering, the process set up by the Supreme Electoral Tribunal was extremely time-consuming, bureaucratic, and costly. It involved each citizen obtaining a birth certificate from often reluctant mayors, and several other documents, culminating with a laminated voter ID card. Obtaining the documents was extremely difficult in a country where technical supplies were short, and where many citizens were poor and semi-literate; but even the well educated had trouble. As the elections approached, hundreds of thousands of people, especially in the zones of former conflict, remained

---

[128] Montgomery, 1995, p. 247.

[129] The expansion of activities was *post facto* approved by the Security Council in S/RES/888, 30 November 1993, demonstrating again that major decisions were flowing from the field up to headquarters.

[130] Montgomery, 1998, p. 124.   [131] Montgomery, 1998, p. 126.

unregistered. But ONUSAL invented mechanisms to respond to the crisis. In some districts, ONUSAL staff performed "'ant work' . . . going to municipalities to look up individual birth certificates," and other similar activities.[132] ONUSAL also set up various means, such as large, day-long registration drives, or *mega-journada*, to register voters quickly and free of charge.[133] In all, during the registration drive, ONUSAL electoral teams made an average of six visits to each of the 262 municipalities. They met with local leaders, explained the registration and voting process to citizens and organizations, collected complaints, and sought to "flatter, cajole, and bully the Supreme Electoral Tribunal to do the job that it was created to do."[134] While for some months it looked as though the entire election process would be delegitimated by the low numbers of people registered to vote, in the end, the electoral division managed to "verify" the registration of 2.3 million people, or some 85 percent of potential voters.[135]

Second, in terms of monitoring the campaigns, while there were some problems of state interference with the media, hundreds of political rallies and meetings were held during the campaign period with few instances of intimidation or violence. Part of this was due to the fact that Special Representative Ramirez-Ocampo persuaded six of the seven presidential candidates to sign a code of conduct or a "Gentlemen's Agreement" to refrain from intimidation, violence, and overly negative campaigning, and to respect the election results and implement the peace accords. This code of conduct was eventually replicated, with the encouragement of ONUSAL regional representatives, in all fourteen of the departments. But the smoothness of the campaigning did not mean that the process was completely non-violent. In fact, it was marred by the politically motivated murders of some fifteen people, including seven FMLN ex-combatants and activists, four ARENA activists, and the brother of an FMLN mayoral candidate, all between October 1993 and February 1994.[136] However, according to the UN human rights division, these killings were different from those committed during the war, as they reflected not the general will of the two major parties, but "fringe elements" that opposed the peace process and the elections in general.[137] In all, most complaints related to the elections were not extremely serious (the most frequent was the charge that campaign posters were being torn down or pasted over), and the "overall mood of the

---

[132] Montgomery, 1995, p. 247.

[133] Salvadoran mayors were allowed to charge from the equivalent of $3 to $10 for voter registration materials. For some Salvadorans, this amounted to a full week's salary.

[134] Montgomery, 1995, p. 247.

[135] *The UN and El Salvador*, 1995, p. 47. A lot of the technical assistance came from experienced staff of the UNHCR, who had prior expertise in producing documents for refugees, internally displaced, and those otherwise undocumented.

[136] *The UN and El Salvador*, 1995, p. 46.   [137] *The UN and El Salvador*, 1995, p. 47.

campaign was calm."[138] It was so calm, that some commented that it was even "unremarkable," and "rather boring."[139]

On the day of the elections, between two and thirty ONUSAL observers monitored each of the 355 polling centers. While there were no serious incidents reported, there were some problems: some polling stations opened late; public transportation to polling sites was sporadic at best; and between 25,000 and 87,000 voters were turned away because of discrepancies between the voting lists and voting cards.[140] In all, about 1,300,000 people voted, approximately 55 percent of the eligible voters. While this number was still about one-third, or 400,000 people more than had voted in the previous elections, turnout was lower than anticipated.[141]

The irregularities reportedly had no impact on the presidential elections, but had some impact on the Assembly and municipal elections. While the FMLN began to contest the results in several dozen municipalities, they eventually relented, and the elections were reported as uncontested. The ARENA party received 49.03 percent of the votes for the presidential race, versus 24.9 percent for the Democratic Convergence-FMLN, forcing a run-off since neither party had received over 50 percent of the vote. In the Legislative Assembly, ARENA won 39 seats, the FMLN 21, and the Christian Democratic Party 18, with the remaining 6 seats divided among smaller parties. In the municipal elections, ARENA won an unexpected 206 out of the 262 Mayorships; the Christian Democratic Party won 29, and the FMLN a surprisingly low 16.[142]

One month later, on April 24, the run-off for the presidential elections went much more smoothly than the first round. Immediately after the first round, ONUSAL drew up a list of improvements that would have to be made in order to legitimate the next round. Under the new leadership of Special Representative Enrique ter Horst, ONUSAL saw through a number of improvements including:

> [improvement in] the arrangement of the voting centres, the use of guides to direct voters to voting places, the display of the Electoral Register, free

---

[138] *The UN and El Salvador*, 1995, p. 48.

[139] Baylora, 1998, p. 24; and Montgomery, 1995, p. 259 respectively.

[140] ONUSAL observers estimated that 25,000 people were unable to vote based on observations at all of the polling sites. The American NGO Hemisphere Initiatives, while not having the same presence in the country, estimates that this number was much higher – around 87,000 (see *The UN and El Salvador*, 1995, p. 52; and Spence et al., 1994, pp. 6–7).

[141] The low turnout seems to have been caused by a number of factors: poor access to the polls, fatigue from overly bureaucratic voting procedures, confusion over voter lists, confusion over where to vote (polling sites in major cities were arranged alphabetically, so people did not vote in their neighborhoods, driving down turnout).

[142] In order for the FMLN to participate in the elections, it had to demobilize and transform itself into a political party over the space of approximately two years. Many observers suggest that this was simply too little time to organize politically. This view is probably somewhat justified, since the FMLN gained considerably in the 1997 elections, even winning the seat of the capital, San Salvador.

public transportation, and the release, early on 24 April, of information on
the results of the elections. Various irregularities were noted as well, but in
general terms the elections again took place without vote manipulation or
serious disturbances of public order.[143]

ARENA's Calderón Sol won the run-off with a landslide 68 percent of the
vote, over the Democratic Convergence–FMLN–Revolutionary National Movement coalition presidential candidate, Rubén Zamora. ONUSAL had sent
863 observers (there were about 500 additional international observers) and
reported that while there were some irregularities, these elections were technically better conducted than the first round.

The overall UN assessment of the elections, however, is not particularly
effusive. The final proclamation was that the elections were "acceptable." This
is in direct contrast to the pre-election hype that was generated in large part
by Special Representative Ramirez-Ocampo's office, against advice from UN
headquarters. These elections were important to El Salvador and the UN, as
they embodied a series of "firsts": the first time in twenty years that an election
would be held in peacetime in El Salvador; the first election for all offices until
2009; the first time since 1932 that all political actors would be represented in
elections; for the UN, it was the first time that human rights were the central
organizing principle for a multidimensional peacekeeping operation. For these
reasons, Special Representative Ramirez-Ocampo had actively taken on the
role of declaring the elections "the elections of the century." In advertising
the "firsts" and associating himself with the success, it has been said that the
Special Representative was looking not primarily to El Salvador and the UN,
but to his future political career in Colombia; indeed, Ramirez-Ocampo left
the mission before the second round of the presidential vote, to engage in
Colombian politics. Some members of the mission have suggested that Ramirez-
Ocampo "tended to view the elections through rose-tinted glasses."[144] But the
agenda at UN headquarters was somewhat different. By April 1994, while much
progress had been made on implementing the Chapultepec Accord, there were
still numerous outstanding tasks to be accomplished, especially in the areas
of police and land reform. Therefore, headquarters wanted to refrain from
emphasizing too strongly the positive outcomes, in order to maintain pressure
on the Salvadoran government to fulfill its promises.

The electoral division began its operation in an "organizational dysfunction" mode, experiencing poor coordination and leadership in two ways. First,
internal to the electoral division, between the head of the operation and the
regional heads, and second, between UN headquarters in New York and the
ONUSAL Special Representative. The direct manifestation of this dysfunction
was in an inability to persuade the Supreme Electoral Tribunal to counteract

[143] *The UN and El Salvador*, 1995, p. 56.
[144] Author interview with a UN official who asked not to be named.

the low voter registration. But since the leaders of ONUSAL, at all levels, agreed on a definition of the central problem (faulty voter lists) and agreed to interpret the mandate as including technical support to increase voter registration, the mission began to move into an organizational learning mode. At the same time, Ramirez-Ocampo did his part in persuading almost all political party heads to agree to abide by the electoral code of conduct, and his successor, ter Horst, took the leadership quickly and effectively, in time for the run-off vote. The liberal mandate interpretation originated in the field, and worked its way through headquarters, and eventually to the Security Council. The result of the efforts of the organizational learning were clear: high levels of voter registration, a largely non-violent campaign period, and uncontested elections.

While the elections were not the culmination of the peace process, they did help to consolidate democratic practices in El Salvador. Poll workers were trained in the technicalities of holding elections; civil society organizations learned how to monitor elections and eventually formed the Civic Education Consortium of Salvadoran Nongovernmental Organizations, which proved decisive in the largely self-monitored 1997 elections; most Salvadoran citizens of voting age obtained voting registration cards, even if not all exercised their right to vote. There were also important political changes that emerged from these elections: the FMLN transformed itself from a guerrilla force into a full-fledged political party, seeking gain through political rather than violent means; and the army and police learned how to provide professional and discrete security for campaigns and elections. It is also undisputed that "the most systematic, decisive, and authoritative venue of international assistance to the elections of 1994 was that of ONUSAL."[145] Some have even argued that "ONUSAL's electoral division saved the elections from certain disaster."[146]

El Salvador since ONUSAL

There is no doubt but that UN intervention in El Salvador augmented the country's prospects for peace.[147] The peace process has not been seriously challenged since the official close of the UN missions in June 1997, and since the end of the war, a "passion for peace seems to have replaced passion for revolution."[148] The root cause of the conflict was seen to be the military's influence over society. This was virtually eliminated after implementation of the peace agreements, with the purging of the top command, the downsizing of the troops, and the restructuring of the forces away from internal security and counteracting guerrilla war, and toward national defense. The cease-fire has not been broken, nor are there fears that this might happen, given that the

[145] Baylora, 1998, p. 19.   [146] Montgomery, 1998, p. 134.   [147] Wood, 2003, p. 257.
[148] Grenier, 2004, p. 325.

FMLN and all major parties have forsworn political or economic gain through violent means.

Political violence is no longer a subject of great concern, but criminal violence is. The growth of violent gangs has become an increasing problem in Salvadoran society and is viewed as stemming in part from the ready availability of arms since the end of the war, and the dislocation of youth as a legacy of the war.[149] There are also some fears of a possible military backlash if gang memberships and crime rates continue to increase. Military resurgence, however, has not yet happened, since the new National Civilian Police force is still functioning independently of the military, and largely within its mandate as set forth in the Chapultepec Accord.

In terms of human rights, aside from increased protections through police and military reforms, judicial reforms designed to improve the administration of justice, including constitutional reforms and a revision of the Criminal Procedure Code, were finally instituted in 1996. And in the years since the signing of the peace accord, Salvadoran dissidents and the press have been enjoying greater freedoms than ever before in Salvadoran history, even though there are still some forces in Salvadoran society seeking to decrease openness and respect for human rights.[150]

While during the UN mission there was tension between the government's promise to allocate considerable funds in order to implement the peace accords, and the stringent fiscal management mandated by the international lending institutions, the Salvadoran economy has been doing well. In the first few years after the war, the economy experienced a "postwar boom," after the privatization of the banking system, reduction of import duties, and the lifting of price controls; this boom, however, leveled out by the middle of 1995. In 2005, the GNP per capita was $5,100 PPP; the GDP real growth rate was over 2 percent; poverty rates had been declining, and there was continuing low inflation, low external debt, and low unemployment (under 10 percent).[151]

El Salvador was not as hard hit by the 1998 Hurricane Mitch or the 2005 Hurricane Stan as other Central American countries, but it was devastated by a series of earthquakes in early 2001. The quakes left approximately 2,000 people dead and 1.5 million people without homes. The damage amounted to an estimated 1.5 billion dollars, and shortly after the quakes, the international community provided approximately $1.3 billion in aid. In general, while the earthquakes have set El Salvador back, the country continues to benefit from external aid and large influxes of capital through labor remittances.[152]

---

[149] Ribando, 2005.   [150] For a thorough discussion, see Ladutke, 2004.

[151] Statistics come from the 2005 *CIA World Factbook*. In March 2001, El Salvador adopted the US dollar as its official currency, alongside the colon. In 2004, El Salvador led most of its Central American neighbors to sign the Central American Free Trade Agreement, favored by the United States and foreign investors.

[152] Remittances in 2004 were estimated at about 16 percent of the GDP.

In terms of electoral performance, which is admittedly only one of a number of factors that determine democratic health in any given country, recent elections have affirmed the strength of the two major parties. In the 2000 elections, the FMLN upset the dominant party by winning a slight majority of thirty-one seats in the Legislative Assembly, while ARENA won twenty-eight; the remaining seats were split among smaller parties. The 1999 and 2004 presidential elections have reaffirmed the strength of the ARENA party, since its candidates won both elections with substantial margins.[153] Overall, while it is unsurprising that the ARENA party has remained strong, given its pre-peace-agreement institutional strengths, the FMLN has become a truly national party, and a significant political force. As one analyst explains, even though voter turnout continues to be low, "In El Salvador today there is a noisy, messy but healthy democratic process. The reconciliation of political elites (if not at the grassroots level of society), has contributed to the growth of a very robust democratic debate."[154]

In sum, despite crime problems and a somewhat mixed, but mainly positive, economic picture, most analysts agree that "the peace process appears to be largely consolidated, producing a transition to democratic rule and significant reform of the state institutions."[155] The overall legacy of the UN involvement in El Salvador appears to have been quite positive, and there is strong doubt that El Salvador will ever return to war, even if levels of violent crime and gang activity may remain troubling.

Conclusion

What was the main source of success of the UN multidimensional peacekeeping mission in El Salvador? While there is no question that the warring parties, helpful states, and Security Council interests played major roles, the evidence clearly demonstrates that the UN Secretariat was largely responsible for its successes, as well as disappointments.

In terms of the "situational difficulty" of ending the civil war and consent of the parties, by the late 1980s and into the early 1990s, the civil war had come to a stalemate. External support for both sides was eroding, both internationally and regionally. However, both sides remained far apart on every single substantive issue to be negotiated in a potential peace deal. Both sides continued to fight,

---

[153] In the 2004 elections, the ARENA candidate's prospects were boosted by rumors of a possible backlash from the United States if the socialist-oriented FMLN-led coalition were to win. Since labor remittances from the United States make up a substantial portion of El Salvador's economy, poor relations with the United States could potentially have a devastating effect on many families.

[154] Teresa Whitfield, interview with the author, UN Headquarters, New York, January 20, 2000.

[155] Stanley and Loosle, 1998, p. 16.

or "spoil," after signing some initial peace deals, and after the deployment of the ONUSAL human rights monitoring mission in May 1991. It was not until ONUSAL military and police observers were deployed that the parties were willing to honor the cease-fire, which began officially in February 1992.

As for Security Council interest, consensus, and intensity, the Council was divided and tended to support different sides during the 1980s. But with the fall of communism, a general consensus arose over allowing the UN Secretariat to take the lead in both the mediation and peace implementation efforts. All votes were unanimous, and the Secretary-General's plans were adopted without modification. This is not to say, however, that the interests manifest by the Council were particularly *intense.*

While funding for ONUSAL was not always readily forthcoming, it was adequate. Over the years, there were very few formal deliberations or statements about the Salvador mission, indicating that ONUSAL simply was not at the top of the priority list for the Security Council. We can therefore say that while there was consensus, there was only a "moderate" level of support for the operation. The fortuitous situational factors and consensual, but only moderately intense interests of the Security Council provide the backdrop for organizational learning within the UN Secretariat's mission.

The operation was able to collect information, especially about human rights abuses, directly from thousands of Salvadorans, and adequately define problems based on this information. The operation also communicated its intentions to Salvadorans through radio, television, newspapers, and posters, even though there was not a separate ONUSAL information program. While there were coordination problems, especially between the CIVPOL and human rights divisions, these were eventually overcome. In terms of the level of organizational engagement, a higher level of UN leadership proved at times to be both necessary and effective. The high level of engagement did not preclude the organization from tending toward an *integrative,* rather than a *colonial,* profile. The human rights, policing, and elections monitoring divisions were especially adept at integrating with, and taking cues from, the population; these divisions even began to take over some malfunctioning institutions of the state.[156] The military division, while extremely effective at implementing its mandate, did have more of a *colonial* profile. Often UN military divisions remain somewhat separate from the population, since their primary engagement is with the local military forces, but given that this division was run by, and primarily composed of, Spanish officers, the *colonial* profile was more pronounced.

---

[156] Salvadorans also trusted the mission, as indicated in a March 1995 Central American University poll, where 50 percent of respondents named ONUSAL as the institution in El Salvador that "did most to protect human rights in El Salvador." *Improvising History,* 1995, p. 4.

In terms of leadership, the leaders of the operation interpreted the mandate broadly, viewing it as a "baseline" or starting point, rather than a "ceiling," or end goal. They also managed to alter incrementally the goals of the warring factions. It is easy to imagine a scenario where the UN mission could have failed, especially if its top negotiators had been less adept at influencing the actions of the two parties. However, all major crises were averted and, over time, virtually all deadlocks were broken. If the UN in general, and de Soto in particular, had not been able to defuse the numerous crises posed by the formerly warring parties, the operation could have not succeeded.

The centralization of political decision-making and mediation at UN head-quarters worked to weaken the office of the Special Representative, who was supposed to be in charge of daily verification activities, including the general political and administrative direction of the operation. The centralization was, however, inextricably interrelated with the fact that the position of the Special Representative changed hands three times, which meant that the historical knowledge, coordination, and legitimacy of the operation remained primarily in one centrally located figure: Alvaro de Soto.

While the political weight of ONUSAL was centered more at organizational headquarters in New York than in El Salvador, this did not preclude the organization from learning over the course of implementing its mandates, which in turn led to the success of the mission. In all, the Security Council played a supportive but not micromanaging role in this mission, which contributed to ONUSAL's ability to function in a comparatively depoliticized and effective manner. In terms of the warring parties, there were numerous occasions when both sides were willing to renege on commitments. But each time, crises were averted from escalating to the point of no return by the work of ONUSAL's leaders. In sum, as one analyst explains, "Although the successes of the peace accords were due first to the commitment of many Salvadoreans, it is inconceivable that the peace process could have advanced as far as it did without ONUSAL."[157]

---

[157] Montgomery, 1995, p. 247.

5

Cambodia: organizational dysfunction, partial learning, and mixed success

Introduction

The United Nations mission in Cambodia was one of the largest in UN history, employing over 87,000 people, and costing approximately $2 billion. The size of the operation was designed to counter the vast problems in Cambodia, a land that had been torn by warfare for over twenty years. This large operation produced mixed results. It was able to alter some of the institutions that enabled the outbreak of war, but this did not mean that the civil war in Cambodia ended during the eighteen-month tenure of UNTAC (United Nations Transitional Authority in Cambodia), or that UNTAC was able to create state institutions that would secure the welfare and prosperity of Cambodian citizens after UNTAC's departure. UNTAC's accomplishments, however, contributed to the eventual demise of the Khmer Rouge, the end of the civil war, the return of hundreds of thousands of refugees, and a shift toward electoral politics, if not more substantially rooted democracy.

International support for the UN's operations was generally consistent throughout the peace process, the signing of the accords, and implementation of the agreements. What was not constant was the ability and behavior of the UN operation. The warring parties generally exhibited a reactive profile: while all voiced consent for the operations after the signing of the Paris Peace Accord, local support for the operations waned as it became clear that the UN Secretariat was unable to fulfill many of the tasks set out for it in the accord. UNTAC began in a state of organizational dysfunction but managed to move into a learning mode in several of its components, as it became better integrated with its environment. In addition, as the organization gained in size and popular legitimacy, it was increasingly able to exert authority over the parties. The organization's ability to learn on the ground allowed it to succeed in implementing parts of its mandate, as well as some tasks that were not specified in the mandate, and to contribute to the creation of more stable, although not fully democratic, Cambodian political institutions.

Situational factors

In all, war in Cambodia lasted for about twenty-one years, from 1970 to 1991. Between 1975 and 1978, between 1 and 1.7 million Cambodians were killed,

131

Close to 2mil deaths

out of a prewar population of approximately 7 million.[1] The deaths were caused by the Maoist Khmer Rouge regime, whose autogenocidal policies killed its own citizens not only by means of the conventional weapons of war, but also by disease, malnutrition, forced labor, starvation, and dislocation. The genocide ended in late 1978, when Vietnam, backed by the Soviet Union, invaded Cambodia, forcing the Khmer Rouge and hundreds of thousands of civilians to flee west to the Thai–Cambodian border.

The causes of the war remain in dispute. However, almost all analysts attest to a combination of factors, which can be broken down into three levels of emphasis: first, some contend that the war and its consequences originated from within Cambodia; second, many focus on dynamics with neighboring states (Vietnam and Thailand in particular); third, others emphasize international manipulations (mainly by the USA, USSR, and China).

First, arguments about the cause of the war that focus primarily on internal processes break down into roughly two types: cultural and institutional. Analysts of both types tend to agree that, as a prominent journalist maintains, "while the United States and Vietnam do share responsibility for much of Cambodia's sorrows, ultimately Cambodians were the victims of their own leaders and their own traditions and history."[2] The war was fundamentally *not* about poverty, ethnicity, or land alienation, as has been the case with many other civil wars. In prewar, royalist Cambodia, 90 percent of the peasants owned enough land on which to subsist.[3] While this number decreased to about 80 percent by 1970, the basic needs of the rural population were for the most part being met, and the decline was not dramatic enough to give rise to peasant revolt.

Given this background, culturalists argue that King Sihanouk was a remarkably paternalistic ruler, treating his population "like children," and the population was, in turn, extremely obedient.[4] Sihanouk, during the time of Khmer Rouge ascendance, was the nominal head of the Khmer Rouge, and while his support for the party eventually proved coerced, most Cambodians were unaware of this. When the secretive, murderous Khmer Rouge regime was

---

[1] Lower estimates are from Jackson, 1989, p. 3; and *The United Nations and Cambodia*, 1995, p. 5. Higher estimates are cited in Kiernan, 1990; Becker, 1997; Coates, 2005 ; Maguire, 2005; and Hinton, 2005.

[2] Becker, 1998, p. xv.   [3] Frieson, 1993, p. 33.

[4] Prince Norodom Sihanouk was named king as an eighteen-year-old by the French colonial government. From 1941 to 1945, Japan occupied Cambodia, after which point the country reverted back to French rule with Sihanouk still king. In 1953, Sihanouk launched a successful "royalist crusade for independence." Two years later, in popular elections, Sihanouk won 99 percent of the vote, consolidated his power, and began persecuting opposition communists and nationalists; his reign became increasingly arbitrary and authoritarian. After a 1970 coup, Sihanouk began to seek support from Chinese, Vietnamese, and Laotian communists against the American-backed regimes in Indochina. After being in exile for much of the war, Sihanouk was again placed in the position of king after the election in 1993 and his son, Prince Norodom Ranariddh, First Prime Minister.

poised to take power, many Cambodians, from peasants to intellectuals to nationalist bureaucrats "had created an unshakable fantasy about the Khmer Rouge . . . [that it] represented something resembling the Yugoslav variant of communism."[5] Many supporters sought the re-enthronement of the King, and they therefore willingly followed the Khmer Rouge until they were taken by surprise in its killing fields. While the majority of peasants owned land, the Khmer Rouge chose the "landlord class" as the target group against which peasants were to rebel. The result was that peasants, for the most part satisfied with sufficient subsistence farming, were nevertheless "drawn to the movement out of duty to reinstate Sihanouk" but were not particularly interested in the revolution.[6]

At its core, the culturalist argument holds that the obedient nature of pre-1970 Cambodian political culture was the downfall of Cambodia.[7] Pierre Lizée attributes the obedience and resultant violence to the prevalence of Theravada Buddhism and a "Hindu Brahamanic cult," which center on social hierarchy and harmony among different parts of society. He maintains that in Cambodia, it is "in fact fundamental that the ruler rule, by violence if necessary, so that the different roles which had to be assumed for the community to be in order could be fulfilled, and so that, then, a higher level of social harmonization could be envisioned."[8] Lizée argues that Cambodia is in effect doomed to violent factionalism, and will never adopt democratic values given its cultural history.[9]

A second group of scholars see the primary cause of the war not in Cambodian political culture, but in an ideological and institutional battle between competing visions of governance. The three primary, competing, and shifting ideological tendencies in Cambodia are the following: royalism (represented by Sihanouk and the nationalists); socialism (represented by two factions, one led by Hun Sen, the leader of the State of Cambodia, and the other by Pol Pot, former head of the Khmer Rouge); and parliamentarianism (represented by Lon Nol in 1970, and the democratic governance structures set up in 1994).[10] This type of argument is not far from that of the culturalists, in that it looks primarily to the domestic roots of violence, but it attempts to account better for change, both ideological and institutional. Many scholars, as well as the international negotiators, prefer the ideological/institutional definition of the war, as it recognizes the possibility of achieving some sort of sustainable compromise in future governing structures.

---

[5] Becker, 1998, p. 3.   [6] Frieson, 1993, p. 46.   [7] Hinton, 2005.
[8] Lizée, 2000, p. 38; see also Lizée, 1993.
[9] Sorpong Peou refutes the culturalist argument by pointing out that democratic values such as tolerance and non-violence have been elements of Cambodian political culture for centuries, and that Lizée and others like him support a theoretical stance that is, in the final analysis, not only empirically erroneous but "patronizing." See Peou, 1997, p. 5.
[10] See Chandler, 1997; see also Pike, 1989; Doyle, 1995, pp. 16–18; and Hinton, 2005.

A second level of analysis looks to the dynamics between Cambodia and neighboring states. Cambodia was, according to this interpretation, ripped apart by the 1960s conflict in Vietnam and Laos, when King Sihanouk refused the insistences of his western-sympathetic Thai and South Vietnamese neighbors (as well as the United States) to take sides against the communists. In the early 1970s, fighting spilling over from Vietnam consumed much of eastern Cambodia. After the end of the American-named "Vietnam War" in 1975, the Indochinese battle changed hands and intensified when the Khmer Rouge came to power and immediately began to fight with capitalist Thailand in the west of the country, and communist Vietnam in the east.[11] In December 1978, the Vietnamese sent more than 100,000 troops to defeat the Khmer Rouge, driving them to the Thai–Cambodian border. On the border, many non-Khmer Rouge were trapped and began to form resistance groups, including the National United Front for an Independent, Neutral, Peaceful and Cooperative Cambodia (FUNCINPEC) and the Khmer People's National Liberation Front (KPNLF). These two groups eventually banded together with the Khmer Rouge to form the Coalition Government of Democratic Kampuchea (referred to hereafter as the Coalition Government), whose primary uniting platform was simply resistance to the Vietnamese-backed People's Republic of Kampuchea (PRK, later known as the State of Cambodia, or SOC). In June of 1980, Thailand began sending Cambodian refugees who had been caught in the battle back to Cambodia. This, coupled with the formation of the Coalition Government incited the PRK to step up its fight against Thailand and the Cambodian resistance groups; the battles would continue until 1986.

A third level of analysis attributes the war to international influences over domestic actors. At almost all stages in the war, fighting would not have been possible without weaponry and training from outside powers. The most notable, documented examples include the following examples: in 1970, the United States helped to bring about a severely destabilizing coup against the government of Price Norodom Sihanouk, abolishing the monarchy and placing Prime Minister Lon Nol in power. Second, the United States' 1970 invasion of Cambodia to expel the North Vietnamese, and the US "secret" bombing of Cambodia in 1973 helped to spur the Khmer Rouge into action.[12] Third, China and France supported the Khmer Rouge and its quasi-alliance with Sihanouk. And finally, the Vietnamese, supported by the Soviet Union, fought on the side

---

[11] Peou, 1997, p. 23.

[12] The US bombing of Cambodia was finally halted by Congress at the end of June 1973, after widespread, popular protests. In that year, the United States had dropped between 250,000 and 500,000 tons of bombs in Cambodia – possibly more than were dropped in Japan during WWII. See Kiernan, 1993, p. 9, and Chandler, 1993. Several years earlier, four students had been killed by the National Guard at Kent State University while protesting against the US bombing of Cambodia.

of the PRK (later SOC) to drive the Khmer Rouge out of Cambodia, placing Heng Samrin in power.[13]

I argue that the interplay of all three levels is important for understanding the causes of the war. I am skeptical of the essentialist features of the cultural argument, preferring to define the internal crisis as one of institutional legitimacy, exacerbated to the point of civil war, and sustained by the involvement of external states, both regional and international. Because of the multiple level causes of the conflict, its management required a multilevel approach. Eventually, only a multinational UN effort could alter the internal and external power dynamics in the direction of conflict resolution.

In the early 1980s, several events took place that would prove critical for ending the war. First, in response to pressure from the Association of Southeast Asian Nations (ASEAN), the United States and China, the fractured opposition united in the Coalition Government against the PRK (and its Vietnamese allies). Second, the Hun Sen regime, Vietnam, and the Soviet Union solidified their bonds against the Coalition Government. Third, the UN General Assembly, representing the international community, condemned the Hun Sen regime and recognized the Coalition Government as the representative body for Cambodia at the UN.[14] But at the same time, the UN *Secretariat* attempted to strike a more neutral path by sending the UN Secretary-General's Special Representative for Humanitarian Affairs in Southeast Asia, Rafeeuddin Ahmed, to attempt to open negotiations.[15]

There were no direct talks between the Coalition Government and the PRK from 1979 to 1987, even though Ahmed and the Indonesian Foreign Minister, Ali Alatas, began to shuttle between the sides in order to clarify positions and search for bases of consensus. The PRK and their Vietnamese allies considered Cambodia to be their possession, as they controlled and administered almost all of it. But the Coalition Government had China, the United States, and the UN General Assembly on their side.

By 1986, several key factors emerged on the battlefield that would help to end the war. According to one scholar, "there appeared to be no clear winner in the war, and the Thai–Cambodian border fell almost silent."[16] At the same time, the economies of Thailand, China, Malaysia, and Singapore had begun their expansion, creating the "Asian economic miracle," and the fighting sides, as well as their external supporters, began to realize that they might have more to gain by stopping the fighting. Meanwhile, the rise of Mikhail Gorbachev in the Soviet

[13] See Kiernan 1993, "Introduction"; and Findlay, 1995, Chapter 1.
[14] The UN General Assembly held an international peace conference on Cambodia in 1981, which was boycotted by the USSR and its allies for appearing anti-Vietnamese. Each year, spurred by ASEAN, the General Assembly would pass resolutions on the Cambodian question, which outlined many of the eventual provisions in the Paris Peace Accord.
[15] Chopra, Minear, and Mackinley, 1994, p. 15.
[16] Peou, 1997, p. 27. Also see Findlay, 1995 p. 3; and Roberts, 2002, p. 115.

Union brought about an end to Soviet financing of the Vietnamese military, and a *rapprochement* between China and the USSR. These world historic events brought all sides closer together.

The peace talks, however, would take several years of difficult negotiations before concluding. The first talks were dubbed mere "cocktail parties" in Jakarta, Indonesia, in July and February of 1989. The Jakarta Informal Meetings brought all of the warring parties together for the first time and gave impetus to bilateral talks between the contending sides. Various subsequent talks between different interested parties moved increasingly from bilateral to multilateral, culminating in the first Paris Peace Conference of August 1989. Vietnam had agreed to withdraw its troops in April, 1989, as a show of good will before the month-long August conference. While some progress was made during the conference, the warring parties deadlocked over power-sharing arrangements during a transitional period before popular elections. Hun Sen refused to allow the Khmer Rouge access to a new governing structure, while the Khmer Rouge continued to insist that Vietnamese forces were still in Cambodia and needed to be removed. More talks were held in Jakarta and Tokyo with little progress. Finally, an Australian-proposed "Framework Document for a Cambodian Settlement" was adopted by the UN Security Council and the General Assembly, after which point the warring factions came under increased international pressure to move forward. The Framework Document envisioned a process whereby the UN, along with a representative Cambodian governing body, would oversee the transition to elections. The Cambodian parties eventually relented, agreeing to join a Supreme National Council (SNC), which would include twelve members representing all four warring factions (with the Coalition Government broken into its three constituent parties), and be chaired by Sihanouk. But disputes arose over representation on the SNC, and open warfare resumed from February through May, 1991.[17]

The fighting did not continue for long, and Sihanouk began to take charge of the negotiations. The first meetings of the SNC without international negotiators were held in Thailand. The SNC made progress on a cease-fire, and an agreement to the cessation of external aid to the different warring factions. Thereafter international talks were held in Beijing, Thailand, Paris, and New York in order to specify the relationship between the UN and the SNC, military arrangements, and the electoral process.

On October 23, 1991, the final Paris Peace Accord was signed by the SNC, representing all four factions, along with the UN Secretary-General, and representatives of sixteen states: the permanent five members of the Security Council (the United States, the United Kingdom, France, the USSR, and China), the six members of ASEAN (Brunei, Indonesia, Malaysia, the Philippines,

---

[17] All sides eventually agreed that the SNC would be comprised of six SOC members, and two from each of the other three parties. Sihanouk was the chair and thirteenth member.

Singapore, and Thailand), Australia, Canada, India, Japan, and the Socialist
Federal Republic of Yugoslavia (as head of the Non-Aligned Movement at the
time). The mandate gave the UN broad authority to oversee implementation
of the accords. While all sides consented to UN authority, FUNCINPEC and
the Buddhist Liberal Democratic party (the KPNLF) were far more enthusiastic about UN involvement than the PRK or the Khmer Rouge. Both of these
dissenting factions, but especially the Khmer Rouge, most likely stood to lose
power in a transition to democracy, and would eventually prove to be "spoilers"
of various parts of the implementation efforts.[18]

By the time of the talks, most of Cambodia had been devastated by the war.
Educated and skilled Cambodians had been major targets of the genocide, and
many of those who survived escaped the war-torn country for better lives elsewhere. The severe "brain drain" left Cambodia – a country with a sizable prewar
intelligentsia – with a largely rural, uneducated, and unskilled population. In
1987, one veteran journalist of the region described Phnom Penh, which had
been a major cosmopolitan cultural center before the war, as "a shocking site . . .
[transformed into] an overgrown rural settlement . . . pigs, poultry, and the
occasional cattle . . . were comfortably roaming the city, even in the center."[19]
However, it is important to note that after coming to power in 1979, the Hun Sen
regime, with the support of Vietnam and the USSR, did control up to 90 percent
of the country and engaged in major communist state-building efforts.[20] While
upon arrival the UN had to embark on significant infrastructure development,
such as rebuilding roads and bridges and clearing mines, according to a World
Bank report at the time, "The situation of public administration in the State of
Cambodia is better than might be expected after the hardships that the country
has endured."[21]

Resolving the war and coming to an agreement about the specific nature of
UN involvement was particularly difficult in Cambodia, given the unusually
high number of both warring factions and interested outside parties. Compounding this numerical problem were the odd ideological bases of the war.
The fighting was not necessarily about capitalism versus communism, for the
Khmer Rouge, a communist organization, was fighting against the PRK communists. The Khmer Rouge were allied with the royalists and supported by
both communist China and capitalist ASEAN and the United States The warring factions defined themselves mainly in opposition to one another, rather
than in terms of ideology. While the PRK/SOC was undoubtedly communist,
and FUNCINPEC unabashedly royalist, these signifiers did not translate into
coherent ideological platforms. The lack of substantive ideological purpose

[18] Stedman, 1997; and Mersiades, 2005, pp. 209–10.   [19] Kamm, 1998, p. 197.
[20] Gottesman, 2003.
[21] World Bank report (1992), p. 219, cited in Kiernan, 1993, p. 28. See also Doyle, 1995,
    p. 18.

would extend through the peace negotiations and the peace implementation. Power-sharing was the central question, whereas other grievances, such as land redistribution, were virtually absent.

While all elements of the causes of the war – internal, regional, and international – have some merit, there is no doubt that once the interests converged of regional and international states that had formerly been fueling different sides of the war, this essentially forced the factions to agree to the Paris Peace Accord. The external cohesion over a desire to see the war end, while fraying over some minor issues, held through to the end of the implementation of the peace accords.

Mandate

The UN operation was to have more power over the civil administration than ever before granted to a peacekeeping mission. Since the UN and most of the interested external parties defined the basic problem causing the war as one of institutional legitimacy, elections were seen to be the best way to install a more legitimate government. The accords outlined a transition process whereby Cambodians would elect a Constituent Assembly; and several months later, after agreeing to a constitution, the Constituent Assembly would convene as a National Assembly. The accords set out many familiar tasks for the UN: monitoring the cease-fire, overseeing the demobilization of at least 70 percent of the troops, overseeing foreign troop withdrawal, coordinating the release of prisoners of war and civilian internees, monitoring police, coordinating and overseeing the return of refugees and displaced persons, coordinating economic assistance, protecting human rights, and creating an environment in which to hold free and fair elections. The new and most important task was not merely the oversight, but the actual administration of the elections. The UN was granted unprecedented power over the electoral process, as well as over the existing civil administrative structures. UNTAC would exercise "direct supervision and control" over most aspects of government, which would be represented by the SNC. In the words of one expert, "between the SNC and UNTAC the balance of authority overwhelmingly lay with UNTAC."[22]

The Special Representative of the Secretary-General, as head of the operation, derived his power primarily from two sources: first, unrestricted access to all administrative operations and information, and second, the ability to reassign or remove troublesome Cambodian personnel. Moreover, under the Paris Peace Accord, the Special Representative was granted a type of veto power over SNC decisions. The SNC and Sihanouk could advise UNTAC, and whenever the body came to a unanimous decision, UNTAC was mandated to abide by it as long as the decision was in keeping with the Paris Peace Accord. However,

[22] Findlay, 1995, p. 13.

the Special Representative of the Secretary-General was the "final arbiter" over the extent to which a decision was in line with the letter and spirit of the accord.

The mandate changed several times over the course of UNTAC's eighteen-month term, which began in March 1992 and ended in September 1993. As it became increasingly evident that the Khmer Rouge, and the State of Cambodia, were "spoiling" the implementation of the Paris Peace Accord, the Security Council voted to impose economic sanctions on the Khmer Rouge, and to set a deadline by which the Khmer Rouge would agree to participate in the elections.[23] The Security Council also repeatedly called on all parties to allow the UN to take administrative control – a charge obviously directed mainly at the SOC. But as it became evident that the demobilization and administrative reform processes were not progressing, the elections became the focal point of all divisions of UNTAC. This de facto shift on the ground was later acknowledged by the Security Council.

Security Council interests

In Cambodia, the *war,* but not the peacekeeping operation, had more directly interested Security Council members than any of the other cases studied in this book. More specifically, during the war, China and the USSR were direct suppliers of weapons and political support to competing factions; moreover, the US military fought directly in Cambodia. In addition, France had been the former colonial power not only in Cambodia, but also in its neighboring states. By the time of the final Paris negotiation, and the implementation of the peace accords, the interests of world powers in Cambodia had essentially converged. But this convergence of interests was not particularly intense, since the very nature of the consensus was primarily about military *disengagement*, rather than a direct engagement in solving the problems that plagued Cambodia.

By the time it came to implement the Paris Peace Accord, major changes in US domestic and foreign policy toward Indochina had come about as a result of US actions in the war in Vietnam. Over 58,000 Americans had perished in the region, many more thousands of Vietnamese and Cambodians had been killed by US troops and bombing raids, and there was little tolerance among politicians, the military, or the American people for anything that would resemble further US military involvement in Cambodia. In the end, a symbolic 49 US military observers were sent with UNTAC, out of a total UN military division of almost 16,000.[24] But before the UN deployed, the United States did play a significant role in ensuring that the UN mission occurred at all. US

---

[23] Security Council Resolutions 766, 21 July 1992, and 793, 30 November 1992.
[24] *The United Nations and Cambodia*, 1995, p. 23; and Schear, 1996, p. 141.

Representative Stephen Solarz convinced Australian Foreign Minister Gareth Evans to help promote the idea of a UN peacekeeping mission with strong UN supervisory powers over the SNC, as a compromise solution to the deadlocked negotiations in late 1989. The United States, along with many other states, was somewhat ambivalent about whom to support in the peace process. The choice was between the lesser of evils. On the one hand, few were enthusiastic about supporting the reforming, although still communist and SOC regime. On the other hand, there was also growing awareness of the Khmer Rouge genocide and thus apprehension about support for a coalition that would include it. The United States remained cautious: "US policy in the mid-1980s was based on a determination to avoid becoming involved. ASEAN, however, was incessant in demanding that the US take a greater role."[25] ASEAN and the United States came to insist on a "comprehensive settlement" as opposed to an incremental one, which would more likely have advanced the positions of both SOC and the Khmer Rouge. It was hoped that a comprehensive settlement, with multinational, UN oversight, would pave the way for a fair election and the possibility that Sihanouk might once again rule, but over a "pluralist democracy."[26]

While China was not enthusiastic about democratization in Cambodia, it, like the United States, changed its position from directly supporting the war to supporting a "comprehensive settlement." In the 1960s, Chinese leaders were angered by Vietnamese communist attempts to create an Indochina Federation, but its anger was tinged by fear when such attempts began to be backed by USSR military might; China sought to avert potential Soviet expansion. In Cambodia, Chinese (and Thai) support enabled Pol Pot and the Khmer Rouge to wage war against the North Vietnamese.[27] By the early 1980s, despite the genocide, the Chinese supported Khmer Rouge inclusion in the Coalition Government because the Chinese felt that the Khmer Rouge were the only viable military threat to the Vietnamese-backed PRK. Moreover, China took the lead in supporting Sihanouk as the most plausible leader to fight the PRK, and Sihanouk also needed China for financial and political support (he remained in exile in Beijing through most of the war). But in the words of one analyst,

> By the late 1980s, it became apparent to Beijing that the Khmer Rouge, however strong their military force and their hatred of the Vietnamese, would be able neither to force Vietnam to withdraw its troops nor to topple the PRK. Once Beijing reached this conclusion, it shifted its policy in favor of a peace settlement in Cambodia, providing the peace process with one of its most crucial players.[28]

China became an active player in the peace process due to a confluence of a number of factors: China's growing interest in rapid economic

[25] Song, 1997, p. 59.   [26] Rodman, 1991.
[27] Findlay, 1995, p. 4; and Chandler, 1997, p. 27.   [28] Song, 1997, p. 55.

development; Chinese desire to be viewed in the international arena as a legitimate regional leader (especially after Tiananmen Square); and China's increasing apprehension over the political costs of supporting the Khmer Rouge. China did not maintain enough influence to prevent the Khmer Rouge from "spoiling" during the peace implementation, but, the end of Chinese financial support for the Khmer Rouge eventually contributed to that party's demise.

With regard to the Soviet Union, as mentioned above, the USSR supported the Vietnamese fight against the Khmer Rouge. In 1976, the USSR used its veto to block a Security Council resolution, which would have condemned Vietnamese incursions into Cambodia; these incursions paved the way for the eventual Vietnamese takeover. But by the mid-1980s, the rise of Gorbachev, and his policies of perestroika and glasnost brought about remarkable changes in Soviet behavior in international relations. The USSR sought a *rapprochement* with China and simultaneously decreased funding for the Vietnamese. By 1991, the economic and political collapse of the Soviet Union spurred a Russian foreign policy of disengagement in the region. While Russian military support for Vietnam and the SOC had essentially dried up, during the Paris negotiations, Russia nevertheless continued to seek to minimize UN control over the SOC, giving that party greater chances of success in eventual elections.

Of the great powers, France, while a supporter of the Coalition Government, attempted to play a more neutral role during both the war and the peace process. In fact, before the first multilateral peace negotiations in 1989, Vietnam and the PRK objected to holding the negotiations at the UN, because the UN had directly condemned their regimes. The only politically acceptable, and easily accessible, location for the negotiations was France.[29] Therefore, the first Paris peace negotiations were co-sponsored by French Foreign Minister Roland Dumas (as well as Foreign Minister Ali Alatas of Indonesia, who provided greater legitimacy through more direct Southeast Asian regional representation). However, during the final stages of the second Paris negotiations, the United States and France clashed over the appointment of the lead UN military officer.[30]

The United Kingdom was the only permanent member of the Security Council to play a minimal role in Cambodia. Other interested actors included Vietnam, Thailand, Japan, Indonesia, and Australia. Vietnam and Thailand, as the neighboring states of Cambodia fueling different sides during the war, sued for

[29] Koh, 1990.
[30] Findlay, 1995, p. 22. This disagreement, however, had more to do with great-power rivalry than with Cambodia. The United States felt that no member of the Security Council should take the lead military role and supported the appointment of Lieutenant General Sanderson of Australia. France felt that it should have the lead role, since it had been intimately involved with the military side of the negotiations. In the end, the Americans and Australians won out.

peace by the end of the Cold War, when they realized that economic progress was more desirable than ideological conquest. Japan sought to assert itself as a regional power and devoted significant financial resources to UNTAC. As Japanese diplomat Yasushi Akashi, the Secretary-General's Special Representative in Cambodia explained, "Japanese interest in Cambodia is extensive and genuine . . . We want to show our sense of international responsibility."[31] Indonesia and Australia had extremely talented negotiators representing their states. Indonesia, the lead power in ASEAN, wanted the Cambodian conflict resolved in order to pursue economic progress in the region. Australia, motivated by similar interests, as well as an interest "in being, and being seen to be, a good international citizen," but with a lesser history of involvement in the war than any of the other actors, was eager to take the initiative in working out the more technical details of peace implementation.[32]

Consensus

After the 1976 USSR use of the veto, the UN Security Council did not take up the issue of Cambodia again until 1990. With the end of the Cold War, national interests of the council members had converged over military disengagement from Cambodia, the removal of the conflict from foreign policy agendas, and the pursuit of economic interests. This convergence enabled the Council to endorse a "comprehensive framework" envisioning a principal role for the UN in the peace implementation.[33] While there were some disagreements between the USSR and China about what a "neutral environment" entailed, and between the United States and France about the leader of the UN military force, differences were resolved through negotiation.

Over the next three years of heavy UN involvement in Cambodia, only once did the Council's unanimity appear to fray, when China abstained on one resolution; all other resolutions were passed unanimously. The abstention came when, after the Khmer Rouge attacked UN personnel attempting to register people to vote in Khmer Rouge-occupied areas, the Council sought to pass a resolution that would either draw the Khmer Rouge back into the election process, or isolate the party if it refused to participate. Resolution 792 of November 30, 1992, set a firm date by which elections would be held and set up international controls "to prevent the supply of petroleum products from reaching areas occupied by any party not complying with the military provisions of the Paris Agreements." China's abstention was made in an attempt to

---

[31] Quoted in Heininger, 1994, p. 35. Note also that Japan changed its constitution in order to participate in this UN peacekeeping operation. Japan eventually sent eight military observers, 75 civilian police, and a 600-member engineering battalion to rebuild two major highways.

[32] Berry, 1997, p. 8.   [33] S/RES/668, 20 September 1990.

demonstrate its willingness to engage with the Khmer Rouge, rather than isolate the group. China remained the most important source of Council influence over the Khmer Rouge, but this influence decreased with diminishing Chinese military support. In the end, China would side with the UN Security Council, rather than with its former ally, the Khmer Rouge.

As one analyst affirmed, "from an international perspective, the Paris Peace Accords represented an unusually robust and unified commitment to peace in Cambodia which was followed through to the end of the transitional period and beyond."[34] In other words, by the early 1990s, there was consensus over both the nature of the problem – state legitimacy – and the method of solving the problem – through a large UN multidimensional peacekeeping operation – which, it was hoped, would pave the way for legitimate, peaceful rule.

Intensity

While there was generally consensus over Security Council interests in Cambodia, the intensity of these interests can be characterized as moderate. By the time of the final peace negotiations in 1991, the agenda of the UN Security Council had become increasingly crowded; of the forty-one resolutions passed that year, only two concerned Cambodia. In 1991, the conflict in Iraq and Kuwait dominated the agenda whereas by 1992, the war in the former Yugoslavia was the most frequent conflict to be considered. In 1992–93, the conflicts in Somalia, Cyprus, the Middle East, Cambodia, Latin America, and Mozambique were the most frequently addressed. A record seventy-three resolutions were passed in 1992, five of which concerned Cambodia; 1993 again saw unprecedented activity on the Council with ninety-two resolutions, six of which concerned Cambodia. Cambodia never dominated the agenda, even though it was frequently discussed. Throughout the operation, only eight statements were made by the President of the Security Council. The Security Council mandates did not differ significantly from the Secretary-General's mandate suggestions, and funds for the operation were generally adequate, even though the United States had already begun to fall behind in the payment of its peacekeeping dues. Taking into account the moderate number of Council actions coupled with generally ample funding for the operation, one could say that the intensity of council interests was moderate to high, hovering closer to the moderate classification.

Organizational change and implementation

UNTAC had adequate external support from the Security Council and interested regional actors. After the signing of the peace accords, it also enjoyed the consent of the warring parties. While these elements could have provided

---

[34] Findlay, 1995, p. 18; see also Akashi, 1994, p. 209.

the grounding on which UNTAC could learn while in the field, this did not occur at the outset. For the first six months, UNTAC was not in a learning mode for several reasons, the most important of which being simply that UNTAC was not fully deployed until almost nine months after the signing of the October accords. Moreover, before the mission was deployed, an interim mission, the United Nations Advance Mission in Cambodia (UNAMIC) was in a state of organizational dysfunction throughout most of its existence, setting an antagonistic tone for relations in Cambodia between the UN and the warring factions.[35]

Once UNTAC was established in Cambodia, over time, several of its components moved from dysfunction to organizational learning. At first, the leadership of UNTAC was unable to handle many of the crises it confronted; the operation was designed with little coordination between its different components; it had difficulty devising ways of integrating with the environment in postwar Cambodia, most specifically, in terms of "controlling" the SOC civilian administration and simply gaining access to the Khmer Rouge occupied areas; and mechanisms for information-gathering and dissemination were inadequate. However, in August of 1992, six months after the start of the operation, and in light of the stalled implementation of the accords, the leadership of UNTAC decided to alter UNTAC's primary goals and the methods to fulfill them. Once this occurred, UNTAC began to move into a learning mode, especially in the elections component, which eventually succeeded in fulfilling its mandate.

This section begins by addressing UNAMIC, the causes of UNTAC's delayed deployment, and the Office of the Special Representative of the Secretary-General. It then turns to evaluations of the fulfillment of tasks set forth for each of the components of UNTAC – Civil Administration, Military, Civilian Police, Human Rights, Information and Education, Repatriation, Rehabilitation, and Elections – and the extent to which each of the components was able to learn in the field.

UNAMIC and organizational dysfunction

In August 1991 the signing of the Paris Peace Accord appeared imminent, and Prince Norodom Sihanouk requested that the UN deploy an early mission to Cambodia as soon as possible after the signing. He and others feared that

---

[35] Note that in the wake of the disastrous start to UNTAG in Namibia, Secretary-General Pérez de Cuéllar made sure that his plan for ONUSAL in El Salvador was ratified by the Security Council two days *before* the final accords were signed, and that ONUSAL was almost fully deployed by the start of the cease-fire. This careful orchestration of the cease-fire, and advanced planning for the overall operation was essentially absent in Cambodia. There had been small fact-finding missions, but these did not speed the process of deployment.

months would pass before UNTAC would be operational, and that fighting might break out in the meantime. Unfortunately, his fears came true.

The Security Council agreed to the idea of an interim operation approximately one and a half months after the request was made, by November 15, and the small 116-person UNAMIC team was operational.[36] UNAMIC was never mentioned in the Paris accords, and it was not given the mandate or the means to deal with the tense situation on the ground in Cambodia. It was also in the field for a long six months before UNTAC was deployed.

UNAMIC was designed as "a survey mission," which was also to "assist in maintaining the cease-fire . . . by, for example, passing messages between the factions and arranging meetings between them."[37] It was also envisioned that the mission would prepare recommendations for UNTAC's size and strategies for deployment, communicate with the SNC, and, with a designated twenty-person staff, seek to promote mine awareness among civilians. By the time UNAMIC was on the ground, it quickly became clear that mines and poor roads were going to be tremendous obstacles to the deployment of UNTAC. Given delays in the deployment of UNTAC and a deteriorating situation on the ground in Cambodia, the Secretary-General requested that the Security Council enhance the mandate of UNAMIC to include mine clearance, road construction, and larger military "good offices," with a staff of 1,090 additional personnel. The Security Council quickly assented.[38]

In the end, UNAMIC did make a significant contribution to UNTAC by gathering estimates of the numbers of troops belonging to the four factions and by de-mining important strategic areas. However, the piecemeal approach to the deployment of UNAMIC and UNTAC had very negative consequences for the peace process in Cambodia. First, it provided a political opening for Sihanouk to criticize the UN and form an alliance between his party and Hun Sen's government, putting himself in the position of head of state before the elections, and antagonizing the Khmer Rouge both at the elite level and by stirring up popular support against the Khmer Rouge. His plan to take over the governing of Cambodia before UNTAC was operational, and before legitimate elections, crumbled by December 1991, but damage to the process had already been inflicted.[39]

Second, the new alliance increased the security fears of the Khmer Rouge, and they hardened their position against the UN. When the nominal leader of the Khmer Rouge, Khieu Samphan, returned to Phnom Penh in late November 1991, an angry mob awaited him. He and his entourage narrowly escaped back

---

[36] S/RES/717, 16 October 1992.
[37] S/RES/718, 31 October 1992; and *The United Nations and Cambodia*, 1995, p. 10.
[38] S/23331, 30 December 1991/add.1, 6 January 1992; and S/RES/728, 8 January 1992.
[39] This argument was made at a conference by John Sanderson, and cited in Findlay 1995, p. 24.

to Bangkok, Thailand, while their new offices in the capital were looted and destroyed. It is important to note that up until this incident, and even afterward for several months, the Khmer Rouge were full participants in the peace process.[40] They had not violated the cease-fire and would not until January 1992. As Sorpong Peou, a Professor of Political Science and a victim himself of the Khmer Rouge, explains,

> Had the UN mission taken quick and adequate action to secure the Khmer Rouge leaders right from the start, the first cease-fire violation could have been avoided . . . It was a matter of perceived insecurity, clouded by the uncertainty caused by UNAMIC's inability to ensure their security, partly due to the small number and slow deployment of its personnel, and partly because of their multiple responsibilities and highly constrained mandate.[41]

Third, after the first violation of the cease-fire in January 1992, UNAMIC simply did not have enough staff to investigate the violation. Once it was clear that the UN could not perform the basic function of monitoring the cease-fire and investigating violations thereof, the Khmer Rouge proceeded increasingly to violate the cease-fire, attack a UNAMIC helicopter, and refuse to allow UNAMIC monitors into Khmer Rouge territory, contrary to promises made in the Paris Peace Accord. This combative attitude toward the UN would escalate over the course of UNTAC's tenure.[42] Moreover, in response to the Khmer Rouge cease-fire violation in February 1992, the SOC launched a new military offensive against the Khmer Rouge. As one diplomat involved in drafting the accords explains: "There was a major screw-up in this whole process, and that is UNAMIC . . . UNAMIC was only an afterthought when the peace accord was drawn up. No one believed it would take so long for UNTAC to be deployed and no one took this interim period as seriously as, in hindsight, we should have."[43]

In sum, after the signing of the accords in October 1991, leaders of the four factions, as well as Cambodians in general, had great expectations for UN assistance in implementing the accords. However, UNTAC was not operational until many months later. The delays in deployment damaged UNTAC before it even began, since the UN had lost the consent of the Khmer Rouge. Sorpong Peou explains most concretely, "If the Khmer Rouge's resolve had been to destroy the peace process at all costs, they would never have signed the peace agreement that exposed them to the international community and to the UN mission in the first place; they would also have likely started their offensive earlier, when UNAMIC was at its most vulnerable stage."[44] This loss of Khmer

---

[40] Mersiades, 2005, p. 210.   [41] Peou, 1997, pp. 183–84.

[42] See Findlay, 1995, pp. 22–26; Chopra, Minear, and Mackinley, 1994, pp. 28–30; and *The United Nations and Cambodia*, 1995, pp. 15–16.

[43] *Far Eastern Economic Review*, February 27, 1992, p. 23.   [44] Peou, 1997, p. 184.

Rouge consent translated into a decrease in UNTAC's ability to manage crises, and an inability to complete many of the tasks that had been set out in the mandate. The organization was in a state of dysfunction even before the main operation had begun.

UNTAC's delayed deployment

The late deployment of UNTAC proved extremely damaging for the operation, forcing it into a state of organizational dysfunction. The delay was caused by several factors. First, France and Australia disagreed over the nationality of the military commander of UNAMIC resulting in lost time. Second, the rainy season in Cambodia extends from May through October, and preparations for inclement weather added time for logistics preparations. But the third and most significant source of delay originated in the Secretariat in New York. The Secretariat bureaucratic mechanisms were overwhelmed by the new tasks they were being asked to perform, and most of the UN's attention was geared toward the brewing conflict in the former Yugoslavia. In addition, Boutros Boutros-Ghali, the new Secretary-General, was confronted with three new, large operations which had been voted into action by the Security Council during his first few months in office, starting in January 1992. It was impossible that he would be able to devote equal amounts of time to all of these operations, and Cambodia suffered as a result. Finally, the budgetary process for approving UNTAC was remarkably slow, especially since this was to be the largest and most expensive UN operation of its time.

The implementation plan for UNTAC was finally presented by the Secretary-General to the Security Council in late February 1992, four months after the signing of the Paris Peace Accord.[45] UNTAC was designed to be an enormous operation, including more than 87,000 employees, over half of whom were Cambodian. There were phenomenal logistical complexities of deploying and managing so many people, who hailed from dozens of different countries, in a territory with a severely war-damaged infrastructure. The staff was to include almost 16,000 military personnel, 5,800 international and local civilians, 3,600 civilian police, and 62,000 Cambodian nationals to assist with monitoring the elections. From the outset, there were severe shortages of vehicles, modular housing and offices, generators, radios, basic office supplies, and even water. Suppliers' capacities were overwhelmed, and the lengthy procurement procedures at the UN meant, for example, that in one provincial office, the civilian administrators did not receive supplies until ten months after the start of UNTAC.[46]

Compounding the logistical problems, the process of advanced planning was disjointed at best, and fatally disabled at worst. Before and after the signing of the

---

[45] S/23613, 19 February 1992.   [46] Heininger, 1994, p. 42.

accords, each component of the operation fielded its own survey missions, with almost no coordination between the components. As General John Sanderson, head of the military division explains, "there was never any strategic planning within UNTAC . . . From the beginning each component conducted a separate survey mission and there was no coordination beforehand to determine the strategic method."[47] This resulted in some divisions being better prepared and more advanced than others. For example, the repatriation and the elections components proved extremely adept at planning for their tasks, and then implementing their mandates. In contrast, the military division had trouble gaining access to information about the numbers and location of troops, causing delays in its ability to plan. In general, while the elections, repatriation, and military components were active in attempting to plan in advance, the human rights, civilian administration, and civilian police divisions received lower priority, and suffered as a result.[48]

Office of the Special Representative of the Secretary-General

In the Paris Peace Accord, there was no mention of the Office of the Special Representative of the Secretary-General (OSRSG). The Implementation Plan rectified the omission, indicating that the office would employ seventy-six people, including support staff.[49] Yasushi Akashi, a career UN diplomat with no prior experience in peacekeeping, was eventually chosen to be the Special Representative of the Secretary-General and head of the operation. This choice was a result of both Sihanouk's wish to have Akashi in the top position, and Japan's growing interest in peacekeeping. While the OSRSG was to be the center of the operation in the field, the mission was structured such that each component reported back to its own headquarters in the capital. This hierarchical and separate reporting structure meant that, especially at the outset, coordination between the components was weak.[50] The feeble coordination was eventually strengthened once Akashi and Sanderson decided to take charge of the whole operation, altering the goals of all components toward fulfillment of the election mandate.

In terms of Akashi's ability to handle crises, many analysts point to an early incident at Pailin when Akashi was turned away from a Khmer Rouge border checkpoint as the primary example of Akashi's "too restrained" and excessively "tactful" style of leadership.[51] However, Akashi did manage to prevent numerous other crises from escalating, especially during the period just prior

---

[47] Sanderson, 1994, p. 22.   [48] Heininger, 1994, Chapter 5.
[49] *The United Nations and Cambodia*, 1995, p. 179.
[50] Chopra, Minear, and Mackinley, 1994, p. 34.
[51] Suntharalingam, 1997, pp. 83 and 104; Kamm, 1998, p. 208.

to the elections, while employing his often self-effacing, but effective style of leadership for the Cambodian context.

Civil administration

The mandate for the civil administration in the Paris Peace Accord indicated that UNTAC was to exercise "control" over five "fields" that could potentially influence the outcome of the elections: foreign affairs, public security, national defense, finance, and information.[52] While the Paris Peace Accord and the UN's implementation plan were careful to indicate that administrative actions of all four factions would be monitored, in fact, since the SOC was in administrative control of the vast majority of the country, most of the UN's preparations would be targeted at the SOC.

As the UN sought to set up its main administrative offices in Phnom Penh and twenty-one provincial offices in the countryside, parallel to the existing administrative structures, it was hampered by the delayed arrival of the director and staff during the summer of 1992. The SOC repeatedly tested the abilities of the UN before it was fully operational, resulting in a "missed opportunity to exert control over SOC," especially in the provinces.[53] While many external observers, as well as the Khmer Rouge, believed that the UN should have attempted to govern the country, Akashi took the position from the outset that "The Paris Agreement says that existing administrative structures have to be maintained. . . . UNTAC cannot replace these structures. Otherwise, the whole country will crumble."[54] The SOC administration included approximately 200,000 staff, whereas at its maximum, UNTAC's civil administration employed only 200 internationals and 600 locals.[55] The numbers alone indicate that the UN was never in a position to truly "control" the SOC administration.

Nevertheless, the Paris Peace Accord stipulated that decision-making authority would revert to the UN if the SNC was unable to act. The consensus structure of SNC meant that it would often be deadlocked, since all factions had veto power. The UN was to exercise control through the issuance of binding directives and codes of conduct, but there was no clear mechanism set up to ensure compliance other than through external diplomatic pressure. In late September 1992, almost one year after the accords had been signed, the Secretary-General's second progress report outlined several mechanisms of UN administrative

[52] A/46/608-S/23177, 30 October 1991, Annex 1, Section B-1.
[53] Heininger, 1994, p. 42. Peou, 1997, and Chopra, Minear, and Mackinley, 1994 also make this argument.
[54] Akashi, quoted in Heininger, 1994, p. 44.
[55] The SOC administration size estimates come from Gottesman, 2003; and Doyle, 1995. The UN's numbers are from S/24578, 21 September 1992, para. 26.

control.[56] However, according to one evaluation, "by the time they [UNTAC] had determined what to do and how to implement the plans, the SOC had become intransigent."[57] While the clarification of methods did assist the field operations in some of its activities, the small size of the component, its late deployment, and an often deadlocked SNC amounted to the unsurprising result that power over administrative structures remained, for the most part, with the SOC.

This is not to say that the UN made no progress in some of its five fields of direct control, and other areas of "optional control." While ultimate control was never achieved, there is no doubt that UNTAC did eventually come to influence some of the behaviors of the SOC administration, even if this meant driving them underground, or forcing the use of oral commands rather than written.[58] More specifically, in the field of foreign affairs, UNTAC established seven-day monitoring at the airport in Phnom Penh, eventually abolishing entry and exit visas for Cambodians and establishing internationally recognized SNC passports. It also established border-control mechanisms to verify that Vietnamese troops were not entering Cambodia, as the Khmer Rouge had charged. In the area of national defense, while Khmer Rouge and SOC fighting continued throughout the tenure of UNTAC, the UN did come to monitor "all incoming and outgoing correspondence of the SOC 'ministry' of defense," which curbed potential abuses relating to the elections, and set up a "code of conduct" between the three cooperating militaries, paving the way for post-election integration. In terms of public security, UNTAC issued an interim traffic code and published a booklet on traffic rules; it also eventually succeeded in drafting a new penal code, and in easing the mistreatment of prisoners. In the area of finance, UNTAC eventually managed to control the distribution of most foreign aid and, more importantly, gained control over currency production and thus inflation. This meant that the potential for hyperinflation was averted, as were rice shortages and government bankruptcy. Finally, in terms of information, UNTAC would eventually establish an Information/Education section within the office of the Special Representative of the Secretary-General, which would prove to be one of the most effective components of the entire operation.

While UNTAC made inroads in some specific areas, it never actually controlled the civilian administration. It did its best to monitor civilian administration activities, and encourage good governance behavior, but by

---

[56] There would be three types: "a posteriori," whereby the UN would review all documentation and administrative decision-making flow charts; "a priori," which entailed the "authority to obtain prior knowledge of all decisions;" and "appraisal," which would be "achieved through the proposal of improvements in the operations of the existing administrative structures. See S/24578, 21 September 1992.

[57] UNTAC civilian administrator, quoted in Heininger, 1994, p. 86.

[58] See McLean, 1994, p. 52; Findlay, 1995, p. 63; and Doyle, 1995, p. 43.

January 1993, it was clear that changes in UNTAC's methods were necessary. The SOC had begun to use government offices in a variety of ways to further its chances in the upcoming elections. UNTAC then established "control teams" which would conduct "raids on local offices suspected of engaging in violent intimidation against Cambodian citizens. Operating without warning, they exposed several instances of SOC intimidation and may have served to deter even more efforts to undermine the freeness and fairness of the election."[59] The control teams reported directly to the Deputy Special Representative of the Secretary-General, Behrooz Sadry. The establishment of these teams, the centralization of reporting, and general redirection of the civil administration activities toward protecting the elections signaled that the civil administration had unofficially adjusted its mandate toward elections monitoring, similar in effect to the eventual official realignment of the military division's mandate, as described below. The re-adjustment of the mandate and methods, however, was not necessarily a sign of organizational learning, as the division never had the means, nor was it structured in such a way as to collect information adequately, coordinate among its units, or integrate with the environment of the SOC civil service.

Military division

UNTAC was never able to fulfill any of the military division's original tasks. As explained above, UNTAC as a whole, including the military division, began in a state of organizational dysfunction, which made task-fulfillment extremely difficult. However, as the operation began to integrate better with its environment and redesign its goals and methods based on the ground-level political situation in Cambodia, the organization began to move into a learning mode, enabling it to implement a new set of tasks.

The original mandate for the military division included many standard responsibilities for multidimensional peacekeeping forces: verification and monitoring of the cease-fire; oversight of the regroupment, cantonment, demilitarization and demobilization of forces; weapons collection and storage; mine-clearance; and verification of the withdrawal of foreign forces.[60]

The UN's attempt to implement its mandate was complicated by several factors. First, the sheer numbers of Cambodian troops – approximately 200,000 regular troops in 650 locations and 250,000 members of militias in almost every Cambodian village were to be guarded by at most 16,000 international troops.[61] Second, there had been little strategic planning for the military component. After his initial survey mission in November–December 1991, UNTAC military

[59] Doyle, 1995, p. 94.
[60] A/46/608-S/23177, 30 October 1991, Annex 1, Section C and Annex 2.
[61] S/23613, 19 February 1993, para. 65.

commander General John Sanderson of Australia went to UN headquarters, uninvited, in order to try to understand better how the New York offices were planning the military component's operation. In New York, he found "no maps of Cambodia, no Khmer-speakers, no operations room, no one able to brief troop-contributing countries on what to expect and what would be expected of them in Cambodia and . . . no concept of how UNTAC's mandate might be translated into operational military terms."[62] Third, and more specifically, the lack of strategic planning meant that logistical planning was severely crippled.[63] At headquarters, very few experts in logistics were available to assist UNTAC. The dislocated planning meant that four out of the five logistics teams that did eventually reach Cambodia arrived only *after* the deployment of all twelve of UNTAC's infantry divisions.[64]

The lack of realistic planning and delayed arrival of the UNTAC military division only inspired fear and insecurity among the members of the four parties who were, in essence, required by the accords to entrust the UN with their lives. When all parties signed the accords, there was an implicit assumption among the outside powers that all sides would abide by their commitments. The UN was the first to break promises by not providing the oversight and security functions detailed in the accords. The SOC responded to the UN Secretariat's breach by reneging on its promises in the area of civilian administration, as described above. In turn, the Khmer Rouge responded to continued SOC administrative control by reneging on its commitments allow the UN to canton and demobilize Khmer Rouge troops.

The hardening of the Khmer Rouge position emerged most visibly on May 30, 1992, when, after blocking the deployment of a Dutch battalion in part of the Khmer Rouge-controlled territory, Akashi and Sanderson decided to visit the area near the Thai border with a large UNTAC convoy, but were also blocked. Rather than attempting to fight their way through, the UN convoy turned back. This event has become the focal point of the controversy over the extent to which the UN should or should not have attempted to use force in order to implement the peace plan. Both Akashi and Sanderson maintain that the UN could not use force in this situation or in others, such as when UNTAC hostages were taken.

Their arguments against the use of force in Cambodia can be divided into three parts. First, UNTAC was not structured to fight a war and had based its legitimacy on the consent of the parties. Moreover, if 200,000 well-trained and equipped Vietnamese troops could not defeat the Khmer Rouge, how would a multinational force of 16,000 accomplish this task? Second, there was no consensus among the external powers to support a military operation; if the UN were to begin fighting, most likely the international as well as domestic conflict would have intensified, rather than diminished. Third, if the mission

---

[62] Findlay, 1995, pp. 117–18.   [63] Ratner, 1995, p. 167.   [64] Heininger, 1994, p. 69.

were to try to coerce compliance, it would not be able to protect the tens of thousands of UNTAC staff, much less other internationals working for NGOs, against counterattacks.

With relations between the UN and the Khmer Rouge already strained, as the military division attempted to move ahead with troop cantonment, the leaders of the Khmer Rouge maintained that they would not comply until the SOC ministries came under better UN control, and until the "foreign forces" were withdrawn from the country. The issue of "foreign forces" arose from an ambiguity in the peace plan. The Khmer Rouge interpreted "foreign forces" to mean all people of Vietnamese descent, whereas the UN interpreted the phrase to apply only to active, uniformed troops and their administrative counterparts. In essence, the Khmer Rouge were requesting that the UN assist in expelling hundreds of thousands of ethnic Vietnamese civilians from Cambodia. UNTAC refused to honor the blatant ethnic discrimination, which in turn worked to alienate the Khmer Rouge further.

Khmer Rouge violations of the cease-fire began on December 27, 1992 with the killing of thirteen ethnic Vietnamese and two Cambodians. Attacks on Vietnamese civilians, UNTAC workers, and supporters of FUNCINPEC and the SOC intensified in January 1993, and continued up to the May 1993 elections.

At the same time, the other parties had been complying with commitments to canton and demobilize their troops. By September 1992, over 50,000 troops, mainly from the SOC, had been cantoned, their arms collected, and demobilization plans were underway.[65] However, since the Khmer Rouge was refusing to cooperate, the UN was unintentionally creating a military vacuum that the Khmer Rouge sought to exploit.[66] The process of demobilization had to be abandoned.

In response, Akashi presented the Secretary-General with a new definition of the basic problem on the ground. He explained:

> I am thus forced to the conclusion that DK [the Khmer Rouge Party] is trying to gain what it could not get either in the battlefield or in the Paris negotiations, that is, to improve its political and military power to such an extent that the other parties will be placed at a distinctive disadvantage when UNTAC leaves.[67]

In light of this new definition of the problem, the UN altered its organization in the field in order to accomplish what it felt was the most important and central task: holding elections. The most major change in the structure of the organization was the realignment of the military division. The initial deployment was designed to oversee cantonment and demobilization of forces in specific military zones. The redeployment abandoned the cantonment bases,

[65] S/24578, 21 September 1992.   [66] *The United Nations and Cambodia*, 1995, p. 206
[67] *The United Nations and Cambodia*, 1995, p. 206.

and placed UNTAC troops in the provincial administrative divisions, in order to support the election efforts of UNTAC's twenty-one provincial offices. This shift in military deployment helped to secure the other sections of the operation and provide badly needed logistical and moral support:

> UNTAC troops provided free medical care in the countryside. They built roads, bridges, and schools and repaired airports. They taught languages and instructed Cambodians in how to purify water and treat intestinal diseases. They sponsored sports and cultural activities, and showed UNTAC videos and films at cantonment sites and other locations. UNTAC military units dug wells and constructed toilets for villages. They even carried out some projects in Khmer Rouge-controlled areas.[68]

In other words, the military division helped to legitimate the UN's presence among Cambodian citizens. Moreover, "The terror campaign did not chase the United Nations out of Cambodia. Instead, it simply delegitimized the Khmer Rouge as a political force."[69] While UNTAC was always careful to encourage the Khmer Rouge leadership to rejoin the political process in Cambodia, in the end, because of Khmer Rouge non-participation in the political process, the Khmer Rouge were denied international donor assistance and private investment, as well as domestic political representation in parliament. Khmer Rouge failures on the political and military fronts inspired infighting within its own organization, and contributed to its eventual demise.

To summarize, while UNTAC enjoyed the "consent" of the parties after the signing of the peace accords, it lost this consent when it proved unable to fulfill its own tasks as set forth in the peace accord. The UN's organizational dysfunction at the outset of the military operation contributed to the unstable environment in Cambodia, by providing a justification for SOC and Khmer Rouge unwillingness to honor commitments. However, it should be stressed that the failure of the military component to canton the factions, disarm them, and reintegrate them did not, as some expected, cause the peace process to fail or the elections to be cancelled. Despite continued fighting, by its mere presence, "the level of conflict during UNTAC's tenure was lower than it had been for years."[70] Moreover, the military component eventually performed a number of tasks that were not in its original mandate, including assisting with voter registration, protecting political party offices, protecting UNTAC civilian staff, patrolling for bandits, providing security at polling stations, and initiating "civic action" projects such as rebuilding roads and schools. While the military component began its operations in a state of organizational dysfunction, its leaders were able to gather information about the nature of the conflict, define problems and set new goals based on new understandings of the problems, coordinate and change the operational design in tandem with other divisions,

---

[68] Heininger, 1994, p. 78.   [69] Heininger, 1994, p. 45.   [70] Heininger, 1994, p. 66.

and exercise leadership in times of crisis. In other words, the component eventually moved into an organizational learning mode and while it was unable to
fulfill its original set of tasks, it did contribute significantly to the success of the
most important task: holding elections.

Civilian police

The civilian police component (CIVPOL) was the poorest functioning of all of
the divisions of UNTAC. It began with the mandate in the Paris Peace Accord not
to monitor, but to "supervise or control" Cambodian police forces.[71] However,
the CIVPOL component was considered of lower importance than others in the
accords, manifest by the fact that it did not merit its own separate article in the
annex on UNTAC's mandate, but was rather listed in the civil administration
section almost as an afterthought. The Secretary-General's implementation
plan attempted to specify the CIVPOL mandate, in that it outlined deployment
plans, touring and information-gathering functions, "on the spot" assessments
of public order needs, possible vocational retraining programs, and, finally,
"other responsibilities relating to the elections and to security requirements
within UNTAC itself."[72] UNTAC's CIVPOL did in the end fulfill some of the
human rights training and election-monitoring tasks, but the component never
came close to fulfilling the basic task of "supervision or control" over the Cambodian police, since CIVPOL was in an almost constant state of organizational
dysfunction.

The CIVPOL division of 3,600 international police was to monitor approximately 54,000 police, most of whom worked for the SOC.[73] Modeled on the
CIVPOL operation in Namibia, the CIVPOL in Cambodia were to be spread
wide throughout the country, with one unit in each of the twenty-one provinces,
and 200 mobile, district-level units. While this plan appeared to be sound, its
execution was wanting. There were a number of basic staffing problems. The
UNTAC Police Commissioner, Klaas Roos, was appointed long after the mission was supposed to be operational; similarly, the component was not fully
staffed until as late as December 1992.[74] Many of the CIVPOL did not speak
Khmer, much less French or English (the two working languages of UNTAC),
many could not drive, and many did not have the six years of prior policing
experience required to participate in the mission.[75]

There were also problems with interpreting the CIVPOL mandate. Unlike in
Namibia, the police in Cambodia were generally poorly trained and organized

---

[71] A/46/608-S/23177, 30 October 1991, Annex 1, Section B, para. 5.
[72] S/23613, 19 February 1992, Section E.
[73] FUNCINPEC and the KPNLF did not have any police. The SOC/Cambodian People's
      Party had about 45,000 and the Khmer Rouge about 9,000.
[74] Heininger, 1994, p. 79.   [75] Doyle, 1995, p. 48.

– something that had not been acknowledged in the mandate. Moreover, large
variations in the quality and policing experiences of the CIVPOL were not
counterbalanced by uniform instructions or training once the officers were
in Cambodia. Given that the CIVPOL were unarmed and did not have the
mandate to arrest suspects after investigating possible crimes, many members
of CIVPOL did not understand what exactly they were to do in Cambodia,
other than simply observe the actions of the existing police. A member of the
Australian Federal Police elaborates:

> In essence they [CIVPOL] were sent into an anarchic nation without law
> and even the most rudimentary of justice systems, let alone general public
> appreciation of the need for it. It was a task that was not only poorly
> articulated but also one set in a structural vacuum. UN police in Cambodia
> had none of the tools that underpin their role in their domestic country:
> no laws, no justice administration, no courts, and no jails.[76]

The CIVPOL mandate was eventually changed to give the force the power of
arrest, and an UNTAC prison to hold suspects was created. However, there was
no legitimate court system set up to prosecute suspected violators of human
rights, thus the CIVPOL investigations and arrests proved largely ineffective.
Moreover, the UNTAC civilian administration was coming under increasing threats, with both politically motivated and petty crime on the rise, and
while the civil administration repeatedly requested protection from CIVPOL,
CIVPOL refused to take on this new function. Their refusal created friction
between the two divisions, and the civil administration eventually turned to
the military division for protection.

In general, the CIVPOL experience in Cambodia was a model of organizational dysfunction. The CIVPOL division never managed to interpret or mold
its mandate to the situation on the ground in Cambodia. While it may have
established some information-gathering mechanisms, it was never clear how
these were to function in relation to the Cambodian police and judiciary systems, much less to the other components of UNTAC. Coordination within
CIVPOL, and between CIVPOL and other components, was poor. Rather than
integrating with the local population, and learning from it, as Findlay explains,
"Unsure of their role, many CIVPOLs ended up either doing very little or
becoming involved in corrupt activities."[77] Members of CIVPOL were accused
of rape, child molestation, creating prostitution rings, and arms trafficking.
The leadership of CIVPOL arrived after the component had deployed, and was
unequipped to manage CIVPOL's problems. The CIVPOL component was one
of the greatest failures of UNTAC. The failure was caused in part by an absence
of major power financial support: "UNTAC's Civilian Police were asked to do
too much, and given too few resources with which to do it."[78] However, many

---

[76] Eaton, 1994, p. 61.   [77] Findlay, 1995, p. 46.   [78] Heininger, 1994, p. 83.

divisions shared similar circumstances. The most critical sources of failure were the lack of preparation, planning, training, leadership, and adaptability on the part of the UN's operation.

Human rights

In the Paris Peace Accord, all four parties agreed to extend to all Cambodians the basic rights outlined in the Universal Declaration of Human Rights, and the UN was given the somewhat vague mandate to "foster respect" for human rights during the transitional period.[79] The accord euphemistically mentioned "policies of the past," but other than this, the recent history of autogenocide was not addressed.[80] Rather than setting up a truth commission or any judicial mechanisms to account for past abuses, the UN was simply to "make provisions for" the following: a human rights education program, "general human rights oversight," and the investigation and possible "corrective action" in response to human rights abuses. The meaning of "corrective action" was not clarified in the accords and led to considerable disagreements within UNTAC over how to interpret the mandate. On the one hand, the leader of the human rights division, Dennis McNamara, advocated a more aggressive approach toward justice; if the Khmer Rouge were not to be brought to justice, then at least the UN should broadly interpret "corrective action" to mean punishment for current human rights abuses. On the other hand, Special Representative Akashi felt that human rights advocacy organizations were setting standards that were too high, and out of sync, with Cambodian reality. He felt that human rights education should come before prosecution.[81]

Pursuing prosecution would have been difficult, considering that the UN was supposed to rely on the Cambodian court system for trying any human rights abuses that the UN had investigated. Since the Khmer Rouge were not participating, and FUNCINPEC and the KPNLF had no judicial systems, any abuses were to be tried in the SOC court system. However, the SOC lacked anything resembling a functioning judicial system, as "judges were often illiterate and owed their position to regime favor."[82]

The Secretary-General's implementation plan took a step toward reconciling the mandate and the SOC judicial system by envisioning punitive action as secondary to a human rights education program:

---

[79] A/46/608-S/23177, 30 October 1991, Part III, Articles 16–17.
[80] A/46/608-S/23177, 30 October 1991, Part III, Article 15. Apparently China would not allow language into the peace accord that dealt directly with past human rights abuses committed in Cambodia, permitting only the phrase that all parties would vow "to take effective measures to ensure that the policies of the past shall never be allowed to return."
[81] Akashi, 1994, p. 210.   [82] Heininger, 1994, p. 97.

> The development and dissemination of a human rights education pro-
> gramme is foreseen as the cornerstone of UNTAC's activities in fostering
> respect for human rights and fundamental freedoms, for all Cambodians
> must fully understand both the content and the significance of those rights
> and freedoms in order to be in a position to know when and how to protect
> them properly.[83]

The means for disseminating the UN's human rights message would include
"printed materials (words and pictures), cultural events and presentations,
radio and television media, videocassette distribution, mobile teaching units,
etc."[84] The "civic education programme" was to stress different clusters of
rights in response to "current events," but was not designed to train lawyers
or judges, since this was deemed too costly and would extend well beyond the
eighteen-month time duration of the UN's mandate. Two additional activities
of the human rights program were first to provide guidelines and codes of
conduct for Cambodian civil servants, including law enforcement officers and
members of the judiciary, and second, to investigate human rights abuses.
While UNTAC was expected to do all of these activities, the implementation
plan foresaw a minuscule office with a staff of ten in Phnom Penh, but none
in provincial offices – human rights educational tasks were to be carried out
by members of the (already overstretched) UN civilian administration and
CIVPOL.[85]

Eventually, two steps were taken in order to better enable UNTAC's human
rights division to implement its mandate. First, the international staff was
increased by twenty-one people – enough to have one human rights officer in
each of the provincial offices. Second, the mission established, after Security
Council approval, a Special Prosecutor's Office of two prosecutors who would
have the power to pursue human rights abusers in SOC courts.[86] Defendants
would be arrested by UNTAC CIVPOL or military, and detained in UNTAC's
International Committee of the Red Cross-rated "four star" prison. However,
the SOC eventually barred human rights cases from its courts, leaving the UN in
the dubious position of holding several prisoners (one of whom had confessed
to killing thirteen Vietnamese for the Khmer Rouge), without the prospect of
a trial.

These steps, while representing some progress, did not alleviate the main
source of tension within the mandate, and within the UNTAC operation. Since
UNTAC could not broach the subject of past abuses, the leaders of the human
rights division sought to hold the SOC regime accountable for ongoing abuses.
The Office of the Special Representative, however, as well as the Civil Administration, were more concerned with gradual institutional reform through working with the SOC.

---

[83] S/23613, 19 February 1992, IIA, para. 12.   [84] S/23613, 19 February 1992, IIA, para. 13.
[85] S/23613, 19 February 1992, IIA, para. 18–22.   [86] S/RES/810, 8 March 1993.

The dilemma between advocating forceful "corrective action" against human rights abusers versus favoring institutional and educational approaches was resolved mainly in favor of the latter. The human rights program oversaw the SNC's ratification of the major international covenants on human rights, as well as the adoption of a new penal code. UNTAC's visits to prisons brought about slightly better physical conditions and the release of several hundred prisoners who had been held without trial. The division investigated and documented over 500 human rights abuse cases, but little further action was taken in these cases even after the establishment of the UN Special Prosecutor's Office.[87] The civic education program eventually managed to train at least sixty judges and lawyers in basic human rights.[88] It also targeted simultaneously the school system, political parties, public officials, and fledgling indigenous human rights groups. It is estimated that by the end of UNTAC's tenure, membership in indigenous human rights groups swelled to 150,000.[89] An International Symposium on Human Rights in Cambodia in December 1992 focused international attention on continuing human rights abuses in Cambodia and laid the foundation for the eventual establishment of a UN Centre for Human Rights in Cambodia after the end of the UNTAC mandate.[90] However, despite the best efforts of UNTAC, as the Secretary-General described in his final progress report, "the human rights situation in Cambodia continues to give rise to deep concern. The persistence of politically and ethnically motivated attacks is obviously a serious threat to the protection of human rights as well as to the creation and maintenance of a neutral political environment."[91]

While this division did accomplish many of the tasks that were elaborated in the Secretary-General's implementation plan, the larger task of fostering respect for human rights in Cambodia was inhibited by a refusal, even in the peace accord, to attempt to come to terms with past abuses, or to establish mechanisms to pursue ongoing human rights abuses. Rather than attempting to foster human rights through the prosecutorial route, the division opted for alternative forms of institutional change, such as education reform, and grass-roots organizing. This route, while less satisfying for those wishing to see the leadership of the Khmer Rouge and some members of the SOC brought to justice, has undoubtedly helped make most Cambodians more aware of international attitudes toward human rights, thus increasing popular expectations of the Cambodian government. For this, outside observers have praised the division's work: "despite weaknesses, UNTAC achieved much on human rights with minimal resources. It was a modest success that, perhaps with a less sweeping mandate and lower expectations, might have seemed more impressive."[92]

---

[87] Asia Watch, 1993.   [88] S/25154, 25 January 1993, Part I, para. 16.
[89] Findlay, 1995, p. 63.   [90] E/CN.4RES/1993/6, 19 February 1993.
[91] S/25719, 3 May 1993, Part I, para. 14.   [92] Heininger, 1994, p. 100.

Information and education

The "info/ed" division was not specified under the Paris Peace Accord as a separate *component* of UNTAC, but over time, it took on the importance of one. The activities of the office were to be shared among several different components – human rights, civil administration, civilian police, military (especially the mine awareness campaign), and elections. The implementation plan recognized that there ought to be centralized coordination of information and education efforts, and that the office "would serve as the sole production point and conduit for information to be disseminated to the Cambodian population by UNTAC."[93]

The office was run by Tim Carney, a US diplomat long familiar with Cambodian politics. He and his staff realized early on the barriers to disseminating information in Cambodia: many members of the international staff did not speak Khmer; the country was rife with rumor, and competing propaganda campaigns; the antiquated radio system reached only about one-half of the country; many Cambodians did not own radios much less television sets; and the literacy rate was low: 48 percent for men, and 22 percent for women. In response, the division recruited "an outstanding group of Khmer-speaking scholars," established far-reaching transmission with the help of Voice of America in Thailand, and distributed 143,000 radios donated by Japanese organizations.[94]

While some top-ranking officials at UN headquarters in New York apparently opposed the idea of the creation of a UN radio station in Cambodia, the staff in the field recognized its importance and insisted on its growth.[95] By September 1992, UNTAC had struck agreements with all factions except the Khmer Rouge for joint cooperation in radio broadcasts, and by November 1992, UNTAC had its own regular broadcasts on the air every day, eventually transmitting for fifteen hours daily. Half-hour broadcasts would provide explanations of many critical facets of the operation: UNTAC's general role and goals, the meaning of international human rights, the registration process for political parties, voter registration, and finally, the mechanics and political purposes of casting a vote. Radio UNTAC would eventually become the most popular and credible radio station in the country.[96] Radio broadcasts were supplemented by dozens of videos displayed in central offices, weekly television news magazine shows, traveling plays and skits, and hundreds of posters, leaflets, flyers, large banners, and advertisements, all in Khmer.

Aside from educational activities about the elections, the division published media guidelines and helped to organize the Media Association of Cambodian

---

[93] S/23613, 19 February 1992, Part III, para. 162.
[94] Doyle, 1995, p. 55; Heininger, 1994, p. 110; and S/25154, 25 January 1993, para. 91.
[95] Findlay, 1995, p. 76.   [96] Lehmann, 1999, p. 65.

Journalists. It also assisted the military division in the mine-avoidance project, and the civilian policing and human rights components with human rights information dissemination. The unit also produced the UNTAC publication *Free Choice,* which, as Ingrid Lehmann explains,

> was initially intended for internal mission communication but, after its fourth issue, was also used for external distribution. It helped greatly in increasing the knowledge of the field staff, who were often facing similar problems, in how their colleagues in other provinces handled such problems. *Free Choice* kept channels of communication open between different parts of UNTAC and contributed to the cohesiveness of the operation.[97]

In terms of gathering information, the info/ed division conducted regular opinion surveys across the entire country in order to "assess the impact of UNTAC's information programme and to monitor the attitude of the people towards UNTAC and its implementation of the peace agreement."[98] As Peter Swarbrick, a top aid to Akashi explains, "We had a staff of Khmer speakers who would go out each day and find out how ordinary people and elites were reacting to the UN operation."[99] The Khmer-speakers in turn explained the meaning of the reactions to members of Akashi's office and helped to devise strategies for how UNTAC operations might better achieve the goal of free and fair elections. The office also helped to gather and interpret information provided by 500 field officers in the UNTAC military division, and drafted "systematic political reports on the activities of the various factions in each of Cambodia's key provinces."[100] After the end of the operation, Akashi reflected that the info/ed division's

> contribution to the success of the mission was invaluable. The assembling of a concentration of Khmer speaking experts provided UNTAC with indispensable information about the thinking of the Cambodian people, especially in the provinces, while the establishment of a Khmer-language radio station and TV studio made it possible for us to get the UNTAC message across to the whole population and to convince voters that democracy was vital and the ballot was secret.[101]

Indeed, even after the rise in political killings leading up to the final casting of the vote, Cambodians had understood that their vote would be secret, alleviating fears of retaliation and ensuring that the vast majority of the population felt free to vote. The info/ed division has since been credited with being directly responsible for high voter turnout.[102] In sum, the info/ed division, while not mandated to perform so many wide-reaching activities, proved in the end to be

---

[97] Lehmann, 1999, p. 75.   [98] S/25154, 25 January 1993, para. 92.
[99] Peter Swarbrick, interview with the author, UN Headquarters in New York, October 14, 1997.
[100] Doyle, 1995, p. 55.   [101] Akashi, 1993.   [102] Lehmann, 1999, p. 76.

one of the most well-functioning divisions, integral to organizational learning and to some of the successful aspects of the operation.

Repatriation

The commitments made by all sides regarding the repatriation of refugees in the early 1989 peace agreement were included almost verbatim in the final Paris Peace Accord of 1991. This indicates a certain enduring consensus – within Cambodia, in the region, among the refugees, and internationally – that the 360,000 Cambodian refugees, most of whom had been living in camps on the Thai border for thirteen years, should return to Cambodia. The accords reflected the idea that Cambodia would not be at peace until its citizens returned, and, more specifically, that elections could not be considered free or fair without the participation of repatriated and resettled Cambodians.[103]

The auspicious and multilevel consensus surrounding repatriation proved to be a sound base from which to plan refugee resettlement. The plan was created, and mandated to be carried out, by the United Nations High Commissioner for Refugees (UNHCR) under the leadership of Sergio Vieira de Mello of Brazil.[104] The UNHCR had for many years been involved with the International Red Cross's management of Cambodian refugee camps. Officials working for both organizations understood well the political, social, and economic positions of the refugees. Headquarters of the UNHCR in Geneva therefore decided to allow the operation to be managed completely from the field – the first time the UNHCR had ever attempted such an organizational configuration.[105] The UNHCR-led repatriation division, while still a component of UNTAC, remained somewhat autonomous from the other components. The division was in fact in the field and functioning long before most of UNTAC's other components, and de Mello managed to avert the worst of the Khmer Rouge spoiling by dealing directly with the faction, convincing its leaders of the non-political, humanitarian nature of the component, and, when necessary, its separateness from the rest of UNTAC.

In terms of the component's mandate, the language used to describe the repatriation process in the Secretary-General's implementation plan is the most crisp, detailed, and clear of the entire thirty-page document, demonstrating a deep and comprehensive understanding of the refugee population and its needs.[106] The program was to be carried out incrementally: mine-free land needed to be identified in Cambodia for resettlement; mass interviewing of the

---

[103] A/46/608-S/23177, 30 October 1991, Annex 4. Estimated costs for the project were to be $92.5 million, raised by the UNHCR and separate from the rest of UNTAC's budget.

[104] de Mello would later become the Secretary-General's Special Representative in East Timor, and then in Iraq, where he was killed in a bomb attack on the UN compound.

[105] Findlay, 1995, p. 52.   [106] S/23613, 19 February 1992, II-F.

refugees needed to be carried out in order to find out where they wanted to settle; food would be provided by international aid groups for up to eighteen months, allowing farmers time to reap harvests; those who did not want to farm would be steered toward other "income-generating activities," with the help of nongovernmental organizations; refugees, many of whom were highly politicized, would need protection from possible attacks as they returned. The return process would occur in stages: refugees would be transported, mainly by truck, to staging areas for documentation, then to reception centres in Cambodia, given start-up kits with household items and money or house-building materials, and then taken to their final destinations. The program would start with a small group of several hundred to test the soundness of the plan. After six months the operations would be re-evaluated and the refugee return flow would gradually increase to accommodate 40,000 returnees per month, in time to register and vote in the elections.

While the plan was very well researched, it was not free from critics or problems. Some charged that too much money had been spent mapping out via satellite potential land in Cambodia to where refugees might be able to return.[107] Others reproached the UNCHR for not coordinating enough with the other UNTAC components early on, especially the military division, which was not deployed in time to protect the first waves of returnees.[108] Still others charged that the refugees were being given start-up kits worth four times the amount of money that the average Cambodian made per year, and that the UN was thus unintentionally creating economic and social divisions.[109]

Although some of these charges may have been in part valid, they stemmed not from the UNHCR's inability, but its remarkable ability to raise funds, plan in advance, and provide for the refugees. More important than the difficulties mentioned above, the Secretary-General's first progress report revealed what would be the division's most difficult problem: finding enough suitable, non-mined land for farming.[110] The shortage of land, as well as continued fighting, were forcing some returnees to become internally displaced, and causing a slow-down in the repatriation process. If the division was going to be able to repatriate the refugees in time for the election, there needed to be a serious re-evaluation of the program. After interviewing numerous refugees about the dilemma, organizers decided to turn to cash grants. Most refugees, while disappointed by the inability of the UNHCR to follow through with its land promises, readily agreed to accept the cash grants.[111]

---

[107] Warner, 1993.
[108] Sadako Ogata, dinner conversation with the author, Stanford CA, March 15, 1999.
[109] Branigin, 1992; and Kamm, 1992.   [110] S/23870, 1 May 1992, Section H.
[111] In all, 88 percent of the 365,000 returnees opted for the cash grants of $50 per adult and $25 per child.

By September 1992, one-third of the refugees in the Thai border camps had been repatriated, and previously unexpected problems with banditry and malaria had been mitigated.[112] The UNHCR had been negotiating returns mainly with the SOC, but also with the other factions including the Khmer Rouge. The UNHCR was able to maintain the consent of the parties by "making sure that all factions were apprised of developments in the repatriation process, which entailed endless dialogue and negotiation, and helped allay their suspicions and gain their cooperation."[113] By December, two-thirds of the people from the camps had been resettled and many had benefited from UNDP–UNHCR jointly managed "quick impact projects." These projects included bridge and road repair, water provision, educational training programs, and the construction of sanitation systems, schools and health centres. Refugees remaining outside of Cambodia were registered to vote while still in the camps. In the several months before the May 1993 elections, the rate of refugee return was increased and the last of the refugees were resettled in April.

While at times the security of refugees seemed in question, eventual cooperation among the UNHCR, CIVPOL, and the military components guaranteed the refugees' physical security, especially when, as elections neared, violence increased. Also as the elections neared, the repatriation component trained local Cambodians in order to take over its offices and continue the management of short-term assistance programs after the eventual departure of the international staff. This division in general exhibited all the signs of first-level organizational learning, by engaging directly with the local population, gathering adequate information from a wide variety of sources, defining problems based on this field-level information, coordinating well with other components and managing crises well. In the end, it succeeded in fulfilling its mandate.

Rehabilitation

In the accords and in most secondary accounts of UNTAC, repatriation and rehabilitation are discussed in tandem with each other.[114] However, the mandates for the two divisions were not at all similar in terms of planning or implementation, and the outcomes of implementation were markedly different: where refugee repatriation was successful, rehabilitation was far less so. For rehabilitation, the UN did not have a direct role, but rather was asked to "launch" and "coordinate" various regional, international and bilateral

---

[112] S/24578, 21 September 1992, Section I-H.

[113] Heininger, 1994, p. 54.

[114] This is most likely because, confusingly, refugee repatriation is listed as a rehabilitation task in the Secretary-General's implementation plan, without reference to UNTAC's refugee return component.

rehabilitation and reconstruction plans.[115] The "Reconstruction Declaration" of the Paris Peace Accord, stipulated that "No attempt should be made to impose a development strategy on Cambodia from any outside source."[116] In other words, development was to be the domain of the new Cambodian government, after the elections, which made UN coordination of aid during UNTAC very difficult.

More specifically, the UN's tasks were to encourage the growth of shorter-term projects in food security, health, housing, training, education, transportation, and public utilities infrastructure. Longer-term projects were to be coordinated after the end of UNTAC's tenure by the International Committee on the Reconstruction of Cambodia, which would be headed by Japan.[117] The Secretary-General's implementation plan named a "Rehabilitation Coordinator" who was given the sizable, underspecified tasks of conducting ongoing assessments, coordinating all aid, and raising funds of almost US $800 million, from voluntary donor contributions. In addition, this office was charged with assisting in the resettlement and reintegration of an estimated 170,000 internally displaced persons (IDPs), 150,000 demobilized troops, and 360,000 refugees.[118]

The UN's rehabilitation office was plagued with operational problems: it quickly lost its first two directors through resignation and dismissal, adding to the already "exceptionally poor planning and administrative confusion."[119] Unlike the other components, the rehabilitation division was so small that it did not have provincial offices, which meant that it had a limited understanding of rural needs.

The mandate and operational difficulties experienced by the rehabilitation division had roots in much deeper political problems. Cambodia had been devastated by decades of war, and much of the fighting had been fueled by external assistance. After the war, external assistance was supposed to benefit the country as a whole, but since the SOC was in administrative control of most of the territory before the elections, the other factions felt that most economic aid to Cambodia would only benefit the SOC's chances in the elections. While the UN did manage to establish a formal mechanism by which the SNC might approve of aid projects, often projects were vetoed by one or more factions.[120] Moreover, even when there were agreements, donors would at times subvert them. For

---

[115] A/46/608-S/23177, 30 October 1991. [116] A/46/608-S/23177, 30 October 1991.

[117] A/47/285-S/24183, 25 June 1992.

[118] In the end, the rehabilitation division did not assist these populations in any significant way. IDPs were not mentioned in any of the subsequent progress reports and were largely left to their own devices. The troops were not demobilized as planned, and the UNHCR took care of the refugees.

[119] Doyle, 1995, p. 50.

[120] A UN "Technical Advisory Committee" had been established to hear donors' proposals and would then present the proposals to the SNC.

example, the Thai government built roads near Khmer Rouge holdouts in order to promote its logging industry; the United States funded various infrastructure projects in FUNCINPEC areas; and Japan assisted in reconstructing a bridge in order to curry favor with the SOC. In other words, various external funders of the war continued to fund their favorite factions in the hope that this would help the faction in the election. The UN had little control over donor actions, which undermined confidence in the UN operation in general. Moreover, the favorite donor projects tended to be large, often hired non-Cambodian workers, and were generally not in rural areas. This meant that average Cambodians did not feel the immediate impact of possible employment with international endeavors, and that the 90 percent of the population living outside of urban areas would not benefit directly from the projects.

The difficult process of approving aid in a politicized context meant that, while US $880 million had been pledged during the June 1992 Tokyo donor's conference, this aid was extremely slow to arrive and be disbursed, which only fueled political tensions in Cambodia. As the last director of the rehabilitation office explained: "We are in a vicious circle here in which the peace process founders in part because the economic component isn't working – and the economic part is not working because the peace process is perceived as foundering . . . Whole regions of Cambodia haven't seen any tangible evidence of reconstruction."[121]

UNTAC, given its questionable rehabilitation mandate, could do little to counteract these processes, but it did manage to bring about some advances. By the summer of 1992, the rehabilitation component had come to realize that Cambodia's natural resources were being exploited, often by the Khmer Rouge and the SOC, for the purposes of continuing the war. The division therefore proposed moratoria on the export of logs, and then minerals and gems, both of which were ultimately passed by the SNC.[122] The division also helped to establish a National Heritage Protection Authority, in order to protect sites such as the palace at Angkor Wat. In all, the rehabilitation division helped the SNC to approve of forty-five large projects, totaling over $366 million; however, only about $100 million of the $880 million pledged at the rehabilitation conference in Tokyo had been disbursed by the end of UNTAC's mandate.[123] In general, the rehabilitation component was in a state of dysfunction from the outset and never managed to recover.

---

[121] Roger Lawrence quoted in Shenon, 1993.
[122] S/24578, 21 September 1992, Section I-I; and S/25154, 25 January 1993, Section I-I. Although exports of these products did decrease, the UN did not gain enough cooperation from the Thai government and its business backers, who were reaping healthy profits from Cambodia's log, mineral, and gem industries. Moreover, the Khmer Rouge would not allow international monitoring in its areas, including those where it was mining or logging.
[123] S/25719, 3 May 1993, Section I-I.

Elections

UNTAC's basic tasks for the overall operation were not prioritized in the Paris Peace Accord. From the outset, Akashi interpreted the mandate as emphasizing above all the elections, and this interpretation grew stronger as other aspects of the operation faltered. For UNTAC to succeed in carrying out its primary electoral task, it was assumed by those who designed and signed the peace accord that other important tasks must first be fulfilled, namely, UN control over the civilian administration and the demobilization of troops. This assumption, however, changed as these responsibilities proved too difficult to perform as originally mandated. The definition of "free and fair" elections was also modified, and came to be understood more in terms of voter participation than an absence of violent conflict.

The basic elements of the mandate for the elections division were set forth in the Paris Peace Accord, and later specified in the Secretary-General's implementation plan. Where the Paris Peace Accord stressed the military aspects of UNTAC, the implementation plan emphasized the electoral functions: "The objective of UNTAC's work would be to facilitate the broadest possible participation of Cambodians in the election of their representatives."[124]

The UN, for the first time in its history, was to hold direct responsibility for conducting elections, instead of monitoring them as it had done in the past. UNTAC first had to draft an electoral law and oversee the repealing of existing laws. The elections division would have to conduct massive educational campaigns about, and then organize for, voter registration, party registration, the political campaign, and the actual vote. In order to further ensure that the elections were free and fair, UNTAC could take "corrective action" in the event of irregularities. For example, members of UNTAC would seek ways of providing equal media and campaigning access to all participating parties. For voters, as the implementation plan summarized, "The voting process would be designed to permit all registered voters to exercise their franchise rights conveniently and in the absence of fear, while preventing fraud."[125]

In terms of the electoral component's structure, the head of the election component, Reginald Austin of Zimbabwe, who had previously supervised the electoral component for UNTAG in Namibia, had been involved with the process from early on, managed to plan for the specific tasks of his division in advance, and was able to re-evaluate and update his mission as the vote neared.[126] UNTAC would require 800 highly mobile, five-person registration teams, and 8,000 seven-person polling teams. The UN electoral division would

---

[124] S/23613, 19 February 1992, Section II-B.   [125] S/23613, 19 February 1992, Section II-B.
[126] Months before the electoral division had been deployed, some of its members had conducted several initial survey missions, producing an extremely detailed operational plan of twenty-six volumes. Heininger, 1994, p. 101.

retain a headquarter staff of 72 people including 12 computer experts, and 126 representatives in the provinces, all of whom were deployed at least a year before the elections. This basic staff would be augmented by 460 UN Volunteers in 200 district offices, and, for the election period, 1,000 international poll supervisors and 50,000 Cambodian election workers. All 1,400 fixed and 200 mobile polling sites were to have a Cambodian presiding officer, which eased language difficulties, cut many costs for the organization, and was intended to leave an enduring legacy of electoral expertise among a sizable group of Cambodians.

The vote would be for parties only (no names would appear on the ballots), by proportional representation in the 120-seat Constituent Assembly, the number of representatives in each district would be determined after voter registration. Parties could be on the ballot if they received 5,000 signatures, and in the end, twenty were eligible to compete. The implementation plan specified that people born in Cambodia, or with one parent born in Cambodia, would be eligible to vote. Voter registration was to take place from October through December 1992, but was extended through January 1993, to ensure that as many people as possible had been registered. In all, about 4 million people registered to vote, or a remarkable 96 percent of the eligible population.

UNTAC's electoral division faced several types of obstacles. Some of the problems the division encountered reached crisis levels, but the organizers were able to avert escalation of the crises through careful political maneuvering. The most significant threats to the electoral process were, first, misleading propaganda, second, continued armed violence, and third, a potential loss of international and local political consensus as a result of the first two types of threats. Each of the three are discussed in turn.

First, both the Khmer Rouge and the Cambodian People's Party began to wage propaganda campaigns against UNTAC. Both parties tried to intimidate the population into believing that the vote would not be secret, and that retribution would ensue if Cambodians did not vote for the correct party. UNTAC responded with a counter-campaign, waged primarily by the info/ed division, to convince Cambodians that their vote would in fact be secret. Among other campaign methods, UNTAC increased its radio-transmitting capabilities, distributed radios, and issued its own all-day broadcasts; it also banned all public meetings until the start of the official campaign.[127] UNTAC upheld its decisions by imposing fines for infractions of its election rules: "some SOC officials lost their right to vote while others paid a fine."[128] UNTAC also sought to "level the playing field" by assisting FUNCINPEC leaders with transportation after SOC denied them access to airports. Similarly, after the SOC denied equal radio

---

[127] The campaign would extend from April 7 to May 19, with a four-day "cooling off" period before the actual voting.
[128] Ratner, 1995, p. 179.

access to the other main contending parties, UNTAC offered its own radio waves to ensure balanced radio access.

Second, outright violence conducted by the Khmer Rouge and the SOC continued throughout UNTAC's tenure. With the approach of the elections, violence against political opponents, civilians, and UNTAC workers increased. UNTAC members were taken hostage on four occasions, and while they were all eventually released, between March and May, thirteen members of UNTAC's civilian and military staff were killed in the line of duty. UNTAC's human rights division estimates that in the time leading up to the elections, beginning in March 1993, there were 200 deaths, 338 injuries, and 144 abductions of Cambodian citizens. Of these, the Khmer Rouge was said to be responsible for 131 deaths, 250 injuries, and 53 abductions; the SOC was responsible for most of the others.[129]

In order to quell the violence, UNTAC sought to increase its visibility throughout the countryside. It deployed peacekeeping troops to 270 different locations, increased patrols to cut down on non-election-related petty crime and violence, deployed CIVPOL and military personnel to party offices to protect buildings and people, and increased the military division's civic action programs. In all, once the official campaign period had begun, approximately 1,500 campaign rallies were held, monitored by UNTAC CIVPOL and military, with little violence. As Peou summarizes:

> While initially diminished . . . UNTAC's authority was gradually enhanced; it acted more and more like Cambodia's sole authority. Not only did it build public confidence in the electoral process through meeting basic needs, civic education, and technical efficiency, but it also promulgated an electoral law and took tough action to enforce it.[130]

Third, in response to the intimidation, propaganda, and violence, the overall pre-election atmosphere in Cambodia was far from the "neutral" environment envisioned in the Paris Peace Accord, which led some parties to withdraw, or threaten to withdraw, their support for UNTAC. For example, after attacks on FUNCINPEC supporters, Prince Sihanouk, who was receiving medical treatment in Beijing at the time, declared that he would no longer cooperate with the UN and that he was going to resign from the SNC because of UNTAC's inability to control the escalating violence. Akashi rushed to China and successfully persuaded the prince to stay in the process.

Akashi was not, however, as eager to try to continue to persuade the Khmer Rouge to give consent, considering the damage that the group had inflicted on UNTAC's mission. After the deaths of yet two more UNTAC elections workers at the hands of the Khmer Rouge, and calls by the Khmer Rouge to halt the

[129] Doyle, 1995, p. 56; and Findlay, 1995, p. 81.   [130] Peou, 1997, p. 205.

elections, Akashi's response was the most critical of all of his public declarations during UNTAC's tenure:

> No party or group has the right to stop these elections... there is no question of cancellation or postponement... [the Khmer Rouge] risks stripping itself of the legitimacy it regained by signing the peace agreement, and has taken a dangerous step toward outlaw status. Let us be clear about what this means: nothing less than international and internal isolation. The world will not forgive the Party of Democratic Kampuchea [Khmer Rouge] for disrupting the Cambodian elections.[131]

Shortly after this statement, complaining of violence against their group, the Khmer Rouge withdrew from the elections and withdrew its representatives from Phnom Penh. Such Khmer Rouge behavior was widely interpreted as preparation for a full-scale attack on Phnom Penh, but as Secretary-General Boutros-Ghali explained, in reflecting on a visit to Cambodia that he had made at the time, "I insisted that the Khmer Rouge was too weak to pose a serious nationwide threat . . . I felt I had no choice but to rely on my political intuition, which told me I was right: The United Nations had to risk going forward with the voting as scheduled."[132] Whether the UN made the decision to go forward because of the Secretary-General's intuition, or because of Special Representative Akashi's, a decision was made to evacuate relatives of those employed in the election effort, while the UN staff would remain to run the elections even in the face of potential full-scale Khmer Rouge attack.

In addition to the Khmer Rouge's withdrawal of support for UNTAC, the Japanese Diet and Australian Parliament considered extracting their members from UNTAC. But after behind-the-scenes intervention by Akashi, both countries remained in support of UNTAC. In a similar near-loss of support, the director of the UN Volunteers (UNVs) threatened to withdraw all 460 volunteers if there were one more death among their ranks.[133] Akashi responded by recalling all UNVs to Phnom Penh for "extensive de-briefing," further security training, and a new plan for inter-component security, whereby CIVPOL and the military division would protect the UNVs and other elections workers.[134] Again, despite efforts to withdraw support for UNTAC, rather than acceding to the withering support and withdrawing from Cambodia, UNTAC attempted to prepare itself for the worst possible scenario: Khmer Rouge attack and a collapse of the peace process. The worst case, however, never materialized. UNTAC's redefinition of the problem, its solution, and organizational realignment proved well founded. UNTAC managed to create a secure, albeit not neutral, environment. This environment was not produced by disarming the

---

[131] United Nations, 1994, p. 10.   [132] Boutros-Ghali, 1999, p. 81.
[133] Akashi, 1994, p. 206.   [134] S/25719, 3 May 1993, para. 31.

factions, but rather, by having the UNTAC military division protect the electoral workers and voters.

The actual election was remarkable for its relative calm. Polling lasted from May 23 to 28. Despite an early onset of the monsoon rains, there was an extremely high turnout: 90 percent of registered voters submitted their votes. Many had to walk long distances, and some were in direct danger of armed attack. However, "Even in the areas of bitter fighting in Kompong Thom, where voters were shelled on their way to polling sites, the turnout was about 80 percent."[135] Some sites had to close for short periods because of fighting, but the vast majority of the polling stations did not experience any outright violence.

The final tally was unexpected, especially for the SOC, which assumed an easy win. FUNCINPEC garnered the most votes, with 45.47 percent, winning fifty-eight assembly seats. The Cambodian People's Party (the SOC's political party) won 38.23 percent and fifty-one assembly seats. The KPNLF's Buddhist Liberal Democratic Party received 3.81 percent, and ten seats; the other seventeen parties split the remainder of the vote.[136] Since there was a constitutional requirement that two-thirds of the parliament were needed to make any major decisions, the two winning sides would be forced to cooperate with one another.

One of the most surprising elements of the poll was that the Khmer Rouge did not wage a full-scale effort to disrupt the election. Most analysts, as well as UN observers, offer several possible reasons why, but all agree that no one actually knows the true reason why the Khmer Rouge did not try to sabotage the vote. Some contend that the Khmer Rouge simply did not have the capacity to wage an all-out attack; however, as Schear and Findlay point out, there is evidence that, since Khmer Rouge armed soldiers were seen near polling sites but not attacking them, there must have been an internal Khmer Rouge decision not to disrupt the vote.[137] Others (including Akashi himself), speculate that Akashi had successfully persuaded Japan and the United States to pressure the Thai government into withdrawing all support for the Khmer Rouge if the Khmer Rouge disrupted the vote.[138] Some contend that China was the country asserting the most pressure, especially after the Khmer Rouge had accidentally killed two Chinese members of UNTAC.[139] Still others claim that the Khmer Rouge made a last-minute decision not to disrupt the vote, and to throw its

---

[135] Doyle, 1995, p. 57. The UN's mobile polling units, which often moved in and out of the most dangerous areas, consisted of trucks equipped with voting booths inside, and surrounded by UNTAC military.

[136] The Molinaka party won one seat, while the other parties did not gain any. See S/25913, 10 June 1993.

[137] Findlay, 1995, p. 85; Schear, 1996. p. 170. In fact, toward the end of the polling week, Khmer Rouge troops began to turn out in fairly large numbers to vote. There were some mobile polling stations that traveled in or near Khmer Rouge occupied areas, but there were no fixed sites in such areas.

[138] Akashi,1993, p. 198.   [139] Doyle, 1995, p. 58.

weight behind FUNCINPEC in the hope that Sihanouk would accept the Khmer Rouge into the new government.[140]

While the Khmer Rouge did not scuttle the elections, the Cambodian People's Party, reeling from its popular loss, did threaten the outcome. The party's first statement before the vote count extolled the freeness and fairness of the elections, but immediately after it became clear that the Cambodian People's Party had not won, the leadership alleged that there were a number of irregularities in the polling and counting process. The Cambodian People's Party requested that UNTAC conduct new polls in seven provinces, including Phnom Penh. Akashi responded by asking for details to support the allegations, and promised that the UN would investigate any wrongdoing; however, no evidence of significant problems was produced. Akashi declared: "The election was free and fair and the Cambodian parties must accept and respect its results in keeping with their commitments under the Paris Agreements."[141] The Security Council, ASEAN, the Interparliamentary Union, and the European Community all strongly backed the results of the election, calling on the Cambodian People's Party to admit defeat and allow Prince Norodom Sihanouk to form a power-sharing government, which would work to bring about national reconciliation.[142] Such a reconciliation, however, did not immediately materialize.

After the Cambodian People's Party's loss, Prince Norodom Sihanouk offered an interim power-sharing arrangement between FUNCINPEC and the Cambodian People's Party until the National Assembly could convene. This arrangement, according to at least one analyst, was scuttled by a lack of US support, sparking a secession in seven eastern Cambodian provinces by members of the Cambodian People's Party.[143] Others argue that the secession was simply a sign that a faction within the Cambodian People's Party was unwilling to accept defeat. Similar to the lack of understanding about why the Khmer Rouge did not disrupt the elections, outsiders may never know the true reason for the secession.

The secession was led by one of Prince Norodom's sons, Cambodian People's Party Deputy Prime Minister Prince Norodom Chakrapong, against another son, FUNCINPEC leader Prince Ranariddh. While Akashi remained publicly silent about this "Byzantine soap opera,"[144] he was reportedly working behind the scenes to help bring about some sort of power-sharing arrangement.[145] His efforts eventually paid off, as the ailing prince Norodom Sihanouk maneuvered a new division of power and reasserted control over the seven eastern provinces. He made himself King, with Prince Ranariddh and Hun Sen Co-Presidents

---

[140] Heininger, 1994, p. 112.   [141] S/25913, 10 June 1993.
[142] S/RES/840, 15 June 1993; S/25971, 18 June 1993; S/25940, 14 June 1993.
[143] Roberts, 1997, pp. 14–15.
[144] This is the journalist Nate Thayer's term. See Thayer, 1993.   [145] Findlay, 1995, p. 92.

during an uneasy summer spent drafting the Cambodian Constitution. Then in September 1993, during the convening of the National Assembly, Cambodia was transformed into a Constitutional Monarchy with Norodom Sihanouk as King, Prince Ranariddh as First Prime Minister, and Hun Sen as Second Prime Minister; cabinet posts were divided primarily between the two parties. Since the Khmer Rouge did not participate in the elections, they had no representatives in the Assembly, which provoked an internal battle within the Khmer Rouge. The new power-sharing arrangement, while possibly not stable, broke the "marriage of convenience" between the Khmer Rouge and Sihanouk/FUNCINPEC.[146] In its wake, thousands of Khmer Rouge troops defected to join the newly unified Cambodian Armed Forces, while Hun Sen laid the groundwork for re-amassing power after the departure of UNTAC.[147]

Cambodia since UNTAC

In the wake of the UNTAC operation, Cambodia has undergone a transition process that is somewhat similar to what has been experienced in other post-communist states. For fourteen years prior to the 1993 election, most of Cambodia was ruled by a Soviet-style replica regime, which imposed a centralized, military driven economy, and a non-democratic, hierarchical political system where the party (the Cambodian People's Party) and state were fused.[148] The transition from the Soviet type of governance has not been to a system where there are coherent ideological positions to which the ruling politicians adhere. Moreover, there is continued fusion of state and party, massive corruption and expansion of patronage networks, and a style of leadership that is based mainly in personal loyalty, even while electoral mechanisms exist that allow citizens to vote in regular elections. Of course, the transition in Cambodia had been made more difficult than in most other communist transitions because of the legacies of foreign intervention, genocide, and civil war.[149]

The civil war did not end while UNTAC was in Cambodia; however, fighting was dramatically reduced during and after UNTAC's presence. The strategy of UNTAC's leaders to exclude the Khmer Rouge from the new political processes because of the group's adherence to violent means worked to undermine the leadership of the Khmer Rouge, and inspired infighting about the overall direction and strategies of the party. The exclusion of the Khmer Rouge from postwar Cambodian political life sowed the seeds for the organization's eventual demise (a feat not even 200,000 Vietnamese troops were able to accomplish in 1979).[150]

---

[146] Heininger, 1994, p. 46.   [147] Brown and Zasloff, 1998, p. 299.   [148] Hughes, 2003.
[149] On the legacies of the genocide, see De Walque, 2004 and Gottesman, 2003.
[150] Pol Pot's death in April 1998 marked the formal death of the Khmer Rouge.

The demise of the Khmer Rouge, and the efforts of UNTAC and donors, however, have not necessarily given rise to freedom and democracy in Cambodia. In 1997, Hun Sen wrested power in a *coup de force* after about 150 people were killed in factional fighting.[151] It is difficult to determine exactly which party began the violence that led to the coup, but there is evidence that the fighting was initiated by a disgruntled Prince Ranariddh who, although holding a majority of seats in the National Assembly, was unable to seize administrative power from Hun Sen.

Hun Sen attempted to legitimate his coup by fulfilling the requirements proposed by international donors to hold parliamentary elections in the summer of 1998. This second round of elections transpired similarly to the first, except that they were less violent, and there were thousands of Cambodians, trained in the 1993 election, who were prepared to organize the technical side of the process. With a turnout slightly higher than in 1993, the Cambodian People's Party won the majority of parliamentary seats with 41.4 percent of the vote and 64 parliamentary seats – almost exactly the same percentage it had garnered in the first elections. However, the opposition vote was divided between FUNCINPEC and the Sam Rainsy Party, with 31.7 percent/forty-three seats for the former, and 14.3 percent/fifteen seats for the latter.[152] Prior to the elections, there were significant problems with equal media access for the competing parties, and intimidation of opposition voters on the part of Hun Sen supporters. After the elections, despite protests from opposition parties and some American journalists, the election was internationally certified as free and fair.[153] The international groups cited high voter turnout and general "enthusiastic support" for the electoral process as the primary indicators of the election's fairness.[154]

In 2003, parliamentary elections were held again, but it took almost a year for a government to form after the elections because the losing parties refused to participate in Hun Sen's increasingly authoritarian-style government. In these elections, Hun Sen's winning Communist People's Party gained just under six percentage points more than the last elections, or 47.3 percent of the vote. The most dramatic numerical result was the downward trajectory of FUNCINPEC, which apparently lost seats not only to the Communist People's Party, but

---

[151] Grant Curtis and Pierre Lizée argue that this was not a "Coup d'Etat," but a "Coup de Force," accompanied by violence, but not a full-scale change in government. Curtis, 1998, p. 49; Lizée, 2000, p. 157.

[152] The remaining votes were divided between thirty-six small parties, none of which gained a seat in Parliament. Local elections were held in January 2002, and the Cambodian People's Party won the vast majority of local posts, after months of intimidating opponents and unequal access to media. These elections were not declared "free and fair" by international observers. Sam Rainsy, a former member of FUNCINPEC and a highly educated, western-oriented leader, has been gaining in popularity in recent years, especially in urban areas.

[153] See Peou, 1999 for a complete discussion.   [154] Peou, 1999, p. 8.

to the Sam Rainsy Party, garnering 20.7 percent of the vote in contrast to the Sam Rainsy Party's 21.9 percent. The pre-election phase was marred by political assassinations, unequal media access, and expanding corruption in the countryside (where the Communist People's Party's patronage networks are strongest). Eventually, FUNCINPEC agreed to form a government with the Communist People's Party, solidifying Hun Sen's hold on power. In the words of one analyst, "elections have become little more than a side-show helping to bolster the electoral-authoritarian regime that Hun Sen has built."[155]

Overall, the existence of electoral politics in Cambodia has not necessarily translated into more broad forms of democratic governance. In addition to the trend toward authoritarian rule, lawlessness, corruption, and banditry are on the rise. The new Cambodian Army "suffers from widespread indiscipline, and lack of professionalism."[156] There was never any UNTAC police retraining, which means that the police force is essentially an extension of the army. In terms of these and other government structures, part of the deal that brought FUNCINPEC into the governing fold with the Communist People's Party was a compromise whereby 200 new ministries were created. In other words, as a way to solve the months-long political impasse, the state has become ever-more bloated, ensuring an oversized apparatus for many years to come, and deepening ties of "patronage at the heart of the Cambodian political system."[157]

Expanding state control has translated directly into a dampening of the ability of opposition parties to mobilize, hindering not only political but also economic growth, which further entrenches the government's position. Eighty percent of the population lives in the countryside, where the Cambodian People's Party claims its main support. The majority of the population survives on subsistence farming, although the textile and tourism sectors are growing. The GDP PPP stands at $1,700, and overall economic growth has been between 4–5 percent per year since 1999, the first full year of peace in Cambodia after thirty years of war.

In terms of legal reforms, the judicial system remains highly politicized, and UN efforts to institute a war crimes tribunal have been met with a myriad of obstacles. In July 2000, the Hun Sen government and the UN agreed to establish a war crimes tribunal to try several dozen high-ranking former members of the Khmer Rouge, but as of this writing the tribunal had not yet produced results.

In terms of Cambodian society, social ills common in many developing nations, especially those in transition from communism and civil war, are expanding. There is no strong or growing middle class to counter the increasing income disparity between rich and poor. Domestic violence and sexual exploitation are on the rise. Several despairing social trends that began during

---

[155] McCargo, 2005, p. 98.   [156] Jeldres, 1997, p. 153.
[157] St. John, 2005, p. 413; and Gottesman, 2003, p. 211.

UNTAC's presence have remained: price distortions, increasing prostitution, and the spread of AIDS.

Cambodia survives today in part because of the massive international donor aid that it receives. While some analysts argue that Cambodia has "been lifted up from the depths of misery and despair and given a better footing as a developing nation" because of international aid, others argue that aid is having more negative effects.[158] They contend that donors have taken over the space that domestic NGOs or political opposition parties should rightly have in the political and economic arenas, and that international aid institutions in effect undermine their own efforts because they recruit the most educated and talented Cambodians to work for them, rather than for Cambodia.[159]

Overall, despite an undeniably distressed general picture, Cambodia is actually faring better than most analysts had predicted in 1995. During UNTAC's tenure in Cambodia, several substantial economic crises were averted: hyperinflation, rice shortages, and government bankruptcy. After UNTAC's departure, there was no severe deflationary pressure as predicted, refugees did not inundate cities after their rice allocations ended, the riel and prices stabilized, and the tax and customs systems continue to function, bringing in revenues for the state. UNTAC's positive institutional legacies include a reformed and functioning border control unit, tax reforms, human rights as a part of the national political dialogue, and thousands of trained Cambodians who monitored the 1998, 2002, and 2003 elections. The number and size of domestic NGOs concerned with human rights have been growing, despite government attempts to crack down on opposition; meanwhile, the ravaging of forests has slowed, due in part to the growth of groups concerned with the environment. It appears that while UNTAC was not able to cure many of Cambodia's ills, it undoubtedly helped to guide Cambodia's transition from war to peace. As one observer explained, "Normality is returning step by step. Kids (some kids, more than before) are going to school; they're growing up; society is cultivating new generations. It is springtime after a winter of the most wretched kind."[160]

Conclusion

The mandate for UNTAC was designed mainly during negotiations between the five permanent member states of the Security Council, and therefore did not derive from, nor was it entirely appropriate for, the context of the Cambodian civil war. The Paris Peace Accord addressed all parties as equals, skipping over the reality that the four parties were on vastly unequal footing at the time of the signing of the final peace accord, especially given that the SOC was in administrative control of most of the country. Moreover, the peace accord

---

[158] Beresford, 2005, p. 137; and St. John, 2005, p. 423.
[159] Sodhy, 2004, p. 171; and Hughes, 2003.   [160] Coates, 2005, p. 326.

presented a transition process with a vision of the best-case scenario. There was no concept of – indeed it was never even discussed – how the UN would or should respond if one or more of the parties did not follow through on its promises, most importantly, during troop demobilization. The authors of the peace agreement knew that they were not directly responsible for its implementation and did not have a clear understanding of the extent of the challenges on the ground in Cambodia. However, rather than imposing preconceived notions of how UNTAC should respond to crises during implementation, members of the Security Council generally supported UNTAC and its leaders' decisions about changes that needed to be made in the mandate. While using the basic ideas and principles embodied in the Paris Peace Accord, UNTAC sought to adjust its mandate – both in terms of means and goals – in order to accomplish more modest but noteworthy achievements.

Some social scientists have charged that the basic ideas of the peace accord, and the institutions it was meant to set up, were so radically antithetical to Cambodian political culture, as well as to the elite patterns of political discourse, that there was no way the peace accord could ever have been implemented in Cambodia.[161] While of course there was little chance of creating a western liberal democracy in Cambodia over the course of eighteen months, the view that democratic reform is impossible in Cambodia is countered by the manifest enthusiasm with which Cambodian citizens have embraced the principles of human rights as well as the most important institution that UNTAC attempted to create: regular elections. Moreover, a prominent scholar of Cambodian origin challenges the notion that the failure of the implementation of the peace agreement was due to an inherently anti-democratic elite and political culture. In referring to early, failed efforts at demobilization, Sorpong Peou explains:

> The cease-fire violations, the political intimidation, and the failure of the disarmament process did not simply derive from the Khmer Rouge's or any other party's tireless thirst for political domination at the expense of others. Underlying the problem in question was the lack of trust among Cambodians themselves and their perception of insecurity derived from the weakness of UN authority: UNTAC was . . . in disarray, operating within a no-man's land of dangers and risks.[162]

In this vein, I have argued in this chapter that UNTAC bore the primary responsibility for the successes and failures of its operations. The UN operation began with UNAMIC and precipitous organizational dysfunction; this dysfunction inspired both the SOC and the Khmer Rouge to renege on promises they had made in the Paris accords. However, UNTAC gradually moved into a learning mode in some of its components. In turn, the move toward

---

[161] See especially St. John, 1995; Curtis, 1998, Chapter 7; and Pierre Lizée, 2000.
[162] Peou, 1997, p. 201.

organizational learning enabled UNTAC to help to bring about some basic
changes in Cambodian political life. Organizational learning was indicated in
components where there were broad mechanisms for information-gathering
and -sharing, most readily exhibited in the info/ed component. Where coordination between some key components was scant at best at the outset of the
operation, under Akashi and Sanderson's leadership, the electoral and military divisions worked to coordinate first with each other, and then with other
divisions, in order to accomplish the newly defined most important task of
holding elections. In terms of the organization's interaction with its environment, UNTAC's authority did not include a monopoly over the legitimate use
of force. The larger the presence of UNTAC, the more effective it became, but
it never wielded state-like powers either to administer the country, or control
violence within Cambodian borders. Its authority was based on the consent
of the factions, its international legitimacy, and its ability to deliver on certain
promises; authority was never derived from UNTAC's ability to coerce, even
though the operation did prove more effective as its military division deployed
in greater numbers. But most importantly, UNTAC's presence and political
strategies led to the eventual demise of the Khmer Rouge.

Not all divisions were able to adapt to, and learn from, their environment, producing mixed results. The repatriation, election, and informa-
tion/education divisions were indisputably the most proficient at learning, and
at fulfilling their mandates. The military and human rights divisions, while not
fulfilling all of the tasks as originally mandated, were able to move into organizational learning modes, producing tangible results in providing security for
the elections, creating goodwill toward UNTAC, and making human rights a
popular cause in Cambodia. The civilian police, rehabilitation, and civilian
administration components were not able to fulfill their primary tasks set forth
in the accords. In general, the failures of these components were directly related
to UNTAC's inability to plan, integrate with and understand the environment,
and manage crises.

By the same token, UNTAC's successes worked to alter three basic institutions
in Cambodia that continue to contribute to the peace that the country enjoys
today. First, the rhetoric, if not always the practice, of human rights guarantees has become common and expected among Cambodian citizens and elites.
Second, civil society organizations, especially those concerning the protection
of human rights, have flourished since UNTAC's departure; this bodes well for
possible democratic change in Cambodia's future. And finally, elections, something completely foreign to Cambodians until the early nineties, have become
a popular new forum for political expression, even if problems remain. These
changes represent some significant positive shifts in the practice of politics in
Cambodia despite the persistence of important economic, political, and social
problems.

6

Mozambique: learning to create consent

Introduction

The United Nations Operation in Mozambique (ONUMOZ) was one of the largest and most ambitious multidimensional peacekeeping operations in Africa of its time: its budget reached toward $1 billion, the mission deployed over 6,000 UN peacekeepers, and the mandate called for an operation that looked much like a transitional authority, with a Special Representative who held executive decision-making authority over all matters concerning peace implementation during the transitional period. ONUMOZ only became fully operational almost a year after the warring parties signed the General Peace Agreement in Rome in the fall of 1992, but managed nevertheless to be success-ful in both implementing its mandate and constructing political institutions that would serve to transform conflicts in Mozambique from militarized dis-putes to peaceful political forms.

The ONUMOZ operation, despite its size and ambitious mandate, was hardly noticed either in the international news media, or, more importantly, by the major powers on the Security Council. The Security Council generally supported ONUMOZ but did not play an active role in the implementation of its tasks. Another necessary but not sufficient source of the successful mandate implementation would be the willingness of the parties to commit to peace. While the parties did eventually agree to a peace deal as well as to institutional changes suggested by ONUMOZ, one would be hard pressed to characterize the two sides as "willing," at least at the outset of the operation. Mozambique had been experiencing warfare within its borders since 1962. War had become a way of life. Political disputes were viewed almost exclusively in terms of zero-sum, violent battles, and it would take a massive, active, and creative multilateral effort to alter such underlying conditions.

ONUMOZ engaged in first-level learning, and also benefited from some second-level learning *between* missions. In terms of second-level learning, mindful of the recent failure in Angola, the leaders of the operation ensured that ONUMOZ would deploy in sufficient numbers to potentially be able to carry out the mandate. But rather than simply attempting to re-create the organiza-tional routines and tasks that had functioned elsewhere, the members of the operation gathered sufficient technical information in Mozambique, defined problems based on local knowledge, coordinated with their counterparts, integrated organizational behavior with the environment, and exercised creative leadership to avert crises and incrementally alter the actions of the warring sides. The operation's members actively sought to create one the of the prior conditions – consent of the warring parties – for success. The organization engaged in first-level learning, which along with the consent of the parties and consensual but not intense Security Council interests, made for the success of the UN peacekeeping operation.

Situational factors

The civil war in Mozambique began in 1977, extended to September 1992, and was thoroughly devastating for the population. It claimed the lives of nearly 1 million people out of a prewar population of approximately 12 million, while over 5 million Mozambicans were displaced both inside and outside the country.[1] According to most analysts, and indeed most of the internal and external actors, the civil war in Mozambique was caused by a convergence of four main factors. First, race- and class-based subjugation of the various peoples in the territory of Mozambique, mainly by Portuguese colonists, followed by the hurried departure of the Portuguese in the 1970s, rendered the country susceptible to internal strife upon independence. Second, Rhodesian Ian Smith supporters, and later defenders of South African apartheid, created a Black Mozambican insurgency against the new socialist Mozambican government. Third, the Mozambican economy was destroyed by a confluence of floods and drought, guerrilla warfare against economic targets, world recession, and ill-fated attempts at East European-style economic reform. And finally, mismanagement on the part of the ruling regime, *Frente de Liberacao de Mocambique* (Mozambique Liberation Front, known as Frelimo) fueled guerilla opposition. The causes turn from the external to the internal, which reflect both the chronological and the multifaceted advances of the conflict. Each of the four elements is addressed below.

First, in terms of Portuguese colonialism and its hurried end, Portuguese explorers first arrived in Mozambique in 1498 in pursuit of a route to India. By the late 1500s, a system of forced labor had been established within Mozambique, and full-scale slave trade developed by the mid-eighteenth century. By the end of the nineteenth century, of all the colonial powers in Africa, Portugal proved the poorest and least well organized. While Mozambique remained a Portuguese possession, British, Dutch, and South Africans came to dominate large sectors of the economy. With the rise of fascist rule in Portugal in the 1930s, rather than undergoing domestic land reform, Portugal encouraged

---

[1] Hanlon, 1991, p. 5; Vines, 1996, p. 1; and Manning, 2002, p. 5. There were approximately 2 million Mozambican refugees, many of whom were in Malawi, but also Tanzania, Zambia, and Zimbabwe. Hume, 1994, p. 20.

tens of thousands of Portuguese peasants to emigrate to Mozambique. Semi-literate, semi-skilled Portuguese came to control most administrative jobs and dominated the Mozambican labor market; no significant educational or training systems were developed for the benefit of the black majority. The systematic exclusion of blacks from political, social, and economic advancement worked to radicalize opposition to colonial rule. According to some development economists, a "zero-sum culture" of power developed; power-sharing was rarely, if ever, contemplated by the Portuguese rulers, and this legacy would prove difficult to overcome.[2]

A protracted war of liberation against Portuguese rule began in 1962, ending thirteen years later with the fall of fascism in Portugal. By the early 1960s, Frelimo emerged as the central anti-colonial resistance movement in Mozambique. With roots in western opposition to fascism and a rhetoric of non-racialism, Frelimo managed to divide whites within Mozambique for a time. Frelimo's first leader, Edward Mondlane, received his doctorate in anthropology from Northwestern University in the United States, and he led the movement until his assassination in 1970.[3] Samora Machel then led the party during Mozambican independence, and the country's turn toward, and eventually away from, socialism, until his death in a plane crash in 1986. Joaquim Chissano, a Paris educated former foreign minister known for his flexibility, pragmatism, and diplomatic polish, then became the leader of Frelimo and eventually the first President of multi-party, democratic Mozambique.[4]

The collapse of the Portuguese regime in 1974 paved the way for Mozambican (and Angolan) independence under the Lusaka Peace Accord. The Accord was signed in haste, leaving political control of Mozambique to Frelimo, with little discussion of political forms other than single-party rule. There were approximately 220,000 Europeans in Mozambique at the time of independence, most of whom feared majority rule, despite Frelimo's conciliatory overtures. The Europeans, mainly of Portuguese origin, fled en masse, destroyed abandoned property in their wake, extracted their capital, and left Mozambique virtually devoid of civil servants, merchants, professionals, and most skilled or semi-skilled workers. Frelimo, with no experience in running a state, and little human or material means to rebuild, searched for methods to unify and sustain the country, but the legacy of colonial rule and its quick end would prove difficult to overcome.[5]

Frelimo turned toward experimentation in rapid development based on East European models. The party sought to create a national identity,[6] advocated

---

[2] Abrahamsson and Nilsson, 1995, Chapter 1; Manning, 2002, Chapter 3.
[3] Intellectuals who supported Frelimo included Albie Sachs, Allen Isaacman, and Ruth First.
[4] Note that all three of Frelimo's leaders came from the southern Shangana tribe, even though Frelimo has gone to great lengths to publicly discourage ethnic group-based expression.
[5] Galli, 2003, pp. 31–38.   [6] Mainly by adopting Portuguese as the national language.

science over tradition, supported the liberation of women,[7] and began massive health and education programs. In terms of the economy, Frelimo national-ized abandoned industries and businesses in a pragmatic attempt to salvage the economy. Conveniently, nationalization coalesced with the socialist ideology.[8] While some of the welfare and labor programs were extremely popular, others were met with opposition. As the government sought to render family farms into "Communal Villages," the Makonde chiefs, especially in the north, resisted, preferring their traditional structures upheld under colonialism.[9] This resis-tance would broaden and intensify in the face of programs akin to Soviet-style collectivization, as explained further below.

In terms of Frelimo's foreign policy, Mozambique joined the non-aligned movement, seeking to avoid a direct coalition with either side in the Cold War. In the Southern African region, Frelimo supported the independence movements: the African National Congress (ANC) in South Africa, SWAPO in Namibia, and the Zimbabwe African National Union (ZANU) in Rhodesia/Zimbabwe. The Frelimo government even went so far as to allow groups, especially from Rhodesia, to stage rebellions from Mozambican territory against the white minority government.

Second, the response in Rhodesia to Mozambique's economic and political moves would prove devastating for Mozambique. This response is arguably the most important cause of the civil war. The racist Ian Smith government, still in power in Rhodesia until 1979, helped to build the *Resistencia Nacional Mocambicana*, or "Renamo." Designed at first as an armed Mozambican group that would provide intelligence about ZANU's activities, the movement grew as it mobilized peasants in the Mozambican countryside by exploiting urban–rural and ethnic divides (the leadership of Renamo was mainly, but not exclusively, composed of members of the Shona-speaking Ndau ethnic group).[10] While seeking intelligence about ZANU, Renamo also sought support from poor farmers by, for example, supplying clothing from Rhodesia, and advocating the maintenance of family farms against the new collectivized farms policies of the government.[11] Renamo also sought support from traditional chiefs whose authority was jeopardized by Frelimo's new, centralized state structures.

---

[7] Indeed, Mozambique was for a short time a model of progressiveness, when in 1977, 28 percent of elected delegates to the Popular Assembly (Mozambique's former parliament) were women. See Newitt, 1995, pp. 547–48.

[8] See Abrahamsson and Nilsson, 1995, Chapter 1; and Pitcher, 2002, p. 51.

[9] Isaacman and Isaacman, 1983, Chapter 7; and Pitcher, 2002, p. 58.

[10] The ethnic dimension of the war is often mentioned in footnotes, since both Frelimo and Renamo made far-reaching efforts to include members of all ethnic groups. As Finnegan (1992, p. 107) explains, "Mozambique contained within its borders no very profound ethnic antagonisms." See also Alden, 1995, p. 125; and Manning, 2002, p. 93. However, regional tensions appear to be growing. Weinstein, 2002, p. 144.

[11] Hanlon, 1990, p. 227.

With the fall of the Smith government and Zimbabwean independence, Renamo was pulled under the wing of the South African Defense Force (SADF) in South Africa. Around this time, South Africa also initiated its policy of "destabilization" in southern Africa, fearing a further erosion of white minority rule. The SADF instructed Renamo in its new mission to destroy mainly non-military, economic and social targets, including markets, schools, hospitals, roads, and bridges, in order to destabilize the Frelimo government. While Renamo's original ideology was purported to be one of an anti-communist, peasant party, these trappings were eventually shed, as the party proved unable to articulate any coherent political platform.[12] As Renamo became better equipped and trained as a fighting force, it came to be known as the "Khmer Rouge" of southern Africa.[13] The group employed such tactics as kidnapping young boys of all ethnic groups, killing their families, educating the children only in weapons use, and then deploying them in the Mozambican countryside to wreak havoc.[14]

Third, in terms of the Mozambican economy, in 1977–78 floods in vital agricultural regions were followed by a five-year drought. It is estimated that 100,000 people died of starvation during this period.[15] The climate-related problems were greatly exacerbated by mismanagement of the local economy. In 1983, the government began its "Operation Production" to reorganize the agricultural sector into communal farms, with centralized organization. Frelimo replaced traditional chiefs with party representatives, imported large and expensive machinery, and essentially forced tens of thousands of unemployed people to work in the fields. The results, especially given the drought conditions, were disastrous.[16] Few Mozambicans were prepared for managerial roles, which had been the domain of the colonists. Moreover, the transportation infrastructure was anything but efficient or united: all major roads ran east–west, none ran north–south, making centralization of the economy difficult if not impossible. As the economy spiraled downward, Mozambique began importing massive amounts of foreign food and other consumer goods – up to four times more than previously, while the cost of imports rose tenfold during the world recession of the early 1980s.[17]

Finally, Frelimo, as mentioned above, was unable to manage the task of governing. It was unprepared to handle the depth of economic despair and

---

[12] Finnegan, 1992, p. 78.

[13] This was the term used in Robert Gersony's 1988 US State Department report, and frequently found in *New York Times* articles.

[14] In 1989, with the rise to power of F. W. de Klerk, most South African funding for Renamo ended. Renamo then moved most of its operations to Malawi and came to be supported by business interests and extremist church groups in South Africa and Portugal, as well as by the Kenyan government. See Hanlon, 1991, pp. 34 and 244; Finnegan, 1992, p. 142; Hume, 1994, p. 11; Vines, 1996, Chapter 3; and Manning, 2002, Chapter 4.

[15] Finnegan, 1992, p. 119; Hume, 1994, p. 10; and Manning, 2002, Chapter 4.

[16] Manning, 2002, p. 122.   [17] Bowen, 1990; and Newitt, 1995, p. 552;.

would not allow other parties political space to organize alternatives. Moreover, during its first few years in power, the government refused to acknowledge that it faced any opposition, much less armed opposition, since it felt that it enjoyed the support of the vast majority of the population for delivering Mozambique from colonial rule. It did not, therefore, place priority on building its army to protect itself from either external or internal threats.

Five years of stalemate

The most widespread fighting of the war came in 1987, with massive destruction and few advances for either side. In the same year, a major international donor conference was held where $330 million was pledged for Mozambican development, and where donors began to press for talks between Frelimo and Renamo. While the stalemate appeared to be "hurting," with sticks and carrots in place, talks would not begin for another three years, and would conclude only after an additional two years of negotiations.

By 1989, the devastating effects of the war on the population were more than evident. Approximately 250,000 children had been orphaned, and the rate of infant mortality was the second highest in the world, with one in three children dying before the age of five.[18] Medical facilities previously serving about half the population had been destroyed.[19] A 1989 study estimated the economic losses at $15 billion, well over five times the 1988 GDP.[20]

Another severe drought struck in 1992, forcing masses of people to flee. Delivery of humanitarian aid was made all the more difficult, since convoys were under Renamo attack: "By late 1992, supply convoys to 74 of Mozambique's 128 districts needed armed escorts to ensure delivery. Numerous trucks were destroyed and many drivers were killed."[21]

The 1992 drought weakened Renamo's internal support in its occupied zones, as the threat of famine was seen to be caused not only by the drought, but also by Renamo's sabotage of the country's infrastructure. Meanwhile, Renamo's external support waned as the movement's tactics proved more and more brutal; at the same time, Frelimo engaged in long-demanded, western-style economic reforms. In 1990, the Frelimo government agreed to a new, multi-party constitution and was engaged in major economic liberalization programs. Moreover in July 1989, four months before the fall of the Berlin Wall, Frelimo had forsaken Marxism as its official ideology. Both the political and economic policies were in direct contrast with Frelimo's earlier, Soviet-style socialist programs. While external, western support for Frelimo rose, internal support did not necessarily follow suit. In the late 1980s, cuts in government spending meant that Frelimo troops would go unpaid for months at a time, which led to mutiny and acts far

---

[18] Machel, 2001.   [19] *The UN and Mozambique*, 1995, p. 12.
[20] Austin, 1994, p. 4.   [21] Austin, 1994, p. 4.

worse. Although Renamo was responsible for the bulk of wartime atrocities, government forces also committed many war crimes, most of which went undetected and unpunished. Such crimes were often committed by unpaid, hungry troops who not infrequently changed their attire and shifted roles between criminality, brutality, and serving with the government.[22]

As internal support for both sides diminished, external support for ending the war increased. The ideological battle, if there indeed had been at least a shadow of one in the late 1970s to early 1980s, had become obsolete. Support from major powers and neighbors fueling different sides of the war had all but ended. As Chester Crocker explains: "By the early 1990s, no external party was prepared to keep sustaining its chosen Mozambican ally; alliances were frayed . . . and donor fatigue had begun to appear; moreover, Mozambique had virtually no resources of its own."[23] However, it is also possible that Renamo could have gone on fighting the guerrilla war almost indefinitely. The group was firmly entrenched in its occupied areas and had become nearly self-sufficient. Moreover, as Hume explains, "although it lacked the military capacity to threaten the cities, Renamo could still maintain its psychological advantage by the threat of disruption and surprise attack."[24] The war was in a stage of protracted stalemate, but it would not end without significant external intervention.

Negotiations

The peace process lasted two years, including twelve rounds of talks. While the process became gradually internationalized in terms of actors, it remained close to the politics of Mozambique. Most aspects of the accord were negotiated by members of the Community of Santo Egidio (commonly known as Sant'Egidio), a Roman Catholic lay organization based in Rome, but the specifics of the accord were not determined primarily by outside powers. In addition, the UN was brought into the process as an observer fairly early, which better enabled the organization to plan its future operational strategy. Both the closeness of the peace process to Mozambican politics and the early, active presence of the UN were direct reflections of the wishes of the Mozambican government. There was never an attempt by the world's great powers to remove the peace process from Mozambique, the nongovernmental organization of Sant'Egidio, or the UN Secretariat, since the Mozambican government generally enjoyed strong international support and was perceived as legitimate.

During the negotiations, Marrack Goulding, the Under Secretary-General in charge of peacekeeping at the time, insisted that "the United Nations should not be expected to accept automatically whatever role might be envisaged by the

---

[22] Finnegan, 1992; and Berman, 1996, p. 54.   [23] Crocker, 1994, p. xi.
[24] Synge, 1997, p. 16.

negotiators."[25] While the UN Secretariat was already overstretched, Goulding and James Jonah, another UN Under Secretary-General, insisted that if the UN were to take on this new responsibility and succeed, the operation would have to be larger and have a more extensive mandate than the failed operation in a similar setting in Angola.[26] More specifically, they indicated that the UN should be charged not only with military and electoral matters, but also with civilian policing and oversight of humanitarian assistance, and "should be central in guiding the peace process."[27] While both of the warring factions expressed concern over the UN's ability to carry out its promises, they both also agreed that the UN would be the best guarantor of the peace.

There were two main points of contention in these talks. First, the government organized the central civil administration, but Renamo had also begun to organize its own parallel civil administration in its occupied zones. This presented a great problem for humanitarian relief organizations, since it was at times difficult to determine which administrative decisions would take precedence. Second, and related to the first problem, Frelimo was reluctant to recognize Renamo as an equal negotiating partner. This dilemma was resolved in part by the willingness of Sant'Egidio to offer its mediation services as an unofficial organization, skirting the issue of official protocol in interstate relations. By the summer of 1992, both sides officially requested UN participation in the implementation of the peace accord, which allowed the process to move to the next stage.

Mandate

The General Peace Agreement for Mozambique was signed in Rome, under the chairmanship of the Italian government on October 4, 1992. The agreement was composed primarily of the seven Protocols that had been painstakingly drafted over the course of the two-year negotiations, and outlined a formula for eight commissions that were to oversee the transition process. Rules established in the General Peace Agreement would take precedence over Mozambican law.[28] The UN was asked to send a large peacekeeping mission and chair the Supervisory and Monitoring Commission, which was in charge of implementing the entire peace agreement. Since the chair of the commissions would essentially have veto power over decisions, ONUMOZ was endowed with formal authority and leverage over the parties.[29]

---

[25] Synge, 1997, p. 19.   [26] Goulding, 2003, p. 198.   [27] Synge, 1997, pp. 20, 21.
[28] The July 1990 Joint Communiqué, the December 1990 Agreement on a Partial Cease-Fire, and the July 1992 Declaration on Humanitarian Assistance were also included as integral parts of the General Peace Agreement.
[29] S/24635, 8 October 1992, Enclosure. The UN was also asked to chair two sub-commissions on cease-fire monitoring and reintegration.

The General Peace Agreement made very specific, detailed provisions for the conduct of the elections.[30] It also specified provisions for the cease-fire, demobilization, withdrawal of foreign forces (from Zimbabwe and Malawi), and the monitoring of the humanitarian corridors. While a lengthy document, the accord was incomplete or not specific on a number of important issues. First of all, there was no indication of where troops would be assembled. Also missing were provisions for justice system and police reforms, human rights protections, economic rehabilitation of people other than former combatants, and a resolution to the issue of the dual civil administration. In addition, the timetable was considered unrealistic. As Hume explained, "Because of defects in the agreements, the process of implementation would have to be constantly . . . accompanied by a process of renegotiation."[31]

The Mozambican government also put direct pressure on the UN to engage in its activities as promptly as possible: "According to Protocol IV, the United Nations is expected to start its functions of verifying and monitoring the cease-fire on the day of entry into force of the General Peace Agreement . . . although . . . it would be our wish to see this monitoring mechanism established in the field as soon as possible."[32] The UN, however, proved unable to organize with such speed. It would be three months before an operational plan was drafted, and about nine months before the peacekeeping troops would be fully deployed.

Several days after the parties signed the peace agreement, UN Secretary-General Boutros-Ghali issued a report to the Security Council conveying the urgency with which the parties had requested UN assistance, and specifying a paltry number of twenty-five military observers "drawn from existing peacekeeping missions" to be sent to Mozambique along with an Interim Special Representative, Aldo Ajello, until the UN could draft a more detailed plan about the specific needs of implementation.[33] Ajello, an Italian diplomat who had been working for UNDP, had not been involved in the negotiations, nevertheless, he would prove to be one of the main forces behind the construction of the implementation plan.

The peace agreement swiftly began to break down as Renamo launched an offensive to take more territory before the arrival of UN troops. The problem of cease-fire breakdown was exacerbated by the increasing insecurity and the threat of mass starvation in the wake of intense drought. The drafting of a specific UN implementation plan was put on hold for a time, as the Secretariat struggled to avert humanitarian disaster by coordinating "special programmes

---

[30] In Angola, in October 1992, Jonas Savimbi refused to acknowledge the election results, claiming that there were not enough monitors in the country to guarantee that the poll was free or fair. This set a fear-inspiring precedent and placed extra weight on the Mozambican election rules, their monitoring, and the provision of guarantees that the results would be free and fair.

[31] Hume, 1994, p. 139.   [32] S/24635, 8 October 1992.   [33] S/24642, 9 October 1992.

of economic assistance to Mozambique."[34] Violations of the cease-fire continued, impeding the delivery of humanitarian aid, and in desperation Italy
submitted a formal request to send its own troops to Mozambique.[35] Finally,
in December 1992, UN Secretary-General Boutros-Ghali proposed an implementation plan for the UN's ONUMOZ mission in Mozambique.

The document outlined a four-part operation plan for the UN – with
political, military, electoral, and humanitarian components – that would be
"based on the strong interrelationship between the four components."[36] The
plan sketched provisions for a large international staff of military and civilian
employees, with an estimated budget of $331.8 million from its inception in
early 1993 until the proposed elections at the end of October 1993. The Security
Council endorsed the plan approximately one week later by a unanimous vote.[37]

Security Council interests

Mozambique was never high on the priority list for any of the major world powers. While Mozambique had declared itself a Marxist state in 1977, after the
failures of importing Soviet-style management, the government began actively
opening to the west in 1982, straddling both sides of the Cold War, but not
garnering much attention. By the time the Mozambican civil war was winding
down, as one of the mediators explains: "Mozambique was, in a way, marginal
to the geopolitical map of the early 1990s. No longer under the influence of
a collapsing communist world, no longer a threat to a changing South Africa
that was abandoning apartheid, Mozambique did not fall under the international spotlight."[38] The international press was by and large uninterested in
the Mozambican peace process.[39] And while regional actors, especially Zimbabwe, but also Kenya and the members of the Southern African Development
Coordination Conference clearly wanted the conflict resolved, there were few
available resources in the region to assist in this process. The interests of the
countries with ample resources, namely the permanent five members of the
Security Council and Italy, are addressed in the following paragraphs.

Western powers were in general divided about whom to support in the
Mozambican civil war, and, perversely, both sides often received support, albeit
from different groups within western nations. While western governments did
not tend to back Renamo overtly, extremist, often religious groups and business
interests around the world came to Renamo's aid in its purported fight against
the anti-church, socialist, one-party policies of Frelimo.[40]

---

[34] A/4/539, 22 October 1992.   [35] *The UN and Mozambique*, 1995, p. 147.
[36] S/24892, 2 December 1992, and S/24892/Add. 1, 9 December 1992.
[37] S/RES/797, 16 December 1992.   [38] Bartoli, 1999, p. 260.
[39] Bartoli (1999, p. 263) explains that this lack of attention made secrecy more possible, and
eventually proved a critical face-saving device for the extremists on both sides.
[40] Newitt, 1995, p. 570; and Manning, 2002, p. 91.

During the first ten years of Frelimo rule, relations with the United States were strained because of Frelimo's ties to the USSR. Moreover, in 1981, Mozambique accused the United States' Central Intelligence Agency of spying on behalf of the US ally, South Africa, after a South African commando attack on a suburb of Maputo. The Mozambican government then expelled six members of the American embassy, and the United States retaliated by withdrawing its embassy altogether. The withdrawal of diplomatic presence and a US ban on aid to Mozambique ended with signing of the 1984 Nkomati accord between South Africa and Mozambique. Under this accord, the United States sought to throw into positive light its policy of "constructive engagement" with South Africa, by drawing Mozambique toward the west, and improving relations between South Africa and its neighbors.[41] On a visit to Washington DC in October 1985, President Machel of Mozambique gained the personal and enthusiastic support of President Reagan of the United States.[42]

As Frelimo made increasing efforts to gain western support, Renamo engaged in similar activities but was unable to persuade many governments. In particular, the US government became increasingly skeptical of Renamo's democratic credentials after Renamo conducted six massacres in 1986–87, the most graphically reported being the Homoine massacre in July 1987 where over four hundred civilians were killed. Moreover, in 1988, a widely read State Department report written by Robert Gersony described Renamo's general behavior toward civilians, including "shooting executions, knife/axe/bayonet killings, burying alive, beating to death, forced asphyxiation, forced starvation, forced drowning, and random shooting at civilians in villages during attacks."[43] The report rendered US Congressional and White House support for Renamo politically impossible.[44] As one analyst explains, "Policy toward Mozambique *was* an anomaly, a glaring exception to the 'Reagan Doctrine,' under which the United States gave aid to insurgents in Nicaragua, Afghanistan, Cambodia, and, most pertinently, Angola . . . The State Department contended that Frelimo's 'turn to the west' was genuine and that Renamo was not, in any case, a legitimate alternative."[45]

After Machel's death, visits by Chissano to Reagan in 1987 and 1990, were followed by US-advocated reforms and greater US aid to the Mozambican government, even though the United States was never one of Mozambique's major donors and enjoyed "a political impact out of proportion to the size of

---

[41] South Africa also officially promised to stop funding and training Renamo insurgents while Mozambique agreed to withdraw its support for the ANC.

[42] Finnegan, 1992, p. 181; and Bartoli, 1999, p. 246. It was also during this time that the Pope began supporting Machel.

[43] Gersony, 1988, p. 25.

[44] Before this report, several conservative members of the US Congress had been advocating greater US support for Renamo.

[45] Finnegan, 1992, p. 181. Italics original.

its aid."[46] After the first meeting, Chissano agreed to multiparty reforms and amnesty for insurgents. After the 1990 trip, Chissano announced that he would meet with Renamo representatives. US aid to Mozambique peaked in 1989–90, when the United States provided over $100 million; at that time, more aid was funneled to Mozambique than to any other country in Southern Africa.[47] US support for the Mozambican government, coupled by encouragement for a negotiated settlement with Renamo, continued through the peace negotiations and implementation of the peace agreement.[48] During the peace negotiations and implementation, the United States provided technical advice and political support but was not particularly active in terms of providing funds for, or trying to orchestrate, the processes.

As for relations between the USSR and Mozambique, they were strong; by the late 1970s, Mozambique was allied with the Soviet bloc. The Soviets more than any other country supplied Mozambique's army, the Mozambican Armed Forces, with heavy weapons, amounting to $600 million in aid annually.[49] But after Frelimo refused to allow the construction of a Soviet military base on its territory, the USSR responded by decreasing its aid.[50] By 1986, with Mozambique's turn to the west, Soviet aid decreased to $200 million per year.[51] As Hanlon explains, even in the early 1980s, "to the Soviet Union, Mozambique was merely a 'Marxist-oriented' country which could provide no military bases and was too far away to be of much interest."[52] With the rise of glasnost and perestroika and collapse of the Soviet economy beginning in 1988, Soviet/Russian aid for Mozambique ceased.

In terms of the United Kingdom, President Machel's first official visit to the UK was in 1983, where Prime Minister Thatcher, thankful to Frelimo for applying pressure on ZANU to accept the UK's peace plan for Zimbabwe, formed a "good personal" relationship with Machel, offered financial support for the Frelimo government, and opened diplomatic channels between Frelimo and US President Reagan.[53] The UK forgave Mozambican debt, donated funds for infrastructure development, and encouraged Mozambique to join the IMF, which it did, accepting IMF and World Bank advice on structural adjustment. In 1987, the UK began supplying and training the Mozambican Armed Forces, and Mozambique enjoyed the status of being the only

---

[46] Hanlon, 1991, p. 62.   [47] Vines, 1996, p. 42.

[48] Hume, 1994, p. xiii; Vines, 1996, p. 49; Bartoli, 1999, p. 261; and Manning, 2002, pp. 91–92.

[49] Hume, 1994, p. 19; and Hall and Young, 1997, p. 139.

[50] What is more, even as early as 1981, despite backing by East Germany, the USSR rejected Mozambique's bid to become part of Comecon.

[51] Note that despite Soviet and Cuban assistance with training the Mozambican army, the Mozambican Armed Forces were never a proficient fighting force.

[52] Hanlon, 1991, p. 28.   [53] Hall and Young, 1997, p. 144.

non-commonwealth African state to receive such assistance.[54] In 1989, during a state visit to the UK, Thatcher encouraged Chissano to hold talks with Renamo.

As with Frelimo's relations with the UK, relations between France and the Mozambican government were very good by the time the peace process got underway, but had started out poor. After Mozambique's independence, the French government and Frelimo had something of an antagonistic relationship because of France's previous support for Portuguese colonial rule. However, Machel and Chissano worked to improve links with France through communications and visits in the early 1980s. By the mid-1980s, France had become Mozambique's second top trading partner and creditor, after Italy.[55] During the peace implementation process, France was an important member of the Supervisory and Monitoring Commission, as well as five other commissions including the one organized to train the new national military force, the Armed Forces for the Defense of Mozambique (FADM).[56] In general, while France was supportive of the peace process, its participation in the process was not particularly remarkable.

The fifth permanent Security Council member, China, trained and advised Frelimo on the art of guerrilla warfare as early as the 1960s. After independence, Frelimo continued to enjoy arms supplies from both China and the Soviet Union despite their rivalry. China, however, was never on the list of top aid donors and did not play much of a role in Mozambican politics after independence.

While Italy was not on the Security Council, it proved the most important external state in the Mozambican peace process. Relations between Italy and Frelimo dated back to 1970, when the Communist Council of Reggio Emilia became the earliest western-based supporter of Frelimo. By the mid-1980s, Italy had become Mozambique's largest trading partner and biggest creditor, and eventually wrote off 40 percent of Mozambique's debt.[57] During the peace process, Italy offered a constructive setting for the negotiations, as the home of Sant'Egidio and the Italian Communist Party; the Italian government meanwhile sponsored many cooperative development projects in Mozambique and provided financial support for the peace talks. Indeed, Italy was the largest donor during the peace process, coordinated the donor's conference on Mozambique, and was the primary contributor to the Trust Fund to transform Renamo from a military organization into a political party.[58]

---

[54] Hall and Young, 1997, p. 145.   [55] Hall and Young, 1997, p. 106.
[56] France formed part of the "troika" of European members, along with the UK and Portugal, all of which were members of this special military commission.
[57] Hall and Young, 1997, p. 143; and Hanlon, 1996, p. 120.
[58] *The UN and Mozambique*, 1995, pp. 111, 123; and Hume, 1994, p. 93.

Consensus

Most of the Security Council resolutions concerning ONUMOZ were merely to extend the mandate. Debates were neither significant nor acrimonious. There was a consensus about the basic nature of the problem. Even if some western countries housed some factions that supported Renamo, while the Soviet Union and China always supported Frelimo, by the end of the Cold War, any official differences were extremely slight.[59] All of the Council's votes were unanimous and continued to remain so through the votes on how best to confront the delays in implementation of the General Peace Agreement. Given all of these factors, the Security Council's interests in Mozambique can be characterized as "consensual" in nature.

In the field, UN Special Representative Aldo Ajello built his strength on the international consensus achieved during and immediately after the negotiations. He maintains that he "took no initiative without first securing their [the local ambassadors'] agreement. Even the draft reports to be presented by the Secretary-General to the Security Council were discussed and agreed on with the ambassadors in Maputo before the reports were sent to New York."[60] In turn, the members of this group of ambassadors rewarded Ajello's efforts to include them by acting in unison, and not making decisions before all had been consulted. This unanimity of action meant that the warring parties were unable to weaken ONUMOZ by playing the favors of major powers off one against the other or the UN.

Intensity

While Security Council interest was consensual, it was not particularly intense. Other major items on the agenda at the time included the faltering peacekeeping operations in Bosnia, Cambodia, Somalia, and Angola. The Council made a mere six statements over three years concerning the situation in Mozambique. During the same period, of the Council's eleven resolutions concerning Mozambique, many were simply to extend or renew the ONUMOZ mandate.[61] The Security Council mandates did not differ from Secretary-General Boutros-Ghali's requests, although there is some indication of self-censorship on the part of the Secretary-General, especially when he requested only twenty-five

---

[59] One minor difference, for example, was in the Council's final assessment of ONUMOZ. Most of the members attributed the success of the operation to the will of the parties and the diplomatic abilities of Ajello, whereas China attributed the success to "the observance of the purposes and principles of the Charter and the adherence to the principles proven effective in traditional peacekeeping operations." *The UN and Mozambique*, 1995, p. 306.

[60] Ajello, 1999, p. 628.

[61] See Security Council Resolutions 879, 29 October 1993; 882, 5 November 1993; 916, 5 May 1994; and 957, 15 November 1994.

military observers to be drawn from other operations for the start-up mission in Mozambique – this number was far too small to have any kind of tangible effect.[62] The Secretariat and Secretary-General requested so few troops early on, because at the time the organization was engaged in more peacekeeping operations than ever before in the history of the organization. The Council and General Assembly did, however, approve of most of the means requested by the Secretary-General, even though the operation weighed heavily on the government of Italy for funding. Over the course of the implementation of ONUMOZ's mandate, several changes in the mandate were proposed by the field operation and accepted by the Security Council. Given the scant Security Council attention to Mozambique, and basically adequate funding, the Security Council's interest intensity can be characterized as "moderate."

Organizational change and mandate implementation

UN peacekeeping in Mozambique can be characterized as a process of mutual and interactive change between the organization and its environment. The leaders of both of the warring sides came to understand and agree with the UN's expectations of them. At the same time, the UN learned from its environment, albeit slowly at first, in order to implement its mandate to achieve peace in Mozambique. While the UN attempted to reach out to the population, it proved most effective at changing the behavior of elites; nowhere is this more remarkably displayed than during and after talks between Ajello and Alfonso Dhlakama, the leader of Renamo.

While the UN was undoubtedly slow in launching its peacekeeping operation, which resulted in greater jockeying for position during the many months of uncertainty after the accords were signed, once the operation was established, it succeeded in accomplishing the basic tasks of its mandate. The UN's success came in part because UN headquarters behaved in a very accommodating manner toward initiatives taken in the field.[63] The flexibility and authority of ONUMOZ was created and fostered by the leadership of Ajello. As he explains, "It is critical to avoid the imposition of an arbitrary dynamic formulated in a political laboratory thousands of miles away. We had to adapt many rules and procedures to the reality in the field, rather than trying to adapt reality to the rules and procedures."[64] While Ajello had not been directly involved in the peace negotiations, he was the primary force behind the drafting of the UN's implementation plan, "skillful[ly] maneuvering to steer the parties to act in their own best interest."[65]

The formulation of the mandate and its implementation were conducted under the fear of failure recently experienced in Angola. This explains the large

---

[62] See S/24642, 9 October 1992, para. 16.   [63] Honwana, 2000, p. 30.
[64] Ajello, 1999, p. 625.   [65] Reed, 1996, p. 301

size of the military division, and the central focus on demobilization, rather than on the elections. Again, Ajello explains:

> The United Nations was not simply to be an observer, but the locomotive moving the entire process forward. If the United Nations had been solely an observer, as in Angola, it would have lacked the power to influence the course of events . . . I made use of all the powers accorded to me by the peace agreement. I was occasionally accused of exceeding these powers, but in reality I was working to ensure that the United Nations played the active role it needed to keep the peace process on track.[66]

ONUMOZ's task was not simple. When the UN arrived, the fighting had stopped but Renamo still controlled some 25 percent of the country. Furthermore, there were several important crises that arose while the UN was on the ground. The crises were resolved through creative changes made by the members of the organization in the field, who were unhindered by potentially restrictive management at UN headquarters. As one analyst explains:

> Once established and funded, the operation took on a life of its own. Much of the political decision-making occurred in Maputo rather than in New York or Western capitals, which were more often informed rather than consulted about the changing needs on the ground. This allowed for greater political flexibility, but ONUMOZ was rarely subjected to close examination by its paymasters.[67]

ONUMOZ was divided into four basic components: political, military, humanitarian, and electoral; a police component was added after the mission was in the field. After a discussion of the efforts to establish ONUMOZ in the field, each division is examined below in terms of the UN's ability to implement its mandate, while also focusing on the indicators of first-level organizational learning and dysfunction.

Establishing ONUMOZ and confronting crises

For many months after the signing of the General Peace Agreement, the UN, Renamo, and the Mozambican government proved unprepared for implementation. In terms of the UN, Ajello was quickly appointed Interim Special Representative of the Secretary-General and he and twenty-five military observers arrived eleven days after the General Peace Agreement's signing. However, the first peacekeepers would not arrive until five months later. The Security Council approved the ONUMOZ operation only three months after the peace agreement signing, and another three more months passed before the General Assembly's Advisory Committee on Administrative and Budgetary Questions approved the budget in March 1993. In all, ONUMOZ was fully deployed with its 6,222 UN

---

[66] Ajello, 1999, p. 623.   [67] Synge, 1997, p. 12.

troops, and 294 unarmed military observers, only in July 1993 – nine months after the signing of the peace agreement.[68]

The UN's lack of speed was due to several factors, most of which were internal to the UN system. First, Ajello's official appointment was held up because of a debate over whether he or Under Secretary-General James Jonah should fill the permanent post of Special Representative. Second, and more importantly, three other large peacekeeping operations in Bosnia, Somalia, and Cambodia were beginning in the spring of 1992, with a total of 70,000 UN peacekeepers; there were simply not enough adequately trained troops, or the accompanying logistical and political support, to start the Mozambique operation quickly. Third, there was some tension between UN headquarters in New York and the humanitarian and development projects already existing in Mozambique led by the United Nations Development Program (UNDP); the newcomers from the Secretariat peacekeeping operation faced uncertain cooperation from their more experienced, but less politically powerful, colleagues, which delayed decisions about divisions of labor.[69] And finally, the processes for procuring basic office equipment and housing were extremely slow.

The late arrival of the UN inspired both sides to attempt to gain more territory on the battlefield, to make new demands, and to attempt to renegotiate points that had already been settled in Rome. While some of the parties' delays were not especially troubling for the UN organizers, since they themselves were not ready to begin the operation, by the time the UN was prepared, both sides were less willing to cooperate fully.

In October 1992, Renamo seized four towns in direct violation of the peace agreement's cease-fire provisions. Ajello, with a staff of five people plus the twenty-five military observers, did not have the organizational capacity in Mozambique to counter the military breach. The government quickly retaliated, regaining three towns, but the fourth was not retaken until November. Eager to avert a resumption of major conflict, Ajello sought to contain the crisis through diplomacy. He called a meeting between himself, the two parties, and ambassadors from the major powers with embassies in Maputo. Ajello describes his move as a gamble, for if Renamo had refused to attend, Ajello's authority would have greatly diminished. But Renamo attended, and both sides agreed again to abide by their cease-fire promises. The cease-fire would hold after this point. This accomplishment would serve Ajello well in the future for garnering external support when needed to confront other crises.

During this same time, Renamo had begun to lobby international aid agencies for support, the International Committee of the Red Cross most noticeably, independently of the Mozambican government, which angered the government because it effectively increased Renamo's international standing.[70] The independent behavior of some international agencies toward Renamo led to

[68] S/25518, 2 April 1993.   [69] Synge, 1997, pp. 12–13, 33.   [70] Manning, 2002, p. 107.

fear on the part of the Mozambican government that the UN would do the same, and the government began to push for a smaller UN force. The government argued that it did not want international agencies such as the UN infringing on Mozambican sovereignty while increasing the international legitimacy of the opposition. Nevertheless, Goulding and Ajello eventually managed to convince Frelimo moderates, who were effectively in charge of the party, of the merits of allowing a larger force.

Meanwhile, Ajello also traveled to the bush to meet with Dhlakama. Ajello explains an important conversation during which he told Dhlakama that everyone knew that Renamo had "muscle," but now came the test of the group's "wisdom." Ajello reasoned further that if Renamo expected to survive into the future, it needed to transform itself such that it could attract young Mozambicans without coercion to its new political organization. While positions in Frelimo apparatuses were already all occupied, Renamo's were empty and needed to be filled with educated Mozambicans.[71] As Ajello asserted, "no bright young people will join Renamo if it is perceived as an organization of bandits. If you do not change this image, you will fail to attract this young generation and you will have no political future."[72] Ajello also made sure that Dhlakama understood that any international sympathy or support shown toward Renamo during the negotiations in Rome would quickly evaporate if the organization did not transform itself. Apparently, the conversation had a profound effect on Dhlakama who continued to repeat "wisdom, not muscle" and did not again disrupt the peace process through military means. It seems that Dhlakama had decided then and there to be recognized and supported by the "international community," represented by Ajello.

But even though Dhlakama had begun to change his behavior, he and his party continued to make new demands. From October 1992 into the spring of 1993, Dhlakama and senior members of Renamo refused to move their headquarters from the bush in Maringue to the capital, Maputo. While the government had made promises to provide housing and office space for Renamo in Maputo, each time provisions were readied, Renamo increased its list of needs. Renamo also insisted that the General Peace Agreement provided for Renamo's own civil administration in the areas that it controlled, whereas the government (and the UN) interpreted the agreement to mean that the government controlled the administration of the whole country. And finally, Renamo began to boycott all of the commissions in March 1993, just as they had begun to function.[73]

[71] Manning, 2002, pp. 108–109.   [72] Ajello, 1999, p. 672.
[73] While Ajello and the government protested against some of Renamo's moves, Ajello knew that in March 1993 the purpose behind the withdrawal to the bush was to train and prepare Renamo officials for their new positions in government. Ajello therefore did not criticize or counteract Renamo during this time. Ajello, 1999, pp. 624–25; Manning, 2002, Chapter 5.

By this point, Ajello had come to understand Dhlakama's motivations and accurately assessed that money could play an important role in steering Dhlakama toward cooperation. In May 1993, Ajello helped to establish a "Trust Fund" for Renamo. Shortly thereafter, Renamo backed down on its various demands and sent delegates to contribute to the commissions.

ONUMOZ's efforts were also hampered at times by government obstructions. After the signing of the peace deal, government cooperation with the UN diminished when the UN deployment proved dangerously unhurried. Most notably, the government refused to sign a status of forces agreement with the UN. This meant that the standard legal provisions for peacekeepers – namely non-payment of taxes and freedom of movement – were not secured. After long negotiations between Ajello and the government, the government finally relented in May 1993, paving the way for the full establishment of ONUMOZ.[74]

Political component

The political component, unlike the others, did not have a specific set of tasks to accomplish; instead, it was to be the power center, uniting the operation. The power of the political component derived formally from the UN's chairmanship of the Supervisory and Monitoring Commission. The commission was somewhat similar in design to a transitional authority, in that it held decision-making influence over all aspects of the implementation process, including the ability to replace or supercede the government in all matters related to the peace accord.

With Ajello serving as chair, the Supervisory and Monitoring Commission was made up of representatives from Frelimo and Renamo, as well as ambassadors from the Organization of African Unity, France, Germany, Italy, Portugal, the UK, and the United States. All decisions of the commission were to be made by consensus. As one analyst further elaborates:

> The Supervisory and Monitoring Commission became the key mechanism for sustaining both momentum and the involvement of the international community. The UN chairmanship of the Supervisory and Monitoring Commission and the other commissions charged with implementing the accords greatly facilitated rapid, objective problem solving. Whenever difficulties were encountered, the Supervisory and Monitoring Commission was able to convene negotiations that succeeded in persuading the parties to adhere to their commitments. This form of collective oversight, involving the two parties, the UN, the OAU, and ambassadors of Mozambique's donor countries, allowed for flexible management and for adjustments.[75]

[74] Ajello, 1999, p. 624; Honwana, 2000, p. 15.
[75] Richard Synge, quoted in *The UN and Mozambique*, 1995, p. 67.

Ajello was at the center of the flexible, but well-coordinated management of ONUMOZ. He was able to gather information, formulate problem definitions, and create sound plans for UN activities. As analysts Hall and Young explain, "Ajello, a forceful speaker and (by all accounts) negotiator, became an important part of the Mozambican political process – pressuring, encouraging and cajoling the various actors involved."[76] Both in his formal role as chair of the Supervisory Commission, and informal role as the central figure in the peace process, Ajello used persuasion and improvisation to steer the process forward.

ONUMOZ was also mandated by the General Peace Agreement to chair two of the seven sub-commissions: the Cease-Fire Commission and the Commission for the Reintegration of Demobilized Soldiers. ONUMOZ was also later asked to chair the Commission for the Formation of the New Army "on the strict understanding that this would not entail any UN obligation to train or establish the armed forces."[77] Mozambicans chaired all other commissions.[78] While the Commission for the Reintegration of Demobilized Soldiers and the Commission for the Formation of the New Army were not particularly active, the Cease-Fire Commission was in charge of overseeing the troop demobilization and proved to be the most effective of all sub-commissions. The Cease-Fire Commission met often, reviewed violations of the cease-fire, and devised solutions.

Military component

Demobilization was the overriding priority of the entire ONUMOZ operation, and while the elections were the last step in the process, they were viewed as being of secondary significance for ending the war and creating the conditions for a lasting peace. Demobilization proved to be a long-drawn-out process of negotiation whereby Ajello and the leaders of the ONUMOZ military division deployed a combination of threats (mainly the withdrawal of international support) and enticements (in the form of trust funds) to steer demobilization to completion. Demobilization was finally achieved under the constant fear of repeating what had happened in Angola, where rather than fully demobilizing, both sides continued to hide unreported troops and weapons as a safety net in case the other were to attack. In Angola, after the disputed UN-monitored elections in September 1992, the well-trained, hidden troops enabled both sides to wage the most devastating episode of the war. From September to November of 1992, when the mandate for ONUMOZ was being drafted, the UN Secretariat and Security Council were well aware of the example of Angola, and attempted

---

[76] Hall and Young, 1997, p. 232.   [77] *The UN and Mozambique*, 1995, p. 33.
[78] The other commissions included the National Police Affairs Commission, the Commission for Information, the Commission for the Territorial Administration, and the National Election Commission.

to construct safeguards against incomplete demobilization and the potential for the resumption of conflict.

The mandate for the military division, detailed in Protocol IV of the General Peace Agreement and in the Secretary-General's implementation plan, was to monitor the cease-fire and demobilization of forces, protect the main roads and corridors, monitor the withdrawal of foreign troops and the disbandment of irregular forces, provide security for UN personnel, and assist with refugee and IDP (internally displaced person) return. The military division would also engage in community relations projects such as building roads, assisting elections monitors, and providing transportation and communication for Renamo and the government, although these activities were not specified in the mandate.

By August 1993, the UN force came to number more than 6,000 military personnel, including 350 UN military observers, five infantry battalions, an engineering company, two field hospitals and all necessary staff for logistics, administration, transportation, and communication. The troops came from over two dozen UN member states, most notably, Bangladesh, Italy, India, Zambia, Uruguay, Botswana, and Portugal.[79] The large size of the military component ostensibly worked as a deterrent against cease-fire violations and provided Ajello with an important source of leverage over both parties.[80]

As the force slowly deployed, the parties were also slow to begin demobilization. A year earlier, during the negotiations in Rome in March 1992, Dhlakama had suggested to the Italian government that his organization would need substantial funding, on the order of $10–12 million, to transform itself from a military operation to a political party.[81] In the General Peace Agreement, absurdly, the government was designated to fund Renamo's transformation into a political organization. Coming as little surprise, government funding for its mortal enemy was not made readily available. Discussions of an international Trust Fund for the transformation of Renamo had been taking place for many months, and in February 1993, Secretary-General Boutros-Ghali, in a letter to the Italian Foreign Minister, agreed to manage such a fund.[82] In all, major donors, most of whom were members of the Supervisory and Monitoring Commission, provided $17.5 million for Renamo's political needs. Dhlakama himself was granted $300,000 per month for the last thirteen months before the October 1994 elections ($3.9 million total), to ensure that he remain in financial control of his organization, with centralized ability to control and allocate resources within his inner circle.[83] Each month Renamo was allotted the funds after Ajello had certified that the organization was fulfilling its duties

---

[79] *The UN and Mozambique*, 1995, p. 43.   [80] Synge, 1997, p. 44.
[81] Hume, 1994, p. 93.
[82] *The UN and Mozambique*, 1995, p. 172. The agreement was later ratified by the Security Council. See S/RES/850, 9 July 1993.
[83] Ajello, 1999, p. 637.

under the peace deal. After initial establishment of the Trust Fund, Dhlakama assented to begin demobilization, even though completion of this task would take many months and more negotiations.

Several crises arose that were quickly laid to rest from June to September of 1993. First, Renamo began to open issues that others thought had been settled. For example, some Renamo and international officials began discussions of creating a transitional authority, rather than continuing with ONUMOZ and the Supervisory and Monitoring Commission. In another example, in September 1993, Renamo began to negotiate directly with South African firms for timber and mineral exports, against previous agreements prohibiting the party from trading independently of the government.[84] Second, and most importantly, Renamo was reluctant to give up its major bargaining chip – its military option – and while in September 1993 Renamo publicly declared its willingness to go along with demobilization, Dhlakama suggested that demobilization need not be completed by the time of the elections. Given the precedent of Angola, the UN refused to make such a concession. Third, both sides were not fulfilling their promises to plan for demobilization. Most significantly, by September 1993, only thirty-four of forty-nine troop assembly sites had been approved. Implementation of the peace agreement was stalled. Ajello therefore called on his international support network.

Ajello's office requested that the UN Secretary-General Boutros-Ghali visit Mozambique at the end of October. During Boutros-Ghali's visit, high-level talks were held in an attempt to reinvigorate the implementation of the General Peace Agreement. Boutros-Ghali appealed to both the citizens and leaders of Mozambique on national television to support the peace operation. Boutros-Ghali used veiled threats of UN withdrawal, and financial inducements of increasing the Trust Fund to convince both sides, especially Renamo, to plan for and begin demobilization. After several rounds of talks, compromises were reached on many outstanding issues: the appointment of an all-Mozambican National Electoral Commission, Cease-Fire Commission rules, and appointments to the Police, Information, and Administration Commissions. More importantly, both sides agreed to begin cantoning their troops by November 1993, in order to complete the process during the first five months of 1994.[85]

The specifics of the demobilization mandate were constructed in line with recommendations made by the Swiss Agency for Development and Cooperation. The Swiss had been conducting extensive research on the Mozambican forces since 1990, including the polling of government troops to find out what

---

[84] Synge, 1997, p. 48.
[85] Honwana, 2000, p. 18. The de facto changes in the implementation schedule needed to be acknowledged officially, and new deadlines secured. All sides agreed that elections could not be held before October 1994. After a four-day "working summit," in October 1993 the Supervisory and Monitoring Commission agreed to a new timetable, which was ratified several days later by the UN Security Council.

they expected of the government upon demobilization, and what activities they would like to engage in after their service. The Swiss suggested a plan whereby troops were to remain on bases no longer than two months in order to be disarmed, registered in a database, and provided with documents, clothing, and some other supplies such as tools and seeds for agricultural workers.[86] After being released, they were given the option of joining the new Mozambican army, the FADM, or accepting what eventually amounted to between eighteen months and two years of pay, distributed in monthly allotments.

While demobilization was to begin in March 1993, it was stalled from the start because neither side had supplied accurate lists of troops, weapons, and bases. Both sides also refused to designate adequate assembly points. The government and Renamo were both suggesting troop assembly points based on wartime strategy, rather than practical conditions such as access to water and roads free of land mines. Renamo, more so than the government, would suggest impractical sites while the government retaliated by delaying its decisions about the assembly areas. In all, the parties were under mutual obligation to establish forty-nine assembly areas – twenty for Renamo and twenty-nine for the government. After the negotiations of September to November 1993, Ajello tired of the delays. He explained to Dhlakama in late 1993 that the UN peacekeepers were his "life insurance," and that if he really wanted to transform his organization into a political party, he would have to agree to remove his troops from the bush and demobilize. Ajello threatened that the UN would otherwise withdraw, sparing the organization the average $1 million cost per day, and suggesting that all international support would be offered to the government. After this, Dhlakama and the government both submitted their final troop assembly location lists.

A Technical Unit and Reintegration Support Scheme were the primary organs in charge of the demobilization and reintegration logistics.[87] The Technical Unit, part of ONUMOZ, prepared the assembly areas, registered soldiers, provided documents, issued clothing and basic living supplies, and transported demobilized soldiers to their destinations.[88] The unit, which was made up of highly skilled individuals seconded from a wide array of international and UN-sister humanitarian organizations, was, as Berman describes, "the embodiment of the institutional know-how and experience which the Swiss Agency for Development and Cooperation had accumulated in its two

---

[86] Synge, 1997, p. 29. Chissano had requested Swiss assistance with unilateral demobilization as early as September 1990. See Berman, 1996, p. 58.

[87] Other programs included the Occupational Skills Development Program, the Information and Referral Service, and the Provincial Fund, all of which were designed to assist soldiers after their initial two years of funding expired.

[88] The International Organization for Migration also provided transportation out of the areas.

years of work prior to the General Peace Agreement and the creation of [ONUMOZ]."[89]

Anticipating difficulties in enticing individual soldiers to demobilize, the almost equally skilled Reintegration Support Scheme coordinated another international "Trust Fund" for demobilized soldiers, which would provide them with eighteen months of salary (after the first six months of salary provided by the government) while troops reintegrated into civilian life. In addition, these subcomponents along with the United Nations Office for Humanitarian Assistance Coordination (UNOHAC) arranged for the provision of jobs as an essential component of ensuring that military officers, who in effect made up the largest part of what could be called a middle class, would be able to maintain the same salaries. Reducing their earning potential would otherwise have given ex-combatants direct incentives either to resume fighting, or engage in crime.[90]

Each assembly area had three to five UN military observers as well as a sizable civilian staff, all of whom were unarmed. Based on lists submitted by Renamo and the government, ONUMOZ expected to demobilize 80,000 government troops and 21,000 Renamo (13,717 government troops had been demobilized before the signing of the peace agreement, and were quickly resettled with minimal UN assistance).[91]

Troop assembly began in December 1993, and at first the arrival of troops at assembly areas proved exceedingly slow. The leaders of both sides were delaying moving their troops to the assembly areas, especially their strongest divisions. But as word of the two years of pay spread, troops began to flock to the areas.

The unanticipated arrival of several thousand extra Renamo troops at Renamo assembly areas resulted in overcrowding and some food shortages. Renamo forces also began to demand greater resources for return to civilian life than previously agreed. Similarly, government troops began rioting, attacking UN personnel and looting food storage sites to protest against what they perceived as long, uncomfortable, and undue captivity.[92] None of the disturbances, however, resulted in troops attacking the weapons storage sites (guarded only by two padlocks), which indicates a certain unwillingness among the troops at that point to return to full-scale fighting.

The housing at the assembly areas was arranged by UNOHAC, which had made the ill-advised decision to teach the soldiers to build their own housing, rather than providing them with inexpensive tents, thinking that this would

---

[89] Berman, 1996, p. 61. See also Alden, 1995, p. 107, who concurs on this point.
[90] UNOHAC was responsible for instituting a countrywide Employment Information and Referral Service for ex-combatants. Ajello, 1999, p. 630. These efforts have been criticized for not being extensive enough. See McMullin, 2004.
[91] S/26034, 30 June 1993, paras. I-7.
[92] Some assembly areas were being overutilized by as much as 400 percent, whereas others were largely vacant. Berman, 1996, p. 68. There were roughly equal numbers of separate disturbances at government and Renamo camps. See Alden, 1995, p. 118.

teach ex-soldiers valuable construction skills. But the need to spend weeks building their own shelter upset the troops. Ajello explains that the "highly intellectualized . . . somewhat patronizing development approach . . . became a source of resentment and even mutiny. It was one of the more serious mistakes we made."[93] UNOHAC in general was accused of employing excessively bureaucratic, slow procedures, and their operations were often sidelined by the faster and more effective units, as explained further in the section on the humanitarian division.

But the primary reason for the most severe delays was that neither side had many soldiers who were willing to join the new FADM, and thus both were reluctant to release soldiers from the assembly areas. As had been previously agreed, the government and Renamo were to conduct "departure surveys" of soon-to-be demobilized troops and share them with each other and with the UN. But since few soldiers were interested in joining the new army, rather than devising better incentives to join the FADM, both sides simply withheld the survey lists. The UN could not release the troops until the lists were shared, and thus the process ran increasingly behind schedule.

In response to the delays, during the summer of 1994 Ajello discovered that "quiet diplomacy did not work" and went directly to the press, criticizing both sides for "playing stupid games."[94] The application of direct, overt pressure, while angering some factions within the government and military, eventually succeeded in moving demobilization forward.

Given delays in demobilization, in order to complete the process ahead of the scheduled elections, thousands of troops were demobilized "on site," without going first to the assembly areas. Of the demobilized troops, about 1 percent opted for further schooling, 50 percent indicated that they wanted to go into agriculture or fishing, 27 percent into trade or transport, and 15 percent into industrial employment.[95] In the end, 67,042 government and 24,648 Renamo troops were registered as demobilized through the UN program, almost five thousand more than originally reported by both sides. Including government troops demobilized before the arrival of the UN, the total demobilization approximated 105,400 troops.[96]

While tens of thousands of troops demobilized, very few opted to join the new FADM. It had been expected that 15,000 from each side would form the national army, but only 12,000 in total chose this option, and of these, only one-third came from the ranks of Renamo.[97] The low number of volunteers was attributed to the successful program of providing two years of reintegration funding.

---

[93] Ajello, 1999, p. 629.   [94] Synge, 1997, p. 47.   [95] Berman, 1996, p. 78.
[96] Troops' names and fingerprints were registered in a computerized database to prevent individuals from being demobilized twice, thus receiving two times the financial allotment.
[97] Ajello, 1999, p. 632.

Troops who decided to join the FADM were trained, as planned, by French, British, Portuguese, and Zimbabwean military, while Italy provided funds for the retraining centers.[98] In April 1994, Renamo, and government command structures were officially disbanded in a ceremony presided over by Ajello, which at the same time formally established the FADM. Command of the FADM is shared jointly by Renamo and government officers who underwent short leadership retraining programs, often in Portugal. Despite the retraining, many charge that the officer corps of the FADM did "not meet some of the basic requirements of military professionalism."[99] It is highly unlikely, however, that this lack of professionalism will lead to a resumption of war.

In terms of disarmament, while the General Peace Agreement mentioned disarmament only in passing, the Secretary-General's implementation plan was fairly explicit about its expectations: "All arms and ammunition not required for the new armed forces would be destroyed under close supervision of the United Nations. A systematic programme for removal of weapons from the civilian population would also be required from the outset."[100] ONUMOZ managed to fulfill only some of these requirements.

During demobilization, the assembly areas were amassing large quantities of armaments, both light and heavy. Given the disturbances at the assembly areas, ONUMOZ officials decided to establish three regional arms depots to store excess weapons until the arms could be destroyed or turned over to the FADM. After demobilization, jointly run government, Renamo and ONUMOZ verification teams searched the country for arms caches in excess of those declared to the Cease-Fire Commission after demobilization. While the government and Renamo proved reluctant to implement fully a post-demobilization arms verification plan, UN verification teams inspected 754 declared and undeclared sites, finding more than 20,000 additional weapons and large quantities of ammunition, on top of the almost 200,000 weapons already collected. Small numbers of weapons and munitions were destroyed, but most were turned over to the new FADM – enough to stock the small army many times over.[101] While these numbers may seem significant, it has been estimated that between 1.5 and 6 million automatic weapons alone were used in Mozambique during the war.[102] However, since peacekeepers were restricted by the Cease-Fire Commission merely to disarming demobilized troops, many weapons in good order remained in the civilian population, entrusted to non-combatants during demobilization, and then presumably recovered by demobilized troops for protection and trade.

The elections in Mozambique were held without disarmament having taken place. Moreover, this came about not despite, but rather with the acceptance

[98] S/1449, 23 December 1994, para. 15.   [99] Honwana, 2000, p. 23.
[100] S/24635, 8 October 1992, Protocol IV; and S/24892, 2 December 1992, para. 22.
[101] S/1449, 23 December 1994, paras. 10–13.   [102] Honwana, 2000, p. 22.

of the UN. The UN understood perhaps better (and certainly sooner) than Dhlakama or Chissano, that the armed forces of the two parties were totally fed up and would not return to war – weapons or no weapons.[103]

After the departure of the UN, Maputo was awash with small weapons, since no effective international or domestic programs had been devised to take care of the problem. Ajello justifies his scant attention to the problem: "Weapons are never the cause of war, they are the instruments . . . My primary objective was to create the conditions for a stable political environment that would render the weapons irrelevant."[104] Ajello did, however, express regret at not pursuing disarmament more thoroughly, since it appears to have contributed to future high crime rates.

Despite the feeble efforts at disarmament, Security Council members visited Mozambique in August 1994 just before elections to declare "cautious optimism" about the peace implementation, and demonstrate international support for Mozambique's transition.[105] In the months before this visit, the 6,000 strong ONUMOZ military division was gradually reduced, in line with the formation and rise of the FADM. In September 1994, on schedule and in time for the elections, there were as few as 240 UN peacekeeping troops in Mozambique; the final withdrawal of UN troops began in mid-November.[106]

Most of the demobilization mandate was fulfilled, which was viewed as the most important accomplishment of the operation, even if disarmament remained incomplete. The cease-fire held; foreign forces from Zimbabwe and Malawi had been verified as withdrawn in June 1993; the UN facilitated the formation of a small FADM; half of the demobilized troops were reintegrated into farming and about half were living on external funding for at least two years. UN personnel were protected, as were refugees and IDPs, as addressed below.

The success of demobilization came about as a result of organizational learning. The early Swiss research into the expectations of troops provided the basis on which the UN's plan was formulated. The failure in Angola created the impetus for continued Security Council and international donor financial support, which provided the preconditions for first-level learning. Ajello's office had a sound understanding of the needs and preferences of the troops, continuously updated by reports from the UN military observers at the dozens of assembly areas. Meanwhile, Ajello negotiated with government and Renamo elites, provided guarantees for their safety, and ensured their political futures, which in turn convinced them, albeit grudgingly, to follow through with their commitments. The UN engaged with its environment in the field, understood the motivations of both regular troops and elites, coordinated with the different

[103] Berman, 1996, p. 42.   [104] Ajello, 1999, p. 639.
[105] S/1009, 29 August 1994.   [106] *The UN and Mozambique*, 1995, p. 45.

sections of the UN, and Ajello provided the leadership necessary to fulfill the most important part of ONUMOZ's mandate.

Police component

The UN's police component (CIVPOL) was created in the middle of the ONU-MOZ operation, in light of the success of demobilization and the realization of the need for greater police-related, rather than military, monitoring. During the peace negotiations, the government was adamantly opposed to the establishment of a UN police force, while Renamo welcomed the idea as an extra means of protection. However, once implementation was underway, the government submitted requests to ONUMOZ to assist with demobilization-related unrest and rising crime, while Renamo complained that the government had been incorporating demobilized troops into its police forces, most importantly, the Presidential Guard. Thus both sides had reason to ask the UN to monitor actions of the police.

The General Peace Agreement made no mention of UN civilian policing, or any international involvement with the Police of the Republic of Mozambique. The Police of the Republic of Mozambique were to function according to the basic principles of democratic policing, and in order to verify adequate behavior, a National Police Affairs Commission was established by the General Peace Agreement, made up of six Renamo, six government, and nine other Mozambican citizens.[107]

Once ONUMOZ was underway, Renamo and the government were at odds about the composition and operation of the National Police Affairs Commission. Moreover, Renamo refused to allow government administrators, including police, into Renamo-controlled zones. Rather than resolving these and other problems among themselves, Chissano and Dhlakama agreed to a UN police monitoring contingent. The Security Council approved in principle, and as late as February 1994, ONUMOZ came up with a mandate and an operational plan for a new, large, 1,444-member, $40 million CIVPOL component as an integral part of ONUMOZ.[108] But the Security Council also stipulated that in order not to increase the overall budget for ONUMOZ, there would have to be a concomitant downsizing of the military component.

ONUMOZ's CIVPOL came to number 1,086 police from twenty-nine countries by September 1994.[109] CIVPOL were to be deployed widely throughout the country, with headquarters in Maputo, a special task force also in Maputo, three regional headquarters, eleven provincial offices, and 180 UN police

---

[107] S/24635, 8 October 1992, Protocol IV, Section V.
[108] Note that in May 1993, after approval by all sides, a small UN CIVPOL operation of 128 was deployed but was largely ineffective due to its minimal mandate and size.
[109] S/1449, 23 December 1994, Section III.

stations in both Renamo- and government-controlled areas. The widely deployed force was expected to fulfill the following tasks: monitor all police activities including those of the Rapid Intervention Police and private security agencies; monitor the extent to which human rights and civil liberties were respected; provide technical support to the National Police Affairs Commission; verify quantities and types of police *matériel*; retrain the Rapid Intervention Police; and monitor the electoral process.[110] CIVPOL officers received human rights and election-monitoring training during their service, which helped to unify the force and clarify its purpose.[111] Moreover, "CIVPOL deployment was timely and helped give ONUMOZ a presence in the remotest and most inaccessible districts in the country throughout the final months of the process, facilitating voter registration and the conduct of the elections themselves."[112] This is not to say, however, that CIVPOL operations were always well functioning.

The problems that CIVPOL faced were of two types: technical and political. First, there were logistical and personnel problems. In many of the police stations there were no living accommodations, water, or electricity, which rendered even rudimentary operations exceedingly difficult. Moreover, the two basic requirements for a UN CIVPOL service in ONUMOZ were the ability to speak English and operate UN vehicles; however, an estimated 36 percent of CIVPOL did not fulfill one or both of these requirements.[113] The second type of problem was political. The Police of the Republic of Mozambique were reluctant to provide any information to the UN police about their activities. In addition, by the time the CIVPOL operation was fully underway, and officers had begun to document human rights and political abuses, there was no adequate judicial system to try cases, and thus no repercussions for offenses that had been reported and documented by the UN.[114] Moreover, corruption among the Police of the Republic of Mozambique appeared to be on the rise, but the UN CIVPOL were not authorized either to reprimand or retrain offending officers. Given the very short period of operation, limited means, and larger problems to tackle, the leadership of ONUMOZ could do little to offset these problems.

There were, however, significant positive effects resulting from the presence of CIVPOL. First, after several months of obstruction, members of CIVPOL "opened up" Renamo-controlled areas, paving the way for government police to enter. Second, they also monitored voter registration, electoral campaigns including political rallies, and the balloting process, all of which contributed to

---

[110] S/89/Add. 1, 28 January 1994; and S/89/Add. 2, 1 February 1994.
[111] Human rights education was conducted by the Office of the UN High Commissioner for Human Rights and was the first of its kind in a peacekeeping operation.
[112] Synge, 1997, p. 120.   [113] Woods, 1998, p. 7.
[114] In all, 511 complaints were investigated by CIVPOL, and 61 were then forwarded to the National Police Affairs Commission, where they languished.

the calm atmosphere surrounding the campaigns and elections. Third, as one analyst summarizes:

> In general, CIVPOL was most effective at policing human rights at posts far from headquarters, where local policemen were less aware of CIVPOL's lack of authority for redress and were fearful of having their misdeeds reported to their superiors. CIVPOL was also more effective in situations where its officers had developed good personal relations with the local police force . . . The relationship between CIVPOL officers and the Mozambique police was complex. It incorporated elements of monitoring, mentoring, joint patrolling, passive observation, and some training.[115]

Woods and others characterize the CIVPOL operation in Mozambique as a qualified success.[116] While the CIVPOL component did engage in some learning – enough to implement the basic tasks of its mandate – the short period of deployment and limited mandate meant that the CIVPOL operation would have little lasting positive effect on policing in Mozambique.[117]

Humanitarian assistance

The difficulties facing humanitarian assistance operations in Mozambique were large and complex. The drought in 1992 was reported to be the worst of the century; mass starvation threatened a population that had been rendered highly vulnerable after thirty years of warfare. Approximately 4 million out of Mozambique's total population of 12 million were internally displaced, 1.8 million had taken refuge in neighboring countries, and between 1.8 and 3.1 million were entirely dependent on external food aid.[118] The Security Council estimated that the humanitarian needs of Mozambique from 1992 till 1994 would come to approximately $616 million, 87 percent of which was to come from international sources. Specific types of aid from various organizations included food, non-food relief supplies (such as blankets, soap, utensils, and tools), and funds to rehabilitate agricultural, health, water, road, education and social welfare systems. The general humanitarian mandate for ONUMOZ encompassed four major areas: (1) the reintegration of former combatants, discussed above in the section on the military component, (2) the return of refugees and internally displaced, (3) de-mining programs, and (4) coordination through a new, temporary coordination mechanism called the UNOHAC. While many parts of the

---

[115] Woods, 1998, p. 9.
[116] See Woods, 1998, p. 11; Ajello, 1999, p. 622; Malan, 1999, p. 176.
[117] McMullin, 2004. Several years after the end of ONUMOZ, the UNDP initiated an extensive $12 million project to train Mozambican police. See Malan, 1999, p. 177.
[118] A/47/539, 22 October 1992.

mandate were fulfilled, all successes cannot be attributed to the peacekeeping operation.

In terms of refugees, the UNHCR was the lead organization in charge of overseeing refugee return, and even though it reported to ONUMOZ, the organization behaved fairly independently in the field. The UNHCR raised its own funds amounting to over $200 million. Like the rest of ONUMOZ, the refugee operation did not become fully operational in the field until the summer of 1993. By this point, thousands of refugees had already begun voluntary repatriations. The UNHCR arranged repatriation accords with the main countries housing Mozambican refugees, including Malawi, South Africa, Swaziland, Tanzania, Zambia, and Zimbabwe and arranged transportation. In the peace agreement, refugees were granted all the rights and freedoms of Mozambican citizens, including the right to vote, and to property restitution. Moreover, in 1993, rain came once again to southern Africa, and Mozambique's harvests were more plentiful than in recent history. The end of the drought and restoration of rights, combined with few cease-fire violations, encouraged refugees and internally displaced people to return.

The UNHCR sought to prepare return areas through the rehabilitation of roads, health facilities, schools, and food production mechanisms. In all, approximately 3 million IDPs, 1.1 million refugees, and 200,000 ex-combatants returned to the places where they wanted to live, many of whom registered to vote in time for the October 1994 elections.[119] This amounted to the largest repatriation of refugees in African history.[120]

While resettlement eventually proved massive, returns to some areas, especially the central provinces of Mozambique, were stalled by the prevalence of land mines. By 1993 more than 10,000 people, mainly civilians, had been killed by land mines in Mozambique, and it was estimated that between 1 and 2 million mines remained in 9,000 areas of the country.[121] De-mining programs, however, fell victim to "inordinate delays."[122] On December 31, 1992, the Supervisory and Monitoring Commission had approved a list of roads to be de-mined as soon as possible. The de-mining, however, was delayed for seven months due mainly to internal rivalries: "The rivalry between DHA [the Department of Humanitarian Affairs] and UNDP in New York over program jurisdiction (a classic case of UN bureaucratic entanglement) played a major part in the confusion and failure to act in clearing landmines."[123] UNDP in particular argued over the wording and control of contracts. Meanwhile, the World Food Programme had arranged its own de-mining program in early

---

[119] S/1449, 23 December 1994, Section IV. At the request of UNHCR, voter registration for refugees was extended until just before the vote.
[120] The UNHCR formally closed its offices in Mozambique in July 1996.
[121] Human Rights Watch, 1994; and S/1009, 29 August 1994, Section I.
[122] S/511, 28 April 1994, Section V.   [123] Synge, 1997, p. 78.

1993 to clear its food and non-food aid delivery channels, circumventing the bureaucratic rivalries.

As life-threatening and embarrassing delays mounted, Secretary-General Boutros-Ghali intervened in May 1994, stripped the UNDP in New York of its $7.5 million de-mining funds and re-allocated the funds to UNOHAC in Maputo, bringing the total de-mining budget to $18.5 million. Shortly thereafter, under a new director, UNOHAC launched an accelerated de-mining program to train Mozambican de-miners, and to facilitate cooperation with de-mining projects already underway.

In the end, private companies, together with bilateral and UN-sponsored de-mining teams, cleared more than 5,790 crucial kilometers of roads by October 1995.[124] The UN also established a Mine Clearance Training Centre, but as the Security Council reported in its 1994 assessment of ONUMOZ, the center was having trouble attracting trainees because at the time it did not have running water or medical facilities; in December 1994, the center did eventually graduate its first 450 Mozambican de-miners.[125] By the end of ONUMOZ, its leaders estimated that the mine-clearing programs would have to extend for another seven to ten years beyond the ONUMOZ mandate. ONUMOZ made preparations for its de-mining equipment to remain in Mozambique along with some members of its staff, and worked to train as many Mozambicans as possible in de-mining and in managing the programs.[126]

The problems with implementing the UNOHAC de-mining mandate reflected broader coordination problems in the unit, even though coordination was supposed to be the most ambitious part of UNOHAC's mandate. UNOHAC's small staff of thirty-five international civil servants was in charge of a multimillion dollar aid budget and was mandated both to coordinate international aid, as well as to implement projects such as de-mining and reintegration of former combatants, which overlapped with the plans of other agencies. UNOHAC, like the rest of ONUMOZ, was slow to establish itself in the field and faced significant resistance as it sought to become the central aid coordinator, especially since its leaders wanted to focus on long-term, rather than short-term aid projects. Many of the main UN humanitarian affiliates such as the World Food Programme, UNICEF, and UNHCR did not want central coordination. Moreover, UNOHAC received little support from the Special Representative, and this relationship deteriorated as UNOHAC failed to produce quick results.[127] UNOHAC's lack of authority, and focus on long-term operations

---

[124] Synge 1997, p. 80.   [125] S/1009, 29 August 1994, Section I.
[126] *The UN and Mozambique*, 1995, p. 53.
[127] When Ajello was in New York negotiating the ONUMOZ mandate, he had supported the establishment of a unified humanitarian assistance program within ONUMOZ, but his top priorities were always the military and political components.

rather than on the short-term needs of the peacekeeping operation meant that Ajello, the donors, and other humanitarian agencies simply came to ignore the office.

In the end, UNOHAC's central coordination and long-delayed, long-term projects were all but abandoned. ONUMOZ represented the first attempt at central coordination for humanitarian aid agencies during a peacekeeping operation, and while the idea appeared sound in principle at headquarters in New York, in practice, it was exceedingly difficult to accomplish.

For the most part, agencies other than UNOHAC implemented the UN's humanitarian mandate. The major humanitarian tasks such as the delivery of food aid, overseeing refugee return, reintegration, and mine clearance were conducted mainly outside the realm of UNOHAC. However, toward the end of the ONUMOZ mandate, with increased funding, UNOHAC did become more functional. While the organization was never able to coordinate the large international aid agencies, Ajello and the UNOHAC director managed to gain authority with NGOs and other UN sub-organizations in the field by holding frequent political and military briefings, and arranging meetings between the UN affiliates, Renamo, and government representatives. Surprisingly, UNOHAC also managed to establish, in accordance with its mandate, trilateral provincial humanitarian assistance committees among the UN, Renamo, and the government. These meetings helped to open areas under Renamo control to the government and paved the way for the territorial reunification of the administration.[128]

UNOHAC in general failed to fulfill its basic coordination mandate. However, the larger, well-established aid agencies, with the help of the major donors, did coordinate amongst themselves, adequately divided the labor in the field, and fulfilled important basic humanitarian tasks. Part of the reason they were able to accomplish their tasks, as Sam Barnes explains, was because "Consensus on what was a priority resulted from discussion in Maputo . . . and not in New York, Geneva or Rome."[129] The accomplishments were extremely important. Most notably, unlike the drought in 1982 when over 100,000 people died, the even more severe 1992 drought did not cause mass starvation because there was adequate aid. Massive numbers of refugees and IDPs returned to their homes. Mines were cleared, and Mozambicans were trained in mine-clearance. Provincial level trilateral cooperation was established, which helped to facilitate other aspects of aid delivery as well as dialogue between international and local officials on opposing sides of the war. The overall organizational picture of UNOHAC is one of organizational dysfunction, but fortunately, other humanitarian organizations filled the vacuum to help implement the mandate.

[128] *The UN and Mozambique*, 1995, p. 48.   [129] Barnes, 1998, p. 16.

Elections, crisis and recovery

Mozambique's first postwar, free elections for the President and the National Assembly (for terms of five years) were to be held from October 27–28, 1994. The President would be elected by an absolute majority, and political parties would be allocated seats in the 250-member National Assembly according to proportional representation, with a 5 percent minimum threshold. Seats would be allocated by province after the registration of voters had taken place.

In order to safeguard against Renamo or Frelimo declaring the elections fraudulent, all steps in the process necessitated the full involvement of both parties as well as international observers. Complex, extensive controls were devised, in the form of large numbers of both domestic and international monitors. Nevertheless, as described below, during the run-up to the elections, fears escalated that Renamo would resume conflict as it became clear that the party had not fully disclosed its arms caches, and, moreover, as it appeared that Dhlakama was unsure of his commitment to leading the smaller party in a multiparty government.

The ONUMOZ electoral component's mandate, as specified in the General Peace Agreement and in the Secretary-General's implementation plan, was to verify the impartial behavior of the all-Mozambican National Elections Commission; verify political parties' freedom of movement, assembly, expression, and fair media access; verify implementation of the electoral process from voter registration to the computation of results; report on irregularities to electoral authorities; and participate in voter education. The component would have a Director's Office in Maputo, three regional offices, and an office in each of the ten provinces. The staff was made up of 158 foreigners and 88 locals, and increased by 2,350 observers during the elections – over two times more observers than were originally envisioned in the implementation plan.[130] The Secretary-General indicated in the implementation plan that aside from verification by the ONUMOZ electoral component, technical assistance (such as civic education, voter registration, and the training of Mozambican electoral officials) would be provided by the UNDP.[131] While the ONUMOZ verification mission proved an essential short-term guarantee against fraud, the UNDP's technical assistance left in its wake a deeper legacy, as it sought to create lasting electoral institutions, rather than merely monitoring behavior.

Aside from the UN observers, the numbers of Mozambicans who were trained and deployed to ensure against electoral fraud were staggering. The

---

[130] The UN's observers included members of the ONUMOZ mission, other UN agencies, members of the diplomatic community in Maputo, and members of the OAU and the EU.

[131] S/24892, 2 December 1992, Section VI. The EU eventually covered 80 percent of the costs, which totaled almost $90 million.

UNDP trained, and the National Elections Commission deployed, 1,600 five-person (8,000 people total) voter registration brigades to the ten provinces and 131 districts of Mozambique; these brigades were "widely praised for their seriousness, dedication, and willingness to endure uncomfortable conditions."[132] Registration brigades were accompanied by 1,600 civic education providers who had been trained by the UNDP and a UN Volunteer staff numbering about 100 people. On polling day, the International Organization for Migration assisted in transporting approximately 52,000 polling officers to each of the 7,244 polling stations. Equipment used for the transportation of all of these electoral workers included over 300 motor vehicles, twenty-six helicopters, and six airplanes.

Stepping back for a moment, it is helpful to address the way in which the electoral procedures were established, in order to understand how the elections functioned. The General Peace Agreement ushered in self-monitoring Mozambican institutions, namely, the National Elections Commission and the Technical Secretariat for the Organization of the Elections. During the year before the elections, negotiations on electoral procedures had been deadlocked for many months. The main issue was the composition of the National Elections Commission, its provincial and district electoral commissions, and the Technical Secretariat. Renamo and the government vied for greater representation on the National Elections Commission and in the Technical Secretariat until the end of November, when compromises were negotiated by Ajello, facilitated in part by a visit from the Secretary-General.[133]

In the lead-up to the elections, while the Technical Secretariat would become mired in partisan disputes, forcing the UNDP to perform many of the technical aspects of the elections, the National Elections Commission functioned remarkably well under the impartial leadership of Dr. Brazao Mazula. While at first the commission was severely divided along party lines, as several observers explain: "the need to reach consensus transformed the election commission from a group of inexperienced partisan politicians into an institution, working together toward a shared goal."[134] This would prove one of the most constructive legacies of the election period.

Another positive legacy came as a result of the civic education and voter registration campaigns. The UNDP, an organization that had long been familiar with development work in Mozambique including educational rehabilitation, was in charge of the civic education campaign. The campaign was extensive

---

[132] Synge, 1997, p. 122.
[133] There were also disputes over voting rights for Mozambicans living abroad. The government wanted them to have voting privileges, while Renamo feared a greater chance of government fraud. In the end, the National Elections Commission decided that there would be no voting rights for Mozambicans living abroad.
[134] Turner, Nelson, and Mahling-Clark, 1998, p. 159.

and multifaceted, given that 67 percent of Mozambicans were illiterate and had never voted in democratic elections. As Synge explains:

> Radio and television programs illustrating the process were popular in towns and cities, as were free newspapers that used comic strips to show the different stages of voting. In the countryside, teams of civic education workers used popular theater, mobile units, and simulated voting to convince people that they could influence the outcome. One of the greatest fears amongst many Mozambicans, that "sorcerers" would know how people would vote, was tackled by simple demonstrations that each ballot would be mixed up with hundreds of others and could therefore not be recognized by anyone during the counting.[135]

The example of sorcerers being a source of fear reveals the extent to which western-based institutions, for many Mozambicans, were foreign and warranted suspicion.[136] The foreign workers in Mozambique were obligated to learn about the ways of Mozambicans before they could ever expect Mozambicans to absorb, celebrate, and claim for their own the institutions that westerners so desperately seemed to want them to have. In the instance of voter education, upon the advice of local anthropologists, dance and theater proved the most well-received educational forms.[137]

Voters were issued photo identity cards by the UNDP, despite protests from the UN's Department of Peacekeeping Operations in New York who thought the project too costly and difficult to implement. The UNDP, with greater field experience and an interest in long-term development in Mozambique, nevertheless issued the cards. These cards would serve as the first official piece of identification for most Mozambicans and arguably helped to foster a sense of unified national identity.

The registration period was extended by two weeks to September 2, in order to register voters in greater numbers in the more remote corners of Mozambique, many of whom were isolated by land mines or local Renamo political intransigence. In the end, 6,363,311 voters were registered, or about 81 percent of the estimated eligible voting population.

The campaign was conducted in an atmosphere of anxiety over whether the peace would hold after the elections. During the campaign period, there was some rock throwing, poster ripping, and inflammatory rhetoric, but in general the battles remained in the realm of words rather than extending into the sphere of physical violence. No official complaints were made about electoral malfeasance even though charges were volleyed in the press.

One of the main sources of disagreement before, during, and after the campaign period was the introduction of discussions for a post-election

[135] Synge, 1997, p. 129.
[136] See West and Mandumbwe, 2005, for a more thorough discussion.
[137] Honwana, 2000, p. 27.

power-sharing arrangement between Chissano and Dhlakama. Dennis Jett, the American Ambassador to Mozambique, was the main supporter of creating a government of national unity, as had been successfully accomplished the year before in South Africa and Malawi. But he did not quietly present the idea first to his colleagues in order to build consensus, in the manner that had been used by foreign diplomats in Mozambique up until that point. Instead, Jett went directly to the press to push Frelimo toward such an agreement. The Frelimo government perceived Jett's heavy-handedness and public chastising as pro-Renamo, and became ever more firmly set against the idea of power-sharing. With generational splits emerging in Frelimo, between the old guard who absolutely refused to consider sharing power with Renamo, and the more pragmatic younger members who were more amenable to the concept, Chissano was effectively backed into a corner and risked the splitting of his party. In the end, he refused to change his position; there would be no post-elections power-sharing. Frelimo justified its position by arguing that in most democracies, the winning party does not absorb the losing party into the executive, and that such a move would in fact be undemocratic. The controversy over the power-sharing arrangements represented the only occasion on which a single, powerful external state split with the international consensus in Maputo, and the tactic backfired.

Aside from the power-sharing controversy, a potentially much more important crisis arose on the first day of polling, October 27, 1994, that could have destroyed the entire peace process. Dhlakama announced his withdrawal from the elections, charging fraud on the part of Frelimo. There was evidence that Dhlakama could have mobilized fighting forces, and fears rose among international observers that despite his apparent shift in outlook, his commitment to an election that he would most likely not win might be uncertain.

As Ajello has argued, three events had transpired to convince Dhlakama that the elections would be fraudulent. First, a fax ostensibly sent by a Brazilian advertising firm working for the government detailed government plans that would ensure that Frelimo would win; second, some irregularities were not fully investigated by the National Elections Commission; and third, during a summit of the front-line states just before the elections, Dhlakama was scheduled to speak before the group but instead sat in his hotel room and was never called to the meeting.[138] After the meeting, the front-line states issued a threatening warning that if the election results were not accepted, they would ensure "appropriate and timely action" to keep the peace.[139] These three events convinced some of Dhlakama's top advisors, and eventually Dhlakama himself, that the elections would be unfair, and that the UN and

---

[138] By this time, the front-line states included Angola, Botswana, Lesotho, Malawi, Mozambique, Namibia, South Africa, Tanzania, Zambia, and Zimbabwe.

[139] *The UN and Mozambique*, 1995, p. 61.

Mozambique's neighbors had agreed to a conspiracy to secure Frelimo's political power.

Ajello responded to Dhlakama's announcement by mobilizing the diplomatic corps in Maputo to visit, call, and fax Dhlakama to convince him that the elections would be closely monitored, and would only be certified free and fair if indeed that was the case. The National Elections Commission, which included seven members of Renamo, unanimously rejected complaints of irregularities and would not accept Dhlakama's refusal to participate. An "ad hoc standing committee" of the Supervisory and Monitoring Commission went into permanent session until Dhlakama eventually agreed to participate in the elections. Dhlakama refused to see Ajello, but he agreed to meet with others, including members of his own party, who coaxed him back into the election within twenty-four hours. In order to save face, Dhlakama agreed to rejoin the process after receiving assurances that the National Elections Commission would monitor closely the elections at all levels, and that all surplus registration cards would be destroyed. Ajello also agreed to arrange a special UN team that would investigate all Renamo complaints. Polling was extended for another day, even though, given the large number of people who continued to vote for him, it appeared that word of Dhlakama's temporary withdrawal had not been widely disseminated.

Other than the crisis with Dhlakama, the three days of elections transpired in a remarkably calm fashion. Transportation and communication for the 2,350 international observers were provided by CIVPOL. Ballots were marked, and voters' hands were stamped with indelible ink to prevent repeat voting. Stations and ballot boxes were well guarded by tens of thousands of international observers and local election monitors; some observers even slept with the ballot boxes to ensure against tampering.

In terms of the atmosphere of the elections, some analysts condemned the elections as being "formalistic" and "lackluster."[140] But the majority described the polling days in more generous terms as calm, and the voters as good humored. The UN itself contended that:

> The overwhelming evidence provided by the international observers showed an election that was conducted peacefully, in which electoral officials followed procedures impartially and efficiently and in which the electorate participated patiently, seriously, and with great dignity. By 31 October, ONUMOZ was able to declare the polling successful. It noted that some 90 percent of the registered voters had cast their ballots.[141]

Over two weeks passed before the election results could be announced, since Renamo insisted that the entire vote be re-counted, and there was extensive

---

[140] Hall and Young, 1997, p. 233.   [141] *The UN and Mozambique*, 1995, p. 63.

haggling over some 200,000 invalid ballots.[142] The final results were issued on November 19 after extensive verification of the results. Chissano became the first democratically elected President with 53 percent of the vote, while Dhlakama won a respectable 34 percent. In the Parliament, Frelimo received 44 percent of the votes or 129 seats, Renamo won 38 percent and 112 seats, and the Democratic Union coalition won just over 5 percent, with 9 seats.[143] The vote was declared free and fair by Ajello, on behalf of the "international community." All parties accepted the results, even though Dhlakama remained unwilling to characterize the elections as fair.

While the parliamentary vote was indeed very close, Frelimo allotted all Cabinet posts and governorships to its own party members, despite complaints from Renamo, the United States, and other countries. In response, Renamo held firm to its areas of administrative control, especially in Sofala province. Dhlakama's party had won a majority of the vote in five of the ten provinces, giving him a solid base as head of the opposition party. Renamo boycotted the first three weeks of parliamentary session, but as party members realized that they were missing out on opportunities to make governing decisions, they rejoined with enthusiasm.

In sum, while it was the UNDP's extensive voter education and registration drives that left the most enduring positive international legacy, ONUMOZ fulfilled well its short-term electoral monitoring mandate. As one analyst noted, "The presence of the ONUMOZ electoral division and its willingness to investigate any complaint, regardless of its plausibility, ensured transparency and built confidence in the process."[144]

ONUMOZ was criticized for pulling out of Mozambique too soon after the elections and the installation of the National Assembly, leaving the tasks of disarmament and de-mining incomplete, as well as several thousand Mozambicans, who had been working for ONUMOZ, unemployed.[145] However, the UN's quick exit was in part designed to help to wean Mozambique of its dependence on external assistance. Before much time had passed, the parties learned to communicate directly with each other, rather than through Ajello (or through the members of Sant'Egidio). The government and opposition had to take responsibility for governing the country, and they eventually did. The elections proved to be transformative, signifying the end of violent politics, even if they also represented only the first step in building a unified and stable state.

---

[142] Ballots with marks that did not appear in the boxes to check were considered invalid, even if the voter had circled or otherwise clearly indicated his or her choice.

[143] Democratic Union, not a particularly popular or well-known party, reportedly won so much of the vote since it was the last party on the ballot, in the same position on the paper as Chissano in the presidential race. Illiterate Chissano supporters had been instructed to mark the last box on the ballot.

[144] Turner, Nelson, and Mahling-Clark, 1998, p. 171.

[145] Synge, 1997, p. 141; and Paris, 2004, Chapter 8.

Mozambique since ONUMOZ

Organizational learning in the ONUMOZ operation helped to end Mozambique's civil war. It also helped to create functioning institutions which ensure that battles remain in the non-violent sphere of politics – there is very little chance of a return to war. [146] Elites have generally become habituated to sharing political space, and resolving disputes through negotiation.[147] Renamo has remained committed to transforming itself from a military into a political organization, even if the party remains driven largely by Dhlakama's personality rather than by institutional structures. Frelimo has continued to gain depth in its institutional structures, and its leaders remain very popular, but the problems of an overlap between state and party remain.[148] Since the end of ONUMOZ, Mozambique has become one of the most-favored donor recipient nations in Africa because of the government's commitments to liberal economic policies. The country has enjoyed growth rates of approximately 10 percent per year and has been dubbed one of the "lion" economies of Africa. Most of Mozambique's formerly crippling external debt has been canceled or rescheduled; inflation rates are generally low; and the GDP per capita (PPP) is about $1,300.[149]

Some analysts of Mozambique do, however, caution that the exuberance over Mozambique's stunning growth rates since the elections, and the unlikely return to war, ignore other pressing problems in Mozambique such as crime, an unbalanced political party system, and economic problems. Crime has become a significant problem in postwar Mozambique. One critic maintains that current criminal activities can be linked back to UN-organized demobilization, disarmament, and reintegration, which focused primarily on building a new, national military and ensuring that former combatants did not return to violent conflict, rather than on preventing former combatants from turning to crime after their demobilization funds ran out.[150] Other critics focus on potential weaknesses in the political system, where increasingly, according to election returns, one party (Frelimo) is becoming more dominant over the other, and where elite-level bargains often take precedence over deeper, more democratic political decision-making mechanisms.[151] Still others focus on the economy and the negative effects of neoliberal privatization policies on the poor. Many anthropologists argue that local communities are being hurt by the changes.[152] Meanwhile, at the elite level of the economy, some observers warn that privatization in general has benefited only a small handful at the expense of the many.

---

[146] See Mozambican Politics Professor, Miguel de Brito, quoted in Walter, 1997, p. 18. See also Synge, 1997, p. 10; Chan and Venancio, 1998, p. 142; and Eaton, Horwood, Niland, 1997, p. 27.

[147] Manning, 2002.   [148] Carbone, 2005.   [149] *CIA World Factbook*, 2005.

[150] McMullin, 2004.   [151] Manning, 2002; Weinstein, 2002; and Carbone, 2005.

[152] Englund, 2002; Galli, 2003; and West and Mandumbwe, 2005.

They also point out that donors have essentially taken the place of citizens, in that the government, which receives half of its budget from donors, must answer more often to donors than to its own people.[153]

However, the government has been obligated to answer to the Mozambican people, at least at a minimum, through the mechanism of regular elections. Since the presidential elections monitored by ONUMOZ in 1994, there have been two subsequent rounds, in 1999 and 2004. In these presidential and parliamentary elections, the electoral machinery that had been set in place by ONUMOZ continued to function. During the campaign periods, neither side mentioned the war, while both focused on improving basic infrastructure and poverty alleviation. In terms of differences in political platforms, Renamo concentrated on exposing Frelimo corruption and strengthening Mozambican cultural traditions, while Frelimo stressed its impressive economic record. Growth remained high, goods were plentiful, foreign investment was pouring in, and inflation remained low. In 1999, Frelimo won 133 parliamentary seats to Renamo's 117. Chissano won the presidential vote by an even narrower margin: 52.3 percent to Dhlakama's 47.7 percent. In 1999, Renamo's ability to receive many votes, despite unequal access to media and other campaign resources, attested to the party's popularity coupled with a broad unease about the ruling party's accession to international economic liberalization policies. It also appeared that UN intervention had helped foster the emergence of a two-party system where Renamo would fulfill the role of the "loyal opposition."

The 2004 elections, however, appeared to solidify the ruling power of Frelimo and reflected increasing infighting within Renamo. Chissano did not stand for re-election, according to legal mandate (which, unlike in some other African countries, was respected). Instead, Frelimo candidate Armando Guebuza ran. Guebuza amassed 63.7 percent of the vote to Dhlakama's much smaller 31.7 percent. In the Parliament, Frelimo won 160 seats to Renamo's 90 – a 27 seat loss for Renamo. International observers cited increasing disaffection with Renamo, as well as heavy rain, which disproportionately affected voter turnout in areas of traditional Renamo support.[154] The post-ONUMOZ elections reflect a troubling and apparently growing ethno-regional division in Mozambique, where Frelimo and people mainly from the south and southern tribes dominate the political and economic picture. While Renamo's ability to transform itself into a political party from a former murder machine is quite extraordinary, its consolidation in recent years has been fraying, while Frelimo only grows stronger. Overall, while Mozambique might certainly be labeled an

---

[153] Pitcher, 2002; Galli, 2003.

[154] Carbone, 2005, pp. 419, 421. While Renamo blamed their low numbers on electoral fraud, no significant irregularities were documented by international observers. Municipal elections in 1998 and 2003, the first of which were boycotted by Renamo, also solidified Frelimo's hold on power at the local level.

"electoral" democracy, it remains far from the western standard of "liberal" democracy.[155]

In terms of the local state administrative apparatuses, the UN did not leave as promising an immediate legacy. ONUMOZ was not a member of the National Commission for State Administration and did not press to become one. Thus when it came to debates about reunification of government and the 25 percent of the country administratively controlled by Renamo, ONUMOZ had little formal leverage. Indeed, Ajello and his staff chose not to tackle this issue, assuming (correctly) that it would be resolved in the process of opening Renamo areas up first to humanitarian assistance, then to elections registration, and finally to the elections and unified governing from Maputo. Upon ONUMOZ's withdrawal, "the status of numerous districts and administrative posts remained undetermined."[156] The double administration served for a short time as Renamo's guarantee of political power after demobilization.[157] But the administration has become unified over time through joint legislation, most notably in debates during 1996–97, when both parties reached a consensus on the municipalities law, in an attempt to devolve power from the center.[158]

In terms of other judicial reforms, the 1990 Constitution, which guarantees all the rights and freedoms that one would expect in a liberal democracy, is still in effect. New media have emerged under this liberal constitution, as have new civil society organizations; one of the most vociferous and popular organizations is the Human Rights League, which has received hundreds of human rights abuse complaints, and has brought about the successful prosecution of police abuse. As for new legislation, aside from the passage of the municipalities law, there were also land law reforms concerning land tenure, leasing, and women's rights to own property. But even while there have been advances on the judicial front, corruption is still a problem, and many members of the judiciary tend not to have a lot of formal education, making deeper and broader institutionalization difficult. Both the positive and the negative trends in judicial reform can be attributed only indirectly to ONUMOZ's tenure in Mozambique.

As for the links between justice, peace, and reconciliation, it would appear to most outsiders that peace has come at the expense of justice. There have been no war crimes tribunals or truth commissions that have attempted to come to terms with the massive human rights abuses of Mozambique's leaders. There are several practical and sociological explanations that attempt to justify and

---

[155] Freedom House scores as of 2005 on the 1 to 7 scale (1 being the most free) stood at 3 for political rights, 4 for civil liberties.

[156] *The UN and Mozambique*, 1995, p. 46.   [157] Walter, 1997.

[158] See Buur and Kyed, 2005. In the National Assembly, since neither Renamo or Frelimo have easily identifiable ideological positions or political platforms, legislators from both parties have been exercising greater independence and forming new alliances. Indeed, regionalism is emerging as a major political trend, since in order to stay in power, representatives in the Assembly compete to allocate scarce state resources to their home areas.

explain why prosecution or the discovery of truth have not been priorities in Mozambique. First, if Mozambique's politicians were to be held accountable for the prosecution of the war, there would be only very few people remaining in government. Second, some analysts long familiar with Mozambique explain that it is the war itself, which is seen as akin to a disease, that is commonly blamed for the suffering, rather than Renamo or Frelimo or the party leaders.[159] Third, since many who committed atrocities "including child soldiers did so as part of military machines they entered under duress, no blanket judgments about culpability are plausible."[160] And finally, as Mozambican anthropologist Joao Honwana explains: "At the level of the individuals . . . the dividing line in the Mozambican conflict was to be found within families and within local communities, rather than between distinct regions, ethnic groups or religious groups."[161] As soldiers returned to their homes, often to the same places where they committed atrocities during the war, indigenous healing and reconciliation ceremonies have taken place in the absence of formal processes of war crimes tribunals or truth commissions. Joao Honwana clarifies:

> A set of different, and arguably more genuine and sustainable, processes of reconciliation is taking shape at the grassroots level in vast areas of the Mozambican countryside. Such processes, protagonized by local communities and former combatants, are mediated by local cosmologies and cultural practices, in which health is viewed as the harmonious relationship among human beings, between people and nature, and between the living and ancestors.[162]

Most notably, Honwana argues that complex indigenous rituals have been remarkably effective at healing, balancing, and restoring meaning to lives traumatized by war. Sara Gibbs offers a similar argument and maintains that the establishment of regular, daily work routines, combined with syncretic healing ceremonies, have gone far to promote reconciliation and should be supported, and better appreciated, by westerners.[163] Thus even though from a typical western perspective the acceptance of war criminals appears to promote impunity and injustice, and that anything less than a drive to prosecute resonates as an excuse to "do nothing," such conceptions do not necessarily hold true for many Mozambicans.[164]

Since the end of the war, Mozambican society has also been healing itself in other ways. Political stability and physical security have been accompanied by significant improvements in living standards. Most schools and hospitals have been rehabilitated, and churches are being rebuilt and widely attended. While there is growing disparity in wealth, growth in both the industrial and the agricultural sectors have meant greater employment for everyone. Funding

---

[159] Bartoli, 1999, p. 265.   [160] Austin, 1994, p. 2.   [161] Honwana, 2000, p. 34.
[162] Honwana, 2000, p. 35.   [163] Gibbs, 1997.   [164] Alden, 2003, p. 352.

for ex-combatants ran out in 1996, but despite predictions of disaster, war
has not returned, and the vast majority of ex-combatants have found other
means of survival.[165] While one could not argue that Mozambique has become
a bastion of liberal democracy and economic prosperity, there is no doubt that
ONUMOZ fostered an environment that has, since its tenure, generally favored
progress and peace in Mozambique.[166]

Conclusion

The accomplishments of ONUMOZ were significant. The cease-fire was maintained. 105,400 troops were demobilized, disarmed as organized forces, and
reintegrated into Mozambican society. Humanitarian relief was delivered,
averting otherwise potentially devastating consequences. Renamo areas that
had been isolated for years were for the first time opened to interactions with
foreign aid workers and eventually with the government. Long-term de-mining
programs were established. The mission recorded the largest return of refugees
and displaced people ever seen before in sub-Saharan Africa. Freely contested
elections were held in which almost 90 percent of the electorate voted, thousands of Mozambican electoral officials were trained, and technical and political
mechanisms were established to ensure the future of regular national elections.

The successes in mandate implementation were, however, tempered by some
failures. Large areas of the country remained plagued by land mines after
ONUMOZ's departure; light weapons were not collected in large enough
numbers; and few ex-combatants were interested in enlisting in the new, unified
Mozambican army, the FADM. While the UN could have played a larger role in
counteracting these phenomena, since they were all included in ONUMOZ's
peacekeeping mandate, there were other problems that ONUMOZ did not even
try to take on and, in retrospect, probably should have. Namely, there was no
overhaul of the police, and little judiciary reform. The resulting rise in crime,
corruption, and state weakness continue to hinder Mozambique's economic,
social, and political development. Nevertheless, Mozambique is unquestion-
ably on the path toward recovery after thirty years of war.

Why was the mission so successful? ONUMOZ began in a state of organizational dysfunction as it struggled with the parties and with the UN bureaucracy
for nine months before becoming operational. During this time, and indeed
throughout the duration of the mission, the major powers generally supported
UN efforts, fearing a repeat of the recent disaster in Angola. This does not mean,
however, that the permanent five members of the Security Council paid much
attention to Mozambique. The Security Council had a reactive profile toward
the situation, rather than initiating directives from headquarters in New York.
The government of Italy was not a member of the Council but played a key

---

[165] Alden, 2003, p. 351.   [166] Manning, 2002, p. 213.

role in providing constant and consistent financial backing for both the peace process and the peacekeeping operation.

While international support did not change in any significant way over time, the mission changed, as did the interests of the warring parties. Over the course of ONUMOZ's two-year tenure in Mozambique, a gradual transformation took place both within the government and in Renamo. Renamo became socialized into the ways of international negotiations and into fulfilling its role as the political party in opposition. The government also came to understand the purposes and advantages of providing space for political opposition, after its previous experience only in one-party rule. Whereas at the outset neither Frelimo or Renamo seemed willing to give up its fight, ONUMOZ enabled both sides to transform the militarized dispute into non-violent political forms.

ONUMOZ was able to bring about this transformation, which was a primary condition for success, because it engaged in first-level organizational learning. The leaders of the mission were able to gather sufficient technical information about how to fulfill their mandate from a wide variety of sources, which in turn enabled them accurately to define problems and organizational responses. In terms of coordination, ONUMOZ made appropriate but difficult decisions about which tasks should be accomplished first, and how to allocate scarce resources for those tasks. The five major components of the mandate – military, police, political, humanitarian, and electoral – were adequately ranked and linked. The linkage required large-scale coordination between dozens of troop-contributing countries and numerous humanitarian aid organizations. While there were certainly internal arguments that inhibited the smooth coordination of humanitarian aid, most were eventually laid to rest.

There was also scant headquarters involvement in the day-to-day operations in the field, since there was a sense at UN headquarters in New York that Special Representative Ajello was in control of the field operation, and that decision-making power could be devolved to him and to ONUMOZ. This freedom allowed Ajello considerable advantage in altering his operations based on ground-level understandings of changes in the conflict. Although ONUMOZ political efforts centered on reconciling warring elites, its military, electoral, and policing divisions were spread wide throughout the country, reaching out to millions of Mozambicans, allowing the operation to have an integrative profile in the country. Finally, ONUMOZ was led by an authoritative and well-respected Special Representative. Ajello was able to unite the interests of the local diplomatic community in Maputo, as well as from officials in the UN Secretariat, his home government of Italy, and the Security Council. His ability to marshal and maintain external support for his operation enabled him to negotiate and devise unorthodox methods, namely the Renamo Trust Fund, to maintain Renamo support for the peace process. Ajello and his supporters incrementally altered the goals of the warring parties and managed crises as they arose, preventing conflicts from overwhelming ONUMOZ's capabilities or escalating into renewed warfare.

First-level learning contributed directly to the successful implementation of the mandate. Moreover, ONUMOZ's ability to fulfill its mandate has left long-term, positive institutional legacies in Mozambique. More than a decade after the first free and fair elections, Mozambique remains at peace, with very little chance of a resumption of war, and with two political parties contending for power through democratic means. These phenomena are a direct legacy of the international peace process and ONUMOZ's tenure in Mozambique.

7

Eastern Slavonia: institution-building
and the limited use of force

Introduction

The battle over Vukovar, the main city in the Eastern Slavonian region of Croatia, was arguably the most brutal and destructive confrontation during the wars in the former Yugoslavia. During the last few months of 1991, out of a prewar Eastern Slavonian population of 135,000, approximately 5,000 were killed, 10,000 wounded, and the city and surrounding region were completely destroyed, mainly by Yugoslav People's Army heavy artillery.[1] Because it was so thoroughly ruined, the city has become known as the "Stalingrad" of the former Yugoslavia.

Five years after the Vukovar battle, in 1996, the UN began a complex, multidimensional peacekeeping mission called the UN Transitional Administration in Eastern Slavonia, Baranja, and Western Sirium (UNTAES). The operation was successful at implementing its basic tasks. Moreover, it allowed Croats and Croatian Serbs time to come to terms with living in the same state, and to engage in a preliminary dialogue about reconciliation. The mission also served as a liaison through which Croatia and Serbia normalized diplomatic relations: "The course and completion of UNTAES neutralized the possibility of a major armed conflict, which could have escalated into a new inter-state (Croatian–Yugoslav) war."[2]

UNTAES was a military and civilian transitional administration.[3] The mission lasted almost two years, cost approximately $480 million, and fielded 5,000 troops, 455 civilian police, and 800 international civilian personnel. The operation functioned under the umbrella of possible NATO military support, if greater force had been necessary, but the mission did not have to fall back on such contingency plans. UNTAES held the monopoly over the use of legitimate force in the region, and it was known for being "willing to flex its military

---

[1] Cohen, 1993, p. 226; Woodward, 1995, p. 178; and Boothby, 1998, p. 9. Serbs and Croats suffered roughly similar numbers of lost lives. "UNTAES Mission Brief," 1997.

[2] Simunovic, 1999, p. 128; see also Boothby, 2004, pp. 38 and 49.

[3] While UNTAES was technically defined as a transitional administration, its tasks could be "described as supervision and oversight, but . . . not governing, which implies the direct control over the actions and affairs of the community." Boothby, 2004, p. 41.

muscle."[4] Moreover, as a transitional administration, it became the central organizer of most state activities, reforming and rebuilding basic institutions that would work to ensure the future multiethnic character of the region.

In this chapter, as in the other case studies, I address first the situational difficulty, arguing that many observers feared failure in this operation, given the difficulty of ending the war in Croatia. I then turn to the interests of the UN Security Council and argue that these interests were consensual, but only moderate in intensity. Finally, I contend that for the most part, the UNTAES operation functioned in a first-level organizational learning mode, which enabled it to implement its mandate successfully. I also maintain that the institutions set in place during the UNTAES administration of the territory have had lasting positive effects on the region, even though some problems remain.

Situational factors

Croatia was one of the wealthier republics of the former Yugoslavia, enjoying a long and beautiful coastline along the Adriatic Sea which, before the war, attracted millions of tourists from both Western and Eastern Europe. Eastern Slavonia, a small territory measuring about thirteen miles east–west and sixty-four miles north–south, is located at the northeastern tip of Croatia, bordering Serbia, Bosnia, and Hungary. Eastern Slavonia, also known today as the Danube region, boasts extremely fertile soil, the productive Djeletovci oil fields, and several important industrial complexes. Its main city, Vukovar, is located on the Danube River, and before 1991, enjoyed lovely Austro-Hungarian architecture and a multiethnic, highly intermarried population. Croatia had a prewar population of approximately 4.7 million people, some 12 percent (over one half million) of whom considered themselves to be ethnic Serbs.[5] The Croatian Serb population had been residing in Croatia for over 500 years, mainly along the rocky, hilly, interior Krajina and Western Slavonian regions that border Bosnia, as well as in Eastern Slavonia.

Eastern Slavonia is the only place where Serbia and Croatia share a border, and thus the most likely place where outright war between Croatia and Serbia could occur. And indeed, war did break out, between Croatia and the Yugoslav People's Army, in the summer of 1991, after Croatia held its first multi-party elections and declared its independence from Yugoslavia.[6]

---

[4] Doyle and Mueller, 1999.

[5] Other minorities include Czechs, Gypsies, Hungarians, Italians, Muslims, Ruthenians, Slovaks, and Ukrainians, comprising a total of about 10 percent of the population. See Minority Rights Group International, 2003, p. 5.

[6] The 1990s war in the former Yugoslavia began in Slovenia, the former Yugoslav republic located to the north of Croatia but lasted only about one week, after the European Union stepped in quickly to negotiate a peace accord. Thereafter violent conflict moved on to Croatia, Bosnia, Macedonia, and Serbia/Kosovo. Of the six former republics only Montenegro was spared major violence.

On June 25, 1991, Germany unilaterally recognized Croatian independence before Croatia had established minority rights guarantees for its ethnic Serb population, much to the dismay not only of the Croatian Serbs, but also to most of the countries in the European Community. Wanting to appear as if its foreign policy were unanimous, the European Community decided to follow the German lead and recognized Croatian (and Slovenian) independence.[7] War between the Yugoslav army and irregular Croatian troops had already begun, and it only worsened with international recognition, angering the Yugoslav government and the Croatian Serb minority (not to mention the Bosnian Serb minority), and emboldening the Croatian government to fight against the Yugoslav army.[8] At the outbreak of the war in Eastern Slavonia, in August 1991, Belgrade provided overt support, in the form of direct Yugoslav People's Army intervention, to the Croatian Serbs living in the region. This high level of support for breakaway Serb regions would not again be replicated to such an extent: "The conventional wisdom held that Belgrade had a far greater stake in Eastern Slavonia than elsewhere in Croatia."[9]

Vicious fighting broke out in Vukovar on August 25, 1991. Croatian Serb forces, backed by the heavy artillery of the Yugoslav People's Army, took the area, as well as the Krajina and Western Slavonia; these territories amounted to almost one-third of Croatia.[10] Approximately 180,000 ethnic Croats were driven, or fled, from the territories under Croatian Serb control, including some 70,000 from Eastern Slavonia.[11]

By the end of 1991, a stalemate had emerged on the Croatian battlefield. The Croatian Serbs were in control of the territories where there were large Croatian Serb populations and had little incentive to try to increase their territorial conquests, while the Croatian government, backed by a weak and nascent army, feared more losses on the battlefield. By early January 1992, both sides were willing to sign a peace deal brokered by UN envoy Cyrus Vance. The deal included a simple, unconditional cease-fire and provisions for UN troops to monitor the cease-fire. By February 1992, the UN Security Council authorized the deployment of the UN Protection Force (UNPROFOR) in Croatia of 12,000 UN peacekeeping troops. UNPROFOR was to be an "interim arrangement to create the conditions of peace and security required for the negotiation of an

---

[7] On these events, see Crawford, 1996.   [8] Stokes, 2005.

[9] Klein, 1997, pp. 1–2. The Yugoslav People's Army did provide support for the Krajina Serbs, but not to the same extent as for those in Eastern Slavonia.

[10] One of the most noted events during this fighting was the massacre at Ovcara, in November 1991. After the fall of Vukovar, over 200 patients from the local hospital were taken at gunpoint by Serb paramilitary members, killed, and buried in a mass grave. This event enraged Croatian and international opinion against the Croatian Serbs, and would become a rallying cry for widespread public revenge against Croatian Serbs.

[11] UNHCR, 1998.

overall settlement of the Yugoslav crisis."[12] The deal established three "UN Protection Areas" – in Eastern Slavonia, Western Slavonia, and Krajina – wherein UN peacekeeping troops would supervise the withdrawal of the Yugoslav People's Army, while also overseeing demilitarization, the return of refugees, and the monitoring of human rights.

UNPROFOR was largely ineffective at fulfilling its mandate. While it did successfully monitor the withdrawal of Yugoslav People's Army forces from Croatia, it was unable to accomplish its other tasks. Sporadic fighting between the two sides continued throughout the UNPROFOR presence, and UNPRO-FOR drew criticism from both sides. By March 1994 another cease-fire agreement was brokered between the Croatian government and the local Serb authorities, and in March 1995, under threats by Croatian President Franjo Tudjman not to ratify the extension of UNPROFOR's mandate, UNPROFOR was "restructured." The follow-on operation, the UN Confidence Restoration Operation for Croatia (UNCRO), was downsized to about 6,500 UN peacekeeping troops who had the mandate to monitor the cease-fire in Croatia as well as the Croatian–Bosnian border.[13]

UNPROFOR and UNCRO were not backed by international consensus and did not have the political means to negotiate a final peace deal. Their presence in effect isolated the Croatian Serbs while enabling the Croatian government to build and train its army in preparation to retake the occupied territory (against the provisions of an international arms embargo).[14]

In May and August 1995, the Croatian Army overran Western Slavonia and the Krajina, respectively, in operations "Flash" and "Storm," resulting in the largest single incidents of ethnic cleansing in the former Yugoslavia up until that time: over 200,000 Croatian Serbs fled, approximately 60,000 to Eastern Slavonia.[15] The UN peacekeepers were unequipped militarily, and they did not have the political mandate, to try to halt the ethnic cleansing. By September 1995, the only remaining territory under question in Croatia was Eastern Slavonia, which "appeared to be the next objective of the triumphant Croatian Army."[16]

The threat of a third Croatian offensive to take Eastern Slavonia "helped to pave the way for a negotiated settlement."[17] After the two earlier offensives, strong international opposition emerged in resistance to a military takeover in Eastern Slavonia, in light of the greater potential for escalation to interstate war between Serbia and Croatia. Outside observers were also dismayed at the

---

[12] S/RES/743, 21 February 1992. When UNPROFOR expanded to Bosnia, its troops would come to number almost 40,000.
[13] UNPROFOR was then divided into three regional peacekeeping operations: UNCRO in Croatia, UNPROFOR in Bosnia, and UNPREDEP in Macedonia.
[14] Burg and Shoup, 1999, p. 91.
[15] UNHCR 1998; and Boothby, 1998, p. 11. In all, between 300,000 and 350,000 Croatian Serbs left Croatia. See Human Rights Watch, 2005.
[16] Lessons Learned Unit, 1998, para. 7, p. 5.   [17] Klein, 1997, p. 2.

ethnic cleansing of the Serbs, and they sought to halt the expulsions, even though Serbs in the countries of the former Yugoslavia had beforehand been viewed as the aggressors, and not a group in need of international protection.[18] Thus, international pressure mounted to find a peaceful solution to the standoff in Eastern Slavonia.

Meanwhile, the exodus of Croatian Serbs from most of the occupied areas also lessened internal pressure from within Croatia for an immediate, violent conclusion to the confrontation. The remaining Croatian Serbs were essentially forced into bargaining, rather than fighting, due not only to the new strength of the Croatian Army, but also because the Croatian Serbs had little support from their "brethren" in Serbia or Bosnia. From August through September 1995, NATO operation "Deliberate Force" crippled the Bosnian Serbs' fighting forces, which had been all but cut off from Belgrade. It was uncertain whether Belgrade might come again to the defense of the Serbs in Eastern Slavonia, but given the region's strategic location, its high Serb population, and natural resources, while Croatian Serbs doubted such an eventuality, international observers felt that this was still a possibility.[19]

In the wake of the extremely destructive fighting in 1991, and the two major Croat offenses in 1995, Eastern Slavonia was in dire straits in the autumn of 1995. The population was estimated at 150,000, 85 percent Serb (including tens of thousands of Serb refugees from other parts of Croatia and Bosnia) and about 8 percent Croat.[20] The economy was devastated, with most of the population unemployed and barely eking out an existence through agricultural activities. The economic degradation was compounded by a severely damaged basic infrastructure. Moreover, almost all males over the age of eighteen were conscripted into the Army of the Serbian Krajina Republic. Those who were not conscripted often joined one of the three menacing and dissolute paramilitary groups – the Serbian "Tigers," "Scorpions," or "Jumping Snakes."

Negotiations

After the two major attacks on Serb-held positions in Croatia, and the subsequent expulsion of the Serb minority, international observers in general and the United States in particular did not want to risk a third offensive that might spark an all-out war between Croatia and Serbia. In addition, "the international community did not wish to see a resumption of conflict in Eastern Slavonia just

[18] In the United States, for example, unofficial support for the rearming of Croatia gave way to official concern over ethnic cleansing of the Croatian Serbs.

[19] Holbrooke, 1998, pp. 238–39.

[20] Lessons Learned Unit, 1998, para. 34, p. 13. Serbs took over houses belonging to Croats while Croats waited in refugee camps outside the UN-controlled zone. The Croats remaining in Eastern Slavonia at this time were usually elderly or married to Croatian Serbs from the region.

at the time when the Dayton Peace Agreement was able to bring war to an end in Bosnia."[21] Viewed in this larger context, there was considerable momentum on all levels to reach a peace agreement. It is necessary to note, however, that foreign countries, and especially the United States, viewed Eastern Slavonia and its problems as merely peripheral to the more important peace process in Bosnia.

The United States was clearly the main international power arbitrating the end of the conflict in Croatia and in Bosnia. The UN and the Contact Group – including France, Germany, Russia, the United Kingdom, and the United States (and later Italy) – were kept informed about negotiations on Eastern Slavonia and the larger Dayton agreement, but aside from the United States, they were not directly involved in the talks, much to their dismay. Holbrooke explained that he found it more complicated to keep the Europeans, as well as the UN, directly involved in the discussions, and therefore all but excluded them during the Bosnia negotiations.[22]

The official negotiators for Eastern Slavonia were Peter Galbraith, US Ambassador to Croatia, and Thorvald Stoltenberg, UN Representative to the International Conference on the Former Yugoslavia. However, in actuality, the major breakthrough on the negotiations occurred in Dayton, Ohio, between Tudjman, representing the Croatian government, and Milosevic, representing the Croatian Serb minority.

Tudjman insisted that the Eastern Slavonia negotiations be resolved at Dayton, before the talks could turn to Bosnia. He wanted to be remembered as the father of his country, which required regaining Eastern Slavonia. While the negotiators were in Dayton, Croatian forces moved closer to Eastern Slavonia on November 9, 1995, threatening forcible takeover if the negotiations did not proceed quickly and in the Croats' favor. The Croatian government, then as now, was torn between its strong desire to be accepted by the west and its anti-liberal aspiration to expel its Croatian Serb minority. According to Richard Holbrooke, Tudjman had three main preferences in November 1995: first, to regain Eastern Slavonia, so that he could be viewed as the father of united Croatia; second, to work to make Croatia ethnically pure; and third, to maintain as much control as possible over the Croat-dominated parts of Bosnia.[23]

Milosevic, on the other hand, had less of a stake in Eastern Slavonia. Although the international observers and Croats feared the possibility of another Yugoslav People's Army offensive in this Serb-dominated, oil-rich border region, according to several observers, Milosevic's main concern was not for the oil or the local Serbs, but to stem the tide of Croatian and Bosnian Serb refugees flooding into Serbia.

---

[21] Boothby, 1998, p. 11.   [22] Holbrooke, 1998, pp. 202, 265.
[23] Holbrooke, 1998, p. 170.

Tudjman and the US State Department negotiators thought that Eastern Slavonia should be negotiated as part of Dayton, and that the transition be overseen by NATO peacekeepers. However, the US Pentagon disagreed, arguing that the US Congress would never approve of funding US troops to be positioned in both Bosnia and Croatia.[24] Moreover, France and the United Kingdom were both reluctant to send troops to Croatia, having had troops stationed in Bosnia already for four years. The UN, instead of NATO, would be called on to oversee the peacekeeping operation.

What came to be known as the "Basic Agreement" had been drafted originally by Galbraith and Stoltenberg, shortened, clarified, and refined at Dayton, and then sent back to Croatia to be signed by the local authorities. This agreement outlined a process by which Eastern Slavonia would be reintegrated into the Croatian state. The length of the UN transitional administration was a major obstacle between the two sides: Tudjman insisted on a one-year mandate, while Milosevic argued on behalf of a three-year term. In the end, a one-year mandate was agreed with the possibility of a twelve-month extension (which was eventually granted).[25] Holbrooke summarizes the outcome:

> For Milosevic, the key to the agreement was that it would be signed far from Dayton by a local Serb leader. While Milosevic wanted credit in Dayton for the breakthrough, he did not want his fingerprints visible in the region. For Tudjman, the results were spectacular: he would get Eastern Slavonia back without a war. For the United States, it meant that we had successfully brought a part of Croatia back to its rightful owner without another war, one that had seemed inevitable only weeks earlier. In so doing, we had also settled an issue that was an absolute prerequisite to the broader peace.[26]

Mandate

Milan Milanovic, head of the Serb negotiating delegation, and Hrvoje Sarinic, head of the Croatian government delegation, signed the Basic Agreement on November 12, 1995, in Erdut, a small Croatian town on the Danube River in Eastern Slavonia.[27] The Basic Agreement was extremely brief – fourteen paragraphs in all – and outlined steps whereby both sides requested the assistance of a UN Transitional Administration that would oversee the peaceful

---

[24] Holbrooke, 1998, p. 221.
[25] Derek Boothby, the UN's Deputy Transitional Administrator in Eastern Slavonia, noted that one year was not enough time for the UN to oversee institutional transformations to guarantee a place for the local Serbs. Derek Boothby, Interview with the author by telephone, April 7, 2001.
[26] Holbrooke, 1998, p. 267.
[27] Galbraith and Stoltenberg also signed the agreement as witnesses.

reintegration of Eastern Slavonia into Croatia.[28] The agreement made provisions for the demilitarization of the region, return of refugees, the establishment of an interim and eventually a permanent police force, oversight of human rights guarantees, restoration of property rights, and elections.[29]

In response to this agreement, UN Secretary-General Boutros Boutros-Ghali issued a two-option proposal to the UN Security Council.[30] His first and preferred option was to have the UN authorize a peacekeeping force that would be constructed by a coalition of member states (in other words, a NATO force), rather than a UN force. Boutros-Ghali did *not* want the UN to have primary responsibility for overseeing the transition to peace in Eastern Slavonia. There was a sense at UN headquarters that the UN was being set up for another fall, similar to what had happened only recently in Srebrenica in Bosnia, and in Croatia with UNCRO. If the UN peacekeepers were given a confusing mandate with few resources to fulfill it, and fighting was to break out again in Croatia, the UN once more would take the blame, not NATO or the western powers. Boutros-Ghali stated explicitly in his report:

> The concept of deterrence by mere presence, as attempted in the "safe areas" in Bosnia and Herzegovina, would be no likelier to succeed on this occasion. Should there be a mismatch between the international force's mandate and its resources, there would be a risk of failure, of international casualties, and of undermined credibility for those who had put the force in the field.[31]

Therefore, Boutros-Ghali was very specific when outlining his proposal for a second option. If the UN were to take on the task of multidimensional peacekeeping in Eastern Slavonia, the force should be large, including 9,300 heavily armed combat and 2,000 logistics troops, adequately funded, and granted a clear mandate to use force if necessary. He also recommended that the operation be led by a single "UN Transitional Administrator," who would report to the Secretary-General, and who would have ultimate authority over both the military and civilian components of the operation.

There was little support among the members of the Security Council and NATO member states to field a NATO peacekeeping operation in Eastern Slavonia, and therefore the major powers favored the second option. Tudjman had expressed his preference to have an American lead the operation. The UN Secretariat and the United States also felt that this would be appropriate. A career

---

[28] Note that, in contrast, the Dayton agreement is hundreds of pages in length and extremely detailed in terms of the specifics of implementation, but almost all of the basic tasks are similar.

[29] The Security Council ratified UN compliance with the requests made in the Basic Agreement in S/RES/1025, 30 November 1995, and requested that the Secretary-General draft an implementation report.

[30] See S/1028, 13 December 1995.   [31] S/1028, 13 December 1995.

diplomat and Major-General in the Air Force Reserves, Jacques Paul Klein, was identified as the potential UN Transitional Administrator.

In November and December 1995, Klein conducted research on Eastern Slavonia and drafted a report detailing what he thought would be necessary in order to guarantee the success of the operation.[32] Klein's report covered his assessment of the preferences of the warring sides, focusing specifically on the least represented group during the peace negotiations, the local Croatian Serbs. Klein "found the local Serbs traumatized by their defeat in Krajina and resigned to a future within a Croatian state" and recommended that "the key was for the UN to show residents that the situation was safe and that Serb dignity would be respected" in order for the Serbs to demilitarize voluntarily and peacefully.[33] He recommended fielding a large peacekeeping force that would "be better able to impose its will on the ground, prevent incidents and infiltrations, and reassure each side that the international community would hold the other to the agreement."[34]

Klein's report received support from all members of the Security Council, especially the United States and Russia. On January 15 1996, the Security Council unanimously authorized the UNTAES operation under UN Charter Chapter VII. The Transitional Administrator would "have overall authority over the civilian and military components," and be responsible for "governing" the territory during the transition.[35] The major powers and potential troop contributors did not want to support the size of the force that the Secretary-General had suggested, and thus the military component was authorized at only 5,000 troops. While few in number, the troops were to be heavily armed, bolstered by the promise of NATO close air support if necessary, and directed to use force in self-defense or to ensure troop freedom of movement.[36]

The military division was to "supervise and facilitate the demilitarization . . . according to the schedule and procedures to be established by UNTAES; monitor the voluntary and safe return of refugees; contribute, by its presence, to the maintenance of peace and security in the region"; and assist, as necessary, with the implementation of the Basic Agreement.[37]

The duties of the civilian component were more extensive. Its tasks included establishing a temporary police force that would train locals, monitoring the prison system, assisting with reforming or establishing various public

---

[32] See Letter to the Secretary-General from Jacques Paul Klein, January 5, 1996.

[33] Letter to the Secretary-General from Jacques Paul Klein, January 5, 1996, pp. 1 and 3.

[34] Letter to the Secretary-General from Jacques Paul Klein, January 5, 1996, p. 3.

[35] S/RES/1037, 15 January 1996. Boothby (2004) argues that the UN was never in fact "governing" the territory but rather overseeing the transition, since there were Serb and Croat administrative structures in place, but in need of reform.

[36] This Chapter VII mandate was nicknamed a "Chinese Chapter VII," since China insisted that the UN's use of force be quite limited.

[37] S/RES/1037, 15 January 1996.

institutions and services, facilitating the return of refugees, organizing elections, assisting with economic development, monitoring respect for human
rights, monitoring de-mining, and having an "active public affairs element."[38]

The tasks were clearly delineated, but not overly specific, and while some
have claimed that the UN mandate "gave unprecedented executive authority
to the Transitional Administrator," others, including this author, argue that
the authority did not, in practice, extend much beyond that of a Special Representative in a typical UN multidimensional peacekeeping operation.[39] But
unlike some other multidimensional operations, the brevity of the Basic Agreement and the subsequent brief but clear mandate from the Security Council
meant that the UN's authority was centralized in the figure of the Transitional Administrator, while at the same time allowing much room for flexibility, and more specific interpretation of the mandate, once the mission became
operational.

Security Council interests

The UN Security Council was by and large not interested in solving all of the
problems of Eastern Slavonia, but rather in resolving the conflict in such a
manner that it would not disrupt the more important peace process in Bosnia.
The Security Council's attention had been focused on Bosnia for three years,
with little success to show for it, and there was some degree of fatigue among
the members in dealing with the former Yugoslavia. In order to carry out the
task-intensive mandate in Eastern Slavonia, the Security Council provided only
about half of what had been requested in terms of numbers of military troops
and hardware.

The mission's main supporter on the Council was the United States, even
though the United States was reluctant to provide the funding to the mission
requested by the Secretary-General. While there was some concern that in
Security Council debates Russia might press for greater concessions to the
Serbs, in the end "the Russian Ambassador told the Serbs that there was 'no
light' between their view and the west's view on the issue of Eastern Slavonia"
(unlike in Bosnia, where Council opinions were divided).[40] Russia, along with
Belgium, provided the main troops for the operation. The other permanent
members of the Council were generally supportive of the mission, including
China, in light of the limited Chapter VII mandate.

---

[38] S/RES/1037, 15 January 1996. After the end of UNTAES, a small contingent of 180 UN
civilian police would stay on for nine months, and OSCE would take over by October 15, 1998, with a mandate to deploy 250 international monitors for an additional
year.
[39] See Doyle and Mueller, 1999; and Boothby, 2004.
[40] Jacques Klein, interview with the author, Sarajevo, June 8, 1998.

Consensus

In the UN Security Council there was general consensus over interests concerning Eastern Slavonia. The focus of the Security Council debates was on how best to end the conflict without great costs to the troop contributors, and without disturbing the Bosnian peace process. The debates were not acrimonious. There was a basic consensus that Eastern Slavonia should remain a part of Croatia, and that its ethnic minority Serb population should be protected and reintegrated into Croatian government and society. All votes were unanimous, and positions did not change over the course of implementation.

Intensity

Eastern Slavonia was never one of the more important items on the Security Council's agenda, paling in comparison to the Bosnia crisis. From 1995 to 1997, many resolutions addressed the territories of the former Yugoslavia, but few were concerned with Eastern Slavonia.[41] By 1998, the focus of the Council had shifted decisively to Africa, with almost half of all resolutions concerning conflicts on the continent. But already in 1995, there were many resolutions regarding the conflicts in Western Sahara, Liberia, the Great Lakes, and Angola. Issues relating to sanctions against Iraq also frequently appeared on the agenda.

As mentioned above, the Security Council allowed for only about half of the troops, and far less funding, than the Secretariat had requested. The Council did, however, make provisions for adequately equipping the troops and providing them with a robust enough mandate to use their weapons. In terms of interest intensity, Security Council interests could generally be characterized as moderately intense: there was adequate funding for the operation, but the Council did not often address the issues of this conflict.[42]

Organizational change and mandate implementation

The UNTAES mission, over the course of twenty months, managed to implement an astonishing array of military and civilian tasks. Over time there was a gradual shift in organizational focus from military to civilian tasks as the

[41] In 1995, of 66 total Security Council resolutions, 1 concerned Eastern Slavonia whereas 24 related to other parts of the former Yugoslavia; in 1996, of 57 resolutions, 3 were about Eastern Slavonia (9 concerned other operations in the former Yugoslavia). In 1997, of 47 Council resolutions, 2 of 13 total resolutions on the former Yugoslavia regarded Eastern Slavonia, and in 1998, of 73 resolutions, 2 concerned Croatia (there were 10 concerning other parts of the former Yugoslavia).

[42] Note also that the ground operation's technical mastery of the situation meant that reports from the field were almost never questioned or open to political debates at UN headquarters, whether in the Secretariat or in the Security Council.

military situation stabilized, and fears on the part of the local Serb population became increasingly rooted in discrimination of an institutional nature.

The civilian and military divisions were established in Croatia by the end of March 1996, approximately three months after ratification of the Security Council's mandate. But the establishment was not always smooth, nor did it always proceed in logical order. For example, funding for UNTAES that had been allocated in January at UN headquarters did not become available in Eastern Slavonia until July.[43] Moreover, various elements of the civilian administration – the Chief Administrative Officer, the Chief Finance Officer, and the staff of the civil-military Integrated Support Services – did not arrive in the field until several months *after* the military divisions had been deployed, even though these units were supposed to provide support for the military components.[44] Part of the reason why the military division was able to set up so quickly was that many of its core troops were already deployed in other parts of Croatia as part of UNCRO, and were simply redeployed to Eastern Slavonia. While US Major-General Jacques Klein, the Transitional Administrator, was frustrated by what he perceived as slow operational establishment, in comparison to other UN multidimensional operations, UNTAES became operational within a relatively short period of time.

In terms of Klein's leadership style, he was in general a very proactive and forceful Transitional Administrator. Given Klein's powerful personality, strong mandate from the Security Council, and the backing of the American government, Klein was able to move the operation forward in ways that very few other leaders could. He wanted to signal early on that UNTAES was not simply a reincarnation of the weak UNCRO operation, and he did this by maintaining a high-profile public image, actively displaying the impressive military hardware granted to the peacekeepers, and talking forcefully with the leaders of both sides. Members of the UNTAES mission have described how Klein would "talk tough" with Milosevic and Tudjman in a manner that few other people could, and that both leaders, rather than objecting either to his style or to the content of his message, would grudgingly agree to his demands.

Part of the reason for the success of the mission, according to many who took part in it, was Klein's approach to the tasks at hand. He viewed the mandate as a "baseline," or minimal set of tasks that the mission should accomplish, rather than as a "ceiling," or a set of ideal goals; he also did not often report to UN headquarters about his plans, much to the dismay of UN officials in New York.[45] Instead, Klein was in frequent contact with the leaders in the region and with the local population. He would shuttle back and forth between Zagreb and

---

[43] Lessons Learned Unit, 1998, p. 7, para. 16.

[44] Lessons Learned Unit, 1998, p. 8, para. 16.

[45] Note that the Security Council resolution authorizing UNTAES indicated that the Secretary-General should report back to the Council on a monthly basis. See S/RES/1037, 15 January 1996, para. 4. But the mission submitted only eight reports during its two years of operation.

Belgrade regularly, in order to obtain agreement from both sides for various initiatives. In terms of contact with the locals, Klein sought to get his message out by going to different churches every Sunday, and then eating salami and drinking *rakija* (plum brandy) with people afterwards to find out how they were doing, what they thought of the UN, what they wanted from the UN, and how they thought this could be realized. He also explained what the UN was trying to accomplish in the region.[46]

In July 1997, Klein was asked to join the leadership of the Office of the High Representative in Sarajevo, the main body overseeing the international operations in Bosnia. Another high-ranking American diplomat, William G. Walker, who was at the time vice-president of the National Defense College, replaced Klein. Walker, who took over the position of UNTAES Transitional Administrator in August 1997 until the end of the operation in January 1998, also enjoyed support from Washington. Walker assumed a "less fiery" leadership style, which many observers characterized as appropriate, given that the most difficult military and civilian tasks had been accomplished, or at least significant steps toward their fulfillment had been set in motion, by the time he came into office.

In terms of the operation's relations with the warring sides, the Croatian government was often unwilling to back UNTAES in the implementation of many of the civilian tasks proposed, or to assist with the peaceful integration of the Serb population into Croatian government and civic life. After six years of war between the two sides, the Croatian government and many in the Croat population were uninterested in guaranteeing the rights of Croatian Serbs. The Croatian government in general wanted the UN operation to end quickly, after early elections, so that the government could reclaim the territories and resettle displaced ethnic Croats back into Eastern Slavonia. On the other side, the Croatian Serbs of Eastern Slavonia were in a difficult position. They were unwanted by Zagreb, and Belgrade was not necessarily going to support them. The only powerful actor that was looking after their rights and helping to construct institutions that would guarantee their future welfare in Croatia was the UN, even though the local Serb leadership at times had trouble recognizing this. The local Serbs had, for six years, set up their own civil administration in their occupied territories in Croatia, called the "Republic of Serbian Krajina." They had established their own governmental systems from health to schools to municipal councils, and it would prove difficult, but not impossible, to integrate these structures into the Croatian government.

Military

The military division was charged with supervising and facilitating the demilitarization of Eastern Slavonia, contributing, "by its presence, to the maintenance

---

[46] Klein, interview with the author, Sarajevo, June 8, 1998.

of peace and security in the area," and promoting "an atmosphere of confidence."[47] The UNTAES military division would also enjoy NATO "close air support" and assistance with the operation's immediate withdrawal, if needed.[48] These somewhat vaguely defined tasks were interpreted as a baseline for action, rather than as maximal goals. In the end, the division accomplished the following tasks: it oversaw the demilitarization of the area, worked toward ex-combat reintegration, expelled a paramilitary organization from the region by force, gathered intelligence information in order to carry out its duties, engaged in de-mining, conducted a weapons buy-back program, and instituted and monitored a "soft border" regime. Each of these activities is addressed below, after a description of the capabilities and general actions of the division.

The military division monopolized the legitimate use of force in the area. With 5,000 troops, abundant heavy arms, and the promise of NATO air power if needed, commander Jozef Schoups and later Willy Hanset, both Belgian Major-Generals, headed the division. The division boasted mechanized infantry battalions from Belgium, Russia, Pakistan, and Jordan; each had its own area of operation. A Polish commando unit backed the battalions while reconnaissance was provided by Argentine troops. In terms of equipment, the division had at its disposal 70 tanks, over 200 armed personnel carriers, a squadron of Ukrainian attack helicopters, and self-propelled heavy artillery. Coming on the heels of the recent NATO airstrikes in operation "Deliberate Force" in Bosnia, the threat of NATO airstrikes was very credible, providing additional military backing for the operation.

The military division's headquarters were co-housed with all of the other UNTAES units, in a field in the back of the Yugoslav People's Army headquarters in Vukovar in April 1996, and the force was fully deployed by May.[49] The troops engaged actively with the local population (unlike the peacekeepers in neighboring Bosnia). The battalions were housed in a central location and generally went out on foot patrol, but also in UN vehicles, with the intent of keeping a high, but not aggressive, UN profile. The troops would patrol, guns pointing up, with orders not to intimidate or harm the local population: "We wanted to give the impression of a strict, no-nonsense peacekeeping force that would provide security to the local Serb population after their forces disarmed."[50] While the regular peacekeeping troops were armed, the more senior UN military observers were not. The 100 military observers were housed and distributed widely around the region. Their primary function was to engage directly with the population, become acquainted with the locals, come to understand which

---

[47] S/RES/1037, 15 January 1996, paras. 10a, 10c, 12.
[48] S/RES/1037, 15 January 1996, para. 14.
[49] The Croatian government had wanted the military division to be housed in Osijek, which was under Croatian government control, but this would have severely jeopardized the division's ability to gain the confidence of the Serb troops and population.
[50] Boothby, interview with the author, April 7, 2001.

individuals or groups might make the transition process difficult, and try to de-escalate conflicts.

Demilitarization was completed on schedule by June 20, 1996, approximately thirty days after the full deployment of the UN peacekeeping troops. The process was generally very smooth, in that the Serb troops had agreed to demobilize and their leaders had decided to abide by the agreement. The Army of the Republic of Serbian Krajina included seven brigades, 15,000 men, and a military police reinforcement brigade of 1,500 men.[51] There were also three paramilitary organizations: the Tigers (with 300–1,000 members), the Jumping Snakes (50–60), and the Scorpions (200–250).[52] While the local forces gave up their heavy weapons and returned to civilian life, the paramilitary organizations had to be run out of the territory, into Serbia proper.

The expulsion of the Scorpions was the most difficult, since they had become entrenched in the Djeletovci oil fields. The band was quickly siphoning off oil in order to buy more weapons at the same time that the UN was trying to disarm. UNTAES senior staff had instructed the leaders of the paramilitary group to leave the region by the morning of May 14, 1996. When that morning came, and there was no apparent movement on the part of the paramilitary troops, the UN peacekeepers first tried diplomatic tactics. Klein then asked Milosevic to intervene. When these efforts failed, the leadership of UNTAES decided to display force. Without much consulting of New York headquarters, Klein ordered the Jordanian battalion to descend on the region in full force, in tanks and armed personnel carriers.[53] Overhead, Ukrainian attack helicopters menaced the Scorpion headquarters. By that afternoon, the Scorpions evacuated to Serbia, but this was not the end of their stand. Over the following several weeks, at night, members of their organization would infiltrate the border and fire on the UNTAES peacekeeping troops. Klein gave the instructions to fire back at the attackers, always using a heavier caliber weapon. While the nightly exchanges escalated for a time, by the end of about three weeks the challenges faded away. The Scorpions were simply outgunned. In August 1996, the oil fields were reopened under INA, the Croatian oil company.

In terms of intelligence, while there was no formalized mechanism by which the operation could gather information, it did devise several other methods. First, because the operation was functioning with the consent of the Croatian government, the government would on occasion provide UNTAES with sensitive information, including confidential lists of weapons caches. Second, the military battalions, military observers, and civilian components collected information in the field, but not in a fully systematic fashion. And finally, UNTAES

---

[51] "UNTAES Mission Brief," p. 3.   [52] "UNTAES Mission Brief," p. 3.

[53] Kofi Annan, at the time the Under Secretary-General for Peacekeeping, was away, so Klein informed Marrack Goulding, who informed the important parties at UN headquarters, but not quickly enough to call the intervention off.

gathered intelligence information through its links with NATO. The military division created a separate Dutch–Belgian cell (both countries are NATO member states) to communicate with NATO's Implementation Force in Bosnia and with NATO headquarters in Brussels. There was also a permanent NATO liaison officer stationed within UNTAES who would attend the daily coordination meetings. This meant that NATO was always informed of important UNTAES activities. In interviews, Klein nevertheless has expressed regret about not having had an intelligence unit. He disliked not having any biographical data on the locals with whom he was working. He explained, "We had nothing. It was terrible . . . you would have thought that governments would be interested in protecting the security of their troops by allowing the UN to have intelligence. But nation states do not want the UN to have intelligence capabilities."[54]

The military division came to be in charge of several other activities, including small arms collection, de-mining, and devising a "soft border" regime between Serbia and Croatia. First, after the troops had been disbanded, the territory was still rife with small arms. The military and civil affairs divisions quickly came to realize that even though they did not have the funding or the specific mandate for small arms collection, this would have to occur in order to secure a safe environment. The mission thus devised a "weapons buy-back program" from October 1996 through August 1997, under which "approximately 10,000 rifles, 7,000 anti-tank rocket launchers, 15,000 grenades, and almost two million rounds of ammunition were removed from civilian hands."[55] The program was funded in large part by the Croatian government but conducted by UNTAES. Members of UNTAES established several sites where they would collect weapons, without asking about their origin, and would return the equivalent value of the weapon in cash to the person turning in the weapon. Many felt that this program contributed significantly to reducing the level of anxiety in the region, and that it greatly eased the potential for future violence.

Second, in terms of de-mining, when UNTAES arrived in the Danube region, it was estimated that there were approximately 800,000 land mines and 100,000 unexploded munitions scattered throughout the territory. Shortly after deployment, UNTAES created a Mine Action Awareness Center in conjunction with UNHCR, the World Bank, and the government of Croatia. The mission employed local Croat and Serb ex-combatants, many of whom had laid the mines themselves, in order to establish a database of where the mines were located. Mine-clearing companies, often made up of Croat and Serb engineers, were then sent into the field for de-mining. The Mine Action Awareness Center also sponsored important mine education programs, in conjunction with UNICEF, reaching tens of thousands of children in the region. While it was estimated that the process of de-mining would take some ten years to

---

[54] Klein, interview with the author, Sarajevo, June 8, 1998.   [55] Boothby, 1998, p. 9.

complete, de-mining was already well underway by the end of the UNTAES mandate.[56]

Finally, the border between Eastern Slavonia and Serbia had been highly porous for the six years when the government of the Republic of Serbian Krajina was in force. The Basic Agreement and the main Security Council resolution authorizing UNTAES did not take into account difficulties surrounding this issue: there were virtually no customs norms, no plan had been set in place for cross-border traffic – which was dominated by "mafia" groups – and Yugoslav and Croatian forces remained stationed on both sides of the Danube. As the "Lessons Learned" report explains:

> There was skepticism at the highest UNTAES management level on the need for a dedicated border-monitoring unit. Because of this skepticism prior to deployment, there had been no real planning to monitor the border, and initially no organizational structure existed, no concept of operations envisioned, no recruitment conducted and no budgetary plans evolved for administration, logistics or equipment support.[57]

This situation changed quickly, however, once the problems of few border controls became evident. Within several months of UNTAES' deployment, a border-monitoring unit was established, and with it came a sharp rise in customs revenue collection, and a drastic decline in illegal goods crossing the border. The UNTAES border-monitoring unit eventually established a "Transitional Customs Service" which integrated elements of the local Serb and Croatian government customs services, paving the way for reform of the customs services. In July 1997, the Security Council recognized the difficulties of not having a formal border agreement between Yugoslavia and Croatia. After several months of negotiations, a "soft border regime" agreement was signed by both sides and finally implemented in December 1997.[58]

To summarize, the UNTAES military division was able to implement its mandate, use limited force, and achieve even more tasks than specified in the mandate, not because of abundant funding, but because it had the consent of the parties and functioned as a learning organization in the field. The leadership was proactive and forceful. The military division devised ways to gather adequate information, defined problems, and fashioned organizational responses to the problems. It coordinated well among its own troops, with other UNTAES components, and with other UN organizations in the field; it also engaged directly with the population, rather than alienating itself from the locals. As the Lessons Learned report on UNTAES boasts: "The mission's successful handling of the

---

[56] Lessons Learned Unit, 1998, pp. 16–17, paras. 45–49.

[57] Lessons Learned Unit, 1998, p. 41, para. 140.

[58] S/59, 22 January 1998, para. 23. An informal agreement on the demilitarization of both sides of the border was put into effect, although the UN was unable to persuade both sides to sign a formal agreement.

demilitarization and disarmament programmes transformed Eastern Slavonia from an armed camp organized for war into a largely peaceful region."[59]

Civilian administration

The civilian administration's mandate included the somewhat under-specified tasks of reintegrating public institutions and assisting with economic development.[60] Almost 800 international civil servants and some 1,700 locals were employed by the civilian administration. The division interpreted its mandate as broadly as possible, and in the end it oversaw the establishment or reform of a surprisingly wide array of institutions. In all, the division set up twenty-four "Joint Implementation Committees" wherein Serb and Croat leaders, along with UNTAES officials, would work out detailed institutional reform programs. The division also secured forty-three separate public agreements, in addition to the Basic Agreement, "for which the Government of Croatia has made itself internationally accountable," and which provided a "comprehensive political and institutional framework of guarantees [so that] the people of the region [might] exercise freely their rights and obligations as equal citizens of Croatia."[61]

Before this operation, there had been no other peacekeeping operation with such a widespread and detailed attempt at institutional reform. As one analyst argues, the Joint Implementation Committees "sought to bring the two sides together to negotiate and agree on the process of transition so as to ensure it would be as inclusive, orderly, and efficient as possible. In many ways the Joint Implementation Committee processes for institutional reform set new precedents and gained important ground for a minority and former 'enemy population' facing reabsorption into a state."[62] Demonstrating how each of these programs came about could be the subject of an entire separate study, and the details can therefore not be covered fully in this chapter. It is, however, important at a minimum to review some of the civilian administration's accomplishments.

First, over one thousand Croatian Serbs in Eastern Slavonia were reintegrated into numerous Croatian public institutions and enterprises, including telephone, postal, railways, water supply, flood control, and road maintenance

---

[59] Lessons Learned Unit, 1998, p. 15, para. 42.

[60] Other areas of responsibility included the establishment of a temporary police force, monitoring the prison system, facilitating the return of displaced persons and refugees, monitoring respect for human rights, assisting with de-mining, establishing a public affairs office, and elections oversight. These tasks were overseen by the various substantive subdivisions discussed in subsequent parts of this chapter.

[61] Lessons Learned Unit, 1998, p. 37, para. 125; and S/953, 4 December 1997, para. 7.

[62] Large, 1999, p. 571.

services, as well as the main Croatian oil company, INA.[63] Second, programs
to increase freedom of movement became increasingly popular, including UN-
sponsored visits, under which 89,000 people traveled between Serbia and Croatia by June 1997; the reintroduction of a bus service between all Croatian cities;
a weekly market that came to be frequented each Saturday by approximately
8,000 Croats and Croatian Serbs; a system of free movement for vehicles with
Croatian license plates; and the opening and repair of most major roads in the
region.[64]

Third, UNTAES established thirty-five document centers for Croatian Serbs
where, by December 1997, over 145,000 citizenship papers and 126,000 passports had been issued. Ten of the centers were also issuing health cards, pen-
sion cards, and other basic legal documents. Unfortunately, by the end of the
UNTAES mandate, some 900 people were still denied papers on the basis of
somewhat suspect "pending criminal charges," many of whom were male and
of fighting age during the conflict.[65]

Fourth, after months of public "persistent encouragement" on the part of
the Transitional Administrator (and the UN Security Council), the Croatian
government instituted a comprehensive program of national reconciliation,
including a multiethnic board that would oversee relevant activities on the
regional, municipal, and local levels. As a result, the previously virulent anti-
Serb media changed its tone, as did some prominent church and political
leaders.[66]

Fifth, ethnic evenhandedness in the standardization of national education
had been a highly contentious issue throughout most of UNTAES' tenure, but
by the end of UNTAES, textbooks describing a distorted history of the conflict
had been recalled, school signs were issued in both Cyrillic and Latin letters,
and many Serb teachers' education diplomas had been recognized. Disagreements persisted, however, over the content of textbooks and exams, school
registration, and the recognition of education diplomas.[67]

Sixth, in terms of pensions, while difficulties remained in recognizing Croatian Serb service from 1991 to 1996 (the time during which many Serb civil
servants were serving in the so-called government of the Republic of Serbian
Krajina), 13,000 partial or full pensions were being paid, by the end of UNTAES'
tenure, with 12 percent of applications denied. Two social welfare centers and

---

[63] S/953, 4 December 1997, para. 12; and S/705, 28 August 1996, para. 21. The oil company
had been taken over by the Yugoslav oil company but was transferred back to Croatia
under the conditions that most of the Croatian Serb employees would be able to retain
their positions.

[64] S/487, 23 June 1997, para. 13; and Lessons Learned Unit, 1998, p. 38, para. 130.

[65] S/487, 23 June 1997, para. 12; and S/953, 4 December 1997, para. 22.

[66] S/953, 4 December 1997, para. 8.   [67] S/953, 4 December 1997, para. 9.

two unemployment centers were in operation in the region by the time of the end of UNTAES.[68]

Seventh, other steps to integrate Serbs and Croats included the following: in terms of the national media, four Serb radio programs were continued, as was one Serb daily television news program; the Croatian National Health Service integrated the medical facilities in the region, full financing was obtained, and 300 previously unrecognized Serb health diplomas were recognized;[69] Croatian Serbs were granted a two-year deferment for military service, possibly extending to four years;[70] four Serb Assistant Ministers and two Serb Senior Advisors were sent abroad for international political training in tolerance and democratic systems, and all became very active in national politics by the end of the UNTAES mandate;[71] a Joint Council of Municipalities, including Croat and Serb representatives, began regular meetings and President Tudjman met with the Council, representing a significant step toward the normalization of national politics.[72] In addition, substantial progress was made toward the ful- fillment of the directive that 40 percent of the members of the judiciary in the region be of ethnic Serb origin.[73]

Finally, in terms of economic activities, UNTAES oversaw the transition of the monetary and financial systems on May 19, 1997. This included the intro- duction of the Croatian Kuna to all regions, the establishment of barter and trade links between the region and the rest of Croatia, and the nationwide establishment of Croatian commercial law, banks, and customs regulations. Members of UNTAES also assisted in developing the registration process for small businesses, and in securing guarantees for formerly socially owned enter- prises so that the government, under the guise of privatization, would not unilaterally terminate or sell Croatian Serb-owned enterprises.[74]

All of these detail-intensive programs were designed to provide institutional guarantees to the Croatian Serbs of Eastern Slavonia. The UNTAES civilian administration was able to see through the written promise and active imple- mentation of these reforms because it, like the military division, functioned as a learning organization in the field. The nine civilian affairs field offices were

---

[68] S/953, 4 December 1997, para. 17; and S/59, 22 January 1998, paras. 11 and 13.

[69] S/59, 22 January 1998, para. 8.

[70] S/953, 4 December 1997, para. 25. The Croatian government did at times call Serbs up for service, and UNTAES expressed "deep concern" over this practice in one of its final reports.

[71] S/59, 22 January 1998, para. 6   [72] S/59, 22 January 1998, para. 6.

[73] S/953, 4 December 1997, para. 23. Note that three of the five Serb lawyers in the region were admitted into the Croatian Bar Association by December 1997.

[74] S/59, 22 January 1998, para. 12. The UN also helped to arrange two international donors meetings where over $59 million was committed for the reconstruction of the area (the Croatian government estimated the need at approximately $1.2 billion). See S/487, 23 June 1997, paras. 19 and 18.

spread wide throughout the territory and accommodated approximately six staff in each. The staff's primary job was to "get to know the school teachers, lawyers, dentists, veterinarians, farmers, and help them with their problems."[75] The staff was generally characterized as very effective, efficient, and well experienced. Klein describes that he "fired many staff members" who were not of high caliber, and that he delegated significant authority to his highly qualified staff. His basic principle was "to hire good people and then let them do their jobs."[76] In terms of coordination, Klein was eager to cooperate with the other organizations on the ground as long as they generally deferred to him and his staff. Every morning, six days a week at 9:00 a.m. there would be meetings between all of the international agencies and major international NGOs, to harmonize plans, share information, divide labor, and set short- and long-term goals.[77] In general, the chain of command was very clear, and there was good inter-agency cooperation (unlike in Bosnia).[78] The UNTAES civil administration managed to maintain the consent of both sides by treating both equally and following through on UN guarantees as pledged in the peace accord and subsequent Security Council resolutions.

After Klein's departure, many of the final stages of implementation fell to Walker, and he and his staff appear to have handled the burden well. After numerous attempts to encourage the Croatian government to comply with certain written promises, Walker initiated a public campaign to ensure that the government follow through on its promises by calling on the media and the Security Council to issue public statements when he deemed necessary.

Police

The mandate for the UN civil police division was to create a Transitional Police Force, define the specifics of its structure and size, train its officers, monitor and train staff in the local prison, and oversee the transition from the Transitional Police Force to the permanent Croatian police force in Eastern Slavonia.[79] The Secretary-General estimated that 600 UN CIVPOL would be necessary to accomplish these tasks, since there would have to be CIVPOL on active duty every day, twenty-four hours per day. But from the beginning, the CIVPOL division of UNTAES encountered problems. It never received adequate funding, and the force came to a maximum strength of only 455 international officers,

---

[75] Boothby, interview with the author, April 7, 2001.

[76] Klein, interview with the author, Sarajevo, June 8, 1998.

[77] Author interviews with Mark Pedersen, Zagreb, May 27, 1998; Richard Wilcox, Sarajevo, June 2 and 3, 1998; and Mark Baskin, Sarajevo, June 4, 11, 15 1998.

[78] Author interviews with Mark Pedersen, Zagreb, May 27, 1998; Richard Wilcox, Sarajevo, June 2 and 3, 1998; Mark Baskin, Sarajevo June 4, 11, 15; and Ripley, 1997, p. 6.

[79] S/RES/1037, 15 January 1996, para. 11a; and S/1028, 13 December 1995, para. 16a.

many of whom were not adequately qualified.[80] Nevertheless, the division did manage to improve the quality of the police force in Eastern Slavonia and set in place institutional guarantees for the future multiethnic make-up of the force.

The UN CIVPOL became operational fairly quickly, and it deployed in each of the twenty police stations throughout the region. By July 1996, the multiethnic Transitional Police Force was established with CIVPOL oversight. The early problems in establishing the Transitional Police Force ranged from difficulties in clearing names of Serb officers with the Croatian government for service in the Transitional Police Force, to obtaining salaries from the Croatian government for the Transitional Police Force, to finding enough fuel and vehicles, and even obtaining uniforms for the force. After several months of negotiations between UNTAES staff and the Croatian government, many of these logistical problems were overcome, but new, possibly more permanent, ones arose.[81] As the Transitional Police Force came into action, it became clear that the force was largely divided along ethnic lines. For example, during political demonstrations, "Serb police officers seemed reluctant to take action against Serb demonstrators [and criminals], and their Croat counterparts adopted the same attitude in dealing with Croatian demonstrators."[82]

In the initial months of the Transitional Police Force, there were far more ethnic Serb than Croat officers. However, over time CIVPOL oversaw a gradual decrease in Croatian Serb officers, with a concomitant increase in Croats and members of other ethnic minority groups. By the end of the UNTAES mandate, there were 815 Croat officers, 811 Serb, and 52 from other ethnic groups. It was hoped that evenly distributed ethnic proportions would create over time a more ethnically united force. All officers underwent a six-week training course at the International Law Enforcement Academy in Budapest, Hungary.[83] After the training, reports of police harassment and favoring members of the same ethnic group decreased. Joint ethnic patrols were instituted throughout the region, and there were reports of increasing camaraderie, especially at the commander level.

In terms of the prison system, there was only one prison in the region, in Beli Manastir. Rather than simply overseeing prison reforms, UNTAES CIVPOL took control of the administration of the prison "with a view to establishing a better integrated prison administration and to monitoring respect for human rights standards in the prison."[84] By the end of the UNTAES mandate, the

---

[80] Some officers were even found guilty of "gross misconduct" and "negligence" and sent home. See Lessons Learned Unit, 1998, para. 60.
[81] When the Croatian government refused to provide funds for the Transitional Police Force uniforms, Jacques Klein turned to the United States for assistance. Within a short time, he had procured uniforms for the entire force from a US clothing company, funded by the US government.
[82] Lessons Learned Unit, 1998, para. 58.
[83] 95 Serb officers attended an additional six-week training course in Erdut.
[84] S/705, 28 August 1996, para. 26.

prison was returned to Croatian authorities after the Croatian staff had been vetted, and undergone human rights training.

In sum, CIVPOL fulfilled its mandate, despite internal problems, recalcitrance on the part of the Croatian government, and unprofessional behavior on the part of some Serb, Croat, and UN officers. It is not clear, however, whether the multiethnic institutions set in place by the force will hold in the future, or fulfill the goal of creating a more integrated society in the region.[85]

Human rights

The Basic Agreement and related Security Council resolution outline a human rights mandate for UNTAES whereby the operation would "monitor the parties' compliance with their commitment . . . to respect the highest standards of human rights and fundamental freedoms."[86] UNTAES was also charged with promoting ethnic confidence. While UNTAES did help to establish a Joint Implementation Committee on Human Rights that worked primarily with the Joint Implementation Committee on Civil Administration, creating a special human rights division within UNTAES was not a top priority of the UNTAES administration. After protests by the Organization for Security and Cooperation in Europe (OSCE) and other human rights organizations, the UNTAES human rights monitoring unit was instituted in August 1997, nineteen months after the beginning of the UNTAES mandate.[87] The human rights monitoring unit was established jointly between UNTAES and the UN Office of the High Commissioner for Human Rights, and it fielded six teams, one each based in five towns in the region, and another at mission headquarters in Vukovar. The teams paid regular visits to local institutions, worked to gather evidence of war crimes, conducted human rights seminars for teachers, school children, members of the judiciary, and middle-level bureaucrats, assisted the UNTAES civilian administration with its documentation production efforts, and held bi-weekly coordination meetings with other human rights groups working in the region.[88] The human rights monitoring unit also enjoyed assistance from the military and CIVPOL divisions in human rights monitoring, building confidence and respect for the rule of law and human rights, and reporting on human rights violations.

Under pressure from the various human rights-interested international bodies in Croatia, the Croatian government signed all of the basic international treaties protecting human and ethnic minority rights. However, throughout the duration of UNTAES and thereafter, a persistent problem that the peacekeeping

[85] Author interviews with Richard Wilcox, Sarajevo, June 2 and 3, 1998.
[86] S/RES/1037, 15 January 1996, para. 12.   [87] Smoljan, 2003, p. 45.
[88] UN High Commissioner for Human Rights, "Human Rights Field Operation in the Former Yugoslavia, Periodic Report," 18 December 1997, paras. 45–50.

mission and all human rights groups protested against, including on several
occasions the UN Security Council, was Croatia's Amnesty Law. The law was
passed under international pressure in May 1996 but contained vague language,
which only served to create confusion, damage confidence-building measures,
and increase insecurity among the local Serb population. One UNTAES report
explained:

> Local Serb residents have cited the lack of a comprehensive amnesty law as
> a major reason why many of them would feel unwelcome and unsafe once
> the region was fully under Croat control. The amnesty issue, therefore,
> goes to the heart of the question of confidence among the local population
> and, by extension, to the restoration and maintenance of the multi-ethnic
> character of the region.[89]

A comprehensive Amnesty Law, excluding all offenses short of war crimes, was
and continues to be seen as a prerequisite for the return of refugees and displaced
persons. No such law was passed by the end of the UNTAES mandate.[90]

The difficulties with the Amnesty Law were seen as part of a pattern of
"administrative discrimination" against the Serb population, characterized by
arbitrary decisions and deliberate misinformation supplied to Serbs, especially
on the part of lower-ranking bureaucrats.[91] It was to this type of discrimination that the UNTAES civilian administration devoted much of its attention.
Administrative discrimination was also combined with low-level harassment,
which increased with greater freedom of movement in the region. Throughout
the duration of UNTAES there were reports of hate speech against Serbs in
the media, harassment, intimidation, physical assault, killings of Serbs, and
looting of Serb property. These human rights violations were not considered
by UNTAES to be serious, high-level abuse, as in times of war, but they were
recognized as damaging to the peace process: "Numerous cases of human rights
violations have been identified. While there is no pattern of gross human rights
violations in the region, the cumulative effect of the violations . . . and discriminatory practices . . . is such that Serbs in the region have little confidence
in the will of the Croatian authorities to protect them after the departure of
UNTAES."[92]

In terms of Croatian government cooperation with the International Tribunal on the Former Yugoslavia, up until the end of UNTAES, the government was not particularly accommodating. While the government did turn
over some Croats suspected of war crimes, it continuously refused to supply

---

[89] S/705, 28 August 1996, para. 14.   [90] S/59, 22 January 1998, para. 18.
[91] S/953, 4 December 1997, para. 21.
[92] S/767, 2 October 1997, para. 37. Even Madeleine Albright, then the US Secretary of State,
made a trip to the region in May 1997 and criticized the Croatian government for not
respecting the rights of the Serb minority in Eastern Slavonia, as well as in other regions
in Croatia.

the International Tribunal with requested documentation. UNTAES and other human rights groups reported a "growing, persistent anti-tribunal campaign within Croatia" including media bias, government withholding of evidence, and general obstruction of the process by the Croatian government.[93]

Although UNTAES was unable to convince the Croatian government to comply fully with its obligations to the International Tribunal, it is interesting to note that UNTAES was the first international body to capture a suspected war criminal. In June 1997, the UNTAES military division apprehended the former Mayor of Vukovar, Slavko Dokmanovic.[94] The proactive actions of this small UN mission can be contrasted with those of the much stronger NATO military force in Bosnia, which has been unwilling to risk arresting war criminals.

Different divisions of UNTAES worked to fulfill the mission's mandate to protect human rights in Croatia, and some progress was evident. However, full guarantees of human rights protection, especially for the minority Serb population, was and remains in the domain of the Croatian government. While UNTAES and human rights groups sought out and won better institutional guarantees for the largest ethnic minority group, international actors were, unsurprisingly, not able to bring about a complete change in Croatian government or societal behavior.[95]

Refugees

UNTAES' mandate called for the operation to facilitate and "monitor the voluntary and safe return of refugees and displaced persons to their home of origin."[96] It also called for UNTAES to try to prevent an outflow of remaining Serbs from Croatia. While UNTAES did not have a separate division for displaced persons and refugee monitoring, several divisions engaged in the return effort, organizing a Joint Working Group with the UNHCR and the Croatian government. The return issue would plague all parties involved throughout the duration of the UNTAES mandate. By the time UNTAES was deployed in Eastern Slavonia, as explained earlier in this chapter, there had been a large influx of Serbs into the region, and a concomitant departure of many Croats. Because it was in UNTAES' mandate to create the conditions for the re-establishment of a multiethnic society in Eastern Slavonia, it was necessary for the organization to devise complex plans whereby displaced Serbs in Eastern Slavonia residing in Croat houses could return to their homes elsewhere in Croatia, so that Croats could return to their homes in Eastern Slavonia, without prompting a new wave of Serb refugees fleeing from Croatia.

[93] S/487, 23 June 1997, paras. 38–40.
[94] Dokmanovic later committed suicide while in jail.
[95] Minority Rights Group International, 2003.
[96] S/RES/1037, 15 January 1996, paras. 11d and 10b.

The UNHCR and UNTAES worked out a collaborative approach for sharing information, staff resources, and logistics teams. The UNHCR chaired the
Joint Implementation Committee on Returns and established various working
groups on village visits, building rehabilitation, and housing issues. Early in
UNTAES' mandate, the UNHCR and UNTAES sponsored several pilot programs, organizing two-way returns: Serbs to Western Slavonia, and Croats to
Eastern Slavonia. UNTAES and the UNHCR secured international funding
for start-up and recovery packages for the displaced, which were designed to
enable primarily displaced Serbs to build new homes in Eastern Slavonia, or to
return to old, often damaged homes in other parts of Croatia. UNTAES and
the UNHCR also sought to organize a single association for displaced Serbs
and Croats, and worked to have discriminatory housing laws rescinded. On
this last point, the UN Security Council also frequently called on the Croatian
government to remove the many legal obstacles to returns.

Unfortunately, the Croatian government was extremely reluctant to assist
in the return process. Shortly after the two large waves of Serb expulsions
from Croatia in the spring and summer of 1995, the government enacted three
main legal obstacles to Serb returns. First, the "Law on the Lease of Flats in
the Liberated Territory" mandated that former inhabitants would irrevocably
lose socially owned apartments that had been vacated and not reclaimed by
December 27, 1995.[97] Most of the Croatian Serb displaced persons were unable
to try to reclaim their apartments until more than a year after they had fled.
Second, the "Law on Temporary Takeover and Administration of Specified
Property" ordered that vacated houses in the formerly occupied territories
be given to new Croat settlers, and the settlers could not be evicted unless
alternative housing was provided for them. Finding such alternative housing
was often exceedingly difficult.[98] Third, the Croatian government also placed
liens on many Serb properties in Western Slavonia and the Krajina, making it
impossible for Serbs to sell their property after fleeing. Aside from the legal
obstacles, the Croatian government was reluctant to provide Serbs with access
to government reconstruction grants, loans, or lost property compensation, all
of which were more readily available for Croats.

Under increasing international pressure, especially from UNTAES, the
UNHCR and the UN Security Council, the Croatian government did eventually give way on some issues. In April 1997, the government opened six
branches of the Office for Displaced Persons and Refugees, and agreed to treat
members of all ethnic groups equally; returns, however, remained extremely
slow. Later that year, parts of the "Law on Temporary Takeovers" were declared
unconstitutional, but instructions for changes in implementation of the law
were reportedly not delivered to municipal authorities even by the end of the

[97] Lessons Learned Unit, 1998, para. 69.   [98] S/767, 2 October 1997, para. 27.

UNTAES mandate.[99] By late 1997, according to Croatian government statistics, 9,000 Serbs and 6,000 Croats had returned to their homes, many "spontaneously."[100] Of the estimated 23,000 displaced people, or 70 percent of the estimated Serb population in Eastern Slavonia registered with the Office for Displaced Persons and Refugees, half of whom indicated that they would like to return to their old homes in Croatia, but as of late 1997, only 3,250 had returned through official means.[101]

In sum, despite concerted efforts on the part of UNTAES, the UNHCR, and the UN Security Council, the Croatian government remained reluctant to allow displaced Serbs to return to their homes. While the UN organizations gathered accurate information, coordinated well with each other, and engaged directly with the local population, no amount of leadership or organizational learning would appear to have been able to change significantly the actions of the Croatian government. By the end of the UNTAES mandate, there had been no concrete mechanisms instituted for Croatian Serbs to return to occupied property, resolve lost property claims, receive just compensation for lost property, or restore lost tenancy rights. There was, however, no large outflow of refugees or displaced persons from Eastern Slavonia, which is attributed to UNTAES as a success.[102] After the end of the UNTAES mandate, the UNHCR, as well as the OSCE, would remain in the country to continue to exert pressure on the Croatian government for reform.

Public affairs

Part of the UNTAES mandate was to "maintain an active public affairs element."[103] The overall message the office sought to convey was: "There is nothing we can do about the past, but together we can help to build a future."[104] The public affairs office of UNTAES was one of the first divisions to be established upon the start of the operation, and it engaged in many different types of outreach efforts, by means of radio, television, and printed publications. Each of these activities is described below.

First, in terms of radio broadcasts, UNTAES Radio was functional within weeks of the establishment of the mission, largely because its operators were able to rely on staff and equipment from UNPROFOR Radio in Zagreb. This relationship did not continue for long, however, because the local staff in Zagreb were unwilling to move to Vukovar. The UNTAES public affairs office subsequently reached an agreement with Radio Vukovar, whereby UNTAES

---

[99] S/953, 4 December 1997, para. 20.   [100] S/953, 4 December 1997, para. 19.
[101] S/767, 2 October 1997, para. 24.
[102] Under UNTAES, there was reportedly a 10 percent emigration from Eastern Slavonia. See S/953, 4 December 1997, para. 6.
[103] S/RES/1037, 15 January 1996, para. 12.   [104] Boothby, 2004, p. 48.

Radio could operate from the Radio Vukovar facilities, utilize its equipment, technicians and engineers, but remain separate from the somewhat biased Radio Vukovar productions.[105] The original Radio UNTAES broadcasts lasted only fifteen minutes per day, but these were quickly increased to seven hours daily. During the April 1997 elections, UNTAES radio sponsored twelve hours daily of programming, which reported on the elections, and on technical aspects of voting procedures. After the elections, broadcasts shifted focus to refugee and displaced persons return, national reconciliation, and economic renewal. Most broadcasts were in local languages and thus came to represent an important news source from Zagreb to Belgrade.

Second, UNTAES TV was operational from February to July 1997. Its half-hour broadcasts on Saturday nights dealt with practical themes, such as registering to vote, obtaining citizenship and other documents, and employment opportunities. UNTAES TV also produced weekday broadcasts that dealt with similar themes, and it was on the air for several hours daily, especially during the weeks leading up to the April elections.[106] Third, the UNTAES public affairs office also produced a thrice-monthly UNTAES Bulletin in both Latin and Cyrillic scripts (in the Croatian and Serbian languages), which covered many of the same substantive issues as the radio and TV programs.

Acting independently of both the local authorities and of UN headquarters, the UNTAES media outreach enjoyed wide access to the local population and served to counter rampant rumors and disinformation that were common in the postwar setting of the former Yugoslavia. The Radio and TV programs frequently featured interviews and call-in shows with senior UNTAES staff, which provided the public with a sense of direct contact with the top decision-makers in the UN operation. The office also sponsored meetings between Serb and Croat media representatives. By the end of the UNTAES mission, there was a marked improvement in the Croatian media coverage of Serbs living in Croatia.

The public affairs portion of the UNTAES mandate was much easier to implement than some of the others parts, because it relied less on the whims of the Croatian government, and more on the dedication and resourcefulness of the UNTAES staff itself. While the various UNTAES media enjoyed popular followings in the northern regions of the former Yugoslavia, the division did not attract as much attention from foreign media, despite attempts to publicize more broadly the successes of the mission.

---

[105] Over time, Radio Vukovar toned down its propaganda, under the influence of UNTAES Radio's frequent messages about national unity. See Lessons Learned Unit, 1998, para. 74.

[106] UNTAES TV also frequently aired American MTV, which became very popular among viewers, and encouraged consideration of its more substantive messages.

Elections

UNTAES was charged not only with monitoring local elections, but also with organizing them, assisting with voting procedures, and certifying the results.[107] The Basic Agreement and the Secretary-General's pre-implementation report did not specify technical aspects – dates, voter lists, eligibility guidelines, municipal boundaries, names of political representatives, or the legal framework – thus UNTAES and the two sides were faced with many further negotiations before elections could be held.

The first negotiations were over the actual date of the elections and were characterized initially by "increasing political posturing and brinksmanship."[108] The Croatian government, especially hard-line members, wanted the elections to be held as soon as possible and suggested very early dates so that the UNTAES operation could depart quickly, paving the way for the Croatian government's takeover of the region. The Serbs generally wanted to delay the elections, but the local Serb leadership was split about the political implications of the elections: Serb extremists did want not the elections to take place at all, hoping to maintain Eastern Slavonia as a separate Serb enclave, while more moderate forces argued that fair elections were the only means of guaranteeing future Serb political representation in Croatia.[109] In the end, the moderates on both sides won out. The date of the elections was set for April 13, 1997, a "late" date in the transition process, but the day that had been previously scheduled for nationwide parliamentary elections. The Croatian government came to realize that holding separate elections for Eastern Slavonia would symbolize the detachment of Eastern Slavonia from the rest of Croatia, and thus it decided that the later date would have to suffice. The UN argued that it needed at least that much time to prepare for the elections.[110] Meanwhile, the moderate Serb leadership was content with the decision, since it left ample time for UNTAES to continue overseeing regional institutional transitions for nine months after the elections.

UNTAES helped to establish a Joint Implementation Committee on Elections, which became the focal forum for debates over the numerous technical details. The Joint Implementation Committee on Elections established a Code

---

[107] S/RES/1037, 15 January 1996, para. 11e.
[108] S/622, 5 August 1996, para. 25.
[109] It is important to note that after the arrest of Dokmanovic in June 1997, there was a formal split in the Serb leadership. Most of the hard-liners left for Serbia. The moderates assumed power in the Danube region and Dr. Vojislav Stanimirovic was sent as a regional representative to the Croatian Parliament.
[110] The UN had sent an electoral assessment team from the Department of Political Affairs to assist UNTAES civil affairs in devising a timetable, as well as legal framework, and budget. But even the extended time frame was criticized as "unrealistic," since there were so many technical problems that needed to be resolved.

of Conduct, appointed Local Elections Commissions, and an Electoral Appeals Commission that included both Serb and Croat jurists. The elections were to be held state-wide for the Parliament (Sabor), as well as county and municipal councils.

The technical difficulties that the electoral bodies faced included disputes over, first, voter eligibility, voter lists, and registration; second, municipal boundaries; and third, political representation. First, in terms of voter eligibility and voter lists, the registration of displaced persons in Eastern Slavonia was inconsistent at best, and the procedures for registration were only finalized approximately one month before the elections. Local Croat officials often appeared to be making arbitrary decisions as to which documents they would accept for displaced persons' voter registration; moreover, voter lists provided by the Croatian government were often inaccurate, as was the 1991 census data upon which the lists were based. In order to formalize procedures and register as many voters as possible, UNTAES extended the deadline for voter registration until just before the elections. The Serb leadership, under the influence of hard-liners, had been dissuading Croatian Serbs from participating in the vote, but several weeks before the elections, the leadership changed its position in favor of participation. The change was due in large part to UNTAES voter registration efforts: "We drove the highways and byways, holding village meetings with 20 to 800 people at each meeting. We would explain again and again through interpreters why it was to the Serbs' advantage to vote in the elections."[111] The Serbs had lost the war, and had only three options for the future: try to fight a war that the Croats would most likely win, become unwanted refugees in Serbia, or remain in Croatia, where many owned property and had family and friends, and band together to form a political block in Croatian politics. By one month before the elections, most Serbs had decided in favor of the third option.

Second, in terms of municipal boundaries, the Croatian government had changed the boundaries in Eastern Slavonia for the 1991–92 elections in order to dilute Serb representation in several communities. For the 1997 elections, the Serb leadership argued on behalf of restoring the old boundaries, while the Croatian government, rather than coming to a decision, simply delayed making a decision at all. In the end, Klein intervened to redraw municipal boundaries, which both sides accepted. Third, in terms of political representation, the local Serb leadership had not nominated representatives for the local elections commissions until less than two months before the elections, which translated into delays for many decisions on the technical aspects of the elections.

For its part, the UN's operation was not conducted flawlessly. The elections division had trouble recruiting staff, and thus came to rely heavily on UN Volunteers. The UN Volunteers often had more experience in elections monitoring than the regular Secretariat staff allotted to UNTAES, which created some

---

[111] Boothby, interview with the author, April 6, 2001.

tension between the two groups. There were also other staffing problems, since some important contracts expired just prior to the elections, leading to the departure of several key elections personnel.

The difficulties and tensions within the UNTAES electoral unit were reflected in some ways on the actual voting day, but the considerable problems encountered during the polling process were by most accounts caused primarily by the Croatian government.[112] UNTAES elections monitors were placed at each of the 193 polling sites in the region, and they communicated with each other by radio. But the placement and communication were not sufficient to avert substantial technical errors. Voting lists generated by the government were often inaccurate and distributed late to the polling sites. Moreover, the ballots, which had been printed by the Croatian government, were distributed throughout the region often in mislabeled boxes, the ballots themselves were misprinted, and inadequate numbers were distributed to the polling stations. The problems with the voter lists and ballots created confusion and delays in opening many polling stations. The technical problems threatened the legitimacy of the elections, and therefore the Transitional Administrator decided to keep the polls open in Eastern Slavonia for a second day; all ballots and polling sites were guarded overnight by UNTAES troops.[113]

Despite the technical problems, the vote transpired in a remarkably calm atmosphere. There were no reports of violence, intimidation, or major fraud. Complaints were investigated and generally quickly resolved. Voter turnout was very high in the region – close to 90 percent, versus 71 percent in the rest of Croatia.[114] Croats who had been displaced from the region cast most of the votes, approximately 70,000. The remaining 60,000 votes were cast mainly by Serbs residing in the region.[115] The Croat ruling party, the Croatian Democratic Union (HDZ), won seventeen seats of the twenty-eight municipalities, and the newly founded Independent Serbian Democratic Party (SDSS) won eleven. In Vukovar, the most important city in the region, the vote was evenly split between the SDSS and HDZ, with each party gaining twelve of the twenty-four seats on the city council.[116]

While elections in Eastern Slavonia were declared sufficiently free and fair, in terms of the national elections, second and third parties were effectively

---

[112] See CSCE, 1997; and *The Economist*, 1997.

[113] CSCE, 1997, p. 8. Voting in Klisa, where there were considerable problems, continued for a third day.

[114] "UNTAES Mission Brief," p. 6, and CSCE, 1997, p. 10.

[115] The CSCE estimates that upwards of 40,000 Serbs in Eastern Slavonia were unable, or chose not, to register to vote. See CSCE, 1997, p. 10.

[116] At the first meeting of the Vukovar Town Assembly, the HDZ attempted to nullify a pre-arranged power-sharing agreement between it and the SDSS. The UNTAES Transitional Administrator intervened to re-establish the power-sharing arrangement, thus averting a potential major conflict. See S/487, 23 June 1997, para. 3.

denied the ability and right to wage effective campaigns. The ruling HDZ party severely limited other parties' access to media and campaign funding, and it resecured a virtual monopoly over the political sphere in Croatia.

While there were undoubtedly significant logistical problems with the vote, namely inadequate information-gathering from the Croatian government, and some poor coordination within UNTAES, these did not completely disrupt the election or alter the results. Both of the contending sides accepted the results as legitimate, which was extremely fortunate for UNTAES. Despite the technical problems, the overriding concern of UNTAES was not technical, but political. The elections represented a key element in the reintegration of Eastern Slavonia into Croatia. The outcome of the elections could potentially have been cause for further fighting, but instead they ushered in a new political arrangement in the region, which in turn greatly helped to stabilize the post-conflict environment. For the first time, the local Serb population was granted a legitimate place in national politics, cementing their position in government for the post-UNTAES future, as well as their commitment to peace.

Croatia since UNTAES

The UNTAES military component began its gradual withdrawal in the summer of 1997. The last of the UNTAES international staff departed Croatia on January 15, 1998, although 180 CIVPOL remained for the next nine months to continue monitoring the transition of the police force, and human rights in general, under the name the "UN Civilian Police Support Group." The OSCE began its sixteen-month follow-on monitoring operation in June 1997, overlapping and coordinating for several months with UNTAES, until it took over the monitoring mission after the departure of the last UN CIVPOL. The OSCE fielded an international staff of 250 to protect human rights and national minorities, assist in the implementation of legislative agreements, and assist with the two-way refugee return programs. While the OSCE operation was fairly small, it managed to exert disproportionate influence because it had the backing of the EU. Croatia, along with many other East European states, has been seeking to join the EU, and thus EU requirements for minority rights guarantees, compliance with the International Criminal Tribunal for the Former Yugoslavia, along with other economic and political reforms have come to dominate political, legal, and economic debates in Croatia.[117]

---

[117] Blitz, 2003; Massari, 2005; Kušić, 2006. For four years, the International Tribunal had demanded that the Croatian government hand over Ante Gotovina, a general in the Croatian Army accused of war crimes. Failure to comply meant that EU accession talks for Croatia were postponed, but in 2005, talks restarted and shortly thereafter, Gotovina was found and arrested in Spain. Croatia hopes to become a member of the EU by 2010.

Since UNTAES, Croatia has remained at peace. The cease-fire has held, troops have remained demobilized, and the humanitarian situation has improved for the majority of the population. Freer and fairer elections than ever before took place after Tudjman's death in December 1999.[118] The January 2000 elections ushered in a new government and a completely new political agenda, with the Social Democratic Party leader, Stjepan Mesic, as President of Croatia, and Drazen Budisa of the Croatian Social Liberal Party as Prime Minister.[119] The new government began a process of formal reconciliation with Croatia's Serbs. In 2000 and 2001, constitutional amendments fundamentally changed the balance of power in Croatia, granting less power to the President, and more to the Parliament. In the 2003 parliamentary elections, the relatively new Serb party from Eastern Slavonia, the Independent Democratic Serbian Party, won three seats in the 152-seat Parliament. Also in those elections, a reformed HDZ regained the lead over the splintering center-left coalition, bringing in a new Prime Minister, Ivo Sanader. Sanader, a conservative who is considered less nationalist or corrupt than previous HDZ leaders, promised to seek to "heal the lingering wounds from the 1990s 'homeland war' by cooperating with ethnic Serbs."[120] He convinced the representatives of the Independent Democratic Serbian Party to join with the reformed HDZ. This new "co-habitation" has meant the ethnic Serb party has been better able to influence the government with minority rights reforms. As some analysts explained: "leading Serbian representatives appear to be satisfied with the policy of the government, but a genuine transformation of the society will probably take years."[121]

Indeed, while societal reconciliation remains a slow process, many legal reforms have been instituted in recent years. Just after the end of UNTAES, in 1998, previously controversial housing and refugee return laws were reformed, although some problems with property rights remained. In 2000 and 2002, new minority rights legislation was enacted that instituted minority representation at all levels of government – national, regional, and local. Croatia also signed all international human and minority rights treaties.

In Eastern Slavonia in particular, institutional guarantees for the integration of the Serb population has meant that Serbs are still employed in state services, the police force is still made up of roughly equal numbers of Serbs and Croats, schools and other public institutions are becoming integrated, and the local governing structures continue to be shared between both communities. There is no doubt that the UN's efforts in Eastern Slavonia have left the region better off than had there been a less-effective international presence. That said, there

---

[118] Tudjman was re-elected President in June 1997 with 61 percent of the vote in rather questionably fair elections. The opposition then began a concerted attempt to form a unified block against the HDZ.

[119] Mesic, 2004. Mesic won a second five-year term in 2005.

[120] Peranic, 2004.   [121] Roter and Bojinovic, 2005, p. 448.

are still problems in the Danube region, especially concerning the economic situation, refugees and displaced persons, and societal-level reconciliation.

First, in terms of the economy, the region has achieved nowhere near the high level of prewar economic activity that it used to enjoy, even though the rest of Croatia is recovering well from the war. Croatia has been enjoying economic growth rates of 3–4 percent per year, low inflation, unemployment under 19 percent, and a GDP per capita PPP of $11,600.[122] In contrast, unemployment in Eastern Slavonia remains comparatively high, and economic recovery slow.[123] Second, in terms of refugees and displaced persons, despite institutional efforts to pave the way to refugee returns, as of 2005, the Croatian government had registered only 122,000 Serb returnees to Croatia (of the 300–350,000 who left during the war); whereas Serbs once made up about 12 percent of the Croatian population, they now make up less than 5 percent.[124] Third, societal-level reconciliation remains at bay, even though there are new Croatian civil society organs that are devoted to protecting human rights and national minorities. The Croatian Helsinki Committee in Vukovar and Human Rights Watch continue to report that there are many human rights violations in the region each year, mainly perpetrated by angry, displaced Croats.

In general, many of the reforms that have taken place in Croatia have come at the insistence of outsiders. UNTAES began the process of institutional reform in Eastern Slavonia, and EU pressure, along with a popular Croatian desire to join the EU, has influenced Croatian officials and citizens to recognize minority rights and move toward reconciliation. While the UN and EU have not been able to bridge some painful societal divides, their efforts have undoubtedly helped to create a more conciliatory climate, along with formal institutions through which Serbs and Croats may regulate future disputes by peaceful means.

Conclusion

UNTAES benefited from both second- and first-level learning. In terms of second-level learning *between* UN peacekeeping missions, the failures of UNPROFOR and UNCRO loomed large in the minds of UN policymakers, especially Secretary-General Boutros-Ghali. The Secretariat feared repeating the same mistake that it had made in the past by allowing the great powers, which were not always in agreement, to charge the peacekeeping operation with numerous responsibilities, both military and civilian, while not supplying the operation with enough financial or political means to fulfill the mandate. Rather than risk another "set-up," the Secretary-General made it clear, in public, that the UN could not be expected to take on the multidimensional tasks of peacekeeping in Eastern Slavonia without the consensual support of the UN

---

[122] Bartlett, 2003, p. 150; and the *CIA World Factbook*, 2005.   [123] Smoljan, 2003.
[124] Human Rights Watch, 2005; *CIA World Factbook*, 2005.

Security Council for a "robust" (Chapter VII) mandate, accompanied by adequate troop numbers, military equipment, and civilian personnel. In the end, even though the Security Council did not provide all of the means requested, the Secretary-General and his staff were adequately supported.

UNTAES was able to fulfill almost all aspects of its mandate in part because it benefited from second-level learning, as well as from favorable situational factors, namely the consent of the warring parties, and consensual but only moderately intense Security Council interests. These last two factors in particular enabled first-level organizational learning to occur within the UNTAES operation. As first-level learning progressed, it bolstered the other two factors. The mission was able to maintain the consent of the warring sides, despite their inclination at times to renege on prior written promises. Moreover, the permanent five members of the Security Council understood that the mission was succeeding in its mandate implementation and therefore did not attempt to second-guess or override field-level policymaking. The United States and Belgium in particular provided critical support for UNTAES but nevertheless left the operation to its own devices in terms of information analysis, grouping problem sets, and setting goals for itself based on its own ground-level expert knowledge. There were few overlapping, parallel, or conflicting mandates between different organizations on the ground, because Klein had executive control over the entire operation, unifying military command structures firmly under civilian command and co-housing the units, making for easier communication and cooperation. The staff of UNTAES engaged directly with the local population and came to understand how to interpret and implement the mandate. The leadership of the mission, and Transitional Administrator Jacques Klein in particular, was appropriately creative and forceful. Once many of the difficult tasks had been accomplished, or at least were well underway, the second Transitional Administrator, William Walker, was able to see through the final phases of UNTAES. These elements amount to first-level organizational learning. The fruits of this learning, in turn, appear to have had lasting positive institutional effects on the region, even if the region remains "uncomfortably" multiethnic, and within Croatia, comparatively poor.[125]

[125] Boothby, 2004, p. 50.

8

East Timor: the UN as state

Introduction

The UN Transitional Administration in East Timor (UNTAET) was the most ambitious UN peacekeeping operation of its time. The mission was unlike most others in that public administration, rather than security, was the most challenging element of the mandate. Not only was UNTAET charged with the tasks of Chapter VII peacekeeping, civilian policing, and humanitarian assistance, but also the governing of an entire country. Whereas historically the UN had attempted to reform or rebuild state structures with the assistance of previously warring political elites, in this case, the UN had to *be* the state and the government. The people who had filled the administrative positions in the repressive Indonesian regime for almost a quarter of a century left East Timor en masse just prior to the beginning of UNTAET, and thus the operation functioned with only the legacy, but not the people, of the previous regime.

Beginning in October 1999 and lasting almost three years, UNTAET was the sovereign authority in East Timor. The structure of UNTAET included three main pillars: (1) governance and public administration, (2) the UN peace-keeping force, and (3) humanitarian assistance and emergency rehabilitation. When considering the size of the local population (approximately 1 million in a country about the size of the small US state of Connecticut), this was a pro-portionately enormous operation, including 9,150 military, 1,640 police, 1,670 international civilian staff (including 486 UN Volunteers), and 1,905 local staff.

The literature on the UN's operations in East Timor provides evidence for two very different stories: an early one of organizational dysfunction, and a later account of organizational learning and success in mandate implementation (although longer-term success is too difficult to determine at this point).[1] This chapter unites the two, in an attempt to form a more complete analysis of the overall success and failure of the operations, especially UNTAET.[2]

---

[1] On failure, see Chopra, 2000 and 2002; and Traub, 2000. On success, see Smith and Dee, 2003; Goldstone, 2004; and Smith, 2004.

[2] Taken together, the international operations in East Timor are as follows: UNAMET (June–August 1999), INTERFET (September 1999–February 2000), UNTAET (October 1999–May 2002), UNMISET (May 2002–May 2005), UNOTIL (May 2005–August 2006), UNMIT (August 2006–).

First, in terms of UNTAET's early dysfunction and difficulties with mandate implementation, second-level "lessons" from previous operations had some significant, but mainly negative, effects on UNTAET. Lessons from Cambodia, the only other Asian country to have had a multidimensional peacekeeping force, and Kosovo, the chronologically closest multidimensional operation, encouraged decreased involvement with the local population, centralization of command, reliance on international as opposed to local staff, and an approach that tended toward the colonial organizational profile, rather than integration. As a result, according to one critic, UNTAET had an early "preoccupation with control at the expense of the local community's involvement in government . . . [and its staff] projected a blunt and bullying style" rather than being accommodating and self-effacing, as would have been warranted, given the comparatively less precarious security context of East Timor.[3]

Even though the security context was not enormously complex (the war ended with the withdrawal of the anti-independence militias along with the Indonesian troops), and Security Council interests remained supportive and consensual throughout the operation, the overall "situational difficulty" score was quite low, and UNTAET began in a state of organizational dysfunction. Contributing to the dysfunction was the short time span in which to plan for the operation, and a poor transfer of accrued knowledge from the UN's previous election-monitoring mission in East Timor, which was sponsored by the Department of Political Affairs.

It took pressure and criticism from the East Timorese, as well as from disaffected UN staff members, to move the organization to integrate better with and learn from its environment. The basic ideas for the most crucial and effective organizational changes originated not with UN headquarters in New York, but rather in the field, in East Timor.

Despite the halting start, after taking initial criticisms seriously, the operation began to engage more fully with the East Timorese, garnering consent for the operation with its policies of "Timorization" (i.e., including East Timorese in governing structures). The mission also enjoyed a certain distance from UN headquarters, which allowed it increasingly to make more decisions based on field-level calculations.[4] As Kofi Annan explained, "the nature and scope of the challenge meant that the United Nations, and all others involved, often had to learn by doing, refining and developing methods whilst implementing the mandate."[5] By the end of May 2002, UNTAET had successfully implemented most aspects of its mandate and was ready to hand over many of the governing responsibilities to an independent, democratically elected East Timorese leadership.

---

[3] Chopra, 2000, pp. 30, 33; see also Chesterman, 2001, p. 72.
[4] Suhrke, 2001, p. 13.   [5] Annan, 2003, p. xxiii.

Situational factors

The small, beautiful Pacific country of Timor-Leste, as it is known today, is prone to natural disasters, is surrounded by a gentle sea to the north and a more volatile sea to the south, and shares about half of an island with Indonesian West Timor.[6] The island is located in the southeastern region of the Indonesian archipelago, and just northwest of the Australian coastline.

Approximately 400 years ago, Timor-Leste was colonized by the Portuguese, who used it mainly as a trading outpost until April 25, 1974, when the authoritarian regime in Portugal fell, and East Timor – like Angola, Mozambique, and the other former Portuguese colonies – gained a rushed independence.[7] In light of the dearth of institutional structures in place to regulate political conflicts, squabbles arose among several political parties, each of which was trying to gain the upper hand in the future governance of East Timor. The main two parties were the Revolutionary Front for an Independent East Timor (Fretilin), which was very popular and had Marxist leanings, and the Democratic Union of Timor, a smaller party representing mainly the landowning elite. As each party sought to wrest control from the other, Indonesia invaded, under the pretense of preventing the creation of a "Cuba of the South Pacific" (ignoring the evidence that Fretilin's connections with Marxism were tenuous).

Less than a year later, Indonesia incorporated the territory as its twenty-seventh province. The United States provided tacit support for the invasion and occupation; more overt military support followed in later years. Australia, as the closest neighbor, was one of the few countries in the world to recognize Indonesian rule as legal in East Timor. And while the UN General Assembly and Security Council did not officially recognize the takeover, little international support flowed to the East Timorese in this new chapter of their struggle for independence.[8]

For twenty-four years, the Indonesian government held Timor-Leste in a brutal iron grip, during which time between one-quarter and one-third of the

---

[6] The name "East Timor" is still used more frequently than Timor-Leste in international contexts, even among East Timorese diplomats. There is a small district of Timor-Leste within West Timor, called the Oecussi enclave.

[7] In 1749, following battles between Portuguese and Dutch colonists, East and West Timor were split, with the West going to the Dutch and the East going to Portugal. From 1942 to 1945, the Japanese occupied East Timor; the territory then reverted back to Portuguese control after the Japanese defeat in WWII and became, officially, a "non-self-governing" territory after the fall of Portuguese rule in 1974. The enclave of Oecussi on the north coast of West Timor was added to East Timor in 1916, as part of a deal between Portuguese and Dutch colonial powers.

[8] See Dunn, 2003; and UN General Assembly Resolution 3485, 12 December 1975; Security Council Resolution 384, 22 December 1975; and Security Council Resolution 389, 22 April 1976.

population, or about 200,000 people, were killed in fighting and famine.[9] The Indonesian military committed "unspeakable crimes . . . bombings, execution, torture, and disappearances, which left no family untouched."[10] Thousands of Timorese fled the territory. Many members of the opposition, fearing incarceration or worse, left for exile in Portugal and elsewhere. The main opposition group Fretilin, and its military wing, the Armed Forces for the National Liberation of East Timor (Falintil), fought the Indonesian occupation.

The East Timorese, as a result of centuries of colonial rule, are 90 percent Roman Catholic, while the Indonesians are primarily Muslim. This was one factor in the war. But the more salient causes lay in the issues of the Cold War – the struggle between communism and democratic capitalism, and external support for the perception of Indonesian support against the spread of communism. Another aspect of the war lay in who would control the gas fields off the coast of East Timor (over which Australia also laid claim). And finally, many international and regional powers were reluctant to support East Timorese independence from Indonesia for fear of inspiring similar movements in their own countries. Many Asian powers supported the Indonesian regime, especially in the UN General Assembly, where they tried – eventually successfully – to remove self-determination in East Timor from the yearly agenda.[11] The Security Council did not again take up the issue until 1999, as discussed in detail below. In the UN system, only the Office of the Secretary-General attempted to keep the issue alive.[12]

By the late 1990s, several events transpired that would move toward eventual East Timorese independence. The Cold War had been over for about a decade, and yet, during most of the 1990s there was no progress toward an end to the conflict. Indeed, during these years, the Indonesian National Military continued to wage major battles against Falintil, even conducting occasional horrific massacres of Timorese civilians, while Falintil fought back through guerrilla means. The Falintil did not have any significant external funding for weapons and supplies, yet battles did not appear to be at a point of a hurting

---

[9] On the killings and numbers, see Kiernan, 2003. Most of the East Timorese population is Catholic, although there is a small Muslim population. There are two major ethnic groups, Austronesian and Papuan, and small Chinese, Arab, and Portuguese minorities. Ethnolinguistically, the population is a mix of more than twenty Austronesian and Melanesian groups, along with a significant admixture of Portuguese. In general, a strong sense of East Timorese national identity, emerging from the long independence struggle, has been more significant than any ethnic, linguistic, or religious cleavages.

[10] Jolliffe, in Cardoso, 2000, p. xi.

[11] See Terrall, 2003, p. 80. However, calls for independence resurfaced when, in November 1991, foreign journalists managed to film a massacre of approximately 270 protesters at the Santa Cruz cemetery in Dili.

[12] See Krieger, 1997, p. xxiv.

stalemate when the negotiations reopened. What changed the situation was the Asian economic crisis in 1997, which in turn brought about the downfall of the Suharto regime in Indonesia in May 1998.

B. J. Habibie, an eccentric and somewhat unpredictable figure, became President of Indonesia and abruptly announced in late January 1999 that the East Timorese could decide for themselves whether they wanted independence or autonomy within Indonesia, in a "popular consultation." From 1983 up until this point, tripartite talks between Indonesia, Portugal, and the UN had been at a standstill. The major East Timorese political parties had united to form the National Council of Timorese Resistance (CNRT), a cohesive political front in favor of independence; however, they were not permitted to represent themselves in these negotiations. Portugal and the UN Secretary-General's office generally supported the East Timorese, against the Indonesian government, in favor of independence. And while the East Timorese continued to be left out of the plans directly, the tripartite negotiations produced an agreement on a UN-monitored East Timorese independence vote in August 1999.[13] A follow-on peacekeeping mission was to help oversee the transition to independence, should the East Timorese vote fall in favor of independence (the Habibie government had been informed, incorrectly, by its advisors that the majority of East Timorese did not want independence). The doubt about the outcome of the election meant that the UN Secretariat was unable to plan adequately for different potential election results. The Indonesian government, supported by the Australian government and others, forbade the deployment of peacekeeping troops alongside the elections monitors, or even planning for a post-election peacekeeping operation. For the "popular consultation," the Indonesian national military was to be in sole charge of security.

This decision would prove catastrophic for the East Timorese several days after they decided overwhelmingly in favor of independence, when members of anti-independence militias went on a "scorched earth" rampage, seeking retribution for the decision in favor of independence. While the Indonesian national military was supposed to be under orders to stop such actions and guard the safety of East Timorese civilians, "the TNI [Indonesian national military] had deep psychological and economic commitments to retaining the twenty-seventh province, where its forces had suffered many casualties and where it remained the preeminent force in business and government."[14] The Indonesian national military forces therefore stood aside, or in some cases even aided in the destruction.

---

[13] See S/513, the 5 May 1999 agreement signed by Indonesia, Portugal, and the UN.
[14] Smith and Dee, 2003, p. 42.

UNAMET

This destruction occurred right before the eyes of the members of a UN mission.[15] It was *not* a peacekeeping mission, but rather an electoral monitoring mission, under the auspices of the UN Department of Political Affairs (although the Department of Peacekeeping Operations was regularly informed of events). The United Nations Mission in East Timor (UNAMET), despite a very short time in which to plan for its operation, had the benefits of an experienced staff, who were generally well versed in the politics of the region, and who often had appropriate language skills. This mission also benefited from being the first of several new operations to begin in 1999, acquiring its basic logistical equipment from the new, well-stocked UN base in Brindisi, Italy. UNAMET enjoyed the support of a large, Japanese-sponsored trust fund and in-kind contributions from Australia. Regional Asian countries were well represented in UNAMET, including staff from Bangladesh, Japan, Malaysia, Nepal, Pakistan, the Philippines, the Republic of Korea, and Thailand. Only India would refuse publicly to lend support for a vote on self-determination.

In late August 1999, the mission appeared, by all accounts, to be progressing well. On the order of 100,000 more people than expected registered to vote including 450,000 East Timorese, and 13,000 Timorese outside of East Timor. Indonesia pledged to remain neutral in the debate between pro-independence and pro-autonomy groups, but "in fact, massive government funds and resources were channeled to the pro-autonomy groups, and indeed the militia."[16] Observers on the ground frequently reported to UN headquarters that conditions for a free and fair ballot did not exist.[17]

Some members of UNAMET lobbied the head of the mission, Ian Martin, to delay the vote.[18] But pressure to stay on schedule came from both below and above, in effect sandwiching the UN mission into conducting the elections. On the ground, elites and citizens alike wanted the vote to go ahead. Xanana Gusmao, the charismatic leader of Fretilin and the united opposition organization, the CNRT, felt that any substantial delay could cause a weakening of international support for the vote, and the possible continuation of Indonesian rule. As one East Timorese man explained, "They've been killing us for twenty-four years. They'll kill us whether we vote or not. This is the only chance we will have to show the world that East Timor wants independence, and we must

---

[15] Most members of UNAMET were evacuated during the operation "Clean Sweep." See Chopra, 2000.

[16] Martin and Mayer-Rieckh, 2005, p. 128.

[17] Apparently, the Australian Secret Intelligence Service had been warning the Howard government of the impending fiasco, but the Australian government chose to ignore the warnings, trusting the word of its ally, the Indonesian government. See Bell, 2000, p. 171.

[18] Smith and Dee, 2003, p. 44; see also Chopra, 2000.

use it."[19] The massive number of East Timorese who took risks to sign up to vote, while anti-independence militias were gathering strength, further attests to a popular desire to vote without delay.

From on high, the UN Secretary-General dispatched an electoral commission to determine whether the Secretariat should support the planned elections. The commission reported that while not ideal, the electoral arrangements were as sound as possible, and that further delay could permanently jeopardize the conducting of the vote. Meanwhile, regional powers and members of the Security Council bilaterally pressured the Indonesian government to contain any possible violence. The vote was to take place in August, regardless of the misgiving of UN staffers.

In the end, the Ballot was delayed to August 30 (by a mere twenty-two days). The poll was largely peaceful, with a 98.6 percent voter turnout. An overwhelming 78.5 percent of East Timorese voted in favor of independence. But just as the celebrations began, the pro-autonomy militias unleashed a three-week, devastating "scorched earth" campaign. They raced through large towns and remote villages, burning all buildings in their wake. Approximately 70 percent of the physical infrastructure was destroyed, and nearly all homes.[20] More than 70 percent of the population was displaced.[21] Most UN international staffers were evacuated, while nine UN members were killed, and the UN compound in Dili came under siege. All administrative services collapsed; and approximately 1,500 East Timorese were killed.[22]

INTERFET

The scale and sweep of the violence caught many international observers off guard. The lead-up to the vote and the vote itself had been largely peaceful. Indonesia had promised to cooperate, and as one UN official in Dili mused, "if the intention had been to prevent East Timor's independence this could have been achieved easily [before the vote] by the late night murder of a few UN Volunteers, or the selective torching of a couple of buildings used by expatriates."[23]

It is unclear, therefore, exactly what the purpose of the violence was. The overwhelmingly pro-independence popular vote had already taken place, which meant the East Timorese could no longer be intimidated into an autonomy agreement. The only explanation was retribution. That, and perhaps the goal

---

[19] Scheiner, 2001, p. 121.   [20] Chopra, 2000, p. 27.
[21] Smith and Dee, 2003, p. 51.   [22] Martin and Mayer-Rieckh, 2005, p. 134.
[23] Chesterman, 2001, p. 12. The militia groups operating in East Timor had apparently not learned from the Hutu power groups and *Interahamwe* in Rwanda, who killed UN peacekeepers in order to provoke western withdrawal, preparing the stage for the genocide.

of sparking a civil war, which would make both sides appear complicit in the fighting, and possibly swing the battles and international sentiment in favor of the security that continued Indonesian occupation might provide. Therefore, the East Timorese leadership, and particularly Xanana Gusmao, forbade Falintil from fighting against the Indonesian militias. Gusmao's pro-independence troops remained cantoned on base while the militias burned and killed. The East Timorese political leadership, realizing their independence fighters were outmatched militarily, took this calculated risk of non-violence to use their weaker position to their benefit. By not fighting back, the East Timorese accentuated their position as victim and hoped the one-sided battle would necessitate international intervention in their favor.

The problem was that there was no readily-available international force. As the head of the UN electoral mission explained, "The UN was prepared neither to respond to the violence and devastation that followed the ballot, nor to the need to rapidly establish a transitional administration."[24] Nor were any other member states of the UN or regional actors. By most counts, it appears that large demonstrations in Australia and elsewhere, protesting a lack of intervention on behalf of the East Timorese, were what finally moved the Australian government to take the lead in establishing a multinational force to stop the violence.[25]

But the Australian government determined that it could not intervene without the consent of the UN, significant support from regional powers, financial support, and the consent of the Indonesian government. This final condition appeared at first almost insurmountable, since the Indonesian government was adamantly opposed to having Australia lead the force, but the Indonesians eventually relented, under US economic and military pressure, satisfied that there would be an Asian Deputy Commander and a significant Asian presence in the force. Remarkably, within a few days, all of the other conditions for Australian intervention were met, and the force deployed by September 20, within one week of the Security Council resolution authorizing the International Force in East Timor (INTERFET).

INTERFET was led by Australia, but it enjoyed the participation of many other countries in the region. The Deputy Force Commander was from Thailand; troops were sent from the Philippines, South Korea, Malaysia, and Fiji; Singapore sent a medical contingent.[26] INTERFET was authorized under Chapter VII to use "all necessary means" to restore order, and had approximately 11,000 troops at the height of its operations. The force succeeded in quickly stopping the violence and in stabilizing the country, paving the way

---

[24] Martin and Mayer-Rieckh, 2005, p. 133.
[25] See Chesterman, 2001, p. 13; Dee, 2001, p. 7; Orford, 2003, p. 1; Simpson, 2004; Scheiner, 2001, p. 110; and Pilger, 2004, p. 14.
[26] Brazil, Canada, France, Germany, Ireland, Italy, New Zealand, Norway, the UK, and the USA also sent troops.

for the deployment of UNTAET, a large, UN multidimensional peacekeeping force and transitional administration.

By the time UNTAET arrived, the situation on the ground was somewhat different from what the majority of peacekeeping operations encounter. Whereas most multidimensional peacekeeping missions must focus on stabilization, demobilization, and disarmament at the outset of the mission, this was not the case in East Timor. With the arrival of INTERFET, most of the pro-autonomy militias fled to West Timor, and the Indonesian military withdrew. But along with the military withdrawal came the departure of the entire state administration in East Timor. The island had been run primarily by Indonesians who had fled. They left an under-educated, under-trained, traumatized population that had no experience with running, much less control over, the governing institutions.[27] In terms of the physical infrastructure, there were no telecommunications technologies outside of Dili, other than some mobile phones.[28] Almost all roads were destroyed, and almost all homes and other structures burned. In the words of Sergio Vieira de Mello, Special Representative of the Secretary-General and Transitional Administrator of UNTAET, "The comprehensiveness of East Timor's destruction – Carthage-like in its sheer awfulness – the assault on life, the climate of fear . . . the destruction or removal of most of East Timor's cultural heritage and institutional memory, the near total dearth of human resources: all of these needed to be dealt with. That was the task of the East Timorese, together with UNTAET."[29]

But on the positive side, both the local population and the elites were favorably predisposed toward the UN. No factions of East Timorese were fighting one another, since they had united as a political force in the CNRT, with Gusmao at the lead. In 1996, East Timorese leaders José Ramos-Horta and Bishop Carlos Filipe Ximenes Belo had won the Nobel Peace prize, and they continued to lobby international actors to support East Timorese human rights. International opinion had been shifting in favor of East Timorese independence, after decades of Timorese political leaders lobbying the UN for intervention on their side, and independence from Indonesia.[30] That day had finally come, and there were high hopes for what the UN might be able to do in East Timor.

Security Council interests

Stepping back for a moment, in 1975, when East Timor was originally slated to gain its independence, the territory had the unfortunate luck of having its future tied up in the Cold War world of great-power politics. The United States was just completing the painful process of extracting itself from Vietnam, and it wanted to maintain alliances with any regime it deemed sympathetic to US

---

[27] Rodrigues, 2003, p. 28.   [28] Smith and Dee, 2003, p. 53, note 9.
[29] Vieira de Mello, 2003, p. 16.   [30] See Bell, 2000, p. 175.

interests in Asia. Indonesia happened to be one such ally.[31] And while the United States and other western powers were generally inclined, at least rhetorically, to support independence from oppressive regimes, this was not the case for East Timor in Indonesia.

The United States had been supporting Indonesia for some years by training and supplying equipment to its armed forces. Given the United States' support for decolonization, Indonesian President Suharto was apparently worried about losing US military assistance if the United States were to oppose Indonesia's annexation of East Timor. The United States, however, under the foreign policy direction of Henry Kissinger, did not do much to contest the move.[32] The UN Security Council voted twice to protest against the infringement on the right to self-determination in East Timor.[33] The United States voted with the Council on the first resolution, but abstained, along with Japan, on the second resolution. While the majority of the members of the Security Council were willing to support East Timor rhetorically, neither of these resolutions declared Indonesian annexation illegal, and neither carried a threat of further sanctions or other consequences.[34]

From this time, through the late 1980s, three permanent members of the Security Council – the United States, France, and the United Kingdom – actively supplied Indonesia with counter-insurgency technologies, strategies, and weapons.[35] While China had originally, although tentatively, expressed support for Fretilin, rumors of arms supplies to the group were not substantiated, and Chinese support for Timorese independence "faded rapidly in the 1970s."[36] The USSR was the only member of the Security Council to vote consistently in favor of East Timorese independence in the General Assembly votes, although there is little evidence of more tangible assistance.

Starting in 1975, a majority of the members of the General Assembly voted each year to support East Timorese independence when the topic was brought up during its annual meetings, until 1982. In that year, Portugal decided not to initiate any more new resolutions, fearing that the majority vote might swing

---

[31] Ayoob, 2004, p. 104.

[32] Dunn, 2003, p. 172. President Gerald Ford and Henry Kissinger had visited Indonesia only one day before the annexation of East Timor, giving the impression of tacit US consent.

[33] See S/RES/384, 22 December 1975; and S/RES/389, 22 April 1976. See also Krieger, 1997, p. xxiii.

[34] As Daniel Patrick Moynihan, the former US Ambassador to the UN, noted in his 1978 memoir: "The United States wished things to turn out as they did, and worked to bring this about. The Department of State desired that the United Nations prove utterly ineffective in whatever measures it undertook. This task was given to me, and I carried it forward with no inconsiderable success." Chomsky, 2001, pp. 138–39.

[35] Scheiner, 2001, p. 109; Greenless and Garran, 2002, p. 248; Cotton, 2004, p. 52.

[36] Taylor, 1999, pp. 49 and 177.

against East Timor.[37] In the General Assembly, as in the Security Council, aside from the issues of great-power politics, language and regional politics also played roles. Portuguese-speaking countries such as Brazil, Mozambique, and Portugal (the former colonial power of all of these countries) were in support of East Timorese independence. But in terms of other members, as Ian Martin explains, Asian and Muslim "solidarity" often worked in favor of the Indonesian government, and against the East Timorese.[38] Or, in the case of Australia, the government felt it was in its strategic regional interest to maintain good relations with its closest neighbor, Indonesia, and thus was reluctant to confront the government over the issue of East Timorese independence.

By the time Suharto fell and Habibie assumed power in the spring of 1998, the calculations of many states had changed. An East Timorese "Support Group" of thirty countries, mainly Asian, had been established at the UN, in addition to a "Core Group" including Australia, Japan, New Zealand, the UK, and the United States. The "Core Group" in particular functioned as an unofficial coordination committee of the "most closely engaged" countries.[39] When the East Timorese voted overwhelmingly in favor of independence in August 1999, and were subsequently brutally punished by pro-autonomy militias, many countries that had previously been unsupportive of East Timor were willing to help in more ways than merely offering rhetoric.

During the height of the violence in East Timor in September 1999, fortuitously, a meeting of the Asia-Pacific Economic Cooperation was taking place in New Zealand. While the forum is generally not concerned with political matters, the New Zealand government moved to include East Timorese independence as part of the agenda.[40] The meeting provided political momentum to help persuade the UN and its powerful member states to act quickly in establishing INTERFET.

Japan and Australia, in particular, took the lead in providing concrete assistance. Both countries had some historical guilt toward the East Timorese – the Japanese, for brutally invading and occupying the island during World War II, and then for supporting the Indonesian government during the Cold War. In the case of Australia, after World War II, many Australians felt they owed a "moral debt" to East Timor, since many East Timorese had protected and supported Australian troops stationed in East Timor in the fight against the

---

[37] The vote in favor of East Timorese self-determination narrowed each year until 1982, when it passed by fifty votes in favor, forty-five against, and forty-nine abstentions. See Krieger, 1997, Document 48, pp. 129–33.

[38] Martin and Mayer-Rieckh, 2005, p. 131.   [39] Martin and Mayer-Rieckh, 2005, p. 127.

[40] President Jiang Zemin of China refused to have the issue become part of the official agenda, for fear of setting a precedent for the future, so the issue was discussed informally during lunch. However, he left the meeting with the tacit agreement that there would be an international intervention force. See Greenless and Garran, 2002, p. 263.

Japanese, and were later "thanked" by Australia in the form of support for the Indonesian annexation of the territory.[41]

Japan became the largest donor supporting Timorese independence and then reconstruction, beginning with a trust fund for INTERFET in the sum of $100 million. The trust fund enabled many poorer Asian and other nations to participate in INTERFET. Japan also hosted the first International Donor's conference for East Timor in December 1999, eventually contributed peacekeeping troops for the first time since several had been killed in Cambodia, and sent the Japanese Engineering Group, which restored water and roads throughout East Timor.[42] While Japan assisted with the finances, Australia focused on military contributions. Australia commanded INTERFET, supplied most of the aviation and logistics support, and its troops made up approximately half of the force.

Whereas during the Cold War, most of the permanent five members of the Security Council provided either tacit or open support for Indonesia, by 1999, this support was fading. However, none of the members would agree to authorize the INTERFET intervention without Indonesian approval. China and Russia, with secessionist movements of their own, even threatened to veto without Indonesian consent.[43] The United States also maintained that it would not agree to any force without consent, and it sought to exert pressure on the Indonesian government through financial and military channels. In terms of financial pressure, after the Asian financial crisis and IMF bailout, Indonesia was greatly indebted to the IMF in general, and to the United States in particular. The United States threatened to use economic sanctions through the IMF and World Bank to induce Indonesia to halt the destruction and to allow the international intervention force.[44] The United States also exerted pressure through warnings from the Chairman of the Joint Chiefs of Staff, the Commander of the Pacific Fleet, and the Secretary of Defense.[45] In the end, Habibie responded to the pressure by requesting the INTERFET intervention.

Consensus

Unlike ever before or since, from May to October 1999, there was a flurry of activity regarding East Timor in the Security Council, with the Council holding eight discussions, and passing six resolutions.[46] All resolutions were passed unanimously, in light of Indonesia's consent for INTERFET, as well as the follow-on peacekeeping operations. There was consensus as to the basic nature of the problem, and debates were not acrimonious. We can therefore

[41] The East Timorese who gave support to the Australian troops during World War II were often brutally punished by Japanese forces. See Bell, 2000, p. 175.
[42] Rodrigues, 2003, p. 25.   [43] Greenless and Garran, 2002, pp. 251, 265.
[44] Dee, 2001, p. 4   [45] Bell, 2000, p. 170.
[46] It had passed none since its second resolution in 1976, and would pass only several more from 2000 to 2005.

determine that there was consensus around Security Council action toward East Timor, both for INTERFET and UNTAET.[47]

Intensity

In 1999, four new, large multidimensional peacekeeping operations were initiated by the Security Council, in East Timor, Kosovo, Sierra Leone, and the Democratic Republic of the Congo. Of the sixty-five resolutions passed, many concerned these operations, as well as the situation in Iraq and Kuwait.

In East Timor, when the fighting broke out after the independence vote, as mentioned above, the Council met frequently to discuss what to do. Since Australia was prepared to lead INTERFET, and Japan to fund the force, the Council had little substance over which its members could disagree. Earlier in the year, the United States had been in favor of sending peacekeepers, along with the electoral-monitoring mission, to be in place before the plebiscite and to help monitor the Indonesian military and the security situation in general, but since Indonesia refused, Australia (which was not a member of the Security Council at the time) along with other members of the Security Council were able to convince the United States not to press the issue.

In terms of tangible contributions, the United States contributed lift capacity to INTERFET, without which the mission could not have deployed rapidly, and France and the UK sent troops for INTERFET.[48] As for the resolutions concerning UNTAET, the mandate for the operation did not arise out of a Secretary-General report. Indeed, from August to December 1999 no official reports were submitted by the Secretary-General. Funding for the peacekeeping operation was adequate, although there was pressure from the beginning to "downsize" the operation to minimize costs.[49] The interest intensity of the Security Council members could be characterized as moderate.

Organizational change and mandate implementation

Aside from external influences from the Security Council and individual states, the East Timorese had developed a complicated relationship with the United Nations over time. According to one historian, there was a general sense that the UN had a history of betrayal of the East Timorese (dating from the independence struggles of the early 1960s), which was reconfirmed after the UN

---

[47] The Security Council votes to establish UNAMET, UNMISET, and UNOTIL in East Timor were also unanimous.

[48] Dee, 2001, p. 20, note 17.

[49] See Suhrke, 2001, pp. 10–11; and Kapila, 2003, p. 60. Any projects that could not be covered by regular peacekeeping assessments were supplemented through bilateral assistance, along with two trust funds organized by the World Bank.

failed to protect the East Timorese during the 1999 scorched earth campaign.[50] But at the same time, as Smith and Dee explain, "During the 24 years of Indonesia's occupation, the UN remained the only realistic hope for achieving self-determination. The East Timorese political leaders were conscious of this reality and were committed to working with the UN."[51]

This commitment started to take a more formal shape in early 1999, when the East Timorese leadership began discussions with the UN Department of Political Affairs (DPA) and the World Bank about assistance with a possible transition to independence.[52] The basic plan was that the DPA-sponsored UNAMET mission would monitor the popular consultation, and would be followed by UNAMET II and III, which would oversee follow-on stages of the political transition to independence and economic development. During these discussions, the East Timorese thought they were communicating with the whole UN system, but in fact, the different UN agencies were not necessarily communicating with one another. After the devastation in September 1999, given the obvious need for a peacekeeping operation to accompany the efforts at political transition and development, many people in the UN system and in East Timor thought the Department of Peacekeeping Operations (DPKO) would become the lead department for the UN's operation. Xanana Gusmao and his colleagues proposed a transitional administration plan for DPKO, whereby a Council of East Timor Transition would be established to work in partnership with the proposed UNTAET operation. His proposal, however, was apparently "ignored by New York."[53]

The disinterest in having Gusmao and his colleagues actively participate in the planning was due to a sense that the DPKO did not want to bias the political process in favor of Fretilin, headed by Gusmao, which was the largest party in the CNRT. Fretilin had not been granted the status that, for example, SWAPO in Namibia had been granted by the UN General Assembly as the "sole and authentic" representative of the Namibian people. Therefore, the exclusion of Gusmao's plan is understandable, to a certain extent.

What was not logical was the Peacekeeping Department's refusal to communicate and plan more effectively with the members of the Department of Political Affairs. DPKO and DPA were at odds as to which department would take the lead role in the operation. As one analyst explains:

> Inter-departmental rivalry over the institutional mandate was reinforced by personality clashes, especially at the top level. The DPKO did not even

---

[50] See Saltford, 2003.   [51] Smith and Dee, 2003, p. 44.

[52] The leadership had previously been in discussions with UNDP, as is often the case in developing nations.

[53] Rodrigues, 2003, p. 29. Moreover, the DPKO planners in New York consulted with many other agencies in the UN system, but not with the UNDP, even though UNDP had already established relations with the East Timorese leadership.

respond to a proposal from the DPA's Under Secretary-General for a joint
planning mission ... Given the tense relations between the two departments,
formalized joint planning or a joint mission seemed impossible.[54]

Eventually, Secretary-General Annan stepped in to settle the intra-UN dispute.
Members of both departments would participate in the planning, but DPKO
would have overall authority.

The "fierce bureaucratic power struggle between DPA and DPKO" had ram-
ifications for the plans and conduct of the operation in the field.[55] The plans
for the multidimensional peacekeeping operation, devised by the members of
the DPKO, were directly shaped by "lessons" from the experiences in Kosovo,
and the most recent experience with multidimensional peacekeeping in Asia
(the UNTAC operation in Cambodia). For example, in the words of one of the
planners, "When the team started planning, it took as a model the plan for the
UN administration in Kosovo . . . it borrowed early decrees and directives from
UNMIK [the United Nations Interim Administration Mission in Kosovo] . . .
The basic principle was: make the structure simple and fully integrated."[56]
However, the overall structure in East Timor was much more simplified than
the one in Kosovo. It was integrated within itself, under UN leadership, unlike
in Kosovo, where different agencies were in charge of the five different "pillars."
But similar to the UNMIK model in Kosovo, locals were not initially permitted
to take part in the governing structures. This decision stemmed in part from
the more detached approach toward the East Timorese taken by DPKO (in
contrast to that of DPA), but also came as a result of previous peacekeeping
experience in Asia. One of the primary "lessons learned" from the operations
in Cambodia was that the UN should strive as much as possible *not* to rely
on local political elites, since the most successful of the divisions in UNTAC
were mainly self-sufficient; they did not need local participation in order to be
successful.

Thus the basic plan for the UNTAET operation centered around three main
UN "pillars," and it did not specify how East Timorese would participate.
UNTAET was not designed to be integrated with Timorese society or the de
facto political structures in East Timor. "From the East Timorese perspective,
it was surprising to see that UNTAET seemed to have done its planning *de
novo*."[57] In other words, the East Timorese felt that DPKO had dreamed up
its own plan, which was more a reflection of past UN experiences and internal
politics than those in East Timor. Even a senior member of the DPKO operation
agreed: "There is little doubt that 'lack of cohesion' within the UN in both New
York and Dili, particularly between DPA/UNAMET and DPKO/UNTAET, was
real and damaging."[58] The "lack of cohesion" complicated relations with the

[54] Suhrke, 2001, p. 6.   [55] Suhrke, 2001, p. 6.   [56] Kawakami, 2003, p. 43.
[57] Azimi and Chang, 2003, p. xxix.   [58] Goldstone, 2004, p. 86.

East Timorese and their integration into the operation. It also contributed to staffing problems in UNTAET.

In the field, many key staff members from UNAMET were either not hired, or not hired quickly enough, by UNTAET. This translated into a significant loss of individually held knowledge of the politics, society, and recent events in East Timor, and therefore an important loss of potential resources for first-level learning on the part of UNTAET as a whole. Moreover the operation in general was understaffed, and many of the most experienced staff were soon sent on to the other operations that began in 1999, most notably the one in Kosovo. Some of the staff who were eventually sent to East Timor were reputed to be of questionable quality: "Part of the problem was that recruitment was largely done at the headquarters level whereas recruitment decisions made at the mission level could have helped ensure a better fit between need and competency."[59] Many of the staff sent to East Timor did not have appropriate language skills, and were reported to be better versed in UN politics than in the regional politics of Asia, or the specifics of East Timor.

In terms of the leadership of the operation, Ian Martin, the head of DPA's operation stayed on as interim head of UNTAET until the Brazilian diplomat, Sergio Vieira de Mello, was hired. Vieira de Mello assumed his post in mid-November 1999. In other words, he was not a part of the UN's historical involvement in East Timor, nor a part of the planning process, since he had previously been deployed in Kosovo. What Vieira de Mello did bring to the operation, however, was a vast experience in UN management, native Portuguese language skills, and political support from key donor countries. Given Vieira de Mello's ties to UN headquarters and to the donor countries, it is not surprising that at first he was criticized for following "a strategy tailored to broader international issues and headquarters perspectives."[60] Vieira de Mello was candid in retrospect about the repercussions of his, and in general, the UN's early approach: "Failure to hit the ground running means that we risk, from the outset, failing to earn legitimacy with the populations we have come to assist."[61] Vieira de Mello's approach changed over time, as his focus, and the operation, gradually shifted from UN headquarters to the field, and the organization moved from a dysfunctional to a learning mode.

Mandate

While mission planning for UNTAET was conducted in DPKO, Security Council Resolution 1272 mandating UNTAET was drafted in haste by the "Friends of the Secretary-General" – Australia, Japan, New Zealand, the UK, and the USA – with little formal input from either the Secretariat or from the East

[59] Azimi and Chang, 2003, p. xxviii.   [60] Suhrke, 2001, p. 12.
[61] Vieira de Mello, 2003, p. 17.

Timorese.[62] The text of the mandate was unprecedented in terms of the authority bestowed upon the Secretariat. Under Chapter VII authorizing "all means necessary," the Transitional Administration was endowed with the overall responsibility for the administration of East Timor, including explicitly all three branches of government: the legislature, executive, and judiciary. The mandate specified six major tasks: (1) "provide security and maintain law and order," (2) "establish an effective administration," (3) "assist in the development of civil and social services," (4) coordinate and deliver humanitarian, rehabilitation, and development assistance, (5) "support capacity building for self-government," and (6) "assist in the establishment of conditions for sustainable development."[63] The Security Council resolution also refers to developing "local democratic institutions" and the administration of justice. In the words of Secretary-General Kofi Annan, the mandate had "inherently open-ended tasks relating to building the very fabric of a nation, tasks which could not be achieved in a transition of a few years, but rather, are the ongoing tasks of development."[64] Never before had a mandate for a peacekeeping mission focused so much on state administrative responsibilities and economic development.

The mandate also specified three major components in the structure of UNTAET: (1) governance and public administration (including a 1,640 international police element), (2) the UN peacekeeping force (with an authorized strength of up to just over 9,000 troops and military observers), and (3) humanitarian assistance and emergency rehabilitation. Unlike previous multidimensional peacekeeping mandates, this one underlined the "importance of including UNTAET personnel with appropriate training . . . including child and gender-related provisions, negotiation and communication skills, cultural awareness and civil-military coordination."[65] It also indicated that there would be cooperation with international financial institutions, but not how the cooperation would be instituted in practice.

More importantly, the mandate did not specify the mechanisms governing the relationship between the UN and the East Timorese leadership, nor how the transition to Timorese governance would occur. This was due in large part to the rushed nature of the pre-mandate deliberations. There was simply no time in the wake of the destruction after the independence vote to negotiate the extremely important factors of how power might be shared, and eventually transferred. Such issues would have to be addressed during the course of the operation. The mandate presented the operation with a central tension:

---

[62] The Security Council documents and progress reports of the Secretary-General all refer to a Secretary-General report dated October 4, 1999, but this report mentions almost nothing about a transitional administration, and no specific plans. It does request "prompt Security Council action on the Secretary-General's report" but there is no publicly available report that specifies and outlines the plans for UNTAET. See S/1999/1025, 4 October 1999.

[63] S/RES/1272, 25 October 1999, p. 2.   [64] Annan, 2003, p. xxiv.

[65] S/RES/1272, 25 October 1999, p. 4.

delivering the services of the state as quickly as possible, while building the capability of others to run the state. The two tasks were not easily integrated with one another, and they required different skills sets: the capacity to administer, as opposed to the ability to teach.

Pillar 1: Governance and public administration / East Timorese Transitional Administration

The primary "pillar" of the operation, Governance and Public Administration, was responsible for fulfilling the majority of the mandate's provisions. Of the three pillars, it was the most comprehensive, including executive and legislative duties, and the civilian police and judicial affairs divisions.[66] This pillar began in a state of organizational dysfunction, but after heavy criticism and self-reflection, its members managed to move it, quite dramatically, into a first-level learning mode. The pillar was criticized from its inception, both from within and without the UN system, for not being well planned, staffed, or integrated with the local East Timorese elite or society. Change within the pillar, in the way it related to the East Timorese, was driven most often by the influence of the East Timorese leadership, which sought a direct stake in the political institutions that were being devised for the country; but most of the staff and leadership of UNTAET also eventually recognized the need for change. The changes took the official form of two major institutional reforms in UNTAET–Timorese relations: the "First Transitional Administration," or the "National Consultative Council" and the "Second Transitional Administration," also called the "National Council."

In terms of the early days of the operation, UNTAET was obliged "to govern and legally rule by decree, while remaining directly accountable to the Security Council, and indirectly and morally, to the populations under its administration."[67] In other words, the Transitional Administration was in no way legally accountable to the East Timorese, nor did it have a formal mechanism governing its relationship with the East Timorese leadership. These central problems began

---

[66] Mandate components 2, 3, and 5 were the primary responsibility of this pillar, including establishing an effective administration, developing civil and social services, and supporting self-governance. The pillar was also responsible for developing democratic institutions, the administration of justice, and maintaining law and order. A Gender Affairs Unit was also established, and it worked to promote the participation of women at all stages of the endeavor. UNTAET recommended that there be 30 percent female representation throughout the new Timorese government. The unit conducted gender orientation sessions with the UNTAET military and police units, as well as with the nascent East Timorese Police Service. According to Vieira de Mello (2003, p. 21), "The results were formidable: a quiet revolution took place. In all state institutions – the police, the civil service, and the Parliament in particular – there are levels of representation by women that would be impressive in countries in which the debate over gender equality is much more advanced."

[67] Boisard, 2003, p. 10.

to be alleviated with the establishment of a National Consultative Council in December 1999. The National Consultative Council included seven representatives of the CNRT, three representatives of pro-autonomy (anti-independence) political groups, one representative of the Catholic Church, and four international members: the Transitional Administrator and three of his staff. The body was supposed to play an advisory role, but in practice it did much more, including reviewing and approving all of UNTAET's regulatory policies.

This effort at sharing responsibilities and communication, however, did not go far enough. One member of the East Timorese leadership, Emilia Pires of the Ministry of Planning and Finance in East Timor, explained that in early 2000 "as the gap between the East Timorese and internationals became wider . . . there was less communication between them leading to more misunderstanding . . . there was also a period when the UN started to be perceived as neo-colonizers by the East Timorese."[68] While the UN sought to recruit and train Timorese to take part in the emerging civil service, Pires reflected further that "Many East Timorese would not join the civil service because they felt it was a UN civil service. They did not understand that UNTAET was setting up the civil service for the East Timorese future government . . . many professional cadres did not join the public service."[69] Vieira de Mello saw a similar picture from the UN's point of view, stating that "[we were] hobbled by our inability to convey to the public at large, as a matter of routine, the nature of our mission and the unprecedented challenges being faced."[70]

The challenges in communication and mutual understanding between UNTAET and the East Timorese stemmed primarily from three sources: technical, linguistic, and cultural. For example, in terms of technical challenges, in a country where approximately 34 percent of the population was illiterate, UNTAET was not able to set up radio broadcasts until eighteen months after the start of the operation. The task was a difficult one, given the challenging physical characteristics of the East Timorese terrain and the lack of existing radio infrastructure; however, eighteen months was a very long time to take in establishing such a critical mechanism for information dissemination.

Second, problems of communication were aggravated not only by technical difficulties, but also by language incompatibility. For example, the central planning meetings of the First Transitional Government were held in English, which most East Timorese Cabinet members did not understand. English was the working language of the UN's operation, but the East Timorese elite would have preferred Portuguese. As one East Timorese politician noted: "All of the Council of Ministers' Meeting for the First Transitional Government were held in English, thereby reducing the effectiveness of the participation of the East Timorese Cabinet Members."[71]

---

[68] Pires, 2003, p. 57.   [69] Pires, 2003, p. 57.   [70] Vieira de Mello, 2003, p. 22.
[71] Rodrigues, 2003, p. 29.

Finally, and most significantly, members of UNTAET and the East Timorese had considerable cultural barriers to overcome. Within UNTAET, as mentioned earlier, staff members were sent from dozens of different countries and were "uneven" in terms of preparation, ability, and cultural sensitivity.[72] At the same time, this mixed UN staff was supposed to set a positive example of bureaucratic efficiency and effectiveness for the new government. Compounding the internal differences within UNTAET was the legacy of a heavy-handed and corrupt Indonesian civil service. UNTAET sought to "re-engineer a bureaucratic culture which, under the Indonesian administration, was characterized by the acronym KKN (corruption, collusion, and nepotism)."[73] The expectation that a multinational peacekeeping operation could overcome, by example and by design, the bureaucratic legacies of two decades of misrule was unrealistic. Nevertheless, the mission sought to make headway by taking incremental institutional steps.

For example, UNTAET staff attempted to reach out to locals, even during the early months of the operation. UNTAET established thirteen district offices, headed by international personnel, but in reaction to East Timorese pressure to include more locals, Timorese deputy district administrators were added to the structure in April 2000, as well as East Timorese deputy heads of departments.

These attempts at reforming UNTAET's institutions did not at first appear to have enough of an effect of decentralizing decision-making authority. Power in UNTAET remained centralized in Dili, and most decisions continued to be made among a small group of international staff members. UNTAET's district administrators "complained of their exclusion from policy decisions," and they argued that unless the decision-making process was reformed, the inclusion of East Timorese as deputy district administrators would be meaningless.[74] When the reforms did not happen quickly enough, Jarat Chopra, the head of the District Administration, resigned and wrote several articles about his experience.[75]

Chopra's very public pressure for reform, and devolution of power and decision-making, was echoed by threats of resignation on the part of the East Timorese leadership (at the time, the threat of resignation was the most effective and direct mechanism for Timorese leaders to push for changes in UNTAET).[76] The leadership also organized the "Tibar Conference" to bring East Timorese and international staff together to reflect on the progress of the mission. As one minister attested: "I believe we came out with a better understanding of each other at the end of the conference."[77] Immediately after the conference,

[72] Martin and Mayer-Rieckh, 2005, p. 136.   [73] Ingram, 2003, p. 89.
[74] Chesterman, 2001, p. 17.   [75] See Chopra, 2000 and 2002.
[76] In December 2000, the East Timorese Cabinet members threatened to resign, citing lack of power, resources or official duties. Ramos Horta and Gusmao both resigned and were immediately reinstated on several occasions. See Chesterman, 2001, p. 20.
[77] Pires, 2003, p. 57.

UNTAET proposed a new formula for joint government, which eventually became the blueprint for the Second Transitional Government. Vieira de Mello explained:

> Through an increasingly inclusive consultation process, we are doing our best . . . to improve our shared understanding of issues . . . we are about to expand the NCC [National Consultative Council] into a more representative body . . . we are establishing District Advisory Councils. We are also strengthening our efforts at communication and outreach to ensure the population at large is abreast of developments . . . Our friends of the East Timorese leadership will agree, I am sure, that despite occasional setbacks, we have now reached a much higher level of mutual understanding and there is a greater sense of common purpose.[78]

Negotiations in June 2000 between UNTAET and East Timorese leaders produced a new governing body, the National Council (also called the "Second Transitional Administration") which would serve as precursor to the eventual Parliament. The National Council had thirty-three members, all of whom were Timorese including the Chairman, and represented a wide cross-segment of East Timorese society. The list included representatives of the thirteen districts; seven members of the CNRT; three members of parties opposed to the CNRT; members of the Catholic, Protestant, and Muslim communities; and representatives from civil society, including women's organizations, youth groups, other Timorese NGOs, professional associations, and labor, business, and farming groups.[79] Xanana Gusmao was elected speaker of the National Council in October 2000. Alongside the National Council, a Cabinet of Transitional Government in East Timor was also founded, and included eight posts: four for East Timorese (Internal Administration, Infrastructure, Economic Affairs, and Social Affairs); and four for international personnel (Police and Emergency Services, Political Affairs, Justice, and Finance). The National Council was endowed with the power to call members of the Cabinet before it for questioning, as well as the ability to initiate, modify, amend, and recommend regulations.

After the establishment of the National Council and the Cabinet, tensions between the East Timorese and UNTAET appear to have lessened, but they were not entirely alleviated. As Timorese began to take on more leadership responsibilities, issues continually emerged, especially concerning how the UN staff would make their own duties obsolete, and the culture and shape of the emerging civil service. UNTAET trod a fine line: on the one hand, members of

---

[78] Vieira de Mello speech to the Lisbon Donors' Meeting on East Timor, June 22–23, 2000. In Chesterman, 2001, p. 20.

[79] The National Council was expanded again three months later to include three new members, one of whom was Jose Ramos-Horta, who took up the post of Cabinet member in charge of Foreign Affairs.

the mission wanted to complete their tasks, which required maintaining control over outcomes, and imparting western notions of bureaucracy and efficiency; but on the other hand, the mission was mandated to train Timorese to take control themselves. Governing mechanisms set up by UNTAET might adhere to strict efficiency and effectiveness standards, but they would most likely not be sustainable if not initiated at least in part by Timorese themselves.

Two aspects of the civil service in particular appear to have been effectively, efficiently, and sustainably developed between UNTAET (with the assistance of the World Bank) and the new East Timorese civil servants: the annual budgetary process, and the national health care system.[80] Other sectors, including, for example, justice and energy/power, were not as well established, while others still, such as education, roads, and private sector development, were for the most part set in motion by the time of independence.[81]

In sum, while the most important pillar of the operation began in a dysfunctional organizational mode, over time, with pressure from the East Timorese and from its own members, the pillar began to change the way it interacted with the East Timorese, and it was able to fulfill many of the tasks it set out to accomplish. Even Vieira de Mello admits that the overall early approach of the operation was misguided and needed to be changed:

> While our consultation in those early days was genuine, our approach towards achieving that failed truly to bring in the East Timorese on all aspects of policy formulation and development . the strategy we eventually developed [a two phase devolution of power] was, I think, the right one; we just had to feel our way, somewhat blindly, towards it, wasting several months in doing so.[82]

The several "wasted" months do not appear to have permanently damaged the ability of the operation to implement its tasks, but the slow movement toward an organizational learning mode did mean that UNTAET created for itself more barriers to success than were necessary.

Civilian police

The CIVPOL division of UNTAET had a fairly broad mandate but began with few resources or staff. It also commanded, at the outset, comparatively little attention from the leadership of UNTAET, since the division reported to a Deputy Special Representative of the Secretary-General, and its commander was not part of the regular weekly planning meetings of UNTAET. It is not surprising, therefore, that the division did not perform particularly well in the beginning, although there was improvement over time.

The CIVPOL was organized as a separate unit from the military division. The physical, logistical, and political separation of the two units was designed

[80] Ingram, 2003, p. 91.   [81] Cliffe and Rohland, 2003, p. 115.
[82] Vieira de Mello, 2003, p. 19.

to be a model for the future East Timorese governing institutions, where civilians, rather than the military, would be connected with policing activity. The purposive separation, while serving important symbolic functions, also had the unintended consequence of poor coordination between the military and police divisions of UNTAET. There was "no joint doctrine or concept for joint operations" between the two units.[83] This meant that there was no permanent coordination in the event of riots, internal unrest, or even electoral-monitoring duties.

There were also internal coordination problems within CIVPOL. Unlike the military division, where units deployed as part of national contingents, the CIVPOL units were most often made up of groups of individual members from different member states. As Vieira de Mello explained:

> The mixing up of 40 different nationalities of police (and thus of training backgrounds, and competencies, policing philosophies and approaches), and the task of this hybrid with establishing an immediate and effective policing presence in a territory to which it is alien both linguistically and culturally, is an approach inherently fraught with risk.[84]

And given those risks, and low staffing numbers, UNTAET's first police commissioner, Chief Superintendent Peter Miller of Canada, was reluctant to establish sub-district stations.[85] This meant that the CIVPOL did not have the institutional profile for adequate interaction with the local population, even in a setting where the security tasks were not particularly problematic.

Staffing problems compounded the difficulties. UN member states have tended to keep their high-quality police officers for duty at home (which is not often the case with military troops); thus not only the number, but the quality of the CIVPOL staff was inadequate. Language difficulties added to the problems. Many of the members of CIVPOL did not have the language skills necessary to communicate well with each other, much less with the East Timorese, and good interpreters were difficult to find in East Timor.[86] In other words, at the outset of the operation, the UN's civilian police were not communicating well with either UNTAET's own military division, with themselves, or with the local population.

In early 2000, Vieira de Mello sought to counteract some of the dysfunction in the CIVPOL division. In terms of the poor quality of staff, he sent CIVPOL members home who did not meet minimum language, driving, or firearm capabilities, and he required of member states that only well-qualified police be sent. By the end of February 2000, less than 500 CIVPOL were in East

---

[83] Smith and Dee, 2003, p. 76.   [84] Vieira de Mello, 2003, p. 20.
[85] Smith and Dee, 2003, p. 74.
[86] Language barriers also inhibited the smooth functioning of the entire policing and judicial process, since different languages were used by different national contingents overseeing the different phases of reporting, investigation, and prosecution. See Azimi and Chang, 2003, p. xxvii.

Timor, even though the force was mandated at 1,640 strong. Vieira de Mello pressed UN headquarters to speed up the hiring processes, and eventually the numbers were augmented to close to the mandated strength. He also instituted a new organizational plan whereby CIVPOL would be deployed according to national contingent, along the lines of the deployment patterns of the military peacekeepers. In turn, "performance improved to a certain degree in the course of the operation."[87]

A police training academy supported by UNTAET opened in Dili in March 2000 and released its first class of graduates in July 2000. The academy was established in order to build up the East Timor Police Service so that the East Timorese could take over policing responsibilities as soon as possible. By the time of the first elections in August 2001, the East Timorese police were established enough that they held responsibility for maintaining law and order; they performed well, and the elections went smoothly. Over time, the primary hindrance to good policing proved to be the lack of an adequate legal system. The slow establishment of this sector spelled significant delays, for example, in prosecuting criminal offenders, because neither the UN nor the East Timorese had adequate structures in place.

Judicial affairs

The tasks confronting UNTAET in the realm of justice were numerous and daunting. After the September 1999 destruction, East Timor was virtually emptied of the personnel required to run a legal system, in terms of both the courts and the prisons. The UNTAET leadership took several steps early on to try to re-create a legal system, including reinstating the primacy of the pre-August 1999 law (minus the elements that contravened basic human rights such as those on antisubversion, social organization, and national security); setting up a UN-run incarceration facility; and establishing a joint UN–East Timorese Transitional Judicial Service Commission.[88] A joint UN–East Timorese Serious Crimes Unit was also established, and it indicted many high-ranking officials for crimes against humanity during the September 1999 rampage, including General Wiranto.[89] The unit began handing down serious indictments for regular crimes, as well as crimes against humanity, in December 2000. In the same month, the Transitional Cabinet approved of a Commission for Truth, Reception, and Reconciliation, which forwarded its first convictions for crimes against humanity in December 2001. In general, UNTAET's strategy in judicial affairs was to train Timorese staff quickly, and turn over the administration of

[87] Martin and Mayer-Rieckh, 2005, p. 134.
[88] The Transitional Judicial Service Commission was made up of three East Timorese and two international staff members.
[89] General Wiranto later became a candidate in the Indonesian elections.

justice to the East Timorese as rapidly as possible. But as one observer noted, "there is no quick way to set up a justice system."[90]

The most important obstacles to success in the realm of the judiciary were rooted not in UN mismanagement, but in the nature of the post-1999 situation in East Timor. While the UN sought to train East Timorese as quickly as possible, "by October 2001, the justice system was still in a nascent state, with only twenty-five East Timorese judges and thirteen prosecutors, most of whom had only secondary education and less than two years of training and experience."[91] There simply was not enough time before independence in May 2002 to train the numbers of people required to run an effective, efficient, and politically independent legal system in East Timor.

Compounding the technical staffing problem was the serious lack of political cooperation on the part of Indonesia in returning, or prosecuting, militia members and others who had committed serious crimes in the 1999 devastation. Most suspects had fled to Indonesia in the wake of the arrival of INTERFET and have been protected there ever since: "the fulfillment of justice for the events in East Timor [are] dependent on Indonesia, which since then has been moving towards that goal at a mere snail's pace."[92] Indonesia did set up some courts to try those accused of serious crimes in East Timor, but as of 2005, of the eighteen accused, seventeen had been acquitted and one was still at large, pending appeal. While in recent years the UN Secretariat has initiated discussions of taking the issues out of the hands of East Timor and Indonesia, and setting up an international tribunal or at least a "Commission of Experts," Indonesia has refused such moves, with the support of China, and most recently, even the East Timorese have not been supportive of the idea. Gusmao in particular has been inclined to try to seek good relations with Indonesia, rather than pressing for prosecution, and has been promoting the avenues of truth, reception, and reconciliation. In other words, judicial processes have progressed slowly, both in terms of setting up the domestic East Timorese legal system, and in terms of prosecuting criminal acts committed during the September 1999 violence.

Pillar 2: UN peacekeeping force

UNTAET's peacekeeping troops were mandated to secure East Timor's borders, maintain order, disarm and demobilize militias, and help to set up a new army, with just under 9,000 peacekeeping troops (although in reality, only about 8,000 were ever deployed). The operation, endowed with UN Charter Chapter VII strength, tended to be less concerned with "force protection" than, for example, the one in Kosovo, and it was "closely and vigorously coordinated."[93] The overall

---

[90] Dunn, 2003, p. 370.   [91] Smith and Dee, 2003, p. 83.   [92] Gorjao, 2002, p. 324.
[93] McNamara, 2003, p. 34.

approach of the peacekeeping troops, their well-oiled internal coordination, as well as coordination and cooperation with other components of UNTAET, contributed significantly to the successful implementation of their mandate.

The peacekeeping force was built on INTERFET's already well-functioning military structure. The presence of INTERFET when UNTAET began meant that there was no security vacuum at the beginning of the operation. And indeed, when UNTAET took over military command in February 2000, 70 percent of INTERFET forces stayed to become UNTAET peacekeepers. By the time UNTAET deployed, the security situation in East Timor had been, for the most part, stabilized by INTERFET. In other words, UNTAET's military division inherited a well-functioning command structure, experienced troops, and a comparatively calm situational profile on the ground in East Timor.

This is not to say, however, that the troops did not confront problems. Beginning in March 2000, and again from July to September 2000, members of different anti-independence militia groups infiltrated East Timor. Several UN peacekeepers were killed, along with several UNHCR staff, and thousands of local Timorese were displaced. The UN Security Council responded by "insisting" that Indonesia stop the attacks, but words were not enough. In September, UNTAET launched two major counterattacks, operations "crocodilo" and "cobra," in cooperation with CIVPOL and other divisions of UNTAET, in order to drive the militia back into West Timor. The commander in charge of the operations, Colonel José Alberto Martins Ferreira, had served as "head of the Military Information cell . . . where he had developed a deep understanding of the militia."[94] Both operations were swift and successful, with no reported loss of civilian life. As Vieira de Mello explained later: "our ability, on the ground, to modify our military's rules of engagement – quickly – as the security situation warranted was vital. Only by doing so were we able, effectively, to address the serious militia incursions of mid-2000 and fulfill one of our core responsibilities: ensuring peace in East Timor."[95] While the UN's operations on the ground worked on the front lines of combating the militia, members of the UN Security Council exerted higher-level pressure on Indonesia to assist in efforts at militia control. In January 2001, the two sources of pressure came together to produce joint UNTAET–Indonesian patrols in problem areas on the border between East and West Timor, greatly reducing the ability of the militias to infiltrate.

In terms of the overall engagement of the military division with the local population, UNTAET's troops and strategies proved exemplary. While the division did not enjoy some of the technical and logistical capabilities that enabled easy mobility for INTERFET, the mission sought to compensate for decreased mobility by using other, more effective means. For example, "some of the contingents became proficient in the language, further gaining the confidence of

---

[94] Smith and Dee, 2003, p. 91.   [95] Vieira de Mello, 2003, p. 18.

the population and enhancing situational awareness."[96] A strong presence of peacekeepers from regional powers narrowed "the gap of cultural misunderstanding between military and civilians."[97] By most assessments, the peacekeeping forces engaged well and appropriately with the local population. The leadership judged that the best way to defeat the militia groups was to make sure that the local population would not provide the groups with support. The head of the UNTAET military operations in mid-2000, Lieutenant General Boonsrang Niumpradit of Thailand, was praised as a "strategist of keen intellect, with an infectious sense of humor and impressive people skills...[who] appreciated that the militias' success would be directly related to their ability to intimidate and win over support from the local population, particularly in remote areas."[98] As movement and activity of the militias diminished, the UNTAET troops began to help increasingly with infrastructure projects – especially UNTAET's military engineers and medical units. Other analysts explain: "The forces seem to have adapted their mission accordingly to the needs of the community, shifting focus gradually and rather effectively from dealing with the militia to winning the hearts and minds of the East Timorese."[99]

Aside from the shift in attention from the militias to greater engagement with the civilian population, UNTAET's military component underwent another important shift in psychological and operational focus. At the outset of the operation, as is customary in UN peacekeeping operations, UNTAET representatives were inclined to treat all sides in the conflict equally in an effort to maintain the impartiality that is essential to the success of most peacekeeping operations. However, "FALINTIL commanders deeply resented the implication that they were in the same category as the militia."[100] Over time, the leadership of UNTAET came to understand that it would need the cooperation and support of Falintil in order to win the favor of the population, and to succeed in implementing the mandate. Therefore, rather than treating Falintil as a group to be disarmed, the majority of troops (several thousand) instead became the core of the East Timorese Defense Force.[101] Falintil members who were not recruited for the new army were demobilized and generally re-integrated successfully through the Falintil Reintegration Assistance Programme, which was run by the International Organization for Migration and funded by the World Bank and USAID. The new East Timorese Defense Force gradually gained in strength and ability over the course of the UNTAET operation, and appeared prepared to engage in its primary duties – deterring militia incursions and other potential sources of aggression, and assisting civilian efforts during natural disasters – upon independence in the spring of 2002.

---

[96] Smith and Dee, 2003, p. 69.   [97] Azimi and Chang, 2003, p. xxvi.
[98] Smith and Dee, 2003, p. 72.   [99] Azimi and Chang, 2003, p. xxvii.
[100] Dunn, 2003, p. 367.   [101] Martin and Mayer-Rieckh, 2005, p. 134.

Pillar 3: Humanitarian assistance and emergency rehabilitation

The humanitarian assistance and emergency rehabilitation pillar was designed to be a temporary arrangement, bridging the gap between early emergency relief operations and longer-term development projects. The pillar was originally coordinated by the UN Office for the Coordination of Humanitarian Affairs (OCHA), and it was eventually handed over to UNTAET, learning on the second level from the UN peacekeeping operation in Mozambique, where humanitarian assistance had not been centrally coordinated. By mid-2000, OCHA was centrally coordinating some 100 humanitarian organizations working on the ground. The groups contributed significantly to all areas of humanitarian assistance – providing emergency food, shelter, and medical care. The pillar had to confront some unforeseen calamities, such as major floods in May 2000, which killed over 80 people, mainly Timorese refugees, and displaced 21,000.[102] While some criticized the work of this pillar for neglecting longer-term development issues early on, it is credited with fulfilling its mandate, and generally being effective and successful.[103]

In terms of refugee returns, by the end of 1999, over half of the 250,000 East Timorese refugees in West Timor had returned. The number of refugees diminished significantly over the course of UNTAET's operation, due in large part to the smooth coordination and cooperation between the UNHCR, international and local church organizations, the UNTAET leadership, and the East Timorese. Xanana Gusmao, in particular, was persuasive as the moral leader in East Timor advocating forgiveness and reception for returning refugees, many of whom either supported, or were perceived to have supported, the anti-independence forces. The refugees who remained in West Timor were often intimidated by anti-independence militia groups who sometimes kept the refugees in West Timor under armed guard, and "activated a malicious propaganda campaign fabricating stories of murder and rape against those returning."[104] UNTAET was at a disadvantage in the face of such campaigns, since they were being conducted in refugee camps in Indonesian West Timor, where UNTAET did not have a mandate to operate. The UNHCR, however, was able to function in West Timor and initiated a number of different types of efforts, such as facilitating "go and see" visits to convince refugees that they could safely return. By the end of UNTAET, while over 200,000 refugees had returned, approximately 50,000 had not.[105] Upon independence, the problem became one for the new East Timorese government, which, while professing an interest in reconciliation with Timorese who were opposed to independence, was not prepared to

---

[102] During the floods, the UNTAET troops assisted in the delivery of humanitarian assistance. Such cooperation helped to demonstrate to the East Timorese people that not all troops in uniform were as brutal as the military forces of the former occupiers.

[103] Martin and Mayer-Rieckh, 2005, p. 135.   [104] Smith and Dee, 2003, p. 85.

[105] S/432, 17 April 2002, para. 31.

put a lot of effort into trying to repatriate the remaining people who were the most reluctant to return. In 2005, the Indonesian government initiated efforts to resettle the remaining refugees upon the end of the UNHCR presence in West Timor.[106] In other words, UNTAET did not completely fulfill its mandate of overseeing refugee return before its end, and the problem remains one that the East Timorese and Indonesian governments must sort out.

Economic and social development

Most of the major social and economic development projects were not directly under UNTAET's purview, but rather the World Bank's. The World Bank established two trust funds for East Timor, and it oversaw projects to rehabilitate such sectors as health, education, agriculture, community development, private development, transport and power, water and sanitation, and microfinance. The World Bank had begun preparing its mission before September 1999, and then in earnest in October/November 1999, when it held a "Joint Assessment Mission" with key East Timorese leaders in order to devise strategies at institution-building that involved East Timorese directly. According to Sarah Cliffe, the Chief of Mission for the World Bank's efforts, the Joint Assessment Mission provided a solid foundation for fruitful working relationships between all parties involved and demonstrated "the importance of following a truly 'joint' approach in planning with both national counterparts and donors."[107] East Timorese were included at all levels of planning and implementation, often with successful results. Targets for accomplishments in each of the sectors were largely met by the time of East Timorese independence.[108]

The greatest achievement was probably in the redevelopment of agriculture. Rice and corn production had returned to pre-1999 levels by the end of the UNTAET operation, and new capabilities in coffee production were being developed. By the spring of 2002, in terms of the other sectors, fishing operations had been largely re-established; water and sanitation services were rehabilitated and augmented; power stations were built and billing services established; enrollment in schools was significantly higher than at pre-1999 levels; and five hospitals and sixty-four community health centers had been built or rebuilt, with another twenty-five centers in progress, providing health care to all areas of East Timor.[109] In terms of a more general economic picture, while the majority of the population was still desperately poor, upon independence, almost 90 percent of the population reported that they were at or above the economic level that they were before the violence in 1999.[110] There were also significant efforts at developing a tourism industry, and the Bayu-Undan oil field was slated to begin production.

---

[106] Madjiah, 2005.   [107] Cliffe, 2003, p. 97.   [108] Cliffe, 2003, p. 115.
[109] S/432, 17 April 2002, paras. 43–57.   [110] S/432, 17 April 2002, para. 42.

One significant economic and social problem that UNTAET and its affiliates did not try to tackle was landownership disputes. Arguing that international staff should not try to weed out such a complicated problem, it was left to the new Timorese government to decide on appropriate dispute resolution mechanisms. And the task was substantial. Much of the territory was claimed by multiple parties – displaced persons, refugees, and other people with claims dating back to Portuguese, and later Indonesian, rule. The problem of land claims is probably the most important one inhibiting greater Timorese social and economic development. Another problem, although not as significant, is the emergence of illegal markets developing in border areas with West Timor. The markets are designed mainly to circumvent East Timor's new tax system and are possibly being used by the anti-independence militia.[111] Overall, however, the World Bank projects in the areas of social and economic development appear to have been initiated and conducted with and by the East Timorese, in conjunction with international assistance, and by the time of independence, most of the mutually agreed-upon goals had been fulfilled.

Elections

Shortly after UNTAET was established, its leadership was faced with a major dilemma that had not been foreseen in the original mandate for the operation: while the UN wanted to answer calls for increased "Timorization," deciding *which* East Timorese to include in the new governing institutions was not always obvious. The members of the largest party, Fretilin, often had the greatest access to UNTAET. Because of this, members of Fretilin and other political parties and NGOs in East Timor encouraged UNTAET to organize elections soon, arguing that if the position of Fretilin was to be dominant, it should at least be made so by a democratic vote, and not by international staff.[112]

Elections were not originally a part of UNTAET's mandate, but Vieira de Mello sought to change this component. In the end, UNTAET helped to arrange and monitor two elections, the first for the Constituent Assembly in August 2001, and then presidential elections in April 2002. The elections paved the way for the smooth drafting of the constitution in March 2002, and independence on May 20, 2002.[113]

Building on the work that had been done on voter registration by the DPA and UNAMET, UNTAET oversaw the civil registration of the East Timorese

---

[111] S/432, 17 April 2002, para. 28. During the time of UNTAET, the military division did work to prevent the emergence of these markets, even though the task was not directly a part of its mandate.
[112] Ingram, 2003, p. 87.
[113] The Constitution and political system took cues from Mozambique and Portugal, with a semi-presidential system wherein the Prime Minister and Cabinet hold executive power while the President holds veto power over legislation and government appointments.

from March to June 2001. The effort resulted in a surprisingly high number of almost 780,000 registered voters, all of whom were issued temporary ID cards.

In terms of voter education, whereas the UN is often in charge of such programs, in this case, in the interest of "Timorization," voter education was placed in the hands of the East Timorese leadership (CNRT). UNTAET staff worried about "authoritarian tendencies" in civic education programs run by the CNRT, which looked at times like "propaganda campaigns."[114] To offset such tendencies, and to encourage a mixed voting system to foster the growth of smaller parties, members of UNTAET encouraged the CNRT to break into its constituent parts, which it did in June 2001.[115]

In the Constituent Assembly elections, Fretilin won in free and fair elections with 57.3 percent of the vote, which translated into fifty-five out of eighty-eight seats. The party won a clear majority, but not enough seats to impose its will on the rest of the future Parliament. There had been some fears of Fretilin seeing itself as paramount to the state, seeking to adopt its party symbols as state symbols.[116] It was therefore fortunate that the party has had to work in coalition with other political parties to draft and approve the Constitution, along with other legislation and national symbols.

In terms of the April 2002 presidential elections, Xanana Gusmao was the obvious, longtime favorite, and he won by a landslide. Francisco da Amaral, the head of Falintil, decided to run in the presidential elections too, not that he stood a chance of winning, but merely, in his own words, "for the sake of democracy."[117] In the area of elections, UNTAET's main legacy for East Timor is to have helped build a solid foundation on which future elections may be held, with an independent electoral commission, and well-trained electoral officers.

Exit strategy, UNMISET, and Timor-Leste after UNTAET

Approximately halfway into the UNTAET mission, the leadership began to plan for its "exit strategy" in a way that would support the new government of Timor-Leste. In Secretary-General Annan's final report on UNTAET, he explained up front that:

> A number of issues that present challenges to the short and longer-term security of the new State have not yet and could not have been fully resolved. These range from border demarcation, return of refugees and regulation of commercial activity in the border area, to strengthening of nascent governmental structures, including law enforcement and the judicial system, as well as the consolidation of the framework for economic and social

[114] Chesterman, 2001, p. 22
[115] The CNRT and UNTAET also developed voter education materials in the Tetum language, and UN Volunteers were particularly helpful with both voter education and turnout.
[116] See Smith, 2004, pp. 150–56.   [117] Dunn, 2003, p. 374.

development. It is therefore essential for the international community to
remain engaged.[118]

The "international community" continued its engagement primarily
through the mechanism of the United Nations Mission of Support in East
Timor (UNMISET) until May, 2005, and then the United Nations Office in
Timor-Leste (UNOTIL), until August, 2006. As UNTAET drew to a close, it
set out to transfer some of its key staff members and areas of knowledge to
UNMISET, while many of its durable goods went to the new government of
Timor-Leste. Indeed, the new Timorese government received more transfers of
goods and assets than any previous peacekeeping operation, which was viewed
as both tangible and symbolic progress in the "Timorization" process.[119]

The UNMISET operation included three primary programs in its mandate:
(1) assistance with core public administrative structures of the East Timorese
government; (2) the provision of interim law enforcement and help with the
development of the East Timorese police; and (3) support for the maintenance
of external and internal security.[120] The operation began with approximately
5,000 military troops, 1,250 civilian police, 120 military observers, and 1,100
civilian personnel, but started downsizing almost immediately, as directed in
subsequent Security Council resolutions. With such a large military component and pared-down mandate, UNMISET was configured to operate much
more like a traditional cease-fire mission than a multidimensional peacekeeping mission, even though the tasks of the judicial system and police reform
were significant.

UNMISET's mandate was supposed to hold for one year but was renewed
for three years. In general, UNMISET is credited with being notably well integrated with the local Timorese population, especially the military component,
which "work[ed] with the local community and, through this relaxed and
open relationship, assist[ed] in breaking the perception of the military as an
occupation force."[121] However, the legacies of Indonesian and colonial misrule
were extremely difficult to overcome, especially in the area of civilian policing.
Aspects of public administration and justice, law enforcement, security and
stability (including the transfer to UNOTIL), the economy, and elections are
explored further below.

---

[118] S/432, 17 April 2002, para. 3.
[119] McNamara, 2003, p. 37. But at the same time, it is not clear whether East Timor will
be able to use a lot of the equipment well into the future. Many of the goods are hi-
tech computers and four-wheel drive vehicles used by international staff, which, without
proper service, will not be sustainable in East Timor's dusty, low-tech environment. See
Ingram, 2003, p. 90.
[120] S/RES/1410, 17 May 2002.   [121] Ishizuka, 2003, p. 52.

Public administration and justice

UNMISET staff assisted their Timorese counterparts in developing "sector investment programmes" in seventeen key areas, setting out development objectives, policies, and programs for implementation during and beyond UNMISET's tenure. Progress was made in developing and institutionalizing procedures in, for example, the areas of banking, finance, health, and education.

By the end of the UNMISET mission, fifty-eight international staff still held key posts for which Timorese counterparts had not yet been fully trained. The main location of these international civil servants, and indeed the primary focus of the public administration division, was in the justice sector. The problems were numerous and difficult to overcome within a short time horizon. Very few judges were prepared to take the bench and a backlog of court cases was growing; people were becoming increasingly disillusioned with the entire justice process, especially for domestic crimes.[122]

Law enforcement

The UNMISET civilian policing component was initially in charge of all policing in East Timor, as was the case with UNTAET, but it gradually shifted its focus from executive policing toward training for regular policing duties, as well as for specialized subjects in East Timorese law enforcement. The staff members of UNMISET's CIVPOL (in contrast to those of UNTAET, at least at the outset) were generally regarded as very well trained and of high quality, and they set a high bar for themselves "to transform the national police into an impartial and professional police service."[123] Training programs were conducted for thousands of regular officers, as well as, for example, for police investigators, police reserve units, a rapid intervention unit, a vulnerable persons unit (especially for gender-based violence), human rights investigators, and a border police unit.[124] In all, seventeen specialized modules were developed. After extensive training, in May 2004, executive power over law enforcement was transferred to the East Timorese.

The East Timorese police, along with their international counterparts, had to combat not only matters related to crime, but also the profound and caustic legacy of police practices under Indonesian rule. While intense technical training by international staff sought to reshape the mind-set of members of the East Timorese police force, reports of police misconduct grew. The rise may have been in part a result of better reporting channels, but undoubtedly, much

---

[122] Note also that in August 2005, a truth commission was set up between East Timor and Indonesia in order to document the violence in 1999, but not human rights abuses before then.

[123] S/99, 18 February 2005, para. 39   [124] S/99, 18 February 2005, paras. 33–37.

of it had to do with the nature of policing in a society where abusive policing practices were common. For this reason, the East Timorese government
requested that dozens of international civilian police advisors remain after the
end of UNMISET.

Security and stability

UNMISET troops played an important role in promoting internal stability
within East Timor. Members of the UNMISET military division sought direct
communication with the local population through "green patrols," where "military personnel patrol local villages promoting positive communication."[125]
Such patrols helped to set a new tone in relations between citizens and the
military. However, there were widespread fears that a total withdrawal could
be very destabilizing.

While East Timor was no longer under threat of invasion from its gigantic
neighbor Indonesia, its long-term security and stability were still hampered
by the presence of some thirty pro-integration militia groups in West Timor,
and a growing gang problem. The militias and gangs have been engaging in
such practices as smuggling and other types of illegal trade, which hurt East
Timor's economic development. There was also something of an emerging fear
of Islamic militant infiltration and their support for pro-Indonesian militias
in East Timor. In 1999, Bin Laden denounced President Habibie of Indonesia for allowing the East Timorese to vote on independence, thus bolstering
worldwide hard-line Islamic support for some of the militias. Indonesia is the
only country that could put a stop to the anti-independence militia activities,
but the UN Secretariat, and members of the Security Council, were reluctant
to apply pressure on Indonesia, since it is the largest Muslim country in the
world, is an important supplier of cheap goods and labor, and was continuing
its process of democratizing. The United States and other world powers fear
undermining or destabilizing the government.

In early 2005, the leaders of East Timor and Secretary-General Annan, citing
continued militia threats on the border with Indonesia, and growing problems
of crime, asked the Security Council to maintain a peacekeeping presence in
East Timor for at least another year. Most members of the Council were in
favor, but the United States insisted that the mission be scaled back, and that
it not include a military component. In April 2005, the UN Security Council
voted unanimously to establish the United Nations Office in Timor-Leste for
one year, beginning with the end of UNMISET. UNOTIL was to comprise a
mere forty-five civilian advisors, seventy-five police advisors and ten human
rights officers, but not peacekeeping troops. The small size of the operation and

---

[125] Ishizuka, 2003, p. 52.

absence of a peacekeeping component sparked fears among the East Timorese and UN staffers that the progress made in East Timor might not hold.

Economy

East Timor is the poorest of all Asian countries, and it has the lowest human development levels of the region.[126] Upon independence in May 2002, unemployment stood at about 80 percent. In that year, many jobs in agriculture were hurt because of a crippling drought, and thus most employment opportunities continued to be linked to the international presence, which was decreasing rapidly. As the education system improved, and more East Timorese graduated from high school and university, there was little concomitant job creation, forcing the best-educated Timorese to look abroad for employment opportunities. Labor remittances became an important new dimension in the economy, but subsistence agriculture continued to be the main source of employment, and the government continued to rely on international aid. In 2005, unemployment had been reduced to 50 percent, the average GDP per capita (PPP) stood at $400, and annual growth at 1 percent.[127]

During UNTAET and UNMISET, the disparities in wealth between the international staff and locals were stark and disturbing: the average international staffer earned between three and ten times more than the average East Timorese citizen (including Timorese working for the international organizations), which in effect began to create a "two-tier economy."[128] Even after the massive international presence left the country, elements of the two-tier economy remained. For example, a small wealthy minority, many of whom were expatriates, continued to enjoy expensive goods and services established during UNTAET's tenure, while the vast majority of the population had no access to such goods and services.[129]

Another major obstacle to greater economic growth and investment lies in the unsolved landownership problems. There are two aspects to the disputes, one internal and the other international. The first concerns domestic land rights, on which there has been little progress since independence.[130] The government has been reluctant to take on the issue because the landownership problem is extremely complex, and solving it could be potentially destabilizing. Therefore, farmers continue to farm where they are, with no guarantees

---

[126] S/99, 18 February 2005, para. 50.   [127] *CIA World Factbook*, "East Timor" 2005.

[128] Terrall, 2003, p. 81.

[129] In addition, during UNTAET, the US dollar became the currency of East Timor, but there were no accompanying coins, which meant that the lowest possibly currency unit was extremely high for most goods purchased by most Timorese. This worked to drive Timorese out of the money economy and into one that relies more on barter.

[130] Interview with Constancio Pinto, Minister Counselor and Deputy Chief of Mission, The Embassy of Timor-Leste, Washington DC, May 17, 2005.

for the future, and people with documented (or other types of) claims to land, whether they are Timorese or Indonesian, have few avenues for developing the land long term. The predicament means that neither domestic nor foreign investors are willing to nurture or develop the land in sustainable ways.

The second major land issue concerns the international boundary between Australia and East Timor. There are significant oil and gas reserves under the seabed that lies between Australia and East Timor. In 1972, the Australians nego-tiated a very favorable deal with Indonesia, giving Australia the lion's share of the reserves. Standard international boundaries lie at the midpoint between the coasts of two countries, but this agreement granted Australia two-thirds of the sea area, thus cutting its poorer neighbor off from most of the reserves. During the pre- and post-independence negotiations on East Timor, several agreements were reached which presumably gave East Timor a 90 percent con-trol over the reserves and paved the way for the opening in February 2004 of the Bayu Undan offshore gas field. The field is expected to earn $32 billion over the course of its life. In April 2005, the East Timorese and Australians came to an agreement whereby East Timor would receive ostensibly 90 percent of the rev-enues from the fields (even though the company developing and exploiting the fields, Phillips Petroleum, is Australian). In exchange, the East Timorese agreed to delay talks on the final boundary until 50 to 100 years from 2005. The dispute between the two countries has to a certain extent soured Australian–Timorese relations.[131]

It remains to be seen whether, and how, the significant profits from the oil fields will change the economy, and possibly the entire society, of East Timor. As it stands now, the "two-tier" economy established during the course of the enormous international efforts to put East Timor on a path toward independence and democracy, coupled by highly concentrated oil wealth, does not bode well for evenly distributed growth and economic development across different sectors of the East Timorese economy and society.

Elections

In December 2004, two districts in Timor-Leste held the first ever local elections. The elections were overseen by East Timorese officials exclusively; voter turnout was high (about 90 percent); and the elections were deemed free and fair, even though Fretilin dominated the voter list: "people voted in an orderly manner, in an atmosphere free of intimidation or interference, in which the secrecy of the ballot was maintained."[132] More orderly, but largely Fretilin-dominated district elections took place throughout Timor-Leste in the summer of 2005.

The next parliamentary elections are scheduled for 2007. In the last elections, the Democratic Party emerged as a new political force in East

[131] Mercer, 2004.   [132] S/99, 18 February 2005, para. 2.

Timor.[133] Led by young, well-educated Timorese intellectuals, the party held seven seats in Parliament, making it the largest opposition party. In terms of future presidential elections, the next round is set for 2007; the charismatic Gusmao may stand for one more term, and given his immense popularity, he might well be encouraged to run again, even though in the last elections he expressed frequent disinterest in becoming President. In recent years, there have been some heated political disputes between Gusmao and the leadership of Fretilin, especially its Prime Minister, Mari Alkatiri. But as one observer explained:

> Despite reports of political infighting between leaders and the emergence of some potentially problematic patronage relationships, democracy in East Timor need fear no serious threat at this time. There is a robustly independent media – including two major daily newspapers and other publications – and much is freely published on a wide range of issues, including critiques of government policy. Moreover, there is no institution in East Timor that looks as though it might challenge democracy.[134]

In other words, many aspects of the new Timorese political, military, economic, and judicial institutions appear to be progressing, but both the East Timorese leadership and members of the UN system agree that external assistance should continue, given the growing threats posed by militias, ex-combatants, gangs, and a weak economy.

Conclusion

UNTAET was an extremely ambitious operation, and after experiencing some significant first-level organizational dysfunction, it gradually moved into a learning mode, which enabled it to implement most of its goals. The UNTAET mandate included the major tasks of providing security, law and order, public administration, humanitarian assistance, and helping the East Timorese to build capacity in self-governance and sustainable economic development. The tasks were inherently open-ended, and they related much more to development than security issues, unlike previous multidimensional peacekeeping operations.

The operation was organized into three main pillars: (1) governance and public administration, (2) the UN peacekeeping force, and (3) humanitarian assistance and emergency rehabilitation. The overall organization into the pillars, under the central command of a UN Special Representative who also held the title of Transitional Administrator, was wise in some important respects. UNTAET was able to coordinate within itself quite well, prioritizing tasks and

[133] Smith, 2004, p. 152.   [134] Smith, 2004, p. 157.

changing priorities as necessitated by changes in the situation on the ground.[135] The operation also enjoyed a certain distance from UN headquarters, which allowed the leadership to make its own decisions. But unfortunately, the focus on tight and centralized control in the field was not accompanied, at least at first, by adequate devolution of power *within* the field operations, especially to the district offices, nor adequate integration with, and inclusion of, the local elites and population. As Roque Rodrigues, Secretary of State for National Defense of East Timor explained: "In all fairness there was a lot of learning to do on both sides: the UN in its new role as the administrative power and we, the East Timorese, in our new role as a liberated people."[136]

And indeed, gradually, this learning did occur. After being excluded from helping to develop the new political processes underway in their own country, the East Timorese leaders became increasingly emboldened and savvy in terms of how to ensure that UNTAET would accomplish what the operation was mandated to do: train East Timorese to eventually take over their own state. At issue was the question of whether the East Timorese were prepared to administer themselves. There is no doubt that in the cases of Mozambique and Angola, liberation in 1974 came too swiftly, before adequate governing mechanisms had been devised, or administrators trained, and civil war came as a result. The East Timorese, sharing the circumstances with the people of Angola and Mozambique of being colonized by Portugal, knew of the turmoil in Angola and Mozambique upon independence, remembered the seeds of East Timor's own nascent civil war on the eve of the Indonesian invasion in 1975, and wanted to avoid the potentially adverse effects of hasty liberation. In 1999, after centuries of Portuguese colonial rule, and twenty-four years of Indonesian domination, the East Timorese did not have the training or expertise to run the state in the manner expected by the UN's international staff, and according to international standards of efficiency, effectiveness, impersonal and even-handed bureaucracy. There appeared to be a genuine willingness on the part of the East Timorese to adopt the international bureaucratic standards and procedures that the UN sought to impart. And while the UN did eventually move into a first-level learning mode, the pressures of the legacy of corrupt and abusive Indonesian rule, and the demands on the part of the UN Security Council to end UNTAET as quickly as possible, conspired against full mandate implementation.

Despite these circumstances, the final successes of UNTAET were deep and significant. The UNTAET civilian administration gradually turned adminis-trative power over to the East Timorese in the form of the First and Second Transitional Administrations. The Second Transitional Administration, a very inclusive body, would become the model for the East Timorese Parliament. The military division of UNTAET, inheriting most of its troops, equipment,

---

[135] Vieira de Mello, 2003, p. 19.   [136] Rodrigues, 2003, p. 28

and smooth-functioning operations from INTERFET, fulfilled its mandate to the letter and beyond. Similarly, the humanitarian assistance and emergency relief programs were well coordinated, delivered necessary relief, and helped as many refugees return to East Timor as possible. The civilian police and judicial affairs were the less-successful components of UNTAET. The main tasks of these divisions carried over to the follow-on UN operation, UNMISET, and were largely completed by the spring of 2005, when the much smaller UN operation, UNOTIL, assumed responsibility for any remaining goals. Overall, the international operations helped to form new governing institutions; rebuilt the East Timorese physical infrastructure; maintained security; trained people in the tasks of governing, policing, lawmaking, and holding elections; and worked to educate the population in the ways of impersonal, non-corrupt governance and electoral politics.

This is not to say, however, that the situation in East Timor is stable enough for the UN to withdraw completely. Anti-independence militias are still active in West Timor, crime rates are on the rise, judges and lawyers still need to be trained, landownership problems have not been solved, economic problems persist, and East Timor's security remains at the mercy of its large and unstable neighbor, Indonesia. Given these circumstances, compounded by the legacy of abusive and corrupt rule, it is too early to determine with finality the extent to which the institutions that the UN sought to create in East Timor will continue to function well into the future, once the UN leaves. But at this point, it is fair to assess the progress in mandate implementation made by UNTAET, in conjunction with the other international missions and the East Timorese, as largely successful.

9

The ongoing multidimensional peacekeeping operations

Introduction

The ongoing multidimensional UN peacekeeping operations represent both continuity and change from the completed missions that I analyzed in the previous chapters of this book. In terms of continuity, the overall argument of the book extends to the current missions in that the three major factors determining success and failure continue to hold – the situational difficulty, great-power interests, and learning or dysfunction in the UN Secretariat's peacekeeping mission. The basic argument also holds that when the powerful members of the Security Council are very interested and involved in UN peacekeeping missions, such missions tend to be less successful. Similarly, when operations are able to move into a first-level learning mode while in action on the ground (facilitated by a devolution of decision-making power from headquarters to the field), this generally leads to success in mandate implementation.

As of the end of 2005, there were eight UN multidimensional peacekeeping operations in the field, employing peacekeepers in numbers not seen since 1993.[1] The operations came in two "waves" and one "ripple." First, in 1999, between June and December of that year, four new multidimensional missions were launched in Kosovo, Sierra Leone, the Democratic Republic of the Congo, and East Timor.[2] There were no major new operations initiated again until September 2003 when, within the space of ten months, another four major, multidimensional missions began in Liberia, Côte d'Ivoire, Burundi, and Haiti. A ripple operation was mandated to begin in Sudan in the spring of 2005. The first wave appears to be the result of a confluence of several peace processes coming to fruition all at the same time, whereas the second wave and ripple are more directly reflective of changes in US and UN policy.

---

[1] The current peace operations in which the UN is not heavily involved – Afghanistan and Iraq – are the ones that undoubtedly garner the most press coverage today. They are not explored in depth here because they are not multidimensional UN peacekeeping missions. However, the implications of the main argument of this book are applied to those cases in the concluding chapter.

[2] The mission in the Congo began very small and gradually grew, unlike the others, which started with larger "footprints."

The vast majority of the newer operations differ from the previous cases discussed in this book in terms of one central, new and general practice: non-UN, militarily robust, peace-enforcement troops often intervened to stop the fighting and enforce the peace, followed by (or in the midst of) more standard UN multidimensional peacekeeping missions.[3] I discuss this new phenomenon, and its indication of second-level learning, in the concluding chapter.

In terms of success and failure, thus far the missions in East Timor, Sierra Leone, Burundi, and to a certain extent Liberia, have been the most successful at mandate implementation, but it is too early to determine whether the peace-keeping operations will have long-term, stabilizing, and democratizing effects in these countries. The operations in Kosovo, Congo, Côte d'Ivoire, and Haiti are not presently in learning modes, although the operation in Kosovo has seen some movement in this direction. These four are also the operations with less successful records at mandate implementation, although given the UN's past experience with turning unsuccessful missions around (after moving into a first-level learning mode), it would be premature to file these missions into the definitive category of failure. The waves and the cases within them are explored in the remainder of this chapter.

The 1999 wave: Kosovo, East Timor, Sierra Leone, and the Congo

The early 1990s were characterized by rapid growth in the multidimensionality of peacekeeping operations, as well as in the number of missions deployed throughout the world. The demise of the Somalia mission in September–October of 1993 sparked the end of the growth period. Widespread apprehension, both in the Security Council and in the Secretariat, about the possibilities for peacekeeping success drove the organization not into a period of fruitful re-examination of the problems, but rather into a pattern of organizational dysfunction. Weak UN peacekeeping forces were already deployed before the episodes of the most extensive killing in 1994–95 in Rwanda, Angola, and Bosnia (Srebrenica); they were also on the ground during much of the fighting in Somalia. While it was not mentioned directly in official Security Council or Secretariat documents, members of both began to wonder about the extent to which weak peacekeeping missions might actually enable, rather than prevent, mass killing. The weak missions, under conditions of first-level organizational dysfunction, were in essence used as tools of war by the parties. They allowed combating forces time to rest, regroup, train, and organize for more concerted

---

[3] The cases include: NATO war fighting and peace-enforcement troops in Kosovo; the Australian-led INTERFET force in East Timor; British stabilization troops in Sierra Leone; the French-led EU mission in Eastern Congo; US marines in Liberia; French stabilization forces in Côte d'Ivoire; and US forces in Haiti. The African Union peacekeeping forces in Burundi and Sudan were tasked with monitoring the cease-fire and assisting in demobilization, but were not designed to stop the fighting.

battle. In response, rather than mustering the reserves to stop the fighting, the UN turned away from peacekeeping: with the exception of the Eastern Slavonia operation in 1996–97, there were no new large, multidimensional peacekeeping missions fielded between 1995 and 1998, and very few new, smaller missions.

By 1999, however, the political tide against peacekeeping shifted again and at the same time, four peace processes were nearing resolution. UN Secretary-General Kofi Annan, the former head of the Department of Peacekeeping Operations (DPKO), had won a second term as Secretary-General and was increasingly garnering support for the UN's endeavors. At the same time, the United States began to make moves toward paying back the significant dues it owed the organization, both for peacekeeping assessments and the regular budget, and after almost a year of congressional obstruction, appointed a US Ambassador to the UN, Richard Holbrooke, who was known for his support of peacekeeping, especially after his important role in the Bosnian peace process. All the while, conflicts around the world continued to take their deadly toll, but four in particular began to lurch toward peace. The advances in the peace processes were supported by a political tide cresting in favor of UN peacekeeping. Within six months, starting in June 1999, four new, large operations began in Kosovo, Sierra Leone, Congo and East Timor. Of these four, the mission in East Timor has essentially concluded, and thus has an entire chapter of this book devoted to it (see Chapter 8). The other operations are still ongoing, although there is increasing pressure, especially from the United States, for financial reasons, to work toward ending the missions in Kosovo, Liberia, and Sierra Leone. I address each case briefly below, highlighting the ways in which first- or second-level learning occurred.

Kosovo

In Kosovo, it is not the UN, but rather NATO that has been in charge of the military side of peacekeeping, while the UN has been in charge of administering the state. In 1999, after Serb forces expelled at gunpoint nearly 1 million Kosovar Albanians from the southern Yugoslav territory of Kosovo, NATO launched operation "Allied Force." The NATO war in Yugoslavia lasted seventy-eight days, beginning in late March, and paved the way for nearly all Kosovar refugees to return. In the summer of 1999, the UN Security Council authorized the United Nations Interim Administration Mission in Kosovo (UNMIK) to administer the province.[4] The mission is designed around "four pillars" and divided between different international organizations. The first pillar, "humanitarian assistance," was headed by the UNHCR until May 2001,

---

[4] See S/RES/1244, 10 June 1999. Note that the Security Council did *not* authorize the NATO operation "Allied Force," but US–UN relations did eventually improve after the divisive actions taken by the Clinton administration.

when it was phased out and replaced by a UN DPKO "police and justice" division. The UN DPKO is also in charge of the second pillar, the "civil administration." Pillar three, "democratization and institution building" is headed by the Organization for Security and Cooperation in Europe (OSCE) and the fourth pillar, "reconstruction and economic development," is managed by the EU. NATO heads what would be a fifth pillar, the Kosovo Force (KFOR), but NATO's forces are not integrated into the UN-centralized civilian command of UNMIK.[5] The problems with the international presence, and the future of Kosovo, are numerous and difficult.

Based on the reflections in this book, and the primary indicators of first-level organizational learning or dysfunction (information, coordination, integration, and leadership), it should come as no surprise that, given the very design of UNMIK, the operation has been operating in a largely dysfunctional mode. The decision to divide the operation, rather than uniting command structures, means that the different wings of UNMIK are often working at cross, or parallel, purposes. The lack of coordination has incurred the rancor of both Kosovar Serbs and Albanians, and demonstrates a significant absence of second-level learning from the operations in Bosnia, where similar problems occurred.[6] As Jacques Klein illustrated colorfully: "You have the pillars and poles and the what have yous – OSCE, KFOR, whyfor – then you wonder why an SRSG has to struggle with organizations which don't like to be controlled because if I don't pay you, you don't work for me."[7] There are also significant coordination problems between the international organizations and NGOs, about 500 of which are currently in operation, as well as *within* NATO's KFOR operation itself.[8] The coordination problems have spilled into other domains, making information-gathering and dissemination difficult, and impeding deeper organizational integration with the local environment. Moreover, the SRSG of UNMIK has changed four times in five years, which means there has not been steady, knowledgeable, effective leadership over the course of the operation.

The first-level organizational dysfunction has also been spurred by the larger political problem of the final status of Kosovo. It is simply not clear what kind of political entity Kosovo is, or will become.[9] While most observers agree that

[5] Unlike, for example, INTERFET in East Timor, which established the peace in East Timor and then turned over command, quite seamlessly, to the UN.
[6] Kosovar Albanians and Serbs continue to attack each other sporadically, and Serbs are most often the victims of the attacks. At times, UN workers have been attacked while NATO peacekeepers have merely observed, reflecting a troubling organizational disconnect.
[7] Klein, 2002.
[8] The NATO peacekeepers are divided by nationality into five regions of Kosovo. The British and Italian forces have generally been quite effective, while the US, French, and German troops have been criticized for paying more attention to "force protection" than to interacting with the locals, learning and respecting the culture, and gathering and disseminating information so as to mitigate conflict. See Mockaitis, 2004.
[9] See Yannis, 2004, for an interesting discussion of this dilemma.

Kosovo will most likely eventually gain independence, possibly in exchange for Serbia's accession to the EU, these outcomes have not been predetermined in the peacekeeping mandate, and have yet to be negotiated.[10] Many Serbs view Kosovo as the cradle of their cultural and religious heritage, and are unwilling to allow the territory to secede. There is also tremendous animosity between the main three Kosovar Albanian political parties, which complicates the negotiation process. The upshot has been that there is a "general sense that no one is in charge, no one is accountable, and there is no political goal. It's 'Alice in Wonderland,'" in the words of one UN staff member.[11]

While there has been progress in some areas of local capacity building, Kosovo has become a European haven for drug running, trafficking in women, money laundering, and other criminal activities.[12] In March 2004, widespread violence broke out between Serbs and Albanians; 19 were killed, 900 injured, hundreds of homes burned (mainly Serb), and thousands of Serbs were displaced.[13] The peacekeepers were unable to prevent the violence, which happened right before their eyes, and many fear that violence might resurface unless something radical changes in the political status of Kosovo.[14] While the UN and NATO operations have helped to freeze most of the fighting, and the parties have made some progress toward fulfilling a series of "standards" or benchmarks that must be met before further discussions about democratization can be held, one would be hard-pressed to argue that the overall operation represents a manifestation of first- or second-level learning, and the results so far have been less than successful. It is possible, however, that once the final status of Kosovo is negotiated, such a decision could provide enough international and domestic political momentum to enable the multilateral and multidimensional peacekeeping efforts to move into a learning mode, and become more successful at solidifying the peace.

Sierra Leone

The multidimensional peacekeeping operation in Sierra Leone (UNAMSIL) appeared early on to be doomed to failure, but unlike UNMIK in Kosovo, after engaging in substantial first-level learning on the ground, and some second-level learning from previous operations, UNAMSIL looks like it will be able to fulfill most aspects of its mandate. In this case, however, mandate fulfillment does not necessarily equate with long-term, successful state-building.

The war in Sierra Leone developed out of corruption and degenerating governmental structures, combined with external meddling stemming from the

---

[10] Kupchan, 2005.   [11] Interview with the author, December 2004, UN headquarters.
[12] Caplan, 2004; Mertus, 2004; von Carlowitz, 2004; Holohan, 2005; and Norris, 2005.
[13] de Vrieze, 2004.
[14] Mertus, 2004; Wood, 2004; Carlucci, 2005; and Holbrooke, 2005.

civil war in neighboring Liberia.[15] In 1996, the infamous President Charles Taylor of Liberia took revenge against Sierra Leone after its government supported the peacekeeping operation of the Economic Community of West African States Monitoring Group (ECOMOG) in Liberia. Interested also in Sierra Leone's diamond riches, Charles Taylor allied with Foday Sankoh, the leader of the supremely destructive Revolutionary United Front (RUF) of Sierra Leone – an organization known for cutting off the hands of innocent civilians to dissuade them from voting in democratic elections.[16] Between 1991 and 2002, over one-third of the population of Sierra Leone, or approximately 2 million people, were displaced, and over 75,000 people were killed in the civil war, which slowly came to an end through external intervention.[17]

Similar to the model in Kosovo, where force was used by a regional organization to create peace, ECOMOG fought to secure the peace in Sierra Leone.[18] But this was only nominally a "regional" as opposed to "single state" enforcement operation, since all but 1,000 of ECOMOG's 13,000 troops came from Nigeria. With the election of Olusegun Obasanjo as President of Nigeria in May 1999, and after the deaths of hundreds of Nigerian troops, Nigeria signaled that it was no longer willing to carry so much of the peacekeeping/peace enforcement burden in Sierra Leone. Five months later, the UN multinational UNAMSIL force was deployed to relieve many of ECOMOG's duties. UNAMSIL began in a state of organizational dysfunction, and, like many of the failed missions, the dysfunction inspired both sides to renege on commitments made in the peace accords.[19] In May 2000, the RUF rebels attacked not only government forces but also UNAMSIL troops, took 100 UN peacekeepers hostage, killed four, and seized UN weapons and vehicles.

Rather than responding as the international community did during the Rwandan genocide, by pulling out its resources, the UK, with the blessing of the UN Security Council, unilaterally sent 750 troops to help to stabilize the capital Freetown, the UN added more peacekeepers, and the Economic Community of West African States (ECOWAS) sent 3,000 troops back in to stabilize other areas (the ECOWAS troops had been trained and equipped by the United States).[20] The rapid response defeated the RUF rebels and paved the way for the UN to resume its multidimensional peacekeeping operation. This did not mean, however, that the UN was able to get back on track immediately. UNAMSIL also had internal, organizational problems. From almost the start of the

[15] Bangura, 2000.
[16] Abdullah, 1998. Sankoh died in jail, reportedly of natural causes, in July 2003.
[17] *CIA World Factbook*, 2005.
[18] But unlike in Kosovo, the regional organization engaged on the side of the government, and against the rebels.
[19] Adebajo and Landsberg, 2000, p. 176.
[20] The UK has since made a twenty-year security commitment to assist Sierra Leone in its transition from war. The guarantee stems in part from Tony Blair's personal commitment to the country, honoring his father's service in Sierra Leone as a schoolteacher.

operation, the military and civilian heads had been at odds with one another. The dispute became public in October of 2000, and ended with India and Jordan withdrawing their substantial numbers of peacekeepers from UNAMSIL. The troops were replaced with nationals from Pakistan and Bangladesh, and the force was expanded several times to reach the number of 17,500 troops with a Chapter VII, peace enforcement mandate. At the same time, UNAMSIL, under the leadership of Nigerian diplomat Oluyemi Adeniji, worked hard to gain the confidence of the local population through setting tangible benchmarks for the mission, and accomplishing many tasks. The operation set as its primary focus the disarmament of more than 70,000 fighters on both sides of the conflict (the RUF and the government-supported Civil Defense Force, also known as Kamajors), which was largely accomplished by 2002, and completed in early 2004. In May 2002, successful, largely peaceful, UN-organized elections were held and Ahmed Tejan Kabbah, a former UN civil servant for twenty years and a person well respected internationally and within Sierra Leone, was re-elected with 70.6 percent of the vote; the next elections are scheduled for 2007.[21] Aside from disarmament and elections, other major tasks included re-integrating former combatants into society through retraining programs and resettling displaced people, both of which have been completed. UNAMSIL has also focused on rebuilding the police force; by the end of 2005, about half of the necessary police had been trained, with expectations that the remaining forces would be trained by Sierra Leoneans.[22]

In terms of the military, the UN has been facing a difficult conundrum: training military forces to be efficient and effective, but not so much so that they become powerful enough to become a threat to the new state, which is a real concern in Sierra Leone, given its history of military coups.[23] In this area, the government and ordinary Sierra Leoneans have been less cooperative with UN plans.[24]

While UNAMSIL has been successful in accomplishing many of its tasks, Sierra Leone remains situated in a very unstable region, and vulnerable to negative neighborhood effects. In addition, corruption, lack of jobs for retrained ex-combatants, and a generally poor economic outlook, mean the security status of Sierra Leone is tenuous: "The country's security structure ... still requires further assistance in capacity building. International support will [remain] critical."[25]

---

[21] Kandeh, 2003.   [22] S/777, 12 December 2005, paras. 31, 32.

[23] Note that private security companies have been used by different governments in Sierra Leone, on the logic that such companies can be effective without the potential threat of a coup.

[24] S/777, 12 December 2005, para. 30.

[25] S/777, 12 December 2005, para. 15. Sierra Leone is also ranked the second least-developed country in the entire world, according to the Human Development Index. See United Nations Development Programme, 2005.

In terms of the indicators of first-level organizational learning, the mission has proven rather effective at gathering and using information appropriately to devise projects in relation to demands on the ground. Coordination within the operation and between it and NGOs has also been comparatively smooth, especially since the shake-up in the peacekeeping force composition. In terms of interactions between UNAMSIL staff and the people of Sierra Leone, the mission (as well as the UN Special Court set up to try perpetrators of war crimes) has been racked by sex abuse scandals. Such scandals have severely damaged not only the image of UNAMSIL and the Special Court, but also the more concrete ability to win the trust of ordinary people. But at the same time, in terms of leadership, the SRSG has been credited with being authoritative without being authoritarian and is working toward devising appropriate disciplinary procedures for peacekeepers who commit crimes. In other words, the operation has, for the most part, moved into a learning mode and has been able to achieve many of its tasks and benchmarks. The completion of the tasks, however, will not necessarily translate into longer-term stability and democratization in Sierra Leone. In this case, first- and second-level learning have contributed to successes so far but are no guarantee that peaceful conditions will hold, considering the difficult situational factors.

Congo

Since World War II, no conflict in the world has caused as much death, destruction, and dislocation as the one in the Democratic Republic of the Congo (DRC). The death toll stands at close to 4 million and is still rising.[26] And yet, the world's response has been tentative at best. While Sierra Leone appears to have benefited from second-level learning from the UN's experience in Rwanda, the DRC, in the words of Secretary-General Annan, "has become a victim of Rwanda. When you approach governments and talk of troops for Congo, they see the catastrophe in Rwanda."[27] Of all the missions fielded in recent years, many observers feel that this one has been marked for failure from the start.[28] The emerging sentiment in and around the UN that peacekeepers should protect civilians (after the debacles in Rwanda, Angola, and Srebrenica) has often not been applied to the civilians trapped in the extremely complicated fighting in the DRC.[29] There is, however, some movement in the direction of increasing external assistance, which may eventually lead toward the end of violent conflict, although peace remains elusive, especially in the eastern regions of North and South Kivu, Ituri, and Katanga.

---

[26] Lacey, 2005b.   [27] Annan, 2002.   [28] Guéhenno, 2002, p. 78.
[29] See the report of the International Commission on Intervention and State Sovereignty, December 2001.

There have been two major peace deals in the DRC in recent years – the Lusaka Accord of July 1999, in which all of the neighboring countries that had sent troops to fight in the DRC agreed to withdraw their forces, and the accord between the government in Kinshasa and the five main armed groups, signed in Sun City, South Africa, in December, 2002.[30] Both accords called for UN assistance with implementation. The United Nations Observer Mission in the Democratic Republic of the Congo (MONUC) began in November 1999 as a small, 500-strong troop-monitoring mission. The DRC has a population of about 50 million people and is approximately the size of all of Western Europe combined, which means the monitoring abilities of such a small mission were limited at best. After literally millions of deaths, and under pressure from humanitarian and human rights groups and from individual members of the UN Secretariat, the Secretary-General and the UN Security Council have agreed periodically over time to ratchet up the size of MONUC to an eventual 16,700 troops. The Secretariat has generally requested far more troops than the Security Council has been willing to mandate. With each troop-level increase, the mission has taken on more responsibilities, including a mandate to protect civilians with the use of force.[31]

Civilians have suffered in the DRC to a degree not experienced elsewhere in the world in recent history. Approximately 1,000 people die each day from fighting, and fighting-induced maladies.[32] Rape as an instrument of war has become common, even of children, and "a climate of general insecurity and lawlessness, of armed groups of uncertain allegiance and intentions" is pervasive, especially in the eastern regions.[33] While there is formally a government led by Joseph Kabila in Kinshasa and in most of the western part of the country, over half of the government's budget is supplied by donors, and those donors are beginning to balk at increasing evidence of financial mismanagement, corruption, and lack of transparency in government transactions – all of which were problems under the long reign of Mobutu Sese Seko and were the main contributing causes of the war in the first place.[34] Some donors are beginning to talk of simply pulling out, rather than trying to exert leverage over the

---

[30] In Lusaka, the governments of Angola, Rwanda, Uganda, and Zimbabwe signed a cease-fire agreement. Each of those countries had sent troops to support opposing sides of the conflict. Many observers view the intent of the neighbors' interventions as efforts to gain economic footholds in the DRC, which is extremely rich in natural resources. See Lemarchand, 2000; Montague, 2002; and Young, 2002.

[31] After expanding several times, the mandate for MONUC includes monitoring the cease-fire and troop withdrawal, maintaining order, DDR, protecting civilians and humanitarian workers, assisting with refugee return, establishing a secure environment, promoting and protecting human rights, and assisting with elections.

[32] This figure has been widely reported. See, for example, Stroehlein, 2005.

[33] S/320, 26 May 2005, para. 20.   [34] Young, 2002.

government.[35] Meanwhile, public services are grinding to a halt, and roads and basic infrastructure are "almost nonexistent."[36] The common ties of culture, community, work, and family that bind society together have become unraveled after almost a decade of fighting and insecurity.

These crippling and mutually reinforcing processes of decline are in some ways being counteracted by efforts at stopping the fighting, advancing more integrative processes, and working toward mending the society.[37] A transitional government has been established as a power-sharing arrangement between the fighting factions, and elections, the first step toward representative government in decades, were scheduled for 2006. The very procedures of conducting a census, issuing identity cards, registering people to vote, and carrying out voter education are seen as progressive and potentially unifying influences in a country that has not had a national census since 1984.[38] And, of course, the peace deals have been signed. But the question of implementation remains.

MONUC is the most direct instrument of international oversight for implementation of the peace accords, and, from the standpoint of one of the field commanders, "is the hardest operation the UN has ever undertaken."[39] The mission is in the process of transforming itself from one of merely cease-fire monitoring to a multidimensional peacekeeping operation with a complex political and military mandate. But the mission has been having trouble devising a coherent strategy to implement its tasks."[40] There is a problem of multiple international actors and a lack of coordination; for example, as explained by one observer, there are too many security sector assistance projects: "army integration projects are taking place under a variety of agencies: Angola, Belgium, South Africa and the UN mission in the Congo are all involved, often without any coordination."[41] The multiplicity of actors disenables all of them, as well as the local actors, and MONUC has not been able to establish itself as the central coordinator.

Moreover, three times in recent history, MONUC has come under sharp international criticism for not being able to control outbreaks of violence – in Kisangani in May 2002, in Ituri in mid-2003, and in Bukavu in May–June 2004. In the case of the violence in Ituri, a French-led European force stepped in for several months to establish security by force, which then paved the way for the UN peacekeepers to return in greater numbers and with a wider mandate to

---

[35] S/320, 26 May 2005, para. 19; and International Crisis Group, 2005, "The Congo's Transition is Failing," p. 3.

[36] S/320, 26 May 2005, para. 2.

[37] See Trefon, 2004 for analyses of the trials of ordinary life in Kinshasa.

[38] The elections preparations are being overseen by the government, with the assistance of MONUC.

[39] Colonel Mahmoud Hussein, Deputy Brigade Commander for Ituri, quoted in Wax, 2005b.

[40] International Crisis Group, 2005, "The Congo's Transition is Failing," p. 23.

[41] Barnes, 2005.

use force.[42] The question of how much force to use has plagued this operation, as it has others. Various humanitarian organizations and think-tanks have condemned the UN for being "overly cautious" even when the UN has a peace-enforcement mandate.[43] But MONUC is in the difficult position of being asked to fight against the very factions that it must also rely on to help implement the peace process. In early 2005, MONUC waged a preventive strike on warring factions in Eastern Congo and nine members of MONUC were killed in a counterattack.[44] While such uses of force could be interpreted as second-level "learning" from Rwanda – where peacekeepers did not fight back after they had been attacked, paving the way for the genocide – it remains to be seen how effective the strategy of the "preventive" use of force will be in the long term.

MONUC has also recently come under a different kind of fire, in the Congolese and international press, for incidents of sex scandals and sexual abuse. As a result of the misconduct, MONUC peacekeepers have been prohibited from "fraternizing" with the local population.[45] This highlights the important dilemma of how peacekeepers ought to behave in post-civil war societies, where extreme poverty and desperation run rampant. On the one hand, UN peacekeepers must interact with, and learn from, locals in order for the organization to learn. But on the other hand, there are few mechanisms in place to ensure that peacekeepers interact in appropriate ways. For peacekeepers who break the law by taking advantage of the disadvantaged, the UN's main recourse is to send offenders home. There is no legal system that governs the behavior of UN military and civilian staff, and legal systems in postwar countries are often not able to cope with prosecuting crimes committed by foreigners.

The failure to articulate and execute a coherent and effective policy on the use of force, combined with the sex scandals and the inability to deal effectively with UN offenders, have worked to tarnish the image of MONUC in the eyes of many Congolese civilians. Thus far, MONUC has demonstrated difficulty with first-level learning, including integrating appropriately with the local environment, coordinating within itself, and exercising decisive and effective leadership. Similarly, on the second level, there is a mixed picture of learning. After Rwanda, there has been pressure to protect civilians in conflicts worldwide, including in the DRC, but how much force to use, who ought to use it, and under what circumstances is still unclear. In addition, a central lesson from Sierra Leone, Mozambique, and other operations has been to disarm before holding elections, but this has not been applied in the DRC. Even if the operations in the DRC are able to engage in learning – on the second or the first levels – it will be extremely difficult to offset the deep situational complexities of the DRC.

---

[42] Mansson, 2005.
[43] International Crisis Group, 2005, "The Congo's Transition is Failing," pp. ii, 24, 25.
[44] Lacey, 2005a.   [45] Wax, 2005a.

To summarize, of all of the operations in the 1999 wave, the one in the DRC looks the least likely to succeed. UNTAET in East Timor has engaged in the most first-level organizational learning and will probably enjoy the long-term reputation as the most successful of the group, even if some problems persist (as discussed in Chapter 8). The result of the operation in Kosovo is too difficult to determine at this point, but if a decision on Kosovo's final status is reached, there may yet be progress in Kosovo despite a lack of first- or second-level learning thus far. And in Sierra Leone, learning and the ensuing success in mandate implementation might not be enough to counteract the difficult state-building tasks that face the country. The slow progress in each of these cases, especially at the beginning of the operations, contributed to another several-year hiatus in launching new peacekeeping missions. But, as explained in the following section, the reluctance to engage in new multidimensional operations did not endure for long.

The 2003–2004 wave and a ripple: Liberia, Côte d'Ivoire, Burundi, Haiti . . . and Sudan

While the 1999 peacekeeping wave was driven mainly by the culmination of several peace processes at once, the 2003–2004 wave was unleashed primarily by a confluence of two other factors: on the one hand, a change in US policy in favor of supporting UN peacekeeping operations, and on the other, an increase within the UN system, both institutional and normative, in favor of an augmented UN role in peacekeeping in civil wars.

In terms of changes in US policy, in 2000, US–UN relations were somewhat strained. As a candidate for the presidency, George W. Bush actively campaigned against the idea of "nation-building" or furthering peacekeeping and peace-building efforts around the globe. In the spring of 2002, the administration even announced the closing of the US Army War College's Peacekeeping Institute, which had opened in 1993 after the disasters in Somalia. The decision to close was clearly not driven by financial considerations, since the annual budget for the institute was very small, but rather was intended to send a message to the US military, the UN, and any countries interested in peacekeeping that this administration was not going to engage in such endeavors.

Furthermore, by the autumn of 2002, pressure to go to war in Iraq created a widening gap between, on the one hand the United States, the United Kingdom, and several other allies; and on the other hand, the majority of the members of the UN General Assembly and the Secretariat. The United States increasingly exerted pressure on the UN to help in the United States' war effort while various institutions and figures in the UN system continued to hold their ground against going to war. In the end, the United States and several allies went to war without authorization from the UN Security Council (in other words, in contravention of international law), and without the support of the UN Secretary-General or the Secretariat. These events marked an all-time low in US–UN relations.

But shortly thereafter, once the war had been "won," and the United States confronted the task of rebuilding a war-torn Iraq, the administration essentially changed its position about nation-building, peacekeeping, and US engagement with the UN. US policy also has had to adjust to new realities of the war on terrorism, after it became clear that al-Qaeda had been training fundamentalist terrorists in such failed states as Afghanistan and, to a certain extent, Somalia. A consensus grew among US policymakers that civil war and state failure could create fertile ground for terrorist training, and that there must be increased efforts to stop such processes. Policymakers also began to realize that allies would be needed to assist with rebuilding states, and with helping to track international terrorists and their networks.

By 2003, the United States and UN made a series of moves toward rapprochement: the United States was voted back onto the Human Rights Commission (from which it had been voted off); the United States opted to rejoin UNESCO (which it had left voluntarily in 1984); the US Senate voted to pay back UN dues which the United States had either not paid, or paid late, for the previous ten years; and the United States began actively pressuring Kofi Annan and the UN Secretariat to help take over the burden of rebuilding Iraq, the tasks of which mirrored very closely those of multidimensional peacekeeping, but with more robust enforcement needs.[46]

While these important changes were underfoot in US–UN relations, ideational change in the UN Secretariat had set in motion significant institutional change within the body. The ideas first emerged in a series of reports, beginning with the scathing, self-critical reports on the UN's roles in the genocides in Rwanda and Srebrenica, through the Secretary-General's Millenium report, the extensive report on the "Responsibility to Protect," and most importantly, the "Brahimi report" on recommended institutional changes in UN peacekeeping.[47] The steady drumbeat of reports indicated that the UN could and should do more to protect civilians in civil wars, which would mean more, and more forceful, peacekeeping. By 2003, the recommendations of the reports, especially those of the Brahimi report, began to become institutionalized. The Department of Peacekeeping Operations was reformed, and grew in size by 50 percent.

[46] Note that Annan, and the Secretariat in general, have held fast against such involvement, especially after the tragic death of one of the Secretariat's top figures, Sergio Vieira de Mello. In other words, the tables in this instance have turned, and the United States is asking favors of the UN, rather than vice-versa.
[47] Annan, 1999; Carlsson, 1999 (also issued as A/54/549, 15 November 1999); A/54, April 2000; International Commission on Intervention and State Sovereignty, 2001; and A/55/503-S/809, 21 August 2000.

The new institutional capacity within DPKO, coupled by Security Council interest in furthering UN peacekeeping, have had the effect of unleashing the most recent wave of peacekeeping operations in Liberia, Côte d'Ivoire, Burundi, and Haiti, and a "ripple" in Sudan in 2005. I address each of these operations briefly below, in chronological order.

Liberia

The United Nations Mission in Liberia (UNMIL) began in late September 2003, in a state of alarming organizational dysfunction, but has slowly been recovering, along with the political (although not yet social or economic) conditions in Liberia. After fourteen years of almost continuous warfare that left approximately 250,000 dead, over 800,000 displaced, and trained tens of thousands of child soldiers, the central figure in the instability, Charles Taylor, fled the country.[48] During the months of August and September 2003, over 14,000 US troops were stationed in ships off the coast of Liberia, ready to step in if necessary, and the Liberian factions signed a peace accord calling for UN oversight of a large, multidimensional peacekeeping mission. Since 1990, there had been various ECOWAS and UN missions in Liberia, but none with as comprehensive a mandate as UNMIL.[49] The Chapter VII mandate was an innovation in peacekeeping, falling somewhere between a typical multidimensional operation and a more intrusive, full-fledged transitional administration. An indigenous, Liberian transitional government was installed by the peace plan, under the leadership of former businessman Gyude Bryant, and the UN's mission was to help this government re-create the state. But the UN did this by installing international, professional technicians in key positions in government who would help create non-corrupt institutions, and train Liberian counterparts. Other than this innovation, the mandate appeared quite standard. It called for the UN to disarm and retrain combatants; protect civilians and assist with refugee resettlement; deliver humanitarian assistance; protect human rights; support police, military, and judicial reform; assist the Liberian transitional government with the re-establishment of the state at both national and local levels; and conduct elections by the end of 2005. The UN eventually fielded a force of almost 16,000 uniformed personnel, over 1,000 civilian police, and nearly 2,000 international, local, and UN Volunteer civilian staff, but it took quite some time for the operation to get up and running.

Five hundred US troops had been helping to keep order during daylight hours (joining their compatriots on the ships at night) in Monrovia while the peace

---

[48] Charles Taylor is credited with sparking the civil war in Sierra Leone, as well as unrest in many of Liberia's neighboring countries. He has been indicted as a war criminal by the Special Court for Sierra Leone.

[49] Howe, 1997; Adebajo, 2002; and Olonisakin, 2003.

process was underway but pledged to leave as soon as the UN mandate came into effect. Stationed previously elsewhere in the country were 3,500 ECOWAS troops who would come under UNMIL authority. However, when the UN mission began, there were simply not enough troops in Liberia to enforce the peace. The US forces left on October 1, and by late October through early November, fighting had broken out, along with a wave of general lawlessness. The extra UN troops had not arrived. There was also no Special Representative of the UN appointed to the operation until late October. Information channels within the nascent UN operation, as well as between the UN and the Liberian population were dysfunctional. "A serious lack of communication, organization, control and coordination was evident within UNMIL and between it and UN agencies."[50] Eventually, it was decided that Jacques Klein of the United States, the tough-talking former head of the operation in Eastern Slavonia, would take over as the SRSG.

Shortly after Klein's arrival, in an instance of second-level learning, Klein and his team decided to draw on the troop demobilization and reintegration strategy used in Mozambique, and to a certain extent, in Eastern Slavonia, where combatants were given cash rewards and provided with retraining in exchange for disarming, demobilizing, and reintegrating into society. While such a strategy appeared to make sense, its early implementation proved disastrous. The program began in early December 2003 before the UN had set up adequate facilities and procedures for disarmament. Within a few days, riots began to break out around the disarmament sites. As one UNMIL official explained, "for the first time since we arrived, riots occurred in Monrovia and it was our fault."[51] The former combatants had not been informed about how the process would work, and demanded more of the UN than the UN could give. The program had to be suspended for two months while adequate facilities were built, cash procured, and information programs launched in order to convey to the Liberian factions what was expected of them, and what could be expected of the UN. While the UN forces and civilian staff were eventually able to quell this episode of unrest, small-scale riots and fighting have continued to break out throughout the course of the operation, often in protest that the UN has not made good on promises to pay former combatants for disarming, or helping to reconstruct the country's infrastructure. Nevertheless, disarmament and infrastructure rebuilding are underway.

The embarrassment of the rocky early start gave Klein and some of the brash staff he took with him from the former Yugoslavia pause for reflection, which in some ways has helped the staff to integrate better within itself, and between UNMIL and the local elites if not Liberian society. Klein also managed to reach out to the Liberians in unique and personal ways. As one Liberian civil society

---

[50] International Crisis Group, 2004, "Liberia and Sierra Leone," p. 4.
[51] International Crisis group, 2004, "Liberia and Sierra Leone," p. 5.

representative explained, "Ordinary Liberians like UNMIL. They see Klein as 'their advocate' and do not want warlords dictating the peace," which is an important indicator of first-level learning.[52]

By the end of November 2004, a total of 100,495 ex-combatants had been disarmed and demobilized, but by December 2005, more than a quarter of them had still not gone through job training and reintegration programs, and funds for creating the new national army were in short supply.[53] The Secretary-General reported that while progress had been made toward mandate implementation, the security situation remained "fragile," with sources of potential unrest stemming from several different groups and areas.[54] The November 2005 elections put in power Ellen Johnson Sirleaf, the first female President of an African nation, and long-time UN civil servant. These elections might be the first step in moving toward better governance, but they are no guarantee of increasing stability in Liberia, given the multitudes of disaffected young and unemployed men who voted against Johnson Sirleaf. Meanwhile, the SRSG Jacques Klein stepped down amidst rumors of scandal, and donors, who supply over half of the current operating budget of the government, expressed a certain "engagement fatigue."[55] Although there has been some first- and second-level learning in the UNMIL operation, these processes are not yet translating into fully successful mandate implementation. The future of Liberia, and UNMIL, remains uncertain.

Côte d'Ivoire

The Ivory Coast, once considered the jewel of Africa, has fallen victim to slow economic descent and rising political violence along with its neighbors, although the violence in Côte d'Ivoire is more clearly ethnic and regional in nature than in Liberia or Sierra Leone, and less tied to resources.[56] The instability began with the death of the country's founding President, Félix Houphouët-Boigny, who ruled from independence in 1960 until 1993. A coup in 1999, the first in Côte d'Ivoire's history, plunged the country into armed conflict, which has increased in intensity and breadth over the last few years through cycles of calm and disquiet.[57] Despite five attempts at coming to lasting peace accords, none of the agreements has had great staying power, even though the ten major contending political organizations have signed several of them. None of the factions is strong enough to win the war outright. France, the former

---

[52] International Crisis Group, 2004, "Liberia and Sierra Leone," p. 6.

[53] S/764, 7 December 2005, para. 39.   [54] S/764, 7 December 2005, para. 21.

[55] Pham, 2005, p. 202. Alan Doss of the UK took over as UN Special Representative after Klein and is reportedly knowledgeable and well respected, having served as Deputy Special Representative of UN peacekeeping missions in Côte d'Ivoire and Sierra Leone.

[56] Akindes, 2005; Palus, 2005; and Toungara, 2001.

[57] Le Pape and Vidal, 2002; and Toualy, 2005.

colonial power with a keen interest in maintaining a functioning international francophone community, is still intensely involved in Ivorian politics, and has intervened militarily to stop the fighting. At the same time, numerous regional and international organizations have been called on to help implement the peace accords, including the United Nations, the African Union, ECOWAS, the European Commission, the International Organization of the Francophone Countries, the Bretton Woods institutions, the Group of Eight countries, and the European Union. In other words, Côte d'Ivoire now suffers from a multiplicity of actors, both domestic and international, none of which has been authoritative enough to secure the peace.

Nominally, the UN is the lead organization in the peace implementation process. UN involvement began with a small monitoring mission in May 2003. In February 2004, under Chapter VII, the Security Council established the United Nations Operation in Côte d'Ivoire (UNOCI) with a multidimensional mandate to assist the Government of National Unity with monitoring troop movement, demobilization and reintegration of troops, repatriation and resettlement, disarmament of militias, protection of UN troops and Ivorian civilians, monitoring an arms embargo, supporting humanitarian aid, facilitating the redeployment of the state administration, helping to protect human rights, monitoring hate radio, and restoring law and order. UNOCI has a civilian staff of about 700 people, along with 6,250 international peacekeepers. But at the same time, 4,000 French troops are stationed in Côte d'Ivoire to monitor the "Zone of Confidence" cease-fire buffer that divides the country between north and south (the country is also divided between east and west, with more violence occurring in the west, especially near the long border with Liberia). Since France is in charge of logistics and support, for both the UN peacekeepers and their own troops, the operations are essentially controlled by France.

In general, the UN peacekeeping operation can be characterized by first-level organizational dysfunction. UN troops lack adequate military assets and there are high vacancy rates among civilian staff. The original Special Representative of the Secretary-General resigned in December 2004, after government forces bombed UN positions and, two days later, French positions along the Zone of Confidence.[58] In the bombings, nine French troops were killed. The Ivorian government claimed the bombings were an accident, however the French troops retaliated by bombing and destroying the entire Ivorian Air Force. The French counterattack was then followed by looting, and widespread attacks on French and foreign nationals.[59]

---

[58] A new Special Representative, Pierre Schori, of Sweden, took up his post in April 2005 and has apparently been having a difficult time with crisis management.

[59] Approximately one-fifth of the population of Côte d'Ivoire is made up of immigrants, mainly from neighboring states.

Since these events, the French troops can no longer claim impartiality, which inhibits their ability to keep the peace, and yet, there are apparently no other troops willing to take their places. Various political parties that began reneging on the peace accords, even before the UN operation began, continue to do so. Most recently, Thabo Mbeki of South Africa has stepped in to try to help restore peace. He has recently been appointed the African Union's High Representative for Elections, with a mandate that is autonomous of the UNOCI elections division. Elections set for 2005 have been postponed. The international organizations involved in Côte d'Ivoire see the elections as vital to restoring order, but at the same time, there has been little movement toward conducting demobilization, disarmament, and reintegration (DDR), before the elections. The perils of conducting elections before adequate DDR has occurred are well known from other cases, but this does not seem to be hindering the drive toward elections. Meanwhile, the economy, human rights protections, and the overall humanitarian situation continue to deteriorate despite the international presence.[60] There are increasing fears that renewed violence in Côte d'Ivoire could spill over and destabilize the fragile peace consolidation processes in neighboring Liberia and Sierra Leone.[61]

In terms of second-level learning, few lessons appear to have been applied with much success in Côte d'Ivoire. The recent consensus that a single powerful country or regional organization should intervene to restore peace and then turn over operations to a UN multidimensional mission – as was the case in Bosnia, Kosovo, East Timor, Sierra Leone, and to a certain extent Liberia – has not proven particularly beneficial in this case. Moreover, the lesson of disarmament before elections is certainly not being applied. In general, the preconditions that would allow the UN operation to move into a learning mode – adequate information sources, centralized coordination, experienced staff, and authoritative leadership – are not present, and there does not appear to be much movement toward changing this state of affairs. The failures of UNOCI stem primarily from the difficult domestic situation in Côte d'Ivoire, but inappropriate (or in the case of France, excessive) interest on the part of the great powers, along with organizational dysfunction in the UN Secretariat's mission, also contribute to the current lack of success.

Burundi

The UN's peacekeeping operation in Burundi (known by its French acronym, ONUB) has been largely successful at implementing its mandate thus far, as well as in helping to lay the foundations of a lasting peace. Indeed, of the many

---

[60] See S/398, 17 June 2005, paras. 42, 54, 61, 85.
[61] See, for example, the International Crisis Group's March 2005 report, "The Worst May Be Yet to Come."

multidimensional missions underway, only the one in Burundi appears to stand a chance of short- and long-term success, despite a long history of instability in the country and in the region.

Since its independence in 1962, Burundi has endured numerous episodes of violence (most notably in 1965, 1972, 1988, and 1993), often between Hutu rebels and the Tutsi-controlled military.[62] The massacres of mainly Hutus in 1972 and 1993 have been termed episodes of "genocide."[63] Beginning with the assassination of the first Hutu President in 1993, the almost constant fighting since then can also be characterized as a civil war, with various and splintering rebel groups fighting for control of the state.[64] Between 1993 and 2003, upwards of 300,000 people were killed in the fighting, with over one-half million made refugees and close to 1 million displaced in a country with a previous population of about 7 million people.[65]

Between 1993 and 2003, many rounds of peace talks, overseen mainly by regional leaders in Tanzania, South Africa, and Uganda, gradually established power-sharing arrangements to satisfy the majority of the contending groups (approximately nineteen political parties in all).[66] African Union (AU) peace-keepers – the first ever mission of this kind for the AU – deployed to help oversee the installation of a transitional government. In June 2004, the UN took over peacekeeping responsibilities from the AU in a signal of growing international support for the already markedly advanced peace process in Burundi. At the outset of the UN mission, 2,500 AU forces, mainly from South Africa, were transferred over to UN, which meant that ONUB was up and running very quickly. The mission's mandate, under Chapter VII of the UN Charter, has been to monitor the cease-fire; carry out disarmament, demobilization, and reintegration of former combatants; support humanitarian assistance and refugee and IDP return; assist with elections; protect international staff and Burundian civilians; monitor Burundi's troublesome borders including halting illicit arms flows; and assist in carrying out institutional reforms including those of the Constitution, judiciary, armed forces, and police.[67] The mission has been allotted 5,650 military personnel, 120 civilian police, and about 1,000 international and local civilian personnel; it has been functioning well with numbers just shy of those indicated in the mandate. It has also benefited from the existence of a fairly functional transitional government, which is in the process of transitioning into a more legitimate, elected entity.

---

[62] Hutus make up about 85 percent of the population, and Tutsis about 15 percent. However, dating back to Belgian colonial rule, when Tutsis were installed in positions of authority in the country, the Tutsi minority has generally enjoyed control over the levers of power. See des Forges, 1999.

[63] Lemarchand, 1996; and Prunier, 2002.   [64] Rwabahungu, 2004.

[65] The population today stands at a little more than 6 million, as a result of the fighting and AIDS. See *CIA World Factbook*, 2005.

[66] Khadiagala, 2003.   [67] S/RES/1545, 21 May 2004.

Although the SRSG, Carolyn McAskie of Canada, was not involved in the peace negotiations, she chairs the Implementation Monitoring Committee, which is the central clearing house and coordinating body in the peace implementation process. Upon her arrival at the beginning of the operation, she reached out to the last rebel holdout group in an attempt to bring it into the fold (something that regional leaders had been less successful at doing), and, through press statements, made it very clear that sexual misconduct among the troops – which had tarnished the reputation of UN peacekeepers in the DRC and Sierra Leone – would not be tolerated in Burundi and would be meet with swift repercussions.[68] The SRSG's former professional experience was mainly in development, which has helped to cement strong links between the processes of both economic and political development.

The main difficulty the operation faced was continued resistance to the peace process by the last holdout rebel group (a Tutsi nationalist organization), despite their earlier willingness to communicate with the SRSG. This organization continued its violent conflict on the outskirts of the capital even with the UN's presence; however, by June 2005, the group had stopped fighting and was brought into the political process. Despite some delays and setbacks, all political parties have accepted a formula for inter-ethnic power-sharing, which means no political party can gain access to government offices unless it is ethnically integrated. The focus of the UN's mission has been to enshrine the power-sharing arrangements in a popularly voted constitution, so that elections may be held, and so that a new government may take the reins of power in the country. Disarmament, demobilization, and reintegration have also been priorities and were proceeding in tandem with elections preparations.[69] In February of 2005, the Constitution was approved with over 90 percent of the popular vote. In May, June, and August of 2005, three separate elections were also held at the local level, for the Parliament, and for the presidency, respectively. All elections were declared satisfactory, despite some upsets in the processes.

The mission has also faced difficulties with refugee returns and securing adequate food supplies for a war-weary population. But on the whole, ONUB has been able to win the trust and confidence of a majority of the formerly warring leaders, as well as of the population at large. The mission has been waging an important information campaign, largely through radio broadcasts, which reach 95 percent of the country, with daily broadcasts and weekly special programs about the role of the UN, particularly in elections and disarmament procedures. It is also engaged in numerous "quick impact" projects including

---

[68] Integrated Regional Information Networks, 2004.

[69] The focus of the mission was at first on elections, but this prioritization of tasks changed in line with the demands on the ground for constitutional reforms to come first, and then elections.

rehabilitating and building schools, orphanages and health clinics; providing sports equipment to youths; and rebuilding infrastructure such as water lines.[70]

In other words, the operation appears to be functioning in a learning mode – gathering and appropriately analyzing information for policy formulation, coordinating within itself and among the other international organizations on the ground, communicating with the local population, resolving crises, and exercising appropriate forms of leadership. Undoubtedly, this first-level learning has been facilitated by second-level learning from other cases (i.e. the operation deployed quickly, and tried not to repeat the mistakes made most recently in the DRC), as well as certain auspicious situational factors, namely, assistance from supportive regional countries, and, more importantly, elite-level negotiation and reconciliation. Some experts on Burundi have argued that this process of elite reconciliation began before the fighting in 1993, when the roots for a consociational democracy were laid.[71] They argue that the sense among the elite in 1993 that the Hutu and Tutsi would be "inevitable partners" paved the way for the cooperation that exists today, at least among elites, in the country.[72] However, this process of elite reconciliation could not have continued in a virtuous cycle in recent years without the assistance of a well-functioning, multidimensional UN peacekeeping operation.

Haiti

In stark contrast to the mission in Burundi, the UN has deployed five missions in Haiti since 1993, none of which has been successful, including the current, multidimensional UN Stabilization Mission in Haiti (MINUSTAH). After so many missions, and so many years of engagement, one might expect some substantial second-level learning to have occurred, at least between the operations in Haiti. But so far, any previous learning has not translated into greater peace and stability in Haiti.[73]

Haiti has had a long history of violent and unstable rule, dating back several hundred years under Spanish and then French colonialism, through its independence in 1804, and up to the present.[74] The thirty-year rein of "Papa Doc" and then "Baby Doc" Duvalier (1956–86) brought some measure of

[70] S/328, 19 May 2005, para. 45.   [71] Ndikumana, 2000; and Sullivan, 2005.

[72] Reyntjens, 1993, pp. 579–80.

[73] A "Discussion Paper on Lessons Learned in Haiti" indicates that the Secretariat is on its way to identifying accurately the problems in Haiti, and potential solutions, but there has been little progress toward translating this analysis into appropriate political and institutional forms. See Khouri-Padova, 2004. There had also been significant advances in planning, management, and coordination between the United States and the UN in the hand-off between the US-led Multinational Force and an earlier UN mission, but this learning has not been able to offset Haiti's subsequent decline. See von Hippel, 2000, Chapter 4.

[74] Pamphile, 2001.

stability, but at a cost of brutal and repressive dictatorship.[75] Racial, economic, and political tensions run deep in Haitian society but have not resulted in civil war.[76] Indeed, the problems in Haiti do not technically amount to a civil war as defined in this book (since the deaths number in the hundreds, not thousands).[77] Rather, the problems are of state failure, general lawlessness, and economic decline.[78]

In response to the breakdown of state structures twice in recent years (in 1995 and 2004), the United States deployed troops to help stabilize the situation, and drove the processes by which the UN deployed follow-on missions to try to promote democratization and economic growth in Haiti.[79] The most recent mission, MINUSTAH, is a Chapter VII "peace-enforcement" mission, and even though the problems in Haiti are somewhat unlike those of the countries where there are civil wars, its mandate reads almost exactly like the mandates of the other multidimensional peacekeeping missions that began in 2004. MINUSTAH is charged with the following tasks: supporting the Haitian Transitional Government in securing a stable environment, including monitoring and restructuring the Haitian National Police "consistent with democratic policing standards"; conducting a "comprehensive and sustainable" DDR program; assisting with the "restoration and maintenance of the rule of law, public safety, and public order"; protecting UN personnel and equipment, and Haitian civilians; organizing municipal, parliamentary, and presidential elections; assisting in re-establishing and extending state authority throughout the country; and safeguarding human rights.[80] At the end of 2005, MINUSTAH included over 7,000 UN troops, almost 2,000 civilian police, about 500 international civilian personnel, 500 local civilian staff and over 160 United Nations Volunteers. The numbers are substantial in a country with 8 million people that is approximately the size of the small US state of Maryland, nevertheless, the state failure and violence in Haiti have been extremely difficult to counteract.[81]

The violence is sometimes related to formal politics, since many of the perpetrators are loyal to ousted President Jean-Bertrand Aristide and his Lavalas party, but at the same time, the widespread fear, lawlessness, and diffuse aggression is often not particularly organized, politically or otherwise. This presents

[75] Leconte, 1999.   [76] Dupuy, 1997.
[77] More people died in 2004 from floods than from fighting.
[78] Rotberg, 2003; Kumar, 2001.
[79] During those years, there was one democratically-elected parliament (in 1995) that was able to govern for about two years. Also during those years, instead of growth, the economy declined at a rate of about 2.5 percent per year. See UN Development Programme, 2005, "Human Development Report."
[80] S/RES/1542, 30 April 2004. Similar to some of the newer mandates, there are also clauses about protecting women and children, and intolerance of misconduct among peacekeepers.
[81] *CIA World Factbook*, 2005, "Haiti."

an important problem to the UN peacekeepers who are trained to deal primarily with former combatants, be they government or rebel forces. The peacekeepers on the ground in Haiti are not trained, nor do they have the mandate, to deal with the most pressing problems facing efforts at political reintegration and state reformation. A prime example of the mandate disconnect is MINUSTAH's DDR program. It covers only "former army and those who were paid to spearhead the cross-border attacks that helped bring about the ouster of Aristide in 2004."[82] In other words, it would appear that the problems of urban gangs, unorganized crime, and the economic, social, and political dislocation that give rise to them, are unsuited to the solution of DDR as it is currently envisioned. What is needed in Haiti is a new type of operation, but such an institutional transformation among international organizations does not appear to be on the horizon any time soon.

The civilian police component would be the most logical unit of the MINUSTAH operation to become a locus for creative thinking about how to combat rampant crime and criminal gangs. This would constitute a form of "police-keeping," as termed by several experts on the matter.[83] But the MINUSTAH civilian police operation, while fairly large in number, is not well composed for the task at hand. Only 80 percent of the authorized police have been deployed, and only 35 percent of those speak French (a mere handful speak Creole, the language of the majority of the population); very few translators are available, thus the possibilities for dispersed integration with the population and low level information-gathering and communication are very limited. Moreover, the leading police-contributing countries are Jordan, Pakistan, Nepal, and China, none of which are known for democratic policing methods (note that the mandate for MINUSTAH specifies that the Haitian police are to be restructured in a manner "consistent with democratic policing standards" – a rather tall, and somewhat hypocritical order given the make-up of MINUSTAH's CIVPOL). Although one might make the argument that authoritarian police tactics are what is necessary in lawless Haiti, given that the Haitian police already regularly kill suspects they have incarcerated, and fire at random on crowds of demonstrators, increased authoritarian practices do not appear to be the key to success.[84]

The question of the appropriate use of force among MINUSTAH's peacekeeping troops has also been very important. Following calls at UN headquarters to use greater force to stem the lawlessness in Haiti, especially on the part of the French, the peacekeeping troops have taken a "robust approach." MINUSTAH has been conducting such activities as re-taking police stations occupied by armed gangs, establishing permanent checkpoints, and

[82] International Crisis Group, 2005, "Can Haiti Hold Elections in 2005?" p. 8.
[83] Day and Freeman, 2005; and Thomas, 2001.   [84] Amnesty International, 2005.

conducting heavily armed patrols in some of the most troubled areas.[85] However, this greater use and display of force has not yet been able to stem the crime, lawlessness, impunity, random violence, and lack of any significant socioeconomic progress.[86]

But the problems of the current UN mission are not simply ones of inappropriate mandate, lack of institutional creativity, and a difficult situation. There has also been a higher-level disagreement about coordination and division of labor at the international level. Like Côte d'Ivoire, Haiti now suffers from a multiplicity of international actors who seek to play an important role in solving the crises (including the UN, the Organization of American States, the United States, France, Canada, Brazil, Chile, Argentina, and South Africa, where Aristide has been living in exile). According to one report, after the deployment of MINUSTAH, it took six months for the UN and the Organization of American States to come to a memorandum of understanding on coordination between the international organizations.[87] Among the members of the Security Council, Russia and China have not been in favor of fielding and paying for UN peacekeeping operations in a situation that is not one of civil war, and in a country that is in the United States' direct sphere of influence – there is a sense that the United States should be taking care of the crises on its own. At the same time, US policy toward Haiti has been inconsistent in content and direction, but consistently heavy-handed.

In other words, there has simply not been much sustained learning in the efforts to help Haiti, either on the first level, or on the second. The lack of learning in the Secretariat, the difficult domestic situation in Haiti, and the unhelpful influence of some Security Council members have all spelled failure for the missions thus far.

Sudan

While Haiti's outlook appears bleak, there is not much more light for Sudan. Sudan was in a state of civil war for most of the second half of the twentieth century, and fighting continues to the present, albeit in different forms and regions from the past. A 21-year war between mainly northern Arab Sunni Muslims, and non-Arab Christian and Animist southern populations claimed the lives of approximately 1.5 million people. Neighboring countries all around Sudan were implicated in the fighting. After many years and rounds of peace talks, the Comprehensive Peace Agreement between northern and southern leaders was signed in January 2005, calling for a multidimensional UN peacekeeping

---

[85] S/313, 13 May 2005, para. 14.
[86] International Crisis Group, 2005, "Update on Haiti for the UN Security Council."
[87] International Crisis Group, 2005, "Can Haiti Hold Elections in 2005?" p. 3.

mission to help implement the accords. In the second half of 2005, the UN struggled to establish the United Nations Mission in Sudan against the backdrop of a separate and much-publicized violent conflict in the western Darfur region of Sudan.[88]

The fighting in Darfur had been going on for years but accelerated rapidly in 2003, and it largely involves Arab nomadic and black pastoral groups (both are mainly Muslim). The Arab militias, backed by the government, have been carrying out horrific campaigns against civilian populations that are seen to support the rebel militias; hundreds of thousands of people have been killed and nearly 2 million have fled the region.[89] The United States and some other countries have termed the fighting genocide, while many others, as well as the UN, have stopped short of using this term.[90]

The United Nations Mission in Sudan patrolling the north/south conflict lines is multidimensional in name but not yet in practice, and has been over-shadowed by higher-level politics in the region and at UN headquarters in New York. The Sudanese government has exploited international disagreement in order to further its own agenda for the country and the Darfur region. The United States favors greater intervention to halt the genocide and ethnic cleansing in Darfur, but at the same time the United States is hindered from pursuing a more forceful diplomatic agenda because it relies on the Sudanese government's support in the war on terror. The UK, a former colonial power in Sudan and the largest European bilateral donor, shares a similar view to that of the United States.[91] China, with significant oil interests in the region, supports the Sudanese government's position that there has been no genocide, and that non-Arab militia rebel groups ignited the conflict; many Arab governments also share this opinion.

On the ground, the United Nations Mission in Sudan has been forbidden by the Sudanese government from fully deploying as mandated, or from extending its mandate to the western Darfur region, amid claims that the UN represents a "foreign occupation." The mission has been understaffed, but must also send monthly reports back to UN headquarters – a guideline that very few missions have to follow, and which signifies little room for maneuver in the field. Meanwhile, the African Union has deployed several thousand peacekeeping troops to Darfur, where there is no peace to keep, and with a mandate that allows them to observe, but not stop, the ethnic cleansing and genocide.[92] Given the lack of consent for UN peacekeeping on the part of the Sudanese government, the conflicting and intense great-power interests, and understaffed AU and

---

[88] S/821, 21 December 2005.   [89] Morrison, and de Waal, 2005, p. 162.
[90] Prunier, 2005.
[91] International Crisis Group. 2005, "The EU/AU Partnership in Darfur: Not Yet a Winning Combination."
[92] Williams, 2005.

UN operations, the prospects for successful peacekeeping in Sudan appear extremely remote.

Conclusion

The ongoing multidimensional peacekeeping missions exhibit some first- and second-level learning, although not as much as one might expect given the extensive experience the UN now has with peacekeeping. In terms of the general causes of success or failure in UN peacekeeping, the short case studies in this chapter focus mainly on factors of the situational difficulty, and learning or dysfunction in the Secretariat's operations. The third element determining success and failure, UN Security Council interests, is addressed where most relevant to the cases, but in this time period, for all cases, a new overriding concern is affecting all of the decisions of the Security Council, either directly or indirectly.

The main concern is international terrorism, although it is often not explicitly discussed in the new peacekeeping mandates, or in many official documents related to the peacekeeping missions. There is no doubt that terrorism, and the "war on terror" are some of the main driving forces in current US, British, Russian, and French foreign policy considerations (although less so for China). It would appear that there has been an interesting, tacit exchange between the UN Secretariat and some of the members of the Security Council (especially the United States), revealing that the Secretariat, which has historically not dealt with matters of terrorism, has begun to entertain Security Council concerns for fighting terrorism, while in return, the Security Council has begun increasingly to endorse the efforts of the Secretariat to extend and improve its peacekeeping practices. An important report issued by the Secretary-General's High-Level Panel on Threats, Challenges, and Change entitled, "A More Secure World" endorses explicitly increased efforts within the UN to fight terrorism, and simultaneously acknowledges that "since the end of the Cold War, peacekeeping and post-conflict peacebuilding in civil wars have become the operational face of the United Nations in international peace and security."[93] Peacekeeping in civil wars is and has been the most important item on the Secretariat's agenda. But by 2003, the number of civil wars was lower than it had been since 1978, while the number of UN peacekeeping and peacebuilding operations in civil wars was the highest in history.[94] In other words, it is not the situation of increasing civil wars that is driving international efforts to end them, but rather, a decision on the part of international actors (namely, the Secretariat in tandem

---

[93] High-Level Panel on Threats, Challenges, and Change, 2004, p. 33.
[94] High-Level Panel on Threats, Challenges, and Change, 2004, p. 33.

with the Security Council) to end civil wars, in part because such conflicts could pose a threat to international peace through enabling terrorist activity to flourish.

The rise of Chapter VII mandates in new peacekeeping missions is a part of this trend, in that it reflects greater Security Council readiness to ensure that peace agreements are implemented, by force, if necessary. Higher troops numbers and multidimensional mandates are also reflections of this trend. The role of the United States, however, has been somewhat ambivalent, which most likely stems in part from the current administration's skepticism about peacekeeping and nation-building. Out of the eight operations discussed in this and the preceding chapter, the United States has had a direct interest in four in particular. It has provided Special Representatives of the Secretary-General for the missions in the Congo and in Liberia, but thus far, greater involvement (as in sending US troops to help with UN peacekeeping) has not occurred.[95] The conflicts in Liberia and Haiti are both considered ones where the United States, given historical and geographic ties, ought to have a major role in conflict resolution. The results of such involvement, however, have been quite mixed, as discussed previously in this chapter.

France is the other major power on the Security Council with direct links to many of the current missions, in that four of the eight are in French-speaking countries (DRC, Côte d'Ivoire, Burundi, Haiti), and France has a direct interest in sustaining countries where the French language is spoken. France's interest in peacekeeping in general is also tied to its historical self-image as a country with a "civilizing mission" in the world. Many French intellectuals and politicians feel that France, and other countries have a "droit d'ingérence," or a "right to intervene" in places where states have broken down and are no longer caring for the basic humanitarian needs of their citizens. Concerns with international terrorism are not as pressing for France as for the United States, but they too play a role in France's interests in UN peacekeeping.

In surveying the current cases, the patterns discussed previously in this book hold, where the most successful missions – namely in East Timor and Burundi – do not have a great power on the Security Council offering well-intentioned, although not always helpful, prescriptions. Among the great powers, domestic processes that determine foreign policy often mirror more closely national self-interest than the interests of the state in need of multidimensional peace-keeping.

In general, the current operations reflect important changes in international relations, especially the foreign policy interests of the United States and France,

---

[95] Generally speaking, the country that supplies the SRSG is often the one the missions turn to in times of need. However, it appears the United States has not been particularly forthcoming for its SRSGs in either the DRC or in Liberia.

as two central members of the Security Council that are driving peacekeeping policy. The more specific trends that relate directly to peacekeeping practices – such as the rise of Chapter VII mandates, non-UN peace-enforcement operations, and the turn away from transitional administrations and back to more standard multidimensional UN peacekeeping operations – are addressed in greater depth in the following, concluding chapter.

10

Conclusion: two levels of organizational learning

In this book I have argued that there are three conditions that are necessary, and jointly they are sufficient, for the successful implementation of UN multidimensional peacekeeping mandates in civil wars. These conditions consist of the consent of the warring parties for the UN operation, consensual but only moderately intense Security Council interests, and first-level organizational learning in the UN Secretariat's peacekeeping operation. I have based this argument on case studies of the ten multidimensional operations, most of which began and ended in the 1990s – the four cases of failure in Somalia, Rwanda, Angola, and Bosnia, and the six successes in Namibia, El Salvador, Cambodia, Mozambique, Eastern Slavonia, and East Timor. The argument also holds for the ongoing missions addressed in Chapter 9: Kosovo, Sierra Leone, Congo, Liberia, Côte d'Ivoire, Burundi, Haiti and Sudan. Most of the book focuses on the devilish details that, taken together, paint a picture of the overall processes that determine the outcomes of peacekeeping operations. In this chapter, however, I address some of the larger implications of my research, and possible new directions in the future of UN multidimensional peacekeeping.

I begin by exploring some of the preconditions that enable first-level learning. This is significant, since first-level learning is one of the most important causes, or "independent variables," that affects peacekeeping outcomes: what lies behind this factor that I otherwise treat as a starting place for explanation? I then analyze the second-level organizational changes at UN headquarters. Based on the past and ongoing cases, it appears that the UN has been inching toward some second-level learning, but not consistently. I address the current major trends in peacekeeping, categorizing them in terms of second-level dysfunction, incremental adaptation, or learning. The main element of learning, I argue, lies in the emerging international division of labor of the use of force: peace-enforcement has become the domain of single states and regional organizations, whereas multidimensional peacekeeping, or state-building remains in the hands of the UN; this division of labor is logical, legitimate, and demonstrates an overall learning trend in peacekeeping. Following this discussion, I investigate the implications of the book's basic argument for the non-UN-led operations in Afghanistan and Iraq. And finally, I address the new ways in which civil wars are ending in the post-Cold War era – in negotiated settlements, rather than in the complete defeat of the losing side(s) – and I explore the extent to which the UN Secretariat might be considered an active agent of this change.

Preconditions for first-level learning

In this book, I have treated first-level organizational learning as an independent variable that is a partial cause of success or failure in UN multidimensional peacekeeping in civil wars. I define first-level organizational learning as the UN's ability to do the following: *gather technical information* from the field in order to develop sound analyses of problems in the post-civil war society; *coordinate* international efforts such that organizational tasks are incrementally and appropriately re-prioritized; *integrate* with the post-civil war environment so that organizational responses and routines derive primarily from field-level considerations rather than higher-level political debates at headquarters; and finally, *exercise leadership* in such a way that fosters the consent of the parties involved, and resolves the many small and large crises that arise in every peace-keeping operation. First-level organizational learning, or its opposite, organizational dysfunction, refer only to peacekeeping operations during the time in which they are being executed, as opposed to second-level organizational learning *between* the missions.

In the introductory chapter, I discussed four preconditions for first-level organizational learning in the field, including widespread mechanisms for gathering information, centralized field coordination, experienced staff with a wide distribution in the field, and well-informed, well-chosen leadership. While these operational features relate directly to the four main indicators of first-level organizational learning, there are several other important types of preconditions for learning that must be explored.

The consent of the warring parties is a necessary but not sufficient factor for success, but it can also be considered a precondition for learning: if the parties do not consent to the peacekeeping operation, there is little chance of deployment to the field, much less learning, once the mission arrives. There is, of course, something of a reciprocal causal relationship between the actions of the peacekeeping operation and the parties. Consent enables the operation to begin, but slow UN deployment often initiates a spiraling erosion of commitments. After the signing of the peace accord, there is a short window of opportunity for the UN to play the role of legitimate guarantor of the peace. When the UN reneges on its commitments to monitor a cease-fire as of a certain date, and its peacekeeping operations do not even arrive until many months after that date has passed, the formerly warring factions have every incentive to return to war, which in turn makes establishing the peacekeeping operation all the more difficult. The missions in Namibia, Cambodia, Mozambique, Sierra Leone, and East Timor all suffered from slow deployment. But after moving into a learning mode, they were able to re-establish consent. However, the operations in Angola, Bosnia, Rwanda, Liberia, Haiti, and the DRC also deployed too slowly, with lasting negative implications for consent, first-level learning, and the possibility of success in mandate implementation.

Fundamentally linked to consent and slow deployment are important processes that occur at Secretariat headquarters before peacekeeping operations begin. Slow deployment has two basic origins. To begin with, the bureaucratic mechanisms at headquarters that are in charge of logistics, procurement, and hiring personnel function inadequately, even now, after the extensive reforms in the wake of the 2000 "Brahimi Report."[1] But more importantly, all peacekeeping operations rely on the kindness of troop contributors to offer not only well-trained, but also well-equipped, troops, in large enough numbers. This generosity is frequently not forthcoming, and often ill-trained and ill-equipped troops are sent on UN missions, despite years of protest on the part of the Secretariat and the establishment of new procedures for training and equipping troops. While the UN Standby Arrangement System has existed for years, thus far, very few countries have signed up for rapid deployment. Well-trained, quickly deployable troops, in large enough numbers to keep the peace, are a precondition for first-level learning.

Finally, appropriate Security Council political support and approval of funding can also be considered preconditions for first-level organizational learning. If the Security Council does not approve of the operation, there is no way that it will be deployed, much less begin to learn. In terms of funding, it is very important to note that abundant funding does not directly translate into success, nor does barely adequate funding translate into failure: the operations in Somalia and Bosnia were extremely well funded, but this funding was accompanied by conflicting political directives that undermined the ability of the peacekeeping operations to function. Conversely, in Eastern Slavonia and Namibia, the operations received much less funding than requested, but both were able to succeed in implementing their mandates, in large part because of first-level organizational learning. These case illustrations do not mean, however, that funding should be cut further; adequate funds can also be considered a precondition for learning.

To summarize, first-level learning originates in several basic areas: the consent of the warring parties, the make-up of the field mission, troop contributors, Secretariat headquarters, and the Security Council. Without appropriate support from all of these elements, missions will be unable to deploy to the field, much less begin to learn once they arrive. Improving preconditions for

---

[1] The official title is "The Report of the Panel on United Nations Peace Operations," August 2000. The report was named after its first author, Algerian diplomat Lakhdar Brahimi. Brahimi is considered to be one of the UN's top peacemakers, having represented the UN in operations in Haiti, Afghanistan, and Iraq. See also "The Brahimi Report and the Future of UN Peace Operations," by Durch et al., 2003. Secretary-General Annan has referred to a "gaping hole" in the UN's peacekeeping machinery. See Annan, 2005, para. 114.

first-level learning are a primary indicator of second-level learning, the subject to which I turn next.

Dysfunction, incremental adaptation, and learning on the second level

There has been a mixed picture of what I term second-level learning in UN peacekeeping. I defined second-level organizational learning in Chapter 1 as learning between peacekeeping missions, at UN headquarters, when change occurs 'in the organization's overall means, structures, and goals, in response to new understandings of problems and their causes.' Second-level organizational dysfunction is indicated when sections of the organization work at cross-purposes with one another, important general insights from one operation are not adequately transferred to other operations, actions are at odds with the fundamental principles of the organization, and there is no systematic evaluation of problems, goals, or methods. Less severe organizational dysfunction, "incremental adaptation," lies in between learning and dysfunction. Incremental adaptation is indicated when programs, policies, and standard operating procedures are transferred from one operation to the next without regard to the new context, or new structures are expanded or added onto old ones, with little regard for the overall picture. The categories are not always clear-cut, but nonetheless, it is possible to make certain judgments about which current trends fit into which categories.

The evidence from the cases in this study paints a general picture of incremental adaptation, punctuated by both organizational dysfunction and learning. Below I present examples of each type, starting with second-level organizational dysfunction, followed by a discussion of incremental adaptation, and finally, some evidence of second-level organizational learning between operations.

Dysfunction

Although there has been a fair amount of first-level organizational learning *within* peacekeeping missions, the same cannot generally be said for second-level learning *between* missions. Over the past decade or so, there have been several surprising cases of non-learning from the past, when one might have expected some improvement, especially during the stage of mandate construction.

For example, the mandates for the missions in Cambodia, Mozambique, and Angola all failed to address the problem of competing post-civil war local administrations, even though it was clear from early in the peace negotiations phase that problems would arise stemming from this issue. The peacekeeping missions were often at a loss as to how to unify severely divided civilian administrations, even though this would prove to be an incredibly important step toward securing a lasting peace. By the time of the Eastern Slavonian operation in Croatia, which began in 1996, the problem of competing administrations (one Croat, one Croatian Serb) was directly tackled by the civil affairs division, since it was clear to the UN, and to both sides, that the conflict would never be resolved without careful attention to the reconstruction of the state's municipal and regional administrations. This realization, however, came only in relation to the operation at hand. In other words, there is no evidence in any of the documents concerning the Eastern Slavonian operation that attention to the local civil administration came in relation to a greater understanding of the general importance of this problem for resolving civil wars. Moreover, the problem of a lack of planning and ideas for how to jump start civil administrations is currently being replicated in, for example, Sierra Leone and Côte d'Ivoire, and was not directly addressed in the mandates for those operations. The problems of merging or re-creating local state institutions have also arisen in the cases of UN transitional administration in Kosovo and East Timor.

The cases of Mozambique and Angola provide similar examples of no learning between cases where it might otherwise have been expected. The ONUMOZ mission in Mozambique was planned and implemented in the wake of the disastrous UNAVEM II operation in Angola. There is no question that ONUMOZ benefited from some serious re-evaluation at UN headquarters about the resources, standard operating procedures, and troop reintegration programs necessary to implement a complex peace deal. However, the learning did not extend beyond the Mozambique operation; it did not even translate back to the UNAVEM III mission in Angola. A similar argument could be made for the numerous operations in Haiti, none of which seems to have been able to implement any significant elements of learning from previous operations.[2]

To give another example of no long-term learning between missions after some initial second-level learning, in the wake of the disastrous start to UNTAG in Namibia, the UN Secretary-General Pérez de Cuéllar made sure that his plan for ONUSAL in El Salvador was ratified by the Security Council before the final peace accords were signed, and that ONUSAL was almost fully deployed by the start of the cease-fire. He argued successfully that cease-fires should not be declared unless there were international monitors in place to ensure compliance. While this looks on the face of it like some evidence of learning, it was not transferred to the *organization* as part of a standard general strategy. When Secretary-General Boutros-Ghali assumed his position, the importance of careful orchestration of the cease-fire to coincide with UN troop deployment, and detailed advanced planning for the overall operation, was essentially lost in the fury to have the UN engage in numerous new multidimensional operations simultaneously. During the tenure of Secretary-General Annan, delayed

---

[2] Some of this lack of learning is of course linked to difficult situations on the ground, but not exclusively.

deployment and poor advanced planning have continued to plague peacekeeping efforts, especially in the subsequent waves of new peacekeeping operations in 1999 and 2003–2004 (see Chapter 9), and despite concerted attempts at reducing deployment times and increasing planning.

Another important trend indicating dysfunction concerns the national origins of peacekeeping troops. During the Cold War, it was common practice that the permanent five (P-5) members of the Security Council did not send their troops to participate in peacekeeping operations because of the politicized and divided nature of the Cold War. This norm changed in Cambodia, when international negotiators actively sought the contribution of P-5 troops as a demonstration to the combatants that the great powers were serious about helping Cambodia in its transition from civil war. Alongside this shift, in the early 1990s, many "middle powers" began increasingly to send their troops on missions for various reasons – often to improve their stature worldwide while promoting humanitarian causes.[3] Today, however, in the wake of the genocides in Rwanda and Srebrenica, the most powerful states, along with the middle powers, have shied away from sending their troops for UN peacekeeping duty. The great powers remain reluctant to send their own troops to peacekeeping theaters under UN auspices, in large part because they have tremendous difficulty in convincing their parliaments to send forces to places that are not at the top of the national security agenda. But as has been argued in this book, the P-5 members of the Security Council tend not to be very good peacekeepers in large part because it is difficult for the great powers to remain impartial while developing field-level capacities for learning. France, Russia, and the United States all have quite negative records.[4] While some observers in and outside of the UN Secretariat lament the absence of P-5 forces from peacekeeping duty, evidence shows that fewer troops from the great powers might actually enable peacekeeping missions to function better in the field because the great powers are less interested in micromanaging from afar troops of other nationalities. What is troubling, however, is the emerging attitude of the "middle-size powers."

The middle powers that regularly used to send troops – Canada, Denmark, Ireland, the Netherlands, Sweden – are shying away from UN peacekeeping duty, preferring instead to contribute, along with the P-5 to "force multipliers," such as trainers, air lift support, structural engineers, communications experts, and the like, rather than actual troops. Meanwhile, the largest share of the

---

[3] Behringer, 2005.

[4] For example, in Rwanda, France was accused of helping the *genocidaires*, and has been having similar problems with impartiality in Côte d'Ivoire. In Bosnia, Macedonia, and elsewhere, US troops have been noted for their passion for "force protection," or making sure that their troops do not get hurt, rather than interacting and integrating with the society, in order to engage in first-level learning. And Russian troops in the former Soviet Union, such as in Georgia and Tajikistan, have not had a reputation for being impartial brokers of the peace.

peacekeeping burden is being shouldered by the Global South. The vast majority of actual UN peacekeeping troops come from the developing world, especially for the missions in Africa.[5] The result is that there is a disturbing new racial and economic divide between those who do the peacekeeping and the "peace-kept" on the one hand, and those who fund and control the operations on the other. This divide reinforces the very economic and social divisions on a world scale that multidimensional peacekeeping is, at least in part, intended to counteract. Rather than sharing the human burden of peacekeeping, people from the developing and developed worlds become more separate and unequal. This trend can be considered one of second-level dysfunction, since the ethical and moral purposes of peacekeeping are contradicted by purposive and divisive peacekeeping policies.[6]

Finally, and most importantly, there has been little evidence at UN head-quarters of a shift in thinking that more attention should be devoted to field operations. Since 1997, shortly after Kofi Annan moved from being the head of the Department of Peacekeeping Operations to taking the reins as UN Secretary-General, there has been an almost continuous effort at reform of various aspects of the UN system, and certainly of peacekeeping. However, all reform efforts have stemmed from, and been directed primarily toward, UN headquarters.[7] Over time, the capacity of the DPKO has expanded dramatically. The department has increased in size by over 50 percent; old offices have been shut down, and new divisions have opened. The changes have made possible an increase in the capacity of the UN to take on new missions, as have been reflected in the waves of new operations in 1999 and 2003–2004, but have the insti-tutional reforms and increased headquarters capacity spelled better precondi-tions for first-level learning, and an increasing possibility of successful mandate implementation? Certainly there have been progressive changes in the under-standing of some important problems, such as the responsibility to protect civilians, as addressed below. However, while the bureaucracy at headquarters has grown bigger, the lack of attention to the specifics involved in the require-ments of first-level learning – greater capacity for information-gathering and analysis in the field, better coordination among units in the field, having an adequately prepared staff on the ground who are given the mandate to interact

---

[5] Whereas the missions in Bosnia, Kosovo, and Afghanistan have many peacekeeping troops from the developed world.

[6] The sex scandals in peacekeeping and, tangentially, the oil-for-food program scandals also represent a disconnect between UN ethics, policy, and action, but in these cases, the offenses were not condoned by the organization, or a component of official policy. The policy of sending troops from the developing world to solve developing-world problems is an explicit policy objective, which overlooks certain ethical dilemmas.

[7] The most recent reform proposed, the establishment of a new UN Peacebuilding Commis-sion to coordinate among units at headquarters, is similar to the other reforms in that it does not focus on the needs of the field.

with citizens in the local environment, and exercising crisis-control leadership by Special Representatives who arrive before peace commitments erode – remains apparent, even in the most recent waves of operations. Spoken plainly, the current peacekeeping missions do not appear to be much better off than the previous ones.[8] If anything, the increase in staff at UN Secretariat headquarters, coupled by an increase in the number of missions, has been accompanied by a decrease in capacity in the field, since the field operations must now answer to more "superiors" at headquarters. It is in the field, in the end, where peacekeeping operations rise and fall. When and if future peacekeeping reform efforts take less of a headquarters perspective, and more of a field-level view, we will undoubtedly witness a decrease in organizational dysfunction.

Incremental adaptation

While dysfunction has been an important part of the picture of second-level organizational change, incremental adaptation has arguably been the norm. Incremental adaptation is indicated when tactics, standard operating procedures, or programs are transferred almost automatically from one context to another. Often the redeployment of any program will be inappropriate for the new context, and thus if the organization is to succeed in implementing its mandate, it must adapt to the new conditions through first-level learning. Reapplying mandates and tactics from one context to the next is precisely what has been occurring since the end of the Cold War in multidimensional peacekeeping. By the 2003–2004 wave of new operations, not only the basic components, but some of the very same language for the new mandates was repeated, even for the mission in Haiti, which had a completely different situational profile (one of state collapse, as opposed to civil war).

Incremental adaptation is evidenced in many ways, but four components in particular provide illustrations of this phenomenon: the civilian police, gender affairs units, elections units, and the peacekeeping "best practices" section. First, civilian policing has not enjoyed great success but has nevertheless become a dimension of every new multidimensional peacekeeping operation. The concept of civilian policing as it is known today was born in Namibia, during the UNTAG operation. UNTAG's CIVPOL division was fairly adept at both inventing and implementing its mandate to monitor and retrain an extremely repressive, but disciplined and well-organized police force. After the end of

---

[8] James Cockayne and David Malone agree. They write: "Contemporary peace operations face many of the same operational challenges as early missions. Weak command and control, inadequate communications and logistical equipment, little prior opportunity for detailed planning, and underequipped and ill-trained military personnel are as much issues today as the were in [Ralph] Bunche's day, if not more so. In at least one area there has been an apparent decline: the promptness with which the UN can deploy the peacekeeping force." See Cockayne and Malone, 2005, p. 333.

UNTAG, the CIVPOL division was transferred to UNTAC in Cambodia almost intact, including the same Dutch chief, and many of the same police observers and trainers. In Cambodia, these same people were given a similar mandate to observe and retrain the local police, but the police in Cambodia were entirely different. Unlike the abusive but generally disciplined police forces in Namibia, the State of Cambodia police were largely untrained, ill-equipped, and spoke Khmer (as opposed to Afrikaans, which is very similar to Dutch). There were no standard policing procedures that could be monitored and evaluated in the same manner as in Namibia. Moreover, all of the problems experienced in UNTAG's CIVPOL (namely a lack of basic training, common languages, and driving skills) were replicated, but with greater intensity, in Cambodia. In the end, the CIVPOL division in Cambodia failed in its efforts to replicate the previously successful program.

Several subsequent attempts at civilian policing, such as in Croatia, Mozambique, and Bosnia, have been somewhat more effective, and there has been some learning. But in the cases of extreme state failure, such as in parts of Sierra Leone, the DRC, and Haiti, a radically new approach to law enforcement, and to the building of law enforcement structures, is needed. The current mandates and methods employed by the multidimensional operations have been transferred to these new, almost completely lawless contexts, with very little success. In places where almost all state structures have broken down, under-trained and under-equipped UN civilian police, who often come themselves from states where authoritarian regimes rule, cannot be expected to help build functioning state institutions and democratic police forces. Part of the problem is simply one of supply: there are very few "good cops" and the states that have them are reluctant to send them abroad, preferring to keep them for use at home. But another important part of the problem is conceptual: is the repeated application of international civilian police a satisfactory response to the general problem of state illegitimacy and breakdown? Thus far, there has been a dearth of creative ideas and practices, which paints a general picture of incremental adaptation in this extremely important aspect of all multidimensional peacekeeping operations. Without a new conception of how to do civilian policing, and who will do it, we can expect UN peacekeeping operations, even the successful ones, to encounter serious problems, including paving the way for increased crime levels after the missions depart the country, as has been the case after almost all operations, even the otherwise successful ones.

Another important and complex dimension of peacekeeping operations and adaptation concerns gender, and the advent of gender affairs offices. There have traditionally been very few women peacekeepers, even though the mission in Namibia made great strides toward "gender mainstreaming" long before such terms became popular.[9] But after the operation in Namibia, issues of gender

[9] Olsson, 2001.

equity, both within peacekeeping operations, and between peacekeepers and local societies, fell to the background.[10] In the operation in Cambodia, UN peacekeepers were accused of creating an important sex-trade industry, and bringing HIV/AIDS to a region where the disease had been previously all but unknown. These types of problems have been replicated in other cases, most egregiously in Kosovo.[11] In a quest to thwart gender inequality and abusive practices, all new peacekeeping operations now include some sort of gender affairs office. It is somewhat ironic, however, that since the inclusion of such components, there have been increasing instances of sexual misconduct among the troops. While this might be a function of better reporting mechanisms, the inclusion of gender divisions and discussions about "gendering" appear to be making only incremental advancement in the problems. As one analyst lamented, "All of this work [on "gender mainstreaming"] may on occasion help a UN staffer, but it does not transform existing practices; it ignores the ways in which those practices are already gendered."[12] While the problems surrounding gender may look like organizational dysfunction, the fact that there has been so much attention to these matters indicates incremental adaptation – new goals are being formulated, and while they might not be satisfied, institutional responses are emerging and being replicated.

A third component of multidimensional peacekeeping that is always included in new operations is an elections unit. Even when other components may fail, UN peacekeeping operations often opt to hold elections as a first step toward exiting the post-civil war environment, even before demobilization, disarmament, and reintegration of troops. This pattern developed first in Cambodia, where the civil administration and military components were faltering, and the mission decided to focus instead on elections as the easiest component of the mandate to fulfill. Several years later, the authoritarian takeover in Cambodia led many analysts to contend that holding elections before a full cease-fire and disarmament was not wise, and could possibly be counterproductive to the long-term goals of peacekeeping and democratization.[13] Concerted attempts to disarm before elections have led to positive results in East Timor, Sierra Leone, Liberia, Burundi, and to a certain extent in Kosovo. However, in Congo, Côte d'Ivoire, and Haiti, the UN has focused on elections before disarmament as a way to solve the conflicts.[14] This strategy has been applied in the past with little success, making its reapplication unlikely to produce desired results.

---

[10] Mendelson, 2005.
[11] The sex trafficking industry run out of Kosovo is the largest in all of Europe. Note that the first "gender affairs office" in a peacekeeping mission was established in the UNMIK mission in Kosovo, in 1999, with a large workload and inadequate support. See Agathangelou and Ling, 2003.
[12] Whitworth, 2004, pp. 185–86.
[13] Snyder, 2000; Kingma, 2002; Reilly, 2002; and Paris, 2004.
[14] The United States has also pursued this strategy in Afghanistan and Iraq, despite warnings against such choices.

A final example of incremental adaptation lies in the UN's institutional capacities for analysis and evaluation of peacekeeping operations. After some of the debacles of the 1993–94 peacekeeping missions, the DPKO established an eight-member Lessons Learned Unit to reflect upon mistakes, in the hope that the UN would not repeat them in the future. The unit had a number of problems (the few reports produced focused primarily on failures, they were not widely read, and were not generally written by people with a background in social science or policy evaluation). After the Brahimi Report, the Lessons Learned Unit was merged in 2001 with the Policy and Analysis Unit to become the Peacekeeping Best Practices Unit (renamed the Peacekeeping Best Practices Section in the summer of 2005). The Peacekeeping Best Practices Section is a remarkable institutional improvement over the Lessons Learned Unit, in that it is actually focused on knowledge management and analysis, produces relevant and timely reports, and conducts training seminars. It also manages a website, where its reports are easily accessible. The very title change to emphasize "best practices" implies learning from successes, not only from failures, which indicates important progress. Some basic problems, however, remain in that this is a small section with only nine professional staff, who have little influence over the rest of DPKO.[15] When the Peacekeeping Best Practices Section's recommendations are visibly and regularly institutionalized in broader peacekeeping practices, especially during the establishment of new missions, this will be an important indication of second-level learning.

Second-level learning

While incremental adaptation has generally been the norm in UN peacekeeping, there has also been some recent and important second-level organizational learning. One example lies in the trend away from taking on the task of full-fledged transitional administrations, and in a greater understanding of the organization's limitations. After the largely failed attempt at taking over the administration of the sizable state in Cambodia, the only other attempts have been in very small territories: Eastern Slavonia, Kosovo, and East Timor. While the operation in Eastern Slavonia went very well, the administration in East Timor was fraught with complications, especially at the outset. And even though the operation in East Timor is considered an overall success, there are lingering accusations, as is also the case with the ongoing operations in Kosovo, that the UN has moved too far in the direction of becoming similar to a colonial power.[16] In turn, the UN has not tried to take on the task of overall civil administrator

[15] Note that in contrast, for example, the World Bank has hundreds of staff engaged in the analysis and evaluation of its programs.
[16] See especially Kimberly Marten's, 2004 *Enforcing the Peace* for a scathing comparison between modern peace-enforcement operations and the colonialism practiced by liberal states in centuries past.

in any of the most recent cases, even though certainly tiny Haiti would on the face of it be a candidate for such an intrusive intervention. Since the operations in East Timor and Kosovo, the most recent discernable trend has been back in the direction of consent-based multidimensional peacekeeping operations in support of a transitional government. It is in these types of operations where the UN has fared best in the past, and it is a sign of learning that the UN is not attempting to take on tasks such as the full administration of a state, for which it has often been ill prepared.

Another example of second-level learning concerns the UN's new strategy of response when its peacekeeping troops are attacked. For instance, when UN peacekeepers in Sierra Leone were attacked, rather than withdrawing the forces as was done in Rwanda, or not really doing anything, as in Bosnia, UN troops under siege in Sierra Leone were augmented by additional UN, ECOWAS, and British troops. The importance placed on strengthening forces, however, was not initially extended to the mission in the DRC, with disastrous consequences in the eastern regions. Later on, however, after much shaming, EU peace-enforcers under the lead of the French government did come to bolster the faltering UN peacekeepers.

These episodes amount to emerging evidence that two important changes have occurred in recent years in the understanding of problems and the goals that the UN sets for itself. The first change concerns the protection of civilians and stems from the scathing, self-critical reports on the UN's failures in Rwanda and Srebrenica, the 2000 Millennium Report, and the 2001 report entitled "The Responsibility to Protect." These reports taken together indicate some very deep soul-searching on the part of members of the UN system, and researchers associated with it, about what the international community writ large ought to do in the face of genocide and crimes against humanity. The new conclusion is that force should be sanctioned if it is used against states committing such crimes, even in violation of state sovereignty. UN Security Council Resolution 1296 (2000) officially expanded the definition of a threat to international peace and security to include the deliberate targeting of civilian populations as well as the denial of humanitarian aid in inter- and intrastate wars. This tremendous shift in thinking had its origins in the genocide convention of 1948 but had not been articulated in the new post-Cold War context until the emergence of these reports and this Security Council resolution.

The shift in overall understanding and goals has also been accompanied by an initial, somewhat unclear shift in the means that should be employed to accomplish those goals. However, the "means" picture is becoming clearer. While many onlookers have been calling for the UN to build its capacity to deploy forces rapidly, at the same time, a certain division of labor has emerged among those who would use force on an international scale, leaving the UN aside. In the final stages of the Bosnian conflict, and then in East Timor, Sierra Leone, Kosovo, Côte d'Ivoire, the DRC, and Liberia, it was not the UN, but other entities – NATO, individual states, or ECOMOG – using force. The swift response to the deteriorating situations in all of these countries can be understood in part as a consequence of the new determination to prevent mass killings.[17] The UN was asked to keep the peace only after there was peace to be kept, unlike in the early 1990s, in Somalia, Rwanda, Bosnia, and El Salvador.[18] The UN Security Council authorized operations in all of the cases listed above under Chapter VII, but it has not been the UN engaging in forceful, military endeavors. Rather, the use of force has been delegated to states or other entities that are inherently better equipped to use force. The UN does not have a standing army, and even efforts to create "stand-by" arrangements have been falling short. The UN's peacekeeping forces may be able to use force in limited circumstances, especially in self-defense, but the restrictions on the UN's use of force have both practical and ethical origins. First, UN peacekeepers are by law a diverse and un-unified bunch, hailing from dozens of countries speaking different languages, and with different backgrounds in military training and standard practices. UN peacekeeping forces are simply not designed to be "fighting machines," and some powerful states, such as the United States, do not want this situation to change. Second, and more importantly, the UN gains enormous moral and ethical legitimacy in the field by not using force. In order to maintain consent for the multidimensional peacekeeping operations, and the legitimacy of the UN as an impartial (but not neutral) arbiter of disputes, it makes sense that the UN should refrain from seeking to use force.[19] The greater realization about when to use force, who should use force, and how it should be done are certainly positive steps toward the betterment of international peacekeeping and can be considered important signs of second-level learning.

The Secretariat as actor and the spread of western institutions

The picture of overall organizational change is multifaceted and nuanced, and while incremental adaptation has been the norm, there have been moves toward both dysfunction and learning. There has also been an important shift in the international role of the UN Secretariat: since the end of the Cold War, the Secretariat has begun to function as something of an international actor. In each case study, I have detailed the ways in which the UN Secretariat is one

---

[17] The determination to prevent genocide has most notably not extended to the victims in the Darfur region in Sudan.

[18] While peacekeeping (human rights monitoring) *before* the establishment of a cease-fire and peace agreement helped to end the war in El Salvador, this was certainly not the case elsewhere.

[19] The UN is supposed to remain impartial in disputes, similar to the role of a judge in a court of law, but not neutral, in the sense that, similar to a judge, it will condemn parties that do not live up to their obligations.

of the primary sources of failure or success in multidimensional peacekeeping operations.

The Secretariat as international actor was part of the Secretary-General Dag Hammarskjold's original vision for the UN:

> The Secretariat too has to negotiate, not only in its own interest, but for the cause of peace and a peaceful development of our world. The weight we carry is not determined by physical force or number of people who form the constituency. It is based solely on trust in our impartiality, our experience and knowledge, our maturity of judgment. Those qualities are our weapons, in no way secret weapons, but as difficult to forge as guns and bombs.[20]

There is indeed mounting evidence that the Secretariat often now functions as something significantly more than a talk shop or the handmaiden of the Security Council, and that it is even beginning to take on state-like qualities. For example, in many peacekeeping operations, members of the Secretariat are in positions to make foreign policy and even life and death decisions for people in states emerging from civil war.

But even more importantly, civil wars in general have been ending differently since the end of the Cold War. Whereas historically, most civil wars ended in the complete elimination, expulsion, or political defeat of the losing side, the very character of how civil wars end has recently been altered: more civil wars now end in negotiated, power-sharing arrangements than in decisive victories.[21] According to several recent reports, the number of civil wars has been declining steadily since a thirty-year high in 1991, mirroring directly a rise in the number of UN peacekeeping missions.[22] The UN Secretariat has been at the forefront of this change, as the primary institutional manifestation of a new international interest in stopping deadly civil wars.

However, unlike Hammarskjold's vision and despite evidence to the contrary, many individuals working within the Secretariat choose not to recognize the power that the organization can potentially wield. For example, a high-ranking UN official explained to this author during an interview that the Secretariat and the Security Council have a similar relationship as that between a secretary and a CEO: the CEO tells the secretary what to do, and he or she does it. But as I have demonstrated over the course of this book, this relationship is much more complex, all the more so since the "secretary" often recommends what his or her orders should be. While it is undoubtedly true that the Security Council is the ultimate decision-maker as to whether to create a peacekeeping mission,

[20] Hammarskjold, 1962, p. 90.
[21] See Doyle and Sambanis, 2000; Walter, 2002; and The High-Level Panel on Threats, Challenges, and Change, 2004, p. 33.
[22] SIPRI, 2003; LaFranchi, 2005.

once this decision is made, no small amount of power is transferred to the Secretariat in order to specify and carry out that decision.

This is not to say, however, that the Secretariat is particularly creative in the institutions that it tries to build in post-civil war contexts. Multidimensional peacekeeping is designed to interpose temporarily an international presence on a post-civil war environment, in order to introduce new institutions to that society. The basic idea of these new institutions comes from the western liberal-democratic tradition, wherein the state has a monopoly over the legitimate use of force, regular multiparty elections take place, minority groups engage in the political process, and more generally, state institutions function in order to manage the welfare of the country's people. In a post-civil war society, none of the basic, structural building blocks for a liberal democracy exist. The state is often in total collapse. The idea of a multilateral organization radically altering the functioning of basic structures that enable civil wars appears on its face to be rather unrealistic, yet this has become the dominant concept for how to end civil wars. Through the mechanism of multinational, multidimensional peacekeeping, the UN and its sponsors seek to transform states emerging from civil conflicts into places of liberal democracy in the western image.

While many efforts bear some fruit, liberal democracy has of course not generally sprouted on the former killing fields. What have arisen are power-sharing arrangements, and often heightened crime rates, along with a certain adherence to some basic principles of human rights, most significantly, the right to elect leaders. Thus far, no viable, internationally legitimized alternative conceptions of desirable governance structures or political ways of life have developed.[23] In other words, all of the basic peace deals are forged with an ideal image that an external (western) liberal democratic system will be placed over the post-civil war society, with the hope that some approximation of the ideal will be created by the overlay of new institutions.

In the end, we are left with a set of very similar institutional blueprints that are transposed onto different contexts (incremental adaptation on a world scale). In this context, the Secretariat functions as both the implementer of directives that it has received, but also an actor, since it is up to the UN organization on the ground to figure out how to interpret the blueprints in such a way that they have a chance of being adapted by local elites. It is also the primary socializing institution that seeks to ensure that the local elites acquire the means by which to understand the blueprints, and allow the introduction of new institutions while shaping them to the needs and traditions of the specific society. In other

---

[23] Fukuyama's predictions of the end of history, many years later, do not sound quite so absurd after all. See Fukuyama, 1989. Michael Pugh sees the absence of alternative ideas as part of a "New York orthodoxy" – the linkage of peacekeeping with the promotion of liberal democratic institutions at part of greater western effort to maintain a system that favors its notions of how the world ought to work. See Pugh, 2004.

words, while the UN Secretariat can be thought of as an actor in peacekeeping, it is still beholden to the dominant conceptions of appropriate forms of conflict resolution, democratization, and how civil wars ought to end.[24]

Implications of the findings of this book for the operations in Iraq and Afghanistan

While UN multidimensional peacekeeping as a solution to civil wars is transferred from one context to the next, similar processes have been occurring in the two major US-led operations, in Afghanistan and Iraq, both of which have dominated the media coverage when it comes to postwar state-building efforts.[25] Both efforts began with essentially unilateral armed interventions on the part of the United States, but later the United States sought to include other partners for state reconstruction.[26] While the operations in Iraq and Afghanistan are not officially termed "multidimensional peacekeeping," the activities of the United States and its allies, in conjunction with, at times, the UN and other international organizations, mirror quite closely the tasks of multidimensional peacekeeping (including, for example, troop demobilization and retraining, civilian policing, humanitarian assistance, state institutional reform, and elections oversight). The operations in Iraq and Afghanistan have been hampered by a similar set of problems: a US military that is set on winning military campaigns that often come at the expense of establishing a positive postwar peace; and an international response to reconstruction that has, at times, come under violent attack, is often uncoordinated, and suffers from financial accountability problems. The US approach in these cases also reflects the potential perils of attempting to micromanage operations from afar, and introducing a colonial, rather than an integrative profile in state-building missions.[27] For the UN, its involvement in both operations reflects an approach advocated in the 2000 "Brahimi Report," that the UN should not take on state-building responsibilities for which it is not prepared or equipped, leaving many tasks to other authorities; the approach has become known as the "light footprint."[28]

The "light footprint" approach was first introduced in Afghanistan by Ambassador Brahimi and Secretary-General Annan, in the wake of the 2001 US war to defeat the Taliban as retribution for its support of al-Qaeda prior to the

---

[24] See Paris, 2004 for a discussion that contemplates possible alternatives to swift economic and political liberalization in the wake of civil conflict.
[25] These cases were not UN-led, and the war in Iraq did not start off as a civil war, thus the cases do not fit the general guidelines for case study choices as presented in Chapter 1. However, these cases are of critical importance to those interested in the broad issues of postwar peacebuilding.
[26] These are typical examples of "democracy by force" a term developed by Karin von Hippel, where US state-building efforts follow a military intervention. See Von Hippel, 2000.
[27] See Marten, 2004.   [28] See Brahimi, 2000.

September 11 attacks.[29] The Taliban, the sons and orphans of former Afghan mujahedeen raised mainly in refugee camps in Pakistan, sought to transform Afghanistan into a devout Muslim state. By the late 1990s, after nearly three decades of war in Afghanistan, the group instituted an extreme version of Sunni Muslim law.[30]

In late 2001, the Taliban were defeated by American forces working with the anti-Taliban "Northern Alliance." The United States was not, however, successful in capturing Osama Bin Laden, as was hotly debated in the news media, primarily because of faulty planning from afar and a lack of sound information on the ground. The US military operations to root out Taliban and al-Qaeda sympathizers continue. The US forces are, gradually over time, engaging in more "goodwill" activities, hoping these will lead to increased trust from Afghans and greater success in military operations. However, as Kimberly Marten explains, "the ham-handed tactics used by American forces in their house-to-house searches for insurgents – tactics that have threatened traditional gender norms by exposing otherwise covered women to the eyes of foreign men – have undercut peacebuilding efforts, making it harder for military forces elsewhere in the country to maintain popular support for their presence."[31] The US operations, in short, are suffering from first-level organizational dysfunction.

In terms of *multilateral* efforts in Afghanistan, the UN's official mission is one of electoral assistance and not in the realm of peacekeeping (the operation is housed under the direction of the UN Department of Political Affairs, not the Department of Peacekeeping Operations). There has been some positive news on the elections front, with successful fall 2004 presidential elections, and somewhat troubled, although noteworthy parliamentary elections in the fall of 2005. There have also been moves toward disarmament, which is led, somewhat counterintuitively, by the United Nations Development Programme. But most of the international peacekeeping efforts – shifting between NATO and EU leadership – have been less successful in part because they are not particularly supported by, or well-coordinated with, the American military efforts that dominate the international presence in most of Afghanistan. Moreover, prisoner abuse scandals, disrespect for Islam, and a reluctance to confront the mounting drug production and trafficking originating in Afghanistan (half of Afghanistan's economy comes from opium production, and it is the number one narcotics-producing country in the world) serve to discredit the operations in both Afghan and international eyes. While the peace process has begun a gradual institutionalization of new, inclusive (except for the Taliban), and

[29] See Vaishnav, 2004.
[30] This version included such anti-liberal practices as amputations and executions for criminals, the banning of "western decadent" television and all images of people, and severe restrictions on the activities of women.
[31] Marten, 2005.

democratic governing structures in Afghanistan, it remains to be seen whether the United States and its partners in Afghanistan will be able to reverse the processes of organizational dysfunction, and failing missions.

The problems in Iraq are similar to those in Afghanistan, but on a much larger scale. The threat of the enigmatic "foreign fighters," splintering domestic groups, and the pull of religious extremism are common to both situations. The United States began its war against Iraq in March 2003, reasoning that the regime of Saddam Hussein was a gathering regional and world threat.[32] Upon the defeat of Iraq, large-scale looting in almost all major cities destroyed much of the infrastructure that the US bombing campaign had not. The end of the war was declared by early May 2003, but since then, the United States, along with several allies, has faced a state-building task of daunting proportions, an ongoing war of counterinsurgency, and budding civil war.

In terms of organizational learning or lack thereof, there have been notable difficulties with advanced planning.[33] The wide-scale looting was unanticipated by the US military, but more importantly, repeated warnings from the US Central Intelligence Agency prior to the war that "an American-led invasion of Iraq would increase support for political Islam and would result in a deeply divided Iraqi society prone to violent internal conflict" were unheeded, along with similar warnings from the US Department of State.[34] Coordination both among the US agencies and between the United States, its allies, and other international agencies working in Iraq has been strained, in large part because of the secretive organizational culture of the Pentagon, but also because the security situation in Iraq has deteriorated, rendering communication difficult. Meanwhile, the leadership of both the civilian and military operations has changed often, and has not been particularly adept at averting conflicts.

But of all the elements of organizational dysfunction, it is probably poor integration with the local environment that is hampering the US efforts more than anything else. The United States has not been able to gain the trust of the Iraqi people in large part because of its overall approach to the local population, resembling more a colonial profile rather than an integrative one. Most members of the US operations are walled-off and carefully guarded from the rest of Iraq in the fortress-like "Green Zone." The main counterinsurgency strategy has been to hunt down and kill insurgents.[35] US troops regularly conduct raids – up to 800 per night – on Iraqi households, searching for evidence of insurgency or leads against insurgents, and arresting dozens of Iraqi men. During these raids, property is often damaged or destroyed, Iraqi men of suspicion are sometimes physically or sexually humiliated by troops, and women are often

---

[32] See President George W. Bush's "State of the Union Address," January, 2003.
[33] See Crocker, 2004; and Packer, 2005.   [34] See Jehl, 2005.
[35] Krepinevich, 2005.

handled in ways deemed inappropriate in Iraqi culture.[36] After the raids, troops regularly offer cooperative families a US 20 dollar bill, which imbues the raids with a certain uncomfortable commercial tinge. American troops are not regularly trained in the language, in cultural sensitivity, or even in basic polite phrases in Arabic.[37] They are sent on daily missions for which they have little understanding or background, which makes it exceedingly difficult for them to gather correct information about the insurgency and foreign fighters, or relay information about the United States' intentions. The horrors of the abuses of often innocent detainees at the Abu Grahib prison offer a very extreme version of inappropriate and self-defeating interactions between Americans and Iraqis; and difficult relations are only more strained by a mounting Iraqi civilian death count that has risen sharply since the beginning of the US-led invasion.

The United States spent between $5 and 10 billion per month on the war effort in Iraq in 2005, whereas the average UN peacekeeping operation in 2005–2006 spent about $23 million per month. This is another example, similar to the operations in Bosnia and Somalia, where high spending levels do not translate into success when not accompanied by field-level organizational learning.

In terms of the UN involvement in Iraq, the members of the entire UN system, along with the Secretary-General, have been reluctant to answer US calls for assistance ever since the death of the UN's Special Representative in Iraq, Sergio Viciro de Mello, in August 2003. As one colleague of his lamented,

> The individual with the most experience in the whole UN system in building or rebuilding governments is no longer with us to take on the task . . . He had started to work his way through the enormously complex dynamics of the Iraqi scene quietly and constructively and in a way that won rather than alienated support. His death in the Baghdad UN compound bombing is one that the whole international community will, and should, be mourning for a long time to come.[38]

Similar to the approach in Afghanistan, but even more so in Iraq, the UN has thus far opted for very little involvement.[39]

In sum, first-level learning is occurring in neither case. Information collection and dissemination efforts are hampered by a severe dislocation between the US forces and the local population. Coordination among the US agencies, and between the US and international counterparts is inconsistent, due in part to mutual distrust and secrecy. Integration with the local society is nearly

---

[36] International Crisis Group, 2004, p. 14; Glanz, 2004.

[37] Unlike British troops, who must undergo cultural sensitivity tests and basic language training before they are deployed. Amos, 2005.

[38] Evans, 2003.

[39] Recent scandals surrounding the UN-run oil-for-food program have only worked to harden the resolve of members of the UN Secretariat not to become more involved in the reconstruction efforts in Iraq.

impossible given the extreme lack of security, and a pronounced absence of positive engagement between foreign troops and the local populations. And finally, the often-shifting civilian and military leadership in both operations has meant that overall strategy as well as short-term crisis problem-solving have been difficult to achieve. The primary insights from this book about UN first-level learning, or lack thereof, hold even for similar operations that are not led by the UN.

Outlook and prospects

Is learning occurring in UN multidimensional peacekeeping? There is undoubtedly a lot of first-level learning, or "learning while doing," and some second-level learning between operations, although second-level organizational dysfunction and incremental adaptation are very important components of the picture. In terms of second-level learning, problems are being re-evaluated in light of a greater understanding of the nature of peacekeeping, and a reconsideration of the value of preventing or stopping crimes against humanity and genocide. However, the major tests will consist of how the reforms are institutionalized in order to complete the process of second-level learning, and whether they will enable first-level learning in future multidimensional peacekeeping operations.

Will Secretariat reform enable greater first-level learning? Will field operations enjoy the free hand that appears necessary in order for them to learn on the ground, and successfully implement their mandates? It is simply too early to be able to judge how the reforms will manifest themselves as the results of the 1999 and 2003–2004 waves of new peacekeeping operations come in. There are reasons for both optimism and pessimism. Pessimism, because there are many tasks to be accomplished and organizational dysfunction has dominated the current picture. However, given that many of the successful multidimensional peacekeeping operations began in a state of organizational dysfunction, but later moved into learning modes and were eventually successful, there is cause for optimism. The results of those operations will offer a better indication of whether the UN, in the issue-area of peacekeeping in civil wars, has been able to learn on the second level, and not simply on the first.

Appendix I

Multidimensionality of mandates of all post-Cold War UN peacekeeping operations in civil wars

Country		Namibia	Angola				W. Sahara	Somalia		Mozambique	Rwanda	Liberia		C. African Rep.	Sierra Leone		Dem. Rep. of Congo	Côte D. Ivoire		Burundi	Sudan
Mission		UNTAG	UNAVEM I	UNAVEM II	UNAVEM III	MONUA	MINURSO	UNOSOM I	UNOSOM II	ONUMOZ	UNAMIR	UNOMIL	UNMIL	MINURCA	UNOMSIL	UNAMSIL	MONUC	MINUCI	UNOCI	ONUB	UNMIS
Date		04/89–05/90	01/89–03/91	03/91–02/95	02/95–06/97	07/97–02/99	04/91–	04/92–05/93	05/93–05/95	12/92–12/94	10/93–05/96	09/93–09/97	09/03–	04/98–02/00	07/98–10/99	10/99–12/05	10/99–	05/03–	04/04–	05/0–	03/05–
Military	Monitor Cease-fire	x	x	x	x	x	x	x	x	x	x	x			x	x	x	x	x	x	x
	Confine to Base			x	x		x			x		x	x							x	
	Peace Enforcement				x				x				x				x	x	x	x	
	Disarmament	x			x				x	x	x	x	x	x	x	x	x		x	x	x
	Demobilization, Reintegration & Retraining											x	x			x			x	x	x
	Retraining	x				x				x											
	Observe Withdrawal	x	x	x	x		x			x		x	x		x	x	x		x	x	x
	De-mine	x			x				x	x	x	x	x				x				
	Safe Areas										x										
	Weapons Collection								x				x	x		x			x		
	Protect Civilians										x		x			x			x		
Displaced Peoples	Refugee Return	x					x		x	x		x	x					x	x	x	x
	Political prisoner return	x					x			x			x							x	
	IDP return										x		x						x	x	
	Protect Refugees										x		x			x			x		x
Humanitarian Assistance	Humanitarian Corridor										x	x	x		x	x					x
	Assist civilians	x						x	x	x	x	x	x	x	x	x	x	x	x		x
	Protect intl workers									x	x					x		x	x		
	Protect children												x			x			x	x	

Country	Mission	Date	General monitoring (Civil)	Elections monitoring (Policing)	Police retraining	Conduct elections	Monitor elections	Oversee elections	Technical assistance	Info./Ed.	Gender Affairs	Constitutional/ judicial reform	National reconciliation	War crimes tribunals	Human rights oversight	Transitional Authority	Good Offices	Miscellaneous
Namibia	UNTAG	04/89–05/90	x	x	x			x	x	x		x	x		x	x	x	
Angola	UNAVEM I	01/89–03/91					(x)											
Angola	UNAVEM II	03/91–02/95	x	x			x					x						
Angola	UNAVEM III	02/95–06/97	x	x	(x)		x						x				x	Civilian Circulation
Angola	MONUA	07/97–02/99	x		x							x			x		x	Confidence Building Measures
W. Sahara	MINURSO	04/91–		x			x											
Somalia	UNOSOM I	04/92–05/93																
Somalia	UNOSOM II	05/93–05/95										x	x					Economic development
Mozambique	ONUMOZ	12/92–12/94	x	x	(x)		x					x	x					
Rwanda	UN/MIR	11/93–05/96	x	x	x		(x)			x			x	x	x		x	
Liberia	UNOMIL	09/93–09/97	x		x		x					x	x		x			Assist HR CSOs
Liberia	UNMIL	09/03–	x		x		x			x	x	x		x		x		Assist state admin
C. African Rep.	MINURCA	04/98–02/00	x	x	x		x		x	x		x					x	
Sierra Leone	UNOMSIL	07/98–10/99	x	x	x							x			x			
Sierra Leone	UNAMSIL	10/99–12/05	x						x					x				Confidence Building Measures
Dem. Rep. of Congo	MONUC	10/99–									x							
Côte D. Ivoire	MINUCI	05/03–															x	Liaison & planning
Côte D. Ivoire	UNOCI	04/06–		x						x		x			x		x	Assist state admin
Burundi	ONUB	05/04–	x					x	x			x			x			
Sudan	UNMIS	03/05–			x		x		x	x	x	x			x		x	

Country		C. America	El Salvador	Guatemala	Cambodia	Cambodia	E. Timor	E. Timor	E. Timor	Bosnia/Croatia	Croatia	Macedonia	Bosnia	Croatia (E. Slavonia)	Croatia (E. Slavonia)	Croatia	Georgia	Tajikistan	Kosovo
Mission		ONUCA	ONUSAL	MINUGUA	UNAMIC	UNTAC	UNTAET	UNMISET	UNOTIL	UNPROFOR	UNCRO	UNPREDEP	UNMIBH	UNTAES	UNPSG	UNMOP	UNOMIG	UNMOT	UNMIK
Date		11/89–01/92	07/91–04/95	01/97–05/97	11/91–03/92	02/92–09/93	10/99–05/02	05/02–05/05	05–	02/92–05/95	05/95–01/96	05/95–02/99	05/95–12/02	01/96–01/97	01/98–10/98	01/96–12/02	08/93–	12/94–05/00	06/99–
Military	Monitor Cease-fire	x	x	x	x		x	x	x	x	x	x		x	x	x	x	x	
	Confine to Base	x		x		x								x			x		
	Peace Enforcement					(x)	x				x			x					
	Disarmament	x	x			x	x			x	x			x		x			
	Demobilization & Reintegration						x												
	Observe Withdrawl	x			x	x	x			x	x			x		x	x		
	De-mine			x	x		x			x			x	x					
	Safe Areas													x					
	Weapons Collection																		
	Protect Civilians					x	x												
Displaced Peoples	Refugee Return			x		x	x			x	x		x	x					x
	Political prisoner return																		
	IDP return					x								x					
	Protect Refugees				x		x												x
Humanitarian Assistance	Humanitarian Corridor									x							x		
	Assist civilians					x	x			x	x		x	x				x	x
	Protect intl workers												x						
	Protect children																		x

	C. America	El Salvador	Guatemala	Cambodia	Cambodia	E. Timor	E. Timor	E. Timor	Bosnia/Croatia	Croatia	Macedonia	Bosnia	Croatia (E. Slavonia)	Croatia (E. Slavonia)	Croatia	Georgia	Tajikistan	Kosovo
Mission	ONUCA	ONUSAL	MINUGUA	UNAMIC	UNTAC	UNTAET	UNMISET	UNGTIL	UNPROFOR	UNCRO	UNPREDEP	UNMIBH	UNTAES	UNPSG	UNMOP	UNOMIG	UNMOT	UNMIK
Date	11/89–01/92	07/91–04/95	01/97–05/97	11/91–03/92	02/92–09/93	10/99–05/02	05/02–05/05	0/–	02/92–02/95	05/95–01/96	05/95–02/99	05/95–12/02	01/96–01/97	01/98–10/98	01/96–12/02	08/93–	12/94–05/00	06/99–
Civil Policing — General monitoring					x	x	x	x	x	x				x				
Elections monitoring		x			x	x						x	x	x				x
Police retraining		x	x			x	x					x	x	x				x
Electoral Assistance — Conduct elections					x	x												
Monitor elections		x											x					x
Oversee elections																		
Technical assistance					x	x							x					x
Info./Ed.						x		x										x
Gender Affairs						x												x
Legal Affairs — Constitutional/judicial reform		x			x	x	x	x				x	x					x
National reconciliation						x							x					
War crimes tribunals									x				x					x
Human rights oversight		x			x	x	x	x		x		x	x					x
Transitional Authority					x	x							x					x
Good Offices		x														x	x	
Miscellaneous		Econ. Land Rights	Socio-econ. Rights			Assist state admin	Assist state admin	Assist state admin		Econ. Development								

Notes on Appendix I

Appendix I presents a breakdown in the first column of the different dimensions of the operations. The dimensions include military operations, refugee assistance, humanitarian assistance, civilian policing, electoral assistance, information/education, gender affairs, legal affairs, transitional authority, and a miscellaneous category including such tasks as economic development programs, assistance for the state's administration, and confidence-building measures. The first row lists the names of the countries where there were and are peacekeeping operations, beginning with Africa, and moving on by regional group to the Americas, Asia, and Europe.

Note that (x) denotes an ambiguous mandate.

Appendix II

Questions for structured-focused comparisons

A) Questions for evaluating the duration of success after the UN multidimensional peacekeeping mission's departure from the host country:
   - After UN withdrawal, was the peace process disrupted in any way, and if so, how?
   - Did the cease-fire hold?
   - Did troops remain demobilized?
   - Did the humanitarian situation improve?
   - Was civilian policing effective? Were there important policing reforms?
   - Did a new constitution and/or legal system come into being?
   - Were the first UN-monitored elections free and fair?
   - Were subsequent elections considered free and fair according to international and internal assessments?
   - Were economic reforms effective?
   - Overall, did UN intervention appear to help or hinder the country's prospects for peace?
B) Situational difficulty questions:
   - What were the sides fighting about?
   - Did the nature of the conflict change over time?
   - Did all sides in the civil war consent to UN assistance to end the conflict?
   - Was there a detailed peace agreement signed by all sides?
   - Were neighboring and regional states supportive of the peace process, or did they continue to fuel different sides of the war?
   - Was there a stalemate?
   - How long had the civil war endured?
   - How many people had been killed, internally displaced, or made refugees compared to the prewar population?
   - What was the state of the governing institutions and physical infrastructure at the time of negotiations and implementation of the peace accords?
C) Questions about Security Council consensus:
   - What was the focus of the Security Council debates?
   - How acrimonious were the debates?
   - Was there consensus about the basic nature of the problem?
   - Were the Council's votes on resolutions unanimous?
   - If not, which countries disagreed and why?

- Did positions or interests change during the peace negotiations or during the implementation period?

D) Questions about Security Council interest intensity:
- What were the other important items on the Security Council agenda at the time?
- How many resolutions and statements did the Security Council issue?
- Did the Security Council mandates differ from the Secretary-General's mandate suggestions?
- Did the Security Council/General Assembly provide the means requested by the Secretary-General for mandate implementation?

Appendix III

Situational difficulty before the start of the UN peacekeeping operation

	Successful cases						Unsuccessful cases			
	Namibia	El Salvador	Cambodia	Mozambique	Croatia/E. Slavonia	E. Timor	Angola	Somalia	Bosnia	Rwanda
Consent of warring parties for UN operation	2	2	0	2	2	2	2	0	0	2
Peace agreement signed by all sides	0	2	2	2	2	0	2	0	0	2
Regional actors	1	1	1	2	1	2	1	2	1	1
Mutually hurting stalemate	1	1	1	1	1	0	1	0	0	0
Fatalities (civil and military)	1	1	0	0	1	1	.5	.5	1	0
Duration of war	0	0	0	0	1	0	0	1	1	1
State of infrastructure	1	.5	0	0	.5	0	0	0	.5	.5
Total (10 easy – 1 difficult)	6	7.5	4	7	8.5	5	6.5	3.5	3.5	6.5

Consent of all warring parties for UN operation
2 = Yes
0 = No

Detailed peace agreement signed by all sides
2 = Yes
0 = No

Regional and non-Security Council states
2 = Supportive
1 = Mixed
0 = Opposed

Mutually hurting stalemate
1 = Yes
0 = No

Fatalities (civil and military)
1 = 1–200,000
.5 = 200,001–500,000
0 = 500,001–1,000,000

Duration of war
1 = Short (less than ten years)
0 = Long (ten or more years)

State of infrastructure
1 = Developed, little damage
.5 = Developed, extensive damage
.5 = Undeveloped, little damage
0 = Undeveloped, extensive damage

BIBLIOGRAPHY

United Nations documents

A/44/971-S/21541, 16 August 1990
A/46/706-S/21931, 8 November 1990
A/45/1055-S/23037, 16 September 1991
A/46/608-S/23177, 30 October 1991
A/46/658-S/2322, 15 November 1991
A/46/864-S/23501, 30 January 1992
A/47/285-S/24183, 25 June 1992
A/47/539, 22 October 1992
A/47/698-S/26033, 2 July 1993
A/51/693, 25 November 1996
A/54/549, 15 November 1999
A/54/2000, 14 April 2000
A/55/503-S/809, 21 August 2000
A/55/502, 20 October 2000
A/55/507, 27 October 2000
A/55/705/Add.1, 27 October 2000

S/RES/384, 22 December 1975
S/RES/389, 22 April 1976
S/RES/439, 13 November 1978
S/RES/435, 12 July 1982
S/RES/530, 20 January 1983
S/RES/629, 16 January 1989
S/RES/640, 29 August 1989
S/RES/643, 31 October 1989
S/RES/668, 20 September 1990
S/RES/693, 20 May 1991
S/RES/714, 30 September 1991
S/RES/728, 8 January 1992
S/RES/729, 14 January 1992
S/RES/743, 21 February 1992
S/RES/766, 21 July 1992

S/RES/717, 16 October 1992
S/RES/718, 31 October 1992
S/RES/793, 30 November 1992
S/RES/797, 16 December 1992
S/RES/810, 8 March 1993
S/RES/819, 6 April 1993
S/RES/824, 6 May 1993
S/RES/832, 28 May 1993
S/RES/836, 3 June 1993
S/RES/840, 15 June 1993
S/RES/844, 18 June 1993
S/RES/850, 9 July 1993
S/RES/872, 5 October 1993
S/RES/879, 29 October 1993
S/RES/882, 5 November 1993
S/RES/888, 30 November 1993
S/RES/912, 21 April 1994
S/RES/916, 5 May 1994
S/RES/918, 17 May 1994
S/RES/925, 8 June 1994
S/RES/929, 22 June 1994
S/RES/946, 30 September 1994
S/RES/957, 15 November 1994
S/RES/1025, 30 November 1995
S/RES/1037, 15 January 1996
S/RES/1118, 30 June 1997
S/RES/1244, 10 June 1999
S/RES/1272, 25 October 1999
S/RES/1410, 17 May 2002
S/RES/1542, 30 April 2004
S/RES/1545, 21 May 2004

S/12636, 10 April 1978
S/12827, 29 August 1978
S/15287, 12 July 1982
S/20346, 22 December 1988
S/20412, 23 January 1989
S/29412, 16 March 1989
S/20566, 4 April 1989
S/20658, 26 May 1989
S/20872, 28 September 1989
S/20883, 6 October 1989
S/23402, 10 January 1992

S/23580, 19 February 1992

S/23613, 19 February 1992

S/23870, 1 May 1992

S/23999/Add.1, 19 June 1992

S/24578, 21 September 1992

S/24635, 8 October 1992

S/24642, 9 October 1992

S/24833, 23 November 1992

S/24892, 2 December 1992

S/24892/Add. 1, 9 December 1992

S/25006, 23 December 1992

S/23331, 30 December 1991/add.1, 6 January 1992

S/25078, 9 January 1993

S/25154, 25 January 1993

S/25241, 4 February 1993

S/25518, 2 April 1993

S/25519, 2 April 1993

S/23999, 21 May 1993

S/25812, 21 May 1993

S/25812/Add.1, 24 May 1993

S/25913, 10 June 1993

S/25940, 14 June 1993

S/25939, 14, 16, 17 June 1993

S/25971, 18 June 1993

S/26005, 29 June 1993

S/26034, 30 June 1993

S/24892, 2 December 1993

S/89, 28 January 1994

S/89/Add.1, 28 January 1994

S/89/Add.2, 1 February 1994

S/470, 20 April 1994

S/511, 28 April 1994

S/561, 11 May 1994

S/565, 13 May 1994

S/1009, 29 August 1994

S/1449, 23 December 1994

S/1028, 13 December 1995

S/622, 5 August 1996

S/705, 28 August 1996

S/487, June 23 1997

S/767, 2 October 1997

S/953, 4 December 1997

S/59, 22 January 1998
S/513, 5 May 1999
S/1025, 4 October 1999
S/203, 10 March 2000
S/432, 17 April 2002
S/724, 9 September 2004
S/99, 18 February 2005
S/273, 26 April 2005
S/313, 13 May 2005
S/328, 19 May 2005
S/320, 26 May 2005
S/376, 7 June 2005
S/398, 17 June 2005
S/764, 7 December 2005
S/777, 12 December 2005
S/821, 21 December 2005

Unpublished UN Report No. 1

Unpublished UN Report No. 2

E/CN.4RES/1993/6, 19 February 1993

Secondary sources

Abdullah, Ibrahim. 1998. "Bush Path to Destruction: The Origin and Character of the Revolutionary United Front/Sierra Leone." *Journal of Modern African Studies*, Vol. 36, No. 2.

Abrahamsson, Hans, and Anders Nilsson. 1995. *Mozambique: The Troubled Transition*. London: Zed Books.

Acuna, Tathiana F. 1995. *United Nations Mission in El Salvador: A Humanitarian Law Perspective*. The Hague: Kluwer Academic Publishers.

Adebajo, Adekeye. 2002. *Liberia's Civil War: Nigeria, ECOMOG, and Regional Security in West Africa*. Boulder: Lynne Rienner.

Adebajo, Adekeye, and Chris Landsberg. 2000. "Back to the Future: UN Peacekeeping in Africa." *International Peacekeeping*, Vol. 7, No. 4.

Adelman, Howard, Astri Suhrke, with Bruce Jones. 1996. "The International Response to Conflict and Genocide: Lessons from the Rwanda Experience – Early Warning and Conflict Management." Copenhagen: Steering Committee of the Joint Evaluation of Emergency Assistance to Rwanda.

Agathangelou, Anna M, and L. H. M., Ling. 2003. "Desire Industries: Sex Trafficking, UN Peacekeeping, and the Neo-Liberal World Order." *Brown Journal of World Affairs*, Vol. 10, No. 1.

Ajello, Aldo. 1999. "Mozambique: Implementation of the 1992 Peace Agreement." In *Herding Cats: Multiparty Mediation in a Complex World*, ed. Chester A. Crocker, Fen Osler Hampson, and Pamela Aall. Washington, DC: US Institute of Peace Press.

Akashi, Yasushi. 1993. "The Challenges Faced by UNTAC." *Japan Review of International Affairs*, Summer.

1994. "Eyewitness: The Challenge of Peacekeeping in Cambodia." *International Peacekeeping*, Vol. 1, No. 2.

Akindes, Francis. 2005. *The Roots of the Military-Political Crises in Côte d'Ivoire*. Uppsala, Sweden: Nordiska Afrikainstitutet.

Alden, Chris. 1995. "The UN and the Resolution of Conflict in Mozambique." *Journal of Modern African Studies*, Vol. 33, No. 1.

2003. "Making Old Soldiers Fade Away: Lessons from the Reintegration of Demobilized Soldiers in Mozambique." *Security Dialogue*, Vol. 33, No. 3.

Allison, Graham T. 1972. *The Essence of Decision*. Boston: Little Brown.

Americas Watch. 1992. *El Salvador's Decade of Terror: Human Rights Since the Assassination of Archbishop Romero*. New Haven: Yale University Press.

Amnesty International. 2005. "Haiti: Arms Proliferation Fuels Human Rights Abuses Ahead of Elections."

Amos, Deborah. 2005. "Car Bomb Explosion Kills 10 People Today in Baghdad." *National Public Radio, Morning Edition*, January 21.

Angola Peace Monitor. 2001. "Monitoring Mechanism Report." *Angola Peace Monitor* 7, January 5.

Angolan Mission Observer. 1999. "United Nations Secretary General Calls for Pullout of MONUA Peacekeepers." Newsletter, February.

Annan, Kofi. 1999. "Report of the Secretary-General Pursuant to General Assembly Resolution 53/35: The Fall of Srebrenica." A/54/549. New York: United Nations.

2000. "Millennium Report: We the Peoples." A/54/2000. New York: United Nations.

2002. "Introductory Comments," *Challenges in Peacekeeping: Past, Present, and Future*. Seminar sponsored by the International Peace Academy and the Peacekeeping Best Practices Unit, Millennium Hotel, New York, NY, October 29.

2003. "Message from the Secretary-General." In *The United Nations Transitional Administration in East Timor: Debriefing Lessons*, ed. Nassrine Azimi and Chang Li Lin. Leiden: Martinus Nijhoff Publishers.

2005. "In Larger Freedom: Towards Development, Security and Human Rights for All." A/59/2005. New York: United Nations.

Anstee, Margaret. 1996. *Orphan of the Cold War: The Inside Story of the Collapse of the Angolan Peace Process, 1992–93*. New York: St. Martin's.

1999. "The United Nations in Angola: Post-Bicesse Implementation." In *Herding Cats: Multiparty Mediation in a Complex World*, ed. Chester Crocker, Fen Osler Hampson, and Pamela Aall. Washington, DC: US Institute of Peace.

Argueta, Manilo. 1983. *One Day of Life*, trans. Bill Brow. New York: Vintage International.

Argyris, Chris, and Donald Schon. 1996. *Organizational Learning: A Theory of Action Perspective*. Reading, MA: Addison-Wesley.

Asia Watch. 1993. "An Exchange on Human Rights and Peace-Keeping in Cambodia." *Asia Watch*, Vol. 5, No. 14.

Austin, Kathi. 1994. "Invisible Crimes: US Private Intervention in the War in Mozambique." Washington, DC: Africa Policy Information Center.

Ayoob, Mohammed. 2004. "Third World Perspectives on Humanitarian Intervention and International Administration." *Global Governance*, Vol. 10, No. 1.

Azimi, Nassrine, and Chang Li Lin, eds. 2003. *The United Nations Transitional Administration in East Timor: Debriefing Lessons*. Leiden: Martinus Nijhoff Publishers.

Baldwin, David. 1993. *Neorealism and Neoliberalism: The Contemporary Debate*. New York: Columbia University Press.

Bangura, Yusuf. 2000. "Strategic Policy Failure and Governance in Sierra Leone." *Journal of Modern African Studies*, Vol. 38, No. 4.

Barash, David, ed. 2000. *Approaches to Peace: A Reader in Peace Studies*. Oxford: Oxford University Press.

Barnes, Lord Patten of. 2005. "Treating the Sickness at the Heart of Africa." *International Herald Tribune*, June 30.

Barnes, Sam. 1998. "Humanitarian Aid Coordination During War and Peace in Mozambique: 1985–1995." Uppsala, Sweden: Nordiska Afrikainstitutet.

Barnett, Michael. 1997. "The UN Security Council, Indifference, and Genocide in Rwanda." *Cultural Anthropology*, Vol. 12, No. 4.

   2002. *Eyewitness to a Genocide: The United Nations and Rwanda*. Ithaca: Cornell University Press.

Barnett, Michael, and Martha Finnemore. 1999. "The Politics, Power, and Pathologies of International Organization." *International Organization*, Vol. 54, No. 1.

Barry, Tom, and Deborah Preusch. 1988. *The Soft War: Uses and Causes of US Economic Aid in Central America*. New York: Grove Press.

Bartlett, William. 2003. *Croatia: Between Europe and the Balkans*. London: Routledge.

Bartoli, Andrea. 1999. "Mediating Peace in Mozambique: The Role of the Community of Sant'Egidio." In *Herding Cats: The Role of Mediation in a Complex World*, ed. Chester Crocker, Fen Osler Hampson, and Pamela Aall. Washington, DC: US Institute of Peace Press.

Bauer, Gretchen. 1998. *Labor and Democracy in Namibia, 1971–1996*. Athens: Ohio University Press; London: J. Currey.

   2004. "The Hand that Stirs the Pot Can also Run the Country: Electing Women to Parliament in Namibia." *Journal of Modern African Studies*, Vol. 42, No. 4.

Baylora, Enrique A. 1998. "El Salvador: From Reactionary Despotism to Partidemocracia." In *Postconflict Elections, Democratization, and International Assistance*, ed. K. Kumar. Boulder: Lynne Rienner.

Becker, Elizabeth. 1997. "On Its Last Legs, the Saddest Cambodian Army." *New York Times*, October 20, A8.

  1998. *When the War Was Over: The Voices of Cambodia's Revolution and Its People*, 2nd edn. New York: Simon and Schuster.

Becker, Heike. 2006. "New Things after Independence: Gender and Traditional Authorities in Postcolonial Namibia." *Journal of Southern African Studies*, Vol. 32, No. 1.

Behringer, Ronald. 2005. "Middle Power Leadership on the Human Security Agenda." *Cooperation & Conflict*, Vol. 40, No. 3.

Bell, Coral. 2000. "East Timor, Canberra and Washington: A Case Study in Crisis Management." *Australian Journal of International Affairs*, Vol. 54, No. 2.

Bennett, Andrew. 1999. *Condemned to Repetition? The Rise, Fall, and Reprise of Soviet-Russian Military Interventionism, 1973–1996*. Cambridge, MA: MIT Press.

Bercovitch, Jacob, and Karl DeRouen. 2005. "Managing Ethnic Civil Wars: Assessing the Determinants of Successful Mediation." *Civil Wars*, Vol. 7, No. 1.

Bercovitch, Jacob, and Jeffrey Langley. 1993. "The Nature of the Dispute and the Effectiveness of International Mediation." *Journal of Conflict Resolution*, Vol. 3, No. 4.

Berdal, Mats. 2005a. *Disarmament and Demobilisation after Civil Wars*. London: Routledge.

  2005b. "The United Nations, Peacebuilding, and the Genocide in Rwanda." *Global Governance*, Vol. 11, No. 1.

Beresford, Melanie. 2005. "Cambodia in 2004: An Artificial Democratization Process." *Asian Survey*, Vol. 45, No. 1.

Berman, Eric. 1996. *Managing Arms in Peace Processes: Mozambique*. Geneva: United Nations Institute for Disarmament Research.

Berry, Ken. 1997. *Cambodia – From Red to Blue: Australia's Initiative for Peace*. Canberra: Allen and Unwin.

Bhatia, Michael. 2003. *War and Intervention: Issues for Contemporary Peace Operations*. Bloomfield, CT: Kumarian.

Biermann, Wolfgang, and Martin Vadset, eds. 1999. *UN Peacekeeping in Trouble: Lessons from the Former Yugoslavia*. Brookfield, VT: Ashgate.

Blitz, Brad. 2003. "Refugee Returns in Croatia: Contradictions and Reform." *Politics*, Vol. 23, No. 3.

Boisard, Marcel. 2003. "Introductory Remarks and Keynote Address." In *The United Nations Transitional Administration in East Timor: Debriefing Lessons*, ed. Nassrine Azimi and Chang Li Lin. Leiden: Martinus Nijhoff Publishers.

Boothby, Derek. 1998. "The UNTAES Experience: Weapons Buy-back in Eastern Slavonia, Baranja, and Western Sirium (Croatia)." Bonn: Bonn International Center for Conversion.

2004. "The Political Challenges of Administering Eastern Slavonia." *Global Governance*, Vol. 10, No. 1.

Bose, Sumantra. 2002. *Bosnia after Dayton: Nationalist Partition and International Intervention.* Oxford: Oxford University Press.

Boulden, Jane. 2001. *Peace Enforcement: The United Nations Experience in Congo, Somalia, and Bosnia.* Westport, CT: Praeger.

Boutros-Ghali, Boutros. 1999. *Unvanquished: A US–UN Saga.* New York: Random House.

Bowden, Mark. 1999. *Black Hawk Down: A Story of Modern War.* New York: Penguin.

Bowen, Merle. 1990. "Economic Crisis in Mozambique." *Current History*, May.

2000. *The State against the Peasantry: Rural Struggles in Colonial and Postcolonial Mozambique.* Charlottesville: University of Virginia Press.

Brahimi, Lakhdar. 2000. "Report of the Panel on United Nations Peace Operations." A/55/305-S/809, 21 August 2000. New York: United Nations.

Branigin, William. 1992. "UN Starts Cambodia Repatriation " *Washington Post*, March 21, A14.

Breslauer, George W., and Philip E. Tetlock, eds. 1991. *Learning in US and Soviet Foreign Policy.* Boulder: Westview Press.

Britt, Thomas, and Amy Adler, eds. 2003. *The Psychology of the Peacekeeper: Lessons from the Field.* Westport, CT: Praeger.

Brockett, Charles. 2005. *Political Movements and Violence in Central America.* New York: Cambridge University Press.

Brown, MacAlister, and Joseph J. Zasloff. 1998. *Cambodia Confounds the Peacemakers 1979–1998.* Ithaca: Cornell University Press.

Brown, Michael, ed. 1996. *The International Dimensions of Internal Conflict.* Cambridge, MA: MIT Press.

Brown, Susan. 1995. "Diplomacy by Other Means." In *Namibia's Liberation Struggle: The Two-Edged Sword*, ed. Colin Leys and John S. Saul. London: James Currey.

Burg, Steven, and Paul Shoup. 2000. *The War in Bosnia-Herzegovina: Ethnic Conflict and International Intervention.* London: M. E. Sharpe.

Burns, Arthur Lee. 1963. *Peace-keeping by UN Forces, from Suez to the Congo.* New York: Praeger.

Burton, John. 1987. *Resolving Deep-Rooted Conflict: A Handbook.* Lanham, MD: University Press of America.

1990. *Conflict: Resolution and Prevention.* New York: St. Martin's.

Bush, George W. 2003. "State of the Union Address." January.

Buur, Lars, and Helene Maria Kyed. 2005. *State Recognition of Traditional Authority in Mozambique: The Nexus of Community Representation and State Assistance.* Uppsala, Sweden: Nordiska Afrikainstitutet.

Byman, Daniel. 2002. *Keeping the Peace: Lasting Solutions to Ethnic Conflicts.* Baltimore: Johns Hopkins University Press.

CIA. World Factbook. 2005. Washington, DC: Central Intelligence Agency.

CSCE. 1997. "The April 1997 Parliamentary, County and Municipal Elections in Croatia." Washington, DC: Commission on Security and Cooperation in Europe.

Call, Chuck. 2002. "Assessing El Salvador's Transition From Civil War to Peace." In *Ending Civil Wars: The Implementation of Peace Agreements*, ed. Stephen Stedman, Donald Rothchild, and Elizabeth Cousens, Boulder: Lynne Rienner.

Callaghan, Jean, and Mathias Schonborn, eds. 2004. *Warriors in Peacekeeping: Points of Tension in Complex Cultural Encounters.* New Brunswick, NJ: Transaction.

Caplan, Richard. 2004. "Partner or Patron? International Civil Administration and Local Capacity-building." *International Peacekeeping*, Vol. 11, No. 2.

Carbone, Giovanni. 2005. "Continuidade na renovação? Ten Years of Multiparty Politics in Mozambique: Roots, Evolution and Stabilisation of the Frelimo-Renamo Party System." *Journal of Modern African Studies*, Vol. 43, No. 3.

Carlsson, Ingvar. 1999. "Report of the Independent Inquiry into the Actions of the United Nations During the 1994 Genocide in Rwanda." S/1999/1257, 15 December. New York: United Nations.

Carlsson, Ingvar, Han Sung-Joo, and Rufus Kupolati. 1999. "Report of the Independent Inquiry into the Actions of the United Nations During the 1994 Genocide in Rwanda." New York: Independent Inquiry, United Nations.

Carlucci, Frank. 2005. "The War We Haven't Finished." *New York Times*, February 22, A19.

Caroll, Faye. 1967. *South West Africa and the United Nations.* Lexington: University of Kentucky.

Cassidy, Robert. 2004. *Peacekeeping in the Abyss: British and American Peacekeeping Doctrine and Practice after the Cold War.* Westport, CT: Praeger.

Chan, Stephen, and Moises Venancio, eds. 1998. *War and Peace in Mozambique.* New York: St. Martin's.

Chandler, David. 1993. *A History of Cambodia*, 2nd edn. Boulder: Westview Press.
   1997. "Three Visions of Politics in Cambodia." In *Keeping the Peace: Multidimensional UN Operations in Cambodia and El Salvador*, ed. Michael Doyle, Ian Johnstone, and Robert Orr. Cambridge, UK: Cambridge University Press.
   2005. "From Dayton to Europe." *International Peacekeeping*, Vol. 12, No. 3.

Chapman, Peter. 1982. "The $16 Million El Salvador Question." *Manchester Guardian Weekly*, February 28.

Chesterman, Simon. 2001. *Just War or Just Peace? Humanitarian Intervention and International Law.* Oxford: Oxford University Press.
   2004. *You, the People: The United Nations, Transitional Administration, and State-Building.* Oxford: Oxford University Press.

Chomsky, Noam. 2001. *A New Generation Draws the Line: Kosovo, East Timor and the Standards of the West*. London: Verso.

Chopra, Jarat. 2000. "The UN's Kingdom of East Timor." *Survival*, Vol. 42, No. 3.

———. 2002. "Building State Failure in East Timor." *Development and Change*, Vol. 33, No. 5.

Chopra, Jarat, Larry Minear, and John Mackinlay. 1994. "United Nations Authority in Cambodia." Providence, RI: Thomas J. Watson Jr. Institute for International Studies, Brown University.

Christopher, Warren. 1993. "New Steps Toward Conflict Resolution in the Former Yugoslavia." Washington, DC: US Department of State, Speech by the Secretary of State.

Citrin, Jack. 1965. *United Nations Peacekeeping Activities: A Case Study in Organizational Task Expansion*. Denver: University of Denver.

Clarke, Walter. 1997. "Failed Visions and Uncertain Mandates in Somalia." In *Learning from Somalia: The Lessons of Armed Humanitarion Intervention*, ed. W. Clarke and J. Herbst. Boulder: Westview Press.

Clarke, Walter, and Jeffrey Herbst, eds. 1997. *Learning from Somalia: The Lessons of Armed Humanitarian Intervention*. Boulder: Westview Press

Claude, Inis L. 1967. *The Changing United Nations*. New York: Random House.

Cliffe, Lionel, ed. 1994. *The Transition to Independence in Namibia*. Boulder: Lynne Rienner.

Cliffe, Sarah, with Claus Rohland. 2003. "Mission Implementation: Developing Institutional Capacities: The East Timor Reconstruction Programme." In *The United Nations Transitional Administration in East Timor: Debriefing Lessons*, ed. Nassrine Azimi and Chang Li Lin. Leiden: Martinus Nijhoff Publishers.

Coate, Roger, ed. 1994. *US Policy and the Future of the United Nations*. New York: Twentieth Century Fund.

Coates, Karen. 2005. *Cambodia Now: Life in the Wake of War*. Jefferson, NC: McFarland.

Cockayne, James, and David Malone. 2005. "The Ralph Bunche Centennial: Peace Operations Then and Now." *Global Governance*, Vol. 11, No. 3.

Cohen, Lenard. 1993. *Broken Bonds: The Disintegration of Yugoslavia*. Boulder: Westview Press.

Collier, David, and James Mahoney. 1996. "Insights and Pitfalls: Selection Bias in Qualitative Research." *World Politics* Vol. 49, No. 1.

Collier, Paul, and Anke Hoeffler. 2005. "Resource, Rents, and Governance." *Journal of Conflict Resolution*, Vol. 49, No. 4.

Costa, Gino. 1995. "The United Nations and the Reform of the Police in El Salvador." *International Peacekeeping*, Vol. 2, No. 3.

Cotton, James. 2004. *East Timor, Australia and Regional Order*. London: Routledge Curzon.

Coulon, Jocelyn. 1998. *Soldiers of Diplomacy: The United Nations, Peacekeeping, and the New World Order*, trans. Phyllis Aronoff and Howard Scott. Toronto: University of Toronto Press.

Cousens, Elizabeth, Chetan Kumar, and Karin Wermester eds. 2000. *Peacebuilding As Politics: Cultivating Peace in Fragile Societies.* Boulder: Lynne Rienner.

Crawford, Beverly. 1995. *Explaining Yugoslavia's Breakup: Institutional Weakness, Economic Crisis, and Identity Politics.* Berkeley: UC Berkeley, Center for German and European Studies.

  1996. "Explaining Defection from International Cooperation: Germany's Unilateral Recognition of Croatia." *World Politics*, Vol. 48, No. 4.

Crocker, Bathsheba. 2004. "Going it Alone, Gone Wrong." In *Winning the Peace: An American Strategy for Post-Conflict Reconstruction*, ed. Robert C. Orr, Washington DC: Center for Strategic and International Studies Press.

Crocker, Chester A. 1992. *High Noon in Southern Africa: Making Peace in a Rough Neighborhood.* New York. W. W. Norton.

  1994. "Foreword." In *Ending Mozambique's War: The Role of Mediation and Good Offices.* Cameron Hume. Washington, DC: US Institute of Peace Press.

Crocker, Chester, Fen Osler Hampson, and Pamela Aall, eds. 2005. *Grasping the Nettle: Analyzing Cases of Intractable Conflict.* Washington, DC: US Institute of Peace Press.

Curtis, Grant. 1998. *Cambodia Reborn? The Transition to Democracy and Development.* Washington, DC: Brookings Institution.

Dale, Richard. 2005. "The Constitution at Work: Ten Years of Namibian Nationhood/Reexamining Liberation in Namibia: Political Culture since Independence." *African Studies Review*, Vol. 48, No. 2.

Dallaire, Romeo. 2004. *Shake Hands with the Devil: The Failure of Humanity in Rwanda.* New York: Carroll and Graf Publishers.

Daniel, Donald C. F., Bradd C. Hayes, with Chantal de Jonge Oudraat. 1999. *Coercive Inducement and the Containment of International Crises.* Washington, DC: US Institute of Peace Press.

Day, Graham, and Christopher Freeman. 2005. "Operationalizing the Responsibility to Protect: The Policekeeping Approach." *Global Governance*, Vol. 11, No. 2.

de Soto, Alvaro. 1999. "Ending Violent Conflict in El Salvador." In *Herding Cats: Multiparty Mediation in a Complex World*, ed. Chester Crocker, Fen Osler Hampson, and Pamela Aall. Washington, DC: US Institute of Peace Press.

de Vrieze, Franklin. 2004. "Kosovo after the March 2004 Crisis." *Helsinki Monitor*, Vol. 15, No. 3.

de Walque, Damien. 2004. "The Long-Term Legacy of the Khmer Rouge Period in Cambodia." *The World Bank Development Research Group*, Policy Research Working Paper No. 3446.

Dee, Moreen. 2001. "Coalitions of the Willing and Humanitarian Intervention: Australia's Involvement with INTERFET." *International Peacekeeping*, Vol. 8, No. 3.

del Castillo, Graciana. 1997. "The Arms-for-Land Deal in El Salvador." In *Keeping the Peace: Multidimensional UN Operations in Cambodia and El Salvador*, ed. M. W. Doyle, Ian Johnstone, Robert C. Orr. Cambridge: Cambridge University Press.

Denitch, Bogdan. 1994. *Ethnic Nationalism: The Tragic Death of Yugoslavia*. Minneapolis: University of Minnesota Press.

des Forges, Alison. 1999. *Leave None to Tell the Story: Genocide in Rwanda*. New York: Human Rights Watch.

Deutsch, Karl W. 1963. *The Nerves of Government*. New York: Free Press.

Dickey, Christopher. 1981. "France, Mexico Recognize Left in El Salvador." *Washington Post*, August 29.

Diehl, Paul F. 1994. *International Peacekeeping*. Baltimore: Johns Hopkins.

Dion, Doug. 1994. *Evidence and Inference in the Comparative Case Study*. Ann Arbor: Michigan.

Dobbins, James, ed. 2004. *The UN's Role in Nation-Building: From the Congo to Iraq*. Santa Monica, CA: Rand.

Doder, Dusko. 1993. "Yugoslavia: New War, Old Hatreds." *Foreign Policy*, Vol. 91, No. 3.

Downs, George, and Stephen Stedman. 2002. "Evaluation Issues in Peace Implementation." In *Ending Civil Wars: The Implementation of Peace Agreements*, ed. Stephen Stedman, Donald Rothchild, and Elizabeth Cousens. Boulder: Lynne Rienner.

Doyle, Michael. 1995. *UN Peacekeeping in Cambodia: UNTAC's Civil Mandate*. New York: International Peace Academy; Boulder: Lynne Rienner.

Doyle, Michael, and Jan Mueller. 1999. "Lessons of a Past Reconstruction Effort in the Balkans." *International Herald Tribune*, July 1, p. 6.

Doyle, Michael, and Nicholas Sambanis. 2000. "International Peacebuilding: A Theoretical and Quantitative Analysis." *American Political Science Review*, Vol. 94, No. 4.

Doyle, Michael, Ian Johnstone, and Robert C. Orr, ed. 1997. *Keeping the Peace: Multidimensional UN Operations in Cambodia and El Salvador*. Cambridge: Cambridge University Press.

Dreyer, Ronald. 1994. *Namibia and Southern Africa: Regional Dynamics of Decolonization 1945–1990*. London: Kegan Paul International.

Druckman, Daniel, and Paul C. Stern. 1997. "Evaluating Peacekeeping Missions." *Mershon International Studies Review* 41.

Dunn, James. 2003. *East Timor: A Rough Passage to Independence*, 3rd edn. Double Bay, New South Wales: Longueville.

Dupuy, Alex. 1997. *Haiti in the New World Order: The Limits of the Democratic Revolution*. Boulder: Westview Press.

Durch, William J. 1996. "Introduction to Anarchy: Humanitarian Intervention and 'State-Building' in Somalia." In *UN Peacekeeping, American Policy, and the Uncivil Wars of the 1990s*, ed. William Durch. New York: St. Martin's.

Durch, William, ed. 1996. *UN Peacekeeping, American Policy, and the Uncivil Wars of the 1990s*. New York: St. Martin's.

Durch, William, and James Schear. 1996. "Faultlines: UN Operations in the Former Yugoslavia." In *UN Peacekeeping, American Foreign Policy, and the Uncivil Wars of the 1990s*, ed. William Durch. New York: St. Martin's.

Durch, William, Victoria Holt, Caroline Earle, and Moira Shanahan. 2003. "The Brahimi Report and the Future of UN Peace Operations." Washington, DC: Henry L. Stimson Center.

Duyvesteyn, Isabelle. 2005. *Clausewitz and African War: Politics and Strategy in Liberia and Somalia*. London: Frank Cass.

Eaton, Chris. 1994. "The Role of Police in Institution Building." In *International Peace Keeping: Building on the Cambodian Experience*, ed. Hugh Smith. Canberra: Australian Defense Studies Centre.

Eaton, Robert, Chris Horwood, and Nora Niland. 1997. "Mozambique: The Development of Indigenous Mine Action Capacities." New York: Department of Humanitarian Affairs, United Nations.

Economist. 1997. "Map-Making Again: Former Yugoslavia: Elections in Serb-Held Eastern Slavonia." *Economist*, April 19.

——— 1999. "Angola: Rocks that Kill: UN Diamond Embargo Difficult to Enforce." *Economist* 351 (8121).

Edelstein, David. 2005. "Occupational Hazards: Why Military Occupations Succeed or Fail." Unpublished book manuscript.

Englund, Harri. 2002. *From War to Peace on the Mozambique-Malawi Borderland*. Edinburgh: Edinburgh University Press for the International African Institute, London.

Etheredge, Lloyd S. 1985. *Can Governments Learn? American Foreign Policy and Central American Revolution*. New York: Pergamon Press.

Evans, Gareth. 2003. "Rebuilding Societies in Crisis: Before and After War." Lecture, Canadian Institute of International Affairs, 75th Anniversary Lecture Series, Toronto, 8 October.

Far Eastern Economic Review, 1992, February 27, p. 23.

Fearon, David, and David Laitin. 2004. "Neotrusteeship and the Problem of Weak States." *International Security*, Vol. 28, No. 4.

Fetherston, A. B. 1994. *Towards a Theory of Peacekeeping*. New York: St. Martin's.

Findlay, Trevor. 1995. *Cambodia: The Legacy and Lessons of UNTAC*. Oxford: Oxford University Press.

——— 2003. *The Use of Force in UN Peace Operations*. Oxford: SIPRI and Oxford University Press.

Finnegan, William. 1992. *A Complicated War: The Harrowing of Mozambique.* Berkeley, CA: University of California Press.

Finnemore, Martha. 1996. *National Interests in International Society.* Ithaca: Cornell University Press.

Fishel, Kimbra L., and Edwin G. Corr. 1998. "UN Peace Operations in El Salvador: The Manwaring Paradigm in a Traditional Setting." In *The Savage Wars of Peace: Toward a New Paradigm of Peace Operations,* ed. J. T. Fishel. Boulder: Westview Press.

Fleitz, Frederick H. 2002. *Peacekeeping Fiascoes of the 1990s: Causes, Solutions, and US Interests.* Westport, CT: Praeger.

Forrest, Joshua. 1998. *Namibia's Post-Apartheid Regional Institutions: The Founding Year.* Rochester, NY: University of Rochester Press.

Fortna, Virginia Page. 2004a. "Does Peacekeeping Keep Peace? International Intervention and the Duration of Peace After Civil War." *International Studies Quarterly,* Vol. 48, No. 2.

2004b. *Peace Time: Cease-Fire Agreements and the Durability of Peace.* Princeton: Princeton University Press.

Fowler, Robert, and Anders Mollander. 2000. "Report of the Panel of Experts on Violations of Security Council Sanctions against Angola." New York: United Nations Security Council.

Freedom House Report. 2005. "Annual Report: Freedom in the World." Available at www.freedomhouse.org.

Friedman, Francine. 2004. *Bosnia and Herzegovina: A Polity on the Brink.* London: Routledge.

Frieson, Kate. 1993. "Revolution and Rural Response in Cambodia, 1970–1975." In *Genocide and Democracy in Cambodia: The Khmer Rouge, the United Nations and the International Community,* ed. Ben Kiernan. New Haven, CT: Yale University Southeast Asia Studies.

Fukuyama, Francis. 1989. "The End of History." *National Interest.* No. 16.

Gagnon, V. P. 1994/95. "Ethnic Nationalism and International Conflict: The Case of Serbia." *International Security,* Vol. 19, No. 3.

2004. *The Myth of Ethnic War: Serbia and Croatia in the 1990s.* Ithaca, NY: Cornell University Press.

Gallagher, Tom. 2005. *The Balkans in the New Millennium: In the Shadow of War and Peace.* New York: Routledge.

Gallarotti, Giulio M. 1991. "The Limits of International Organization: Systematic Failure in the Management of International Relations." *International Organization,* Vol. 45, No. 2.

Galli, Rosemary. 2003. *People's Spaces and State Spaces: Land and Governance in Mozambique.* New York: Lexington Books.

Galtung, Johan. 1976. *Peace, War and Defense: Essays in Peace Research,* Vol. II. Oslo: International Peace Research Institute.

Geisler, Gisela. 2005. "A Second Liberation: Lobbying for Women's Political Representation in Zambia, Botswana and Namibia." *Journal of Southern African Studies*, Vol. 32, No. 1.

George, Alexander. 1979. "The Causal Nexus between Cognitive Beliefs and Decision-Making Behavior: The 'Operational Code' Belief System." In *Psychological Models in International Politics*, ed. L. Falkowski. Boulder: Westview Press.

George, Alexander, and Andrew Bennett. 2005. *Case Studies and Theory Development in the Social Sciences*. Cambridge, MA: MIT Press.

George, Alexander, and Timothy McKeown. 1985. "Case Studies and Theories of Organizational Decisionmaking." *Advances in Information Processing in Organizations*. Vol. 2.

Gersony, Robert. 1988. "Summary of Mozambican Refugee Accounts of Principally Conflict-Related Experience in Mozambique." Washington, DC: US Department of State, Bureau for Refugee Programs.

Gettleman, Marvin E., Patrick Lacefield, Louis Menashe, David Mermelstein, eds. 1986. *El Salvador: Central America in the New Cold War*. New York: Grove Press.

Gibbs, Sara. 1997. "Postwar Reconstruction in Mozambique: Reframing Children's Experiences of Trauma and Healing." In *Rebuilding Societies After Civil War*, ed. Krishna Kumar, Boulder: Lynne Rienner.

Glanz, James. 2004. "Scouring Iraq for Enemies, Finding Farmers and Mud." *New York Times*, October 10.

Goldstone, Anthony. 2004. "UNTAET with Hindsight: The Peculiarities of Politics in an Incomplete State." *Global Governance*, Vol. 10, No. 1.

Gonçalves, Euclides. 2006. "Local Powers and Decentralisation: Recognition of Community Leaders in Mocumbi, Southern Mozambique." *Journal of Contemporary African Studies*, Vol. 24, No. 1.

Gorjao, Paulo. 2002. "The Legacy and Lessons of the United Nations Transitional Administration in East Timor." *Contemporary Southeast Asia*, Vol. 24, No. 2.

Gottesman, Evan. 2003. *Cambodia After the Khmer Rouge*. New Haven: Yale University Press.

Goulding, Marrack. 2003. *Peacemonger*. Baltimore, MD: Johns Hopkins University Press.

Gourevitch, Philip. 1998. "Genocide Fax." *New Yorker*, May 11.

Greenless, Don, and Robert Garran, ed. 2002. *Deliverance: The Inside Story of East Timor's Fight for Freedom*. Crows Nest, NSW, Australia: Allen and Unwin Pty, Limited.

Grenier, Yvon. 2004. "The Rise and Fall of Revolutionary Passions in El Salvador: Some Lessons for the Study of Radical Political Movements." *Journal of Human Rights*, Vol. 3, No. 3.

Groth, Siegfried. 1995. *Namibia: The Wall of Silence*. Wuppertal, Germany: Peter Hammer Verlag.

Guéhenno, Jean-Marie. 2002. "On the Challenges and Achievements of Reforming UN Peace Operations." *International Peacekeeping*, Vol. 9, No. 2.

Gutman, Roy. 1993. *A Witness to Genocide: The 1993 Pulitzer Prize-winning Dispatches on the "Ethnic Cleansing" of Bosnia*. New York: Macmillan.

Haas, Ernst B. 1986. *Why We Still Need the United Nations*. Berkeley: UC Berkeley, Institute of International Studies.

——— 1990. *When Knowledge is Power*. Berkeley: University of California Press.

Haas, Ernst B., Robert L. Butterworth, and Joseph S. Nye. 1972. *Conflict Management by International Organizations*. Morristown, NJ: General Learning Press.

Haas, Peter. 1992. "Introduction: Epistemic Communities and International Policy Coordination." *International Organization*, Vol. 46, No. 1.

Hall, Margaret, and Tom Young. 1997. *Confronting Leviathan: Mozambique since Independence*. Athens, OH: Ohio University Press.

Hammarskjold, Dag. 1962. *Servant of Peace: A Selection of the Speeches and Statements of the Secretary-General of the United Nations, 1953–1961*. New York: Harper and Row.

Hampson, Fen Osler. 1996a. *Nurturing Peace: Why Peace Settlements Succeed or Fail*. Washington DC: US Institute of Peace Press.

——— 1996b. "The Pursuit of Human Rights: The United Nations in El Salvador." In *UN Peacekeeping, American Policy, and the Uncivil Wars of the 1990s*, ed. W. J. Durch. New York: St. Martin's and Henry J. Stimson Center.

Hanlon, Joseph. 1990. *Mozambique: The Revolution under Fire*. London: Zed Books.

——— 1991. *Mozambique: Who Calls the Shots?* London: James Currey.

——— 1996. *Peace without Profit: How the UN Blocks Rebuilding in Mozambique*. Oxford: James Currey.

Hare, Paul. 1998. *Angola's Last Best Chance for Peace: An Insider's Account of the Peace Process*. Washington, DC: US Institute of Peace Press.

——— 2005. "Angola: The End of an Intractable Conflict." In *Grasping the Nettle: Analyzing Cases of Intractable Conflict*, ed. Chester Crocker, Fen Osler Hampson, and Pamela Aall. Washington, DC: US Institute of Peace Press.

Harlech-Jones, Brian. 1997. *A New Thing? The Namibian Independence Process, 1989–1990*.Windhoek: EIN Publications.

Hawk, Kathleen Hill. 2002. *Constructing the Stable State: Goals for Intervention and Peacebuilding*. Westport, CT: Praeger.

Heininger, Janet. 1994. *Peacekeeping in Transition: The United Nations in Cambodia*. New York: Twentieth Century Fund Report.

Heuva, William. 2001. *Media and Resistance Politics in Namibia: The Alternative Press in Namibia, 1960–1990*. Basel, Switzerland: Schlettwein Publishing.

High-Level Panel on Threats, Challenges, and Change. 2004. "A More Secure World:
    Our Shared Responsibility." New York: United Nations.
Hillen, John. 1998. *Blue Helmets: The Strategy of UN Military Operations*. London:
    Brassey's.
Hinton, Alexander. 2005. *Why Did They Kill? Cambodia in the Shadow of Genocide*.
    Berkeley: University of California Press.
Hirsch, John, and Robert Oakley. 1995. *Somalia and Operation Restore Hope: Reflec-
    tions on Peacemaking*. Washington: US Institute of Peace Press.
Hodges, Tony. 2004. *Angola: Anatomy of an Oil State*, 2nd edn. Oxford: James
    Currey.
Holbrooke, Richard. 1998. *To End a War*. New York: Random House.
    2005. "New Course for Kosovo." *Washington Post*, April 20, A25.
Holiday, David, and William Stanley. 1993. "Building the Peace: Preliminary Lesson
    from El Salvador." *Journal of International Affairs*, Vol. 46, No. 2.
Holohan, Anne. 2005. *Networks of Democracy: Lessons from Kosovo for Afghanistan,
    Iraq and Beyond*. Stanford: Stanford University Press.
Honwana, Joao. 2000. "Implementing Peace Agreements in Civil Wars: The Case of
    Mozambique." Unpublished workshop paper, Stanford: Stanford University.
Howard, Lise. 2002. "UN Peace Implementation in Namibia: The Causes of Suc-
    cess." *International Peacekeeping*, Vol. 9, No. 1.
Howe, Herbert. 1997. "Lessons of Liberia: ECOMOG and Regional Peacekeeping."
    International Security, Vol. 21, No. 3.
Hughes, Caroline. 2003. *The Political Economy of Cambodia's Transition*. New York:
    RoutledgeCurzon.
Human Rights Watch. 1994. "Landmines in Mozambique." New York: Human
    Rights Watch.
    1999. "Angola Unravels: The Rise and Fall of the Lusaka Peace Process." New
    York: Human Rights Watch.
    2005. "Overview of Human Rights Issues in Croatia." New York: Human Rights
    Watch.
Hume, Cameron. 1994. *Ending Mozambique's War: The Role of Mediation and Good
    Offices*. Washington, DC: US Institute of Peace Press.
Humphreys, Macartan. 2005. "Natural Resources, Conflict, and Conflict
    Resolution: Uncovering the Mechanisms." *Journal of Conflict Resolution*,
    Vol. 49, No. 4.
Improvising History: A Critical Evaluation of the UN Observer Mission in El Salvador.
    1995. Lawyers Committee for Human Rights, New York.
Ingram, Sue. 2003. "Missions Implementation: Developing Institutional Capac-
    ities." In *The United Nations Transitional Administration in East Timor:
    Debriefing Lessons*, ed. Nassrine Azimi and Chang Li Lin. Leiden: Martinus
    Nijhoff Publishers.
Integrated Regional Information Networks (IRIN). 2004. "Interview with Carolyn
    McAskie, Head of the New UN Mission." Nairobi.

Inter Press Service, December 16, 1993.

International Commission on Intervention and State Sovereignty. 2001. "The Responsibility to Protect." New York.

International Crisis Group. 2004. "Liberia and Sierra Leone: Rebuilding Failed States." Dakar/Brussels.

International Crisis Group. 2004. "What Can the US Do in Iraq?" *Middle East Report* No. 34, 22 December.

International Crisis Group. 2005. "Can Haiti Hold Elections in 2005?" Port-au-Prince/Brussels.

International Crisis Group. 2005. "The Congo's Transition is Failing: Crisis in the Kivus." Nairobi/Brussels.

International Crisis Group. 2005. "The EU/AU Partnership in Darfur: Not Yet a Winning Combination." Nairobi/Brussels.

International Crisis Group. 2005. "The Worst May Be Yet to Come." Brussels.

International Crisis Group. 2005. "Update on Haiti for the UN Security Council." New York.

Isaacman, Allen, and Barbara Isaacman. 1983. *Mozambique: From Colonialism to Revolution, 1900–1982.* Boulder: Westview Press.

Ishizuka, Katsumi. 2003. "Peacekeeping in East Timor: The Experience of UNMISET." *International Peacekeeping*, Vol. 10, No. 3.

Jablonsky, David, and James McCallum. 1999. "Peace Implementation and the Concept of Induced Consent in Peace Operations." *Parameters: US Army War College*, Vol. 29, No. 1.

Jabri, Vivienne. 1990. *Mediating Conflict: Decision-Making and Western Intervention in Namibia.* Manchester: Manchester University Press.

Jackson, Ben. 1996. "Letter from Angola: United Nations' Relations with UNITA." *New Statesman and Society*, Vol. 9, No. 394.

Jackson, Karl D. 1989. *Cambodia: 1975–1978: Rendezvous with Death.* Princeton, NJ: Princeton University Press.

Jackson, Michael. 2004. *In Sierra Leone.* Durham: Duke University Press.

James, Alan. 1990. *Peacekeeping in International Politics.* London: Macmillan.

Jaster, R. 1985. *South Africa in Namibia: The Botha Strategy.* London: Macmillan.

Jehl, Douglas. 2005. "Report Says White House Ignored CIA on Iraq Chaos." *New York Times*, October 13, p. A10.

Jeldres, Julio. 1997. "Cambodia's Fading Hopes." *Journal of Democracy*, Vol. 7, No. 1.

Jett, Dennis. 1999. *Why Peacekeeping Fails.* New York: St. Martin's.

Jockel, Joseph. 1994. *Canada and International Peacekeeping.* Washington, DC: Center for International Strategic and International Studies.

Johansen, Robert C. 1994. "UN Peacekeeping: How Should We Measure Success?" *Mershon International Studies Review* 38.

Johnstone, Ian. 1995. *Rights and Reconciliation: UN Strategies in El Salvador*, ed. International Peace Academy. Boulder: Lynne Rienner.

Jolliffe, Jill. 2000. "Foreword." In *The Crossing: A Story of East Timor*, ed. Luís Cardoso. London: Granta Books.

Kamm, Henry. 1992. "Return of Refugees to Cambodia Takes Longer than Planned." *New York Times*, April 12, p. A22.

1998. *Cambodia: Report from a Stricken Land*. New York: Arcade Publishing.

Kandeh, Jimmy. 2003. "Sierra Leone's Post-Conflict Elections of 2002." *Journal of Modern African Studies*, Vol. 41, No. 2.

Kapila, Mukesh. 2003. "Setting-up of UNTAET: Post-UNAMET Planning, Drafting Resolutions and Finance." In *The United Nations Transitional Administration in East Timor: Debriefing Lessons*, ed. Nassrine Azimi and Chang Li Lin. Leiden: Martinus Nijhoff Publishers.

Kaplan, Robert. 1994. *Balkan Ghosts: A Journey Through History*. New York: Vintage.

Karns, Margaret. 1987. "Ad Hoc Multilateral Diplomacy: The United States, the Contact Group, and Namibia." *International Organization*, Vol. 41, No. 1.

Kawakami, Takahisa. 2003. "Setting-up of UNTAET: Post-UNAMET, Planning, Drafting Resolutions, and Finance." In *The United Nations Transitional Administration in East Timor: Debriefing Lessons*, ed. Nassrine Azimi and Chang Li Lin. Leiden: Martinus Nijhoff Publishers.

Keohane, Robert O. 1984. *After Hegemony: Cooperation and Discord in the World Political Economy*. Princeton: Princeton University Press.

Khadiagala, Gilbert. 2003. "Case Study: Burundi." In *Dealing with Conflict in Africa: The United Nations and Regional Organizations*, ed. J. Boulden. New York: Palgrave Macmillan.

Khouri-Padova, Lama. 2004. "Discussion Paper: Haiti, Lessons Learned." New York: Peacekeeping Best Practices Unit, United Nations Department of Peacekeeping Operations.

Kiernan, Ben. 1990. "The Genocide in Cambodia, 1975–1979." *Bulletin of Concerned Asian Scholars*, Vol. 20, No. 2.

2003. "The Demography of Genocide in Southeast Asia: The Death Tolls in Cambodia, 1975–79, and East Timor, 1975–80." *Critical Asian Studies*, Vol. 35, No. 4.

Kiernan, Ben, ed. 1993. *Genocide and Democracy in Cambodia: The Khmer Rouge, the United Nations and the International Community*. New Haven: Yale University Southeast Asia Studies.

King, Charles. 2005. "The Uses of Deadlock: Intractability in Eurasia." In *Grasping the Nettle: Analyzing Cases of Intractable Conflict*, ed. Chester Crocker, Fen Osler Hampson, and Pamela Aall. Washington, DC: US Institute of Peace Press.

Kingma, Kees. 2002. "Demobilization, Reintegration and Peacebuilding in Africa." *International Peacekeeping*, Vol. 9, No. 2.

Kleiboer, Marieke. 1994. "Ripeness of Conflict: A Fruitful Notion?" *Journal of Peace Research*, Vol. 31, February.

Klein, Jacques Paul. 1996. "Letter to the Secretary-General of the United Nations: My Visit to Croatia and Serbia, December 28–31." New York: United Nations.

    1997. "The Prospects for Eastern Croatia: The Significance of the UN's Undiscovered Mission." *RUSI Journal*, Vol. 142. No. 2.

    2002. "Comments: What Does it Take to Make UN Peacekeeping Operations Succeed?" Speech delivered at *Challenges in Peacekeeping: Past, Present, and Future.* Seminar sponsored by the International Peace Academy and the Peacekeeping Best Practices Unit, Millennium Hotel, New York, October 29.

Koh, Tommy. 1990. "The Paris Conference on Cambodia: A Multilateral Negotiation that 'Failed.'" *Negotiation Journal*, Vol. 6, No. 1.

Koven, Ronald. 1981. "France Planning to Condemn Communist Role in El Salvador." *Washington Post*, February 19.

Kowalchuk, Lisa. 2004. "The Salvadoran Land Struggle in the 1990s: Cohesion, Commitment, and Corruption." In *Landscapes of Struggle: Politics, Society, and Community in El Salvador*, ed. Lauria-Santiago, Aldo and Leigh Binford. Pittsburgh, PA: University of Pittsburgh Press.

Krasno, Jean, Bradd Hayes, and Donald Daniel, eds. 2003. *Leveraging for Success in United Nations Peace Operations.* Westport, CT: Praeger.

Krepinevich, Andrew F., Jr. 2005. "How to Win in Iraq." *Foreign Affairs*, Vol. 84, No. 5.

Krieger, Heike, ed. 1997. *East Timor and the International Community: Basic Documents.* Cambridge: Cambridge University Press.

Kumar, Chetan. 2001. "Peacebuilding in Haiti." In *Peacebuilding as Politics: Cultivating Peace in Fragile Societies*, ed. Elizabeth Cousins and Chetan Kumar, with Karin Wermester. Boulder: Lynne Rienner.

Kupchan, Charles. 2005. "Yielding to Balkan Reality." *Foreign Affairs*, Vol. 84, No. 6.

Kušić, Siniša. 2006. "Croatia: Advancing Political and Economic Transformation." *Journal of Southeast European & Black Sea Studies*, Vol. 6, No. 1.

LaFranchi, Howard. 2005. "A Welcome Surprise: War Waning Globally." *Christian Science Monitor*, October 18.

Lacey, Marc. 2005a. "Militia Fighters Kill 9 U.N. Peacekeepers in Congo as Instability Continues." *New York Times*, February 26, p. A6.

    2005b. "Beyond the Bullets and Blades." *New York Times*, March 20, Section 4, p. 1.

Ladutke, Lawrence. 2004. *Freedom of Expression in El Salvador: The Struggle for Human Rights and Democracy.* Jefferson, NC: McFarland and Company.

Laitin, David D. 1999. "Somalia: Civil War and International Intervention." In *Civil Wars, Insecurity, and Intervention*, ed. B. Walter and J. Snyder. New York: Columbia University Press.

Lalande, Serge. 1995. "Somalia: Major Issues for Future UN Peacekeeping." In *New Dimensions of Peacekeeping*, ed. Daniel Warner. London: Martinus Nijhoff. Publishers.

"Land, Peace, and Participation: The Development of Post-War Agricultural Policy in El Salvador and the Role of the World Bank." 1997. Washington, DC: Washington Office on Latin American Affairs.

Large, Judith. 1999. "Kafka Meets Machiavelli: Post-war, Post-transition Eastern Slavonia." *Development in Practice*, Vol. 9, No. 5.

Last, David. 1997. *Theory, Doctrine and Practice of Conflict De-Escalation in Peacekeeping*. Cornwallis Park, NS Canada: Canadian Peacekeeping Press.

——— 2003. "From Peacekeeping to Peacebuilding." *Online Journal of Peace and Conflict Resolution*. Vol. 5, No. 1.

Lauria-Santiago, Aldo, and Leigh Binford, eds. 2004. *Landscapes of Struggle: Politics, Society, and Community in El Salvador*. Pittsburgh, PA: University of Pittsburgh Press.

Le Billon, Philippe. 2005. *Fuelling War: Natural Resources and Armed Conflict*. New York: Routledge for the International Institute for Strategic Studies, London.

Le Pape, Marc, and Claudine Vidal, eds. 2002. *Côte d'Ivoire: l'année terrible, 1999–2000*. Paris: Karthala.

LeVine, Mark. 1997. "Peacemaking in El Salvador." In *Keeping the Peace: Multidimensional UN Operations in Cambodia and El Salvador*, ed. Michael W. Doyle, Ian Johnstone, and Robert C. Orr. Cambridge: Cambridge University Press.

Leconte, Frantz, ed. 1999. *En Grandissant Sous Duvalier: L'Agonie d'un Etat-Nation*. Paris: L'Harmattan.

Lederach, John Paul. 1997. *Building Peace: Sustainable Reconciliation in Divided Societies*. Washington, DC: US Institute of Peace Press.

Leeuw, Frans, Ray C. Rist, Richard C. Sonnichsen, eds. 1994. *Can Governments Learn? Comparative Perspectives on Evaluation and Organizational Learning*. New Brunswick: Transaction Publishers.

Lehmann, Ingrid A. 1999. *Peacekeeping and Public Information: Caught in the Crossfire*. London: Frank Cass.

Lemarchand, Réné. 1996. *Burundi: Ethnic Conflict and Genocide*. Cambridge: Cambridge University Press.

——— 2000. "The Crisis in the Great Lakes." In *Africa in World Politics: The African State System in Flux*, ed. John Harbeson and Donald Rothchild. Boulder: Westview Press.

Lessons Learned Unit. 1998. "United Nations Transitional Administration in Eastern Slavonia, Baranja, and Western Sirium (UNTAES): Lessons Learned." New York: Department of Peacekeeping Operations.

Levitt, Barbara, and James G. March. 1988. "Organizational Learning." *Annual Review of Sociology* 14.

Levy, Jack. 1994. "Learning and Foreign Policy: Sweeping a Conceptual Minefield." *International Organization* 48, No. 2.

Leys, Colin, and John S. Saul, eds. 1995. *Namibia's Liberation Struggle: The Two-Edged Sword.* London: James Currey.

Licklider, Roy, ed. 1993. *Stopping the Killing: How Civil Wars End.* New York: New York University Press.

Lieber, Robert. 2005. *The American Era: Power and Strategy for the 21st Century.* New York: Cambridge University Press.

Lizée, Pierre. 1993. "The Challenge of Conflict Resolution in Cambodia." *Canada Defense Quarterly*, September.

2000. *Peace, Power and Resistance in Cambodia.* London: Macmillan.

Lungo, Mario Ucles. 1996. *El Salvador in the Eighties: Counterinsurgency and Revolution.* Philadelphia: Temple University Press.

Lyons, Terrence, and Ahmed Samatar. 1995. *Somalia: State Collapse, Multilateral Intervention, and Strategies for Political Reconstruction.* Washington, DC: Brookings Institution.

Machel, Graca, 2001. *The Impact of War on Children.* London: Hurst.

MacKinnon, Michael G. 2000. *The Evolution of US Peacekeeping Policy Under Clinton: A Fairweather Friend?* London: Frank Cass.

Madjiah, Lela. 2005. "What Could Be Worse than East Timor Refugee Camps?" *Jakarta Post*, April 28.

Magas, Branka. 1993. *The Destruction of Yugoslavia: Tracking the Break-Up 1980–92.* London: Verso.

Maguire, Peter. 2005. *Facing Death in Cambodia.* New York: Columbia University Press.

Malan, Mark. 1999. "Peacebuilding in Southern Africa: Police Reform in Mozambique and South Africa." *International Peacekeeping*, Vol. 6, No. 4.

Malone, David. 2004. *The UN Security Council: From the Cold War to the 21st Century.* Boulder: Lynne Rienner.

Managing Arms in Peace Processes: Nicaragua and El Salvador. 1997. New York and Geneva: United Nations Institute for Disarmament Research.

Mandela, Nelson. 2002. *The Politics of Peace in Mozambique: Post-Conflict Democratization, 1992–2000.* Westport, CT: Praeger.

2004. *In His Own Words.* New York: Little Brown.

Mansson, Katarina. 2005. "Use of Force and Civilian Protection: Peace Operations in the Congo." *International Peacekeeping*, Vol. 12, No. 4.

March, James G. 1988. *Decisions and Organization.* London: Basil Blackwell.

Marnika, Maurice. 1996. "The Rules of the Game: The Three Guiding Principles of Peacekeeping." *Peacekeeping & International Relations*, Vol. 25, No. 1.

Marten, Kimberly Zisk. 2004. *Enforcing the Peace: Learning from the Imperial Past.* New York: Columbia.

2005. "In Building Nations, Establish Security, Then Democracy." *Chronicle of Higher Education*, Vol. 51, No. 28.

Martin, Ian, and Alexander Mayer-Rieckh. 2005. "The United Nations and East Timor: From Self-Determination to State-Building." *International Peacekeeping*, Vol. 12, No. 1.

Martin, Lisa. 1992. *Coercive Cooperation: Explaining Multilateral Economic Sanctions.* Princeton, NJ: Princeton University Press.

Mason, David T., and Patrick J. Fett. 1996. "How Civil Wars End: A Rational Choice Approach." *Journal of Conflict Resolution*, Vol. 40, December.

Massari, Maurizio. 2005. "Do All Roads Lead to Brussels? Analysis of the Different Trajectories of Croatia, Serbia-Montenegro and Bosnia-Herzegovina." *Cambridge Review of International Affairs*, Vol. 18, No. 2.

Mayall, James. 1996. *The New Interventionism: 1991–1994.* Cambridge: Cambridge University Press.

McCargo, Duncan. 2005. "Cambodia: Getting Away with Authoritarianism?" *Journal of Democracy*, Vol. 16, No. 4.

McCormick, David. 1997. "From Peacekeeping to Peacebuilding: Restructuring Police and Military Institutions." In *Keeping the Peace: Multidimensional UN Operations in Cambodia and El Salvador*, ed. Michael W. Doyle, Ian Johnstone, and Robert C. Orr. Cambridge: Cambridge University Press.

McHenry Donald. 1990. "Foreword." *Nation Building: The UN and Namibia.* Washington, DC: National Democratic Institute for International Affairs.

McLean, Lyndall. 1994. "Civil Administration in Transition: Public Information and the Neutral Political/Electoral Environment." In *International Peacekeeping: Building on the Cambodian Experience*, ed. Hugh Smith. Canberra: ADSC.

McMullin, Jaremey. 2004. "Reintegration of Combatants: Were the Right Lessons Learned in Mozambique?" *International Peacekeeping*, Vol. 11, No. 4.

McNamara, Dennis. 2003. "Introductory Remarks and Keynote Address." In *The United Nations Transitional Administration in East Timor: Debriefing Lessons*, ed. Nassrine Azimi and Chang Li Lin. Leiden: Martinus Nijhoff Publishers.

McNulty, Mel. 1997. "France's Role in Rwanda and External Military Intervention: A Double Discrediting." *International Peacekeeping*, Vol. 4, No. 3.

Mearsheimer, John. 2003. *The Tragedy of Great Power Politics.* New York: W. W. Norton and Co.

Mendelson, Sarah. 2005. *Peacekeepers and Human Trafficking in the Balkans.* Washington, DC: CSIS Press.

Menkhaus, Ken. 1997. "International Peacebuilding and the Dynamics of Local and National Reconciliation in Somalia." In *Learning from Somalia: The Lessons of Armed Intervention*, ed. W. Clarke and J. Herbst. Boulder: Westview Press.

2004. *Somalia: State Collapse and the Threat of Terrorism.* Adelphi Paper 364. New York: Oxford University Press.

Mercer, David. 2004. "Dividing Up the Spoils: Australia, East Timor, and the Timor Sea." *Space and Polity*, Vol. 8, No. 3.

Mersiades, Michael. 2005. "Peacekeeping and Legitimacy: Lessons from Cambodia and Somalia." *International Peacekeeping*, Vol. 12, No. 2.

Mertus, Julie. 2004. "Improving International Peacebuilding Efforts: The Example of Human Rights Culture in Kosovo." *Global Governance*, Vol. 10, No. 3.

Mesic, Stipe. 2004. *The Demise of Yugoslavia: A Political Memoir*. Budapest, Hungary: Central European University Press.

Mill, John Stuart. 1843. *A System of Logic: Ratiocinative and Inductive*. New York: Harper.

Minear, Larry, Colin Scott, and Thomas G. Weiss. 1996. *The News Media, Civil War, and Humanitarian Action*. Boulder: Lynne Rienner.

Mingst, Karen A., and Margaret P. Karns, eds. 2006. *The United Nations In the Post-Cold War Era*. 3rd edn. New York: Westview Press.

Minority Rights Group International. 2003. "Minorities in Croatia." London.

Mockaitis, Thomas. 2004. "Civil-Military Cooperation in Peace Operations: The Case of Kosovo." Carlisle, PA: US Army War College, Strategic Studies Institute.

Montague, Dena. 2002. "Stolen Goods in the Democratic Republic of the Congo." *SAIS Review*. Vol. 22, No. 1.

Montgomery, Tommie Sue. 1995. *Revolution in El Salvador: From Civil Strife to Civil Peace*, 2nd edn. Boulder: Westview Press.

1998. "International Missions, Observing Elections, and the Democratic Transition in El Salvador." In *Electoral Observation and Democratic Transitions in Latin America*, ed. K. Middlebrook. La Jolla: Center for US–Mexican Studies, University of California, San Diego.

Morillon, Philippe. 1993. *Croire et oser: chronique de Sarajevo*. Paris: Balland.

Morrison, Alex, and James Kiras, eds. 1996. *UN Peace Operations and the Role of Japan*. Cornwallis Park, NS Canada: Canadian Peacekeeping Press.

Morrison, J. Stephen, and Alex de Waal. 2005. "Can Sudan Escape its Intractability?" In *Grasping the Nettle: Analyzing Cases of Intractable Conflict*, ed. Chester Crocker, Fen Osler Hampson, and Pamel Aall. Washington, DC: US Institute of Peace Press.

Moxon-Browne, Edward, ed. 1998. *A Future for Peacekeeping?* Boulder: St. Martin's.

Murray, Kevin, with Ellen Coletti and Jack Spence. 1994. "Rescuing Reconstruction: The Debate on Post-War Economic Recovery in El Salvador." Cambridge, MA: Hemisphere Initiatives.

Murray, Kevin, with Tom Barry. 1995. *Inside El Salvador*. Albuquerque, NM: Interhemispheric Resource Center Press.

Ndikumana, Leonce. 2000. "Towards a Solution to Violence in Burundi: A Case for Political and Economic Liberalization." *Journal of Modern African Studies*, Vol. 38, No. 3.

Nevins, Joseph. 2005. *A Not-So-Distant Horror: Mass Violence in East Timor.* Ithaca, NY: Cornell University Press.

Newitt, Malyn. 1995. *A History of Mozambique.* Bloomington: Indiana University Press.

Norris, John. 2005. *Collision Course: NATO, Russia, and Kosovo.* Westport, CT: Praeger.

Ntchatcho, Herman. 1993. "Political Amnesty and Repatriation of Refugees in Namibia." In *African Yearbook of International Law,* ed. Abdulqawi Yusuf. London: Martinus Nijhoff Publishers.

Nujoma, Sam. 2001. *Where Others Wavered.* Bedford, UK: Panaf Books.

Official Gazette Extraordinary of South West Africa. 1980. "Proclamation by the Administrator General for the Territory of South West Africa. No. AG8." Windhoek, April 24.

Oliver, Ian. 2005. *War and Peace in the Balkans: The Diplomacy of Conflict in the Former Yugoslavia.* New York: I. B. Tauris.

Olonisakin, 'Funmi. 2003. "Case Study: Liberia." In *Dealing with Conflict in Africa: The United Nations and Regional Organizations,* ed. Jane Boulden. New York: Palgrave Macmillan.

Olsson, Louise. 2001. "Gender Mainstreaming in Practice: The United Nations Transitional Assistance Group in Namibia." *Journal of International Peacekeeping,* Vol. 8, No. 2.

Orford, Anne. 2003. *Reading Humanitarian Intervention: Human Rights and the Use of Force in International Law.* Cambridge: Cambridge University Press.

Orr, Robert, ed. 2004. *Winning the Peace: An American Strategy for Post-Conflict Reconstruction.* Washington, DC: Center for Strategic and International Studies Press.

Otaala, Barnabas, ed. 2003. *Government Leaders in Namibia Respond to the HIV/AIDS Epidemic.* Windhoek: University of Namibia Press.

Otunnu, Olara A., and Michael W. Doyle, eds. 1998. *Peacemaking and Peacekeeping for the New Century.* New York: Rowman and Littlefield.

Oudraat, Chantal. 1996. "The United Nations and Internal Conflict." In *The International Dimensions of Internal Conflict,* ed. Michael Brown. Cambridge, MA: MIT Press.

Owen, David. 1995. *Balkan Odyssey.* New York: Harcourt, Brace, and Company.

Packer, George. 2005. *The Assassin's Gate: America in Iraq.* New York: Farrar, Straus, and Giroux.

Palus, Nancy. 2005. "Ivory Coast's People Choose a New Leader, à la Yugoslavia." *Christian Science Monitor,* Vol. 92, No. 237.

Pamphile, Leon. 2001. *Haitians and African Americans: A Heritage of Tragedy and Hope.* Gainesville: University Press of Florida.

Papp, Daniel. 1993. "The Angolan Civil War and Namibia: The Role of External Intervention." In *Making War and Waging Peace: Foreign Intervention in Africa,* ed. David R. Smock. Washington, DC: US Institute of Peace Press.

Paris, Roland. 2004. *At War's End: Building Peace after Civil Conflict.* New York: Cambridge University Press.

Peou, Sorpong. 1997. *Conflict Neutralization in the Cambodia War: From Battlefield to Ballot-Box.* Kuala Lumpur: Oxford University Press.

Peranic, Barbara. 2004. "Croatia's Nationalist Government Makes Concessions to Serbs." *Transitions Online,* January 19.

Pérez de Cuéllar, Javier. 1997. *Pilgrimage for Peace: A Secretary-General's Memoir.* New York: St. Martin's.

Perito, Robert. 2004. *Where is the Lone Ranger When We Need Him? America's Search for a Postconflict Stability Force.* Washington, DC: US Institute of Peace Press.

Pham, John-Peter. 2005. *Liberia: Portrait of a Failed State.* New York: Reed Press.

Pike, Douglas. 1989. "The Cambodian Peace Process: Summer of 1989." *Asian Survey* 29.

Pilger, John. 2004. Column. *New Statesman,* April 5.

Pillar, Paul. 1983. *Negotiating Peace: War Termination as a Bargaining Process.* Princeton: Princeton University Press.

Pires, Emilia. 2003. "Setting-up of UNTAET: Post-UNAMET, Planning, Drafting Resolutions, and Finance." In *The United Nations Transitional Administration in East Timor: Debriefing Lessons,* ed. Nassrine Azimi and Chang Li Lin. Leiden: Martinus Nijhoff Publishers.

Pitcher, Anne. 2002. *Transforming Mozambique: The Politics of Privatization, 1975–2000.* Cambridge: Cambridge University Press.

Popkin, Margaret. 1994. "Justice Impugned: The Salvadoran Peace Accords and the Problem of Impunity." Cambridge, MA: Hemisphere Initiatives.

____. 1995. "El Salvador: A Negotiated End to Impunity?" In *Impunity and Human Rights in International Law and Practice,* ed. N. Roht-Arriaza. New York: Oxford University Press.

Power, Samantha. 2002. *A Problem from Hell: America and the Age of Genocide.* New York: Basic Books.

Preston, Julia. 1994. "Boutros-Ghali, U.N. General Widen Rift; Balkan Forces Commander Said to Challenge His Boss." *Washington Post,* January 12, A15.

Price, Robert. 1991. *Apartheid State in Crisis: Political Transformation in South Africa, 1975–1990.* Oxford: Oxford University Press.

____. 2002. *The Rwanda Crisis: A History of Genocide.* London: Hurst.

Prunier, Gerard. 1995. *The Rwanda Crisis: History of a Genocide.* New York: Columbia University Press.

____. 1997. "The Experience of European Armies in Operation Restore Hope." In *Learning from Somalia: The Lessons of Armed Intervention,* ed. W. Clarke and J. Herbst. Boulder: Westview Press.

____. 2005. *Darfur: The Ambiguous Genocide.* London: Hurst.

Pugh, Michael. 2004. "Peacekeeping and Critical Theory." *International Peacekeeping,* Vol. 11, No. 1.

Pugh, Michael, ed. 1996. "The UN, Peace and Force." Special Edition of *International Peacekeeping*. Vol. 3, No. 4.

Ragin, Charles. 1987. *The Comparative Method*. Berkeley: University of California Press.

Rathbun, Brian. 2004. *Partisan Interventions: European Party Politics And Peace Enforcement In The Balkans*. Ithaca: Cornell University Press.

Ratner, Steven R. 1995. *The New UN Peacekeeping: Building Peace in Lands of Conflict after the Cold War*. New York: St. Martin's.

Reed, Pamela L. 1996. "The Politics of Reconciliation: The United Nations Operation in Mozambique." In *UN Peacekeeping, American Policy, and the Uncivil Wars of the 1990s*, ed. William J. Durch. New York: St. Martin's.

Reilly, Benjamin. 2002. "Post-Conflict Elections: Constraints and Dangers." *International Peacekeeping*, Vol. 9. No. 2.

"Reluctant Reforms: The Cristiani Government and the International Community in the Process of Salvadoran Post-War Reconstruction." 1993. Washington, DC: Washington Office on Latin America.

Reyntjens, Filip. 1993. "The Proof of the Pudding Is in the Eating: The June 1993 Elections in Burundi." *Journal of Modern Africa Studies*, Vol. 31, No. 4.

Rhode, David. 1997. *Endgame: The Betrayal and Fall of Srebrenica, Europe's Worst Massacre since World War II*. Boulder: Westview Press.

Ribando, Clare. 2005. "Gangs in Central America." Washington, DC: Congressional Research Services.

Rikhye, Indar Jit. 1984. *The Theory and Practice of Peacekeeping*. London: C. Hurst & Co. for the International Peace Academy.

Ripley, Tim. 1997. "A Fragile Peace Emerges from the Rubble of Eastern Slavonia." *Jane's Intelligence Review*, Vol. 9, No. 7.

Roberts, David. 1997. "More Honoured in the Breech: Consent and Impartiality in the Cambodian Peacekeeping Operation." *International Peacekeeping*, Vol. 4, No. 1.

   2002. "Political Transition and Elite Discourse in Cambodia, 1991–99." *Journal of Communist Studies & Transition Politics*, Vol. 18, No. 4.

Rodman, Peter. 1991. "Supping with the Devils." *National Interest*, Vol. 25, Fall.

Rodrigues, Roque. 2003. "Introductory Remarks and Keynote Address." In *The United Nations Transitional Administration in East Timor: Debriefing and Lessons*, ed. Nassrine Azimi and Chang Li Lin. Leiden: Martinus Nijhoff Publishers.

Rotberg, Robert. 1995. "Elections in Namibia Point Toward Stability." *Christian Science Monitor*, January 25.

   2003. *Haiti's Turmoil: Politics and Policy Under Aristide and Clinton*. Cambridge, MA: World Peace Foundation.

Rotberg, Robert, ed. 2000. *Peacekeeping and Peace Enforcement in Africa: Methods of Conflict Prevention*. Washington, DC: Brookings Institution.

Roter, Petra, and Ana Bojinovic. 2005. "Croatia and the European Union: A Troubled Relationship." *Mediterranean Politics*, Vol. 10, No. 3.

Rothchild, Donald. 1997. *Managing Ethnic Conflict in Africa: Pressures and Incentives for Cooperation.* Washington, DC: Brookings Institution.

Rousseau, David. 2005. *Democracy and War: Institutions, Norms, and the Evolution of International Conflict.* Stanford: Stanford University Press.

Ruggie, John Gerard. 1994. "Peacekeeping and US Interests." *Washington Quarterly*, Vol. 14, No. 4.

1998. "What Makes the World Hang Together? Neo-Utilitarianism and the Social Constructivist Challenge." *International Organization*, Vol. 52, No. 4.

Rwabahungu, Marc. 2004. *Au Coeur des Crises Nationales au Rwanda et au Burundi: La Lutte pour les Ressources.* Paris: L'Harmattan.

SIPRI Yearbook. 2003. *Armaments, Disarmament, and International Security.* Oxford: Oxford University Press.

Sahnoun, Mohamed. 1994. *Somalia: Missed Opportunities.* Washington, DC: US Institute of Peace Press.

St. John, Ronald. 1995. "The Political Economy of the Royal Government of Cambodia." *Contemporary Southeast Asia*, Vol. 17, December.

2005. "Democracy in Cambodia – One Decade, US$5 Billion Later: What Went Wrong?" *Contemporary Southeast Asia: A Journal of International & Strategic Affairs*, Vol. 27, No. 3.

Saltford, John. 2003. *The United Nations and the Indonesian Takeover of West Papua: The Anatomy of Betrayal, 1962–1969.* London: Routledge Curzon.

Sambanis, Nicholas. 2001. "Do Ethnic and Nonethnic Civil Wars Have the Same Causes?" *Journal of Conflict Resolution*, Vol. 45, No. 3.

Sanderson, John. 1994. "UNTAC: Successes and Failures." In *International Peace Keeping: Building on the Cambodia Experience*, ed. Hugh Smith. Canberra: Australian Defence Studies Centre.

Saul, John and Colin Leys. 2003. "Truth, Reconciliation, Amnesia: The 'ex-Detainees' Fight for Justice. In *Re-examining Liberation in Namibia: Political Culture Since Independence*, ed. Henning Melber. Stockholm: Nordiska Afrikainstitutet.

Schear, James. 1996. "Riding the Tiger: The United Nations and Cambodia's Struggle for Peace." In *UN Peacekeeping, American Policy, and the Uncivil Wars of the 1990s*, ed. William Durch. New York: St. Martin's.

Scheiner, Charles. 2001. "The United States: From Complicity to Ambiguity." In *The East Timor Question: The Struggle for Independence from Indonesia*, ed. Paul Hainsworth and Stephen McCloskey, preface by José Ramos-Horta. New York: St. Martin's.

Schnabel, Albrecht. 2002. "Post-Conflict Peacebuilding and Second-Generation Preventive Action." *International Peacekeeping.* Vol. 9, No. 2.

Schwartz, Benjamin. 1992. *American Counterinsurgency Doctrine and El Salvador: The Frustrations of Reform and the Illusions of Nation Building.* Los Angeles: RAND.

Shenon, Philip. 1993. "Most Cambodians See Nothing of Aid." *New York Times*, February 21, A10.

Silber, Laura, and Allan Little. 1996. *Yugoslavia: Death of a Nation.* New York: Penguin Books.

Simmons, Beth. 1994. *Who Adjusts? Domestic Sources of Foreign Economic Policy during the Interwar Years.* Princeton: Princeton University Press.

Simon, Herbert. 1983. *Reason in Human Affairs.* Stanford: Stanford University Press.

Simpson, Brad. 2004. "Solidarity in an Age of Globalization: The Transnational Movement for East Timor and U.S. Foreign Policy." *Peace and Change*, Vol. 29, Nos. 3–4.

Simunovic, Pjer. 1999. "A Framework for Success: Contextual Factors in the UNTAES Operation in Eastern Slavonia." *International Peacekeeping*, Vol. 6, No. 1.

Skocpol, Theda and Margaret Somers. 1980. "The Uses of Comparative History in Macrosocial Inquiry." *Comparative Studies in Society and History*, Vol. 22, No. 2.

Smith, Anthony. 2004. "East Timor: Elections in the World's Newest Nation." *Journal of Democracy*, Vol. 15, No. 2.

Smith, Michael, with Moreen Dee. 2003. *Peacekeeping in East Timor: The Path to Independence.* Boulder: Lynne Rienner.

Smoljan, Jelena. 2003. "Socio-economic Aspects of Peacebuilding: UNTAES and the Organization of Employment in Eastern Slavonia." *International Peacekeeping*, Vol. 10, No. 2.

Smyth, Frank. 1992. "In El Salvador, Both Sides Say That New Year Pact Will End Long Civil War." *Christian Science Monitor*, January 6, 4.

Snyder, Jack. 2000. *From Voting to Violence: Democratization and Nationalist Conflict.* New York: Norton.

Sodhy, Pamela. 2004. "Modernization and Cambodia." *Journal of Third World Studies*, Vol. 21, No. 1.

Sokalski, Henryk J. 2003. *An Ounce of Prevention: Macedonia and the UN Experience in Preventive Diplomacy.* Washington, DC: US Institute of Peace Press.

Song, Jin. 1997. "The Political Dynamics of the Peacemaking Process in Cambodia." In *Keeping the Peace: Multidimensional UN Operations in Cambodia and El Salvador*, ed. Michael Doyle, Ian Johnstone, and Robert Orr. Cambridge: Cambridge University Press.

Spence, Jack, David Dye, Mike Lanchin, Geoff Thale, with George Vickers. 1997. "Chapultepec: Five Years Later: El Salvador's Political Reality and Uncertain Future." Cambridge, MA: Hemisphere Initiatives.

Spence, Jack, David Dye, and George Vickers, with Garth David Cheff, Carol Lynne D'Archangelis, Pablo Galarce, and Ken Ward. 1994. "El Salvador: Elections of the Century – Results, Recommendations, Analysis." Cambridge, MA and San Salvador: Hemisphere Initiatives.

Stanley, William. 1996. *The Protection Racket State: Elite Politics, Military Extortion and Civil War in El Salvador.* Philadelphia: Temple University Press.

Stanley, William and Charles T. Call. 1997. "Building a New Civilian Police Force in El Salvador." In *Rebuilding Societies after Civil War: Critical Roles for International Assistance*, ed. K. Kumar. Boulder: Lynne Rienner.

Stanley, William and David Holiday. 1997. "Peace Mission Strategy and Domestic Actors: UN Mediation, Verification, and Institution-Building in El Salvador." *International Peacekeeping*, Vol. 4, No. 2.

Stanley, William, and Robert Loosle. 1998. "El Salvador: The Civilian Police Component of Peace Operations." In *Policing the New World Disorder: Peace Operations and Public Security*, ed. Robert Oakley, Michael Dziedzic, and Eliot Goldberg. Washington, DC: National Defense University Press.

Stanley, William, George Vickers, and Jack Spence, eds. 1993. "Risking Failure: The Problems of the New Civilian Police in El Salvador." Cambridge MA: Hemisphere Initiatives, the Washington Office on Latin America, and the Unitarian Universalist Service Committee.

Stedman, Stephen John. 1991. *Peacemaking in Civil War: International Mediation in Zimbabwe, 1974–1980*. Boulder: Lynne Rienner.

   1997. "Spoiler Problems in Peace Processes." *International Security*, Vol. 22, No. 2.

Steenkamp, Willem. 1989. *South Africa's Border War 1966–1989*. Gibraltar: Ashanti.

Stokes, Doug. 2003. "Countering the Soviet Threat? An Analysis of the Justifications for US Military Assistance to El Salvador, 1979–92." *Cold War History*, Vol. 3, No. 3.

Stokes, Gale. 2005. "From Nation to Minority: Serbs in Croatia and Bosnia at the Outbreak of the Yugoslav Wars." *Problems of Post-Communism*, Vol. 52, No. 6.

Strobel, Warren. 1997. *Late-Breaking Foreign Policy: The News Media's Influence on Peace Operations*. Washington, DC: US Institute of Peace Press.

Stroehlein, Andrew. 2005. "In Congo, 1,000 Die Per Day: Why Isn't It a Story?" *Christian Science Monitor*, June 14.

Suhrke, Astri. 2001. "Peacekeepers as Nation-Builders: Dilemmas of the UN in East Timor." *International Peacekeeping*, Vol. 8, No. 4.

Sullivan, Daniel. 2005. "The Missing Pillars: A Look at the Failure of Peace in Burundi through the Lens of Arend Lijpart's Theory of Consociational Democracy." *Journal of Modern Africa Studies*, Vol. 43, No. 1.

Sullivan, Michael. 2005. "The Parliamentary Election in Cambodia, July 2003." *Electoral Studies*, Vol. 24, No. 1.

Suntharalingam, Nishkala. 1997. "The Cambodian Settlement Agreements." In *Keeping the Peace: Multidimensional UN Operations in Cambodia and El Salvador*, ed. Michael Doyle, Ian Johnstone, and Robert Orr. Cambridge, UK: Cambridge University Press.

Suzman, James. 2003. "Minorities in Independent Namibia." London: Minority Rights Group International.

Synge, Richard. 1997. *Mozambique: UN Peacekeeping in Action.* Washington, DC: US Institute of Peace Press.

Taylor, John. 1999. *East Timor: The Price of Freedom.* London: Zed Books.

Terrall, Ben. 2003. "The UN in East Timor: Lessons for Iraq?" *Radical Society*, Vol. 30, Nos. 3–4.

Tetlock, Philip, and Charles McGuire. 1985. "Cognitive Perspectives on Foreign Policy." In *Political Behavior Annual*, ed. S. Long. Boulder: Westview Press.

Thakur, Ramesh, and Carlyle A. Thayer. 1995. *UN Peacekeeping in the 1990s.* Boulder: Westview Press.

Thakur, Ramesh, and Albrecht Schnabel, eds. 2002. *United Nations Peacekeeping Operations Ad Hoc Missions, Permanent Engagement.* Tokyo: United Nations University Press.

Thayer, Nate, 1993. "Unsettled Land." *Far Eastern Economic Review*, February 27

Thomas, Timothy. 2001. "IT Requirements for 'Policekeeping'." *Military Review*, Vol. 81, No. 5.

Thornberry, Cedric. 2004. *A Nation Is Born: The Inside Story of Namibia's Independence.* Windhoek, Namibia: Gamsberg Macmillan Publishers.

Tonny, Knudsen, and Carsten Laustsen, eds. 2006. *Kosovo between War and Peace: Nationalism, Peacebuilding and International Trusteeship.* London: Frank Cass.

Torres-Rivas, Edelberto. 1997. "Insurrection and Civil War in El Salvador." In *Keeping the Peace: Multidimensional UN Operations in Cambodia and El Salvador*, ed. Michael W. Doyle, Ian Johnstone, and Robert C. Orr. Cambridge: Cambridge University Press.

Toualy, Georges. 2005. *Réflexion sur la crise ivoirienne: vivre en paix dans un état-nation souverain.* Paris: L'Harmattan.

Toungara, Jeanne Maddox. 2001. "Ethnicity and Political Crisis in Côte d'Ivoire." *Journal of Democracy.* Vol. 12, No. 3.

Traub, James. 2000. "Inventing East Timor." *Foreign Affairs*, Vol. 79, No. 4.

Trefon, Theodore. 2004. *Reinventing Order in the Congo: How People Respond to State Failure in Kinshasa.* London: Zed Books.

Turner, Michael, Sue Nelson, and Kimberly Mahling-Clark. 1998. "Mozambique's Vote for Democratic Governance." In *Rebuilding Societies after Civil War: Critical Roles for International Assistance*, ed. Krishna Kumar. Boulder: Lynne Rienner.

UNHCR. 1998. "Country Profile, Croatia." Geneva: United Nations High Commissioner for Refugees.

United Nations. 1994. *The United Nations in Cambodia: A Vote for Peace.* New York: United Nations.

United Nations. 1995. *Comprehensive Report on Lessons-Learned from United Nations Operations in Somalia April 1992–March 1995.* New York: United Nations, Lessons Learned Unit, Department of Peacekeeping Operations.

The United Nations and Cambodia, 1991–1995. 1995. New York: Department of Public Information, United Nations.

The United Nations and El Salvador. 1990–1995. 1995. New York: United Nations.

The United Nations and Mozambique, 1992–1995. 1995. New York: United Nations.

The United Nations and Somalia, 1992–1996. 1996. New York: United Nations.

United Nations. 1996. *The Blue Helmets: A Review of United Nations Peacekeeping.* New York: United Nations Department of Public Information.

United Nations. 1997. "Angola-UNAVEM III." New York: United Nations, Department of Public Information.

United Nations Development Programme. 2005. "Human Development Report."

"UNTAES Mission Brief." 1997. Zagreb: United Nations.

US Department of State. 1998. "Background Notes: El Salvador."

US Department of Energy. 2005. "Crude Oil and Total Petroleum Import Countries." Washington, DC: Energy Information Agency.

Urquhart, Brian. 1987. *A Life in Peace and War.* London: Weidenfield and Nicolson.

Vaccaro, Matthew J. 1996. "The Politics of Genocide: Peacekeeping and Disaster." In *UN Peacekeeping, American Policy, and the Uncivil Wars of the 1990s,* ed. William Durch. New York: St. Martin's.

Vaishnav, Milan. 2004. "Afghanistan: The Chimera of the Light Footprint." In *Winning the Peace: An American Strategy for Post-Conflict Reconstruction,* ed. Robert C. Orr, Washington, DC: Center for Strategic and International Studies Press.

Vance, Cyrus. 1983. *Hard Choices.* New York: Simon and Schuster.

Vickers, George. 1992. "The Political Reality After Eleven Years of War." In *Is there a Transition to Democracy in El Salvador?* ed. Joseph Tulchin with Gary Bland. Boulder: Lynne Rienner.

Vieira de Mello, Sergio. 2003. "Introductory Remarks and Keynote Address." In *The United Nations Transitional Administration in East Timor: Debriefing and Lessons,* ed. Nassrine Azimi and Chang Li Lin. Leiden: Martinus Nijhoff Publishers.

Vines, Alex. 1996. *RENAMO: From Terrorism to Democracy in Mozambique?* London: James Currey.

von Carlowitz, Leopold. 2004. "Crossing the Boundary from the International to the Domestic Legal Realm: UNMIK Lawmaking and Property Rights in Kosovo." *Global Governance,* Vol. 10, No. 3.

von Hippel, Karin. 2000. *Democracy by Force: US Military Intervention in the Post-Cold War World.* Cambridge: Cambridge University Press.

Wachtel, Andrew. 1998. *Making a Nation, Breaking a Nation: Literature and Politics in Yugoslavia.* Stanford: Stanford University Press.

Walter, Barbara. 1997. "Designing Transitions from Violent Civil War." University of California: Institute on Global Conflict and Cooperation.

———. 2002. *Committing to Peace: The Successful Settlement of Civil Wars.* Princeton: Princeton University Press, 2002.

Walter, Barbara F., and Jack Snyder, eds. 1999. *Civil Wars, Insecurity, and Intervention.* New York: Columbia University.

Waltz, Kenneth. 1979. *Theory of International Politics.* New York: Random House.

Warner, Nick. 1993. "Cambodia: Lessons of UNTAC for Future Peacekeeping Operations." Canberra: International Seminar on UN Peacekeeping at the Crossroads.

Waugh, Colin. 2004. *Paul Kagame and Rwanda: Power, Genocide and the Rwandan Patriotic Front.* Jefferson, NC: McFarland and Company.

Wax, Emily. 2005a. "Congo's Desperate 'One-Dollar UN Girls'." *Washington Post*, A1.

2005b. "In Congo, Peace Eludes Its UN Peacekeepers." *Washington Post*, March 28, A12.

Weiland, Heribert, and Matthew Braham, eds. 1994. *The Namibian Peace Process: Implications and Lessons for the Future:* Arnold Bergstraesser Institut.

Weinstein, Jeremy. 2002. "Mozambique: A Fading UN Success Story." *Journal of Democracy,* Vol. 13, No. 1.

Weiss, Thomas G., ed. 1995. *The United Nations and Civil Wars.* Boulder: Lynne Rienner.

Wendt, Alexander. 1999. *Social Theory of International Politics.* Cambridge: Cambridge University Press.

Werner, Suzanne, and Amy Yuen. 2005. "Making and Keeping Peace." *International Organization,* Vol. 59, No. 2.

Wesley, Michael. 1997. *Casualties of the New World Order: The Causes of Failure of UN Missions to Civil Wars.* Boulder: St. Martin's.

West, Harry, with Agostinho Mandumbwe. 2005. *Kupilikula: Governance and the Invisible Realm in Mozambique* Chicago: University of Chicago Press.

Whitfield, Teresa. 1994. *Paying the Price: Ignacio Ellacuría and the Murdered Jesuits of El Salvador.* Philadelphia: Temple University Press.

forthcoming. *Friends Indeed: The United Nations, Groups of Friends, and the Resolution of Conflict.* Washington, DC: Institute of Peace Press.

Whitworth, Sandra. 2004. *Men, Militarism, and UN Peacekeeping.* Boulder: Lynne Rienner.

Williams, Paul. 2005. "Military Responses to Mass Killing: The African Union Mission in Sudan." *International Peacekeeping,* Vol. 13, No. 2.

Williams, Philip J., and Knut Walter. 1997. *Militarization and Demilitarization: El Salvador's Transition to Democracy.* Pittsburgh: University of Pittsburgh Press.

Wohlforth, William C. 2003. *Cold War Endgame: Oral History, Analysis, Debates.* University Park: Pennsylvania State University Press.

Wood, Elisabeth. 1995. "Economic Change, Civil War, and Democracy in El Salvador: Rural Social Relations in Revolution and Reconstruction." Ph.D. thesis, Stanford University, Stanford.

2000. *Forging Democracy from Below: Contested Transitions in South Africa and el Salvador.* New York: Cambridge University Press.

2003. *Insurgent Collective Action and Civil War in El Salvador*. New York: Cambridge University Press.

Wood, Nicholas. 2004. "Kosovo Smolders After Mob Violence." *New York Times*, March 24, 2004.

Woodhouse, Tom, and Oliver Ramsbotham, eds. 2000. *Peacekeeping and Conflict Resolution*. London: Frank Cass.

Woods, James. 1997. "US Government Decisionmaking Process During Humanitarian Operations in Somalia." In *Learning from Somalia: The Lessons of Armed Intervention*, ed. W. Clarke and J. Herbst. Boulder: Westview.

1998. "Mozambique: The CIVPOL Operation." In *Policing the New World Disorder: Peace Operations and Public Security*, ed. Robert Oakley, Michael Dziedzic, and Eliot Goldberg. Washington, DC: Institute for National Strategic Studies, National Defense University.

Woodward, Susan. 1995. *Balkan Tragedy: Chaos and Dissolution After the Cold War*. Washington, DC: Brookings Institution.

World Bank. 2005. "Private Solution for Infrastructure in Angola." A Country Framework Report.

Wren, Christopher. 1989. "Rebel Hunters in Namibia Train for Less Violent Times as Ordinary Police." *New York Times*, January 9, A3.

1990. "Outjo Journal: UN Namibia Team Makes Some Unlikely Friends." *New York Times*, January 19, p. A4.

Wright, Clive. 2004. "Tackling Conflict Diamonds: The Kimberley Process Certification Scheme." *International Peacekeeping*, Vol. 11, No. 4.

Wright, Michael, and Caroline Rand Herron. 1981. "Two Allies Go their Own Way on El Salvador." *New York Times*, August 30, 2.

Yannis, Alexandros. 2004. "The UN as Government in Kosovo." *Global Governance*, Vol. 10, No. 1.

Yearbook of the United Nations. 1989. Vol. 43. New York: United Nations.

1993. Vol. 47. New York: United Nations.

Young, Crawford. 2002. "Contextualizing Congo Conflicts: Order and Disorder in Postcolonial Africa." In *The African Stakes of the Congo War*, ed. John F. Clark. New York: Palgrave Macmillan.

Zartman, I. William. 1985. *Ripe for Resolution: Conflict and Intervention in Africa*. New York: Oxford University Press.

Zartman I. William, ed., 1995. *Elusive Peace: Negotiating an End to Civil Wars*. Washington, DC: Brookings Institution.

Zartman, I. William, and J. Lewis Rasmussen, ed. 1997. *Peacemaking in International Conflict: Methods and Techniques*. Washington, DC: US Institute of Peace Press.

INDEX